# 2015 COLLEGE FOOTBALL
# COACHES
# ALMANAC™
## AND PREVIEW

### THE ULTIMATE GUIDE TO COLLEGE FOOTBALL COACHES AND THEIR TEAMS FOR 2015

Darrin Donnelly

For the latest college football coaching news, rumors, rankings, and trends, visit:

# CoachesAlmanac.com

# Contents

## THE POWER FIVE PROGRAMS

## Big Ten Preview

## Big Ten East Division

## Big Ten West Division

## Big 12 Preview

## The Big 12

## Pac-12 Preview

## Pac-12 North Division

## Pac-12 South Division

## SEC Preview

## SEC East Division

## SEC West Division

# THE MID-MAJOR PROGRAMS

## Independent

## MAC Preview

## MAC East Division

## MAC West Division

## Mountain West Preview

## MWC Mountain Division

## MWC West Division

## Sun Belt Preview

## The Sun Belt

## Overtime

# Introduction

In college football, head coaches are synonymous with the programs they lead. And for good reason.

Perhaps more than any other sport, the outcome of a college football game, the success of a college football team's season, or the state of an entire college football program depends on the head coach. They're responsible for evaluating talent, recruiting that talent to play for them, developing that talent over four to five years, and motivating that talent to reach its highest potential on a daily basis. They're responsible for roughly 2,000 offensive and defensive play-calls throughout the season – with each and every call waiting to be scrutinized and second-guessed by anyone and everyone. As the face of the program wherever they go, a head coach is also largely responsible for the business side of the game.

The buck stops with the head coach and the pressure is greater than ever in today's era of big-time college football.

It's the coaches who make or break their programs and that's why the *College Football Coaches Almanac and Preview* (the *CFCA*, for short) was created. This big book gives you everything you need to know about every major college football coach in America heading into 2015.

The *CFCA* is for college football fans who want to know more – a *lot* more – about the coaches behind each program.

It's for those who want to know which offensive and defensive schemes a coach implements and whether he has the right players in place to run it in 2015. Want to know if any changes are being made to a team's overall system, like switching from a pro-style offense to the Air Raid, or if a coach is simply making a philosophical change, like focusing more on the run than the pass? This book has the answers you're looking for.

The *CFCA* is for college football enthusiasts who want to know the stories behind the coaches. How did these coaches work their way up? How has their background shaped them? What ties do they have to other coaches, schools, and communities? Who were their mentors? What season-by-season results have they achieved? It's all in this book.

What about a coach's job status? How much does he get paid compared to other coaches? How safe is his job right now? Which coaches are rumored to be looking for better opportunities? Which assistants are in line for head coaching gigs? And why would some coaches be better fits at different schools? These are the questions this book answers.

The *CFCA* also breaks down all the key staff changes that occurred in the offseason, explaining why those changes were made and how they will impact the team's offensive and defensive strategies going forward.

In short, this book is the ultimate guide to college football coaches and their teams heading into 2015.

Before you dive into the 2015 edition of the *CFCA*, there are a few things you should know about the information provided...

**Offensive and Defensive Schemes**

An important part of this book is identifying the base offensive and defensive schemes a coach is trying to implement. College football has so much diversity when it comes to the Xs and Os behind each team's strategy and I wanted to make sure this book served as an easy reference for anyone interested in quickly understanding a coach's system of choice.

The days of a team lining up in a single formation with only slight variations throughout the game are long gone. Pretty much every offense and defense could accurately be called "multiple" as they adjust often in the modern age of college football. However, every team has a *base* philosophy that it adapts from as needed.

In determining the base offense and defense, a few points need to be made.

A "pro-style" offense is a fairly broad label that should be clarified. It refers to an offense that looks a lot like a typical NFL-style offense. It's an offense that uses multiple formations (everything from shotgun spread formations to two-back, two-TE sets), relies on a pro-style QB (strong arm, required to make key pre-snap decisions, doesn't need to be a running threat), and will implement FBs and blocking TEs as needed. For the purposes of this book (and ongoing references at

CoachesAlmanac.com), the standard "pro-style" label refers to a *balanced* pro-style offense (aiming for a 50-50/55-45 run-pass ratio). Otherwise, distinctions are made between a *run-first* pro-style offense, which refers to a more physical pro-style offense that relies heavily on a bruising rushing attack, and a *pass-first* pro-style offense, which refers to a system that likes to air it out early and often, but is usually capable of shifting gears quickly when necessary. Distinctions between these styles have been made throughout this book.

Similarly, a "spread" offense shouldn't be labeled as such simply because a team prefers to run a lot of shotgun. On one end of the spectrum, there's the Air Raid offense, which spreads a defense out, throws the ball up to 80% of the time, and doesn't require a mobile QB. On the other end, there's the run-first spread-option offense, which is usually implemented as a hurry-up offense, runs the ball 60% of the time or more, and requires a dual-threat QB. This book distinguishes between each of these styles. If an offense is refereed to simply as "the spread" – with no further distinction – it should be considered a *balanced* spread attack that tries to balance out the passing game with some read option and power running.

Distinctions are also made on the defensive side of the ball. Most teams will make adjustments between four-man and three-man fronts depending on the situations they face. In the modern era of wide-open college football, every team can slip into a nickel package (five DBs) as needed. However, whether a team *bases* out of a 4-3 or 3-4, for example, makes a big difference in what a team is trying to accomplish and how they're going to recruit players. It also matters whether a team prefers to run an attacking, blitz-heavy defense or a bend-but-don't-break, read-and-react scheme. As necessary, this book aims to clarify these differences for each team.

### Job Security Grades

The job security grade listed is based on the following scale.

**A:** Job is extremely safe. Many of the A-graded coaches have just received a contract extension. In the case of A-graded new hires, the hiring was largely approved by an excited fan base.

**B:** Job is safe, but the coach has taken a step back and/or is dealing with a fan base that is growing a bit restless. In the case of new hires who receive a B grade, it means the coach is walking into an impatient situation and/or the fan base is somewhat skeptical of the hire.

**C:** Coach is on the hot seat and will be fighting for his job in 2015.

**D:** A scorching hot seat. Coaches with a D grade survived speculation that they would be replaced *last* season. The coach enters 2015 lucky to still be running the program.

The intention of this grading scale is to give an accurate representation of the coach's standing with his program as he heads into the 2015 season. It should *not* be viewed as an opinion on who should or shouldn't be fired or as a prediction for what the future holds for a coach. Personally, I believe colleges today tend to fire coaches way too quickly, but that's only my opinion. The grades in this book are based on the reality of the situation.

## Rumors

Rumors mentioned in the Rumor Mill section of each coach entry are just that: *rumors*. They shouldn't all be viewed as cold, hard facts.

Having said that, paying attention to coaching rumors is part of following college football. Coaches don't typically announce to the public that they're eyeing another job. Likewise, athletic directors obviously don't like to publicize their growing impatience with a current coach or who they're interested in hiring as a replacement. Therefore, it's important (and a lot of fun!) to follow these rumors when evaluating a coach's future.

## Salaries

Most coach salaries listed in this book are based on what the coach was paid in 2014 as reported by a reputable media source (see the Acknowledgments section of this book). If a coach has just signed a new contract extension, the publicized 2015 salary is listed instead of last season's salary. If a coach's salary is listed with an asterisk next to it, it means his salary was not made public (usually because the school is a private institution) and the figure is based on estimates found elsewhere (again, see the Acknowledgments section of this book).

### Recruiting

Unless otherwise noted, all references to the national or conference ranking for a recruiting class refer to the composite ranking listed by *247Sports*, which bases its rankings on the *combined* ratings listed by several other major recruiting services. The result is the most comprehensive and unbiased ranking system that I'm aware of.

### Predictions

Every college football preview needs to include predictions and the *CFCA* is no different. Like most preseason predictions, the projected final standings for each conference and the preseason Top 25 are based on things like past performance, returning personnel, 2015 schedules, etc. However, what makes the predictions here a bit different than those you'll find elsewhere is that they're based more heavily on the coaches. Historical coaching trends, coaching staff changes, and schematic overhauls are the main factors for these predictions.

### Never-Ending Updates

Finally, the content in this book – coach rankings, rumors about new jobs, job security grades, schematic changes, recruiting wars, etc. – will change as coaches and teams evolve throughout the season. You can follow these important changes throughout the season at **CoachesAlamanac.com** and on Twitter at: **@CoachesAlmanac**.

Also, if you have any question about the information in this book or if there is anything you want to see more of or less of in next year's edition of the *College Football Coaches Almanac and Preview*, I want to hear from you. Shoot me an email at **info@coachesalmanac.com** or just send me a message on Twitter.

To receive FREE updates by email on the latest coaching news, rumors, rankings, contract changes, and emerging college football trends, sign up at:

# CoachesAlmanac.com/Updates

# The 2015 Preseason Coach Rankings

What follows is a ranking for all 128 FBS head coaches. The rankings are not based *solely* on wins, losses, and lifetime achievements. Those factors are certainly taken into account, but the ranking system is based primarily on answering one key hypothetical question: *If you were an athletic director who could hire any coach for your program and you were guaranteed to have him at a high-energy level for the next five years, who would you hire?*

When evaluated in light of this question, concerns such as salary commanded, interest in other schools (or the NFL), and the age of the coach can be disregarded.

The ranking is based largely on how high a level each coach is currently coaching (and recruiting) at. Lifetime achievements are an important factor, but more recent results carry a heavier weighting.

Obviously, a list like this is bound to create plenty of debate and you can join in on that debate at **CoachesAlmanac.com**, where these rankings will be updated throughout the season.

## The 2015 Preseason CFCA Coach Rankings:

1. **Urban Meyer** – Ohio State (142-26 in 13 seasons)
2. **Nick Saban** – Alabama (177-59-1 in 19 seasons)
3. **Jimbo Fisher** – Florida State (58-11 in 5 seasons)
4. **Bob Stoops** – Oklahoma (168-44 in 16 seasons)
5. **Les Miles** – LSU (131-50 in 14 seasons)
6. **Mark Dantonio** – Michigan State (93-48 in 11 seasons)
7. **Mark Richt** – Georgia (136-48 in 14 seasons)
8. **Jim Harbaugh** – Michigan (58-27 in 7 seasons)
9. **Gus Malzahn** – Auburn (29-10 in 3 seasons)
10. **Art Briles** – Baylor (89-62 in 12 seasons)
11. **Bill Snyder** – Kansas State (187-94-1 in 23 seasons)
12. **Steve Spurrier** – South Carolina (226-85-2 in 25 seasons)

13. **Gary Patterson** – TCU (132-45 in 14 seasons)

14. **Brian Kelly** – Notre Dame (216–77–2 in 24 seasons)

15. **Frank Beamer** – Virginia Tech (273-138-4 in 34 seasons)

16. **Gary Pinkel** – Missouri (186-103-3 in 24 seasons)

17. **David Shaw** – Stanford (42-12 in 4 seasons)

18. **Paul Johnson** – Georgia Tech (165-74 in 18 seasons)

19. **Chris Petersen** – Washington (100-18 in 9 seasons)

20. **Mark Helfrich** – Oregon (24-4 in 2 seasons)

21. **Kevin Sumlin** – Texas A&M (63-28 in 7 seasons)

22. **Dabo Swinney** – Clemson (61-26 in 7 seasons)

23. **Hugh Freeze** – Ole Miss (54-22 in 6 seasons)

24. **Brett Bielema** – Arkansas (78-39 in 9 seasons)

25. **Charlie Strong** – Texas (43-23 in 6 seasons)

26. **Mike Gundy** – Oklahoma State (84-44 in 10 seasons)

27. **Jim Mora** – UCLA (29-11 in 3 seasons)

28. **James Franklin** – Penn State (31-21 in 4 seasons)

29. **Jerry Kill** – Minnesota (148-96 in 21 seasons)

30. **Bobby Petrino** – Louisville (92-34 in 10 seasons)

31. **Todd Graham** – Arizona State (77-41 in 9 seasons)

32. **Rich Rodriguez** – Arizona (146-98-2 in 21 seasons)

33. **Mike Leach** – Washington State (96-68 in 13 seasons)

34. **David Cutcliffe** – Duke (84-77 in 13 seasons)

35. **Dan Mullen** – Mississippi State (46-31 in 6 seasons)

36. **Butch Jones** – Tennessee (62-40 in 8 seasons)

37. **George O'Leary** – UCF (133-93 in 19 seasons)

38. **Steve Sarkisian** – USC (43-33 in 6 seasons)

39. **Gary Anderson** – Oregon State (49-38 in 7 seasons)

40. **Kyle Whittingham** – Utah (85-43 in 10 seasons)

41. **Jim McElwain** – Florida (22-16 in 3 seasons)

42. **Dave Doeren** – NC State (34-18 in 4 seasons)

43. **Pat Narduzzi** – Pittsburgh (First Year Head Coach)

44. **Tommy Tuberville** – Cincinnati (148-85 in 19 seasons)

45. **Larry Fedora** – North Carolina (55-36 in 7 seasons)

46. **Dana Holgorsen** – West Virginia (28-23 in 4 seasons)

47. **Mike Riley** – Nebraska (93-80 in 14 seasons)

48. **Bryan Harsin** – Boise State (19-7 in 2 seasons)

49. **Pat Fitzgerald** – Northwestern (60-53 in 9 seasons)

50. **Doc Holliday** – Marshall (40-25 in 5 seasons)

51. **Skip Holtz** – Louisiana Tech (101-84 in 15 seasons)

52. **Steve Addazio** – Boston College (27-23 in 4 seasons)

53. **Tim DeRuyter** – Fresno State (27-14 in 3 seasons)

54. **Troy Calhoun** – Air Force (59-44 in 8 seasons)

55. **Mike Bobo** – Colorado State (First Year Head Coach)

56. **Kirk Ferentz** – Iowa (127-106 in 19 seasons)

57. **Kyle Flood** – Rutgers (23-16 in 3 seasons)

58. **Matt Wells** – Utah State (19-9 in 2 seasons)

59. **Justin Fuente** – Memphis (17-20 in 3 seasons)

60. **Ken Niumatalolo** – Navy (57-35 in 7 seasons)

61. **Bronco Mendenhall** – BYU (90-39 in 10 seasons)

62. **Ruffin McNeill** – East Carolina (38-27 in 5 seasons)

63. **Paul Chryst** – Wisconsin (19-19 in 3 seasons)

64. **Mark Stoops** – Kentucky (7-17 in 2 seasons)

65. **Sonny Dykes** – California (28-33 in 5 seasons)

66. **Al Golden** – Miami (FL) (55-56 in 9 seasons)

67. **Tom Herman** – Houston (First Year Head Coach)

68. **Chad Morris** – SMU (First Year Head Coach)

69. **Randy Edsall** – Maryland (94-100 in 15 seasons)

70. **Dave Clawson** – Wake Forest (93-90 in 15 seasons)

71. **David Bailiff** – Rice (69-68 in 11 seasons)

72. **Larry Coker** – UTSA (83-38 in 10 seasons)

73. **Willie Fritz** – Georgia Southern (146-65 in 18 seasons)

74. **Mark Hudspeth** – Louisiana-Lafayette (103-37 in 11 seasons)

75. **Kliff Kingsbury** – Texas Tech (12-13 in 2 seasons)

76. **Jeff Brohm** – Western Kentucky (8-5 in 1 season)

77. **Philip Montgomery** – Tulsa (First Year Head Coach)

78. **Frank Solich** – Ohio (130-75 in 16 seasons)

79. **Bobby Wilder** – Old Dominion (52-20 in 6 seasons)

80. **Mike London** – Virginia (47-43 in 7 seasons)

81. **Darrell Hazell** – Purdue (20-30 in 4 seasons)

82. **Terry Bowden** – Akron (151-87-2 in 21 seasons)

83. **Mike MacIntyre** – Colorado (22-39 in 5 seasons)

84. **Rick Stockstill** – Middle Tennessee (57-55 in 9 seasons)

85. **Craig Bohl** – Wyoming (108-40 in 12 seasons)

86. **Lance Leipold** – Buffalo (109-6 in 8 seasons)

87. **Rod Carey** – Northern Illinois (23-6 in 2 seasons)

88. **P.J. Fleck** – Western Michigan (9-16 in 2 seasons)

89. **Dennis Franchione** – Texas State (210-126-2 in 29 seasons)

90. **Tim Beckman** – Illinois (33-41 in 6 seasons)

91. **Kevin Wilson** – Indiana (14-34 in 4 seasons)

92. **Matt Rhule** – Temple (8-16 in 2 seasons)

93. **Willie Taggart** – South Florida (22-38 in 5 seasons)

94. **Jeff Monken** – Army (42-24 in 5 seasons)

95. **Matt Campbell** – Toledo (26-13 in 3 seasons)

96. **Scott Shafer** – Syracuse (10-15 in 2 seasons)

97. **Neal Brown** – Troy (First Year Head Coach)

98. **Curtis Johnson** – Tulane (12-25 in 3 seasons)

99. **Dan McCarney** – North Texas (78-112 in 16 seasons)

100. **Paul Rhoads** – Iowa State (29-46 in 6 seasons)

101. **Dino Babers** – Bowling Green (27-13 in 3 seasons)

102. **Rocky Long** – San Diego State (97-89 in 15 seasons)

103. **Brian Polian** – Nevada (11-14 in 2 seasons)

104. **Blake Anderson** – Arkansas State (7-6 in 1 season)

105. **Sean Kugler** – UTEP (9-16 in 2 seasons)

106. **Derek Mason** – Vanderbilt (3-9 in 1 season)

107. **Joey Jones** – South Alabama (40-35 in 7 seasons)

108. **Mark Whipple** – Massachusetts (124-68 in 17 seasons)

**109. Bob Diaco** – Connecticut (2-10 in 1 season)

**110. Chuck Martin** – Miami (OH) (76-17 in 7 seasons)

**111. Scott Satterfield** – Appalachian State (11-13 in 2 seasons)

**112. Pete Lembo** – Ball State (109-56 in 14 seasons)

**113. Bob Davie** – New Mexico (46-51 in 8 seasons)

**114. Ron Turner** – FIU (47-80 in 11 seasons)

**115. Charlie Partridge** – Florida Atlantic (3-9 in 1 season)

**116. Todd Monken** – Southern Miss (4-20 in 2 seasons)

**117. Norm Chow** – Hawaii (8-29 in 3 seasons)

**118. David Beaty** – Kansas (First Year Head Coach)

**119. Chris Creighton** – Eastern Michigan (141-56 in 18 seasons)

**120. John Bonamego** – Central Michigan (First Year Head Coach)

**121. Tony Sanchez** – UNLV (First Year Head Coach)

**122. Ron Caragher** – San Jose State (53-37 in 8 seasons)

**123. Todd Berry** – Louisiana-Monroe (56-93 in 13 seasons)

**124. Brad Lambert** – Charlotte (10-12 in 2 seasons)

**125. Paul Haynes** – Kent State (6-17 in 2 seasons)

**126. Doug Martin** – New Mexico State (33-73 in 9 seasons)

**127. Trent Miles** – Georgia State (21-59 in 7 seasons)

**128. Paul Petrino** – Idaho (2-21 in 2 seasons)

For instant coaching news, the latest coaching buzz, and some great motivation from college football's greatest coaches, follow us on Twitter at:

# @CoachesAlmanac

# Preseason Top 25 Team Rankings

The preseason Top 25 rankings that follow are predictions for how these teams will *end* the 2015 season. They don't necessarily represent where a team deserves to *start* the 2015 season. These rankings are largely based on coaching performance and trends, coaching staff changes, returning personnel, and this season's schedules.

A quick note about schedules. When predicting how a team's season will play out, the favorability of a schedule obviously plays a crucial role. However, as the College Football Playoff committee made clear in 2014, a schedule that is *too* favorable can and will hurt a team's ranking.

The Top 4 teams in this Top 25 are the predicted participants in the College Football Playoff.

## The 2015 Preseason Team Rankings:

1. **Ohio State** – The Buckeyes are loaded with returning talent and they're the clear favorites to repeat as National Champions.

2. **Alabama** – Though Nick Saban may be light on returning starters, he still has more stock-piled talent than any other team in the country. Whoever survives the brutal SEC West should have a spot reserved for them in the playoffs.

3. **Oregon** – The Ducks are loaded with speed and athleticism once again. The question on everyone's mind: how quickly will they adjust to the post-Marcus Mariota era?

4. **Baylor** – Baylor is here to stay and will once again be in the running for a Big 12 title and a spot in the College Football Playoff. However, the Bears will need to go undefeated. If they end up with one loss, the CFP committee could pass them over due to their weak nonconference schedule.

5. **Michigan State** – While all the hype in the state of Michigan may be about Jim Harbaugh's return to Ann Arbor, Mark Dantonio has a team capable

of challenging Ohio State for the Big Ten East. Even if they lose to the Buckeyes, a one-loss Spartan team could still be in position to earn a playoff spot *if* they have a nonconference win over Oregon on their resume.

6.  **Auburn** – With Will Muschamp now building a defense to go along with Gus Malzahn's explosive offense, the Tigers could be scary good for years to come.

7.  **Notre Dame** – This will be the most talented Notre Dame team Brian Kelly has had and the Irish have a schedule that sets up nicely for a championship run.

8.  **Oklahoma** – History tells us not to bet against Bob Stoops after a disappointing season.

9.  **TCU** – The Horned Frogs have the starting talent to win a National Championship (especially on offense), but do they have the *depth* to survive the season with a big target on their back?

10. **Florida State** – The Seminoles enter 2015 with a lot more uncertainty than they've had the past two years, but they're still the ACC's top team until proven otherwise.

11. **LSU** – Overall, the Tigers have one of the most-talented teams in the nation, but Les Miles still needs to settle on a QB.

12. **Ole Miss** – Though questions remain at QB, there's enough talent on this Ole Miss team to compete for an SEC title. Four SEC West teams are in the Top 12 and all four have a good shot at making the playoffs. The problem is that these schools look poised to beat each other up, which means only one team from college football's toughest division will likely land in the playoffs.

13. **Clemson** – The Clemson offense is loaded. If one of the nation's top defensive coordinators, Brent Venables, can get his inexperienced (but talented) Tiger defense up to speed, Clemson should make a playoff run.

14. **Georgia** – As long as the transition to a new offensive coordinator goes smoothly, the Bulldogs should be the favorite to win the SEC East.

15. **UCLA** – Jim Mora needs to find a QB quickly, but the Bruins are loaded with talent and could make a playoff run if they survive the difficult Pac-12 South.

16. **Stanford** – David Shaw has a talented team that could surprise the Pac-12 in 2015.

17. **Tennessee** – On paper, it looks like the Vols are a year away from an SEC title run, but this team just might join the party a year earlier than expected.

18. **Georgia Tech** – Paul Johnson's option attack will continue to cause problems for whoever the Yellow Jackets play.

19. **Arizona State** – Todd Graham is quietly building a dynasty in the desert. This is a team that could surprise the nation by winning the Pac-12 and landing in the playoffs.

20. **Arkansas** – Like Tennessee, the Razorbacks look to be a year away from making an SEC title run, but Brett Bielema's team should still be a disruptive force in college football's toughest division.

21. **USC** – The Trojans are dark-horse National Championship contenders, but the Pac-12 South will be tough to survive for a team still trying to build depth.

22. **Oklahoma State** – The top of the Big 12 may be crowded, but Mike Gundy has a team that could sneak in to the title race.

23. **Minnesota** – Be ready for Jerry Kill's team to take advantage of the fact that Big Ten West foes Wisconsin and Nebraska are transitioning to new head coaches.

24. **Texas A&M** – It would be unwise to overlook a team led by offensive guru Kevin Sumlin and one of the best defensive coaches in the game; newly-added defensive coordinator John Chavis.

25. **Michigan** – Jim Harbaugh's debut season at Michigan will be with a team that is much more talented than last year's 5-7 record indicates.

I want to hear from you. Got an opinion on the coach rankings or preseason Top 25? Have some suggestions for what you'd like to see in next year's *College Football Coaches Almanac and Preview*? Don't hesitate to let me know.

Email: **info@coachesalmanac.com**

Twitter: **@CoachesAlmanac**

# The Best of the Best

## The 2014 CFCA National Coach of the Year:
## Urban Meyer, Ohio State

Lou Holtz used to tell his teams to expect at least three major crises throughout each season. How they responded to those adversities, Holtz said, would determine the success of their season. In 2014, Urban Meyer overcame crisis after crisis as he led Ohio State to the National Championship. The job Meyer did in 2014 may have been one of the greatest coaching performances in the history of college football. It all culminated with Ohio State relying on a third-string QB to win the first-ever College Football Playoff National Championship despite the fact that pollsters had the Buckeyes ranked No. 5 before the playoffs began.

## The 2014 CFCA Comeback Coach of the Year:
## Gary Patterson, TCU

After going 7-6 in 2012 and 4-8 in 2013, some started questioning whether Gary Patterson was capable of transitioning TCU to the Big 12. In 2014, Patterson silenced his critics with a dominating 12-1 season and a No. 3 finish in the polls.

## The 2014 CFCA Mid-Major Coach of the Year:
## Willie Fritz, Georgia Southern

As the gap between the Power 5 schools and the non-Power 5 schools widens in this modern era of college football, it's important to recognize the top performances from the "Mid-Major" level. Last year's top Mid-Major coaching performance belonged to Willie Fritz. In his debut season at Georgia Southern, he was given the task of transitioning the Eagles from the FCS level to the FBS. He responded with an undefeated Sun Belt conference championship and a 9-3 overall record that included near-victories against NC State and Georgia Tech.

## 2014 Conference-by-Conference Coaches of the Year:

(As chosen by each conference's coaches and/or selected media members.)

**The American:** Justin Fuente, Memphis (10-3 overall, 7-1 in the AAC)

**ACC:** Paul Johnson, Georgia Tech (11-3 overall, 6-2 in the ACC)

**Big Ten:** Jerry Kill, Minnesota (8-5 overall, 5-3 in the Big Ten)

**Big 12:** Gary Patterson, TCU (12-1 overall, 8-1 in the Big 12)

**Conference USA:** Doc Holliday, Marshall (13-1 overall, 7-1 in C-USA)

**MAC:** P.J. Fleck, Western Michigan (8-5 overall, 6-2 in the MAC)

**Mountain West:** Jim McElwain, Colorado State (10-2 overall, 6-2 in the MWC)

**Pac-12:** Rich Rodriguez, Arizona (10-4 overall, 7-2 in the Pac-12)

**SEC:** Gary Pinkel, Missouri (11-3 overall, 7-1 in the SEC)

**Sun Belt:** Willie Fritz, Georgia Southern (9-3 overall, 8-0 in the Sun Belt)

## Other 2014 Major Coaching Awards:

**AFCA FBS Coach of the Year:** Gary Patterson, TCU

**AP Coach of the Year:** Gary Patterson, TCU

**Paul "Bear" Bryant Coach of the Year:** Gary Patterson, TCU

**Bobby Dodd Coach of the Year:** Nick Saban, Alabama

**Home Depot Coach of the Year:** Gary Patterson, TCU

**Eddie Robinson Coach of the Year:** Gary Patterson, TCU

**Sporting News Coach of the Year:** Gary Patterson, TCU

**Walter Camp Coach of the Year:** Gary Patterson, TCU

**Woody Hayes Trophy:** Gary Patterson, TCU

**AFCA Assistant Coach of the Year:** Gary Campbell, Oregon RB coach

**Broyles Award (top assistant):** Tom Herman, Ohio State offensive coordinator

**Other Broyles Award Finalists:** Oregon offensive coordinator Scott Frost, Alabama offensive coordinator Lane Kiffin, TCU co-offensive coordinator Doug Meacham, Missouri defensive coordinator Dave Steckel

**AFCA FCS Coach of the Year:** Sean McDonnell, New Hampshire

**AFCA Division II Coach of the Year:** John Wristen, Colorado State-Pueblo

**AFCA Division III Coach of the Year:** Lance Leipold, Wisconsin-Whitewater

**AFCA NAIA of the Year:** Mark Henninger, Marian University

# 2015 ACC PREVIEW

## Five Things You Need to Know about the ACC in 2015:

**The Battle at the Top:** On paper, this may look like a rebuilding year for **Jimbo Fisher**, but he's still got the most talented team in the ACC. Until somebody proves they can knock off the kings of the conference, **Florida State** is the favorite to win a fourth-straight ACC title.

**New to the ACC: Pitt** hired **Pat Narduzzi** to replace **Paul Chryst**, who left for **Wisconsin.** Narduzzi looks like the perfect fit for the Panthers. He brings a high-energy persona to a program that could use some liveliness, he's a defensive genius, and his offensive scheme should fit perfectly with the personnel he's inheriting. Best of all, after its last two coaches treated Pitt like a stepping-stone job, it looks like the Panthers may have found a head coach who *wants* to be the face of this program for years to come. Don't be surprised to see Pitt contending for a Coastal Division title right away.

**Coach on the Rise: Dave Doeren** is quietly building a contender at **NC State**. The Wolfpack may not be ready to knock off ACC heavyweights **Florida State** and **Clemson** just yet, but they could slip into the Atlantic Division's third-place spot in 2015.

**Keep an Eye On: Clemson** defensive coordinator **Brent Venables** has taken Clemson's defense from the bottom-half of the ACC to the top of the nation in just three years. In 2015, he'll be asked to deliver one of the best coaching performances of his career as the Tigers have just three returning starters on defense. If Clemson is going to knock off **Florida State** in the Atlantic Division, Venables will have to overachieve with this inexperienced defense.

**Coaches on the Hot Seat:** It looks like **Virginia's Mike London, Miami's Al Golden, Syracuse's Scott Shafer,** and **North Carolina's Larry Fedora** will all be fighting for their jobs this season.

## 2015 Projected Standings for the ACC:

| Atlantic Division: | Coastal Division: |
| --- | --- |
| 1. Florida State | 1. Georgia Tech |
| 2. Clemson | 2. Pittsburgh |
| 3. NC State | 3. Virginia Tech |
| 4. Louisville | 4. North Carolina |
| 5. Boston College | 5. Duke |
| 6. Wake Forest | 6. Miami (FL) |
| 7. Syracuse | 7. Virginia |

# Ranking the ACC's Coaches:

1. **Jimbo Fisher** – Florida State (58-11 in 5 seasons)
2. **Frank Beamer** – Virginia Tech (273-138-4 in 34 seasons)
3. **Paul Johnson** – Georgia Tech (165-74 in 18 seasons)
4. **Dabo Swinney** – Clemson (61-26 in 7 seasons)
5. **Bobby Petrino** – Louisville (92-34 in 10 seasons)
6. **David Cutcliffe** – Duke (84-77 in 13 seasons)
7. **Dave Doeren** – NC State (34-18 in 4 seasons)
8. **Pat Narduzzi** – Pittsburgh (First Year Head Coach)
9. **Larry Fedora** – North Carolina (55-36 in 7 seasons)
10. **Steve Addazio** – Boston College (27-23 in 4 seasons)
11. **Al Golden** – Miami (FL) (55-56 in 9 seasons)
12. **Dave Clawson** – Wake Forest (93-90 in 15 seasons)
13. **Mike London** – Virginia (47-43 in 7 seasons)
14. **Scott Shafer** – Syracuse (10-15 in 2 seasons)

# 2014 ACC Coach of the Year:
(Selected by the ACC coaches)
Paul Johnson, Georgia Tech

# 2014 ACC Standings:

| Atlantic Division | (Conference) | (All Games) |
|---|---|---|
| #5 Florida State | 8-0 | 13-1 |
| #15 Clemson | 6-2 | 10-3 |
| #24 Louisville | 5-3 | 9- 4 |
| Boston College | 4–4 | 7–6 |
| NC State | 3–5 | 8–5 |
| Syracuse | 1–7 | 3–9 |
| Wake Forest | 1–7 | 3–9 |
| | | |
| Coastal Division | | |
| #8 Georgia Tech | 6–2 | 11–3 |
| Duke | 5–3 | 9–4 |
| North Carolina | 4–4 | 6–7 |
| Pittsburgh | 4–4 | 6–7 |
| Miami (FL) | 3–5 | 6–7 |
| Virginia Tech | 3–5 | 7–6 |
| Virginia | 3–5 | 5–7 |

*Championship Game*: Florida State 37, Georgia Tech 35

**2014 ACC Bowl Record**: 4-7 (8th place among all 10 conferences)

# Boston College Eagles – Steve Addazio

## Coach Ranking: #52

**Overall Record:** 27-23 in 4 seasons
**Record at Boston College:** 14-12 in 2 seasons
**2014 Results:** 7-6, 4-4 in the ACC (4th in the ACC Atlantic)
**Returning Starters in 2015:** 3 on offense, 6 on defense
**Salary:** $1.75 Million*     **Age:** 56       **Job Security Grade:** A

**COACH'S BIO:**
Steve Addazio grew up in Farmington, Connecticut, and was a four-year starter on the offensive line at Central Connecticut State (FCS) from 1978-1981. He began his coaching career in 1985 as the OL coach under **Paul Pasqualoni** at Western Connecticut State. From 1988-1994, he served as the head coach at Cheshire High School in Connecticut. There, he built a nationally-ranked program that once won 34-straight games and three-straight state championships. He rejoined the college coaching ranks as Pasqualoni's OL coach at Syracuse from 1995-1998. He then served under **Bob Davie** at Notre Dame from 1999-2001 before joining **Gerry DiNardo**'s staff at Indiana, where he worked his way up to offensive coordinator in 2004. In 2005, he was hired by **Urban Meyer** to coach the OL at Florida and was promoted to assistant head coach and OC in 2009. Addazio was hired as Temple's head coach in 2011 and spent two seasons there before accepting the job at Boston College. He inherited a BC team that had gone 2-10 the year before he was hired.

**2014 REVIEW:**
The 2014 season was supposed to be a major rebuilding year for the Eagles. They had just nine returning starters and had to replace Heisman Trophy finalist Andre Williams at RB and four-year starter Chase Rettig at QB. Instead, Addazio led Boston College to its second-straight bowl game while knocking off No. 9 USC and falling just short of upset wins against Clemson and Florida State.

**2014 RESULTS:   7-6 (4-4 in the ACC)**        **Final Ranking: NR**

| | | |
|---|---|---|
| at Massachusetts | W 30–7 | (30,479) |
| Pittsburgh | L 20–30 | (30,083) |
| #9 USC | W 37–31 | (41,632) |
| Maine | W 40–10 | (28,676) |
| Colorado State | L 21–24 | (33,632) |
| at NC State | W 30–14 | (49,125) |
| #24 Clemson | L 13–17 | (42,038) |
| at Wake Forest | W 23–17 | (26,439) |
| at Virginia Tech | W 33–31 | (55,729) |
| Louisville | L 19–38 | (33,565) |
| at #1 Florida State | L 17–20 | (82,300) |
| Syracuse | W 28–7 | (30,267) |
| vs. Penn State (Pinstripe Bowl) | L 30–31 OT | (49,012) |

**OFFENSE:**

Addazio and his staff entered 2014 with major issues on the offensive side of the ball. They had to not only replace a four-year starter at QB and a 2,000-yard rusher at RB, but six other starters as well. Addazio and second-year offensive coordinator **Ryan Day** responded by implementing the spread-option offense and relying on dual-threat QB **Tyler Murphy** to rack up rushing yards out of the pistol and shotgun formations. The plan worked brilliantly and the Eagles ran for more than 3,300 yards, which ranked them No. 15 in the nation in rushing. Though the BC passing attack finished last in the ACC, the spread option scored enough points to get this team into a bowl game. This year, the Eagles will once again be welcoming many new faces. For the second year in a row, Addazio will have to replace eight offensive starters, including his QB. On top of that, OC Ryan Day has left to take a job as QB coach for the Philadelphia Eagles. The new OC is **Todd Fitch**, who was the WR coach and passing game coordinator for BC the previous two seasons. Fitch previously served as an OC for **Skip Holtz** at Connecticut, East Carolina, and South Florida. The Eagles are expected to continue running the spread-option offense, but it will be tough to match last season's rushing numbers while replacing their *entire* offensive line.

**DEFENSE:**

The Boston College defense stepped up big last season. In 2013, this unit ranked dead last in the ACC in total defense. Last year, the Eagles climbed to No. 3 in the conference. With six returning starters, the defense should be the strength of this year's team. Addazio's defensive coordinator is **Don Brown**. Entering his third year at BC, Brown has a long and distinguished coaching resume. As a head coach, he built UMass into an FCS national power in the mid-2000s. Before arriving at Boston College, Brown turned Connecticut into a Top 20 defense. Based out of the 4-3, Brown runs an attacking defense that likes to blitz and is particularly stout against the run. Last year's squad was the nation's No. 2 defense in rushing yards allowed, behind only Michigan State.

**RECRUITING:**

Boston College's 2014 recruiting class, which relied heavily on the New England region, was ranked No. 12 in the ACC and No. 60 nationally. Though the overall class ranking wasn't impressive, **Elijah Robinson**, a dual-threat QB out of New Jersey, enrolled in the spring and he has the talent to compete for the starting QB spot this fall.

**RUMOR MILL:**

Addazio, who was Florida's OC under **Urban Meyer**, was rumored to be a candidate for the open Florida job that went to **Jim McElwain**. He was also mentioned as a candidate for the Michigan job that went to **Jim Harbaugh**. In December, Boston College responded by giving Addazio a six-year contract extension that will now run through the 2020 season.

**2015 OUTLOOK:**

**Sept. 5**   **Maine Black Bears** – The Eagles will open the season with back-to-back FCS opponents. BC beat Maine by 30 last year and the Black Bears finished the season at 5-6.

**Sept. 12**   **Howard Bison** – This FCS team also won just five games last year. Addazio is 4-0 against FCS schools and should be 6-0 after this game.

**Sept. 18**   **Florida State Seminoles** – Last year, Florida State kicked a field goal in the final seconds to beat BC. It's worth noting that the Eagles upset No. 9 USC in their third of the year game last season.

**Sept. 26**   **Northern Illinois Huskies** – Boston College is 13-1 against the MAC. The lone loss occurred back in 1966.

**Oct. 3**   **at Duke Blue Devils** – The last time these teams played (2011), Duke won 20-19.

**Oct. 10**   **Wake Forest Demon Deacons** – Addazio is 2-0 against Wake Forest.

**Oct. 17**   **at Clemson Tigers** – BC gave up a fourth-quarter lead in last year's loss to Clemson. Addazio is still looking for his first win against the Tigers.

**Oct. 24**   **at Louisville Cardinals** – These two teams are tied for the fewest returning starters in the ACC with just nine, but by this point in the season that should no longer be such a big factor.

**Oct. 31**   **Virginia Tech Hokies** – Addazio is 2-0 against the Hokies, but this year's Virginia Tech team should be much stronger.

**Nov. 7**   **NC State Wolfpack** – The Eagles haven't lost to NC State since Addazio was hired. Both these programs are on the rise and trying to break into the upper level of the Atlantic Division. That makes this a *MUST-WIN* game for BC.

**Nov. 21**   **vs. Notre Dame Fighting Irish (in Boston)** – Notre Dame head coach Brian Kelly grew up in Boston and Addazio coached on ND's staff from 1999-2001. This game will be played at Fenway Park.

**Nov. 28**   **at Syracuse Orange** – Addazio is 1-2 against Syracuse, which includes a loss while he was at Temple.

**BOTTOM LINE:**
Boston College was 15 points away from winning 11 games last year. Of course, losses are losses – no matter how close – and the Eagles finished just above .500 for the second-consecutive season. With an offense full of new faces, it'll be tough for BC to take the next step and win eight games. But with another strong defense expected, 2015 could be a lot like 2014 and the success of this season will depend on how the Eagles finish out close games.

## Steve Addazio's Year-by-Year Coaching Record:

### Temple: 13-11 (7-8 in the MAC and the Big East)
2011   9–4 (5–3)          **Final Ranking: NR**
       Beat Wyoming 37-15 in the New Mexico Bowl.
2012   4–7 (2–5)          **Final Ranking: NR**
       Temple joins the Big East.

### Boston College: 14-12 (8-8 in the ACC)
2013   7–6 (4–4)          **Final Ranking: NR**
       Lost to Arizona 19-42 in the AdvoCare V100 Bowl.
2014   7–6 (4–4)          **Final Ranking: NR**
       Lost to Penn State 30-31 in OT in the Pinstripe Bowl.

# Clemson Tigers – Dabo Swinney

## Coach Ranking: #22

**Overall Record:** 61-26 in 7 seasons
**Record at Clemson:** 61-26 in 7 seasons
**2014 Results:** 10-3, 6-2 in the ACC (2nd in the ACC Atlantic)
**Returning Starters in 2015:** 7 on offense (including QB), 3 on defense
**Salary:** $3.2 Million      **Age:** 45      **Job Security Grade:** A

COACH'S BIO:

Dabo Swinney grew up in the Birmingham suburb of Pelham, Alabama. In 1989, he walked on as a WR at Alabama. He eventually earned a scholarship and lettered for three years (1990-1992) under **Gene Stallings**. Swinney was a member of the 1992 National Championship team and he was named to the Academic All-SEC team twice. Swinney joined Stallings' coaching staff as a graduate assistant in 1993 and was promoted to WR/TE coach in 1996. He kept that position under **Mike Dubose** from 1997-2000. Dubose's entire Alabama staff was fired after the 2000 season and Swinney spent the next two years working in the real estate business. He returned to coaching in 2003 when his former Alabama position coach, **Tommy Bowden**, hired him to be Clemson's WR coach. In 2008, Bowden resigned six games into the season and Swinney was named interim head coach. After leading the Tigers to three-straight wins to close out the regular season, Swinney was formally named Clemson's head coach in December of 2008. In seven seasons, he's led the Tigers to three division titles and one ACC championship.

2014 REVIEW:

The 2014 season was supposed to be a "rebuilding year" for Clemson as Swinney had to replace several key players. Though the Tigers went 0-3 against ranked opponents, they did hit the 10-win mark and beat archrival South Carolina for the first time since 2008. Winning 10 games during a "rebuilding year" is a good sign that Swinney is creating an elite-level program at Clemson.

| 2014 RESULTS: 10-3 (6-2 in the ACC) | Final Ranking: #15 | |
|---|---|---|
| at #12 Georgia | L 21–45 | (92,746) |
| South Carolina State | W 73-7 | (81,672) |
| at #1 Florida State | L 26–23 OT | (82,316) |
| North Carolina | W 50–35 | (79,155) |
| NC State | W 41–0 | (78,459) |
| Louisville | W 23–17 | (81,500) |
| at Boston College | W 17–13 | (42,038) |
| Syracuse | W 16–6 | (80,031) |
| at Wake Forest | W 34–20 | (28,846) |
| at #24 Georgia Tech | L 6–28 | (49,378) |
| Georgia State | W 28–0 | (77,693) |
| South Carolina | W 35–17 | (82,720) |
| vs. Oklahoma (Russell Athletic Bowl) | W 40–6 | (40,071) |

## OFFENSE:

Clemson's offense will have seven starters back in 2015, including dual-threat QB **Deshaun Watson** (who will be returning from the torn ACL he suffered as a true freshman last year). What the Tigers won't have back is their offensive coordinator, **Chad Morris**. After four seasons running Clemson's offense, Morris will be the new head coach at SMU. This is a big loss for the Tigers, but Morris was bound to become a head coach at some point. Clemson tried hard to keep him. In 2014, Morris made $1.3 million, which tied him with LSU's **Cam Cameron** as the highest-paid OC in college football. Morris ran a **Gus Malzahn**-inspired up-tempo, balanced spread attack while at Clemson and despite having to "rebuild" the Tiger offense last year, he still racked up more than 400 yards a game. To fill the big shoes left by Morris' departure, Swinney will be using two co-OCs in 2015. **Jeff Scott** (last year's WR coach) and **Tony Elliott** (last year's RB coach) will continue to run the same offense installed by Morris, though they do plan to pare down the playbook a bit and focus on perfecting the essential components of this system. With a more experienced unit and a healthy Watson at QB, this offense should be one of the ACC's best as long as the transition to new OCs goes smoothly.

## DEFENSE:

**Brent Venables** has established himself as one of the nation's top defensive coordinators. After 13 seasons as Oklahoma's co-DC and then sole DC, Venables arrived at Clemson in 2012. He inherited a defense that ranked near the back of the ACC and in three years built it into one of the nation's best. In 2014, Clemson had the nation's No. 1 defense in yards allowed. Venables' base defense is a 4-3, but he designates a "Nickel-Sam" LB who can quickly shift from a Sam LB role to a Nickel DB role based on the defense called and the offensive alignment. This allows the defense to quickly transition from a 4-3 to a 4-2-5 at any moment during the game. With just three starters returning, Venables will face a big challenge in 2015, but he's the type of DC who has proven he can reload fast and Clemson has stockpiled plenty of top-level talent to work with.

## RECRUITING:

Swinney's reputation as a top recruiter is one of the reasons he was promoted to interim head coach back in 2008. Starting with Swinney at the top and trickling down the chain of command, Clemson's coaches have established themselves as some of the best recruiters in the nation and the 2015 class was their best class yet. The Tigers' 2015 recruiting class was ranked No. 8 nationally and second only to Florida State in the ACC. A school-record 15 of Clemson's 25 signees got an early start by enrolling in the spring.

## RUMOR MILL:

When Florida fired **Will Muschamp** during the season last year, rumors quickly swirled that Swinney was a target for the job and that the interest was mutual. Swinney shot down the rumors and reiterated that he's firmly committed to Clemson. After the 2014 season, Clemson gave Swinney an eight-year contract extension and a raise of $1.1 million. His contract currently runs through the 2021 season.

**2015 OUTLOOK:**

**Sept. 5**     **Wofford Terriers** – The Tigers will ease into the season with an in-state FCS opponent. Swinney is 7-0 in games against South Carolina-based FCS schools and he beat Wofford 35-27 in 2011.

**Sept. 12**     **Appalachian State Mountaineers** – Last year was Appalachian State's first season as an FBS school. The Mountaineers went 7-5. Clemson is 8-0 all-time against teams from the Sun Belt Conference.

**Sept. 17**     **at Louisville Cardinals** – The Tigers will have just five days to turn around and open ACC play on the road on a Thursday night. This won't be an easy task.

**Oct. 3**     **Notre Dame Fighting Irish** – This will be just the third meeting ever between these two schools and it should make for an electric environment in Death Valley. Notre Dame is one of the most experienced teams in the nation with 19 starters returning in 2015.

**Oct. 10**     **Georgia Tech Yellow Jackets** – Though the Tigers have gone 2-1 against Georgia Tech's flexbone offense since Venables arrived as DC, the Yellow Jackets won this matchup convincingly last year. Swinney is 3-5 against Paul Johnson.

**Oct. 17**     **Boston College Eagles** – Swinney is 6-1 against Boston College and he's never lost to the Eagles at home.

**Oct. 24**     **at Miami Hurricanes** – Clemson hasn't played Miami since 2010. Swinney is 1-1 against the Hurricanes.

**Oct. 31**     **at NC State Wolfpack** – Swinney has won three straight against NC State by a combined score of 129-62.

**Nov. 7**     **Florida State Seminoles** – Florida State has defeated Clemson each of the last three years and it has cost the Tigers the Atlantic Division title all three seasons. Swinney has got to find a way to knock off the current kings of the ACC. If the Tigers want to return to the ACC Championship, they *MUST WIN* this game.

**Nov. 14**     **at Syracuse Orange** – Clemson is 2-0 against Syracuse since the Orange joined the ACC. The last time the Tigers traveled to Syracuse, they won 49-14 in 2013.

**Nov. 21**     **Wake Forest Demon Deacons** – Swinney is a perfect 6-0 against this Atlantic Division foe.

**Nov. 28**     **at South Carolina Gamecocks** – Last year's win over South Carolina broke Swinney's five-game losing streak against this in-state rival. Clemson needs to build on that momentum.

**BOTTOM LINE:**
The two biggest issues facing Clemson in 2015 will be how the offense handles the departure of OC Chad Morris and how quickly DC Brent Venables can get his inexperienced defense rolling. The schedule is set up to allow the Tigers to ease into the season with its first two games, but the honeymoon will end quickly after that. Though Clemson looks to be a year or two away from having a CFP-caliber season, this team still has the talent to compete for an ACC crown in 2015.

## Dabo Swinney's Year-by-Year Coaching Record:

<u>Clemson: 61-26 (39-14 in the ACC)</u>

2008   **4–3 (3–2)**          **Final Ranking: NR**
Terry Bowden resigned after six games and Swinney was named interim head coach.
Swinney was formally named head coach prior to the bowl game.
Lost to Nebraska 21-26 in the Gator Bowl.

2009   **9–5 (6–2)**          **Final Ranking: #24**
ACC Atlantic Division Champions.
Lost to #12 Georgia Tech 34-39 in the ACC Championship Game.
Beat Kentucky 21-13 in the Music City Bowl.

2010   **6–7 (4–4)**          **Final Ranking: NR**
Lost to South Florida 26-31 in the Meineke Car Care Bowl.

2011   **10–4 (6–2)**          **Final Ranking: #22**
ACC Champions.
Swinney named Bobby Dodd National Coach of the Year.
Beat #5 Virginia Tech 38-10 in the ACC Championship Game.
Lost to #23 West Virginia 33-70 in the Orange Bowl.

2012   **11–2 (7–1)**          **Final Ranking: #9**
ACC Atlantic Division Co-Champions.
Beat #9 LSU 25-24 in the Chick-fil-A Bowl.

2013   **11–2 (7–1)**          **Final Ranking: #7**
Beat #7 Ohio State 40-35 in the Orange Bowl.

2014   **10–3 (6–2)**          **Final Ranking: #15**
Beat Oklahoma 40-6 in the Russell Athletic Bowl.

# Florida State Seminoles – Jimbo Fisher

## Coach Ranking: #3

**Overall Record:** 58-11 in 5 seasons
**Record at Florida State:** 58-11 in 5 seasons
**2014 Results:** 13-1, 8-0 in the ACC (ACC Champions)
**Returning Starters in 2015:** 4 on offense, 7 on defense
**Salary:** $5 Million        **Age:** 49        **Job Security Grade:** A

COACH'S BIO:
Jimbo Fisher grew up in West Virginia and played QB for three seasons at Salem College (Division II). After being named an All-American as a junior, Fisher followed his head coach, **Terry Bowden**, to Division III Samford College for his senior season in 1987. Fisher was named the Division III Player of the Year. After one season in the Arena League, Fisher joined Bowden's Samford coaching staff as a graduate assistant in 1989. He was promoted to offensive coordinator in 1991 and followed Bowden to Auburn in 1993, where he would serve as the QB coach through 1998. Fisher served as **Rick Minter**'s OC at Cincinnati in 1999 and then as **Nick Saban**'s OC at LSU from 2000-2004. When Saban left for the NFL, Fisher stayed at LSU and served as **Les Miles**' OC for two more seasons. From 2007-2009, Fisher was **Bobby Bowden**'s OC at Florida State and in 2010, he took over as head coach for the Seminoles. In five seasons as head coach, he has won three ACC titles and a National Championship.

2014 REVIEW:
After winning the National Championship in 2013 and having the Heisman Trophy winner return as QB, anything less than a national title repeat in 2014 was going to be a disappointment for the Seminoles. Despite several close calls and off-the-field distractions, Florida State racked up 13-straight wins before falling to Oregon in the CFP semifinals.

| 2014 RESULTS:   13-1 (8-0 in the ACC) | Final Ranking: #5 | |
|---|---|---|
| vs. Oklahoma State (in Arlington, Texas) | W 37–31 | (61,521) |
| The Citadel | W 37–12 | (81,294) |
| #22 Clemson | W 23–17 OT | (82,316) |
| at NC State | W 56–41 | (57,583) |
| Wake Forest | W 43–3 | (82,327) |
| at Syracuse | W 38–20 | (43,295) |
| #5 Notre Dame | W 31–27 | (82,431) |
| at Louisville | W 42–31 | (55,414) |
| Virginia | W 34–20 | (82,325) |
| at Miami (FL) | W 30–26 | (76,530) |
| Boston College | W 20–17 | (82,300) |
| Florida | W 24–19 | (82,485) |
| vs. #12 Georgia Tech (ACC Championship) | W 37–35 | (64,808) |
| vs. #3 Oregon (CFP Semifinal) | L 20–59 | (91,322) |

## OFFENSE:

After two years as a starter and losing just one game during that stretch, Heisman Trophy-winning QB **Jameis Winston** left college early for the NFL. The biggest question facing the Florida State offense heading into 2015 is how they'll replace one of the most prolific QBs in school history. Talented Notre Dame graduate transfer **Everett Golson** might be the answer, but he'll walk into a very difficult job. Under Jimbo Fisher (who handles Florida State's play-calling himself), the Seminoles run a multiple-set pro-style offense that has a reputation for being one of the most complicated systems in the nation. Golson transferred in May, which means he'll only have a few months to learn Fisher's complex offense. To make matters even more difficult, the Seminoles must replace four starters on the offensive line – all four of whom were named to the All-ACC team last season. There's no denying that Fisher is one of the top offensive minds in the game, but he'll be tackling a major rebuilding task with this offense in 2015.

## DEFENSE:

**Mark Stoops** served as Florida State's defensive coordinator from 2010-2012 and produced one of the top defenses in the country. In 2011 and 2012, Florida State led the ACC in points allowed. Stoops' 2012 squad also finished No. 2 in the nation in total defense. Stoops left to become the head coach at Kentucky in 2013 and his replacement was **Jeremy Pruitt**, who had been **Nick Saban**'s DB coach at Alabama. Picking up right where Stoops left off, Pruitt's 2013 defense was one of college football's best, finishing the season ranked No. 1 in the nation in points allowed. Georgia convinced Pruitt to take over its defense in 2014 and that meant Fisher had to find a new DC for the third-straight year. This time, Fisher hired from within and promoted **Charles Kelly** from LB coach and special teams coordinator to DC. Kelly didn't make any major changes to the 3-4/4-3 blend the Seminoles ran under Pruitt, but the FSU defense fell from No. 1 in the ACC to No. 11 in total defense last year. The Seminoles struggled badly in the postseason as they gave up 465 yards to Georgia Tech in the ACC Championship Game and 639 yards to Oregon in the CFP semifinals. New to the staff in 2015 is DE/OLB coach **Brad Lawing**, who spent the last two years as **Will Muschamp**'s assistant head coach and DL coach at Florida.

## RECRUITING:

For the sixth year in a row, Fisher signed the ACC's top-rated recruiting class. The 2015 class included four five-star prospects and was ranked No. 3 nationally. Fisher also reeled in the nation's most-coveted graduate transfer in former Notre Dame QB Everett Golson, who chose Florida State over Alabama, Florida, Georgia, and LSU.

## RUMOR MILL:

Fisher was rumored to be a top target for the Texas job after the 2013 season and this past offseason, Fisher acknowledged that he was contacted by an NFL team to gauge his interest in making a move to the pros. In December, Florida State gave Fisher an eight-year contract extension that will run through the 2022 season. Fisher will make a minimum of $5 million in 2015 and receive a guaranteed raise of $100,000 each successive year. With this new contract, Fisher is now one of the highest paid coaches in the country.

**2015 OUTLOOK:**

**Sept. 5**    **Texas State Bobcats** – This Sun Belt Conference team went 7-5 last season. The Bobcats are coached by former TCU, Alabama, and Texas A&M coach Dennis Franchione.

**Sept. 12**    **South Florida Bulls** – These Florida schools have met just twice before; a USF win in 2009 and a Florida State win, under Fisher, in 2012.

**Sept. 18**    **at Boston College Eagles** – Florida State will open ACC play on a Friday night against BC. Fisher is 5-0 against the Eagles.

**Oct. 3**    **at Wake Forest Demon Deacons** – The Seminoles are 26-6-1 against Wake Forest and Fisher is 4-1 in this series.

**Oct. 10**    **Miami Hurricanes** – Since Fisher became Florida State's head coach, the Seminoles are a perfect 5-0 in this heated rivalry.

**Oct. 17**    **Louisville Cardinals** Florida State is 13-2 all-time against Louisville. The Cardinals have just nine returning starters in 2015, tied with Boston College for the fewest in the ACC.

**Oct. 24**    **at Georgia Tech Yellow Jackets** – This will be a rematch of last year's ACC Championship Game and these teams met in the 2012 ACC Championship as well. Fisher led the Seminoles to close victories in both of those previous matchups.

**Oct. 31**    **Syracuse Orange** – Florida State has defeated Syracuse the previous two seasons by a combined score of 97-23.

**Nov. 7**    **at Clemson Tigers** – The Seminoles escaped with an OT victory in this game last year and the 2015 matchup could decide who wins the Atlantic Division. Fisher is 4-1 against Clemson coach Dabo Swinney. If Florida State wants to win its fourth-straight ACC title, it *MUST WIN* this road game.

**Nov. 14**    **NC State Wolfpack** – The Seminoles have won both games against NC State since Dave Doeren took over the program in 2013. Before those two wins, Fisher was 1-2 against the Wolfpack.

**Nov. 21**    **Chattanooga Mocs** – Florida State is following the lead of several SEC powers by scheduling an FCS opponent in November. Chattanooga went 10-4 last year and finished No. 8 in the FCS rankings.

**Nov. 28**    **at Florida Gators** – Fisher is 4-1 against this in-state rival and now that Florida has a new head coach in Jim McElwain, it's important for Fisher to keep dominating this rivalry.

**BOTTOM LINE:**
Florida State ended the 2014 season with its first loss since November of 2012. With the 29-game winning streak snapped and lots of holes to fill this season, 2015 may be the biggest test of Fisher's short career as a head coach. The Seminoles have recruited plenty of elite-level talent and until another team proves it can stop Florida State's dominance of the ACC, it would be unwise to bet against a fourth-straight conference championship for Fisher.

## Jimbo Fisher's Year-by-Year Coaching Record:

### Florida State: 58-11 (34-6 in the ACC)
2010    10–4 (6–2)              **Final Ranking: #16**
ACC Atlantic Division Champions.
Lost to #12 Virginia Tech 33-44 in the ACC Championship Game.
Beat #19 South Carolina 26-17 in the Chick-fil-A Bowl.
2011    9–4 (5–3)              **Final Ranking: #23**
Beat Notre Dame 18-14 in the Champs Sports Bowl.
2012    12–2 (7–1)              **Final Ranking: #8**
ACC Champions.
Beat Georgia Tech 21-15 in the ACC Championship Game.
Beat #16 Northern Illinois 31-10 in the Orange Bowl.
2013    14–0 (8–0)              **Final Ranking: #1**
National Champions.
ACC Champions.
Beat #20 Duke 45-7 in the ACC Championship Game.
Beat #2 Auburn 34-31 in the BCS National Championship Game.
2014    13–1 (8–0)              **Final Ranking: #5**
ACC Champions.
Beat #12 Georgia Tech 37-35 in the ACC Championship Game.
Lost to #3 Oregon 20-59 in the CFP Semifinal Game.

# Louisville Cardinals – Bobby Petrino

## Coach Ranking: #30

**Overall Record:** 92-34 in 10 seasons, 3-10 in 1 NFL season
**Record at Louisville:** 50-13 in 5 seasons
**2014 Results:** 9-4, 5-3 in the ACC (3rd in the ACC Atlantic)
**Returning Starters in 2015:** 5 on offense (including QB), 4 on defense
**Salary:** $3 Million        **Age:** 54        **Job Security Grade:** A

**COACH'S BIO:**
Bobby Petrino grew up in Helena, Montana, and played QB for his hometown college, Carroll (NAIA), from 1980-1982. His father, **Bob Petrino, Sr.**, was Carroll's head coach at the time. After spending 1983 as a graduate assistant on his father's staff at Carroll, Petrino began a college coaching career that would include stops under **Mike Price** at Weber State (Division 1-AA), **John L. Smith** at Idaho, Utah State, and Louisville, **Bruce Snyder** at Arizona State, **Chris Ault** at Nevada, and **Tommy Tuberville** at Auburn. He also spent four years as the QB coach and then offensive coordinator under **Tom Coughlin** with the NFL's Jacksonville Jaguars. In 2003, Petrino landed his first head coaching job at Louisville. In four seasons, he won two conference titles. Petrino then left for the NFL. He didn't survive his first season with the Atlanta Falcons and resigned after a 3-10 start. He was hired by Arkansas in 2008 and after guiding the Razorbacks to a Top 5 finish in 2011, he was fired following an embarrassing off-the-field incident. Petrino returned to coaching in 2013 with a one-year stint at Western Kentucky. He was rehired by Louisville in 2014 to replace **Charlie Strong**, who left to accept the Texas job.

**2014 REVIEW:**
It was a season of change for Louisville in 2014. The Cardinals debuted in the ACC with a new coach and having to replace **Teddy Bridgewater** at QB. Louisville handled all the change about as well as can be expected and finished in the Top 25.

| 2014 RESULTS:   9-4 (5-3 in the ACC) | Final Ranking: #24 | |
|---|---|---|
| Miami (FL) | W 31–13 | (55,428) |
| Murray State | W 66–21 | (50,179) |
| at Virginia | L 21–23 | (34,816) |
| at FIU | W 34–3 | (10,826) |
| Wake Forest | W 20–10 | (51,463) |
| at Syracuse | W 28–6 | (37,569) |
| at Clemson | L 17–23 | (81,500) |
| NC State | W 30–12 | (50,227) |
| #2 Florida State | L 31–42 | (55,414) |
| at Boston College | W 38–19 | (33,565) |
| at Notre Dame | W 31–28 | (80,795) |
| Kentucky | W 44–40 | (55,118) |
| vs. #13 Georgia (Belk Bowl) | L 14–37 | (45,671) |

## OFFENSE:

Petrino has a reputation for installing explosive offenses that throw the ball down the field often. During his four seasons at Arkansas, he threw the ball more than he ran it and the result was the SEC's top offense in scoring, passing, and total yards during his final season there (2011). However, Petrino had to alter his pass-first philosophy at Louisville last year. Recognizing that the team's strength was on defense and that the QB spot was unstable, Petrino took a more conservative approach and ran the ball 54% of the time in 2014. To get back to the days of running his big-play offense, Petrino must find a QB he can rely on. Three different players started at QB last season and the position isn't any more settled heading into 2015. The Cardinals must also replace three All-ACC offensive linemen. What this all means is that it may be at least another year before the aggressive style of offense Petrino is known for returns to Louisville. Returning for his second season as the offensive coordinator will be **Garrick McGee**, who was Petrino's OC at Arkansas before spending two years as UAB's head coach.

## DEFENSE:

Louisville paid big bucks to hire **Todd Grantham** away from Georgia to become the Cardinals' defensive coordinator last year. His $1 million salary made him the sixth-highest-paid assistant coach in all of college football in 2014. Grantham earned his pay as he built a defense that finished the year ranked No. 6 in the nation in yards allowed. The Oakland Raiders tried to hire Grantham away from Louisville after the season, but he decided to stay with the Cardinals. Louisville responded by reworking Grantham's current contract. He'll now earn as much as $1.4 million annually for the remainder of his four-year contract. Grantham runs a 3-4 base defense and uses a fiery style to motivate his team. He'll face a big challenge this season as he must replace seven starters on defense. He has particularly big holes to fill on the defensive line and in the secondary, but blue-chip transfers from Georgia, **Shaq Wiggins** and **Josh Harvey-Clemons,** will help immediately replenish the secondary.

## RECRUITING:

Petrino's 2015 recruiting class was ranked No. 7 in the ACC and No. 32 in the nation. The highest-rated signee was DE **Devonte Fields**. After a spectacular 2013 season at TCU, Fields was voted the Big 12's preseason Defensive Player of the Year heading into 2014, but he was dismissed by the school following allegations of domestic violence. He spent last year in junior college and was rated the No. 4 juco prospect in the nation. Petrino defended his signing of Fields by stating, "I believe in second chances and sometimes third chances. … You do your research, and you try to make sure that if you have an opportunity to give a young man a second chance, I believe that you should do it." Petrino also faced controversy when he pulled a prospect's scholarship offer two days before Signing Day. The prospect's high school coach said Petrino is now banned from recruiting at his school.

## RUMOR MILL:

In August before the 2014 season kicked off, *Sports Illustrated* reported that there was "serious friction" between Petrino and DC Todd Grantham. Both coaches laughed off the report and denied they were feuding.

**2015 OUTLOOK:**

**Sept. 5**    **vs. Auburn Tigers (in Atlanta)** – The Cardinals will open the season with a major test against Auburn. These coaching staffs should be familiar with each other due to Petrino's experience at Arkansas and DC Grantham's at Georgia. Louisville is 5-1 in its last six games against SEC schools. The one loss occurred in last year's bowl game against Georgia.

**Sept. 12**    **Houston Cougars** – This won't be an easy nonconference game for Louisville. Houston has a new head coach in former Ohio State OC Tom Herman.

**Sept. 17**    **Clemson Tigers** – It'll be a five-day turnaround for both Louisville and Clemson when they open up ACC play on a Thursday night. If the Cardinals want to compete for the Atlantic Division title, they must start conference play off with a win at home. That makes this a *MUST-WIN* game for Petrino.

**Sept. 26**    **Samford Bulldogs** – Samford is an FCS school that went 7-4 last year. Petrino is 6-0 all-time against FCS schools.

**Oct. 3**    **at NC State Wolfpack** – Louisville is 4-1 all-time against the Wolfpack.

**Oct. 17**    **at Florida State Seminoles** – The Cardinals are 2-13 all-time against the Seminoles. Petrino needs to reverse that trend fast if the Cardinals hope to compete for Atlantic Division titles.

**Oct. 24**    **Boston College Eagles** – Last year's matchup marked the first time these schools had played each other since 1998. Louisville holds a 4-3 edge in the all-time series.

**Oct. 30**    **at Wake Forest Demon Deacons** – It will be another short week for the Cardinals as they'll have to play this Friday-night game six days after the BC game. Petrino is 2-0 against Wake Forest, including his 2007 Orange Bowl victory over the Demon Deacons.

**Nov. 7**    **Syracuse Orange** – Dating back to his first stint at Louisville, Petrino is 4-0 against the Orange.

**Nov. 14**    **Virginia Cavaliers** – Four turnovers contributed to last year's loss to Virginia, a loss that ended up costing Louisville a 10-win season.

**Nov. 21**    **at Pittsburgh Panthers** – This will be another Big East reunion for Louisville. This series is tied at 8-8 and Petrino went 2-0 against the Panthers during his first tenure at Louisville.

**Nov. 28**    **at Kentucky Wildcats** –A pregame scuffle involving players *and* coaches last year shows just how heated this rivalry has gotten. Louisville has now won four in a row in this series, but Kentucky leads the all-time series 14-13. With Mark Stoops building up his program, it's important for Petrino to extend the winning streak in this in-state battle.

**BOTTOM LINE:**

Louisville has just nine returning starters, which ties them with Boston College for the fewest in the ACC. Unfortunately for the Cardinals, they won't have the luxury of easing into the season with a soft early schedule. On paper, it looks like 2015 may be a "rebuilding year," but there's enough talent here for Petrino to sneak up on some ACC opponents and put Louisville in the Atlantic Division title race.

## Bobby Petrino's Year-by-Year Coaching Record:

### Louisville: 41-9 (24-6 in Conference USA and the Big East)
2003   9–4 (5–3)          Final Ranking: NR
          Lost to #14 Miami (OH) 28-49 in the GMAC Bowl.
2004   11–1 (8–0)        Final Ranking: #6
          C-USA Champions.
          Beat #10 Boise State 44-40 in the Liberty Bowl.
2005   9–3 (5–2)          Final Ranking: #19
          Louisville joins the Big East.
          Lost to #12 Virginia Tech 24-35 in the Gator Bowl.
2006   12–1 (6–1)        Final Ranking: #5
          Big East Champions.
          Beat #15 Wake Forest 24-13 in the Orange Bowl.

### Atlanta Falcons: 3-10 (0-0 in the NFL Playoffs)
2007   3-10 (0-0)        4th in the NFC South
          Petrino resigned with three games left on the schedule.

### Arkansas: 34-17 (17-15 in the SEC)
2008   5–7 (2–6)          Final Ranking: NR
2009   8–5 (3–5)          Final Ranking: NR
          Beat East Carolina 20-17 in OT in the Liberty Bowl.
2010   10–3 (6–2)        Final Ranking: #12
          Lost to #6 Ohio State 26-31 in the Sugar Bowl.
2011   11–2 (6–2)        Final Ranking: #5
          Beat #11 Kansas State 29-16 in the Cotton Bowl.

### Western Kentucky: 8-4 (4-3 in the Sun Belt)
2013   8-4 (4-3)          Final Ranking: NR

### Louisville: 9-4 (5-3 in the ACC)
2014   9–4 (5–3)          Final Ranking: #24
          Lost to #13 Georgia in the Belk Bowl.

# NC State Wolfpack – Dave Doeren
## Coach Ranking: #42

**Overall Record:** 34-18 in 4 seasons
**Record at NC State:** 11-14 in 2 seasons
**2014 Results:** 8-5, 3-5 in the ACC (5th in the ACC Atlantic)
**Returning Starters in 2015:** 7 on offense (including QB), 8 on defense
**Salary:** $2.2 Million      **Age:** 43      **Job Security Grade:** A

COACH'S BIO:
Dave Doeren grew up in the Kansas City suburb of Shawnee, Kansas, where he played football and golf at Bishop Miege High School. In college, he played LB at Drake (FCS) and was named an Academic All-American in 1993. After one year as an assistant high school coach in Kansas, Doeren returned to Drake as the LB coach. In 1997, he was promoted to defensive coordinator. From 1998-1999, he served as a graduate assistant on **Paul Hackett's** staff at USC and then spent two years coaching DBs at Montana. Doeren was hired by **Mark Mangino** to be the LB coach and recruiting coordinator at Kansas in 2002 and he was promoted to co-DC in 2005. When **Brett Bielema** took over as Wisconsin's head coach in 2006, he hired Doeren to be the Badgers' co-DC. By 2008, Doeren was promoted to the sole DC position. Northern Illinois hired Doeren to be its new head coach in 2011. He won two-straight MAC championships and led the Huskies to an Orange Bowl berth before accepting the NC State job in 2013.

2014 REVIEW:
After a four-game midseason skid pushed NC State's ACC losing streak to 12 games (the most in school history), Doeren righted the ship and led the Wolfpack (the third-youngest team in the nation last year) to victories in four of their final five games. Capping the season off with the school's first bowl victory since 2011 allows Doeren to carry some positive momentum into 2015.

| 2014 RESULTS:   8-5 (3-5 in the ACC) | Final Ranking: NR | |
|---|---|---|
| Georgia Southern | W 24–23 | (54,273) |
| Old Dominion | W 46–34 | (55,390) |
| at South Florida | W 49–17 | (27,269) |
| Presbyterian | W 42–0 | (54,408) |
| #1 Florida State | L 41–56 | (57,583) |
| at Clemson | L 0–41 | (78,459) |
| Boston College | L 14–30 | (49,125) |
| at Louisville | L 12–30 | (50,227) |
| at Syracuse | W 24–17 | (40,787) |
| #24 Georgia Tech | L 23–56 | (54,653) |
| Wake Forest | W 42–13 | (55,353) |
| at North Carolina | W 35–7 | (53,000) |
| vs. UCF (St. Petersburg Bowl) | W 34–27 | (26,675) |

**OFFENSE:**

At Northern Illinois, Doeren ran an offense that he described as a blend between Oregon's and Wisconsin's. He prefers to have a dual-threat QB who can run out of the spread, but he also wants an offense that can line up and run downhill power plays that set up the play-action pass. During his first season at NC State, Doeren had to adjust his preferred offensive style to the personnel, which had been built into a pass-first team by the previous staff. In 2014, the Wolfpack offense looked more like the system Doeren prefers. Junior **Jacoby Brissett** proved he could be a dual-threat QB and racked up 529 rushing yards to go along with his 2,606 passing yards. With Brissett back and six other starters, this offense should only get better in 2015. Doeren's third-year offensive coordinator is **Matt Canada**, who served as Northern Illinois' OC in 2011 and Wisconsin's in 2012. A notable addition to the offensive staff will be **George McDonald** as WR coach. McDonald began last season as Syracuse's OC, but he was demoted midseason when the Orange decided to move the offense away from the up-tempo style McDonald had implemented the previous year.

**DEFENSE:**

Doeren has got to improve NC State's defense if this program is going to take the next step and start competing for Atlantic Division titles. The Wolfpack have finished 13th in the ACC in points allowed each of the past two seasons. **Dave Huxtable** will enter his third season as NC State's defensive coordinator and with eight starters back, this is the year big improvements will be expected. Huxtable has more than three decades of coaching experience and he led the nation's No. 17 defense as the DC at Pitt in 2012. He runs a 4-2-5 hybrid system that requires the nickelback to have many of the same responsibilities a typical outside LB would have, especially against the run.

**RECRUITING:**

Doeren's 2015 recruiting class was NC State's highest-rated class in seven years. It was ranked No. 30 nationally and No. 6 in the ACC. The 23-man class was once again heavy with in-state talent. Signees from the state of North Carolina included two four-star RBs, a four-star offensive tackle, and a four-star DE.

**RUMOR MILL:**

This past offseason, NC State rewarded Doeren with a two-year contract extension and a $400,000-a-year raise. His contract with the Wolfpack now runs through 2019. If Doeren continues on the successful path he's on, expect this young coach to quickly become a top candidate for some big-time job openings.

**NOTEWORTHY:**

The addition of WR coach George McDonald should add a boost to NC State's recruiting efforts. McDonald was named one of the top recruiters in the nation by *Rivals.com* in 2012.

## 2015 OUTLOOK:

**Sept. 5**  **Troy Trojans** – NC State is 3-0 all-time against Sun Belt teams, including last year's one-point win over Georgia Southern.

**Sept. 12**  **Eastern Kentucky Colonels** – Doeren is 4-0 against FCS teams. Eastern Kentucky went 9-4 last year and finished No. 18 in the FCS rankings.

**Sept. 19**  **at Old Dominion Monarchs** – This will be Old Dominion's first home game against a Power 5 school. The Monarchs went 6-6 last season, their first year as an FBS team.

**Sept. 26**  **at South Alabama Jaguars** – The Jaguars have just five returning starters in 2015, tied for the fewest in all of college football. This game should cap another 4-0 nonconference start for NC State.

**Oct. 3**  **Louisville Cardinals** – If NC State is going to surprise the Atlantic Division this season, it needs to get off to a strong start in divisional play. NC State is 1-4 all-time against Louisville.

**Oct. 9**  **at Virginia Tech Hokies** – This Friday-night game is a tough draw from the Coastal Division as the Hokies are expected to be a much better team than they were last year. NC State has lost its last three games to Virginia Tech.

**Oct. 24**  **at Wake Forest Demon Deacons** – The last time Doeren took the Wolfpack to Wake Forest, they left with a 28-13 loss in 2013. He can't let that happen again this season.

**Oct. 31**  **Clemson Tigers** – Clemson has won 10 of the last 11 games in this series.

**Nov. 7**  **at Boston College Eagles** – Doeren is 0-2 against the Eagles and this is a team he needs to regularly beat if he wants NC State to establish itself in the upper half of the division.

**Nov. 14**  **at Florida State Seminoles** – The last time NC State beat Florida State was in 2012, when the Seminoles were ranked No. 3 in the nation.

**Nov. 21**  **Syracuse Orange** – NC State is 7-1 all-time against the Orange. New Wolfpack WR coach George McDonald was Syracuse's OC for the first five games of last season.

**Nov. 28**  **North Carolina Tar Heels** – Last year's convincing win over the Tar Heels broke a two-game losing streak for the Wolfpack in this series. With the recruiting wars for in-state talent getting tighter between these two rivals, it's becoming even more important to own this series. That makes this a *MUST-WIN* game for Doeren.

## BOTTOM LINE:

If you're looking for a dark horse team that might sneak into the Atlantic Division title race earlier than expected, NC State is that team. Doeren is quickly establishing himself as one of the top young coaches in college football and the Wolfpack looks like a team ready to take the next step. A 10-win season is not out of the question for NC State in 2015.

## Dave Doeren's Year-by-Year Coaching Record:

#### Northern Illinois: 23-4 (15-1 in the MAC)
2011    11–3 (7–1)            **Final Ranking: NR**
          MAC Champions.
          Beat Ohio 23-20 in the MAC Championship Game.
          Beat Arkansas State 38-20 in the GoDaddy.com Bowl.
2012    12–1 (8–0)            **Final Ranking: #16**
          MAC Champions.
          Beat #18 Kent State 44-37 in 2OT in the MAC Championship Game.
          Northern Illinois lost to #13 Florida State 10-31 in the Orange Bowl, but Doeren had already left to accept the NC State job.

#### NC State: 11-14 (3-13 in the ACC)
2013    3–9 (0–8)             **Final Ranking: NR**
2014    8–5 (3–5)             **Final Ranking: NR**
          Beat UCF 34-27 in the St. Petersburg Bowl.

# Syracuse Orange – Scott Shafer
## Coach Ranking: #96

**Overall Record:** 10-15 in 2 seasons
**Record at Syracuse:** 10-15 in 2 seasons
**2014 Results:** 3-9, 1-7 in the ACC (T-6th in the ACC Atlantic)
**Returning Starters in 2015:** 8 on offense (including QB), 3 on defense
**Salary:** $1.4 Million*    **Age:** 48    **Job Security Grade:** C

**COACH'S BIO:**
Scott Shafer grew up in the Northeast Ohio town of Painesville and after one year of attending Ohio University, he transferred to Baldwin-Wallace (Division III), where he played QB from 1987-1989. He started coaching as a graduate assistant on **Bill Mallory**'s Indiana staff in 1991. After coaching DBs at Rhode Island from 1993-1995, Shafer joined **Joe Novak**'s staff at Northern Illinois and worked his way up to the defensive coordinator position, which he held from 2000-2003. He spent 2004 as **Ron Turner**'s DB coach at Illinois before serving as **Bill Cubit**'s DC at Western Michigan from 2005-2006. In 2007, **Jim Harbaugh** hired Shafer to be his assistant head coach and DC at Stanford. Shafer then spent one season as **Rich Rodriguez**'s DC at Michigan before being hired by **Doug Marrone** as Syracuse's DC in 2009. When Marrone took the Buffalo Bills job following the 2012 season, Shafer was promoted to head coach.

**2014 REVIEW:**
Coming off of Shafer's 7-5 debut season in 2013 and with an experienced team heading into 2014, there were high hopes for last year's Orange. Instead, injuries and an anemic offense led to an ugly step back for this program.

| 2014 RESULTS:   3-9 (1-7 in the ACC) | Final Ranking: NR | |
|---|---|---|
| #12 (FCS) Villanova | W 27–26 2OT | (41,189) |
| at Central Michigan | W 40–3 | (25,531) |
| Maryland | L 20–34 | (40,511) |
| vs. #8 Notre Dame (in East Rutherford, NJ) | L 15–31 | (76,802) |
| Louisville | L 6–28 | (37,569) |
| #1 Florida State | L 20–38 | (43,295) |
| at Wake Forest | W 30–7 | (25,107) |
| at #20 Clemson | L 6–16 | (80,031) |
| NC State | L 17–24 | (40,787) |
| #22 Duke | L 10–27 | (39,331) |
| at Pittsburgh | L 7–30 | (32,549) |
| at Boston College | L 7–28 | (30,267) |

**OFFENSE:**
Syracuse wanted to continue running an up-tempo offense and further utilize the running ability of dual-threat QB **Terrel Hunt** last season, but things didn't go as planned. Hunt broke his leg in the Louisville game and the offense never regained its rhythm. Offensive coordinator **George McDonald** was demoted after the Louisville game and he was replaced by QB coach **Tim Lester**. With Lester calling the shots, offensive production continued to decline. In the final game of the season against Boston College, Syracuse managed just 136 yards of total offense, which was a fitting end to a season where the Orange ended up ranked No. 121 nationally in scoring offense. Despite expectations that Syracuse would continue running a fast-paced, no-huddle offense in 2014, the Orange slowed things down and actually ran 16% *fewer* plays. In fact, Wake Forest was the only ACC team that ran fewer plays than Syracuse last season. Offensive changes are expected in 2015 and while Shafer and his staff are keeping quiet about exactly what those changes will be, it's expected to more of a multiple-set pro-style system. When Lester was the head coach and OC at Elmhurst College (Division III) from 2008-2012, he'd often run a "12 Personnel" power offense featuring one back and two TEs. Having a healthy Hunt at QB and seven other returning starters should help this offense improve on last year's ugly performance.

**DEFENSE:**
As poor as the offense was in 2014, Syracuse stayed competitive in most games thanks to the strength of its defense. Shafer has a reputation for building strong defenses and last year's squad ranked No. 27 nationally in yards allowed. The Orange run an aggressive 4-3 base defense, but Shafer and his staff will give multiple looks depending on the offense they're going up against. It's not uncommon to see Syracuse shift into a 3-4 or even a 3-3-5. The defensive coordinator is **Chuck Bullough**. Before taking over as Shafer's DC in 2013, Bullough was the LB coach for the Cleveland Browns under **Pat Shurmur** from 2011-2012. Before that, Bullough was the DC at UCLA under **Rick Neuheisel**. Shafer and Bullough will face a difficult task in 2015 as this inexperienced group must find eight new starters. Expect to see the Syracuse defense go through some growing pains early in the year.

**RECRUITING:**
Though Shafer signed a rather large class with 27 signees, his 2015 recruiting class was ranked last in the ACC and No. 64 nationally. This is not a good sign, especially for a coach who needs a quick infusion of talent.

**RUMOR MILL:**
**Doug Marrone** led Syracuse to eight wins in 2012 and the program has been slipping backwards since his departure. While a transitional period is fully expected with most new coaches, three-win seasons are not going to cut it for a program that wants to prove it can compete in the ACC. On top of that, Syracuse has a new athletic director and new ADs are often quicker to fire coaches they didn't personally hire. With that in mind, Shafer needs to start racking up wins fast. Anything less than six or seven wins in 2015 probably means a coaching change.

**2015 OUTLOOK:**

**Sept. 4**     **Rhode Island Rams** – This FCS school went 1-11 in 2014. Shafer was the DB coach at Rhode Island from 1993-1995.

**Sept. 12**    **Wake Forest Demon Deacons** – Shafer is 2-0 against Wake Forest.

**Sept. 19**    **Central Michigan Chippewas** – Getting to 3-0 before the LSU game would be huge for a team that desperately needs a bowl trip. Syracuse is 20-5 all-time against the MAC, including last year's win over CMU.

**Sept. 26**    **LSU Tigers** – Since 2002, Syracuse has played just one SEC opponent (a win over Missouri in 2012).

**Oct. 10**     **at South Florida Bulls** – Syracuse is 2-6 against this former Big East foe. The Orange beat the Bulls the last time these teams met in 2012. Shafer and USF head coach Willie Taggart coached together on Jim Harbaugh's staff at Stanford in 2007.

**Oct. 17**     **at Virginia Cavaliers** – Virginia has finished last in the Coastal Division for each of the past three seasons. The Orange need to pick up at least one ACC road win and this is their best opportunity.

**Oct. 24**     **Pittsburgh Panthers** – The Panthers have dominated this series in recent years, winning nine of the last 10 meetings. Shafer and new Pitt head coach Pat Narduzzi coached together for six seasons at Rhode Island and Northern Illinois.

**Oct. 31**     **at Florida State Seminoles** – This will be the first game of a very difficult three-game stretch for Syracuse. Shafer lost his previous two games against Florida State by a combined 74 points.

**Nov. 7**     **at Louisville Cardinals** – Louisville owns a 7-6 edge in this series.

**Nov. 14**    **Clemson Tigers** – Despite gaining just 170 yards against the Tigers last season, Syracuse forced four turnovers and kept the game tight for three quarters.

**Nov. 21**    **at NC State Wolfpack** – The loss to NC State stung last year as it broke the Wolfpack's longest conference losing streak in school history. Syracuse is now 1-7 all-time against NC State.

**Nov. 28**    **Boston College Eagles** – If things go well for Syracuse early in the year, a bowl game may be riding on this regular-season finale. If that's the case, this will obviously be a *MUST-WIN* game for Shafer.

**BOTTOM LINE:**
Shafer enters 2015 on the hot seat, but the schedule sets up nicely for Syracuse to build some early momentum. Though they'll be outmatched against LSU, this team has a chance to reach five wins *before* the brutal Florida State-Louisville-Clemson stretch. Getting off to a fast start will be critical for Shafer and the Orange.

## Scott Shafer's Year-by-Year Coaching Record:

**Syracuse: 10-15 (5-11 in the ACC)**

2013    7–6 (4–4)            **Final Ranking: NR**
        Beat Minnesota 21-17 in the Texas Bowl.

2014    3–9 (1–7)            **Final Ranking: NR**

# Wake Forest Demon Deacons – Dave Clawson

## Coach Ranking: #70

**Overall Record:** 93-90 in 15 seasons (9 seasons in FCS)
**Record at Wake Forest:** 3-9 in 1 season
**2014 Results:** 3-9, 1-7 in the ACC (T-6th in the ACC Atlantic)
**Returning Starters in 2015:** 9 on offense (including QB), 7 on defense
**Salary:** $1.8 Million*     **Age:** 48     **Job Security Grade:** A

COACH'S BIO:
Dave Clawson grew up in the Niagara Falls suburb of Youngstown, New York, and played both football and basketball at Williams College (Division III) from 1985-1988. After two-year stops as an assistant at Albany (FCS) and Buffalo, Clawson was named RB coach at Lehigh (FCS) in 1993 and was promoted to offensive coordinator in 1994. He served as Villanova's (FCS) OC from 1996-1998 and took over as head coach at Fordham (FCS) in 1999. He led Fordham to its first ever playoff appearance in his fourth season. In 2004, Clawson became the head coach at Richmond (FCS) and turned the Spiders into a Top 5 team in four years. He left Richmond to become **Phillip Fulmer**'s OC at Tennessee in 2008. A year later, he was named Bowling Green's head coach and won the MAC championship in his fifth season. After the 2013 season, Wake Forest hired Clawson to replace **Jim Grobe**.

2014 REVIEW:
Clawson inherited a young team coming off of five-straight losing seasons. As expected, Wake Forest struggled through another losing season as the program transitioned to a new staff and system. The glimmer of hope came in Week 11 when the Demon Deacons knocked off Virginia Tech with a 6-3 overtime win.

| 2014 RESULTS:   3-9 (1-7 in the ACC) | Final Ranking: NR | |
|---|---|---|
| at Louisiana–Monroe | L 10–17 | (21,003) |
| Gardner–Webb | W 23–7 | (26,925) |
| at Utah State | L 24–36 | (20,345) |
| Army | W 24–21 | (28,123) |
| at Louisville | L 10–20 | (51,463) |
| at #1 Florida State | L 3–43 | (82,327) |
| Syracuse | L 7–30 | (25,107) |
| Boston College | L 17–23 | (26,439) |
| #19 Clemson | L 20–34 | (28,846) |
| at NC State | L 13–42 | (55,353) |
| Virginia Tech | W 6–3 2OT | (27,820) |
| at Duke | L 21–41 | (22,247) |

## OFFENSE:

Wake Forest entered 2014 with just *one* senior starter on offense and a true freshman, **John Wolford**, won the starting position at QB. With such a young and inexperienced team, it's easy to understand why the Demon Deacons had the nation's *worst* total offense last season. The good news is that 2014's young squad will enter 2015 as one of the ACC's most experienced offenses with nine starters returning. Under **Jim Grobe**, Wake Forest ran a spread-option attack that utilized dual-threat QBs. Clawson and offensive coordinator **Warren Ruggiero** are reworking the offense into a multiple-set system that worked well for them at Bowling Green. In 2013, while running the ball about 60% of the time, Bowling Green averaged 34.8 points a game (27th in the nation) and had the MAC's second-ranked passing offense and third-ranked rushing offense. It's that kind of pro-style offense that Clawson and Ruggiero want to establish at Wake Forest. To do that, they'll need to find a running game. The Demon Deacons averaged less than 40 rushing yards a game in 2014. This offensive overhaul will take time, but after fielding the nation's worst offense last year, *any* improvement will be worth cheering about in 2015.

## DEFENSE:

**Mike Elko** was Clawson's defensive coordinator for the five years they were at Bowling Green and he's continuing in that role at Wake Forest. Elko built Bowling Green into one of the nation's top defenses, ranking No. 10 nationally in total defense and No. 5 nationally in points allowed his final season there (2013). In his first season at Wake Forest, Elko transitioned the defense from a 3-4 to a 4-2-5. This unit ranked No. 9 in the ACC in yards allowed and No. 12 in the ACC in points allowed. While those numbers may not look all that impressive, it's important to remember that this defense was on the field way too long due to the offense's struggles. This was a young group last year and they'll have seven starters back in 2015.

## RECRUITING:

After his first recruiting class landed at the bottom of the ACC, Clawson's second effort was a notch better. It was ranked No. 11 in the ACC and No. 52 nationally.

## RUMOR MILL:

When **Brett Bielema** left Wisconsin following the 2012 season, Clawson was reportedly the Badgers' No. 2 candidate behind **Gary Anderson**, who was hired at that time. When Anderson left Wisconsin in December of last year, Clawson's name immediately came up as a candidate once again. Clawson was also rumored to be a candidate for the UConn job that went to **Bob Diaco** after the 2013 season.

## NOTEWORTHY:

When Clawson became Fordham's head coach, he was just 31, making him the nation's youngest Division I head coach. At Clawson's three previous stops as a head coach, he pulled off a 10-win season with each team by Year 4.

**2015 OUTLOOK:**

**Sept. 3**     **Elon Phoenix** – This Thursday-night game should be an easy start to the season for Wake Forest. Elon, an FCS program, went 1-11 last year.

**Sept. 12**     **at Syracuse Orange** – These teams tied for last place in the Atlantic Division in 2014. Taking a step out of the ACC cellar starts with winning this game. If progress is going to be made in 2015, this is a *MUST-WIN* game for Clawson and the Demon Deacons.

**Sept. 19**     **at Army Black Knights** – Last year's three-point win over Army didn't come easy and this year the Deacons must travel to West Point.

**Sept. 26**     **Indiana Hoosiers** – Clawson faced Kevin Wilson's Indiana team while coaching Bowling Green in 2013. The Hoosiers won 42-10.

**Oct. 3**     **Florida State Seminoles** – Wake Forest has lost its last three games to Florida State by a combined score of 154-6.

**Oct. 10**     **at Boston College Eagles** – The Deacons were held to just 19 rushing yards against BC last year and still managed to come within a TD of winning this game. The Eagles have won six of the last eight games in this series.

**Oct. 17**     **at North Carolina Tar Heels** – The last time Wake Forest played this in-state opponent, the Deacons won 28-27 in 2012.

**Oct. 24**     **NC State Wolfpack** – The previous year's loser has rebounded with a win seven-straight times in this back-and-forth series. NC State won last year, which means the Deacons are due for a win this year if that trend continues.

**Oct. 30**     **Louisville Cardinals** – Wake Forest was held to just 100 total yards and negative-22 rushing yards in its 10-point loss to Louisville last season.

**Nov. 14**     **at Notre Dame Fighting Irish** – Notre Dame blanked Wake Forest 38-0 the last time the Demon Deacons traveled to South Bend in 2012.

**Nov. 21**     **at Clemson Tigers** – Wake Forest will try to break a six-game losing streak against the Tigers. Clemson leads this series with an all-time record of 62-17-1 against the Deacons.

**Nov. 28**     **Duke Blue Devils** – Clawson beat Duke back in 2006 when he was coaching Richmond, an FCS school. Duke was the only ACC opponent Wake Forest gained more than 300 yards of offense against last year, but the Blue Devils still won by 20 points.

**BOTTOM LINE:**

Clawson knows how to turn programs around. His record proves that. But each turnaround takes time and though Wake Forest fans deserve to be impatient after six-straight losing seasons, it will likely take another year or two before the Demon Deacons can pull off a winning season. Two conference wins in 2015 would be a step in the right direction.

## Dave Clawson's Year-by-Year Coaching Record:

### Fordham: 29-29 (1-1 in the Division 1-AA Playoffs)
1999    0–11 (0-0)              Final Ranking: NR
2000    3–8 (0-0)               Final Ranking: NR
2001    7–4 (0-0)               Final Ranking: NR
        Clawson named Patriot League Coach of the Year.
2002    10–3 (1-1)              Final Ranking: #12
        Patriot League Champions.
        Clawson named 1-AA National Coach of the Year.
        Clawson named Patriot League Coach of the Year.
        Lost to Villanova 10-24 in the Division 1-AA quarterfinals.
2003    9–3 (0-0)              Final Ranking: NR

### Richmond: 29-20 (3-2 in the Division 1-AA/FCS Playoffs)
2004    3–8 (0-0)              Final Ranking: NR
2005    9–4 (1-1)              Final Ranking: #8
        Atlantic 10 Conference Champions.
        Clawson named 1-AA National Coach of the Year.
        Clawson named Atlantic 10 Coach of the Year.
        Lost to #3 Furman 20-24 in the Division 1-AA quarterfinals.
2006    6–5 (0-0)              Final Ranking: NR
2007    11–3 (2-1)             Final Ranking: #4
        CAA Conference Co-Champions.
        Clawson named CAA Coach of the Year.
        Lost to #5 Appalachian State 35-55 in the FCS semifinals.

### Bowling Green: 32-31 (24-17 in the MAC)
2009    7–6 (6–2)             Final Ranking: NR
        Lost to Idaho 42-43 in the Humanitarian Bowl.
2010    2–10 (1–7)            Final Ranking: NR
2011    5–7 (3–5)             Final Ranking: NR
2012    8–5 (6–2)             Final Ranking: NR
        Lost to #24 San Jose State 20-29 in the Military Bowl.
2013    10–3 (7–1)            Final Ranking: NR
        MAC Champions.
        Beat #16 Northern Illinois 47-27 in the MAC Championship Game.
        Bowling Green lost to Pittsburgh 27-30 in the Little Caesars Pizza Bowl, but
        Clawson had already left to accept the Wake Forest job.

### Wake Forest: 3-9 (1-7 in the ACC)
2014    3–9 (1–7)             Final Ranking: NR

# Duke Blue Devils – David Cutcliffe

## Coach Ranking: #34

**Overall Record:** 84-77 in 13 seasons
**Record at Duke:** 40-48 in 7 seasons
**2014 Results:** 9-4, 5-3 in the ACC (2nd in the ACC Coastal)
**Returning Starters in 2015:** 6 on offense, 7 on defense
**Salary:** $1.8 Million      **Age:** 60      **Job Security Grade:** A

**COACH'S BIO:**
A native of Birmingham, Alabama, David Cutcliffe was a student assistant for **Bear Bryant**'s staff while attending Alabama. After graduating in 1976, he spent four years as a high school assistant coach and two years as a high school head coach. In 1982, Cutcliffe joined **Johnny Majors**' staff at Tennessee. When Majors was forced to resign in 1991, **Phillip Fulmer** took over as Tennessee's head coach and kept Cutcliffe as the QB coach. In 1993, Cutcliffe was promoted to offensive coordinator and he held that position through the 1998 season. Cutcliffe accepted the Ole Miss head coaching job at the end of the 1998 season and coached there until 2004. He was fired after his lone losing season at Ole Miss. Cutcliffe was hired to join **Charlie Weis**' first staff at Notre Dame, but health concerns forced him to resign and take the 2005 season off. He returned to the sidelines in 2006 and spent two more seasons as Tennessee's OC. Cutcliffe became Duke's head coach in 2008 and in 2013 he was named the National Coach of the Year after leading the Blue Devils to their only 10-win season in school history.

**2014 REVIEW:**
Duke followed-up its 2013 Coastal Division championship with a runner-up finish in 2014. A late-season loss to archrival North Carolina cost the Blue Devils their second-straight trip to the ACC Championship Game.

| 2014 RESULTS:   9-4 (5-3 in the ACC) | Final Ranking: NR | |
|---|---|---|
| Elon | W 52–13 | (31,213) |
| at Troy | W 34–17 | (21,331) |
| Kansas | W 41–3 | (25,203) |
| Tulane | W 47–13 | (20,197) |
| at Miami (FL) | L 10–22 | (44,559) |
| at #22 Georgia Tech | W 31–25 | (44,281) |
| Virginia | W 20–13 | (28,131) |
| at Pittsburgh | W 51–48 2OT | (39,293) |
| at Syracuse | W 27–10 | (39,331) |
| Virginia Tech | L 16–17 | (30,107) |
| North Carolina | L 20–45 | (33,941) |
| Wake Forest | W 41–21 | (22,247) |
| vs. #15 Arizona State (Sun Bowl) | L 31–36 | (47,809) |

**OFFENSE:**
Last season, Cutcliffe had to replace offensive coordinator **Kurt Roper**, who left to take the same position at Florida following a 2013 season where he was named a Broyles Award finalist. Cutcliffe promoted WR coach **Scottie Montgomery** to OC and Duke didn't miss a beat in 2014. Averaging roughly 32 points a game (just as they had the previous two seasons), the Blue Devils scored the fourth-most points in the ACC. Cutcliffe and Montgomery will have a more difficult job this year as Duke must replace two-year starter **Anthony Boone** at QB and top WR **Jamison Crowder**, who had more than 1,000 receiving yards in each of the last three seasons. Duke runs an up-tempo pro-style offense that achieved a near 50-50 balance between the run and pass in 2014. Cutcliffe is a brilliant offensive coach who has shown the ability to adapt his offense quickly to his players' strengths.

**DEFENSE:**
Duke's offense gets a lot of attention, but the Blue Devil defense has made tremendous strides over the past two seasons. In 2012, Duke's defense was the worst in the ACC in points allowed. By 2014, the Blue Devils had climbed to No. 4 in the ACC (tied with Louisville) in that category. Former Cornell head coach **Jim Knowles** has been Duke's defensive coordinator since 2011 and he operates out of a 4-2-5 scheme. Having four returning starters back at DB, including All-Americans **Jeremy Cash** and **DeVon Edwards**, is a welcomed scenario for a defense built around athleticism in the secondary. If Knowles can rebuild the d-line, which loses three senior starters from 2014, this "bend-but-don't-break" defense should continue its improvement trend.

**RECRUITING:**
Considering that Duke is best known for its basketball program and its strict academic standards, Cutcliffe is doing an outstanding job signing players who can compete for ACC titles. Ranked as the 10th-best class in the ACC and No. 50 nationally, the 2015 recruiting class was Cutcliffe's highest-rated group since he arrived at Duke. California-based four-star LB **Ben Humphreys** chose Duke over schools like Miami (FL), Wisconsin, Nebraska, and Arizona State.

**RUMOR MILL:**
Louisville reportedly contacted Cutcliffe during its coaching search to replace **Charlie Strong** (the school eventually hired **Bobby Petrino**) and rumors circulated this past offseason that Michigan contacted Cutcliffe during its coaching search (Cutcliffe denied those rumors and the Wolverines hired **Jim Harbaugh**). In 2012, Duke awarded Cutcliffe with a contract extension that currently runs through June of 2019.

**NOTEWORTHY:**
After Cutcliffe was fired by Ole Miss in 2004, it was reported that one of the reasons for his firing was because he refused to fire any of his assistants following the disappointing season.

**2015 OUTLOOK:**

**Sept. 3**   **at Tulane Green Wave** – Cutcliffe is 4-0 all-time against Tulane, including two wins while he was at Ole Miss.

**Sept. 12**   **North Carolina Central Eagles** – This will be Duke's fourth game against this in-state FCS opponent since 2009. Cutcliffe won the three previous games in this series by a combined score of 148-31.

**Sept. 19**   **Northwestern Wildcats** – The last time these schools met, Northwestern gave Cutcliffe a 24-20 loss in his first season at Duke (2008).

**Sept. 26**   **Georgia Tech Yellow Jackets** – The last three Coastal Division titles have been won by either Duke or Georgia Tech. Oddly, the *loser* of this game over the past two seasons has won the division. Both these coaches arrived in the ACC in 2008. Last year was Cutcliffe's first win over Paul Johnson's Yellow Jackets. He's 1-6 overall.

**Oct. 3**   **Boston College Eagles** – Duke hasn't played Boston College since 2011. Cutcliffe is 1-1 against the Eagles.

**Oct. 10**   **at Army Black Knights** – The last time these schools met, Army beat Cutcliffe in 2010. Playing Georgia Tech earlier in the season should help prepare Duke's defense for Army's triple-option offense.

**Oct. 24**   **at Virginia Tech Hokies** – Cutcliffe is 1-6 against Frank Beamer and the Hokies. The one victory occurred the last time they played in Blacksburg, in 2013.

**Oct. 31**   **Miami Hurricanes** – The Hurricanes have given Cutcliffe trouble over the years. He's just 1-6 against Miami.

**Nov. 7**   **at North Carolina Tar Heels** – Last year's loss to North Carolina broke Duke's two-game winning streak in this series and also ended up costing the Blue Devils the Coastal Division title. This will be Cutcliffe's *MUST-WIN* game in 2015 as Duke looks for payback in this rivalry.

**Nov. 14**   **Pittsburgh Panthers** – Pitt beat Duke by three points in 2013 and Duke returned the favor with a three-point win last year. The Panthers could be a surprise team in the Coastal Division and if that's the case, this late-season game could have big division-race consequences.

**Nov. 21**   **at Virginia Cavaliers** – Cutcliffe has dominated this series since arriving at Duke. He's 6-1 against Virginia and has won each of the last three games against Mike London and the Cavaliers.

**Nov. 28**   **at Wake Forest Demon Deacons** – After losing his first three games against Wake Forest, Cutcliffe has won the last four games in this series.

**BOTTOM LINE:**
Many wondered if 2013's Coastal Division Championship was a fluke season for the Blue Devils. Cutcliffe proved that it wasn't by following up 2013 with a nine-win season and a second-place finish in the division. The big question in 2015 will be whether Duke takes a step back with a new QB leading the offense. If the transition goes smoothly, there's no reason to think the Blue Devils won't be right back in the Coastal Division hunt. The next step for Cutcliffe will be to start *consistently* beating Georgia Tech, Virginia Tech, and Miami. He currently owns an identical 1-6 record against all three of those Coastal Division programs.

## David Cutcliffe's Year-by-Year Coaching Record:

<u>Ole Miss: 44-29 (25-23 in the SEC)</u>
1998   1–0 (0–0)                Final Ranking: NR
       Cutcliffe got an early start on the job and coached Ole Miss to its 35-15 win
       over Texas Tech in the Independence Bowl.
1999   8–4 (4–4)                Final Ranking: #22
       Beat Oklahoma 27-25 in the Independence Bowl.
2000   7–5 (4–4)                Final Ranking: NR
       Lost to West Virginia 38-49 in the Music City Bowl.
2001   7–4 (4–4)                Final Ranking: NR
2002   7–6 (3–5)                Final Ranking: NR
       Beat Nebraska 27-23 in the Independence Bowl.
2003   10–3 (7–1)               Final Ranking: #13
       SEC West Division Co-Champions.
       Beat #21 Oklahoma State 31-28 in the Cotton Bowl Classic.
2004   4–7 (3–5)                Final Ranking: NR

<u>Duke: 40-48 (20-36 in the ACC)</u>
2008   4–8 (1–7)               Final Ranking: NR
2009   5–7 (3–5)               Final Ranking: NR
2010   3–9 (1–7)               Final Ranking: NR
2011   3–9 (1–7)               Final Ranking: NR
2012   6–7 (3–5)               Final Ranking: NR
       Cutcliffe named ACC Coach of the Year.
       Lost to Cincinnati 34-48 in the Belk Bowl.
2013   10–4 (6–2)              Final Ranking: #22
       ACC Coastal Division Champions.
       Cutcliffe named National Coach of the Year.
       Cutcliffe named ACC Coach of the Year.
       Lost to #1 Florida State 7-45 in the ACC Championship Game.
       Lost to #20 Texas A&M 48-52 in the Chick-fil-A Bowl.
2014   9–4 (5–3)               Final Ranking: NR
       Lost to #15 Arizona State 31-36 in the Sun Bowl.

# Georgia Tech Yellow Jackets – Paul Johnson

## Coach Ranking: #18

**Overall Record:** 165-74 in 18 seasons (5 seasons in Division 1-AA)
**Record at Georgia Tech:** 58-35 in 7 seasons
**2014 Results:** 11-3, 6-2 in the ACC (ACC Coastal Division Champions)
**Returning Starters in 2015:** 5 on offense (including QB), 8 on defense
**Salary:** $2.6 Million     **Age:** 58     **Job Security Grade:** A

COACH'S BIO:
Paul Johnson grew up in Newland, North Carolina, and attended Western Carolina University. He didn't play football in college and immediately began his coaching career after graduating. He spent four seasons as an offensive coordinator at the high school and junior college levels. In 1983, he was hired by **Erk Russell** to be the DL coach at Georgia Southern (Division 1-AA). Johnson was promoted to OC in 1985. In his two seasons as OC, Georgia Southern won back-to-back 1-AA National Championships. Johnson then spent eight seasons as **Bob Wagner**'s OC at Hawaii and two seasons as **Charlie Weatherbie**'s OC at Navy. In 1997, he was named head coach at Georgia Southern and led the Eagles to two National Championships in five seasons. In 2002, Johnson took over a Navy program that had gone 1-20 over the previous two seasons and after a 2-10 debut season, he led the Midshipmen to five-straight winning seasons. He was hired by Georgia Tech in 2008 and has won four Coastal Division titles in seven seasons. Johnson won the 2009 ACC Championship, but the title was later vacated due to NCAA sanctions.

2014 REVIEW:
Georgia Tech was the surprise team of the ACC last season. Expected to finish near the back of the Coastal Division, the Yellow Jackets won the division and finished the season ranked in the Top 10 for the first time since 1998. Johnson was named the ACC Coach of the Year for the third time.

| 2014 RESULTS:   11-3 (6-2 in the ACC) | Final Ranking: #7 | |
|---|---|---|
| Wofford | W 38-19 | (45,403) |
| at Tulane | W 38-21 | (30,000) |
| Georgia Southern | W 42-38 | (53,173) |
| at Virginia Tech | W 27-24 | (62,318) |
| Miami (FL) | W 28-17 | (52,221) |
| Duke | L 25-31 | (44,281) |
| at North Carolina | L 43-48 | (53,000) |
| at Pittsburgh | W 56-28 | (44,734) |
| Virginia | W 35-10 | (46,657) |
| at North Carolina State | W 56-23 | (54,653) |
| #19 Clemson | W 28-6 | (49,378) |
| at #9 Georgia | W 30-24 OT | (92,746) |
| vs. #4 Florida State (ACC Championship) | L 35-37 | (64,808) |
| vs. #7 Mississippi State (Orange Bowl) | W 49-34 | (58,211) |

**OFFENSE:**
Georgia Tech is the only Power 5 program that runs the flexbone triple-option offense. With the success the Yellow Jackets have had with this offense, it makes one wonder why more teams don't implement it. Paul Johnson is his own offensive coordinator and it'd be hard to argue that there's anyone better at calling plays for this offense. In 2014, Georgia Tech led the ACC in rushing for the seventh-consecutive season. For the third time in Johnson's seven seasons, the Yellow Jackets also led the ACC in scoring. They averaged 37.9 points a game (No. 12 nationally) and 342 rushing yards a game (No. 2 nationally). Since Johnson arrived at Georgia Tech, the Yellow Jackets have been one of the nation's Top 10 rushing teams every season. Johnson runs the ball about 80% of the time and relies on a steady dose of classic triple-option football and counters off of the option look. When the Jackets do throw the ball, they go deep. Last season, Georgia Tech was ranked No. 3 nationally in yards per pass attempt (9.3 yards per attempt) and No. 1 in the ACC. Having a tough QB who can run hard and make split-second decisions is the key to this offense. Junior QB **Justin Thomas** will return as the starter in 2015 after rushing for 1,086 yards and passing for 1,719 yards last year. The RBs must be replaced, but Georgia Tech will have four starters back on the offensive line. Johnson says he'd like to see the passing game improve in 2015. With Thomas back at QB and an experienced o-line, expect Georgia Tech to once again field one of the nation's most difficult offenses to defend.

**DEFENSE:**
Georgia Tech's defense thrived on forcing turnovers in 2014. The Jackets ranked No. 2 in the ACC and No. 17 nationally in turnovers gained. However, aside from forcing turnovers, the defense struggled to slow down opponents. This group finished next to last in the ACC in yards allowed and No. 10 in points allowed. However, last year's squad was inexperienced and they made big improvements as the season went on. After giving up 429 yards a game during the first eight weeks of the season, the Jackets gave up 308 yards a game in their final four games of the regular season. Defensive coordinator **Ted Roof** is hoping to carry that momentum into 2015. With eight starters back, they should be able to. Roof, a former Georgia Tech LB and the former head coach at Duke, will enter his third season as Tech's DC after previous DC stints at Penn State, Auburn, and Minnesota. He transitioned the defense from a 3-4 to a 4-3 when he arrived here in 2013 and this experienced group should all be on the same page in 2015.

**RECRUITING:**
Johnson keeps his recruiting efforts primarily focused on his home state of Georgia and neighboring Florida. With so much talent in these two states, it's hard to argue with Johnson's strategy. The 2015 recruiting class was Johnson's highest-rated class since 2010. It was ranked No. 8 in the ACC and No. 43 nationally.

**RUMOR MILL:**
Prior to the 2014 season, it was reported that Johnson was unhappy at Georgia Tech, but he quickly denied those rumors. After the 2014 regular season, Georgia Tech gave Johnson a four-year contract extension, which will now run through the 2020 season.

**2015 OUTLOOK:**

| | |
|---|---|
| Sept. 3 | **Alcorn State Braves** – Georgia Tech will open the season on a Thursday night against an FCS team that went 10-3 last year. |
| Sept. 12 | **Tulane Green Wave** – The Jackets passed for a season-low 15 yards in their win against Tulane last year. |
| Sept. 19 | **at Notre Dame Fighting Irish** – In 2007, when Johnson was at Navy, he led the Midshipmen to their first win over Notre Dame since 1963. This will be his first time coaching against the Irish since coming to Georgia Tech. While at Navy, Johnson went 1-5 against Notre Dame. |
| Sept. 26 | **at Duke Blue Devils** – Last year's loss to Duke broke Johnson's 10-game winning streak against the Blue Devils, which dated back to his days at Navy. Johnson is 10-2 all-time against Duke. |
| Oct. 3 | **North Carolina Tar Heels** – Last season's loss to North Carolina broke Johnson's five-game winning streak against the Tar Heels. |
| Oct. 10 | **at Clemson Tigers** – The Georgia Tech defense had its best game of the season against Clemson last year, holding the Tigers to just 190 yards of total offense in a 28-6 win. Johnson is officially 4-3 against Clemson, but he's 5-3 if you count his vacated victory in the 2009 ACC Championship Game. |
| Oct. 17 | **Pittsburgh Panthers** – Johnson is 3-0 against Pitt, including a 2007 victory when he was still at Navy. Tech racked up a season-high 612 yards and 56 points against Pitt last year. |
| Oct. 24 | **Florida State Seminoles** – This will be a rematch of last year's ACC Championship Game. Johnson is 2-2 against the Seminoles and both losses occurred in ACC Championships. |
| Oct. 31 | **at Virginia Cavaliers** – Georgia Tech has a three-game winning streak going against the Cavaliers. |
| Nov. 12 | **Virginia Tech Hokies** – This Thursday-night showdown could be for the Coastal Division title. Johnson is 2-5 against Frank Beamer. |
| Nov. 21 | **at Miami Hurricanes** – Last year's win against the Canes broke a five-year losing streak for the Jackets in this series. Dating back to their previous schools, Johnson and Al Golden are 3-3 against each other. |
| Nov. 28 | **Georgia Bulldogs** – Last season's overtime win against Georgia was Johnson's first in this series since 2008. Johnson is actually 2-6 all-time against the Bulldogs, but one of those losses occurred while he was coaching Georgia Southern back in 2000. They call this rivalry, "Clean, Old-Fashioned Hate," and a win this year would prove 2014 was no fluke. As it often is, this is a *MUST-WIN* game for the Jackets. Johnson is 6-7 against the SEC since arriving at Georgia Tech. |

**BOTTOM LINE:**
Since coming to Georgia Tech, Johnson has won or tied for the Coastal Division title more often than not. With eight starters back on defense and Justin Thomas back at QB, the Yellow Jackets are the favorites to repeat as division champs and get back to the ACC title game.

## Paul Johnson's Year-by-Year Coaching Record:

### Georgia Southern: 62-10 (14-3 in the Division 1-AA Playoffs)
1997    **10-3 (1-1)**          **Final Ranking: #8**
Johnson named Southern Conference Coach of the Year.
Lost to #3 Delaware 7-16 in the Division 1-AA quarterfinals.
1998    **14-1 (3-1)**          **Final Ranking: #2**
Johnson named Southern Conference Coach of the Year.
Lost to #1 UMass 43-55 in the Division 1-AA National Championship Game.
1999    **13-2 (4-0)**          **Final Ranking: #1**
Division 1-AA National Champions.
Johnson named Division 1-AA National Coach of the Year.
Beat #2 Youngstown State 59-24 in the Division 1-AA National Championship Game.
2000    **13-2 (4-0)**          **Final Ranking: #1**
Division 1-AA National Champions.
Johnson named Division 1-AA National Coach of the Year.
Beat #2 Montana 27-25 in the Division 1-AA National Championship Game.
2001    **12-2 (2-1)**          **Final Ranking: #3**
Lost to #2 Furman 17-24 in the Division 1-AA semifinals.

### Navy: 45-29 (Independent)
2002    **2-10 (Ind.)**          **Final Ranking: NR**
2003    **8-5 (Ind.)**          **Final Ranking: NR**
Lost to Texas Tech 14-38 in the Houston Bowl.
2004    **10-2 (Ind.)**          **Final Ranking: #24**
Johnson named Bobby Dodd National Coach of the Year.
Beat New Mexico 34-19 in the Emerald Bowl.
2005    **8-4 (Ind.)**          **Final Ranking: NR**
Beat Colorado State 51-30 in the Poinsettia Bowl.
2006    **9-4 (Ind.)**          **Final Ranking: NR**
Lost to #23 Boston College 24-25 in the Meineke Car Care Bowl.
2007    **8-4 (Ind.)**          **Final Ranking: NR**
Navy lost to Utah 32-35 in the Poinsettia Bowl, but Johnson had already left to accept the Georgia Tech job.

### Georgia Tech: 58-35 (37-19 in the ACC)
2008    **9-4 (5-3)**          **Final Ranking: #22**
ACC Coastal Division Co-Champions.
Johnson named ACC Coach of the Year.
Lost to LSU 3-38 in the Chick-fil-A Bowl.
2009    **10-3 (7-1)**          **Final Ranking: #13**
ACC Coastal Division Champions.
Johnson named ACC Coach of the Year.
Beat Clemson 39-34 in the ACC Championship Game, but the win was later vacated due to NCAA sanctions.
Lost to #11 Iowa 14-24 in the Orange Bowl.

## Georgia Tech (continued)

2010    6–7 (4–4)                Final Ranking: NR
        Lost to Air Force 7-14 in the Independence Bowl.
2011    8–5 (5–3)                Final Ranking: NR
        Lost to Utah 27-30 in OT in the Sun Bowl.
2012    7–7 (5–3)                Final Ranking: NR
        ACC Coastal Division Champions.
        Lost to Florida State 15-21 in the ACC Championship Game.
        Beat USC 21-7 in the Sun Bowl.
2013    7–6 (5–3)                Final Ranking: NR
        Lost to Ole Miss 17-25 in the Music City Bowl.
2014    11–3 (6–2)               Final Ranking: #7
        ACC Coastal Division Champions.
        Johnson named ACC Coach of the Year.
        Lost to #4 Florida State 35-37 in the ACC Championship Game.
        Beat #7 Mississippi State 49-34 in the Orange Bowl.

# Miami Hurricanes – Al Golden

## Coach Ranking: #66

**Overall Record:** 55-56 in 9 seasons
**Record at Miami:** 28-22 in 4 seasons
**2014 Results:** 6-7, 3-5 in the ACC (T-5th in the ACC Coastal)
**Returning Starters in 2015:** 5 on offense (including QB), 6 on defense
**Salary:** $2.25 Million      **Age:** 46      **Job Security Grade:** D

**COACH'S BIO:**
Al Golden grew up in Colts Neck, New Jersey, and was a two-year starter at TE for Penn State. He spent the 1992 season with the New England Patriots and began his coaching career as the offensive coordinator at Red Bank (N.J.) Catholic High School in 1993. From 1994-1996, he served as a graduate assistant on **George Welsh**'s staff at Virginia and was hired as **Tom Obrien**'s LB coach at Boston College in 1997. After three seasons with the Eagles, Golden returned to his alma mater and coached LBs under **Joe Paterno** at Penn State in 2000. From 2001-2005, he was **Al Groh**'s defensive coordinator at Virginia. Temple hired Golden to be its new head coach in 2006 and he led the Owls to their first bowl game in 30 years in 2009. Miami hired Golden in 2011 to replace **Randy Shannon**.

**2014 REVIEW:**
After a 9-4 season in 2013, it looked like the Hurricanes were turning the corner and ready to compete for a Coastal Division title in 2014. Instead, they closed out the year with a four-game losing streak, which gave Al Golden his first losing season since becoming Miami's head coach.

| 2014 RESULTS: 6-7 (3-5 in the ACC) | Final Ranking: NR | |
|---|---|---|
| at Louisville | L 13–31 | (55,428) |
| Florida A&M | W 41–7 | (48,254) |
| Arkansas State | W 41–20 | (41,519) |
| at #24 Nebraska | L 31–41 | (91,585) |
| Duke | W 22–10 | (44,559) |
| at Georgia Tech | L 17–28 | (52,221) |
| Cincinnati | W 55–34 | (43,953) |
| at Virginia Tech | W 30–6 | (64,007) |
| North Carolina | W 47–20 | (51,702) |
| #2 Florida State | L 26–30 | (76,530) |
| at Virginia | L 13–30 | (44,750) |
| Pittsburgh | L 23–35 | (61,106) |
| vs. South Carolina (Independence Bowl) | L 21–24 | (38,242) |

**OFFENSE:**
Miami runs a balanced pro-style offense that has run the ball 53% of the time in each of the two seasons since bringing in **James Coley** to be the offensive coordinator (in 2013). Before coming to Miami, Coley was the OC at his alma mater, Florida State, under **Jimbo Fisher**. Last year, true freshman **Brad Kaaya** stepped into the starting role at QB and passed for nearly 3,200 yards. He was named the ACC Rookie of the Year and should be even more comfortable with Miami's system as a sophomore. However, Kaaya's three top targets – WR **Phillip Dorsett**, TE **Clive Walford**, and RB **Duke Johnson** – are all headed to the NFL. In 2014, those three combined for 1,968 receiving yards and Johnson added 1,652 rushing yards. The Hurricanes must also replace three starters on the offensive line. Kaaya showed that he's the real deal at QB last season, but with just four returning starters he'll be asked to shoulder much more of the offense in 2015. There's plenty of young talent on this roster, but it'll be tough for Coley and Golden to quickly replace the playmakers they're losing.

**DEFENSE:**
**Mark D'Onofrio** was Golden's teammate at Penn State and he's been Golden's defensive coordinator since 2006, when they were at Temple. D'Onofrio entered 2014 under fire after his squad finished near the bottom of the NCAA in yards allowed the previous two seasons. He answered his critics with a big turnaround last year. The Miami defense rose from No. 90 nationally in yards allowed in 2013 to No. 14 in 2014. It could be tough to continue that level of play this year as the Hurricanes must replace five starters, including three-time All-ACC MLB **Denzel Perryman**, who was the heart of Miami's 4-3 defense and led the team in tackles each of the past two seasons.

**RECRUITING:**
Miami's recruiting class may have taken a step back from the superstar class of 2014 (which was ranked No. 12 in the nation), but the 2015 class still landed at No. 3 in the ACC (No. 26 nationally). That's a fairly strong class especially when you consider there were loud rumors that Golden might be fired after last season.

**RUMOR MILL:**
What a difference a year can make in this profession. After a 2014 season in which the Hurricanes climbed back into the Top 10 for the first time since 2009, Miami fans worried in the offseason that Golden would be heading back to his alma mater to take the Penn State job (a job that eventually went to **James Franklin**). By October of 2015, sentiment had changed and some disgruntled fans went so far as to fly a banner over Sun Life Stadium that read: "Fire Al Golden, Save The U." There were rumors in December that Golden was about to be fired, but no changes were made. Though Golden's current contract runs through 2019, this is likely a make-or-break season for the fifth-year coach.

**NOTEWORTHY:**
After four seasons as Miami's head coach, Golden's 28-22 record is the exact same record previous Hurricanes coach **Randy Shannon** compiled in his four seasons. Shannon was fired after going 7-5 in his fourth and final year with the Hurricanes.

**2015 OUTLOOK:**

**Sept. 5**   **Bethune-Cookman Wildcats** – Miami played this in-state FCS opponent in 2011 and 2012, winning both games by a combined score of 83-24. Bethune-Cookman went 9-3 in 2014.

**Sept. 11**   **at Florida Atlantic Owls** – This Friday-night matchup will mark the second time these cross-town schools have played each other. Miami beat FAU 34-6 in 2013. The Owls went 3-9 last year.

**Sept. 19**   **Nebraska Cornhuskers** – The Hurricanes should be 2-0 heading into this game and this will be an opportunity for Golden to quickly quiet his critics by avenging last year's 10-point loss to the Huskers.

**Oct. 1**   **at Cincinnati Bearcats** – Miami is 11-1 all-time against Cincinnati, with the lone loss occurring back in 1947. The Hurricanes racked up 621 yards of offense against the Bearcats last year.

**Oct. 10**   **at Florida State Seminoles** – The Hurricanes have lost five straight to the archrival Seminoles and this is the type of game that could be a job-saver if Golden pulls off the win. For that reason, this is Golden's _MUST-WIN_ game. Miami OC James Coley played for FSU and he coached there from 2008-2012 (he was Jimbo Fisher's OC from 2010-2012).

**Oct. 17**   **Virginia Tech Hokies** – Miami shut down Virginia Tech with a 30-6 win last season, but the Hokies should be a better team in 2015. Golden is 2-2 against Frank Beamer.

**Oct. 24**   **Clemson Tigers** – This is a tough draw from the Atlantic Division. The last time these teams played, Miami won 30-21 in 2010. The three meetings before that all went into overtime.

**Oct. 31**   **at Duke Blue Devils** – Golden is 3-1 against Duke, but the lone loss occurred the last time Miami traveled to Durham, in 2013.

**Nov. 7**   **Virginia Cavaliers** – The Hurricanes have had trouble getting up for their annual game against Virginia and Golden is 1-3 against Mike London's Cavaliers.

**Nov. 14**   **at North Carolina Tar Heels** – Golden is 3-1 against North Carolina. Last year's 47-20 win was more lopsided than the scoreboard indicated as Miami led 44-6 midway through the $3^{rd}$ quarter.

**Nov. 21**   **Georgia Tech Yellow Jackets** – Since coming to Miami, Golden is 3-1 against Paul Johnson. Dating back to Golden's time at Temple and Johnson's time at Navy, this coaching series is tied at 3-3.

**Nov. 27**   **at Pittsburgh Panthers** – This game will be played the Friday after Thanksgiving. Miami has won 16 of the last 18 games against this former Big East foe, but the series is tied at 1-1 since Pitt joined the ACC.

**BOTTOM LINE:**
With a fan base growing impatient that Miami hasn't returned to the elite level of college football, Al Golden will be fighting for his job in 2015. The Coastal Division is fairly wide open and the Hurricanes have shown they can beat anyone in the division, but this coaching staff will need to quickly break in some new offensive playmakers if this team is going to reach the nine or 10 wins that may be required to save Golden's job.

## Al Golden's Year-by-Year Coaching Record:

<u>Temple: 27-34 (20-12 in the MAC)</u>
| | | |
|---|---|---|
| 2006 | 1–11 (Ind.) | Final Ranking: NR |
| 2007 | 4–8 (4–4) | Final Ranking: NR |

Temple, formerly an Independent program, joins the MAC.

| | | |
|---|---|---|
| 2008 | 5–7 (4–4) | Final Ranking: NR |
| 2009 | 9–4 (7–1) | Final Ranking: NR |

MAC East Division Co-Champions.
Lost to UCLA 21-30 in the EagleBank Bowl.

| | | |
|---|---|---|
| 2010 | 8–4 (5–3) | Final Ranking: NR |

<u>Miami (FL): 28-22 (16-16 in the ACC)</u>
| | | |
|---|---|---|
| 2011 | 6–6 (3–5) | Final Ranking: NR |

Miami did not accept a bowl invitation due to a self-imposed postseason ban.

| | | |
|---|---|---|
| 2012 | 7–5 (5–3) | Final Ranking: NR |

Miami was ineligible for a bowl game and for the ACC Championship due to a self-imposed postseason ban. Had the Hurricanes been eligible for an ACC title, they would have been co-champions of the Coastal Division.

| | | |
|---|---|---|
| 2013 | 9–4 (5–3) | Final Ranking: NR |

Lost to #18 Louisville 9-36 in the Russell Athletic Bowl.

| | | |
|---|---|---|
| 2014 | 6–7 (3–5) | Final Ranking: NR |

Lost to South Carolina 21-24 in the Independence Bowl.

# North Carolina Tar Heels – Larry Fedora

## Coach Ranking: #45

**Overall Record:** 55-36 in 7 seasons
**Record at North Carolina:** 21-17 in 3 seasons
**2014 Results:** 6-7, 4-4 in the ACC (T-3rd in the ACC Coastal)
**Returning Starters in 2015:** 10 on offense (including QB), 7 on defense
**Salary:** $1.8 Million      **Age:** 52      **Job Security Grade:** C

**COACH'S BIO:**

Larry Fedora was born in College Station, Texas, and he was an All-American WR at Austin College (NAIA). He got his start in coaching as a graduate assistant there in 1986. Fedora then spent four seasons as an assistant coach at Garland High School in Texas. In 1991, he joined **Grant Teaff's** staff at Baylor and was an assistant there for six seasons, even as **Chuck Reedy** took over as head coach in 1993. He served as **Fisher DeBerry's** passing game coordinator and WR coach at Air Force from 1997-1998. Fedora then served as the offensive coordinator at Middle Tennessee from 1999-2001. In 2002, he joined **Ron Zook's** staff at Florida and worked his way up to OC by 2004. From 2005-2007, Fedora served as **Mike Gundy's** OC at Oklahoma State. He was named Southern Miss' head coach in 2008 and won the Conference USA Championship in his fourth and final year there. North Carolina hired Fedora in 2012, replacing interim head coach **Everett Withers**.

**2014 REVIEW:**

With some preseason predictions calling for North Carolina to win the Coastal Division, 2014 was supposed to be the year the Tar Heels stepped up to the ACC's top level. Those high hopes faded quickly when a 70-41 loss to ECU kicked off a four-game losing streak. Though Fedora rallied his team and pulled off notable wins against Georgia Tech and Duke, the season ended on a negative note with ugly back-to-back losses.

| 2014 RESULTS:   6-7 (4-4 in the ACC) | Final Ranking: NR | |
|---|---|---|
| Liberty | W 56–29 | (51,000) |
| San Diego State | W 31–27 | (58,000) |
| at East Carolina | L 41–70 | (51,082) |
| at Clemson | L 35–50 | (79,155) |
| Virginia Tech | L 17–34 | (60,000) |
| at #6 Notre Dame | L 43–50 | (80,795) |
| Georgia Tech | W 48–43 | (53,000) |
| at Virginia | W 28–27 | (45,200) |
| at Miami (FL) | L 20–47 | (51,702) |
| Pittsburgh | W 40–35 | (53,000) |
| at #25 Duke | W 45–20 | (33,941) |
| NC State | L 7–35 | (53,000) |
| vs. Rutgers (Quick Lane Bowl) | L 21–40 | (23,876) |

**OFFENSE:**

Fedora runs an up-tempo spread offense that achieved a run-pass balance of almost exactly 50-50 in 2014. Though the fast-paced North Carolina offense averaged 33.2 points a game (third in the ACC), it screeched to a halt at times last season. Against NC State, for example, the Tar Heels gained just 207 total yards in an embarrassing 35-7 loss. If inconsistency was the problem in 2014, having 10 starters back on offense – including QB **Marquise Williams** and all five starters on the offensive line – should alleviate that issue in 2015. Williams is a true dual-threat QB. He passed for more than 3,000 yards and rushed for nearly 800 yards as a junior last season. Last year was Fedora's first season as a head coach without **Blake Anderson** on his staff. Anderson, who had spent the previous four seasons as Fedora's OC at Southern Miss and North Carolina, left to become the head coach at Arkansas State. Fedora promoted from within and decided to use two co-offensive coordinators in 2014: WR coach **Gunter Brewer** and OL coach **Chris Kapilovic**. With Williams and nine other starters back in 2015, this offense is poised to be the most explosive Fedora has fielded since coming to UNC.

**DEFENSE:**

When a coach is known for being an offensive guru, as Fedora is, it's common for his defense to struggle. North Carolina has fallen into that trap. Last year's defense, despite having seven starters back, finished last in the ACC in both total defense and points allowed. In fact, UNC gave up the most points and yards in program history. Fedora recognizes that while a great offense might light up the scoreboard, a great defense is required to reach an elite level as a program. Following the same path being taken by other offensive masterminds like **Kevin Sumlin** at Texas A&M and **Gus Malzahn** at Auburn, Fedora is sending a clear message that defense will become a bigger priority. He's bringing in **Gene Chizik** to be his new defensive coordinator. Chizik has a long and distinguished resume as one of the top DCs in the game and he won a National Championship as Auburn's head coach in 2010. Fedora also added **John Papuchis** to his staff as the LB coach. Papuchis spent the last three seasons as Nebraska's DC under **Bo Pelini**. Last year, the Tar Heels ran a 4-2-5 system, but Chizik and company are installing a new 4-3 scheme. This group has seven starters returning and while the transition to a new system may take a little time, expect to see significant improvements made by this group in 2015.

**RECRUITING:**

For the third year in a row, Fedora landed a Top-30 recruiting class. The 2015 class was ranked No. 4 in the ACC and it included one of the nation's top DEs, **Jalen Dalton**, who enrolled in the spring and could contribute right away.

**RUMOR MILL:**

Fedora won eight games in his debut season with the Tar Heels, but his record has been trending downward since. The grumblings have begun and Fedora enters 2015 on the hot seat.

**NOTEWORTHY:**

North Carolina signed **Gene Chizik** to a three-year deal worth $700,000 per year, which makes him one of the top-paid assistant coaches in the country.

**2015 OUTLOOK:**

**Sept. 3**  **vs. South Carolina Gamecocks (in Charlotte, NC)** – As a coach entering the season on the hot seat, one of the fastest ways Fedora can silence his critics is by opening up the season with a Thursday-night win over Steve Spurrier and the Gamecocks. This game will set the tone for the year, which makes it a *MUST-WIN* matchup for the Tar Heels. North Carolina has lost five of its last six games against South Carolina.

**Sept. 12**  **North Carolina A&T Aggies** – North Carolina A&T is an FCS school that went 9-3 last year.

**Sept. 19**  **Illinois Fighting Illini** – North Carolina has lost its last three games against Big Ten teams, including last season's bowl loss to Rutgers.

**Sept. 26**  **Delaware Blue Hens** – This is the second FCS school UNC will face in 2015. Fedora is 5-0 against FCS teams. Delaware went 6-6 last year.

**Oct. 3**  **at Georgia Tech Yellow Jackets** – Fedora's defense has given up an average of 46.3 points a game the last three times they've faced Paul Johnson's flexbone offense. Last year was Fedora's lone win against Georgia Tech in those three meetings.

**Oct. 17**  **Wake Forest Demon Deacons** – The last time these in-state schools met, Fedora's Tar Heels lost by one point in 2012.

**Oct. 24**  **Virginia Cavaliers** – Dating back to his time at Southern Miss, Fedora is a perfect 5-0 against Virginia.

**Oct. 29**  **at Pittsburgh Panthers** – It will be a short turnaround week for the Tar Heels as they travel to Pittsburgh for a Thursday-night game. Fedora is 2-0 against the Panthers.

**Nov. 7**  **Duke Blue Devils** – Last year's win against Duke was Fedora's first in three tries.

**Nov. 14**  **Miami Hurricanes** – Miami is another Coastal Division foe Fedora has a losing record against, at 1-2. The Tar Heels were held to just 6 rushing yards in last year's loss to the Hurricanes.

**Nov. 21**  **at Virginia Tech Hokies** – If things go the way UNC fans hope, this game could end up being for the Coastal Division title. Fedora is 1-2 against Frank Beamer and the Hokies.

**Nov. 28**  **at NC State Wolfpack** – North Carolina was embarrassed by the Wolfpack in last year's 35-7 loss. Fedora is 2-1 in this rivalry.

**BOTTOM LINE:**
Fedora enters the year in a unique situation. Though he's on the hot seat after a disappointing 2014, he's got a team capable of quickly quieting his critics. North Carolina is loaded with returning talent and if the new all-star defensive coaching staff can make positive changes right away, as they should, North Carolina has a legitimate shot at playing for an ACC Championship. It's worth noting that Fedora's breakout season at Southern Miss also occurred during Year 4 of his tenure.

## Larry Fedora's Year-by-Year Coaching Record:

### Southern Mississippi: 34-19 (20-12 in Conference USA)
2008   7-6 (4-4)         **Final Ranking: NR**
        Beat Troy 30-27 in OT in the New Orleans Bowl.
2009   7-6 (5-3)         **Final Ranking: NR**
        Lost to Middle Tennessee 32-42 in the New Orleans Bowl.
2010   8-5 (5-3)         **Final Ranking: NR**
        Lost to Louisville 28-31 in the Beef 'O' Brady's Bowl.
2011   12-2 (6-2)        **Final Ranking: #19**
        Conference USA Champions.
        Beat #7 Houston 49-28 in the C-USA Championship Game.
        Beat Nevada 24-17 in the Hawaii Bowl.

### North Carolina: 21-17 (13-11 in the ACC)
2012   8-4 (5-3)         **Final Ranking: NR**
        North Carolina was ineligible for a bowl game and for the ACC Championship due to NCAA sanctions. Had the Tar Heels been eligible for an ACC title, they would have been co-champions of the Coastal Division.
2013   7-6 (4-4)         **Final Ranking: NR**
        Beat Cincinnati 39-17 in the Belk Bowl.
2014   6-7 (4-4)         **Final Ranking: NR**
        Lost to Rutgers 21-40 in the Quick Lane Bowl.

# Pittsburgh Panthers – Pat Narduzzi

## Coach Ranking: #43

**Overall Record:** 0-0
**2014 Results:** Pittsburgh went 6-7, 4-4 in the ACC (T-3$^{rd}$ in the Coastal)
Narduzzi was Michigan State's defensive coordinator from 2007-2014
**Returning Starters in 2015:** 8 on offense (including QB), 7 on defense
**Salary:** $2 Million*      **Age:** 49      **Job Security Grade:** A

COACH'S BIO:
Pat Narduzzi grew up about an hour from Pittsburgh in Youngstown, Ohio. His father, **Bill Narduzzi**, was the head coach at Youngstown State (Division II and 1-AA) from 1975-1985 and Pat played LB for him as a freshman in 1985. When Youngstown State didn't renew his father's contract after the 1985 season, Narduzzi transferred to Rhode Island (Division 1-AA) and was a three-year starter at LB there. He coached for three seasons at Miami (OH) and then returned to his alma mater to coach LBs at Rhode Island from 1993-1997. He was promoted to defensive coordinator in 1998 and would stay in that position for two seasons. From 2000-2002, he was the LB coach for **Joe Novak** at Northern Illinois. Narduzzi then served one season as the DC for **Terry Hoeppner** at Miami (OH) before **Mark Dantonio** hired him to be Cincinnati's DC in 2004. He followed Dantonio to Michigan State in 2007 and spent eight seasons leading one of the nation's top defenses. Narduzzi won the Broyles Award as the nation's top assistant coach in 2013. Pittsburgh will be his first stint as a head coach.

2014 REVIEW:
In his third and final season as Pitt's head coach, **Paul Chryst** led the Panthers to their seventh-straight bowl game. However, 2014 was also Pitt's third 6-7 season in four years. Chryst left to take the Wisconsin job prior to the Panthers' bowl game, a game they lost by giving up 29 fourth-quarter points.

| 2014 RESULTS:   6-7 (4-4 in the ACC) | Final Ranking: NR | |
|---|---|---|
| Delaware | W 62–0 | (40,549) |
| at Boston College | W 30–20 | (30,083) |
| at FIU | W 42–25 | (10,147) |
| Iowa | L 20–24 | (48,895) |
| Akron | L 10–21 | (40,059) |
| at Virginia | L 19–24 | (43,307) |
| Virginia Tech | W 21–16 | (43,125) |
| Georgia Tech | L 28–56 | (44,734) |
| #24 Duke | L 48–51 2OT | (39,293) |
| at North Carolina | L 35–40 | (53,000) |
| Syracuse | W 30–7 | (32,549) |
| at Miami (FL) | W 35–23 | (61,106) |
| Houston (Armed Forces Bowl) | L 34–35 | (37,888) |

**OFFENSE:**

Narduzzi plans to implement a run-heavy pro-style offense similar to what **Paul Chryst** was already running at Pitt. The Panthers ran the ball 66% of the time in 2014 and averaged 435 total yards a game, which was 3rd best in the ACC. Narduzzi has hired **Jim Chaney** to be his offensive coordinator. Chaney spent the last two seasons as **Brett Bielema**'s OC at Arkansas and he shares Narduzzi's vision for installing a blue-collar offense designed to run the ball often, but multiple enough to stretch the defense with the deep pass. Last year at Arkansas, Chaney's offense ran the ball 61% of the time and produced two 1,100-yard rushers. This year at Pitt, he'll have plenty of weapons to work with. The Panthers will return eight starters, including the ACC Player of the Year in junior RB **James Connor**, one of the nation's top WRs in junior **Tyler Boyd**, and four starters back on the offensive line. The transition to the new staff shouldn't be too extreme and with so much talent returning, Pitt could have one of the most potent offenses in the ACC.

**DEFENSE:**

As the defensive coordinator at Michigan State the past eight seasons, Narduzzi built one of the top defenses in the nation. The Spartans gave up an average of just 17 points a game over the last three seasons and they led the Big Ten in total defense for three of the last four years. Narduzzi achieved this success with an innovative defense specifically designed to shut down modern spread offenses and still adapt to pro-style rushing offenses. The base defense is a 4-3 Cover 4 system that has the corners play mostly press coverage. This gives the defense a nine-in-the-box look. The safeties also play closer to the line of scrimmage than most teams and they're asked to make in-play coverage adjustments based on what the offense does. They'll play zone coverage against shorter underneath passing routes, but switch to man coverage against deeper routes. Narduzzi's DC will be **Josh Conklin**, a Broyles Award nominee last year at Florida International. At FIU, he ran an attacking-style defense that made a name for itself by creating turnovers (ranked No. 5 nationally) and scoring on defense (ranked No. 2 nationally). Pitt will have seven starters back on defense and though the transition to a new system may take some time, this squad should quickly improve from last year's performance, which ranked 11th in the ACC in points allowed.

**RECRUITING:**

When a new coaching staff comes in, initial recruiting classes are usually small in size. That's exactly what happened at Pitt as Narduzzi signed the smallest class in the ACC with just 14 recruits. This class was ranked No. 13 in the ACC and No. 61 nationally.

**RUMOR MILL:**

Narduzzi has been a hot head coaching candidate for the past couple years. After the 2013 season, he was considered a top candidate to replace **Charlie Strong** at Louisville and he reportedly turned down a $2 million offer from UConn. Pitt didn't release details on Narduzzi's contract, but it seems safe to assume that he'll receive a salary that at least matches the $2 million offered by UConn. Narduzzi's $900,000 salary in 2014 made him the Big Ten's highest-paid assistant coach.

**2015 OUTLOOK:**

**Sept. 5**    **Youngstown State Penguins** – Narduzzi's father was the head coach at Youngstown State from 1975-1985. The Penguins are now coached by former Nebraska head coach Bo Pelini, another Youngstown native who Narduzzi should be quite familiar with after their days in the Big Ten.

**Sept. 12**    **at Akron Zips** – Akron beat Paul Chryst's Panthers last year, which broke a five-game winning streak Pitt had against the MAC. Akron is coached by former Auburn head coach Terry Bowden. New Pitt OL coach John Peterson was Bowden's assistant head coach last season.

**Sept. 19**    **at Iowa Hawkeyes** – Pitt has gone 2-11 in its last 13 games against the Big Ten. Iowa has won the last two meetings in this series. The Panthers gave up a fourth-quarter lead in last year's game against the Hawkeyes.

**Oct. 3**    **at Virginia Tech Hokies** – Though the Panthers have won five of their last six games against this former Big East opponent, starting ACC play on the road in Blacksburg won't be easy.

**Oct. 10**    **Virginia Cavaliers** – This game has been won by the home team each of the last two seasons. Pitt is 4-3 all-time against Virginia.

**Oct. 17**    **at Georgia Tech Yellow Jackets** – The Panthers gave up 465 rushing yards to the Yellow Jackets last season and the 56 points scored by Georgia Tech were the most ever by an opponent at Heinz Field. It'll be very interesting to see how Narduzzi's defense handles the Georgia Tech flexbone offense.

**Oct. 24**    **at Syracuse Orange** – The Panthers easily beat the Orange last season. Pitt has won nine of its last 10 games against Syracuse.

**Oct. 29**    **North Carolina Tar Heels** – Pitt will have a short week to prepare for this crucial Thursday-night game. The Panthers have lost two straight to the Tar Heels and if they're going to rise above the .500 level in the ACC, they've got to start winning games like this one.

**Nov. 7**    **Notre Dame Fighting Irish** – Pitt beat the 24th-ranked Irish when these teams last met at Heinz Field in 2013. When Cincinnati hired Brian Kelly to be its head coach after the 2006 season, they passed over Narduzzi who had been Cincinnati's DC at the time.

**Nov. 14**    **at Duke Blue Devils** – Pitt suffered a heartbreaking loss in double OT last year against the Blue Devils.

**Nov. 21**    **Louisville Cardinals** – This all-time series is tied at 8-8. Narduzzi was rumored to be a top candidate for the Louisville job when the Cardinals hired Bobby Petrino after the 2013 season.

**Nov. 27**    **Miami Hurricanes** – This game will be played the Friday after Thanksgiving and it will likely have a big impact on what type of bowl game the Panthers go to. That makes this a *MUST-WIN* game for Narduzzi in Year 1.

**BOTTOM LINE:**
You never know exactly how a team will respond to a new staff, but Narduzzi seems like the perfect fit for this program and the Panthers have the talent to surprise the rest of the ACC this year. If Narduzzi picks up momentum early, this team should a legitimate contender for the Coastal Division title.

# Virginia Cavaliers – Mike London

## Coach Ranking: #80

**Overall Record:** 47-43 in 7 seasons (2 seasons in FCS)
**Record at Virginia:** 23-38 in 5 seasons
**2014 Results:** 5-7, 3-5 in the ACC (7th in the ACC Coastal)
**Returning Starters in 2015:** 5 on offense (including QB), 5 on defense
**Salary:** $2.3 Million      **Age:** 54      **Job Security Grade:** D

**COACH'S BIO:**
It's hard not to root for a coach with a story like Mike London's. After playing DB at Richmond (Division 1-AA) from 1979-1982 and spending one season with the NFL's Dallas Cowboys, London spent five years working as a police officer and detective on Richmond, Virginia's street crimes unit. He was nearly killed when a criminal once tried to shoot him at close range, but the loaded gun malfunctioned and didn't fire. He's also responsible for saving the life of one of his daughters, who had a rare bone marrow disorder. London donated his bone marrow, which was a perfect match for his daughter despite the 10,000-to-1 odds that it would be. In 1989, London began a college coaching career that would include stops at Boston College under **Tom O'Brien**, Virginia under **Al Groh**, the NFL's Houston Texans under **Dom Capers**, and Richmond under **Dave Clawson**. London was hired as the head coach at Richmond in 2008 and won the FCS National Championship in his first season. He became Virginia's head coach in 2010 and was named the ACC Coach of the Year in 2011.

**2014 REVIEW:**
Virginia rebounded somewhat from its disastrous 2-10 season in 2013, but the Cavaliers still finished 2014 with a losing record for the fourth time in five seasons.

| 2014 RESULTS:   5-7 (3-5 in the ACC) | Final Ranking: NR | |
|---|---|---|
| #7 UCLA | L 20–28 | (44,749) |
| #17 (FCS) Richmond | W 45–13 | (34,533) |
| #21 Louisville | W 23–21 | (34,816) |
| at #21 BYU | L 33–41 | (59,023) |
| Kent State | W 45–13 | (33,526) |
| Pittsburgh | W 24–19 | (43,307) |
| at Duke | L 13–20 | (28,131) |
| North Carolina | L 27–28 | (45,200) |
| at Georgia Tech | L 10–35 | (46,657) |
| at #2 Florida State | L 20–34 | (82,325) |
| Miami (FL) | W 30–13 | (39,112) |
| at Virginia Tech | L 20–24 | (60,431) |

## OFFENSE:

Virginia runs a balanced pro-style offense that rushed the ball slightly more than it passed it in 2014. This offense has been stuck in the back half of the ACC in scoring each of the five seasons London has been here. Virginia's offensive coordinator is former Colorado State head coach **Steve Fairchild**. His style is heavily influenced by the NFL. He was the OC for the Buffalo Bills and the St. Louis Rams, and he served as the senior offensive assistant for the San Diego Chargers before coming to Virginia. The lack of a consistent running threat hurt this offense last season. The Cavaliers rushed for less than 40 yards in three of its final four games of 2014. London has added **Dave Borbely** to the staff as the new OL coach. Borbely was **Charlie Strong**'s OL coach and running game coordinator at Louisville from 2010-2013. Though only five starters are back for Virginia in 2015, they'll have three starting offensive linemen returning and junior QB **Greyson Lambert**, who missed a few games last year due an ankle injury.

## DEFENSE:

Virginia made big improvements on defense in 2014. After the Cavaliers gave up more points than any other school in the ACC in 2013, they moved up to No. 6 in the conference last year. Nationally, Virginia's defense made an impressive one-year jump from 99th to 33rd in points allowed. Experience was a big reason for that turnaround and having a second year in defensive coordinator **Jon Tenuta**'s 4-3 system also paid off. This year, Tenuta must replace six starters, including all three LBs. Tenuta, a former DB for the Cavaliers, has been a DC at Kansas State, Ohio State, Georgia Tech, and Notre Dame. He was rumored to be a head coaching candidate for the Michigan State job that eventually went to **Mark Dantonio**.

## RECRUITING:

After a monster recruiting class in 2014, which included the nation's No. 1-rated safety and No. 1-rated DT, the 2015 class took a step back and landed at No. 9 in the ACC and No. 48 nationally. The decline wasn't too surprising considering that the speculation regarding whether London would be fired continued well into November last season. London makes his talent-rich home state of Virginia a top priority in recruiting and this strategy has paid off.

## RUMOR MILL:

After winning a total of six games from 2012-2013, there was some speculation that London needed to take the Cavaliers to a bowl game in 2014 to save his job. He fell one win short of bowl eligibility and there were rumors that London might be fired late last season. Virginia AD **Craig Littlepage** issued a statement prior to the Virginia Tech game declaring that London would remain the head coach at Virginia. London will enter Year 6 of his tenure the same way he did the last two: on the hot seat. Though he has two years remaining on his contract, a fourth-straight losing season would likely mean the end of the London era at Virginia.

## NOTEWORTHY:

**Tom O'Brien**, the former head coach at Boston College and NC State, spent the last two seasons as Virginia's TE coach and associate head coach for offense. This offseason, O'Brien announced his retirement.

**2015 OUTLOOK:**

**Sep. 5**   **at UCLA Bruins** – This will be a tough way to open the season. The Bruins have 18 starters back from a team that finished No. 10 last year. UCLA scored three defensive TDs to sneak by the Cavaliers in 2014.

**Sep. 12**   **Notre Dame Fighting Irish** – Week 2 matches Virginia up with another tough opponent loaded with experience as the Irish return 19 starters from last year's 8-5 team.

**Sep. 19**   **William & Mary Tribe** – London is 3-0 against this in-state FCS school, including two wins while he was at Richmond.

**Sept. 25**   **Boise State Broncos** – This Friday-night game caps off a very difficult nonconference schedule. Virginia is 2-4 all-time against the MWC and Boise State finished 12-2 last year.

**Oct. 10**   **at Pittsburgh Panthers** – With such a difficult nonconference schedule, it'll be crucial for Virginia to get off to a fast start in ACC play. London is 1-1 against Pitt.

**Oct. 17**   **Syracuse Orange** – The only break Virginia gets in this year's schedule is replacing Florida State with Syracuse from the Atlantic Division. This will be the first meeting between these schools since Syracuse joined the ACC. The all-time series is tied at 2-2.

**Oct. 24**   **at North Carolina Tar Heels** – London is 0-5 against the Tar Heels.

**Oct. 31**   **Georgia Tech Yellow Jackets** – Virginia has got to figure out a way to run the ball against Georgia Tech. Over the last three years against Tech, the Cavaliers have rushed for a *total* of just 188 yards. London is 1-4 against Paul Johnson and the Yellow Jackets.

**Nov. 7**   **at Miami Hurricanes** – London is 4-1 against the Hurricanes. The lone loss occurred the last time the Cavaliers played at Miami, in 2013.

**Nov. 14**   **at Louisville Cardinals** – Virginia upset Louisville last year by capitalizing off of four Cardinal turnovers.

**Nov. 21**   **Duke Blue Devils** – London has lost his last three games against Duke. The Cavaliers lost last year's game despite outgaining the Blue Devils by 131 yards.

**Nov. 28**   **Virginia Tech Hokies** – London is 0-5 against Frank Beamer and the Cavaliers have lost 11-straight games to their in-state rival. Like last year, a bowl berth may once again be riding on this game. Bowl berth or not, simply breaking the losing streak against the rival Hokies could be enough to save London's job. This is a *MUST-WIN* game for London and his team.

**BOTTOM LINE:**
With just 10 returning starters and only one game on the schedule that Virginia will certainly be favored in (against FCS opponent William & Mary), it's going to be very difficult for London to reach six wins and bowl eligibility. Another five-win season could be enough to keep his job *if* one of those wins includes the season finale against archrival Virginia Tech.

## Mike London's Year-by-Year Coaching Record:

### Richmond: 24-5 (5-1 in the FCS Playoffs)
2008    13–3 (4-0)              Final Ranking: #1
        FCS National Champions.
        London named FCS National Coach of the Year.
        Beat #5 Montana 24-7 in the FCS Championship Game.
2009    11–2 (1-1)              Final Ranking: #4
        Lost to #5 Appalachian State 31-35 in the FCS quarterfinals.

### Virginia: 23-38 (11-29 in the ACC)
2010    4–8 (1–7)              Final Ranking: NR
2011    8–5 (5–3)              Final Ranking: NR
        London named ACC Coach of the Year.
        Lost to Auburn 24-43 in the Chick-fil-A Bowl.
2012    4–8 (2–6)              Final Ranking: NR
2013    2–10 (0–8)             Final Ranking: NR
2014    5–7 (3–5)              Final Ranking: NR

# Virginia Tech Hokies – Frank Beamer

## Coach Ranking: #15

**Overall Record:** 273-138-4 in 34 seasons (6 seasons in Division 1-AA)
**Record at Virginia Tech:** 231–115–2 in 28 seasons
**2014 Results:** 7-6, 3-5 in the ACC (T-5th in the ACC Coastal)
**Returning Starters in 2015:** 8 on offense (including QB), 8 on defense
**Salary:** $2.7 Million        **Age:** 68        **Job Security Grade:** B

**COACH'S BIO:**
Frank Beamer grew up in Hillsville, Virginia, and was a three-year starter at CB for Virginia Tech from 1966-1968. He spent three seasons as a high school assistant coach and then began a college coaching career with stops at Maryland under **Jerry Claiborne**, The Citadel under **Bobby Ross**, and Murray State under **Mike Gottfried**. After two years as Murray State's defensive coordinator, Beamer was promoted to head coach. He spent six seasons at Murray State and was then hired to replace **Bill Dooley** as Virginia Tech's head coach in 1987. In 28 seasons leading the Hokies, he's gone to 22-consecutive bowl games, he's won eight conference championships, he's been named the conference coach of the year five times, and he was named the National Coach of the Year in 1999. With 273 victories, Beamer is college football's winningest active FBS coach.

**2014 REVIEW:**
Though Virginia Tech stumbled to a third-straight mediocre record in 2014, the Hokies were the only team to defeat the eventual National Champions and lost five games by a touchdown or less. Had Virginia Tech been able to close out a few of those close games, Beamer would have easily captured his 14th season of 10 or more wins.

**2014 RESULTS:   7-6 (3-5 in the ACC)**          **Final Ranking: NR**

| | | |
|---|---|---|
| #19 (FCS) William & Mary | W 34-9 | (62,722) |
| at #8 Ohio State | W 35-21 | (107,517) |
| East Carolina | L 21-28 | (63,267) |
| **Georgia Tech** | L 24-27 | (62,318) |
| Western Michigan | W 35-17 | (59,625) |
| **at North Carolina** | W 34-17 | (60,000) |
| **at Pittsburgh** | L 16-21 | (43,125) |
| **Miami (FL)** | L 6-30 | (64,007) |
| **Boston College** | L 31-33 | (55,729) |
| **at #19 Duke** | W 17-16 | (30,107) |
| **at Wake Forest** | L 3-6 2OT | (27,820) |
| **Virginia** | W 24-20 | (60,431) |
| vs. Cincinnati (Military Bowl) | W 33-17 | (34,277) |

**OFFENSE:**

In 2013, Beamer brought in **Scott Loeffler** to be his new offensive coordinator and make some fundamental changes to Virginia Tech's offensive style. For years prior, the Hokies ran an offense designed for dual-threat QBs like **Michael Vick**, **Tyrod Taylor**, and **Logan Thomas**, but during the past two seasons, Loeffler has been transitioning Virginia Tech to a West Coast pro-style offense. So far, the change hasn't been too successful as the Hokies' scoring offense has finished 12th in the ACC in each of those two seasons. With eight starters back, including pro-style senior QB **Michael Brewer** (now in his second season as the starter in Loeffler's system), the pressure is on for this offense to start putting up some better numbers. Before joining Beamer's staff in 2013, Loeffler was Auburn's OC during **Gene Chizik**'s final season there.

**DEFENSE:**

Defensive coordinator **Bud Foster** and Frank Beamer have a long history together. Foster was originally hired by Beamer at Murray State in 1981. Foster has been Virginia Tech's DC since 1995 and he's the only coach ever to be named a Broyles Award finalist, which goes to the nation's top assistant coach, *four* times. (He won the Broyles Award in 2006.) Foster is widely considered one of the best DCs in all of college football and the Hokies have finished second in the ACC in points allowed for each of the past four seasons. Foster's "Lunch Pail Defense" is an attacking-style system that led the nation in sacks per pass attempt last season. He implements an adaptable four-man-front defense that gives offenses fits with its ability to seamlessly shift from a 4-2-5 base to a 4-3 to a 4-4 with eight in the box. The Hokies will have eight starters back in 2015 and this group should be one of the top defenses in the nation. With a salary of $1.4 million in 2014, Foster was college football's highest-paid assistant coach last season.

**RECRUITING:**

Though Virginia Tech still landed the nation's No. 29 recruiting class (No. 5 in the ACC), the seven- and eight-loss seasons may be catching up with the Hokies as they've been trending slightly lower in the nation's recruiting rankings over the past few years.

**RUMOR MILL:**

Any claims that Beamer – a future Hall of Famer and the winningest active coach in FBS – is on the hot seat are *way* premature, but three-consecutive mediocre seasons have created a sense of urgency for Virginia Tech to climb back into ACC title contention.

**NOTEWORTHY:**

Bud Foster's name comes up often as a head coaching candidate, but this past offseason **Kevin Sumlin** and Texas A&M made a serious run at bringing in Foster as their new DC (A&M eventually hired **John Chavis** away from LSU). Foster admitted the speculation wasn't a rumor and told the *Roanoke Times*, "It was probably as close as I've ever been to leaving (Virginia Tech)."

**2015 OUTLOOK:**

**Sept. 7**      **Ohio State Buckeyes** – This Labor Day showdown will start the season off with a bang as the Hokies try to knock off the defending National Champions. Last year, Virginia Tech gave Ohio State its only loss of the season.

**Sept. 12**     **Furman Paladins** – Virginia Tech has won its last three games against FCS schools by a combined score of 187-32. Furman went 3-9 last year.

**Sept. 19**     **at Purdue Boilermakers** – Beamer is 2-1 all-time against the Big Ten. He's 19-4 if you include recent Big Ten additions Rutgers and Maryland.

**Sept. 26**     **at East Carolina Pirates** – These two teams have met in seven of the last eight seasons and Virginia Tech has gone 5-2 during that stretch. Beamer is 12-7 all-time against ECU, with one of those losses occurring while he was at Murray State.

**Oct. 3**      **Pittsburgh Panthers** – Though Beamer is 8-6 all-time against Pitt, he's gone 1-5 over the last six games in this series.

**Oct. 9**      **NC State Wolfpack** – This Friday night game will mark the first meeting between these two schools since 2010. Beamer has won his last three games against the Wolfpack.

**Oct. 17**     **at Miami Hurricanes** – This rivalry has carried over from the Big East and it's one of those games that can always go either way. Beamer is 13-11 against the Hurricanes.

**Oct. 24**     **Duke Blue Devils** – Beamer is 10-1 against Duke with the lone loss occurring the last time the Blue Devils came to Blacksburg, in 2013.

**Oct. 31**     **at Boston College Eagles** – Virginia Tech had won five straight against Boston College before Steve Addazio was hired. The Hokies have lost both games since Addazio became head coach of the Eagles.

**Nov. 12**     **at Georgia Tech Yellow Jackets** – Bud Foster's defense has had a knack for slowing down Georgia Tech's dominant running game. Over the last three seasons, the Jackets have averaged 317.5 rushing yards a game against all opponents. Against Virginia Tech, they've averaged 190.3 rushing yards; a 40% decline from their average rushing output. This Thursday-night matchup could end up deciding the Coastal Division title, which makes it a *MUST-WIN* game for Beamer and the Hokies.

**Nov. 21**     **North Carolina Tar Heels** – Beamer has gone 9-2 against North Carolina since joining the ACC and one of those losses (2009) was later vacated by UNC.

**Nov. 28**     **at Virginia Cavaliers** – The Hokies have dominated this rivalry in recent years. Beamer has won his last 11 games against the Cavaliers.

**BOTTOM LINE:**
If the offense finally starts clicking, this could be the year Virginia Tech breaks back into the national spotlight. A tough nonconference schedule with Ohio State and ECU won't make the path to 10 wins easy, but having 16 starters back means the Hokies should be able to pull out more of those close games they struggled with last season.

## Frank Beamer's Year-by-Year Coaching Record:

### Murray State: 42-23-2 (0-1 in the Division 1-AA Playoffs)
1981    8–3 (0-0)                  Final Ranking: #9
1982    4–7 (0-0)                  Final Ranking: NR
1983    7–4 (0-0)                  Final Ranking: NR
1984    9–2 (0-0)                  Final Ranking: #13
1985    7–3–1 (0-0)                Final Ranking: #17
1986    7–4–1 (0-1)                Final Ranking: #18
    Lost to Eastern Illinois 21-28 in the first round of the Division 1-AA playoffs.

### Virginia Tech: 231–115-2 (121–49 in the Big East and ACC)
1987    2–9 (Ind.)                 Final Ranking: NR
1988    3–8 (Ind.)                 Final Ranking: NR
1989    6–4–1 (Ind.)               Final Ranking: NR
1990    6–5 (Ind.)                 Final Ranking: NR
1991    5–6 (1–0)                  Final Ranking: NR
    Virginia Tech, formerly an Independent program, joins the Big East. (The Big East did not play full conference schedules until 1993.)
1992    2–8–1 (1–4)                Final Ranking: NR
1993    9–3 (4–3)                  Final Ranking: #20
    Beat #21 Indiana 45-20 in the Independence Bowl.
1994    8–4 (5–2)                  Final Ranking: #24
    Lost to Tennessee 23-45 in the Gator Bowl.
1995    10–2 (6–1)                 Final Ranking: #9
    Big East Co-Champions.
    Beamer named Big East Coach of the Year.
    Beat #9 Texas 28-10 in the Sugar Bowl.
1996    10–2 (6–1)                 Final Ranking: #12
    Big East Co-Champions.
    Beamer named Big East Coach of the Year.
    Lost to #6 Nebraska 21-41 in the Orange Bowl.
1997    7–5 (5–2)                  Final Ranking: NR
    Lost to #7 North Carolina 3-42 in the Gator Bowl.
1998    9–3 (5–2)                  Final Ranking: #19
    Beat Alabama 38-7 in the Music City Bowl.
1999    11–1 (7–0)                 Final Ranking: #2
    Big East Champions.
    Beamer named National Coach of the Year.
    Beamer named Big East Coach of the Year.
    Lost to #1 Florida State 29-46 in the BCS National Championship Game.
2000    11–1 (6–1)                 Final Ranking: #6
    Beat #16 Clemson 41-20 in the Gator Bowl.
2001    8–4 (4–3)                  Final Ranking: #18
    Lost to #24 Florida State 17-30 in the Gator Bowl.
2002    10–4 (3–4)                 Final Ranking: #14
    Beat Air Force 20-14 in the San Francisco Bowl.

## Virginia Tech (continued)

**2003**   **8–5 (4–3)**          **Final Ranking: NR**
Lost to California 49-52 in the Insight Bowl.

**2004**   **10–3 (7–1)**         **Final Ranking: #10**
Virginia Tech leaves the Big East and joins the ACC.
ACC Champions.
Beamer named ACC Coach of the Year.
Lost to #3 Auburn 13-16 in the Sugar Bowl.

**2005**   **11–2 (7–1)**         **Final Ranking: #7**
ACC Coastal Division Champions.
Beamer named ACC Coach of the Year.
Lost to Florida State 22-27 in the ACC Championship Game.
Beat #16 Louisville 35-24 in the Gator Bowl.

**2006**   **10–3 (6–2)**         **Final Ranking: #18**
Lost to Georgia 24-31 in the Chick-fil-A Bowl.

**2007**   **11–3 (7–1)**         **Final Ranking: #9**
ACC Champions.
Beat #12 Boston College 30-16 in the ACC Championship Game.
Lost to #8 Kansas 21-24 in the Orange Bowl.

**2008**   **10–4 (5–3)**         **Final Ranking: #14**
ACC Champions.
Beat #20 Boston College 30-12 in the ACC Championship Game.
Beat #12 Cincinnati 20-7 in the Orange Bowl.

**2009**   **10–3 (6–2)**         **Final Ranking: #10**
Beat Tennessee 37-14 in the Chick-fil-A Bowl.

**2010**   **11–3 (8–0)**         **Final Ranking: #15**
ACC Champions.
Beat #20 Florida State 44-33 in the ACC Championship Game.
Lost to #5 Stanford 12-40 in the Orange Bowl.

**2011**   **11–3 (7–1)**         **Final Ranking: #17**
ACC Coastal Division Champions.
Lost to #21 Clemson 10-38 in the ACC Championship Game.
Lost to #13 Michigan 20-23 in OT in the Sugar Bowl.

**2012**   **7–6 (4–4)**          **Final Ranking: NR**
Beat Rutgers 13-10 in OT in the Russell Athletic Bowl.

**2013**   **8–5 (5–3)**          **Final Ranking: NR**
Lost to #17 UCLA 12-42 in the Sun Bowl.

**2014**   **7–6 (3–5)**          **Final Ranking: NR**
Beat Cincinnati 33-17 in the Military Bowl.

# Notre Dame Fighting Irish – Brian Kelly

## Coach Ranking: #14

**Overall Record:** 216–77–2 in 24 seasons (13 seasons in Division II)
**Record at Notre Dame:** 45-20 in 5 seasons
**2014 Results:** 8-5 (Independent)
**Returning Starters in 2015:** 9 on offense (including QB), 10 on defense
**Salary:** $4 Million*       **Age:** 53       **Job Security Grade:** B

COACH'S BIO:
Brian Kelly grew up in Boston and considered following in his father's footsteps as a politician before choosing to pursue a career in coaching. Kelly played LB and was named a captain for Assumption College (Division II). After graduating, he joined the school's coaching staff and served as defensive coordinator from 1983-1986. Kelly joined Grand Valley State's (Division II) staff in 1987 and was promoted to head coach in 1991. He spent 13 seasons at Grand Valley State and won Division II National Championships in 2002 and 2003. He then spent three years as Central Michigan's head coach before a three-year stint at Cincinnati, where he led the Bearcats to Big East titles in 2008 and 2009. Kelly was hired by Notre Dame in 2010 and he currently has the third-most wins of any active FBS coach.

2014 REVIEW:
Kelly lost his offensive and defensive coordinators to head coaching positions before the season 2014 began. He lost four starters who declared early for the NFL draft and lost five more key players (three starters) due to academic suspensions just three weeks before the season opener. Yet, the Irish stormed out to a 6-0 start and a No. 5 ranking before falling to No. 2 Florida State in the final seconds of a marque showdown. After that, the Irish were decimated by injuries and turnovers as they dropped their last four games of the regular season. An upset win over LSU in the Music City Bowl helped salvage the year and raise expectations heading into 2015.

| 2014 RESULTS:   8-5 | Final Ranking: NR | |
|---|---|---|
| Rice | W 48–17 | (80,795) |
| Michigan | W 31–0 | (80,795) |
| vs. Purdue (in Indianapolis) | W 30–14 | (56,832) |
| vs. Syracuse (in East Rutherford, NJ) | W 31–15 | (76,802) |
| #14 Stanford | W 17–14 | (80,795) |
| North Carolina | W 50–43 | (80,795) |
| at #2 Florida State | L 27–31 | (82,431) |
| vs. Navy (in Landover, MD) | W 49–39 | (36,807) |
| at #11 Arizona State | L 31–55 | (65,870) |
| Northwestern | L 40–43 OT | (80,795) |
| #24 Louisville | L 28–31 | (80,795) |
| at USC | L 14–49 | (79,586) |
| vs. #22 LSU (Music City Bowl) | W 31–28 | (60,149) |

**OFFENSE:**
Notre Dame's spread attack improved from the 74th-ranked scoring offense in 2013 to the 40th-ranked squad in 2014. The Irish passing attack led the way, finishing the season ranked No. 19 in the nation. What hurt this offense was the lack of a consistent rushing threat and the high number of turnovers. Though Kelly will continue to handle the play-calling, he's bringing in **Mike Sanford** from Boise State to be his new offensive coordinator and QB coach. Sanford, 33, is considered one of the top young coaches in America. Reportedly, Ohio State, Vanderbilt, and Oregon State also tried to hire him. At Boise State, Sanford's offense ranked No. 9 nationally in scoring and while he has plenty of expertise when it comes to the spread system Kelly likes to run, Sanford also likes to implement a power running game to balance out his offense. Last year, QB **Everett Golson** was benched late in the season following a string of turnovers and **Malik Zaire** stepped in and led the Irish to their upset win over LSU. Golson decided to transfer after his demotion and Zaire, who is more of a rushing threat, will take over as the fulltime QB. With four starters returning on the offensive line and several blue-chip RBs to hand the ball off to, the Irish running game should improve in 2015. Last year's OC, **Mike Denbrock**, remains on the staff as associate head coach and WR coach. Denbrock turned down the head coaching job at Central Michigan to stay at Notre Dame.

**DEFENSE:**
**Brian VanGorder** was hired as the defensive coordinator in 2014, replacing **Bob Diaco**, who left to become the head coach at Connecticut. VanGorder, who had spent 2013 as the LB coach for **Rex Ryan's** New York Jets, brought in a high-energy style and replaced Diaco's 3-4 defense with a 4-3 system. Statistically, Notre Dame's defense was ugly in 2014. The Irish finished the year ranked 84th in points allowed. However, this squad was annihilated by injuries in the second half of the season. *Nine* defensive starters were lost to injuries in 2014 and three others were lost to academic suspension. With this in mind, it's surprising the Irish defense held up as well as it did. With 10 starters returning and added depth, this defense should be vastly improved in 2015.

**RECRUITING:**
Kelly landed a recruiting class that barely missed the Top 10 this offseason and he did a good job *re*-recruiting current players by convincing DT **Sheldon Day** and OT **Ronnie Stanley** to forego the NFL draft and return to Notre Dame in 2015. After Signing Day, recruiting coordinator and RB coach **Tony Alford** left the Irish to join **Urban Meyer** at Ohio State. This move stings as Alford was recognized as a top-notch recruiter during his six years at Notre Dame. However, new OC Mike Sanford has already established himself as an outstanding recruiter and should help cancel out the loss of Alford.

**RUMOR MILL:**
There were rumors that last season's academic suspensions frustrated Kelly to the point that he was looking to make a move to the NFL. In May, Kelly told *Sports Illustrated* the opposite was true and that his commitment to Notre Dame has only been strengthened. Kelly interviewed for the Philadelphia Eagles job after the 2012 season and his name comes up frequently as a candidate for NFL jobs.

**2015 OUTLOOK:**

**Sept. 5**    **Texas Longhorns** – Two historic programs kick off the season in what will likely be one of the most-watched games of the college football season. This will be Kelly's first meeting with Charlie Strong, who coached the DL at Notre Dame under Holtz and Davie from 1995-1998.

**Sept. 12**    **at Virginia Cavaliers** – The Irish went 2-2 against ACC schools last year and this year they'll be playing six ACC opponents. Virginia has had just one winning season since 2008.

**Sept. 19**    **Georgia Tech Yellow Jackets** – Since coming to Notre Dame, Kelly is 7-1 against teams that run the flexbone triple-option offense. Georgia Tech's Paul Johnson is a master coach of this offense.

**Sept. 26**    **Massachusetts Minutemen** – Though this should be an easy win for the Irish, it's sandwiched between Notre Dame's two toughest ACC opponents, which makes this game a potential "letdown" moment.

**Oct. 3**    **at Clemson Tigers** – Notre Dame hasn't played Clemson since the 1970s and this should be the most hostile environment the Irish walk into this season.

**Oct. 10**    **Navy Midshipmen** – After losing to Navy during his first season at Notre Dame, Kelly has one four straight against the Midshipmen.

**Oct. 17**    **USC Trojans** – The Irish were embarrassed by their rivals last season and this year's rematch has the potential to be a Top-10 showdown. Kelly is 3-2 against the Trojans. As it usually is, this will be a *MUST-WIN* game for Notre Dame.

**Oct. 31**    **at Temple Owls** – The Irish opened the 2013 season with a 28-6 win over Temple and this matchup should go similarly.

**Nov. 7**    **at Pittsburgh Panthers** – Pitt's new head coach, Pat Narduzzi, was a leading candidate for the Cincinnati head coaching job that opened up in 2006. That job ended up going to Brian Kelly. Narduzzi became the defensive coordinator at Michigan State where he led one of the top defenses in college football from 2007-2014.

**Nov. 14**    **Wake Forest Demon Deacons** – The Irish blew out Wake Forest 38-0 in 2013, which was the last time they came to South Bend for the season's home finale.

**Nov. 21**    **vs. Boston College Eagles (at Fenway Park in Boston)** – Brian Kelly returns to his hometown in dramatic fashion as the Irish and Eagles will play the first football game in Fenway Park since 1968. BC head coach Steve Addazio was an assistant at Notre Dame under Bob Davie from 1999-2001.

**Nov. 28**    **at Stanford Cardinal** – Kelly is 2-2 against Stanford head coach David Shaw and their last three meetings have been decided by a touchdown or less.

**BOTTOM LINE:**
With 19 starters returning, this should be Brian Kelly's best team since he came to Notre Dame. A more balanced offense and an experienced defense should set the Irish up for a legitimate playoff run in 2015.

## Brian Kelly's Year-by-Year Coaching Record:

### Grand Valley State: 118-35-2 (11-4 in the Division II Playoffs)
1991    9–3 (0-1)              **Final Ranking: NA**
Lost to Texas A&M Commerce 15-36 in first round of Division II playoffs.
1992    8–3 (0-0)              **Final Ranking: NA**
1993    6–3–2 (0-0)            **Final Ranking: NA**
1994    8–4 (0-1)              **Final Ranking: NA**
Lost to Indiana (PA) 27-35 in first round of Division II playoffs.
1995    8–3 (0-0)              **Final Ranking: NA**
1996    8–3 (0-0)              **Final Ranking: NA**
1997    9–2 (0-0)              **Final Ranking: NA**
1998    9–3 (0-1)              **Final Ranking: NA**
Lost to Slippery Rock (PA) 21-37 in first round of Division II playoffs.
1999    5–5 (0-0)              **Final Ranking: NA**
2000    7–4 (0-0)              **Final Ranking: NA**
2001    13–1 (3-1)             **Final Ranking: NA**
Lost to North Dakota 14-17 in Division II National Championship Game.
2002    14–0 (4-0)             **Final Ranking: NA**
Division II National Champions.
Kelly named Division II Coach of the Year.
Beat Valdosta State 31-24 in Division II National Championship Game.
2003    14–1 (4-0)             **Final Ranking: NA**
Division II National Champions.
Kelly named Division II Coach of the Year.
Beat North Dakota 10-3 in Division II National Championship Game.

### Central Michigan: 19-16 (15-16 in the MAC)
2004    4–7 (3-5)              **Final Ranking: NR**
2005    6–5 (5-3)              **Final Ranking: NR**
2006    9–4 (7-1)              **Final Ranking: NR**
MAC Champions.
Beat Ohio 31-10 in MAC Championship Game.
Central Michigan beat Middle Tennessee 31-14 in the Motor City Bowl, but
Kelly had already left to accept the Cincinnati job.

### Cincinnati: 34-6 (17-4 in the Big East)
2006    1–0 (0–0)             **Final Ranking: NR**
Kelly got an early start on the job and coached Cincinnati to its 27-24 win
over Western Michigan in the International Bowl.
2007    10–3 (4-3)             **Final Ranking: #17**
Kelly named Big East Coach of the Year.
Beat Southern Mississippi 31-21 in the Papajohns.com Bowl.
2008    11–3 (6-1)             **Final Ranking: #17**
Big East Champions.
Kelly named Big East Coach of the Year.
Lost to #19 Virginia Tech 7-20 in the Orange Bowl.

## Cincinnati (continued)

2009    12–0 (7–0)              **Final Ranking: #4**
        Big East Champions.
        Kelly named Big East Coach of the Year.
        Cincinnati lost to Florida in the Sugar Bowl 24-51 and finished the season
        ranked #8, but Kelly had already left to accept the Notre Dame job.

## Notre Dame: 45-20 (Independent)

2010    8–5 (Ind.)             **Final Ranking: NR**
        Beat Miami (FL) 33-17 in the Sun Bowl.
2011    8–5 (Ind.)             **Final Ranking: NR**
        Lost to #25 Florida State 14-18 in the Champs Sports Bowl.
2012    12–1 (Ind.)            **Final Ranking: #3**
        Kelly named National Coach of the Year.
        Lost to #2 Alabama 14-42 in the BCS National Championship Game.
2013    9–4 (Ind.)             **Final Ranking: #20**
        Beat Rutgers 29-16 in the Pinstripe Bowl.
2014    8–5 (Ind.)             **Final Ranking: NR**
        Beat #22 LSU 31-28 in the Music City Bowl.

Your Source for College Football Coaching News, Rumors, Rankings, and Trends:

# CoachesAlmanac.com

# 2015 BIG TEN PREVIEW

## Five Things You Need to Know about the Big Ten in 2015:

**The Battle at the Top:** It may not have the same ring as Woody vs. Bo, but Urban vs. Jim will be college football's must-watch coaching matchup of 2015 as **Jim Harbaugh** takes over at **Michigan** and tries to knock off **Urban Meyer** and the defending National Champions. And get ready for some epic recruiting battles between these fierce competitors. All hype aside, though, **Ohio State** is the clear Big Ten favorite and **Michigan State** is next in line.

**New to the Big Ten:** The top two programs in the West Division, **Wisconsin** and **Nebraska**, both hired new coaches for 2015. While these hires make sense from a "good fit" perspective – **Mike Riley's** personality is expected to mesh better with the Nebraska administration and **Paul Chryst** is returning to his hometown of Madison – these hires were, frankly, a bit underwhelming for such big-time programs. Riley and Chryst can prove the skeptics wrong quickly by finishing 2015 right where their predecessors left off; at the top of the Big Ten West.

**Coach on the Rise:** **Jerry Kill** is building a legitimate Big Ten contender in **Minnesota**. With **Wisconsin** and **Nebraska** both transitioning to new head coaches in 2015, the door is wide open for Kill to take the next step and win the West.

**Keep an Eye On:** After eight years as **Michigan State's** defensive coordinator, **Pat Narduzzi** has left to become a head coach. This year, co-DCs **Harlon Barnett** and **Mike Tressel** will try to fill the *big* shoes left by Narduzzi, who built one of college football's most dominating defenses at Michigan State.

**Coaches on the Hot Seat:** As many as five Big Ten coaches may be fighting for their jobs in 2015: **Illinois'** Tim Beckman, **Maryland's** Randy Edsall, **Iowa's** Kirk Ferentz, **Purdue's** Darrell Hazell, and **Indiana's** Kevin Wilson. Interestingly, all five coaches have good reasons to be hopeful about 2015 and could quickly quiet their critics with a strong season.

## 2015 Projected Standings for the Big Ten:

**East Division:**
1. Ohio State
2. Michigan State
3. Michigan
4. Penn State
5. Indiana
6. Rutgers
7. Maryland

**West Division:**
1. Minnesota
2. Wisconsin
3. Nebraska
4. Iowa
5. Northwestern
6. Illinois
7. Purdue

## Ranking the Big Ten's Coaches:

1. **Urban Meyer** – Ohio State (142-26 in 13 seasons)
2. **Mark Dantonio** – Michigan State (93-48 in 11 seasons)
3. **Jim Harbaugh** – Michigan (58-27 in 7 seasons)
4. **James Franklin** – Penn State (31-21 in 4 seasons)
5. **Jerry Kill** – Minnesota (148-96 in 21 seasons)
6. **Mike Riley** – Nebraska (93-80 in 14 seasons)
7. **Pat Fitzgerald** – Northwestern (60-53 in 9 seasons)
8. **Kirk Ferentz** – Iowa (127-106 in 19 seasons)
9. **Kyle Flood** – Rutgers (23-16 in 3 seasons)
10. **Paul Chryst** – Wisconsin (19-19 in 3 seasons)
11. **Randy Edsall** – Maryland (94-100 in 15 seasons)
12. **Darrell Hazell** – Purdue (20-30 in 4 seasons)
13. **Tim Beckman** – Illinois (33-41 in 6 seasons)
14. **Kevin Wilson** – Indiana (14-34 in 4 seasons)

## 2014 Big Ten Coach of the Year:
(Selected by the Big Ten coaches and media members)
Jerry Kill, Minnesota

## 2014 Big Ten Standings:

| East Division | (Conference) | (All Games) |
| --- | --- | --- |
| #1 Ohio State | 8–0 | 14–1 |
| #5 Michigan State | 7–1 | 11–2 |
| Maryland | 4–4 | 7–6 |
| Rutgers | 3–5 | 8–5 |
| Michigan | 3–5 | 5–7 |
| Penn State | 2–6 | 7–6 |
| Indiana | 1–7 | 4–8 |
| | | |
| West Division | | |
| #13 Wisconsin | 7–1 | 11–3 |
| Minnesota | 5–3 | 8–5 |
| Nebraska | 5–3 | 9–4 |
| Iowa | 4–4 | 7–6 |
| Illinois | 3–5 | 6–7 |
| Northwestern | 3–5 | 5–7 |
| Purdue | 1–7 | 3–9 |

*Championship Game*: Ohio State 59, Wisconsin 0

**2014 Big Ten Bowl Record:** 6-5 (4th place among all 10 conferences)

# Indiana Hoosiers – Kevin Wilson

## Coach Ranking: #91

**Overall Record:** 14-34 in 4 seasons
**Record at Indiana:** 14-34 in 4 seasons
**2014 Results:** 4-8, 1-7 in the Big Ten (7th in the Big Ten East)
**Returning Starters in 2015:** 6 on offense (including QB), 6 on defense
**Salary:** $1.3 Million    **Age:** 53    **Job Security Grade:** D

**COACH'S BIO:**
Kevin Wilson grew up in the small town of Maiden, North Carolina. He walked on as an offensive lineman at North Carolina and earned a scholarship after two seasons. After graduating, he joined **Dick Crum**'s staff and served as a graduate assistant at UNC from 1984-1986. After two small-college stops as an assistant, Wilson became the head coach at Fred T. Foard High School and posted a winless record in his one and only season there (1989). He returned to college coaching as **Randy Walker**'s OL coach at Miami (OH) in 1990. He worked his way up to offensive coordinator by 1992 and followed Walker to Northwestern in 1999, where he would serve as OC until 2001. In 2002, Wilson was hired by **Bob Stoops** to become the co-OC at Oklahoma and he was named the sole OC in 2006. Wilson won the Broyles Award, which goes to the nation's top assistant coach, in 2008. He was hired as Indiana's head coach in 2011, replacing **Bill Lynch**.

**2014 REVIEW:**
Wilson had Indiana on an upward trajectory heading into 2014 with one win, four wins, and five wins in the previous three seasons. That upward trend stalled out last year as the Hoosiers won just four games. However, the season did have two highlights: an upset win over 18th-ranked and eventual SEC East champion Missouri and a victory over in-state rival Purdue for the second year in a row.

**2014 RESULTS:    4-8 (1-7 in the Big Ten)**     Final Ranking: NR

| | | |
|---|---|---|
| Indiana State | W 28–10 | (38,006) |
| at Bowling Green | L 42–45 | (23,717) |
| at #18 Missouri | W 31–27 | (66,455) |
| Maryland | L 15–37 | (44,313) |
| North Texas | W 49–24 | (40,457) |
| at Iowa | L 29–45 | (68,590) |
| #8 Michigan State | L 17–56 | (44,403) |
| at Michigan | L 10–34 | (103,111) |
| Penn State | L 7–13 | (42,683) |
| at Rutgers | L 23–45 | (47,492) |
| at #7 Ohio State | L 27–42 | (101,426) |
| Purdue | W 23–16 | (40,079) |

**OFFENSE:**
Wilson brought his up-tempo spread offense to Indiana in 2011 and made steady progress with it during his first three seasons. In 2013, the Hoosiers had the Big Ten's second-highest-scoring offense and they led the Big Ten in passing yards. That offense took a big step back in 2014 as the pass offense slid from first to worst in the conference. Why the setback? A season-ending injury to starting QB **Nate Sudfeld** midway through the year triggered a fast decline in offensive firepower. Indiana averaged 32.3 points a game with Sudfeld as the starter and just 17.8 points a game without him. Sudfeld is back for his senior season in 2015 and he'll have three returning starters on the offensive line to protect him. The Hoosiers are hoping transfers from jucos and UAB (which shut down its football program) will step in quickly to fill voids at the RB and WR positions. Co-offensive coordinators **Kevin Johns** and **Greg Frey** have been on Wilson's staff since he arrived at Indiana.

**DEFENSE:**
After finishing last in the Big Ten in total defense from 2011-2013, Wilson brought in former Ohio head coach (2001-2004) and Wake Forest defensive coordinator (2011-2013) **Brian Knorr** to be his new DC in 2014. Knorr stepped in and shifted the Hoosiers from a 4-3 to a 3-4 defense. The move helped as Indiana went from giving up 528 yards a game in 2013 to 434 yards a game last year (an impressive difference of nearly 100 yards a game). The Hoosiers hope to continue that defensive progress this year, but the secondary must replace both starting CBs. LB coach **William Inge** will serve as the co-DC for the third year in a row. Inge has established himself as one of the Big Ten's top recruiters.

**RECRUITING:**
Indiana's recruiting class just missed the Top 50 nationally and finished No. 9 in the Big Ten. That's somewhat remarkable when you consider this is a team that hasn't had a winning season since 2007 and the Hoosiers are trying to recruit with their head coach on the hot seat. Wilson and his staff have shown they can recruit outside of the Midwest. The 2015 class included seven players from the Southern states of Florida and Georgia.

**RUMOR MILL:**
The Hoosiers have had just one winning season in the past 20 years and this program is desperate for a bowl trip. Wilson will enter 2015 firmly on the hot seat and failing to make a bowl game will likely cost him his job. If Wilson does get fired, he should instantly become a hot candidate for any big-time OC job openings as he's still considered one of the better offensive coaches in the game. It's worth noting that former Indiana head coach **Cam Cameron** (1997-2001) is currently the third-highest-paid assistant coach in the nation and the $1.5 million salary he'll receive at LSU puts his pay above Wilson's for 2015.

**NOTEWORTHY:**
This will be Wilson's fifth year at Indiana. He'll become the first coach to make it to a fifth year with the school since Cam Cameron did it in 2001. (Cameron was fired after going 5-6 during that 2001 season.) When Wilson was hired, he was given a seven-year contract.

## 2015 OUTLOOK:

**Sept. 5**     **Southern Illinois Salukis** – Wilson is 4-0 against FCS schools. Southern Illinois went 6-6 as an FCS team last year.

**Sept. 12**     **FIU Golden Panthers** – Florida International went 4-8 last year, but the Panthers have 16 starters back heading into 2015. That makes FIU a potentially dangerous early-season opponent. Former Illinois coach Ron Turner will be entering his third season as FIU's head coach.

**Sept. 19**     **Western Kentucky Hilltoppers** – WKU has 16 starters back and the Hilltoppers won their final five games of 2014 to finish 8-5. Wilson and the Hoosiers can't afford to take this opponent lightly.

**Sept. 26**     **at Wake Forest Demon Deacons** – Second-year Wake Forest head coach Dave Clawson was Bowling Green's head coach in 2013 when Wilson and the Hoosiers beat the Falcons 42-10. Current Indiana DC Brian Knorr was on Wake Forest's staff from 2008-2013. This road game is probably Indiana's toughest nonconference matchup and getting off to a 4-0 start would be huge for a team desperately trying to become bowl eligible. That makes this a *MUST-WIN* game for Wilson and the Hoosiers.

**Oct. 3**     **Ohio State Buckeyes** – Indiana open Big Ten play against the defending National Champions. The Hoosiers haven't defeated Ohio State since 1988. Wilson has lost his four games against the Buckeyes by an average of 15 points each.

**Oct. 10**     **at Penn State Nittany Lions** – Wilson is 1-3 against Penn State, but the Hoosiers lost by just six points against the Nittany Lions in 2014.

**Oct. 17**     **Rutgers Scarlet Knights** – Indiana's got to pull off two or three games like this one if it wants to go bowling.

**Oct. 24**     **at Michigan State Spartans** – Wilson has struggled badly against Michigan State. He's 0-4 against the Spartans and he's lost those games by an average of more than 27 points each.

**Nov. 7**     **Iowa Hawkeyes** – The last time Iowa came to Bloomington, the Hoosiers pulled off a 27-24 victory in 2012.

**Nov. 14**     **Michigan Wolverines** – Indiana is 9-54 all-time against the Wolverines and Michigan is currently on a 19-game winning streak in this series.

**Nov. 21**     **at Maryland Terrapins** – If things go the way Wilson hopes, Indiana should be fighting for bowl eligibility heading into these final two road games of the season.

**Nov. 28**     **at Purdue Boilermakers** – Wilson is on a two-game winning streak against this in-state rival, but the Boilermakers are showing signs of improvement under Darrell Hazell, who will be in his third year as Purdue's head coach.

## BOTTOM LINE:

Indiana hasn't gone undefeated in the nonconference since Wilson arrived. If the Hoosiers can do that in 2015 and get off to a 4-0 start – a feat that looks doable with this year's schedule – they'll have a legitimate shot at reaching the six wins necessary for bowl eligibility. If that happens, Wilson should save his job.

Kevin Wilson's Year-by-Year Coaching Record:

<u>Indiana: 14-34 (6-26 in the Big Ten)</u>
| 2011 | 1–11 (0–8) | Final Ranking: NR |
| 2012 | 4–8 (2–6) | Final Ranking: NR |
| 2013 | 5–7 (3–5) | Final Ranking: NR |
| 2014 | 4–8 (1–7) | Final Ranking: NR |

# Maryland Terrapins – Randy Edsall

## Coach Ranking: #69

**Overall Record:** 94-100 in 15 seasons
**Record at Maryland:** 20-30 in 4 seasons
**2014 Results:** 7-6, 4-4 in the Big Ten (3rd in the Big Ten East)
**Returning Starters in 2015:** 6 on offense, 4 on defense
**Salary:** $2 Million        **Age:** 57        **Job Security Grade:** C

**COACH'S BIO:**
Growing up in Glen Rock, Pennsylvania, Randy Edsall was an all-state football, basketball, and baseball player in high school. He was a QB at Syracuse from 1976-1979, where his offensive coordinator was **Tom Coughlin**. After graduating, Edsall began coaching and was an assistant coach at Syracuse from 1980-1990. When Coughlin was hired as Boston College's head coach in 1991, he hired Edsall to be his DB coach. Edsall followed Coughlin to the NFL's Jacksonville Jaguars and coached there from 1994-1997. He returned to college as Georgia Tech's defensive coordinator under **George O'Leary** in 1998 and he was hired as Connecticut's head coach in 1999. At UConn, Edsall successfully led the program's transition from Division 1-AA (FCS) to 1-A (FBS). By the end of his 12-year tenure with the Huskies, Edsall had won two Big East titles in his final four seasons. In 2011, he was hired by Maryland, where he would eventually lead the program's transition from the ACC to the Big Ten.

**2014 REVIEW:**
Last year marked Maryland's first season in the Big Ten. Though preseason expectations were low, the Terrapins finished third in the Big Ten's East Division, behind only Ohio State and Michigan State. Edsall's Terps had never finished higher than fifth while in the ACC's Atlantic Division.

**2014 RESULTS:   7-6 (4-4 in the Big Ten)**        **Final Ranking: NR**

| | | |
|---|---|---|
| James Madison | W 52–7 | (45,080) |
| at South Florida | W 24–17 | (28,915) |
| West Virginia | L 37–40 | (48,154) |
| at Syracuse | W 34–20 | (40,511) |
| at Indiana | W 37–15 | (44,313) |
| #20 Ohio State | L 24–52 | (51,802) |
| Iowa | W 38–31 | (48,373) |
| at Wisconsin | L 7–52 | (80,336) |
| at Penn State | W 20–19 | (103,969) |
| #12 Michigan State | L 15–37 | (51,802) |
| at Michigan | W 23–16 | (101,717) |
| Rutgers | L 38–41 | (36,673) |
| vs. Stanford (Foster Farms Bowl) | L 21–45 | (34,780) |

**OFFENSE:**

Under offensive coordinator **Mike Locksley**, Maryland would prefer to run a traditional pro-style offense, but Locksley has shown a willingness to adapt to his QB's talents. Last year's QB, senior **C.J. Brown**, was the team's leading rusher with 539 yards on the ground. Maryland had an experienced offense with nine returning starters last season. This year, they lose five of those starters, including Brown. Finding a quality replacement at QB will be the priority in 2015. **Caleb Rowe** is expected to be the starter, but he missed the spring recovering from a torn ACL. The Terps need to find a consistent rushing threat from a position other than QB. Last year, Maryland ranked 111th nationally in rushing yards.

**DEFENSE:**

It will be a season of change for the Maryland defense in 2015. Despite having nine starters back last year, this defense underachieved and the Terps finished 12th in the Big Ten in total defense and 97th nationally. In an effort to right the ship, Maryland is switching from a 3-4 to a 4-3 scheme and a new defensive coordinator will be leading this change. Last year's inside LB coach **Keith Dudzinski** is the new DC. He's taking over for **Brian Stewart**, who left to become the DB coach at Nebraska. Dudzinski will have his work cut out for him as Maryland returns just four starters on defense, the fewest in the Big Ten. With the installation of a new defensive scheme and an inexperienced front seven, this year's squad might actually take a *further* step back after last year's disappointing performance.

**RECRUITING:**

Every year it seems that Maryland – somewhat quietly – lands a recruiting class that ranks near the Top 40 nationally and 2015 was no different. Though the Terps didn't land a superstar prospect like the five-star offensive tackle, **Damian Prince**, they signed in 2014, the 2015 class still held its own with a finish at No. 8 in the Big Ten and No. 44 nationally. For the second year in a row, the trenches were the priority for Edsall as his top-rated recruits were once again linemen.

**RUMOR MILL:**

The job Edsall did building up UConn's program made him a hot coaching candidate just a few years ago. When **Charlie Weis** was fired at Notre Dame after the 2009 season, Edsall's name came up as a candidate for the job. During his first year at Maryland, Edsall was a rumored candidate for the NFL's Jacksonville Jaguars opening. Since that time, though, most of the rumors swirling around Edsall have been about whether he can hold onto his job at Maryland. Though he's now taken the Terps to back-to-back bowl games, it's worth remembering that Maryland fired **Ralph Friedgen** after going 9-4 and being named the ACC Coach of the Year in 2010. Edsall needs to break out of the .500 range and he can't afford a step back in Year 5 of his tenure here.

**NOTEWORTHY:**

Not surprisingly, Edsall has found the Big Ten to be a more physical conference than the ACC and the team made some strength and conditioning changes this offseason. Edsall says his players this year will be, "bigger, thicker guys than you have seen before."

## 2015 OUTLOOK:

**Sept. 5**   **Richmond Spiders** – Since taking over at Maryland, Edsall is 4-0 against FCS schools. Richmond coach Danny Rocco was the DL coach at Boston College when Edsall was the DB coach there. The Spiders made it to the second round of the FCS playoffs in 2014 and finished 9-5.

**Sept. 12**   **Bowling Green Falcons** – Bowling Green has won back-to-back MAC East titles and knocked off Indiana last season. This team shouldn't be taken too lightly.

**Sept. 19**   **South Florida Bulls** – Dating back to his time at UConn, Edsall is 5-4 against USF. Last year's win over the Bulls was his first game with USF since coming to Maryland.

**Sept. 26**   **at West Virginia Mountaineers** – Edsall is 1-3 against West Virginia since arriving at Maryland and he went 1-6 against the Mountaineers while at UConn.

**Oct. 3**   **Michigan Wolverines** – This will be the first Big Ten game of the Harbaugh era at Michigan. The Terps can expect a more motivated Michigan team than the one they beat late in the season last year.

**Oct. 10**   **at Ohio State Buckeyes** – This will be the Maryland football team's first trip ever to Columbus.

**Oct. 24**   **Penn State Nittany Lions (in Baltimore)** – "Let the rivalry begin," Edsall declared right after last year's win against Penn State. This game got chippy in 2014 and the Nittany Lions will be looking for revenge this year. If they want to stay in the top half of the Big Ten East, this will be a *MUST-WIN* game for Edsall and the Terps.

**Oct. 31**   **at Iowa Hawkeyes** – Maryland went an impressive 5-1 in road games last season and they'll need to win a game like this one if they want to make sure they keep moving forward as a Big Ten program.

**Nov. 7**   **Wisconsin Badgers** – The Badgers handed Maryland a 52-7 beating last year.

**Nov. 14**   **at Michigan State Spartans** – For the Terps to take the next step and start competing for the Big Ten East Division title, they'll need to pick up a win against either Ohio State or Michigan State. That will be a very tall order in 2015.

**Nov. 21**   **Indiana Hoosiers** – If the Terps are going to match or improve on last year's 7-6 record, they must win these final two games of the season.

**Nov. 28**   **at Rutgers Scarlet Knights** – Last year marked the first season of Big Ten play for these two schools and they both proved they could compete in their new conference. This year will be tougher as Rutgers and Maryland each have just 10 starters returning in 2015, the fewest in the Big Ten. Of course, by this point in the season, inexperience should no longer be a major issue.

## BOTTOM LINE:

With Penn State and Michigan expected to be better in 2015, it's going to be very hard for Edsall and the Terps to match last year's third-place finish in the Big Ten East. In fact, it may be hard to reach the six wins necessary for bowl eligibility.

## Randy Edsall's Year-by-Year Coaching Record:

### Connecticut: 74-70 (22-26 in the Big East)
1999    4–7 (1-AA)          **Final Ranking: NR**
UConn's final year in Division 1-AA.
2000    3–8 (Ind.)          **Final Ranking: NR**
UConn joins Division 1-A as an Independent program.
2001    2–9 (Ind.)          **Final Ranking: NR**
2002    6–6 (Ind.)          **Final Ranking: NR**
2003    9–3 (Ind.)          **Final Ranking: NR**
2004    8–4 (3–3)          **Final Ranking: NR**
UConn joins the Big East.
Beat Toledo 39-10 in the Motor City Bowl.
2005    5–6 (2–5)          **Final Ranking: NR**
2006    4–8 (1–6)          **Final Ranking: NR**
2007    9–4 (5–2)          **Final Ranking: NR**
Big East Co-Champions.
Lost to Wake Forest 10-24 in the Meineke Car Care Bowl.
2008    8–5 (3–4)          **Final Ranking: NR**
Beat Buffalo 38-20 in the International Bowl.
2009    8–5 (3–4)          **Final Ranking: NR**
Beat South Carolina 20-7 in the PapaJohns.com Bowl.
2010    8–5 (5–2)          **Final Ranking: NR**
Big East Co-Champions.
Edsall named Big East Coach of the Year.
Lost to #9 Oklahoma 20-48 in the Fiesta Bowl.

### Maryland: 20-30 (10-22 in the ACC and Big Ten)
2011    2–10 (1–7)          **Final Ranking: NR**
2012    4–8 (2–6)          **Final Ranking: NR**
2013    7–6 (3–5)          **Final Ranking: NR**
Lost to Marshall 20-31 in the Military Bowl.
2014    7–6 (4–4)          **Final Ranking: NR**
Maryland leaves the ACC and joins the Big Ten.
Lost to Stanford 21-45 in the Foster Farms Bowl.

# Michigan Wolverines – Jim Harbaugh

## Coach Ranking: #8

**Overall Record:** 58-27 in 7 seasons (3 seasons in FCS), 44-19 in 4 NFL seasons
**2014 Results:** Michigan went 5-7, 3-5 in the Big Ten (T-4th in the East)
With the San Francisco 49ers, Harbaugh went 8-8
**Returning Starters in 2015:** 9 on offense, 7 on defense
**Salary:** $5 Million       **Age:** 51       **Job Security Grade:** A

**COACH'S BIO:**
Jim Harbaugh was born in Toledo, Ohio, but moved around often as his father, **Jack Harbaugh**, was a football coach for several different teams, including stints as an assistant at Michigan and Stanford. Harbaugh played QB for **Bo Schembechler** at Michigan from 1983-1986 and then spent 14 years in the NFL, playing for the Chicago Bears (mostly under **Mike Ditka**) from 1987-1993 and the Indianapolis Colts from 1994-1997. From 1994-2001, while still playing in the NFL, Harbaugh was an unpaid assistant coach for his father at Western Kentucky. After his NFL career ended, he served as **Bill Callahan**'s QB coach with the Oakland Raiders from 2002-2003. Harbaugh surprised many by accepting the head coaching job at the University of San Diego, a small FCS program, in 2004. After going 29-6 in three years at San Diego, Harbaugh became the head coach at Stanford in 2006. Inheriting a 1-11 team, he turned the Cardinal into a national power in just four seasons. Harbaugh spent the last four years coaching the San Francisco 49ers, where he won the NFC West twice and made it to the Super Bowl in 2012.

**2014 REVIEW:**
A losing record with ugly losses to Notre Dame, Michigan State, and Ohio State ensured that 2014 was **Brady Hoke**'s fourth and final season at Michigan. The Wolverines knew they had to make a big hire for Hoke's replacement and bringing in Harbaugh, a former Michigan QB and one of the hottest names in all of coaching, is about as big as it can get for this program.

| 2014 RESULTS:   5-7 (3-5 in the Big Ten) | Final Ranking: NR | |
|---|---|---|
| Appalachian State | W 52–14 | (106,811) |
| at #16 Notre Dame | L 0–31 | (80,795) |
| Miami (OH) | W 34–10 | (102,824) |
| Utah | L 10–26 | (103,890) |
| Minnesota | L 14–30 | (102,926) |
| at Rutgers | L 24–26 | (53,327) |
| Penn State | W 18–13 | (113,085) |
| at #8 Michigan State | L 11–35 | (76,331) |
| Indiana | W 34–10 | (103,111) |
| at Northwestern | W 10–9 | (42,429) |
| Maryland | L 16–23 | (101,717) |
| at #7 Ohio State | L 28–42 | (108,610) |

**OFFENSE:**

In 2014, Michigan finished last in the Big Ten in total offense and 115th nationally. The Wolverines averaged just 20.9 points a game. To put that number in perspective, rivals Ohio State and Michigan State both averaged more than 40 points a game. The offensive woes were the major cause of **Brady Hoke**'s troubles last year. Though Jim Harbaugh ran a lot of read-option with the San Francisco 49ers last year, his base offense at Michigan is expected to look more like the physical pro-style system he ran at Stanford. The Cardinal averaged 40.3 points a game in Harbaugh's final year there (2011). Harbaugh did it with a run-first pro-style system at Stanford, running the ball about 60% of the time. His offensive coordinator at Michigan will be **Tim Drevno**. Though Drevno spent last season as USC's running game coordinator and OL coach, he and Harbaugh have a long history together. Drevno was Harbaugh's OC at the University of San Diego and he remained on Harbaugh's staff coaching TEs and then the OL at Stanford and San Francisco before moving to USC in 2014. Since Brady Hoke was trying to implement a pro-style offense as well, the transition to Harbaugh's system shouldn't be too difficult. With nine starters back, there is talent here, but the Wolverines will have to find the right QB to run this offense.

**DEFENSE:**

Defense wasn't the problem last season as the Wolverines finished the year ranked No. 7 nationally in yards allowed. Michigan's new defensive coordinator will be **D.J. Durkin**, who spent the last five years as the LB coach at Florida, first under **Urban Meyer** and then **Will Muschamp**. In 2013 and 2014, Durkin also served as Florida's DC. Before his stint at Florida, he was Harbaugh's DE coach and special teams coordinator at Stanford from 2007-2009. Michigan ran a 4-3 last season and transitioning to the 4-3/3-4 blend Durkin and Muschamp ran at Florida shouldn't be a problem. It will be especially helpful that Michigan's DC from last year, **Greg Mattison**, is staying on the staff as the DL coach. Mattison is a seasoned veteran who served under Urban Meyer as co-DC at Florida and under **John Harbaugh** (Jim's brother) as LB coach and then DC for the Baltimore Ravens from 2008-2010. Mattison spent the last four seasons as Michigan's DC. Having seven returning starters will help ensure that this defense continues to be one of the best in the Big Ten.

**RECRUITING:**

Even though Michigan hired a nationally-recognized coach, the late start in recruiting (Harbaugh wasn't hired until December 30th) hurt Harbaugh's first class. Michigan signed just 14 recruits, which tied for the smallest recruiting class in all of college football. Harbaugh did sign six four-star prospects, which is why this tiny class still ranked No. 38 nationally.

**RUMOR MILL:**

Now that Michigan has their man, the biggest worry is that Harbaugh will be pulled back to the NFL in a few years. Michigan is doing all it can to make sure that doesn't happen. The school signed Harbaugh to a seven-year contract worth a *minimum* of $40.1 million.

**2015 OUTLOOK:**

**Sept. 3**  **at Utah Utes** – The Harbaugh era will kick off on a Thursday night. Michigan is currently on a five-game losing streak against Pac-12 schools, which includes last year's loss to the Utes.

**Sept. 12**  **Oregon State Beavers** – Oregon State will also be breaking in a new head coach this year. Gary Anderson left Wisconsin to take over the Beavers, who went 5-7 last year and have just 11 starters back this year.

**Sept. 19**  **UNLV Rebels** – The Rebels also have a new head coach in Tony Sanchez, who spent the last six years running one of the nation's most dominant high school programs at Bishop Gorman in Las Vegas. UNLV was 2-11 last year.

**Sept. 26**  **BYU Cougars** – These two schools have only met once before, in the 1984 Holiday Bowl. The Cougars won that game 24-17 and were voted National Champions that year. BYU has gone 8-5 in each of the last three seasons.

**Oct. 3**  **at Maryland Terrapins** – Michigan is 3-1 all-time against Maryland. The lone loss occurred last season. Harbaugh needs to pull this one off as he starts the Big Ten schedule on the road.

**Oct. 10**  **Northwestern Wildcats** – Michigan has won the last three meetings in this series, but all three have been close calls. Last year, the Wolverines won 10-9 and the two games before that went into OT.

**Oct. 17**  **Michigan State Spartans** – Though Michigan has dominated this series historically, the tables have turned since Mark Dantonio took over at Michigan State. The Wolverines have lost six of the last seven in this rivalry. That's a trend Harbaugh needs to reverse quickly.

**Oct. 31**  **at Minnesota Golden Gophers** – Last year's loss to Minnesota was only the second time the Wolverines have lost to the Gophers in their last 24 meetings.

**Nov. 7**  **Rutgers Scarlet Knights** – Last year's loss to Rutgers was the first meeting between these two programs. The Scarlet Knights went 8-5 last season.

**Nov. 14**  **at Indiana Hoosiers** – Michigan is 54-9 all-time against Indiana and the Wolverines currently have a 19-game winning streak going against the Hoosiers.

**Nov. 21**  **at Penn State Nittany Lions** – Michigan's five-point win against Penn State last year snapped a four-game losing streak for the Wolverines in this series.

**Nov. 28**  **Ohio State Buckeyes** – There's always big anticipation for this game and with two of the biggest names in the football coaching world set to collide for the first time, the buildup will be even bigger this year. As it always is, this is a *MUST-WIN* game for Michigan.

**BOTTOM LINE:**
With 16 starters back, the most of any school in the Big Ten, Jim Harbaugh should be able to start Michigan's turnaround quickly. If Harbaugh can find the right QB and get his players to buy into his vision quickly, the Wolverines should be competing for the Big Ten East title in his debut season.

## Jim Harbaugh's Year-by-Year Coaching Record:

### University of San Diego: 29-6 (2-0 in FCS Postseason Games)
2004   7–4 (0-0)               **Final Ranking: NR**
2005   11–1 (1-0)             **Final Ranking: NR**
       Pioneer League Champions.
       Beat Morehead State 47-40 in the Pioneer League Championship Game.
2006   11–1 (1-0)             **Final Ranking: #20**
       Pioneer League Champions.
       Beat Monmouth 27-7 in the Gridiron Classic.

### Stanford: 29-21 (21-15 in the Pac-10)
2007   4–8 (3–6)               **Final Ranking: NR**
2008   5–7 (4–5)               **Final Ranking: NR**
2009   8–5 (6–3)               **Final Ranking: NR**
       Lost to Oklahoma 27-31 in the Sun Bowl.
2010   12–1 (8–1)             **Final Ranking: #4**
       Beat #12 Virginia Tech 40-12 in the Orange Bowl.

### San Francisco 49ers: 44-19-1 (5-3 in the NFL Playoffs)
2011   13-3 (1-1)             **NFC West Champions**
       Lost to the New York Giants 17-20 in OT in the NFC Championship Game.
2012   11-4-1  (2-1)          **NFC West Champions**
       Lost to Baltimore 31-34 in Super Bowl XLVII.
2013   12-4 (2-1)             **2nd in the NFC West**
       Lost to Seattle 17-23 in the NFC Championship Game.
2014   8-8 (0-0)              **3rd in the NFC West**

# Michigan State Spartans – Mark Dantonio

## Coach Ranking: #6

**Overall Record:** 93-48 in 11 seasons
**Record at Michigan State:** 75-31 in 8 seasons
**2014 Results:** 11-2, 7-1 in the Big Ten (2nd in the Big Ten East)
**Returning Starters in 2015:** 6 on offense (including QB), 7 on defense
**Salary:** $5.6 Million      **Age:** 59      **Job Security Grade:** A

**COACH'S BIO:**
Mark Dantonio was born in Texas and grew up in Zanesville, Ohio where his father was a high school basketball coach. Dantonio was an all-state safety in high school and played DB at South Carolina under **Jim Carlen**. In 1980, Dantonio began working his way up the coaching ladder with graduate assistant stops at Ohio, Purdue, and then on **Earle Bruce**'s staff at Ohio State. In 1986, **Jim Tressel** hired Dantonio to be his defensive coordinator at Youngstown State (FCS). After five seasons there, Dantonio served as Kansas' DB coach under **Glen Mason** from 1991-1994. In 1995, **Nick Saban** hired Dantonio to be his DB coach at Michigan State, a role he would keep for six years, even when Saban left for LSU in 2000. Dantonio reunited with Tressel as Ohio State's DC in 2001 and helped lead the Buckeyes to the 2002 National Championship. He left to become the head coach at Cincinnati in 2004. After three years in Cincinnati, he was hired as Michigan State's head coach in 2007. Dantonio has won two Big Ten conference titles and four division titles in his eight years at Michigan State.

**2014 REVIEW:**
Michigan State's two losses in 2014 came against the two teams that made it to the CFP National Championship; Ohio State and Oregon. The Spartans ended the season on a high note with a 21-point fourth-quarter rally to upset No. 4 Baylor.

| 2014 RESULTS:  11-2 (7-1 in the Big Ten) | Final Ranking: #5 | |
|---|---|---|
| #6 (FCS) Jacksonville State | W 45-7 | (75,127) |
| at #3 Oregon | L 27-46 | (59,456) |
| Eastern Michigan | W 73-14 | (73,846) |
| Wyoming | W 56-14 | (74,227) |
| #17 Nebraska | W 27-22 | (75,923) |
| at Purdue | W 45-31 | (40,217) |
| at Indiana | W 56-17 | (44,403) |
| Michigan | W 35-11 | (76,331) |
| #13 Ohio State | L 37-49 | (76,409) |
| at Maryland | W 37-15 | (51,802) |
| Rutgers | W 45-3 | (70,902) |
| at Penn State | W 34-10 | (99,902) |
| vs. #4 Baylor (Cotton Bowl Classic) | W 42-41 | (71,464) |

## OFFENSE:

The Spartans operate out of a run-first pro-style offense that strives for a 60/40 split between running and passing. Proving that you can still rack up big points with a traditional-style offense, Michigan State finished seventh in the nation in points per game last year. The Spartans return six starters on offense in 2015 and for the 40% of the time they throw the ball, they'll have the luxury of relying on QB **Connor Cook**, who returns for his senior season after passing for more than 3,200 yards in 2014 while maintaining a 3-to-1 touchdown-to-interception ratio. For the third year in a row, the offense will be directed by co-offensive coordinators **Jim Bollman** and **Dave Warner**. As long as the Spartans can find an adequate replacement for RB **Jeremy Langford**, who rushed for more than 1,500 yards last year, they should once again field one of the Big Ten's top offenses in 2015.

## DEFENSE:

Michigan State runs one of college football's most innovative and effective defenses. Though it looks like a traditional 4-3 Cover 4 system, the Spartan defense is unique in that the corners usually play press coverage (with nine in the box most of the time) and the safeties, who also play closer to the line of scrimmage than most teams, must make in-play coverage adjustments – zone coverage for shorter underneath passing routes and man coverage for deeper routes. This defense was specifically designed to shut down college football's modern spread offenses and it has done exactly that. Michigan State's defense has given up an average of just 17 points a game over the last three seasons and the Spartans have led the Big Ten in total defense for three of the last four years. However, the backbone of this dominating defense for the past eight years has been **Pat Narduzzi**, Dantonio's defensive coordinator since he was first hired back at Cincinnati in 2004. Narduzzi is now leaving to become the head coach at Pittsburgh. Dantonio promoted from within to fill the void left by Narduzzi. DB coach **Harlon Barnett** (a former All-American DB at Michigan State) and LB coach **Mike Tressel** (the nephew of former Ohio State coach **Jim Tressel**) will be co-DCs in 2015. Both coaches have been on Dantonio's staff since he was originally hired at Cincinnati.

## RECRUITING:

Michigan State landed the Big Ten's No. 3-ranked recruiting class in 2015 and out-recruited in-state rival Michigan for the first time since Dantonio became head coach. Though the Spartans focused mostly on signing Midwest talent, they did bring in a four-star CB from Texas in this class. That's a sign that Michigan State's brand is starting to reach national status.

## RUMOR MILL:

Dantonio has been mentioned as a candidate for some high-profile job openings (including the Texas opening that went to **Charlie Strong**) over the past few years, but he maintains that he sees Michigan State as, "the destination, not a stop." The school is doing everything it can to make sure Dantonio continues to feel that way. In 2014, he was the nation's second-highest-paid coach, behind only **Nick Saban** at Alabama.

**2015 OUTLOOK:**

**Sept. 4**  **at Western Michigan Broncos** – The Spartans kick the season off on a Friday night. Dantonio is 3-0 against Western Michigan, but this will be his first road game against the Broncos, a team that went 8-5 last year.

**Sept. 12**  **Oregon Ducks** – Last year's 46-27 loss to Oregon looked much worse on the scoreboard than it actually was (the Spartans had a two-score lead midway through the third quarter). The Ducks have just 12 starters back this year and must replace Heisman-winning QB Marcus Mariota.

**Sept. 19**  **Air Force Falcons** – This will be the first-ever meeting between these two schools and it'll be interesting to see how Michigan State's defense handles Air Force's triple-option offense.

**Sept. 26**  **Central Michigan Chippewas** – Since arriving at Michigan State, Dantonio is 9-1 against MAC teams. His only loss came to Central Michigan back in 2009.

**Oct. 3**  **Purdue Boilermakers** – Dantonio is a perfect 6-0 against Purdue.

**Oct. 10**  **at Rutgers Scarlet Knights** – Dating back to his time at Cincinnati, Dantonio is 2-1 against Rutgers.

**Oct. 17**  **at Michigan Wolverines** – Dantonio hasn't been shy about his dislike for the Wolverines. He's 6-2 against his in-state rivals and with Jim Harbaugh taking over as Michigan's head coach, this is a *MUST-WIN* game for Dantonio and the Spartans.

**Oct. 24**  **Indiana Hoosiers** – Michigan State has dominated this series in recent years. Dantonio is 6-0 against the Hoosiers and he has won those games by an average margin of more than three TDs each.

**Nov. 7**  **at Nebraska Cornhuskers** – The Spartans have gone 2-2 against the Huskers since they joined the Big Ten.

**Nov. 14**  **Maryland Terrapins** – Dantonio is 3-0 against Randy Edsall, with two of those victories occurring when Dantonio was at Cincinnati and Edsall was at Connecticut.

**Nov. 21**  **at Ohio State Buckeyes** – This game will likely decide the Big Ten East Division championship. Dating back to his time at Cincinnati, Dantonio is 2-6 against Ohio State. He's gone 2-2 against the Buckeyes since Jim Tressel resigned.

**Nov. 28**  **Penn State Nittany Lions** – Dantonio is 3-3 against Penn State, but one of those losses occurred while he was at Cincinnati.

**BOTTOM LINE:**
Michigan State has won 11 games or more in four of the last five seasons. As long as the defense doesn't take a major step back with the departure of longtime defensive coordinator Pat Narduzzi, the Spartans should once again be the biggest challenge to Ohio State in the Big Ten East. If they can beat Oregon at home in the nonconference schedule, the showdown with Ohio State could be a battle of unbeaten teams with a playoff spot on the line.

## Mark Dantonio's Year-by-Year Coaching Record:

### Cincinnati: 18-17 (11-11 in Conference USA and the Big East)
2004    7–5 (5–3)          **Final Ranking: NR**
Beat Marshall 32-14 in the Fort Worth Bowl.
2005    4–7 (2–5)          **Final Ranking: NR**
Cincinnati leaves Conference USA and joins the Big East.
2006    7–5 (4–3)          **Final Ranking: NR**
Cincinnati beat Western Michigan 27-24 in the International Bowl, but Dantonio had already left to accept the Michigan State job.

### Michigan State: 75-31 (45-19 in the Big Ten)
2007    7–6 (3–5)          **Final Ranking: NR**
Lost to #14 Boston College 21-24 in the Champs Sports Bowl.
2008    9–4 (6–2)          **Final Ranking: #24**
Lost to #16 Georgia 12-24 in the Capital One Bowl.
2009    6–7 (4–4)          **Final Ranking: NR**
Lost to Texas Tech 31-41 in the Alamo Bowl.
2010    11–2 (7–1)        **Final Ranking: #14**
Big Ten Co-Champions.
Dantonio named Big Ten Coach of the Year.
Lost to #15 Alabama 7-49 in the Capital One Bowl.
2011    11–3 (7–1)        **Final Ranking: #10**
Big Ten Legends Division Champions.
Lost to #15 Wisconsin 39-42 in the Big Ten Championship Game.
Beat #18 Georgia 33-30 in 3OT in the Outback Bowl.
2012    7–6 (3–5)          **Final Ranking: NR**
Beat TCU 17-16 in the Buffalo Wild Wings Bowl.
2013    13–1 (8–0)        **Final Ranking: #3**
Big Ten Champions.
Dantonio named Big Ten Coach of the Year.
Beat #2 Ohio State 34-24 in the Big Ten Championship Game.
Beat #5 Stanford 24-20 in the Rose Bowl.
2014    11–2 (7–1)        **Final Ranking: #5**
Beat #4 Baylor 42-41 in the Cotton Bowl.

# Ohio State Buckeyes – Urban Meyer

## Coach Ranking: #1

**Overall Record:** 142-26 in 13 seasons
**Record at Ohio State:** 38-3 in 3 seasons
**2014 Results:** 14-1, 8-0 in the Big Ten, NATIONAL CHAMPIONS
**Returning Starters in 2015:** 8 on offense (including QB), 7 on defense
**Salary:** $5.8 Million     **Age:** 51     **Job Security Grade:** A

**COACH'S BIO:**
Urban Meyer grew up in the Northeast Ohio town of Ashtabula and spent two years playing minor league baseball before graduating from Cincinnati. He got his coaching start at St. Xavier High School in Cincinnati under legendary coach **Steve Rasso** and then spent 1986 and 1987 as a graduate assistant at Ohio State under **Earle Bruce**. From there, Meyer worked his way up the coaching ranks with stops at Illinois State and Colorado State. From 1996-2000, Meyer coached WRs at Notre Dame under **Lou Holtz** and **Bob Davie**. In 2001, Meyer became the head coach at Bowling Green and after two winning seasons, he accepted the head coaching job at Utah. He went 22-2 at Utah and was then hired by Florida. With the Gators, Meyer won two National Championships in six years and was named the Coach of the Decade by both *Sports Illustrated* and *The Sporting News* in 2009. He resigned for health reasons and took the 2011 season off before returning to the sidelines at Ohio State in 2012. In 2014, he won the first-ever CFP National Championship.

**2014 REVIEW:**
The 2014 season at Ohio State will go down in college football history as one of the greatest coaching performances ever. Meyer bounced back from a surprising loss to Virginia Tech early in the year and overcame injuries to *two* starting QBs as he led the Buckeyes to the National Championship.

| 2014 RESULTS: 14-1 (8-0 in the Big Ten) | Final Ranking: #1 | |
|---|---|---|
| vs. Navy (in Baltimore) | W 34-17 | (57,579) |
| Virginia Tech | L 21-35 | (107,517) |
| Kent State | W 66-0 | (104,404) |
| Cincinnati | W 50-28 | (108,362) |
| at Maryland | W 52-24 | (51,802) |
| Rutgers | W 56-17 | (106,795) |
| at Penn State | W 31-24 2OT | (107,895) |
| Illinois | W 55-14 | (106,961) |
| at #7 Michigan State | W 49-37 | (76,409) |
| at Minnesota | W 31-24 | (45,778) |
| Indiana | W 42-27 | (101,426) |
| Michigan | W 42-28 | (108,610) |
| vs. #11 Wisconsin (Big Ten Championship) | W 59-0 | (60,229) |
| vs. #1 Alabama (CFP Semifinal) | W 42-35 | (74,682) |
| vs. #2 Oregon (CFP National Championship) | W 42-20 | (85,689) |

**OFFENSE:**
Urban Meyer is one of the creators of the modern spread-option offense. Operating out of a shotgun spread formation, Meyer likes to balance out his passing attack with a lot of read option from a dual-threat QB. His offense also includes a steady power running game, which is why Meyer has started referring to it as the "power spread" offense. With the right talent (which Ohio State certainly has), this offense is one of college football's most difficult to defend. For the past two seasons, Ohio State has ranked in the Top 5 nationally in scoring and the Buckeyes have done it with a balanced attack (3,967 rushing yards and 3,707 passing yards in 2014). That production shouldn't taper off anytime soon. Ohio State has three of the top QBs in the nation to choose from (senior **Braxton Miller**, junior **Cardale Jones**, and sophomore **J.T. Barrett**) along with seven other starters returning on offense for 2015, including junior RB **Ezekiel Elliott**, who rushed for nearly 1,900 yards last season. This team is loaded with talent. The Buckeyes do lose offensive coordinator and 2014 Broyles Award winner (given to the nation's top assistant coach) **Tom Herman**, who accepted the head coaching job at Houston. Herman had been Meyer's OC during all three years of his tenure at Ohio State. Meyer was able to retain last year's co-OC **Ed Warinner**, who reportedly turned down an offer to become Kansas' head coach. Key additions to the staff will be co-OC **Tim Beck**, who served as Nebraska's OC under **Bo Pelini** from 2011-2014, and new assistant head coach and RB coach **Tony Alford**, who spent the last six years on Notre Dame's staff under **Brian Kelly** and **Charlie Weis**.

**DEFENSE:**
Ohio State finished No. 19 nationally in total defense last year, up from 47th in 2013. With seven starters back, this 4-3 defense should once again be one of the nation's stingiest. The top-notch defensive staff includes **Luke Fickell** at defensive coordinator (a role he's been in since 2005 at Ohio State, including a 2011 stint as head coach of the Buckeyes), co-DC **Chris Ash** (who spent three years as **Brett Bielema**'s DC at Wisconsin and Arkansas before coming to OSU in 2014), and assistant head coach and DL coach **Larry Johnson** (who spent 18 years at Penn State before joining the Buckeyes in 2014).

**RECRUITING:**
For the fifth year in a row, Ohio State signed one of the nation's Top-10 recruiting classes. Once again, the Buckeyes landed several of the Midwest's elite recruits, but also brought in some blue-chip talent from SEC territory.

**RUMOR MILL:**
The morning after winning his third National Championship, Urban Meyer was asked by a reporter if he was interested in making the jump to the NFL. Meyer's response: "Not right now." The open-ended answer gave Ohio State fans some reasonable unease. The Browns, Cowboys, and Dolphins have reportedly shown past interest in Meyer. Ohio State responded by giving Meyer a big raise and a three-year contract extension, which will now pay him an average of $6.5 million a year. That average salary will make Meyer the second-highest-paid coach in college football, behind only **Nick Saban**. The new contract runs through the 2020 season and includes a $2 million buyout if Meyer were to leave for another job.

## 2015 OUTLOOK:

**Sept. 7**  **at Virginia Tech Hokies** – The Buckeyes will kick off the season on Labor Day night against the only team that beat them in 2014. With 16 starters back, the Hokies are expected to be a much better team than they were last year. Meyer is 7-3 against ACC schools.

**Sept. 12**  **Hawaii Rainbow Warriors** – Ohio State will play this game just five days after its season-opener. Hawaii went 4-9 last year.

**Sept. 19**  **Northern Illinois Huskies** – The Huskies won the MAC last season and they're 23-6 under current head coach Rod Carey. Ohio State is 23-0 all-time against MAC schools.

**Sept. 26**  **Western Michigan Broncos** – This will be the first-ever meeting between these two schools. Western Michigan has lost 13-straight games against the Big Ten. Current Broncos head coach P. J. Fleck was a graduate assistant at Ohio State in 2006 under Jim Tressel.

**Oct. 3**  **at Indiana Hoosiers** – Ohio State hasn't lost to Indiana since 1988, but the last time the Buckeyes played in Bloomington, they snuck out with a three-point win in 2012.

**Oct. 10**  **Maryland Terrapins** – Last year's 52-24 win by Ohio State marked the first ever meeting between these two schools. Maryland returns just 10 starters in 2015.

**Oct. 17**  **Penn State Nittany Lions** – Penn State nearly knocked off the Buckeyes in a double-OT thriller last season. Instead, Ohio State won its third-straight game in this series. Dating back to his time at Florida, Meyer is 4-0 against Penn State.

**Oct. 24**  **at Rutgers Scarlet Knights** – Ohio State's 56-17 win over Rutgers last year marked the first time these schools have played each other. Rutgers is tied with Maryland for having the fewest number of returning starters in the Big Ten with just 10 coming back in 2015.

**Nov. 7**  **Minnesota Golden Gophers** – Ohio State is on a nine-game winning streak against Minnesota. Last year's seven-point win over the Gophers was Meyer's first game against Minnesota.

**Nov. 14**  **at Illinois Fighting Illini** – Meyer is 3-0 against Illinois and he's won those three games by average margin of 32 points each.

**Nov. 21**  **Michigan State Spartans** – This will be the first of the two biggest games on Ohio State's schedule; games that are expected to decide the Big Ten East Division title. Meyer is 2-1 against Mark Dantonio, who was Jim Tressel's DC at Ohio State from 2001-2003.

**Nov. 28**  **at Michigan Wolverines** – Like it is every year, this is Ohio State's *MUST-WIN* game of the season. It will also mark the first meeting between two of the game's biggest names in coaching: Urban Meyer and Jim Harbaugh. Meyer is 3-1 against Michigan, but the lone loss occurred back when he was at Florida (2007).

## BOTTOM LINE:
With 15 starters back and elite talent at every position, anything less than repeating as National Champions will be a disappointment for Ohio State.

## Urban Meyer's Year-by-Year Coaching Record:

**Bowling Green: 17-6 (11-5 in the MAC)**
2001    8–3 (5–3)                Final Ranking: NR
        Meyer named MAC Coach of the Year.
2002    9–3 (6–2)                Final Ranking: NR

**Utah: 22-2 (13-1 in the MWC)**
2003    10–2 (6–1)               Final Ranking: #21
        Mountain West Champions.
        Meyer named MWC Coach of the Year.
        Beat Southern Miss 17-0 in the Liberty Bowl.
2004    12–0 (7–0)               Final Ranking: #4
        Mountain West Champions.
        Meyer named National Coach of the Year.
        Meyer named MWC Coach of the Year.
        Beat #20 Pittsburgh 35-7 in the Fiesta Bowl.

**Florida: 65-15 (36-12 in the SEC)**
2005    9–3 (5–3)                Final Ranking: #12
        Beat #25 Iowa 31-24 in the Outback Bowl.
2006    13–1 (7–1)               Final Ranking: #1
        National Champions.
        SEC Champions.
        Beat #8 Arkansas 38-28 in the SEC Championship Game.
        Beat #1 Ohio State 41-12 in the BCS National Championship Game.
2007    9–4 (5–3)                Final Ranking: #13
        Lost to Michigan 35-41 in the Capital One Bowl.
2008    13–1 (7–1)               Final Ranking: #1
        National Champions.
        SEC Champions.
        Beat #1 Alabama 31-20 in the SEC Championship Game.
        Beat #2 Oklahoma 24-14 in the BCS National Championship Game.
2009    13–1 (8–0)               Final Ranking: #3
        SEC East Division Champions.
        Lost to #2 Alabama 13-32 in the SEC Championship Game.
        Beat #4 Cincinnati 51-24 in the Sugar Bowl.
2010    8–5 (4–4)                Final Ranking: NR
        Beat Penn State 37-24 in the Outback Bowl.
        Meyer resigned after the season for health reasons.

## Ohio State: 38-3 (24-0 in the Big Ten)

**2012**   **12–0 (8–0)**         **Final Ranking: #3**
Due to NCAA sanctions, Ohio State was ineligible for postseason play and the Big Ten conference championship.

**2013**   **12–2 (8–0)**         **Final Ranking: #10**
Big Ten Leaders Division Champions.
Lost to #10 Michigan State 24-34 in the Big Ten Championship Game.
Lost to #12 Clemson 35-40 in the Orange Bowl.

**2014**   **14–1 (8–0)**         **Final Ranking: #1**
National Champions.
Big Ten Champions.
Meyer named National Coach of the Year by the *CFCA*.
Beat #11 Wisconsin 59-0 in the Big Ten Championship Game.
Beat #1 Alabama 42-35 in the CFP Semifinal Game.
Beat #2 Oregon 42-20 in the CFP National Championship Game.

# Penn State Nittany Lions – James Franklin

### Coach Ranking: #28

**Overall Record:** 31-21 in 4 seasons
**Record at Penn State:** 7-6 in 1 season
**2014 Results:** 7-6, 2-6 in the Big Ten (6th in the Big Ten East)
**Returning Starters in 2015:** 9 on offense (including QB), 6 on defense
**Salary:** $4.3 Million    **Age:** 43    **Job Security Grade:** A

COACH'S BIO:
James Franklin grew up in Langhorne, Pennsylvania and played QB at East Stroudsburg (Division II) from 1991-1994. After graduating with a psychology degree, he started working his way up the coaching ranks with stops that included Washington State under **Mike Price**, Maryland under **Ralph Friedgen**, and the Green Bay Packers under **Mike Sherman**. In 2006, he became the offensive coordinator at Kansas State under **Ron Prince**, a position he held for two years. Franklin reunited with Friedgen at Maryland and served as the Terrapins' assistant head coach and OC from 2008-2010. He became Vanderbilt's head coach in 2011 and in his second season, the Commodores finished the year ranked in the Top 25 for the first time since 1948. He was hired by Penn State in 2014 to replace **Bill O'Brien**, who left to accept the head coaching job with the NFL's Houston Texans.

2014 REVIEW:
After having one head coach for 46 years, Penn State kicked off 2014 with its fourth head coach in four years (that includes **Tom Bradley**'s stint as interim head coach near the end of 2011). Though Franklin's debut season included six conference losses (the most for Penn State since 2004), it ended on a high note with the Nittany Lions winning their first bowl game since 2009.

| 2014 RESULTS:   7-6 (2-6 in the Big Ten) | Final Ranking: NR | |
|---|---|---|
| vs. UCF (in Dublin, Ireland) | W 26–24 | (53,304) |
| Akron | W 21–3 | (97,354) |
| at Rutgers | W 13–10 | (53,774) |
| Massachusetts | W 48–7 | (99,155) |
| Northwestern | L 6–29 | (102,910) |
| at Michigan | L 13–18 | (113,085) |
| #12 Ohio State | L 24–31 2OT | (107,895) |
| Maryland | L 19–20 | (103,969) |
| at Indiana | W 13–7 | (42,683) |
| Temple | W 30–13 | (100,173) |
| at Illinois | L 14–16 | (35,172) |
| #10 Michigan State | L 10–34 | (99,902) |
| vs. Boston College (Pinstripe Bowl) | W 31–30 OT | (49,012) |

**OFFENSE:**

Scoring just 20.6 points a game in 2014, Penn State finished last in the Big Ten in scoring offense. The problem wasn't talent; it was depth, as the NCAA's scholarship limitations (which have now been lifted) have taken their toll on this program. The Nittany Lions entered 2014 with just one returning starter on the offensive line and that inexperience showed. Penn State gave up 44 sacks and QB **Christian Hackenberg** (often under pressure) threw 15 interceptions compared to just 12 TD passes. There wasn't much help from the running game. Averaging just 2.9 yards a carry, the Nittany Lions had to pass the ball more often than they ran it in 2014. That's not the goal of the run-first pro-style offense Franklin and offensive coordinator **John Donovan** prefer to run. At Vanderbilt, they were able to run the ball closer to 60% of the time. The offense should improve in 2015 as Penn State returns nine starters, including four offensive linemen. Hackenberg, an extremely talented pro-style QB, is back for his junior year and third season as the starter. Donovan and Franklin have coached together since Franklin became Maryland's OC back in 2008.

**DEFENSE:**

While the offense scored the least amount of points in the Big Ten last year, the defense *allowed* the least amount of points in the conference. In fact, Penn State ranked No. 7 in the nation in points allowed last year. That stellar performance wasn't a big surprise as Vanderbilt ranked in the Top 25 nationally in total defense during all three of Franklin's years there. Defensive coordinator **Bob Shoop** and co-DC **Brent Pry** came with Franklin to Penn State and their 4-3 defense has picked up right where it left off at Vandy. Six starters return on this side of the ball in 2015 and the defense should be stout once again.

**RECRUITING:**

Franklin has earned a reputation as one of the better recruiters in the country and now that the scholarship sanctions have been lifted at Penn State, he isn't wasting any time restocking this program with talent. His 2015 class ranked No. 2 in the Big Ten and No. 14 nationally. Replenishing the offensive line is clearly a priority for the Nittany Lions and Franklin signed three four-star offensive tackles, including juco transfer **Paris Palmer**, who could step in and start right away.

**RUMOR MILL:**

Franklin was one of the hottest coaching candidates in college football when Penn State hired him last year. He was reportedly targeted by USC and Texas, as well as the NFL's Cleveland Browns, Washington Redskins, and Houston Texans (who eventually hired **Bill O'Brien**). Penn State made Franklin the nation's eighth-highest-paid coach in 2014 and his six-year contract guarantees him a *minimum* of $25.5 million. Even with the big contract, expect Franklin's name to continue coming up as an NFL target each offseason.

**2015 OUTLOOK:**

**Sept. 5**    **at Temple Owls** – Penn State is 39-3-1 all-time against this in-state foe and Temple hasn't defeated the Nittany Lions since 1941.

**Sept. 12**    **Buffalo Bulls** – Buffalo has a new head coach in Lance Leipold. He spent the last eight seasons as the head coach at Wisconsin–Whitewater, where he went 109-6 and won six Division III National Championships.

**Sept. 19**    **Rutgers Scarlet Knights** – Penn State finished below Rutgers in the East Division standings last season. Franklin can't let that happen again in 2015.

**Sept. 26**    **San Diego State Aztecs** – Both these teams went 7-6 last year and this will be Penn State's first ever game against the Aztecs. San Diego State coach Rocky Long was Brady Hoke's DC at SDSU before stepping into the head coaching position when Hoke left for Michigan.

**Oct. 3**    **Army Black Knights** – These two schools met regularly in the '50s, '60s, and '70s, but their last game against each other was in 1979. Franklin coached Vanderbilt to a 44-21 win over Army in 2011.

**Oct. 10**    **Indiana Hoosiers** – Penn State is 17-1 all-time against Indiana. The only loss occurred in 2013.

**Oct. 17**    **at Ohio State Buckeyes** – The Nittany Lions took the Buckeyes into double OT last year, but couldn't pull off the upset. Penn State is 13-17 all-time against Ohio State and the defending National Champions have a three-game winning streak going in this series.

**Oct. 24**    **at Maryland Terrapins (in Baltimore)** – Maryland pulled off a one-point win last year in a heated battle between these two bordering schools. Whether one wants to declare it a new "rivalry" or not, the Nittany Lions need to send a message in this series and this will be a *MUST-WIN* game for Franklin in 2015.

**Oct. 31**    **Illinois Fighting Illini** – This should be the first of two winnable games against West Division opponents, but Penn State lost both of these cross-division matchups last year.

**Nov. 7**    **at Northwestern Wildcats** – Last year's loss to Northwestern broke a six-game winning streak the Nittany Lions had in this series. Franklin is 0-2 against Northwestern, including a 2012 loss he suffered while at Vanderbilt.

**Nov. 21**    **Michigan Wolverines** – The five-point loss in Ann Arbor last year broke the Nittany Lions' four-game winning streak against the Wolverines.

**Nov. 28**    **at Michigan State Spartans** – The 24-point loss to Michigan State last year was the most lopsided defeat of the season for Penn State. This game will be a good indicator of how much progress Franklin makes in 2015.

**BOTTOM LINE:**
Penn State lost four games by seven points or less last year. The Nittany Lions will need to swing those types of games in the other direction this year and with 15 starters back and improving depth, they should be able to do that. Eight or nine is a reasonable goal for this team and reaching 10 wins for the first time since 2009 is not out of the question.

## James Franklin's Year-by-Year Coaching Record:

**Vanderbilt: 24-15 (11-13 in the SEC)**

2011   6–7 (2–6)                    Final Ranking: NR
       Lost to Cincinnati 24-32 in the Liberty Bowl.

2012   9–4 (5–3)                    Final Ranking: #20
       Beat NC State 38-24 in the Music City Bowl.

2013   9–4 (4–4)                    Final Ranking: #23
       Beat Houston 41-24 in the BBVA Compass Bowl.

**Penn State: 7-6 (2-6 in the Big Ten)**

2014   7-6 (2-6)                    Final Ranking: NR
       Beat Boston College 31-30 in OT in the Pinstripe Bowl.

# Rutgers Scarlet Knights – Kyle Flood

## Coach Ranking: #57

**Overall Record:** 23-16 in 3 seasons
**Record at Rutgers:** 23-16 in 3 seasons
**2014 Results:** 8-5, 3-5 in the Big Ten (T-4th in the Big Ten East)
**Returning Starters in 2015:** 5 on offense, 5 on defense
**Salary:** $1.25 Million **Age:** 44 **Job Security Grade:** A

COACH'S BIO:
Kyle Flood was born and raised in Queens, New York. In college, he was an all-conference lineman and team captain at Iona (Division 1-AA). After graduating, he returned to his high school, St. Francis Prep, to coach the offensive and defensive lines from 1993-1994. In 1995, he made the move to college coaching and joined the staff at Long Island-C.W. Post (Division II) as the OL coach for two seasons. He went to Hofstra (Division 1-AA) in 1997, coached there for five years, and was hired by Delaware (Division 1-AA) as the assistant head coach, recruiting coordinator, and OL coach in 2002. After four years at Delaware (including a Division 1-AA National Championship season in 2003), Flood was hired by **Greg Schiano** to become Rutgers' OL coach in 2005. He worked his way up to the assistant head coach position under Schiano and when Schiano left to accept the head coaching job with the Tampa Bay Buccaneers after the 2011 season, Flood was named head coach of the Scarlet Knights.

2014 REVIEW:
After Rutgers lost six of its final eight games in 2013, Flood entered the 2014 season on the hot seat. A 5-1 start quickly quieted his critics, but a lopsided three-game losing streak brought back the hot-seat chatter. Flood regrouped his team and finished out the season strong, winning three of his final four games, including the bowl game against North Carolina.

| 2014 RESULTS: 8-5 (3-5 in the Big Ten) | Final Ranking: NR | |
|---|---|---|
| vs. Washington State (in Seattle) | W 41–38 | (30,927) |
| Howard | W 38–25 | (48,040) |
| Penn State | L 10–13 | (53,774) |
| at Navy | W 31–24 | (33,655) |
| Tulane | W 31–6 | (48,361) |
| Michigan | W 26–24 | (53,327) |
| at #13 Ohio State | L 17–56 | (106,795) |
| at #16 Nebraska | L 24–42 | (91,088) |
| Wisconsin | L 0–37 | (52,797) |
| Indiana | W 45–23 | (47,492) |
| at #10 Michigan State | L 3–45 | (70,902) |
| at Maryland | W 41–38 | (36,673) |
| vs. North Carolina (Quick Lane Bowl) | W 40–21 | (23,876) |

**OFFENSE:**

Former Maryland head coach **Ralph Friedgen** came out of retirement last year and returned to coaching as Rutgers' offensive coordinator. Friedgen's balanced pro-style attack helped Rutgers land near the middle of the Big Ten in rushing, passing, and scoring. However, after the season, Friedgen decided that one year back on the sidelines was enough and he has resumed his retirement. Stepping in as the new OC is **Ben McDaniels**, who was the WR coach here in 2014. Before that, McDaniels spent three seasons as an assistant in the NFL, including 2012 and 2013 as **Greg Schiano**'s offensive assistant at Tampa Bay. With his NFL background, it's unlikely that the Scarlet Knights' offensive scheme will change much from the traditional pro-style system they ran last year. What will change are the faces on this offense as Rutgers has just five offensive starters returning, the fewest in the Big Ten. McDaniels will be the sixth OC in six years at Rutgers and he is the younger brother of New England Patriots OC and former Denver Broncos head coach **Josh McDaniels**.

**DEFENSE:**

Last year was **Joe Rossi**'s first season as defensive coordinator. He was Rutgers' special teams coordinator the two seasons before taking over as DC. Rossi runs a 4-3/3-4 hybrid defense that likes to utilize multiple stunts and blitzes. The Knights struggled with this strategy in 2014, finishing 10th in the Big Ten in points allowed. Only five defensive starters return in 2015, which means Rossi will once again have his hands full in trying to slow down the Big Ten East's scoring machines like Ohio State and Michigan State.

**RECRUITING:**

Rutgers landed a better recruiting class in 2015 compared to 2014, but it still came in at No. 55 nationally and No. 11 in the Big Ten. Flood and the Knights continue to lose New Jersey's top talent to out-of-state programs. Schools like Penn State, Notre Dame, Michigan, and Alabama swooped in and picked off the talent-rich state's elite prospects in 2015. The top New Jersey prospect signed by Rutgers was rated outside of the state's Top 10 for the second year in a row. To put that in perspective, in Schiano's last recruiting class (2011), he signed four of New Jersey's Top-10 recruits. Flood must make it a priority to keep more in-state talent at Rutgers in future recruiting classes.

**RUMOR MILL:**

Flood fought his way off the hot seat in 2014 and earned himself a raise and contract extension. Rutgers bumped his salary up from $950,000 to $1.25 million and extended his contract by two years, through the 2018 season.

**NOTEWORTHY:**

Making the jump from the AAC to the Big Ten was expected to be a long and difficult transition for Rutgers, but Flood and the Scarlet Knights surprised many with their eight-win season last year. The 2014 performance showed right away that Rutgers is capable of competing in this conference. As the Big Ten revenue starts to flow into this program, this will be a team to watch closely over the next few years.

**2015 OUTLOOK:**

**Sept. 5**     **Norfolk State Spartans** – Rutgers beat this FCS school 38-0 in 2013. We should see a similar result in 2015. Norfolk State, 4-8 last year, hasn't had a winning season since 2011.

**Sept. 12**     **Washington State Cougars** – The Scarlet Knights surprised many with their season-opening win over Washington State last year and the Cougars will be looking for revenge this season. Facing Mike Leach's Air Raid offense this early in the season will present Rutgers' inexperienced secondary with a difficult challenge.

**Sept. 19**     **at Penn State Nittany Lions** – Rutgers threw five interceptions in last year's three-point loss to Penn State. The Knights are 2-23 all-time against the Nittany Lions.

**Sept. 26**     **Kansas Jayhawks** – Kansas is rebuilding its program with a new coach and just eight total starters returning in 2015. This matchup should extend Rutgers' winning streak against the Big 12 to three games.

**Oct. 10**     **Michigan State Spartans** – Michigan State dominated this matchup last season. Rutgers fans can only hope that getting the Spartans at home will make for a more competitive game this year.

**Oct. 17**     **at Indiana Hoosiers** – Rutgers needs to beat Indiana again this year if it wants to maintain a position near the middle of the Big Ten East standings.

**Oct. 24**     **Ohio State Buckeyes** – Similar to the situation with Michigan State, the Knights are hoping that getting the Buckeyes at home will keep this game less lopsided in 2015.

**Oct. 31**     **at Wisconsin Badgers** – This will be the first of two very tough draws from the Big Ten West and it will mark Rutgers' first trip to Madison in school history.

**Nov. 7**     **at Michigan Wolverines** – Rutgers pulled off a crucial upset over Michigan last season. Michigan should be a much stronger team than it was in 2014.

**Nov. 14**     **Nebraska Cornhuskers** – This second matchup with the Big Ten West won't be much easier than the first (against Wisconsin).

**Nov. 21**     **at Army Black Knights** – Flood won his previous matchup against Army with a 28-7 victory in 2012. Rutgers is 21-18 all-time in this series.

**Nov. 28**     **Maryland Terrapins** – Both these teams joined the Big Ten last year and for that reason, it's important for Rutgers to own this series. A bowl berth may be on the line when these teams meet. This will be the *MUST-WIN* game for Flood and the Scarlet Knights.

**BOTTOM LINE:**
The Big Ten East is only getting stronger at the top, Rutgers will once again face the conference's toughest cross-division schedule with games against Nebraska and Wisconsin from the West, and the Knights are tied for having the fewest returning starters in the Big Ten. Considering these factors, a step back from eight wins is expected, but a fifth-straight bowl trip is still a realistic goal for Rutgers.

## Kyle Flood's Year-by-Year Coaching Record:

<u>Rutgers: 23-15 (11-12 in the Big East, AAC, and Big Ten)</u>
2012    9–4 (5–2)                Final Ranking: NR
        Big East Co-Champions.
        Lost to Virginia Tech 10-13 in OT in the Russell Athletic Bowl.
2013    6–7 (3–5)                Final Ranking: NR
        The Big East becomes the America Athletic Conference.
        Lost to Notre Dame 16-29 in the Pinstripe Bowl.
2014    8–5 (3–5)                Final Ranking: NR
        Rutgers leaves the AAC and joins the Big Ten.
        Beat North Carolina 40-21 in the Quick Lane Bowl.

# Illinois Fighting Illini – Tim Beckman

## Coach Ranking: #90

**Overall Record:** 33-41 in 6 seasons
**Record at Illinois:** 12-25 in 3 seasons
**2014 Results:** 6-7, 3-5 in the Big Ten (5th in the Big Ten West)
**Returning Starters in 2015:** 8 on offense (including QB), 7 on defense
**Salary:** $2.0 Million       **Age:** 50       **Job Security Grade:** C

**COACH'S BIO:**
Sharing two characteristics of many future coaches, Tim Beckman was born in Northeast Ohio and his father was a longtime football coach. After starting his college career at Kentucky, Beckman transferred to the University of Findlay (NAIA), where he played LB for Hall of Fame coach **Dick Strahm**. Beckman started his coaching career in 1988 as a graduate assistant at Auburn under **Pat Dye**. He worked his way up through small colleges before landing the defensive coordinator and assistant head coach position at Bowling Green in 1998. During his seven years at Bowling Green, he served under head coaches **Gary Blackney**, **Urban Meyer**, and **Gregg Brandon**. Beckman then spent 2005-2006 as the CB coach under **Jim Tressel** at Ohio State and he followed that up with a two-year stint as **Mike Gundy**'s DC at Oklahoma State. He was hired as Toledo's head coach in 2009 and led the Rockets to a division title in his third season. Beckman was hired by Illinois in 2012.

**2014 REVIEW:**
After starting Big Ten play with three-straight losses, including a home loss to Purdue, it looked like Beckman's third season might be his last at Illinois. Instead, he rallied his team with late-season wins against Penn State and Northwestern and took the Illini to a bowl game for the first time since 2011. Though Illinois finished with a losing record once again, Beckman saved his job by earning a bowl berth in 2014.

| 2014 RESULTS:   6-7 (3-5 in the Big Ten) | Final Ranking: NR | |
|---|---|---|
| #24 (FCS) Youngstown State | W 28-17 | (36,234) |
| Western Kentucky | W 42-34 | (38,561) |
| at Washington | L 19-44 | (62,325) |
| Texas State | W 42-35 | (41,019) |
| at #21 Nebraska | L 14-45 | (91,255) |
| Purdue | L 27-38 | (45,046) |
| at Wisconsin | L 28-38 | (80,341) |
| Minnesota | W 28-24 | (44,437) |
| at #13 Ohio State | L 14-55 | (106,961) |
| Iowa | L 14-30 | (50,373) |
| Penn State | W 16-14 | (35,172) |
| at Northwestern | W 47-33 | (31,137) |
| vs. Louisiana Tech (Heart of Dallas Bowl) | L 18-35 | (31,297) |

**OFFENSE:**

Beckman brought the up-tempo spread offense to Illinois when he arrived in 2012 and after some initial transition issues, the Illini have climbed from the bottom of the Big Ten to the middle of the conference in total offense. The passing attack leads the way for offensive coordinator **Bill Cubit**'s version of the spread. Illinois had the Big Ten's second-best pass offense last season. However, as we've seen across the nation in recent years, the no-huddle spread attack works best when there is a serious rushing threat and it's the running game that Cubit needs to quickly improve. The Illini finished 114th nationally in rushing yards. An effort is being made to improve the running game and Illinois ran a lot of plays out of the I-formation in the spring. With eight starters back, including junior QB **Wes Lunt** (who missed several games due to injuries last season), this offense should be better in 2015. Before Cubit became the OC and QB coach at Illinois in 2013, he spent eight seasons as Western Michigan's head coach and went 51-47.

**DEFENSE:**

**Tim Banks** has been the Illini's defensive coordinator since Beckman arrived in 2012. However, Banks will share the DC duties with **Mike Phair** in 2015. Phair spent the last 13 seasons working in the NFL. Most recently, he was the DL coach at Tampa Bay in 2014 and before that he was the DL coach for the Chicago Bears from 2011-2013. Beckman is hoping the addition of Phair as co-DC and DL coach will instantly improve what was the Big Ten's worst defense in 2014. While the overall system isn't expected to change much from the multiple-set scheme Banks has been running, Phair's expertise up front should help generate a better pass rush and run defense. Illinois had the nation's 114th-ranked rushing defense last season. This defense gave up 34 points a game in 2014 and if it can't improve in 2015, it will likely mean other losing season for the Illini.

**RECRUITING:**

Beckman once again targeted the junior colleges to bring in recruits who might be able to contribute right away. Seven juco signees and four-star RB **Ke'Shawn Vaughn** (who chose Illinois despite also having offers from schools like Ohio State, Notre Dame, and Wisconsin) pushed the 2015 recruiting class to No. 7 in the Big Ten and No. 47 in the nation. This was Beckman's highest-rated recruiting class since his debut class in 2011.

**RUMOR MILL:**

As far as win totals go, Beckman has Illinois moving in the right direction with two wins in 2012, four in 2013, and six in 2014. However, Beckman is still searching for his first winning season at Illinois. In the spring, a former player accused Beckman and his staff of mistreatment and the university launched an investigation. Several current and former players quickly spoke out in defense of Beckman. Still, ugly allegations combined with three-straight losing seasons have put Beckman firmly on the hot seat heading into 2015.

**NOTEWORTHY:**

Previous Illinois head coach **Ron Zook** was fired after back-to-back bowl seasons in 2010 and 2011. Beckman's current contract runs through 2016.

**2015 OUTLOOK:**

**Sept. 4** **Kent State Golden Flashes** – Illinois will kick off the season on a Friday night. Beckman is 2-0 against MAC teams and Kent State finished 2-9 last year. Beckman and current Kent State head coach Paul Haynes coached the secondary together at Ohio State in 2005 and 2006.

**Sept. 12** **Western Illinois Fighting Leathernecks** – Beckman is 7-0 against FCS schools. Western Illinois finished 5-7 in 2014.

**Sept. 19** **at North Carolina Tar Heels** – Illinois has not played against an ACC school since 1999. Both these teams finished 6-7 last year. UNC head coach Larry Fedora was the OC at Oklahoma State when Beckman was the DC there in 2007.

**Sept. 26** **Middle Tennessee Blue Raiders** – Illinois went 1-1 against Conference USA teams last season. Middle Tennessee is 0-5 all-time against the Big Ten. The Blue Raiders went 6-6 in 2014.

**Oct. 3** **Nebraska Cornhuskers** – Beckman is 0-2 against Nebraska, but this will be the first time the Huskers have traveled to Champaign since joining the Big Ten.

**Oct. 10** **at Iowa Hawkeyes** – If Beckman is going to improve on last year's six wins, he's got to pull off a road win against a middle-of-the-pack Big Ten team.

**Oct. 24** **Wisconsin Badgers** – The Illini are just 1-9 against the Badgers in their last 10 meetings. Beckman is 0-3 against Wisconsin.

**Oct. 31** **at Penn State Nittany Lions** – The Illini had their best defensive performance of the season in last year's upset win over the Nittany Lions. They'll need another strong defensive showing to knock off an improved Penn State team on the road.

**Nov. 7** **at Purdue Boilermakers** – Beckman can't let Purdue get the best of him for the second year in a row.

**Nov. 14** **Ohio State Buckeyes** – Beckman was Urban Meyer's DC when Meyer was the head coach at Bowling Green. Dating back to his time at Toledo, Beckman is 0-5 against Ohio State.

**Nov. 21** **at Minnesota Golden Gophers** – Last year's win against Minnesota broke a three-game losing streak in this series for Illinois. Dating back to their time as head coaches in the MAC, Beckman and Jerry Kill have an even 2-2 record against each other.

**Nov. 28** **vs. Northwestern Wildcats (in Chicago)** – Beckman may have saved his job with last year's win over this in-state rival as the victory made Illinois bowl eligible. That could be the case again this season, which makes this a *MUST-WIN* game for Beckman. This year's matchup will be played at Soldier Field in Chicago.

**BOTTOM LINE:**

For the third year in a row, the preseason storyline is the same: Illinois has the potential to be a pretty good team *if* the defense can drastically improve. It's doubtful that another six-win season will be enough for Beckman to hold onto his job. He needs to find a way to get to eight wins, which won't be easy with games against Ohio State and Penn State from the East Division.

## Tim Beckman's Year-by-Year Coaching Record:

<u>Toledo: 21-16 (17-7 in the MAC)</u>
2009    5–7 (3–5)              Final Ranking: NR
2010    8–5 (7–1)              Final Ranking: NR
        Lost to Florida International 32-34 in the Little Caesars Pizza Bowl.
2011    8–4 (7–1)              Final Ranking: NR
        MAC West Division Co-Champions.
        Toledo beat Air Force 42-41 in the Military Bowl, but Beckman had already
        left to accept the Illinois job.

<u>Illinois: 12-25 (4-20 in the Big Ten)</u>
2012    2–10 (0–8)             Final Ranking: NR
2013    4–8 (1–7)              Final Ranking: NR
2014    6–7 (3–5)              Final Ranking: NR
        Lost to Louisiana Tech 18-35 in the Heart of Dallas Bowl.

# Iowa Hawkeyes – Kirk Ferentz

## Coach Ranking: #56

**Overall Record:** 127-106 in 19 seasons (3 seasons in FCS)
**Record at Iowa:** 115-85 in 16 seasons
**2014 Results:** 7-6, 4-4 in the Big Ten (4th in the Big Ten West)
**Returning Starters in 2015:** 5 on offense, 7 on defense
**Salary:** $4.1 Million      **Age:** 60      **Job Security Grade:** D

COACH'S BIO:
After a successful high school career in Pittsburgh, Pennsylvania, Kirk Ferentz played LB at Connecticut from 1974-1976. He made the academic all-conference team while at UConn and joined the Huskies' coaching staff as a graduate assistant in 1977. He spent two years as a high school assistant coach and English teacher before joining **Jackie Sherrill**'s staff at Pittsburgh in 1980. From 1981-1989, Ferentz coached the OL at Iowa under **Hayden Fry**. He then spent three years as the head coach at Maine (Division 1-AA) before **Bill Belichick** hired him to be the OL coach for the Cleveland Browns. Ferentz coached the OL for six seasons with the Cleveland/Baltimore NFL franchise. When Hayden Fry retired after his 20th season at Iowa, the Hawkeyes hired Ferentz to be their new head coach in 1999. Ferentz won a share of the Big Ten title in 2002 and 2004 and he's been named the Big Ten Coach of the Year three times.

2014 REVIEW:
For the fifth year in a row, Iowa finished the season unranked. Despite having a fairly soft schedule where the Hawkeyes played just one ranked FBS opponent, Ferentz's team never caught any sustained momentum and once again failed to break into the Top 25. Iowa has not been ranked since November of 2010.

| 2014 RESULTS:   7-6 (4-4 in the Big Ten) | Final Ranking: NR | |
|---|---|---|
| #9 (FCS) Northern Iowa | W 31–23 | (66,805) |
| Ball State | W 17–13 | (64,210) |
| Iowa State | L 17–20 | (70,585) |
| at Pittsburgh | W 24–20 | (48,895) |
| at Purdue | W 24–10 | (36,603) |
| Indiana | W 45–29 | (68,590) |
| at Maryland | L 31–38 | (48,373) |
| Northwestern | W 48–7 | (66,887) |
| at Minnesota | L 14–51 | (49,680) |
| at Illinois | W 30–14 | (50,373) |
| #14 Wisconsin | L 24–26 | (68,610) |
| Nebraska | L 34–37 OT | (66,897) |
| vs. Tennessee (TaxSlayer Bowl) | L 28–45 | (56,310) |

## OFFENSE:

Iowa's traditional pro-style offense strives for nearly equal balance between the run and the pass. In recent years, this offense has been criticized for being too plain and lulling fans to sleep. The Hawkeyes tried to pick up the pace in 2014, but the results were still disappointing. For the third year in a row, the Iowa offense ranked outside the Top 70 nationally in scoring. This offseason, Ferentz promoted his son and OL coach, **Brian Ferentz**, to the position of running game coordinator. However, offensive coordinator **Greg Davis** will continue to call plays for the Iowa offense. Davis will be entering his fourth season as the OC and he's facing some pressure due to Iowa's offensive struggles since his hiring in 2012 (he took over at that time for **Ken O'Keefe**, who had been Iowa's OC for 13 years). **Jake Rudock**, who spent the last two years as the starting QB, is transferring to Michigan after losing his starting position to **C.J. Beathard** in the offseason. Beathard has the talent to make plays with his feet and perhaps that dual-threat ability can recharge an offense that has struggled to find big playmakers for several years now.

## DEFENSE:

The Hawkeyes will have seven starters back on a defense that finished No. 22 in the nation in yards allowed last season. Defensive coordinator **Phil Parker** has been on this staff since Ferentz was hired and he'll enter his fourth year as the DC. He runs a 4-3 scheme that shifts into nickel packages when necessary. Iowa's pass defense was the nation's seventh best in 2014 and three of last year's starting DBs will return in 2015. The defense should once again be Iowa's strength.

## RECRUITING:

For the third year in a row, Iowa's recruiting class finished near the back of the Big Ten and ranked No. 58 nationally. Though the Hawkeyes continue to attract quality linemen, this program is struggling to sign elite-rated talent at the speed positions.

## RUMOR MILL:

In 2009, Ferentz was rumored to be a top candidate for the Kansas City Chiefs head coaching job and Iowa responded by locking him up with a contract that now runs through 2020. Those once-common rumors about Ferentz being a top NFL candidate have quieted in recent years. Last season, Ferentz made $4.1 million, which made him college football's ninth-highest-paid coach in 2014. Though Iowa finished 2009 ranked in the Top 10, it's been four years since the Hawkeyes have been ranked *at all*. Those aren't the results you'd expect from one of the highest-paid coaches in America and it's why *ESPN.com* recently named Ferentz college football's most overpaid coach. Though his contract still has six years left on it, impatience is running extremely high in Iowa City. Rumor has it that Ferentz would have already been replaced if his contract wasn't so expensive for Iowa to get out of.

## NOTEWORTHY:

In the offseason, Ferentz and his staff visited five other schools looking for ways to improve the Iowa program in all aspects.

**2015 OUTLOOK:**

Sept. 5     **Illinois State Redbirds** – Iowa has scheduled an FCS opponent in each of the past seven seasons. The Hawkeyes have gone 7-0 in those games.

Sept. 12     **at Iowa State Cyclones** – Ferentz has lost three of the last four games against in-state rival Iowa State (he's 7-9 all-time) and a loss to the Cyclones again this year would likely ensure another mediocre season for the Hawkeyes. This is a *MUST-WIN* game for Iowa. The last time the Hawkeyes went 4-0 in the nonconference was 2009, which was also the last time they finished the season ranked.

Sept. 19     **Pittsburgh Panthers** – Pitt's new head coach is former Michigan State DC Pat Narduzzi, so he knows Iowa's offense well. Last year, Iowa beat Pitt by four on the road.

Sept. 26     **North Texas Mean Green** – North Texas' head coach is former Iowa State head coach Dan McCarney. McCarney also played for and coached at Iowa. While at Iowa State, McCarney went 5-3 against Ferentz.

Oct. 3     **at Wisconsin Badgers** – Ferentz has lost his last three games against Wisconsin. He's 6-8 all-time against the Badgers.

Oct. 10     **Illinois Fighting Illini** – These teams have only played each other once in the past six years and that was last season's 30-14 Iowa win.

Oct. 17     **at Northwestern Wildcats** – Ferentz is 4-5 against Pat Fitzgerald, but he's won three of the last four meetings, including last year's 48-7 blowout win.

Oct. 31     **Maryland Terrapins** – This *should* be a softer draw from the East Division, but Maryland beat Iowa last year.

Nov. 7     **at Indiana Hoosiers** – This game should also be a soft draw from the Big Ten East. Ferentz has won five of his last six games against the Hoosiers.

Nov. 14     **Minnesota Golden Gophers** – Ferentz is 10-6 all-time against Minnesota, but he's 2-2 against the Gophers since Jerry Kill became their head coach. Minnesota might be the Big Ten team benefiting the most from Iowa's recent slide.

Nov. 21     **Purdue Boilermakers** – Ferentz is 2-0 against Darrell Hazell and he'll look to keep that streak intact with this home finale.

Nov. 27     **at Nebraska Cornhuskers** – This game will be played the Friday after Thanksgiving. Ferentz is 1-5 against the Huskers. With Nebraska transitioning to a new head coach, this is a good opportunity for Ferentz to turn things around in this series.

**BOTTOM LINE:**
The way the schedule lines up, Ferentz has a chance to quiet his critics in 2015. The four nonconference games and two East Division games are all winnable. And with Nebraska and Wisconsin transitioning to new head coaches, the West Division looks wide open. If the Hawkeyes can build some early momentum, they just might be able to pull off a nine or 10-win season and return to the Top 25.

## Kirk Ferentz's Year-by-Year Coaching Record:

### Maine: 12-21 (0-0 in the Division 1-AA Playoffs)
| | | |
|---|---|---|
| 1990 | 3–8 (0-0) | Final Ranking: NR |
| 1991 | 3–8 (0-0) | Final Ranking: NR |
| 1992 | 6–5 (0-0) | Final Ranking: NR |

### Iowa: 115-85 (68-60 in the Big Ten)
| | | |
|---|---|---|
| 1999 | 1–10 (0–8) | Final Ranking: NR |
| 2000 | 3–9 (3–5) | Final Ranking: NR |
| 2001 | 7–5 (4–4) | Final Ranking: NR |

Beat Texas Tech 19-16 in the Alamo Bowl.

**2002**  **11–2 (8–0)**  **Final Ranking#8**
Big Ten Co-Champions.
Ferentz named National Coach of the Year.
Ferentz named Big Ten Coach of the Year.
Lost to #5 USC 17-38 in the Orange Bowl.

**2003**  **10–3 (5–3)**  **Final Ranking: #8**
Beat #17 Florida 37-17 in the Outback Bowl.

**2004**  **10–2 (7–1)**  **Final Ranking: #8**
Big Ten Co-Champions.
Ferentz named Big Ten Coach of the Year.
Beat #12 LSU 30-25 in the Capital One Bowl.

**2005**  **7–5 (5–3)**  **Final Ranking: NR**
Lost to #16 Florida 24-31 in the Outback Bowl.

**2006**  **6–7 (2–6)**  **Final Ranking: NR**
Lost to #18 Texas 24-26 in the Alamo Bowl.

**2007**  **6–6 (4–4)**  **Final Ranking: NR**

**2008**  **9–4 (5–3)**  **Final Ranking: #20**
Beat South Carolina 31-10 in the Outback Bowl.

**2009**  **11–2 (6–2)**  **Final Ranking: #7**
Ferentz named Big Ten Coach of the Year.
Beat #9 Georgia Tech 24-14 in the Orange Bowl.

**2010**  **8–5 (4–4)**  **Final Ranking: NR**
Beat #14 Missouri 27-24 in the Insight Bowl.

**2011**  **7–6 (4–4)**  **Final Ranking: NR**
Lost to #19 Oklahoma 14-31 in the Insight Bowl.

**2012**  **4–8 (2–6)**  **Final Ranking: NR**

**2013**  **8–5 (5–3)**  **Final Ranking: NR**
Lost to #14 LSU 14-21 in the Outback Bowl.

**2014**  **7–6 (4–4)**  **Final Ranking: NR**
Lost to Tennessee 28-45 in the TaxSlayer Bowl.

# Minnesota Golden Gophers – Jerry Kill

## Coach Ranking: #29

**Overall Record:** 148-96 in 21 seasons (14 seasons in Division II & FCS)
**Record at Minnesota:** 25-26 in 4 seasons
**2014 Results:** 8-5, 5-3 in the Big Ten (T-2nd in the Big Ten West)
**Returning Starters in 2015:** 6 on offense (including QB), 7 on defense
**Salary:** $2.1 Million  **Age:** 54  **Job Security Grade:** A

COACH'S BIO:
Jerry Kill grew up in the small town of Cheney, Kansas, and played LB at Southwestern College (NAIA) from 1979-1982. He coached as the defensive coordinator under **Dennis Franchione** at Pittsburg State (NAIA) from 1985-1987. Kill then spent two seasons as the head coach at Webb City High School and won a Missouri state championship in 1989. He returned to Pittsburg State and served as the offensive coordinator under **Chuck Broyles** from 1991-1993 (a stretch that included a Division II National Championship). Kill became the head coach at Saginaw Valley State (Division II) in 1994 and then left for the same position at Emporia State (Division II) in 1999. He served as the head coach at Southern Illinois (Division 1-AA/FCS) from 2001-2007 and became the head coach at Northern Illinois in 2008. In his third year at Northern Illinois, he led the Huskies to a MAC West Division title and was hired by Minnesota in 2011.

2014 REVIEW:
The upward trend continued for Minnesota in 2014 as the Golden Gophers finished the season with a winning record in the Big Ten for the first time since 2003. Before the Wisconsin game, Minnesota broke into the Top 25 for the first time since November of 2008. Kill was named the Big Ten Coach of the Year in 2014.

| 2014 RESULTS:   8-5 (5-3 in the Big Ten) | Final Ranking: NR | |
|---|---|---|
| #16 (FCS) Eastern Illinois | W 42–20 | (44,344) |
| Middle Tennessee | W 35–24 | (47,223) |
| at TCU | L 7–30 | (43,958) |
| San Jose State | W 24–7 | (47,739) |
| at Michigan | W 30–14 | (102,926) |
| Northwestern | W 24–17 | (49,051) |
| Purdue | W 39–38 | (51,241) |
| at Illinois | L 24–28 | (44,437) |
| Iowa | W 51–14 | (49,680) |
| #8 Ohio State | L 24–31 | (45,778) |
| at #21 Nebraska | W 28–24 | (91,186) |
| at #14 Wisconsin | L 24–34 | (80,341) |
| vs. #16 Missouri (Citrus Bowl) | L 17–33 | (48,624) |

**OFFENSE:**

Minnesota runs a multiple-set offense designed to produce a dominating rushing attack. While the Gophers will sometimes line up in two-back, two-TE sets aimed at running the ball downhill and setting up the play-action pass, they'll also line up in the spread and run plenty of option when they have the personnel to do it. While the formations are varied, the goal is the same: Minnesota wants to run the ball first and run the ball often. This philosophy appears to be working. Each year since Kill's arrival, the Gophers' rushing attack has become more potent. Minnesota averaged just 135 rushing yards a game in 2010, the year before Kill was hired. Last year, the Gophers racked up 215 rushing yards a game, which ranked No. 30 nationally. Offensive coordinator and assistant head coach **Matt Limegrover** has been Kill's OC for the past 14 years and his biggest challenges for 2015 will be finding adequate replacements for RB **David Cobb** (1,629 rushing yards in 2014) and TE **Maxx Williams** (who left for the NFL with two years of college eligibility remaining). For an offense that ran the ball 70% of the time last year, Minnesota will benefit from having an experienced offensive line returning in 2015. In the offseason, Minnesota installed the no-huddle offense, which will allow the Gophers to change things up and go up-tempo when they feel it's needed.

**DEFENSE:**

Minnesota's 4-3 defense finished a respectable No. 34 nationally in points allowed last season and though Kill has made it clear that his priority on defense is stopping the run, the Gophers had the nation's 18th-best pass defense in 2014. With three starters back in the secondary, that pass defense should again be a strength in 2015. Continuity is a theme on Kill's staff. His defensive coordinator and associate head coach is **Tracy Claeys**, who has been Kill's DC for the past 16 seasons.

**RECRUITING:**

None of Kill's recruiting classes have cracked the Top 10 in the conference and that was again the case last year as the 2015 class was rated No. 13 in the Big Ten and No. 61 nationally. If the wins continue under Kill, facility upgrades will likely follow, which should improve this program's recruiting efforts.

**RUMOR MILL:**

As Kill continues to succeed, he's attracting attention from other programs. There was speculation this offseason that Kill was considered for the openings at Nebraska and Michigan before the schools hired **Mike Riley** and **Jim Harbaugh**, respectively. After the 2014 season, Minnesota gave Kill a contract extension and a raise of nearly $1 million. His current contract runs through the 2018 season.

**NOTEWORTHY:**

Kill has had to overcome some serious health concerns during his career. In 2005, he was diagnosed with kidney cancer. He underwent surgery and has been cancer free for nine years now. In 2013, he took a leave of absence during the season after suffering a series of seizures. Kill committed himself to gaining control over his epilepsy and didn't have any seizures in 2014. Despite being ridiculed by some for his struggle with epilepsy, Kill has been a courageous voice of inspiration against the ignorance of those who don't understand this condition.

**2015 OUTLOOK:**

Sept. 3   **TCU Horned Frogs** – This Thursday-night game will be a matchup between two longtime coaching friends. Kill was Gary Patterson's best man at his wedding. Both Patterson and Kill grew up in Kansas and coached under Dennis Franchione at Pittsburg State. Minnesota has lost its last five games against Big 12 opponents.

Sept. 12   **at Colorado State Rams** – The Gophers are 7-0 all-time against Mountain West teams. Colorado State is breaking in a new head coach in former Georgia OC Mike Bobo.

Sept. 19   **Kent State Golden Flashes** – Kill is 2-0 against MAC teams since coming to Minnesota.

Sept. 26   **Ohio Bobcats** – The last time the Gophers lost to a MAC team was in 2010, when Kill's Northern Illinois team beat the Gophers.

Oct. 3   **at Northwestern Wildcats** – Last year's win over Northwestern was Minnesota's second in a row against the Wildcats. Controlling this series will go a long way toward opening up the West Division for Minnesota.

Oct. 10   **at Purdue Boilermakers** – After last year's one-point win in this game, the Gophers know they can't take Purdue lightly.

Oct. 17   **Nebraska Cornhuskers** – These two teams tied for second in the West Division last year. Minnesota has now won two in a row against Nebraska. With the Huskers transitioning to a new head coach, the Gophers should be able to extend their winning streak in this series.

Oct. 31   **Michigan Wolverines** – Last year's win over Michigan broke a six-game losing streak for Minnesota in this series. With Jim Harbaugh now coaching the Wolverines, expect this to be a tougher opponent in 2015.

Nov. 7   **at Ohio State Buckeyes** – Minnesota has lost nine-straight games against Ohio State, but last year's seven-point loss was the closest margin in this series since 2001.

Nov. 14   **at Iowa Hawkeyes** – Last year's blowout victory over Iowa sent a clear message that Minnesota may be passing the Hawkeyes in Big Ten prestige. This game could have West Division title implications.

Nov. 21   **Illinois Fighting Illini** – The surprising loss to Illinois last year was Minnesota's first in this series since 2009. Kill will need to be careful here and make sure his team isn't looking ahead to Wisconsin.

Nov. 28   **Wisconsin Badgers** – A trip to the Big Ten championship was on the line when these two rivals met last season. Minnesota has lost 11 straight in this series and if the Gophers are finally ready to take the next step and win a division title, they *MUST WIN* this game.

**BOTTOM LINE:**
Jerry Kill has this program heading in the right direction and after coming within one game of a West Division title last year, making it to the Big Ten Championship Game will be the goal this year. Regardless of whether Minnesota wins the Big Ten West, one thing Kill needs to do in 2015 is win a bowl game. He's 0-5 all-time in bowl games.

## Jerry Kill's Year-by-Year Coaching Record:

### Saginaw Valley State: 38-14 (0-0 in the Division II Playoffs)

| 1994 | 6–4 (0-0) | Final Ranking: NR |
|------|-----------|-------------------|
| 1995 | 7–3 (0-0) | Final Ranking: NR |
| 1996 | 7–3 (0-0) | Final Ranking: NR |
| 1997 | 9–2 (0-0) | Final Ranking: NR |
| 1998 | 9–2 (0-0) | Final Ranking: NR |

### Emporia State: 11-11 (0-0 in the Division II Playoffs)

| 1999 | 5-6 (0-0) | Final Ranking: NR |
|------|-----------|-------------------|
| 2000 | 6-5 (0-0) | Final Ranking: NR |

### Southern Illinois: 55-32 (4-5 in the Division 1-AA Playoffs)

2001    1–10 (0-0)          Final Ranking: NR

2002    4–8 (0-0)           Final Ranking: NR

2003    10–2 (0-1)          Final Ranking: #9
Gateway Conference Co-Champions.
Lost to Delaware 7-48 in first round of the Division 1-AA playoffs.

2004    10–2 (0-1)          Final Ranking: #9
Gateway Conference Champions.
Lost to Eastern Washington 31-35 in first round of the Division 1-AA playoffs.

2005    9–4 (1-1)           Final Ranking: #7
Gateway Conference Co-Champions.
Lost to Appalachian State 24-38 in the Division 1-AA quarterfinals.

2006    9–4 (1-1)           Final Ranking: #7
Lost to Montana 3-20 in the Division 1-AA quarterfinals.

2007    12–2 (2–1)          Final Ranking: #3
Lost to Delaware 17-20 in the Division 1-AA semifinals.

### Northern Illinois: 23-16 (18-6 in the MAC)

2008    6–7 (5–3)           Final Ranking: NR
Lost to Louisiana Tech 10-17 in the Independence Bowl.

2009    7–6 (5–3)           Final Ranking: NR
Lost to South Florida 3-27 in the International Bowl.

2010    10–3 (8–0)          Final Ranking: NR
MAC West Division Champions.
Kill named Eddie Robinson National Coach of the Year.
Lost to Miami (OH) 21-26 in the MAC Championship Game.
Northern Illinois beat Fresno State 40-17 in the Humanitarian Bowl, but Kill had already left to accept the Minnesota job.

## Minnesota: 25-26 (13-19 in the Big Ten)

2011    3–9 (2–6)                Final Ranking: NR
2012    6–7 (2–6)                Final Ranking: NR
        Lost to Texas Tech 31-34 in the Meineke Car Care Bowl of Texas.
2013    8–5 (4–4)                Final Ranking: NR
        Kill took a seven-game leave of absence due to health issues during this season. Kill's longtime defensive coordinator Tracy Claeys was the acting head coach during the seven-game stretch Kill missed. Minnesota went 4-3 during those seven games.
        Lost to Syracuse 17-21 in the Texas Bowl.
2014    8–5 (5–3)                Final Ranking: NR
        Kill named Big Ten Coach of the Year.
        Lost to #16 Missouri 17-33 in the Citrus Bowl.

# Nebraska Cornhuskers – Mike Riley

## Coach Ranking: #47

**Overall Record:** 93-80 in 14 seasons, 14-34 in 3 NFL seasons, 40-32 in 4 CFL Seasons, 11-9 in 2 WLAF Seasons

**2014 Results:** Nebraska went 9-4, 5-3 in the Big Ten (T-2nd in the West) At Oregon State, Riley went 5-7, 2-7 in the Pac-12

**Returning Starters in 2015:** 6 on offense (including QB), 6 on defense

**Salary:** $2.7 Million    **Age:** 62    **Job Security Grade:** B

COACH'S BIO:

Mike Riley was born in Wallace, Idaho, but attended high school in Corvallis, Oregon, where his father was an assistant coach for Oregon State. Riley played DB for **Bear Bryant** at Alabama from 1971-1974. After college, he immediately began his career in coaching. He landed his first head coaching job with the CFL's Winnipeg Blue Bombers in 1987. He won two Grey Cups (CFL titles) in his four seasons at Winnipeg. He then spent two seasons coaching San Antonio in the now-defunct World League (WLAF). Riley returned to the college game as **John Robinson**'s offensive coordinator at USC in 1993 and held that position until he was hired as Oregon State's head coach in 1997. He left Oregon State to take the San Diego Chargers job in 1999. He was fired after three seasons in San Diego and spent 2002 as an assistant with the New Orleans Saints. He returned to Oregon State in 2003 and served as the head coach through 2014. He surprised many last year by leaving Oregon State to accept the Nebraska job.

2014 REVIEW:

**Bo Pelini** was fired by Nebraska after finishing second in the Big Ten West in 2014. Pelini won nine or more games in all seven of his seasons at Nebraska. Riley won nine or more games in four of his 14 seasons at Oregon State.

| 2014 RESULTS: 9-4 (5-3 in the Big Ten) | Final Ranking: NR | |
|---|---|---|
| Florida Atlantic | W 55–7 | (91,441) |
| McNeese State | W 31–24 | (91,082) |
| at Fresno State | W 55–19 | (41,031) |
| Miami (FL) | W 41–31 | (91,585) |
| Illinois | W 45–14 | (91,255) |
| at #10 Michigan State | L 22–27 | (75,923) |
| at Northwestern | W 38–17 | (47,330) |
| Rutgers | W 42–24 | (91,088) |
| Purdue | W 35–14 | (91,107) |
| at #22 Wisconsin | L 24–59 | (80,539) |
| Minnesota | L 24–28 | (91,186) |
| at Iowa | W 37–34 OT | (66,897) |
| vs. #24 USC (Holiday Bowl) | L 42–45 | (55,789) |

**OFFENSE:**

Nebraska had no trouble putting up points in 2014. The Huskers were 13th in the nation in scoring offense and their 38 points a game trailed only Ohio State and Michigan State in the Big Ten. Nebraska did it with a power spread offense similar to Ohio State's. With that in mind, it's not too surprising that last year's Husker offensive coordinator **Tim Beck** has joined **Urban Meyer**'s staff at Ohio State as the new co-OC for the Buckeyes. Mike Riley will be bringing a new offense to Nebraska. While at Oregon State, he ran a pass-first pro-style offense. Riley's OC will be **Danny Langsdorf**. Though Langsdorf was the QB coach for **Tom Coughlin**'s New York Giants last year, he and Riley have a long history of working together. He spent nine seasons (2005-2013) as Riley's OC at Oregon State. In Langsdorf's last two seasons at Oregon State, the Beavers averaged 33.7 points a game. Though the Huskers will have six starters returning, including dual-threat QB **Tommy Armstrong**, it will likely take some time to transition from the power spread to a pass-first offense.

**DEFENSE:**

**Mark Banker** will be Nebraska's new defensive coordinator. Banker served as Oregon State's DC for each of the past 14 seasons under Riley. The Beavers finished 98th in the nation last year in points allowed, but Banker should have more talent to work with at Nebraska. Banker will install a 4-3 look on defense. Because the Huskers have relied more on five-DB sets in recent years, depth may be a problem at the LB spot. Expect Banker and his defensive staff to run more nickel-package sets if they can't find enough quality LBs to run the 4-3 scheme. The Huskers finished ninth in the Big Ten in points allowed last year and Nebraska fans are hoping the new system on defense will quickly improve those numbers.

**RECRUITING:**

Riley's first recruiting class came in at No. 4 in the Big Ten and No. 31 nationally. This was an impressive first class for a coach who many thought would struggle with recruiting in the Big Ten. Riley's last class at Oregon State (2014) was ranked No. 63 nationally.

**RUMOR MILL:**

Rumor has it that Bo Pelini was fired less because of his record (he averaged 9.6 wins a season and won four division titles) and more because of his volatile personality and tense relationship with the Nebraska administration. With that in mind, it's not too surprising to see the Huskers hiring a coach like Riley, whose laid-back nice-guy persona is considered by many to be the polar opposite of Pelini's. By firing Pelini when they did, Nebraska will have to continue paying him roughly $130,000 a month until a $6.5 million buyout is met. Meanwhile, Pelini has returned to his hometown to become the new head coach at Youngstown State (FCS), where he'll earn a salary of roughly $215,000 a year.

**NOTEWORTHY:**

Riley signed a five-year contract worth $2.7 million a year with the Huskers. At Oregon State, he was the lowest-paid coach in the Pac-12, making $1.5 million in 2014. Nebraska paid Pelini $3.1 million in 2014.

## 2015 OUTLOOK:

**Sept. 5**    **BYU Cougars** – This will be Nebraska's first-ever meeting with BYU and it won't be an easy way to start the season. At Oregon State, Riley went 1-2 against coach Bronco Mendenhall and his Cougars. BYU went 8-5 last year and has 14 starters returning in 2015.

**Sept. 12**    **South Alabama Jaguars** – South Alabama has just five returning starters, which is tied for the fewest in the nation. Nebraska is 7-0 all-time against teams from the Sun Belt Conference.

**Sept. 19**    **at Miami Hurricanes** – The Hurricanes will be looking for revenge after last year's loss in Lincoln. Nebraska is 6-5 all-time in this series.

**Sept. 26**    **Southern Miss Golden Eagles** – This game will mark the third time in four years these two schools have met. Southern Miss went 3-9 last year, which was its third-straight losing season. Nebraska is 5-1 all-time against the Eagles.

**Oct. 3**    **at Illinois Fighting Illini** – It'll be important for Nebraska to get off to a strong start as it opens Big Ten play. The Huskers are 2-0 against Illinois since joining the Big Ten.

**Oct. 10**    **Wisconsin Badgers** – Wisconsin and Nebraska were the top two teams in the Big Ten West last year. This year, they both have new head coaches who know each other well. Paul Chryst spent nine years coaching on Riley's staffs. If the Huskers want to compete for the West Division title, they *MUST WIN* this game.

**Oct. 17**    **at Minnesota Golden Gophers** – These two teams tied for second in the Big Ten West last year and Nebraska has lost its last two games against the Gophers. Riley must reverse this trend quickly, especially since Minnesota is looking like a program on the rise.

**Oct. 24**    **Northwestern Wildcats** – The Cornhuskers enter this matchup with a three-game winning streak against the Wildcats.

**Oct. 31**    **at Purdue Boilermakers** – Over the past two seasons, Nebraska has outscored Purdue 79-21.

**Nov. 7**    **Michigan State Spartans** – This game is obviously a tough draw from the Big Ten East. Last season, the Huskers scored 19 fourth quarter points and nearly pulled off the upset in East Lansing.

**Nov. 14**    **at Rutgers Scarlet Knights** – Even though Nebraska should be the more talented team, this has the potential to be a "letdown" game for the Huskers as it's sandwiched between the toughest game on the schedule and the season-ending rivalry game against Iowa. Riley needs to keep his team motivated for this one.

**Nov. 27**    **Iowa Hawkeyes** – This new rivalry will once again be played the Friday after Thanksgiving. The Huskers are 3-1 against the Hawkeyes since joining the Big Ten, including last year's overtime victory.

## BOTTOM LINE:

With new coaches, new offensive and defensive systems, and plenty of new faces on the depth chart, this will be a year of transition for Nebraska. Matching last season's nine wins would be an impressive first-year performance for Mike Riley, but seven or eight wins is a more realistic expectation for the Huskers in 2015.

## Mike Riley's Year-by-Year Coaching Record:

Winnipeg Blue Bombers: 40-32 (6-2 in the CFL Playoffs)
| | | |
|---|---|---|
| 1987 | 12-6 (0-1) | **East Division Champions** |

Lost to Toronto 3-19 in the Division Finals.
| | | |
|---|---|---|
| 1988 | 9-9 (3-0) | **2nd in the East Division** |

CFL Champions.
Beat BC 22-21 in the Grey Cup game.
| | | |
|---|---|---|
| 1989 | 7-11 (1-1) | **3rd in the East Division** |

Lost to Hamilton 10-14 in the Division Finals.
| | | |
|---|---|---|
| 1990 | 12-6 (2-0) | **East Division Champions** |

CFL Champions.
Beat Edmonton 50-11 in the Grey Cup game.

San Antonio Riders: 11-9 (0-0 in the WLAF Playoffs)
| | | |
|---|---|---|
| 1991 | 4-6 (0-0) | **2nd in North American West** |
| 1992 | 7-3 (0-0) | **3rd in the North American West** |

Oregon State: 8-14 (2-14 in the Pac-10)
| | | |
|---|---|---|
| 1997 | 3–8 (0–8) | **Final Ranking: NR** |
| 1998 | 5–6 (2–6) | **Final Ranking: NR** |

San Diego Chargers: 14-34 (0-0 in the NFL Playoffs)
| | | |
|---|---|---|
| 1999 | 8-8 (0-0) | **3rd in the AFC West** |
| 2000 | 1-15 (0-0) | **5th in the AFC West** |
| 2001 | 5-11 (0-0) | **5th in the AFC West** |

Oregon State: 85-66 (56-49 in the Pac-10/Pac-12)
| | | |
|---|---|---|
| 2003 | 8–5 (4–4) | **Final Ranking: NR** |

Beat New Mexico 55-14 in the Las Vegas Bowl.
| | | |
|---|---|---|
| 2004 | 7–5 (5–3) | **Final Ranking: NR** |

Beat Notre Dame 38-21 in the Insight Bowl.
| | | |
|---|---|---|
| 2005 | 5–6 (3–5) | **Final Ranking: NR** |
| 2006 | 10–4 (6–3) | **Final Ranking: #21** |

Beat Missouri 39-38 in the Sun Bowl.
| | | |
|---|---|---|
| 2007 | 9–4 (6–3) | **Final Ranking: #25** |

Beat Maryland 21-14 in the Emerald Bowl.
| | | |
|---|---|---|
| 2008 | 9–4 (7–2) | **Final Ranking: #18** |

Riley named Pac-10 Coach of the Year.
Beat #18 Pittsburgh 3-0 in the Sun Bowl.
| | | |
|---|---|---|
| 2009 | 8–5 (6–3) | **Final Ranking: NR** |

Lost to #14 BYU 20-44 in the Las Vegas Bowl.
| | | |
|---|---|---|
| 2010 | 5–7 (4–5) | **Final Ranking: NR** |
| 2011 | 3–9 (3–6) | **Final Ranking: NR** |
| 2012 | 9–4 (6–3) | **Final Ranking: #19** |

Lost to Texas 27-31 in the Alamo Bowl.

<u>Oregon State (continued)</u>

2013    7–6 (4–5)                **Final Ranking: NR**
        Beat Boise State 38-23 in the Hawaii Bowl.
2014    5–7 (2–7)                **Final Ranking: NR**

# Northwestern Wildcats – Pat Fitzgerald

## Coach Ranking: #49

**Overall Record:** 60-53 in 9 seasons
**Record at Northwestern:** 60-53 in 9 seasons
**2014 Results:** 5-7, 3-5 in the Big Ten (6th in the Big Ten West)
**Returning Starters in 2015:** 6 on offense, 10 on defense
**Salary:** $2.5 Million*      **Age:** 40      **Job Security Grade:** B

COACH'S BIO:
It's almost as though Pat Fitzgerald was born to be the football coach at Northwestern. He grew up in the Chicago suburb of Orland Park and was an All-American LB for the Wildcats under **Gary Barnett** in the mid-1990s. He was named the Big Ten Defensive Player of the Year in 1995 and 1996 while also becoming the first player ever to win both the Nagurski Trophy and Bednarik Award *twice* (both awards are given to the nation's top defensive player). After college, Fitzgerald spent one year as a graduate assistant at Maryland under head coach **Ron Vanderlinden**, who had been Northwestern's defensive coordinator when Fitzgerald played there. He then reunited with Gary Barnett as an assistant at Colorado in 1999. Fitzgerald spent the 2000 season as the LB coach at Idaho under **Tom Cable** before returning to his alma mater in 2001. He served as the DB coach and then LB coach and recruiting coordinator on **Randy Walker**'s staff for five seasons. When Walker died of a heart attack prior to the 2006 season, Fitzgerald was named the Wildcats' new head coach at the age of 31. In 2008, Fitzgerald was inducted into the College Football Hall of Fame in honor of his playing career.

2014 REVIEW:
Last year was a head-scratcher of a season for Northwestern as the Wildcats managed to score upset wins against teams like Wisconsin and Notre Dame, but also found a way to get blown out by Iowa and drop its season finale against in-state rival Illinois. As a result of this inconsistent performance, Northwestern missed a bowl game for the second year in a row.

| 2014 RESULTS:    5-7 (3-5 in the Big Ten) | Final Ranking: NR | |
|---|---|---|
| California | L 24–31 | (34,228) |
| Northern Illinois | L 15–23 | (41,139) |
| Western Illinois | W 24–7 | (32,016) |
| **at Penn State** | W 29–6 | (102,910) |
| **#17 Wisconsin** | W 20–14 | (42,013) |
| **at Minnesota** | L 17–24 | (49,051) |
| Nebraska | L 17–38 | (47,330) |
| **at Iowa** | L 7–48 | (66,887) |
| **Michigan** | L 9–10 | (42,429) |
| at #18 Notre Dame | W 43–40 OT | (80,795) |
| **at Purdue** | W 38–14 | (30,117) |
| Illinois | L 33–47 | (31,137) |

**OFFENSE:**

Northwestern has been running the shotgun spread offense since **Randy Walker** installed it back in 2000. Once a high-powered scoring machine, this offense has fizzled out over the past two seasons. The Wildcats finished 101st nationally in points per game last year. That performance was especially disappointing when you consider the fact that this offense had *nine* returning starters in 2014. Offensive coordinator **Mick McCall** will be entering his eighth season at that position. He knows he's got to get this offense back on track and that means finding ways to get sophomore RB **Justin Jackson** more touches. As a true freshman in 2014, Jackson rushed for 1,187 yards. McCall also needs to find a quality replacement for departing QB **Trevor Siemian**, who started the last three seasons for the Wildcats. There was a time when Northwestern was associated nationwide with its innovative high-octane offense, but that's no longer the case. If the Wildcats are going to start competing for West Division titles, McCall has got to revive this stale offense.

**DEFENSE:**

The Wildcats run a 4-3 defense that finished near the middle of the Big Ten in points allowed last season. While respectable, Fitzgerald and defensive coordinator **Mike Hankwitz** are expecting bigger things in 2015. Ten starters return, which means the defense should be the strength of this Northwestern team. Before arriving at Northwestern in 2008, Hankwitz was **Gary Barnett**'s DC at Colorado from 2004-2005 and **Brett Bielema**'s DC at Wisconsin from 2006-2007.

**RECRUITING:**

Fitzgerald's 2014 recruiting class included three of Illinois' top seven prospects. The in-state star power helped Northwestern land at No. 8 in the Big Ten recruiting rankings, something that is not easy to do for a school that puts such an emphasis on academics. The Wildcats were not so lucky in 2015 as Fitzgerald landed just one of the state's Top-10 recruits and failed to sign a single four-star recruit (after signing four in 2014). As a result, Northwestern's 2015 class dropped back to No. 10 in the Big Ten and No. 53 nationally.

**RUMOR MILL:**

Michigan reportedly pursued Fitzgerald after the 2010 season, but the Wolverines ended up hiring **Brady Hoke** and Northwestern stepped up to give Fitzgerald a 10-year contract extension. Fitzgerald's contract currently runs through the 2020 season. Though Fitzgerald remains a popular figure at Northwestern, the 2014 Wildcats should have been better than their 5-7 record. If Northwestern misses a third-straight bowl game in 2015, Fitzgerald's seat may start warming up.

**NOTEWORTHY:**

When Fitzgerald was named head coach at Northwestern, the 31-year-old was the youngest head coach in college football. Entering his 10th season at Northwestern, he is the second-longest tenured coach in the Big Ten (behind only Iowa's **Kirk Ferentz**). Fitzgerald's 60 victories makes him the all-time winningest coach in Northwestern football history.

**2015 OUTLOOK:**

**Sept. 5**   **Stanford Cardinal** – For the third year in a row, Northwestern will kick off the season against a Pac-12 foe. Fitzgerald went 1-1 in the 2013-2014 series against Cal, the only two times he's coached against the Pac-12.

**Sept. 12**   **Eastern Illinois Panthers** – Northwestern last played Eastern Illinois in 2011, a game the Wildcats won 42-21. Fitzgerald is 11-1 against FCS schools. Eastern Illinois went 5-7 in 2014.

**Sept. 19**   **at Duke Blue Devils** – Duke has won 29 games over the past two seasons. Fitzgerald is 4-1 against the ACC with the only loss coming against Duke in 2007.

**Sept. 26**   **Ball State Cardinals** – Last year's loss to Northern Illinois was Fitzgerald's first to a MAC school. He's 8-1 overall against the MAC. Ball State has won two of its last three games against Big Ten schools.

**Oct. 3**   **Minnesota Golden Gophers** – Though Fitzgerald is 5-3 against Minnesota, he's lost the last two against Jerry Kill's Gophers.

**Oct. 10**   **at Michigan Wolverines** – Last year, after scoring a TD with three seconds left, Fitzgerald went for the two-point conversion instead of kicking the extra point and sending the game into OT. The conversion failed and Michigan won 10-9. Fitzgerald is now 1-6 against the Wolverines with the only win occurring back in 2008.

**Oct. 17**   **Iowa Hawkeyes** – Last year's 41-point loss to Iowa was Fitzgerald's most lopsided defeat in what has otherwise been a fairly tight series. The Wildcats have now dropped two straight to the Hawkeyes.

**Oct. 24**   **at Nebraska Cornhuskers** – Fitzgerald is 1-3 against Nebraska with the lone win occurring in 2011, when the Huskers first joined the Big Ten. With this being a transition year for Nebraska, Northwestern will have a decent shot at pulling off a much-needed win on the road in this game.

**Nov. 7**   **Penn State Nittany Lions** – Last season's convincing 29-6 win over Penn State brought Fitzgerald's record to 2-0 against James Franklin (he also beat Franklin in 2012, when Franklin was at Vanderbilt). The Nittany Lions should be a tougher opponent this year.

**Nov. 14**   **Purdue Boilermakers** – Fitzgerald is 3-3 against the Boilermakers and he needs to make sure he owns this series now that these teams are in the same division.

**Nov. 21**   **at Wisconsin Badgers** – Northwestern pulled off the upset against the Badgers in 2014. It was Wisconsin's only regular season conference loss.

**Nov. 28**   **vs. Illinois Fighting Illini (in Chicago)** – This rivalry will be played at Soldier Field in 2015. Last year's loss to the Illini cost Northwestern a bowl game and that makes this a *MUST-WIN* game for Fitzgerald and the Wildcats. Fitzgerald is 5-4 against Illinois.

**BOTTOM LINE:**
Having two tough opponents on the nonconference schedule (Stanford and Duke) and drawing Michigan and Penn State (two teams that should be better than they were last year) from the East Division will make reaching six wins and bowl eligibility very challenging for the Wildcats in 2015.

Pat Fitzgerald's Year-by-Year Coaching Record:

<u>Northwestern: 60-53 (30-42 in the Big Ten)</u>
| | | |
|---|---|---|
| 2006 | 4–8 (2–6) | Final Ranking: NR |
| 2007 | 6–6 (3–5) | Final Ranking: NR |
| 2008 | 9–4 (5–3) | Final Ranking: NR |

Lost to #25 Missouri 23-30 in OT in the Alamo Bowl.

| | | |
|---|---|---|
| 2009 | 8–5 (5–3) | Final Ranking: NR |

Lost to Auburn 35-38 in OT in the Outback Bowl.

| | | |
|---|---|---|
| 2010 | 7–6 (3–5) | Final Ranking: NR |

Lost to Texas Tech 38-45 in the TicketCity Bowl.

| | | |
|---|---|---|
| 2011 | 6–7 (3–5) | Final Ranking: NR |

Lost to Texas A&M 22-33 in the Meineke Car Care Bowl of Texas.

| | | |
|---|---|---|
| 2012 | 10–3 (5–3) | Final Ranking: #16 |

Beat Mississippi State 34-20 in the Gator Bowl.

| | | |
|---|---|---|
| 2013 | 5–7 (1–7) | Final Ranking: NR |
| 2014 | 5–7 (3–5) | Final Ranking: NR |

# Purdue Boilermakers – Darrell Hazell

## Coach Ranking: #81

**Overall Record:** 20-30 in 4 seasons
**Record at Purdue:** 4-20 in 2 seasons
**2014 Results:** 3-9, 1-7 in the Big Ten (7th in the Big Ten West)
**Returning Starters in 2015:** 8 on offense (including QB), 7 on defense
**Salary:** $2.1 Million      **Age:** 51      **Job Security Grade:** B

COACH'S BIO:
Darrell Hazell grew up in Cinnaminson, New Jersey, and was a team captain and all-conference WR in college at Muskingum (Division III). After graduating in 1986, Hazell immediately began working his way up the coaching ladder. He started with stops as an assistant at smaller colleges like Oberlin, Eastern Illinois, and Penn, and then worked his way up through the mid-major level with stops at Western Michigan and Army. In 1999, he was hired by **Don Nehlen** to be West Virginia's RB coach. In 2001, he joined **Greg Schiano**'s staff as the WR coach at Rutgers and was promoted to assistant head coach in 2003. **Jim Tressel** hired Hazell to be Ohio State's WR coach in 2004 and promoted him to assistant head coach in 2005. In 2011, Kent State hired Hazell to be its new head coach. Inheriting a program with just one winning season (2001) since 1987, Hazell led the Golden Flashes to an 11-win season in 2012 and was named the MAC Coach of the Year. Purdue hired Hazell to replace **Danny Hope** in 2013.

2014 REVIEW:
"Progress" is a relative term and though Purdue won just three games in 2014, it was a step forward from 2013's 1-11 season. Beating Illinois and losing competitive games to Minnesota and Indiana by a combined eight points shows that this team is headed in the right direction.

| 2014 RESULTS:   3-9 (1-7 in the Big Ten) | Final Ranking: NR | |
|---|---|---|
| Western Michigan | W 43–34 | (37,031) |
| Central Michigan | L 17–38 | (36,410) |
| vs. #11 Notre Dame (in Indianapolis) | L 14–30 | (56,832) |
| #16 (FCS) Southern Illinois | W 35–13 | (31,434) |
| Iowa | L 10–24 | (36,603) |
| at Illinois | W 38–27 | (45,046) |
| #8 Michigan State | L 31–45 | (40,217) |
| at Minnesota | L 38–39 | (51,241) |
| at #17 Nebraska | L 14–35 | (91,107) |
| #25 Wisconsin | L 16–34 | (35,068) |
| Northwestern | L 14–38 | (30,117) |
| at Indiana | L 16–23 | (40,079) |

**OFFENSE:**
In Hazell's final season at Kent State (2012), his team relied heavily on the running game and ranked No. 18 in the nation in rushing yards. With that strategy, the Golden Flashes racked up 33 points a game. Promising to adapt to the talent he inherits at Purdue, Hazell's offense has evolved into a pass-first, one-back system over the past two seasons. However, that fundamental transition from a run-first offense to a pass-first offense has not translated to better results. The Boilermakers threw the ball more than they ran it last year, but still came in at No. 103 nationally in passing yards. More importantly, Purdue has been stuck near the back of the Big Ten in scoring each of the past two seasons. In 2014, they averaged less than 24 points a game. While adjusting to the personnel is an essential part of good coaching, it seems clear that Hazell needs to bring in the type of players who can establish a quality running game. Hazell's offensive coordinator is **John Shoop**. Before coming to Purdue in 2013, Shoop spent five seasons as the OC at North Carolina under **Butch Davis** and **Everett Withers**. Purdue has eight starters returning, but Shoop needs to decide on a QB. Last year, sophomores **Austin Appleby** and **Danny Etling** shared time at the position, but neither pulled away as the clear QB of the future for this team.

**DEFENSE:**
Purdue runs a 3-4 defensive scheme with **Greg Hudson** entering his third year as defensive coordinator. Hudson's defense made progress last year as it went from allowing 460 yards a game in 2013 to allowing 416 yards a game in 2014. Though an improvement, that defense still ranked in the bottom half of the nation, at No. 82 in yards allowed and No. 99 in points allowed. Now entering the third year with this system, it's time for the defense to step up and make some serious progress. With seven starters back, the Boilermakers should continue to improve on this side of the ball.

**RECRUITING:**
Though it looks like this program is headed in the right direction, Hazell hasn't been able to convince potential recruits of that notion. For the third-straight year, Hazell signed one of the lowest-rated recruiting classes in the Big Ten. The 2015 class was ranked last in the conference and No. 65 in the nation.

**RUMOR MILL:**
Purdue fired **Danny Hope** after going 22-27 and leading the Boilermakers to two-straight bowl games. With that in mind, it's not surprising to see some speculation that Hazell's seat is already hot going into 2015. However, such speculation is probably premature. Hazell hit the reset button on this program in Year 1 and scored his first Big Ten victory in Year 2. This will be a crucial season for Hazell and his rebuilding job, but managing to win even four or five games with the tough 2015 schedule should be enough to convince critics that this program is headed in the right direction under his leadership. The amazing job Hazell did at Kent State is enough to warrant some patience here.

**2015 OUTLOOK:**

| | |
|---|---|
| Sept. 6 | **at Marshall Thundering Herd** – Opening up the season on the road against a team that went 13-1 and won Conference USA last year is not ideal. Hazell and Marshall head coach Doc Holliday worked on the same staff at West Virginia in 1999. |
| Sept. 12 | **Indiana State Sycamores** – Hazell led the Boilermakers to a 20-14 win over Indiana State in 2012, which was Purdue's only win that season. |
| Sept. 19 | **Virginia Tech Hokies** – The Hokies went 7-6 last year and are expected to have a big bounce-back season in 2015. |
| Sept. 26 | **Bowling Green Falcons** – Hazell went 2-0 against Bowling Green while at Kent State. Purdue has struggled with the MAC in recent years. The Boilermakers have gone 4-4 in their last eight games against MAC opponents. Bowling Green went 8-6 and won the MAC East last season. |
| Oct. 3 | **at Michigan State Spartans** – Since arriving at Purdue, Hazell has gone 0-2 against the Spartans, losing both those games by 14 points each. |
| Oct. 10 | **Minnesota Golden Gophers** – Purdue has gone 2-4 in its last six meetings with Minnesota. |
| Oct. 17 | **at Wisconsin Badgers** – The Boilermakers have a nine-game losing streak in this series and traveling to Madison will make breaking that streak even more difficult. |
| Oct. 31 | **Nebraska Cornhuskers** – The last time Purdue welcomed Nebraska to West Lafayette, the Huskers walked out with a 44-7 victory in 2013. |
| Nov. 7 | **Illinois Fighting Illini** – Hazell beat Illinois on the road last year for his only conference win of the season. Hazell and Illinois head coach Tim Beckman coached on the same staff at Ohio State from 2005-2006. |
| Nov. 14 | **at Northwestern Wildcats** – This is the type of game Hazell must find a way to win if Purdue is going to climb into the middle-tier of the Big Ten West. |
| Nov. 21 | **at Iowa Hawkeyes** – The Boilermakers were held to just 156 total yards in their 14-point loss to Iowa last season. |
| Nov. 28 | **Indiana Hoosiers** – Purdue had a three-point lead midway through the fourth quarter in this game last year, but couldn't hold on for the win. Hazell is 0-2 against this in-state rival, which makes this his *MUST-WIN* game of 2015. |

**BOTTOM LINE:**
The schedule isn't going to make it easy for Hazell and the Boilermakers to improve on last year's three wins. Virginia Tech will obviously be a tough nonconference opponent, but Marshall (last year's C-USA champions) and Bowling Green (last year's MAC East champions) won't be cupcakes either. Drawing Michigan State from the Big Ten East only adds to the difficult road ahead for Purdue. With that in mind, winning four or five games would be a decent accomplishment for a program still rebuilding.

## Darrell Hazell's Year-by-Year Coaching Record:

### Kent State: 16-10 (12-4 in the MAC)
2011    5–7 (4–4)         Final Ranking: NR
2012    11–3 (8–0)       Final Ranking: NR
          MAC East Champions.
          Hazell named MAC Coach of the Year.
          Lost to #19 Northern Illinois 37-44 in double OT in the MAC Championship Game.
          Lost to Arkansas State 13-17 in the GoDaddy.com Bowl.

### Purdue: 4-20 (1-15 in the Big Ten)
2013    1–11 (0–8)       Final Ranking: NR
2014    3–9 (1–7)        Final Ranking: NR

# Wisconsin Badgers – Paul Chryst

## Coach Ranking: #63

**Overall Record:** 19-19 in 3 seasons
**2014 Results:** Wisconsin went 11-3, 7-1 in the Big Ten (Big Ten West Champions)
At Pittsburgh, Chryst went 6-6, 4-4 in the ACC
**Returning Starters in 2015:** 5 on offense (including QB), 8 on defense
**Salary:** $2.3 Million      **Age:** 49      **Job Security Grade:** B

COACH'S BIO:
Paul Chryst is a Madison, Wisconsin, native who played QB for the Badgers from 1986-1988. The son of a college football coach, Chryst quickly followed in his father's footsteps after graduating from Wisconsin and joined the West Virginia staff as an assistant under **Don Nehlen** in 1989. Chryst then made several stops as an assistant at the college level and in the pros (with the World League and the CFL). From 1997-1998, he served as Oregon State's offensive coordinator under **Mike Riley**. He followed Riley to the NFL in 1999 and spent three seasons as San Diego's TE coach. After spending 2002 as Wisconsin's TE coach under **Barry Alvarez**, Chryst again reunited with Mike Riley and served as his OC at Oregon State from 2003-2004. He returned to Wisconsin in 2005 and was the OC under Alvarez and then **Brett Bielema** until 2011. Pittsburgh hired Chryst to be its head coach in 2012, replacing **Todd Graham**. After three years at Pitt, Chryst has returned to his hometown and alma mater to become the head coach at Wisconsin.

2014 REVIEW:
After winning the Big Ten West Division, second-year head coach **Gary Anderson** shocked Wisconsin fans by leaving the program to accept the head coaching job at Oregon State. Former head coach and current AD Barry Alvarez served as the interim head coach in the Badgers' Outback Bowl victory over Auburn.

| 2014 RESULTS:   11-3 (7-1 in the Big Ten) | Final Ranking: NR | |
|---|---|---|
| vs. #13 LSU (in Houston) | L 24–28 | (71,599) |
| Western Illinois | W 37–3 | (77,125) |
| Bowling Green | W 68–17 | (79,849) |
| South Florida | W 27–10 | (78,111) |
| at Northwestern | L 14–20 | (42,013) |
| Illinois | W 38–28 | (80,341) |
| Maryland | W 52–7 | (80,336) |
| at Rutgers | W 37–0 | (52,797) |
| at Purdue | W 34–16 | (35,068) |
| #11 Nebraska | W 59–24 | (80,539) |
| at Iowa | W 26–24 | (68,610) |
| #22 Minnesota | W 34–24 | (80,341) |
| vs. #6 Ohio State (Big Ten Championship) | L 0–59 | (60,229) |
| vs. #19 Auburn (Outback Bowl) | W 34–31 OT | (44,023) |

## OFFENSE:

With RB **Melvin Gordon** in its backfield, Wisconsin relied heavily on the running game in 2014. The Badgers' rushing offense averaged 320 yards a game and was ranked No. 1 in the Big Ten and No. 4 in the nation. Chryst is bringing in **Joe Rudolph** as his offensive coordinator and associate head coach. Rudolph has been coaching with Chryst since 2008, when the two coached together on **Brett Bielema**'s Wisconsin staff. Rudolph served as Chryst's OC for all three seasons in Pittsburgh and these two shouldn't have any trouble adapting to Wisconsin's run-first culture. Last year at Pitt, the Panthers ran the ball twice as often as they passed it in their run-heavy pro-style offense and this system produced the nation's No. 16 rushing attack. The biggest priority for the new regime is finding a replacement at RB for Gordon, who decided to forego his final year of college eligibility and enter the NFL Draft after rushing for the second-most yards *ever* in an FBS season. Junior RB **Corey Clement** will do his best to fill those big shoes. Clement rushed for 949 yards as Gordon's backup last year. Wisconsin will also have to replace three starters on the offensive line, which means that one of college football's most impressive rushing attacks is likely due for a step back in 2015.

## DEFENSE:

Chryst was able to retain **Dave Aranda** at Wisconsin and Aranda will now be entering his third season as the defensive coordinator here. This is a big plus for Chryst's staff. During Aranda's first two seasons as Wisconsin's DC, the Badgers had the Big Ten's No. 2-ranked defense in both scoring defense and total defense. Last year, his 3-4 defense finished No. 4 nationally in total defense and pass defense. This year's squad should once again be the strength of this team. The Badgers have eight starters back on defense, including all four DBs. With Aranda and all that talent returning, expect Wisconsin to field what may be the Big Ten's – perhaps even the nation's – best defense in 2015.

## RECRUITING:

Though his first recruiting class was somewhat small with just 20 signees, Chryst managed to bring in the Big Ten's No. 5-rated class (one spot ahead of Jim Harbaugh's first class at Michigan). This class ranked No. 34 nationally and included pro-style QB **Alex Hornibrook**, who had originally committed to Pitt but followed Chryst to Wisconsin, and four-star RB **Jordan Stevenson**, a recruit out of Dallas who chose Wisconsin over closer warm-weather schools like Alabama, Arkansas, Texas, and Oklahoma State.

## RUMOR MILL:

Wisconsin is glad to welcome back a hometown coach who spent time working for both Barry Alvarez and Brett Bielema, but Chryst will be under immediate pressure to prove he has what it takes to keep the Badgers at the top of the Big Ten West. His .500 record in three seasons at Pittsburgh didn't exactly make Chryst a hot coaching candidate outside of Madison.

**2015 OUTLOOK:**

**Sept. 5**    **vs. Alabama Crimson Tide (in Arlington, TX)** – Paul Chryst and the Badgers kick the season off against the defending SEC champions. Wisconsin went 1-1 against the SEC last year, including a four-point loss to LSU in a season-opening "kickoff" game in Houston.

**Sept. 12**   **Miami (OH) RedHawks** – Wisconsin is 29-1 all-time against MAC schools, though Chryst went 0-1 against the MAC last season at Pitt with a 21-10 loss to Akron. The RedHawks went 2-10 last season and they return just 12 starters in 2015.

**Sept. 19**   **Troy Trojans** – This Sun Belt school went 3-9 last year and they'll have a new head coach this season in Neal Brown, who was Kentucky's OC in 2014.

**Sept. 26**   **Hawaii Rainbow Warriors** – New Wisconsin DB coach Daronte Jones spent the last three seasons on Hawaii's staff and was the assistant head coach there in 2014. The Badgers are 6-2 all-time against Mountain West schools.

**Oct. 3**     **Iowa Hawkeyes** – This is one of the most even rivalries in the Big Ten. The Badgers are 44-42-2 all-time against the Hawkeyes and they enter 2015 having won the last three games in this series. At Pitt, Chryst lost to Iowa last season, 24-20.

**Oct. 10**    **at Nebraska Cornhuskers** – Chryst spent nine years coaching with new Nebraska head coach Mike Riley at Oregon State, with the San Diego Chargers, and with the San Antonio Riders (World League). This game could end up deciding the West Division champion once again, which makes it a *MUST-WIN* game for Wisconsin. The Badgers are 3-1 against the Huskers since Nebraska joined the Big Ten.

**Oct. 17**    **Purdue Boilermakers** – Wisconsin enters this matchup with a nine-game winning streak against Purdue.

**Oct. 24**    **at Illinois Fighting Illini** – The Badgers have dominated this series in recent years, winning nine of the last 10 meetings.

**Oct. 31**    **Rutgers Scarlet Knights** – Wisconsin stomped Rutgers 37-0 on the road last year. While at Pitt, Chryst beat Kyle Flood and the Scarlet Knights 27-6 in 2012.

**Nov. 7**     **at Maryland Terrapins** – Last year, Wisconsin blew out Maryland 52-7 in the first ever meeting between these two schools.

**Nov. 21**    **Northwestern Wildcats** – The Wildcats shocked the Badgers last year, giving them their only conference loss of the regular season.

**Nov. 28**    **at Minnesota Golden Gophers** – This game will mark the 125th meeting of this historic rivalry. Wisconsin currently owns an 11-game winning streak in this series.

**BOTTOM LINE:**
With a loaded defense and a favorable Big Ten schedule (drawing Maryland and Rutgers from the Big Ten East), the Badgers will be expected by many to repeat as West Division champs even though they'll likely struggle through some growing pains early in the season on offense.

## Paul Chryst's Year-by-Year Coaching Record:

**Pittsburgh: 19-19 (10-13 in the Big East and ACC)**

2012   6–7 (3–4)                Final Ranking: NR
Lost to Ole Miss 17-38 in the BBVA Compass Bowl.

2013   7–6 (3–5)                Final Ranking: NR
Pittsburgh joins the ACC.
Beat Bowling Green 30-27 in the Little Caesars Bowl.

2014   6–6 (4–4)                Final Ranking: NR
Pittsburgh lost to Houston 34-35 in the Armed Forces Bowl, but Chryst had already left to accept the Wisconsin job. The interim head coach was Joe Rudolph, who is now Wisconsin's OC.

To receive FREE updates by email on the latest coaching news, rumors, rankings, contract changes, and emerging college football trends, sign up at:

# CoachesAlmanac.com/Updates

# 2015 BIG 12 PREVIEW

## Five Things You Need to Know about the Big 12 in 2015:

**The Battle at the Top:** The Big 12 schedule-makers have set the conference up for a November to remember. The top four teams – **Baylor, Oklahoma, Oklahoma State**, and **TCU** – don't play each other until the final month of the season. Baylor and TCU are picked by most to be the favorites in this conference, but it's hard to bet against **Bob Stoops'** track record of winning Big 12 titles after disappointing seasons.

**New to the Big 12: Kansas** hired Texas A&M WR coach **David Beaty** to be its new head coach and his $800,000 base salary will make him the lowest-paid coach in the Power 5. Either the Jayhawks have found an "under-the-radar" coach to lead their team or the Kansas football program couldn't afford a "high-in-demand" coach after having to pay expensive buyouts to fire **Mark Mangino, Turner Gill**, and **Charlie Weis**.

**Coach on the Rise: Dana Holgorsen** isn't going down without a fight and he deserves some credit for the job he did in 2014. Despite entering the season on a scorching hot seat, he took **West Virginia** back to a bowl game and landed the Big 12's fourth-best recruiting class. Don't be surprised if the Mountaineers pull off another conference-rattling upset or two in 2015.

**Keep an Eye On:** The Air Raid offense has fully invaded the Big 12. With **Bob Stoops** bringing it back to **Oklahoma** and **David Beaty** installing it at **Kansas**, seven of the Big 12's 10 teams – **Baylor, Kansas, Oklahoma, Oklahoma State, Texas Tech, TCU**, and **West Virginia** – will run a version of the Air Raid system in 2015. When an offensive scheme gets this popular, you can be assured that defensive coordinators will soon find more effective ways to slow it down.

**Coaches on the Hot Seat: Iowa State's Paul Rhoads** enters 2015 on the hottest seat in the Big 12. Despite a bounce-back season in 2014, **Dana Holgorsen's** seat is still warm at **West Virginia. Kliff Kingsbury** isn't on the hot seat just yet, but he needs to quickly prove that an ugly 2014 was just a short-term setback for **Texas Tech**.

## 2015 Projected Standings for the Big 12:

1. Baylor
2. Oklahoma
3. TCU
4. Oklahoma State
5. Texas
6. Kansas State
7. West Virginia
8. Texas Tech
9. Iowa State
10. Kansas

## Ranking the Big 12's Coaches:

1.  **Bob Stoops** – Oklahoma (168-44 in 16 seasons)
2.  **Art Briles** – Baylor (89-62 in 12 seasons)
3.  **Bill Snyder** – Kansas State (187-94-1 in 23 seasons)
4.  **Gary Patterson** – TCU (132-45 in 14 seasons)
5.  **Charlie Strong** – Texas (43-23 in 6 seasons)
6.  **Mike Gundy** – Oklahoma State (84-44 in 10 seasons)
7.  **Dana Holgorsen** – West Virginia (28-23 in 4 seasons)
8.  **Kliff Kingsbury** – Texas Tech (12-13 in 2 seasons)
9.  **Paul Rhoads** – Iowa State (29-46 in 6 seasons)
10. **David Beaty** – Kansas (First Year Head Coach)

## 2014 Big 12 Coach of the Year:
(Selected by the Big 12 coaches)
Gary Patterson, TCU

## 2014 Big 12 Standings:

|                  | (Conference) | (All Games) |
| ---------------- | ------------ | ----------- |
| #7 Baylor        | 8–1          | 11–2        |
| #3 TCU           | 8–1          | 12–1        |
| #18 Kansas State | 7–2          | 9–4         |
| Oklahoma         | 5–4          | 8–5         |
| Texas            | 5–4          | 6–7         |
| West Virginia    | 5–4          | 7–6         |
| Oklahoma State   | 4–5          | 7–6         |
| Texas Tech       | 2–7          | 4–8         |
| Kansas           | 1–8          | 3–9         |
| Iowa State       | 0–9          | 2–10        |

**2014 Big 12 Bowl Record:** 2-5 (10th place among all 10 conferences)

# Baylor Bears – Art Briles

## Coach Ranking: #10

**Overall Record:** 89-62 in 12 seasons
**Record at Baylor:** 55-34 in 7 seasons
**2014 Results:** 11-2, 8-1 in the Big 12 (Big 12 Co-Champions)
**Returning Starters in 2015:** 8 on offense, 9 on defense
**Salary:** $4 Million*      **Age:** 59      **Job Security Grade:** A

COACH'S BIO:
The son of a high school football coach, Art Briles was an all-state QB in Rule, Texas, before playing WR in college for **Bill Yeoman** at Houston from 1974-1977. After college, Briles began his coaching career as a high school assistant and became the head coach at Hamlin High in 1984, when he was just 28. After two successful seasons at Hamlin and two not-so-successful seasons at Georgetown High, Briles was hired at Stephenville High in 1988. Evolving from a run-first veer offense in his early coaching days, Briles' innovative shotgun spread system created a Texas high school dynasty at Stephenville. During his 12 seasons there, he won 135 games and four state championships while developing six Division 1 QBs. In 2000, Briles was hired by **Mike Leach** to be Texas Tech's RB coach and in 2003 he became Houston's head coach. He spent five seasons at Houston and went to four bowl games. Baylor hired Briles in 2008 and in 2013 he won the school's first Big 12 championship. He followed that up with a share of the Big 12 title in 2014.

2014 REVIEW:
Before Briles arrived at Baylor, the school posted 12-straight losing seasons and hadn't finished a year ranked in the Top 25 since 1986. In 2014, Briles led the Bears to their second-consecutive Big 12 Championship and a Top-10 finish for the first time since 1951. Though 2014 marked Baylor's highest final ranking in school history, the Bears failed to make the playoffs and felt snubbed by the CFP committee.

| 2014 RESULTS:   11-2 (7-1 in the Big 12) | Final Ranking: #7 | |
|---|---|---|
| SMU | W 45-0 | (45,733) |
| Northwestern State | W 70-6 | (45,034) |
| at Buffalo | W 63-21 | (24,714) |
| at Iowa State | W 49-28 | (51,776) |
| at Texas | W 28-7 | (93,727) |
| #9 TCU | W 61-58 | (46,803) |
| at West Virginia | L 27-41 | (60,758) |
| Kansas | W 60-14 | (47,574) |
| at #16 Oklahoma | W 48-14 | (85,048) |
| Oklahoma State | W 49-28 | (47,179) |
| vs. Texas Tech (in Arlington, TX) | W 48-46 | (54,179) |
| #9 Kansas State | W 38-27 | (47,934) |
| vs. #7 Michigan State (Cotton Bowl) | L 41-42 | (71,464) |

**OFFENSE:**
Art Briles is one of four active coaches who have recently made the transition from running a top-level high school program to running a top-level major college program in a relatively short period of time. Like the other three members of this unique group – **Gus Malzahn**, **Hugh Freeze**, and **Todd Graham** – Briles runs a no-huddle, up-tempo, shotgun-spread offense. For the past two seasons, Baylor has had the nation's top offense in both scoring and total yards. The Bears have done it on the ground and through the air. In 2013, Baylor had the Big 12's top rushing team and second-best passing team. In 2014, the Bears had the Big 12's top passing offense and the second-best rushing offense. And Baylor does it all at hyper-speed. Last year, the Bears were the nation's second-ranked team in number of offensive plays. Add it all up and you have an offense that opposing coaches have stopped trying to shut down; they're simply hoping to *slow* it down. Of course, with that kind of success, it's only a matter of time before an offensive coordinator gets handed the keys to his own program and after 17 years with Briles (dating all the way back to their time together at Stephenville High), **Philip Montgomery** is leaving to become the head coach at Tulsa. This will be a significant change for Baylor since Montgomery has handled the play-calling duties for the past three seasons. His replacement is Art Briles' 32-year-old son, **Kendal Briles**, who has been at Baylor since his father's arrival. He served as the Bears' WR coach and passing game coordinator from 2012-2014. Having eight starters back should make the transition a bit easier, but the Bears will have to replace two-time All-American QB **Bryce Petty**. Baylor will still have plenty of weapons in 2015, but with a new OC and QB, a slight step back in offensive production is to be expected.

**DEFENSE:**
Entering his fifth season as Baylor's defensive coordinator is **Phil Bennett**. A veteran coach with 37 years of experience (including a stint as SMU's head coach from 2002-2007), Bennett inherited a Baylor defense ranked 10th in the Big 12 in total defense when he arrived in 2011. Since that time, he's engineered a solid turnaround. While the Bears ranked a respectable fourth in the Big 12 in both yards and points allowed last season, their main focus is forcing turnovers and getting the ball back in the hands of their high-powered offense. With just four starters back last year, Baylor forced the second most turnovers in the Big 12. This year, nine starters are back and the Bears expect that experience to pay big dividends for this nickel-based defense.

**RECRUITING:**
After landing the Big 12's No. 3-rated recruiting class (behind Oklahoma and Texas) for three-straight years, the 2015 class fell back to No. 5 in the conference. The size of this class played a factor. With just 19 signees, Baylor was tied for the smallest recruiting class in the Big 12.

**RUMOR MILL:**
At the end of the 2013 season, Briles was rumored to be a top candidate for the Texas job (which went to **Charlie Strong**), but Baylor stepped in and gave Briles a big raise and a 10-year contract extension, which will now run through the 2023 season.

**2015 OUTLOOK:**

**Sept. 4**  **at SMU Mustangs** – The Bears will kick the season off with a Friday-night game in Dallas. SMU has a new head coach in Chad Morris, who spent the last four seasons as Clemson's OC. Dating back to his time at Houston, Briles is 4-1 against the Mustangs.

**Sept. 12**  **Lamar Cardinals** – Since coming to Baylor, Briles is 7-0 against FCS schools and he's won those games by an average margin of 41 points.

**Sept. 26**  **Rice Owls** – Briles is 6-1 all-time against the Owls and 2-0 since he arrived at Baylor. Rice went 8-5 last season, but they have just 10 starters returning in 2015.

**Oct. 3**  **vs. Texas Tech Red Raiders (in Arlington, TX)** – They call this annual game the "Texas Shootout" and the high-scoring matchup has lived up to its billing. Briles is 4-3 in this series and he has won the last four games in this rivalry by an average score of 57-42.

**Oct. 10**  **at Kansas Jayhawks** – Since arriving at Baylor, Briles is a perfect 5-0 against the Jayhawks. Though Kansas has a new head coach in David Beaty, the rebuilding job will take some time.

**Oct. 17**  **West Virginia Mountaineers** – West Virginia gave Baylor its only regular season loss last year and cost the Bears a trip to the playoffs. Briles is 1-2 in this series and these two fast-paced offenses like to pile up the points. Both teams have averaged more than 50 points each in their last three meetings.

**Oct. 24**  **Iowa State Cyclones** – Briles is 3-2 against Paul Rhoads. The last time the Bears played Iowa State in Waco (2013), they won 71-7.

**Nov. 5**  **at Kansas State Wildcats** – Playing in Manhattan on a Thursday night will be a tough environment, but Briles is an impressive 4-1 against Hall of Famer Bill Snyder.

**Nov. 14**  **Oklahoma Sooners** – Baylor embarrassed the Sooners in Norman last year 48-14 and Oklahoma will be looking for revenge this year. With the way the schedules line up for both schools, this could be a battle of unbeaten teams. Briles is 3-5 against Stoops, but he's won the last two meetings.

**Nov. 21**  **at Oklahoma State Cowboys** – Since arriving at Baylor, Briles is 2-5 against Oklahoma State and he's never won in Stillwater.

**Nov. 27**  **at TCU Horned Frogs** – This renewed rivalry is heating up and the Big 12 schedule-makers are hoping this late-November game is for the conference championship. That makes this a *MUST-WIN* game for Briles, who is 3-2 against TCU since coming to Baylor.

**Dec. 5**  **Texas Longhorns** – Though he's 4-3 overall in this series, Briles has gone 4-1 in his last five meetings with Texas.

**BOTTOM LINE:**
Over the past four seasons, no offense has dominated college football the way Baylor's has. Even though the Bears will have a new offensive coordinator and QB in 2015, one shouldn't expect the Bears to slow down too much. With 17 starters back, Baylor is set up nicely for a third-straight Big 12 title run. And this time, Briles is hoping that a Big 12 title includes a playoff berth.

## Art Briles' Year-by-Year Coaching Record:

__Houston: 34-28 (24-16 in Conference USA)__
2003   7–6 (4–4)                **Final Ranking: NR**
       Lost to Hawaii 48-54 in the Hawaii Bowl.
2004   3–8 (3–5)                **Final Ranking: NR**
2005   6–6 (4–4)                **Final Ranking: NR**
       Lost to Kansas 13-42 in the Fort Worth Bowl.
2006   10–4 (7–1)               **Final Ranking: NR**
       C-USA Champions.
       Beat Southern Miss 34-20 in the C-USA Championship Game.
       Lost to South Carolina 36-44 in the Liberty Bowl.
2007   8–4 (6–2)                **Final Ranking: NR**
       C-USA West Division Co-Champions.
       Houston lost to TCU 13-20 in the Texas Bowl, but Briles had already left to
       accept the Baylor job.

__Baylor: 55-34 (33-27 in the Big 12)__
2008   4–8 (2–6)                **Final Ranking: NR**
2009   4–8 (1–7)                **Final Ranking: NR**
2010   7–6 (4–4)                **Final Ranking: NR**
       Lost to Illinois 14-38 in the Texas Bowl.
2011   10–3 (6–3)               **Final Ranking: #12**
       Beat Washington 67-56 in the Alamo Bowl.
2012   8–5 (4–5)                **Final Ranking: NR**
       Beat #17 UCLA 49-26 in the Holiday Bowl.
2013   11–2 (8–1)               **Final Ranking: #13**
       Big 12 Champions.
       Lost to #15 UCF 42-52 in the Fiesta Bowl.
2014   11–2 (8–1)               **Final Ranking: #7**
       Big 12 Co-Champions.
       Lost to #7 Michigan State 41-42 in the Cotton Bowl.

# Iowa State Cyclones – Paul Rhoads

## Coach Ranking: #100

**Overall Record:** 29-46 in 6 seasons
**Record at Iowa State:** 29-46 in 6 seasons
**2014 Results:** 2-10, 0-9 in the Big 12 (10th in the Big 12)
**Returning Starters in 2015:** 6 on offense (including QB), 9 on defense
**Salary:** $1.8 Million    **Age:** 48    **Job Security Grade:** D

**COACH'S BIO:**
Paul Rhoads followed his father, a member of the Iowa High School Football Coaches Hall of Fame, into coaching. Rhoads grew up in Ankeny, Iowa, and played DB at Missouri Western (NAIA) from 1985-1988. After college, he immediately began a coaching career with stops at Utah State, Ohio State (under **John Cooper**), and Pacific. From 1995-1999, he was an assistant on **Dan McCarney's** staff at Iowa State. From 2000-2007, he established himself as one of the top defensive coordinators in the Big East while serving under **Walt Harris** and then **Dave Wannstedt** at Pittsburgh. Rhoads spent one season (2008) as **Tommy Tuberville's** DC at Auburn before he was hired as the head coach at Iowa State in 2009, replacing **Gene Chizik**, who had just left to accept the Auburn head coaching job.

**2014 REVIEW:**
Rhoads led Iowa State to three bowl games in his first four seasons, but fell to 3-9 in 2013. A bounce-back year was needed in 2014. Instead, Iowa State opened the year with a humbling 20-point loss to an FCS school. Though they knocked off in-state rival Iowa, the Cyclones failed to win a Big 12 game for the first time since 2008. Injuries devastated Iowa State last season. Only *four* starters made it from the start of the year to the end of the year without missing games due to injuries.

**2014 RESULTS:  2-10 (0-9 in the Big 12)**    **Final Ranking: NR**

| | | |
|---|---|---|
| #2 (FCS) North Dakota State | L 14–34 | (54,800) |
| #20 Kansas State | L 28–32 | (54,800) |
| at Iowa | W 20–17 | (70,585) |
| #7 Baylor | L 28–49 | (51,776) |
| at #21 Oklahoma State | L 20–37 | (52,608) |
| Toledo | W 37–30 | (52,281) |
| at Texas | L 45–48 | (92,017) |
| #19 Oklahoma | L 14–59 | (50,784) |
| at Kansas | L 14–34 | (33,288) |
| Texas Tech | L 31–34 | (50,877) |
| West Virginia | L 24–37 | (50,059) |
| at #3 TCU | L 3–55 | (45,242) |

**OFFENSE:**

Each year since Rhoads was hired, the Iowa State offense has ranked ninth or worse in the Big 12 in scoring. With 10 returning starters back and a new offensive coordinator in former Kansas head coach **Mark Mangino**, Iowa State's spread offense was supposed to finally work its way out of the Big 12's cellar in 2014. While the Cyclones did manage to finish eighth in scoring instead of ninth in the conference, they finished 99th nationally. This season, fifth-year senior **Sam Richardson** returns as the starting QB after passing for 2,669 yards and rushing for 421 yards in 2014. The Cyclones will have six starters back and while they need a big-play RB to step up, going into their second season with Mangino's system should mean better production from this offense.

**DEFENSE:**

Paul Rhoads was hired by Iowa State as a defensive-minded coach. However, that defensive expertise hasn't translated to performance on the field. In total defense, the Cyclones finished last in *all* of college football last year, giving up more than 528 yards a game. Iowa State runs a 4-3 defense led by **Wally Burnham**, the 73-year-old coaching veteran who has more than 40 years of coaching experience. Burnham has been Rhoads' defensive coordinator since he arrived in 2009. The defense can't get any worse than last season and a squad that was young and injury-laden in 2014 should be experienced and motivated in 2015. The Cyclones will have nine starters back on defense and they're expecting big things from DT **Demond Tucker**, an incoming juco transfer who was previously named the NJCAA Defensive Player of the Year.

**RECRUITING:**

It's always been tough to recruit at Iowa State, which is overshadowed by in-state rival Iowa and nearby Midwest powers like Nebraska and Kansas State. It's even tougher to recruit when your head coach spends most of the season on the hot seat. Rhoads signed the ninth-ranked recruiting class in the Big 12 and landed at No. 71 nationally. He did manage to sign six juco recruits who will hopefully be able to contribute quickly. DT Demond Tucker was one of the top-rated juco players in the country at his position.

**RUMOR MILL:**

After the 2011 season, Iowa State gave Rhoads a 10-year contract extension. It may be tough for Rhoads to keep his position for the entire term of that contract. Over the past two seasons, Rhoads has gone 5-19. An unusually high number of injuries hampered the Cyclones each of the past two seasons and that's probably a contributing reason why Rhoads was retained for 2015. It's worth remembering that Iowa State fired Dan McCarney after he went 4-8 in 2006. Rhoads will enter 2015 on the hottest seat in the Big 12.

**NOTEWORTHY:**

Rhoads was born just 10 minutes from Iowa State's stadium. His enthusiasm and personable style have made this hometown coach extremely popular with many Iowa State fans.

## 2015 OUTLOOK:

**Sept. 5**    **Northern Iowa Panthers** – Iowa State has gone 2-1 against this in-state FCS school since the Rhoads era began. The last time they played (2013), Northern Iowa won 28-20.

**Sept. 12**    **Iowa Hawkeyes** – Rhoads is 3-3 in this important rivalry and last year's win over the Hawkeyes may have saved his job. This is a *MUST-WIN* game for the Cyclones. If they can pull it off for the second year in a row, they'll have a legitimate shot at starting the season 4-0.

**Sept. 19**    **at Toledo Rockets** – Iowa State beat the Rockets at home last season and now they'll travel to Toledo for a rematch. Rhoads is 3-0 against MAC teams.

**Oct. 3**    **Kansas Jayhawks** – The Jayhawks' win over Iowa State last season was their only Big 12 win of the year. As a result, the Cyclones finished last in the Big 12 standings. Rhoads is 4-2 against KU and he's never lost to the Jayhawks in Ames.

**Oct. 10**    **at Texas Tech Red Raiders** – Iowa State is on a three-game losing streak in this series.

**Oct. 17**    **TCU Horned Frogs** – The last time these teams played in Ames (2013), TCU snuck out with a four-point win.

**Oct. 24**    **at Baylor Bears** – When Iowa State last traveled to Waco (2013), the Bears pummeled the Cyclones 71-7. Rhoads is 2-3 against Art Briles.

**Oct. 31**    **Texas Longhorns** – Though Rhoads is on a four-game losing streak to Texas, the last two losses were by a *combined* four points.

**Nov. 7**    **at Oklahoma Sooners** – The Sooners have dominated this series. Rhoads is 0-5 against Oklahoma and he's lost those games by an average margin of 34 points each.

**Nov. 14**    **Oklahoma State Cowboys** – The last time Oklahoma State traveled to Ames in November, the Cyclones upset the No. 2-ranked Cowboys in double OT. That game marked Rhoads' only win against Oklahoma State.

**Nov. 21**    **at Kansas State Wildcats** – Rhoads was hired at Iowa State the same year Bill Snyder returned to K-State. Despite some close games, Rhoads is 0-6 against Snyder.

**Nov. 28**    **at West Virginia Mountaineers** – When the Cyclones traveled to Morgantown in 2013, they came away with a triple-OT victory. That was Rhoads' only win against West Virginia.

## BOTTOM LINE:

Paul Rhoads is on the hottest seat in the Big 12 and if he wants to hold onto his job, he'll probably need to make it to a bowl game in 2015. To end his two-year bowl drought and get this program headed back in the right direction, it's crucial that Rhoads and the Cyclones get off to a fast start. Their first four games are all winnable and a 4-0 start would put them in a great position to reach six wins and bowl eligibility.

## Paul Rhoads' Year-by-Year Coaching Record:

<u>Iowa State: 29-46 (14-38 in the Big 12)</u>
2009    7–6 (3–5)               Final Ranking: NR
        Beat Minnesota 14-13 in the Insight Bowl.
2010    5–7 (3–5)               Final Ranking: NR
2011    6–7 (3–6)               Final Ranking: NR
        Lost to Rutgers 13-27 in the Pinstripe Bowl.
2012    6–7 (3–6)               Final Ranking: NR
        Lost to Tulsa 17-31 in the Liberty Bowl.
2013    3–9 (2–7)               Final Ranking: NR
2014    2–10 (0–9)              Final Ranking: NR

# Kansas Jayhawks – David Beaty
## Coach Ranking: #118

**Overall Record:** 0-0

**2014 Results:** Kansas went 3-9, 1-8 in the Big 12 (9th in the Big 12)

Beaty was Texas A&M's WR coach from 2012-2014

**Returning Starters in 2015:** 4 on offense (including QB), 4 on defense

**Salary:** $800,000          **Age:** 44          **Job Security Grade:** B

**COACH'S BIO:**

David Beaty grew up in Garland, Texas, and was a four-year starting WR at Lindenwood College (NAIA) in St. Charles, Missouri. After graduating in 1994, Beaty started his coaching career as an assistant high school coach in Texas. He became the head coach at North Dallas High School in 2001 and then served as the head coach of MacArthur High in Irving, Texas, from 2002-2005. His five-year high school record was 39-15. Beaty made the move to the college level in 2006 when he became the WR coach at Rice under **Todd Graham**. He then served as WR coach under **Mark Mangino** at Kansas from 2008-2009. After a season as the offensive coordinator at Rice, Beaty returned to Kansas as **Turner Gill**'s co-OC in 2011. When Gill was fired, Beaty joined **Kevin Sumlin**'s staff at Texas A&M and served as the WR coach from 2012-2014 and also as A&M's recruiting coordinator during the 2013 and 2014 seasons.

**2014 REVIEW:**

**Charlie Weis** didn't make it to midseason of his third year as Kansas' head coach. After the Jayhawks' 23-0 loss to Texas, KU fired Weis. Linebacker coach **Clint Bowen** stepped in as interim head coach for the remainder of the season and managed one win in his eight tries. However, the Jayhawks nearly knocked off No. 5 TCU in the final home game of the season. Kansas has now lost 48 games since 2010; the school's most losses *ever* over a five-year period.

| 2014 RESULTS:   3-9 (1-8 in the Big 12) | Final Ranking: NR | |
|---|---|---|
| SE Missouri State | W 34–28 | (36,574) |
| at Duke | L 3–41 | (25,203) |
| Central Michigan | W 24–10 | (34,822) |
| Texas | L 0–23 | (36,904) |
| at West Virginia | L 14–33 | (52,164) |
| #16 Oklahoma State | L 20–27 | (31,985) |
| at Texas Tech | L 21–34 | (54,071) |
| at #12 Baylor | L 14–60 | (47,574) |
| Iowa State | W 34–14 | (33,288) |
| #5 TCU | L 30–34 | (30,889) |
| at #23 Oklahoma | L 7–44 | (84,908) |
| at #11 Kansas State | L 13–51 | (53,439) |

**OFFENSE:**
Kansas hired **Charlie Weis** with the expectation that his offensive expertise would quickly improve the struggling Jayhawks. Instead, Kansas finished dead last in the Big 12 in scoring each of the past three seasons. In fact, KU's offense has finished last in the Big 12 every year since **Mark Mangino** was fired after the 2009 season. Last year, the Kansas offense finished 118th nationally in both scoring and total yards. David Beaty will replace Weis' pro-style offense with the Air Raid system. While KU fans are hoping Beaty can inject this offense with some firepower, don't expect to see a fast turnaround as the Jayhawks return just four starters on offense – the fewest in the Big 12. Beaty hired **Rob Likens** to be his offensive coordinator. Likens spent 2010-2014 as **Sonny Dykes'** assistant head coach at Louisiana Tech and Cal. With Likens as the passing game coordinator last season, Cal finished sixth nationally in passing yards.

**DEFENSE:**
When Weis was fired after four games last year, LB coach **Clint Bowen** took over as interim head coach. Though he went just 1-7, the Jayhawks looked more competitive and enthusiastic when Bowen was in charge. Kansas strongly considered hiring Bowen as the new head coach. Instead, Bowen is being retained as the assistant head coach and defensive coordinator. Kansas runs a 3-3-5 defense and, like the offense, returns just four starters in 2015.

**RECRUITING:**
It's always tough for an incoming head coach to bring in a top recruiting class. It's even tougher when that incoming head coach is taking over a program that hasn't had a winning season in seven years. Kansas landed a class that ranked last in the Big 12 and 72nd nationally. However, it should be noted that Beaty has a good reputation as a recruiter, especially with his ties to the state of Texas. During his two seasons as recruiting coordinator at Texas A&M, Beaty helped land the nation's No. 5- and No. 9-ranked classes.

**RUMOR MILL:**
Before settling on David Beaty as its new head coach, rumor has it that the Jayhawks offered the job to **Ed Warinner**, the current co-offensive coordinator at Ohio State who served as Mark Mangino's OC at Kansas from 2007-2009. Warinner reportedly turned down KU's offer and chose to stay at Ohio State. Former Nebraska OC **Tim Beck** was also said to be in the running, but instead accepted a position to join Warinner as co-OC at Ohio State.

**NOTEWORTHY:**
Beaty's salary of $800,000 is by far the lowest in the Big 12 (the next lowest is **Paul Rhoads'** $1.8 million salary at Iowa State). However, Beaty's contract includes many performance incentives that could push his pay above $1.5 million. One such incentive is that Beaty will be paid an additional $25,000 for *each* Big 12 victory. Outgoing coach Charlie Weis was paid $2.5 million a year and Weis will continue to receive that salary through 2016.

## 2015 OUTLOOK:

**Sept. 5**    **South Dakota State Jackrabbits** – Kansas opened the 2011 season against this FCS school and scored its only victory of the year against the Jackrabbits. South Dakota State finished 9-5 in 2014, which included a 38-18 loss to Missouri to open the season. This is a *MUST-WIN* game for the Jayhawks. Losing the season-opener to an FCS school could mean a winless first year for Beaty.

**Sept. 12**    **Memphis Tigers** – This won't be the pushover nonconference opponent Kansas may have hoped for when it scheduled this game. The Tigers went 10-3 last year and finished the season ranked No. 25.

**Sept. 26**    **at Rutgers Scarlet Knights** – The last time the Jayhawks played a Big Ten team, they beat Minnesota in the 2008 Insight Bowl. Rutgers finished 8-5 last season and went 4-2 at home.

**Oct. 3**    **at Iowa State Cyclones** – Last year's win over Iowa State kept Kansas out of last place in the Big 12 standings. The Jayhawks are 1-4 in their last five meetings with the Cyclones. Former Kansas head coach Mark Mangino is now the offensive coordinator at Iowa State.

**Oct. 10**    **Baylor Bears** – Kansas last beat Baylor in 2007, the year before the Bears hired Art Briles. These two programs have gone in opposite directions since that time.

**Oct. 17**    **Texas Tech Red Raiders** – Kansas is 1-15 all-time against Texas Tech. The Jayhawks' only win occurred in 2001.

**Oct. 24**    **at Oklahoma State Cowboys** – The Jayhawks are 1-6 against Oklahoma State head coach Mike Gundy and the Cowboys have won the last five games in this series.

**Oct. 31**    **Oklahoma Sooners** – Oklahoma head coach Bob Stoops is a perfect 10-0 against the Jayhawks.

**Nov. 7**    **at Texas Longhorns** – Since the Big 12 was formed, Kansas has *never* defeated Texas. The Jayhawks are 2-12 all-time against the Longhorns and their last victory occurred in 1938.

**Nov. 14**    **at TCU Horned Frogs** – Kansas had a 10-point lead over TCU midway through the third quarter last year, but the Jayhawks couldn't hold on for the upset. Since joining the Big 12, Kansas is the only conference foe TCU has gone undefeated against.

**Nov. 21**    **West Virginia Mountaineers** – KU's upset win over West Virginia in 2012 was the only Big 12 victory of the Charlie Weis era.

**Nov. 28**    **Kansas State Wildcats** – Since Bill Snyder's 2009 return, the Jayhawks are 0-6 in this rivalry and they've lost the last five meetings by an average margin of 38 points each.

## BOTTOM LINE:

With a new head coach and the fewest returning starters in the Big 12, don't expect a fast start for this turnaround effort. It's hard to say this about a team that has averaged nearly 10 losses a season for the past five years, but things may get *worse* before they get better for the Jayhawks.

# Kansas State Wildcats – Bill Snyder

## Coach Ranking: #11

**Overall Record:** 187-94-1 in 23 seasons
**Record at Kansas State:** 187-94-1 in 23 seasons
**2014 Results:** 9-4, 7-2 in the Big 12 (3rd in the Big 12)
**Returning Starters in 2015:** 6 on offense, 6 on defense
**Salary:** $3 Million        **Age:** 75        **Job Security Grade:** A

**COACH'S BIO:**
Bill Snyder grew up in Missouri and played DB at William Jewell College from 1959-1962. He began his coaching career as an assistant at the high school level before spending the 1966 season as a graduate assistant under **John McKay** at USC. Snyder then spent seven years as a high school head coach in California before returning to the college level as an assistant in 1974. In 1979, he was hired by **Hayden Fry** to be Iowa's offensive coordinator and QB coach, a position he held until he left to become the head coach at Kansas State in 1989. Snyder inherited what was widely considered to be the worst major college football program in America and turned it into a national power. He retired from the sidelines after the 2005 season, but returned as head coach of the Wildcats in 2009. Snyder has been named the Big 8/Big 12 Coach of the Year seven times and this past offseason, he became just the fourth coach ever to be inducted into the College Football Hall of Fame while still actively coaching.

**2014 REVIEW:**
Heading into the TCU game in November, Kansas State had worked its way up to No. 7 in the country and had a shot at making the playoffs. The loss to TCU followed by back-to-back losses to close out the year put a damper on Snyder's 23rd season at K-State. The Wildcats' No. 18 final ranking marked the third time in Snyder's six seasons since returning to the sidelines that his team finished in the Top 20.

**2014 RESULTS:   9-4 (7-2 in the Big 12)**          **Final Ranking: #18**

| | | |
|---|---|---|
| Stephen F. Austin | W 55–16 | (52,830) |
| at Iowa State | W 32–28 | (54,800) |
| #5 Auburn | L 14–20 | (53,046) |
| UTEP | W 58–28 | (52,899) |
| Texas Tech | W 45–13 | (52,726) |
| at #11 Oklahoma | W 31–30 | (85,019) |
| Texas | W 23–0 | (52,879) |
| Oklahoma State | W 48–14 | (53,746) |
| at #6 TCU | L 20–41 | (48,012) |
| at West Virginia | W 26–20 | (47,683) |
| Kansas | W 51–13 | (53,439) |
| at #5 Baylor | L 27–38 | (47,934) |
| vs. #14 UCLA (Alamo Bowl) | L 35–40 | (60,517) |

**OFFENSE:**

K-State runs a multiple-set pro-style offense that likes to line up in the shotgun and add in some option, especially if the QB is a good runner. In the late 1990s, Snyder started running more option out of the shotgun-spread look and **Urban Meyer** credits Snyder's innovation as an instrumental component in what would become the spread-option offense Meyer is now known for. Since Snyder's return to coaching in 2009, he's used two co-offensive coordinators. **Dana Dimel**, the former head coach at Wyoming and Houston, is primarily in charge of the running game while **Del Miller** is primarily in charge of the passing game. In this age of hurry-up offenses, the Wildcats tend to take their time at the line of scrimmage and they're not afraid to slow down the game with a ball-control strategy. This has proven to be an efficient system. Though K-State ranked 74th in the nation in total offensive plays last year, it ranked No. 23 in points per game, proving that you don't have to run a hyper-speed offense to rack up big points. With a new QB and just six starters back, the 2015 offense will have trouble matching last year's scoring output. Four of those returning starters are on the o-line, so don't be surprised to see this team rely more on the run in 2015.

**DEFENSE:**

**Tom Hayes** will enter his 33rd season of coaching this year. Hayes was named K-State's defensive coordinator in 2012 and since that time, the Wildcats' 4-3 base defense has ranked in the top three of the Big 12 in points allowed each year. In the pass-happy Big 12, stopping the passing game is a priority and K-State fielded the conference's second best pass defense in 2014. With three returning starters in the secondary, the Wildcat pass defense should be a strength again this year.

**RECRUITING:**

K-State's 2015 recruiting class was ranked near the bottom of the Big 12, finishing at No. 8 in the conference. In the past, Snyder was known for his heavy reliance on junior college transfers. That was not the case in 2015 as this class included just one juco player, which marked the smallest number of juco players signed by Snyder since 1992. Snyder acknowledged that it has gotten much tougher to recruit top juco players in recent years as other major programs have followed K-State's lead in targeting "under-the-radar" talent at junior colleges.

**RUMOR MILL:**

Snyder's contract has a rollover provision that renews each season, essentially ensuring that he will be K-State's head coach for as long as he wants to be. That leaves two questions: how long will Snyder (who will turn 76 during the 2015 season) continue coaching, and who will take over the job when he retires? The favorite for the job right now is whispered to be Snyder's son, **Sean Snyder**, who is currently the Wildcats' associate head coach and special teams coordinator. Other potential candidates include Clemson DC **Brent Venables**, a Kansas native who played for and coached under Snyder in the 1990s, and current Ohio State co-OC **Tim Beck**, who was a graduate assistant on Snyder's staff from 1991-1992.

**2015 OUTLOOK:**

**Sept. 5**     **South Dakota Coyotes** – Two years ago, K-State lost its home opener to FCS powerhouse North Dakota State. South Dakota is nowhere near the same threat NDSU was. The Coyotes went 2-10 last season.

**Sept. 12**     **at UTSA Roadrunners** – The last time the Wildcats played a non-Power 5 school on the road was in Snyder's return season of 2009, when they lost to Louisiana-Lafayette 15-17.

**Sept. 19**     **Louisiana Tech Bulldogs** – This team could be more dangerous than many expect. Skip Holtz's Bulldogs went 9-5 last season and won the West Division of C-USA.

**Oct. 3**     **at Oklahoma State Cowboys** – Though Snyder is 11-5 all-time against Oklahoma State, he's 2-3 since returning to the sidelines in 2009.

**Oct. 10**     **TCU Horned Frogs** – TCU head coach Gary Patterson is a K-State graduate and rumor has it that in 2008 he was nearly hired by the Wildcats to replace Ron Prince. Instead, Snyder returned for a second tenure. Snyder is 2-1 against Patterson.

**Oct. 17**     **Oklahoma Sooners** – Oklahoma head coach Bob Stoops was a member of Snyder's staff at K-State from 1989-1995. Oklahoma is the only current Big 12 team that has a winning record against Snyder, at 12-8.

**Oct. 24**     **at Texas Longhorns** – Last year's 23-0 win over Texas marked the only shutout loss of Charlie Strong's career. Snyder is 6-3 all-time against the Longhorns.

**Nov. 5**     **Baylor Bears** – Baylor spoiled K-State's national title hopes in 2012 and has now won three straight against the Cats. Snyder will try to end that streak in this Thursday-night showdown. If K-State wants to compete for another Big 12 title, this will be a *MUST-WIN* game.

**Nov. 14**     **at Texas Tech Red Raiders** – Snyder has now won four in a row against Texas Tech, but the Red Raiders have 17 starters back and should be an improved team in 2015.

**Nov. 21**     **Iowa State Cyclones** – The Wildcats are a perfect 6-0 against the Cyclones since Snyder returned to coaching in 2009, but these games are usually tight. Only one of the last six games in this series has been decided by more than a touchdown.

**Nov. 28**     **at Kansas Jayhawks** – Snyder has dominated this in-state rivalry with a 19-4 record against the Jayhawks throughout his career. Since his 2009 return, he's 6-0 against KU and he's won the last five meetings by an average margin of 38 points each.

**Dec. 5**     **West Virginia Mountaineers** – K-State is 3-0 against West Virginia since the Mountaineers joined the Big 12 in 2012.

**BOTTOM LINE:**
With just 12 starters returning in 2015, expectations won't be particularly high for the Wildcats. But then again, expectations haven't been all that high since Snyder's return and K-State has managed to win 51 games and a Big 12 championship during those six seasons. Though it doesn't look like the Cats will have the firepower to compete for a Big 12 title this year, another eight- or nine-win season is expected.

## Bill Snyder's Year-by-Year Coaching Record:

<u>Kansas State: 187-94-1 (109-71-1 in the Big 12/Big 8)</u>

1989    1–10 (0–7)        Final Ranking: NR

1990    5–6 (2–5)        Final Ranking: NR
Snyder named Big 8 Coach of the Year.

1991    7–4 (4–3)        Final Ranking: NR
Snyder named Big 8 Coach of the Year.

1992    5–6 (2–5)        Final Ranking: NR

1993    9–2–1 (4–2–1)        Final Ranking: #18
Snyder named Big 8 Coach of the Year.
Beat Wyoming 52-17 in the Copper Bowl.

1994    9–3 (5–2)        Final Ranking: #16
Lost to Boston College 7-12 in the Aloha Bowl.

1995    10–2 (5–2)        Final Ranking: #6
Beat #25 Colorado State 54-24 in the Holiday Bowl.

1996    9–3 (6–2)        Final Ranking: #17
The Big 8 expands and becomes the Big 12.
Lost to #5 BYU 15-19 in the Cotton Bowl.

1997    11–1 (7–1)        Final Ranking: #7
Beat #14 Syracuse 35-18 in the Fiesta Bowl.

1998    11–2 (8–0)        Final Ranking: #9
Snyder named National Coach of the Year.
Snyder named Big 12 Coach of the Year.
Big 12 North Division Champions.
Lost to #10 Texas A&M 33-36 in double OT in the Big 12 Championship Game.
Lost to Purdue 34-37 in the Alamo Bowl.

1999    11–1 (7–1)        Final Ranking: #6
Big 12 North Division Co-Champions.
Beat Washington 24-20 in the Holiday Bowl.

2000    11–3 (6–2)        Final Ranking: #8
Big 12 North Division Champions.
Lost to #1 Oklahoma 24-27 in the Big 12 Championship Game.
Beat #21 Tennessee 35-21 in the Cotton Bowl.

2001    6–6 (3–5)        Final Ranking: NR
Lost to #18 Syracuse 3-26 in the Insight.com Bowl.

2002    11–2 (6–2)        Final Ranking: #6
Snyder named Big 12 Coach of the Year.
Beat Arizona State 34-27 in the Holiday Bowl.

2003    11–4 (6–2)        Final Ranking: #13
Big 12 Champions.
Beat #1 Oklahoma 35-7 in the Big 12 Championship Game.
Lost to #7 Ohio State 28-35 in the Fiesta Bowl.

2004    4–7 (2–6)        Final Ranking: NR

2005    5–6 (2–6)        Final Ranking: NR
Snyder retires at the conclusion of the season.

## Kansas State (continued)

2009    6–6 (4–4)                Final Ranking: NR
        Snyder returns as Kansas State's head coach.
2010    7–6 (3–5)                Final Ranking: NR
        Lost to Syracuse 34-36 in the Pinstripe Bowl.
2011    10–3 (7–2)               Final Ranking: #15
        Snyder named Big 12 Coach of the Year.
        Lost to #7 Arkansas 16-29 in the Cotton Bowl.
2012    11–2 (8–1)               Final Ranking: #11
        Snyder named Big 12 Coach of the Year.
        Big 12 Champions.
        Lost to #5 Oregon 17-35 in the Fiesta Bowl.
2013    8–5 (5–4)                Final Ranking: NR
        Beat Michigan 31-14 in the Buffalo Wild Wings Bowl.
2014    9–4 (7–2)                Final Ranking: #18
        Lost to #14 UCLA 35-40 in the Alamo Bowl.

# Oklahoma Sooners – Bob Stoops

## Coach Ranking: #4

**Overall Record:** 168-44 in 16 seasons
**Record at Oklahoma:** 168-44 in 16 seasons
**2014 Results:** 8-5, 5-4 in the Big 12 (T-4th in the Big 12)
**Returning Starters in 2015:** 7 on offense (including QB), 6 on defense
**Salary:** $5.1 Million      **Age:** 54      **Job Security Grade:** B

**COACH'S BIO:**
Bob Stoops grew up in Youngstown, Ohio, and played high school football for his father, **Ron Stoops**, a longtime defensive coordinator at Cardinal Mooney High. In college, he was a four-year starter at DB under **Hayden Fry** at Iowa. After graduating, Stoops immediately joined the Iowa staff as a graduate assistant in 1983. After five years on Iowa's staff, he spent 1988 as an assistant at Kent State and was then hired by **Bill Snyder**, who had just left Iowa to become Kansas State's head coach, in 1989. Stoops coached DBs for two years and was then promoted to co-DC for K-State – a position he would hold from 1991-1995. In 1996, **Steve Spurrier** hired Stoops to be Florida's DC. The Gators won a National Championship in Stoops' first year there. After three years in Florida, Stoops was hired as Oklahoma's head coach in 1999. He won a National Championship in 2000 and his .792 winning percentage ranks him second to only **Urban Meyer** among active FBS head coaches. Stoops has won eight Big 12 championships at Oklahoma.

**2014 REVIEW:**
After going 11-2 and scoring a convincing Sugar Bowl win over Alabama in 2013, the Sooners entered 2014 with national title hopes and a No. 4 ranking in the preseason polls. The season would turn out to be one of the most disappointing of the Stoops era at Oklahoma with low points including a blowout loss at home against Baylor and a 40-6 whipping at the hands of Clemson in the bowl game to end the year.

**2014 RESULTS:    8-5 (5-4 in the Big 12)**          **Final Ranking: NR**

| | | |
|---|---|---|
| Louisiana Tech | W 48–16 | (85,063) |
| at Tulsa | W 52–7 | (29,357) |
| Tennessee | W 34–10 | (85,622) |
| **at West Virginia** | W 45–33 | (61,908) |
| **at #25 TCU** | L 33–37 | (47,394) |
| **vs. Texas** (in Dallas) | W 31–26 | (92,100) |
| **#14 Kansas State** | L 30–31 | (85,019) |
| **at Iowa State** | W 59–14 | (50,784) |
| **#10 Baylor** | L 14–48 | (85,048) |
| **at Texas Tech** | W 42–30 | (59,014) |
| **Kansas** | W 44–7 | (84,908) |
| **Oklahoma State** | L 35–38 OT | (85,312) |
| vs. #18 Clemson (Russell Athletic Bowl) | L 6–40 | (40,071) |

**OFFENSE:**
When Stoops was first hired at Oklahoma, he brought in **Mike Leach** to be his offensive coordinator and the high-flying Air Raid offense was introduced to what was then a run-heavy conference. Interestingly, while Big 12 teams like Baylor, TCU, West Virginia, Oklahoma State, and Texas Tech have piled up the points with variations of the wide open offense Leach brought to the conference, the Sooners have become more of a running team in recent years. In fact, Oklahoma finished near the bottom of the Big 12 in passing yards over the past two seasons. Stoops wants to reverse this trend and go back to the Air Raid. This offseason, he replaced co-OCs **Josh Heupel** and **Jay Norvell** with **Lincoln Riley**. After playing QB for Mike Leach at Texas Tech and spending seven years as an assistant on Leach's staff, Riley spent the last four seasons as the OC at East Carolina. There, his Air Raid offense broke more than 50 school records. Last year, ECU was ranked No. 3 nationally in passing yards and No. 5 nationally in total offense. Riley is bringing the Air Raid offense back to Norman. Now the question is, will junior QB **Trevor Knight** be able to master it or will the Sooners be relying on a new QB in 2015?

**DEFENSE:**
Bob Stoops' brother, **Mike Stoops**, has been Oklahoma's DC and associate head coach since returning to Norman in 2012 after an eight-year stint as Arizona's head coach. Widely regarded as two of the top defensive minds in the game, the Stoops brothers have built this Sooner program on defense. Though Oklahoma led the Big 12 in rushing defense last year, its pass defense fell from No. 1 in 2013 to No. 9 in the conference in 2014. This sharp decline was troubling, especially for a squad that had nine starters back. This offseason, Bob Stoops hired **Kerry Cooks** as the secondary coach to help fix the pass defense's problems. This is a strong hire. Cooks spent the last three seasons as Notre Dame's co-DC and CB coach.

**RECRUITING:**
**Charlie Strong** and Texas got the best of the Sooners in the Red River recruiting war of 2015, but not by much. The Sooners landed the nation's 15th-ranked class. While Stoops is still one of college football's top recruiters, the reemergence of Texas A&M has clearly created more competition for talent in the Southwest. Stoops hasn't been able to land a Top-10 class since A&M hired **Kevin Sumlin**.

**RUMOR MILL:**
Every year it seems Stoops is rumored to be on his way to whatever high-profile coaching job is available. Over the years, he's been linked to openings at Ohio State and the Cleveland Browns because he grew up in Ohio, openings at Notre Dame because he's Irish-Catholic, and openings at Florida because he spent three years as the DC there. Last year, the Michigan job was thrown in with renewed Florida rumors. The end result has always been the same: Stoops sticks with the Sooners.

**NOTEWORTHY:**
Stoops has an excellent track record of bouncing back from adversity. The 2014 season marked only the fourth time Stoops has failed to win at least 10 games. The previous three times this occurred, Stoops rebounded the next year with 11 wins or more and a Big 12 championship.

**2015 OUTLOOK:**

Sept. 5     **Akron Zips** – Akron is vastly overmatched in this season opener, but Terry Bowden's Zips did upset Pittsburgh in a nonconference road game last season.

Sept. 12    **at Tennessee Volunteers** – Stoops is 5-4 against the SEC. If you include former Big 12 members Missouri and Texas A&M, Stoops is 24-7 against current SEC teams. This year's Tennessee squad should be much more talented than the team OU beat 34-10 last year.

Sept. 19    **Tulsa Golden Hurricane** – Stoops knows it's important to dominate this in-state mid-major opponent. He's 8-0 against Tulsa with a 38-point average margin of victory.

Oct. 3      **West Virginia Mountaineers** – West Virginia hasn't beat Oklahoma since joining the Big 12. Stoops' only loss to the Mountaineers came in the Fiesta Bowl at the end of the 2007 season.

Oct. 10     **vs. Texas Longhorns (in Dallas)** – Stoops is 10-6 in the Red River Rivalry and should be the favorite again this year as Texas continues to rebuild.

Oct. 17     **at Kansas State Wildcats** – Though Stoops is 8-3 against his former mentor, Bill Snyder, the Wildcats have won two of the last three meetings in this series.

Oct. 24     **Texas Tech Red Raiders** – Oklahoma has won its last three games against Texas Tech by an average margin of 14 points each. Stoops is 11-5 overall in this series, but 7-1 when playing Texas Tech at home.

Oct. 31     **at Kansas Jayhawks** – Stoops is a perfect 10-0 against the Jayhawks. Expect him to pick up win number 11 this year.

Nov. 7      **Iowa State Cyclones** – Just like the KU series, Stoops is a perfect 10-0 against Iowa State and should make it 11-0 in 2015.

Nov. 14     **at Baylor Bears** – Before Baylor hired Art Briles, Stoops was 9-0 against the Bears. He's gone 1-3 against Briles over the past four seasons. Baylor is loaded with 17 starters back and if the Bears win again this year, they would become the first team ever to beat a Stoops-coached team three years in a row. That makes this a *MUST-WIN* game for the Sooners.

Nov. 21     **TCU Horned Frogs** – Last season marked the first time TCU beat Oklahoma since joining the Big 12. Stoops' all-time record against TCU is 3-2.

Nov. 28     **at Oklahoma State Cowboys** – Stoops is 12-4 in this rivalry, but he's dropped two of the last four against the Cowboys.

**BOTTOM LINE:**
Stoops has a history of having big seasons just when the college football world starts to count Oklahoma out. If the Sooners can knock off Tennessee in Knoxville, they'll have a good shot at being 9-0 when they head into the crucial November stretch against Baylor, TCU, and Oklahoma State. If the Air Raid offense is reignited quickly in Norman, this could be a season where the Sooners surprise a lot of people by storming their way into the playoffs.

## Bob Stoops' Year-by-Year Coaching Record:

<u>Oklahoma: 168-44 (104-28 in the Big 12)</u>
**1999**  7-5 (5-3)              **Final Ranking: NR**
Lost to Ole Miss 25-27 in the Independence Bowl.
**2000**  13-0 (8-0)            **Final Ranking: #1**
National Champions.
Big 12 Champions.
Stoops named National Coach of the Year.
Stoops named Big 12 Coach of the Year.
Beat #8 Kansas State 27-24 in the Big 12 Championship Game.
Beat #3 Florida State 13-2 in the BCS National Championship Game.
**2001**  11-2 (6-2)            **Final Ranking: #6**
Beat Arkansas 10-3 in the Cotton Bowl.
**2002**  12-2 (6-2)            **Final Ranking: #5**
Big 12 Champions.
Beat #12 Colorado 29-7 in the Big 12 Championship Game.
Beat #7 Washington State 34-14 in the Rose Bowl.
**2003**  12-2 (8-0)            **Final Ranking: #3**
Big 12 South Division Champions.
Stoops named National Coach of the Year.
Stoops named Big 12 Coach of the Year.
Lost to #12 Kansas State 7-35 in the Big 12 Championship Game.
Lost to #2 LSU 14-21 in the BCS National Championship Game.
**2004**  12-1 (8-0)            **Final Ranking: #3**
Big 12 Champions.
Beat Colorado 42-3 in the Big 12 Championship Game.
Lost to #1 USC 19-55 in the BCS National Championship Game.
**2005**  8-4 (6-2)             **Final Ranking: #22**
Beat #6 Oregon 17-14 in the Holiday Bowl.
**2006**  11-3 (7-1)            **Final Ranking: #11**
Big 12 Champions.
Stoops named Big 12 Coach of the Year.
Beat #19 Nebraska 21-7 in the Big 12 Championship Game.
Lost to #9 Boise State 42-43 in OT in the Fiesta Bowl.
**2007**  11-3 (6-2)            **Final Ranking: #8**
Big 12 Champions.
Beat #1 Missouri 38-17 in the Big 12 Championship Game.
Lost to #11 West Virginia 28-48 in the Fiesta Bowl.
**2008**  12-2 (7-1)            **Final Ranking: #5**
Big 12 Champions.
Beat #19 Missouri 62-21 in the Big 12 Championship Game.
Lost to #1 Florida 14-24 in the BCS National Championship Game.
**2009**  8-5 (5-3)             **Final Ranking: NR**
Beat #19 Stanford 31-27 in the Sun Bowl.

**Oklahoma (continued)**

2010   12–2 (6–2)          Final Ranking: #6
       Big 12 Champions.
       Beat #13 Nebraska 23-20 in the Big 12 Championship Game.
       Beat #25 Connecticut 48-20 in the Fiesta Bowl.

2011   10–3 (6–3)          Final Ranking: #15
       Beat Iowa 31-14 in the Insight Bowl.

2012   10–3 (8–1)          Final Ranking: #15
       Big 12 Co-Champions.
       Lost to #10 Texas A&M 13-41 in the Cotton Bowl.

2013   11–2 (7–2)          Final Ranking: #6
       Beat #3 Alabama 45-31 in the Sugar Bowl.

2014   8–5 (5–4)           Final Ranking: NR
       Lost to #18 Clemson 6-40 in the Russell Athletic Bowl.

# Oklahoma State Cowboys – Mike Gundy

## Coach Ranking: #26

**Overall Record:** 84-44 in 10 seasons
**Record at Oklahoma State:** 84-44 in 10 seasons
**2014 Results:** 7-6, 4-5 in the Big 12 (7th in the Big 12)
**Returning Starters in 2015:** 8 on offense (including QB), 8 on defense
**Salary:** $3.5 Million    **Age:** 48    **Job Security Grade:** A

COACH'S BIO:
Mike Gundy grew up in Midwest City, Oklahoma, and was a four-year starting QB at Oklahoma State from 1986-1989. He's the school's all-time leading passer with 7,997 passing yards. He joined **Pat Jones'** coaching staff at Oklahoma State in 1990 and worked his way up to offensive coordinator by 1994, a position he retained when **Bob Simmons** was hired in 1995. Gundy then spent 1996 on **Chuck Reedy's** staff at Baylor before a four-year stint at Maryland under **Ron Vanderlinden**. In 2001, Gundy returned to Oklahoma State as **Les Miles'** offensive coordinator. When Miles left to become LSU's head coach after the 2004 season, Gundy became head coach of the Cowboys. In 10 seasons, he has led Oklahoma State to nine-straight bowl games and more victories than any other coach in school history.

2014 REVIEW:
With just four starters back on both sides of the ball, 2014 was fully expected to be a rebuilding year for Oklahoma State. After a 5-1 start in which the Cowboys climbed to No. 15 in the polls, they suffered through a brutal five-game losing streak (losing by an average of 27 points a game during that stretch). However, Gundy regrouped his team and knocked off archrival Oklahoma to close out the regular season and then went on to beat Washington in the Cactus Bowl. Gundy and his staff deserve a lot of credit for regaining some momentum late in the year after such an ugly stretch midway through the season. Amazingly, 21 freshmen played for the Cowboys last season.

**2014 RESULTS:   7-6 (4-5 in the Big 12)**      **Final Ranking: NR**

| | | |
|---|---|---|
| vs. #1 Florida State (in Arlington, TX) | L 31–37 | (61,521) |
| Missouri State | W 40–23 | (51,562) |
| UT-San Antonio | W 43–13 | (54,577) |
| **Texas Tech** | W 45–35 | (55,958) |
| **Iowa State** | W 37–20 | (52,608) |
| at Kansas | W 27–20 | (31,985) |
| at #12 TCU | L 9–42 | (43,214) |
| #22 West Virginia | L 10–34 | (59,124) |
| at #11 Kansas State | L 14–48 | (53,746) |
| Texas | L 7–28 | (52,495) |
| at #5 Baylor | L 28–49 | (47,179) |
| at #18 Oklahoma | W 38–35 OT | (85,312) |
| vs. Washington (Cactus Bowl) | W 30–22 | (35,409) |

**OFFENSE:**

Oklahoma State runs an Air Raid offense that has regularly ranked near the top of the nation in scoring during Gundy's tenure. That offensive production took a big step back in 2014, falling from 13th nationally in scoring to 76th. Inexperience heading into the season and injuries to two starting QBs created season-long inconsistency issues. Junior QB **Daxx Garman** took over for an injured **J.W. Walsh** in week two and after going 4-4 in his eight starts (2,041 passing yards, 12 TDs, 12 INTs), he too was lost for the year after suffering a concussion against Texas. His replacement was freshman **Mason Rudolph**, who led the Cowboys to an upset win over Oklahoma and a bowl victory over Washington. Rudolph is expected to be the starter in 2015 with competition from Walsh and incoming freshman **John Kolar**. Garman decided to transfer out of the program. With eight starters back this year and a lot of excitement about Rudolph, this offense should get back to its old ways of piling up the points. Offensive coordinator **Mike Yurcich** will be entering his third season at that position for Oklahoma State. Three of Gundy's previous four OCs have gone on to head coaching positions: **Todd Monken** at Southern Miss, **Dana Holgorsen** at West Virginia, and **Larry Fedora** at North Carolina.

**DEFENSE:**

**Glen Spencer** took over as sole defensive coordinator for the Cowboys in 2013 and had instant success. Operating out of a 4-3 system, Spencer turned Oklahoma State into the Big 12's No. 1 defense in points allowed and he was named a finalist for the Broyles Award, which goes to the nation's top assistant coach. But with just four returning starters in 2014, a step back was expected and the Cowboys fell to seventh in the Big 12 in points allowed. November was particularly ugly as Oklahoma State gave up 42 points a game during a three-game stretch that month. The Cowboys' pass defense was atrocious as they finished the year ranked 113th nationally in passing yards allowed. This year should be a much different story as eight starters are back, including all four DBs.

**RECRUITING:**

Though Gundy signed a relatively small class of just 20 recruits, he still managed to land in the Top 40 nationally and at No. 6 in the Big 12. The Cowboys made the secondary a priority with DBs accounting for one-quarter of the 2015 recruiting class.

**RUMOR MILL:**

At one point last year, Mike Gundy was whispered to be a top candidate for the Florida head coaching job. Rumors circulated that the interest was mutual and that Gundy himself was pursuing the position. Nothing came of such rumors and Florida hired **Jim McElwain**. Gundy's current contract with Oklahoma State runs through 2019.

**NOTEWORTHY:**

This offseason, Gundy added two coaches to his staff who were coaching in the NFL last year. **Greg Adkins** spent the last two seasons coaching TEs for the Buffalo Bills and **Marcus Arroyo** spent 2014 coaching QBs for the Tampa Bay Buccaneers.

**2015 OUTLOOK:**

Sept. 3     **at Central Michigan Chippewas** – The Cowboys will open the season with a Thursday-night road game in what will be Gundy's first meeting ever with a MAC school. Central Michigan went 7-6 last year and they have a new head coach in John Bonamego, who spent the last two seasons as special teams coordinator for the Detroit Lions.

Sept. 12     **Central Arkansas Bears** – Gundy is 8-0 all-time against FCS schools.

Sept. 19     **UTSA Roadrunners** – For the third year in a row, Oklahoma State will play UT-San Antonio. The Cowboys outscored the Roadrunners 99-48 in their previous two meetings. UTSA has just five starters back in 2015.

Sept. 26     **at Texas Longhorns** – Gundy is 3-7 against Texas and those three victories occurred the last three times these teams played in Austin.

Oct. 3     **Kansas State Wildcats** – Gundy is 4-3 all-time against the Wildcats and he's a perfect 3-0 at home in this series.

Oct. 10     **at West Virginia Mountaineers** – West Virginia head coach Dana Holgorsen was Mike Gundy's OC at Oklahoma State in 2010. Gundy is 1-2 against his former assistant and WVU has won the last two games in this series.

Oct. 24     **Kansas Jayhawks** – Gundy is 6-1 against Kansas. The Jayhawks have a new coach and just eight returning starters (the lowest in the Big 12).

Oct. 31     **at Texas Tech Red Raiders** – Oklahoma State is riding a six-game winning streak against Texas Tech and Gundy is 8-2 all-time against the Red Raiders.

Nov. 7     **TCU Horned Frogs** – These teams were both ranked in the Top 15 when they met last season, but TCU embarrassed the Cowboys 42-9. If OSU wants to make a run at a Big 12 title, it starts with this *MUST-WIN* game.

Nov. 14     **at Iowa State Cyclones** – Gundy is 5-2 against Iowa State, but both losses occurred on trips up to Ames in 2011 and 2008.

Nov. 21     **Baylor Bears** – Gundy is 5-2 against Baylor coach Art Briles and though the Bears have won two of the last three meetings, Gundy has never lost to Baylor at home.

Nov. 28     **Oklahoma Sooners** – Last year's upset win over No. 18 Oklahoma was Gundy's second win in 10 tries against the archrival Sooners. This one should be another heated matchup. Mike Gundy's brother, Cale Gundy, is Oklahoma's assistant head coach, recruiting coordinator, and inside WRs coach.

**BOTTOM LINE:**
After winning 41 games in the four years prior to 2014, Oklahoma State took a step back last season with a young and inexperienced team. But, what was "young and experienced" last year is "grown-up and dangerous" this year. A weak nonconference schedule will allow OSU to work out any kinks prior to the Big 12 opener against Texas. Don't be surprised if the Cowboys push their way back into Big 12 title contention this year.

## Mike Gundy's Year-by-Year Coaching Record:

<u>Oklahoma State: 84-44 (49-35 in the Big 12)</u>
2005    4–7 (1–7)            Final Ranking: NR
2006    7–6 (3–5)            Final Ranking: NR
        Beat Alabama 34-31 in the Independence Bowl.
2007    7–6 (4–4)            Final Ranking: NR
        Beat Indiana 49-33 in the Insight Bowl.
2008    9–4 (5–3)            Final Ranking: #16
        Lost to #15 Oregon 31-42 in the Holiday Bowl.
2009    9–4 (6–2)            Final Ranking: #25
        Lost to Ole Miss 7-21 in the Cotton Bowl.
2010    11–2 (6–2)           Final Ranking: #10
        Big 12 South Co-Champions.
        Gundy named Big 12 Coach of the Year.
        Beat Arizona 36-10 in the Alamo Bowl.
2011    12–1 (8–1)           Final Ranking: #3
        Big 12 Champions.
        Gundy wins the Bear Bryant Award for Coach of the Year.
        Beat #4 Stanford 41-38 in OT in the Fiesta Bowl.
2012    8–5 (5–4)            Final Ranking: NR
        Beat Purdue 58-14 in the Heart of Dallas Bowl.
2013    10–3 (7–2)           Final Ranking: #17
        Lost to #9 Missouri 31-41 in the Cotton Bowl.
2014    7–6 (4–5)            Final Ranking: NR
        Beat Washington 30-22 in the Cactus Bowl.

# TCU Horned Frogs – Gary Patterson

## Coach Ranking: #13

**Overall Record:** 132-45 in 14 seasons
**Record at TCU:** 132-45 in 14 seasons
**2014 Results:** 12-1, 8-1 in the Big 12 (Big 12 Co-Champions)
**Returning Starters in 2015:** 10 on offense (including QB), 5 on defense
**Salary:** $4 Million*       **Age:** 55       **Job Security Grade:** A

**COACH'S BIO:**
Gary Patterson grew up in the small Kansas town of Rozel and played SS and LB at Kansas State in the early 1980s. He started his coaching career as a graduate assistant for the Wildcats in 1982 and then landed a job as the LB coach at Division 1-AA Tennessee Tech (1983-1984), where the offensive coordinator was **Dennis Franchione**. After Franchione became a head coach, Patterson reunited with him as LB coach for Division II Pittsburg State in 1988 and then as his DC at New Mexico from 1996-1997. Patterson served the same role at TCU when Franchione was head coach from 1998-2000. When Franchione left to accept the Alabama job, Patterson was hired as head coach of the Horned Frogs. In 14 seasons at TCU, Patterson has won five conference championships and he's been named the National Coach of the Year twice.

**2014 REVIEW:**
TCU averaged 11 wins per year in its seven seasons prior to joining the Big 12. After joining the Big 12 in 2012, the Horned Frogs stumbled to 7-6 and 4-8 seasons. Many wondered if TCU was in over its head in the Big 12. Patterson answered those concerns in a big way in 2014 with a 12-1 season and a share of the Big 12 championship. The Frogs entered the season unranked and finished No. 3. For his performance, Patterson was named the Big 12 Coach of the Year, the AP National Coach of the Year, and the *CFCA* Comeback Coach of the Year.

| 2014 RESULTS:   12-1 (8-1 in the Big 12) | Final Ranking: #3 | |
|---|---|---|
| Samford | W 48–14 | (40,094) |
| Minnesota | W 30–7 | (43,958) |
| at SMU | W 56–0 | (23,093) |
| #4 Oklahoma | W 37–33 | (47,394) |
| at #5 Baylor | L 58–61 | (46,803) |
| #15 Oklahoma State | W 42–9 | (43,214) |
| Texas Tech | W 82–27 | (45,122) |
| at #20 West Virginia | W 31–30 | (61,190) |
| #7 Kansas State | W 41–20 | (48,012) |
| at Kansas | W 34–30 | (30,889) |
| at Texas | W 48–10 | (96,496) |
| Iowa State | W 55–3 | (45,242) |
| vs. #9 Ole Miss (Peach Bowl) | W 42-3 | (65,706) |

**OFFENSE:**

In 2013, TCU entered the season ranked No. 20 and ended up 4-8, the worst season of Patterson's career. The lack of offensive production was a major reason for this poor performance. TCU finished 2013 ranked 106th nationally in total offense. To fix the offensive woes, Patterson brought in **Doug Meacham** and **Sonny Cumbie** to be his new co-offensive coordinators (while still keeping previous OCs and longtime assistants **Jarrett Anderson** and **Rusty Burns** on the staff). Prior to joining TCU, Meacham coached the Air Raid offense as TE/inside receivers coach at Oklahoma State and he served as Houston's OC in 2013. Cumbie played QB for Air Raid mastermind **Mike Leach** from 2000-2004 and served as Texas Tech's co-OC in 2013. Adding Meacham and Cumbie to the staff resulted in one of the most dramatic turnarounds you'll ever see in offensive production. The 2014 Horned Frogs climbed to No. 5 nationally in total offense and No. 2 in scoring. With 10 starters back, including dual-threat QB and Heisman finalist **Trevone Boykin**, expect TCU to once again field one of the nation's most explosive offenses.

**DEFENSE:**

Since Patterson has been at TCU, the Horned Frogs have consistently had one of the nation's top defenses. Last year was no different as TCU led the Big 12 in points allowed and yards allowed. A big reason for TCU's success has been longtime defensive coordinator **Dick Bumpas** and his 4-2-5 system. However, after 11 years as TCU's DC (including four years as a finalist for the Broyles Award, which goes to the nation's top assistant coach), Bumpas is retiring. Patterson is promoting from within to replace Bumpas. Safeties coach **Chad Glasgow** (who was Texas Tech's DC in 2011) and LB coach **DeMontie Cross** will serve as co-DCs for TCU in 2015. Replacing a longtime assistant like Bumpas is a concern, but Patterson has always called the defensive plays himself, which should make this transition less of an issue. The bigger concern is that just five starters are returning on this side of the ball and TCU loses six of its top seven tacklers from last season.

**RECRUITING:**

It was disappointing to see that TCU couldn't parlay last year's success into a stronger recruiting class. For the second year in a row, TCU's class was ranked seventh in the Big 12 and last among the conference's Texas schools. However, Gary Patterson has a well-established reputation for finding under-the-radar talent and getting more out of less with one of the nation's top strength programs.

**RUMOR MILL:**

Patterson has been mentioned as a candidate for multiple high-profile jobs over the years, but TCU is doing what it needs to do to keep him. This past offseason, TCU gave Patterson a long-term contract extension that runs through 2019.

**NOTEWORTHY:**

TCU led the nation in interceptions and finished second in turnovers gained last season. The Frogs have ranked in the Top 20 nationally for each of the last three seasons in turnovers gained.

**2015 OUTLOOK:**

**Sept. 3**   **at Minnesota Golden Gophers** – TCU opens the season on a Thursday night against a team they beat by 23 points in Fort Worth last year. Patterson is 4-2 all-time against current Big Ten schools. Minnesota coach Jerry Kill served as Patterson's best man at his wedding.

**Sept. 12**   **Stephen F. Austin Jacks** – TCU played Stephen F. Austin back in 2008. The Frogs beat this FCS school 67-7.

**Sept. 19**   **SMU Mustangs** – Patterson is 11-2 in the "Battle for the Iron Skillet" rivalry and he's won the last three meetings by a combined score of 128-33.

**Sept. 26**   **at Texas Tech Red Raiders** – TCU racked up 82 points and 785 yards in last season's blowout win against Tech. Those 82 points were the most ever scored by one team in a Big 12 conference game. Current TCU co-OC Sonny Cumbie is a former Red Raiders QB and was an assistant coach there from 2009-2013.

**Oct. 3**   **Texas Longhorns** – Patterson is 2-2 all-time against Texas and 2-1 since joining the Big 12 in 2012.

**Oct. 10**   **at Kansas State Wildcats** – Patterson is 1-2 against his alma mater. He was reportedly a top candidate to replace Ron Prince there after the 2008 season, but K-State instead hired Bill Snyder for a second tenure.

**Oct. 17**   **at Iowa State Cyclones** – Counting a Houston Bowl victory in 2005, Patterson is 3-1 all-time against Iowa State.

**Oct. 29**   **West Virginia Mountaineers** – TCU eked out a one-point win in Morgantown last year and the Mountaineers will be looking for payback in this Thursday-night showdown.

**Nov. 7**   **at Oklahoma State Cowboys** – This will be TCU's third visit to Stillwater in four years. The Frogs lost their previous two trips there. Current TCU co-OC Doug Meacham played on the o-line for Oklahoma State back in the 1980s and he was an assistant coach there for 11 years.

**Nov. 14**   **Kansas Jayhawks** – The Jayhawks nearly pulled off the upset against TCU last year. Instead, Patterson extended his record to 3-0 against KU.

**Nov. 21**   **at Oklahoma Sooners** – This is the first of two giant end-of-the-year Big 12 showdowns for TCU. Patterson is 2-3 all-time against Bob Stoops.

**Nov. 27**   **Baylor Bears** – This season finale could be for the Big 12 championship. Though Patterson is 4-3 all-time against Baylor, he's 2-3 since Art Briles took over as head coach there. This matchup has become college football's best new rivalry and it's a *MUST-WIN* game for TCU.

**BOTTOM LINE:**
The Horned Frogs ended 2014 red hot and their 42-3 thumping of Ole Miss in the Peach Bowl sent a message to the nation to watch out for this team in 2015. TCU's offense could be even better than last year's record-breaking unit and while the defense is inexperienced, Patterson has a history of reloading fast on that side of the ball. TCU should be the favorite in its first 10 games of the season. It's what this team does in the final two games that will determine whether they make the playoffs and close in on the school's first National Championship since 1938.

## Gary Patterson's Year-by-Year Coaching Record:

TCU: 132-45 (82-31 in C-USA, the MWC, and the Big 12)

2000    0-1 (0-0)          Final Ranking: #18

Dennis Franchione left to accept the Alabama job prior to the bowl game and Patterson coached the Frogs in a 21-28 loss to Southern Miss in the Mobile Alabama Bowl.

2001    6-6 (4-3)          Final Ranking: NR

TCU leaves the WAC and joins Conference USA.

Lost to Texas A&M 9-28 in the GalleryFurniture.com Bowl.

2002    10-2 (6-2)        Final Ranking: #22

C-USA Co-Champions.

Patterson named C-USA Coach of the Year.

Beat Colorado State 17-3 in the Liberty Bowl.

2003    11-2 (7-1)        Final Ranking: #24

Lost to #19 Boise State 31-34 in the Fort Worth Bowl.

2004    5-6 (3-5)          Final Ranking: NR

2005    11-1 (8-0)        Final Ranking: #9

TCU leaves C-USA and joins the Mountain West Conference.

MWC Champions.

Patterson named MWC Coach of the Year.

Beat Iowa State 27-24 in the Houston Bowl.

2006    11-2 (6-2)        Final Ranking: #21

Beat Northern Illinois 37-7 in the Poinsettia Bowl.

2007    8-5 (4-4)          Final Ranking: NR

Beat Houston 20-13 in the Texas Bowl.

2008    11-2 (7-1)        Final Ranking: #7

Beat #9 Boise State 17-16 in the Poinsettia Bowl.

2009    12-1 (8-0)        Final Ranking: #6

MWC Champions.

Patterson named National Coach of the Year.

Patterson named MWC Coach of the Year.

Lost to #6 Boise State 10-17 in the Fiesta Bowl.

2010    13-0 (8-0)        Final Ranking: #2

MWC Champions.

Beat #4 Wisconsin 21-19 in the Rose Bowl.

2011    11-2 (7-0)        Final Ranking: #13

MWC Champions.

Louisiana Tech 31-24 in the Poinsettia Bowl.

2012    7-6 (4-5)          Final Ranking: NR

TCU leaves the MWC and joins the Big 12.

Lost to Michigan State 16-17 in the Buffalo Wild Wings Bowl.

2013    4-8 (2-7)          Final Ranking: NR

2014    12-1 (8-1)        Final Ranking: #3

Big 12 Co-Champions.

Patterson named the Comeback Coach of the Year by the *CFCA*.

Patterson named Big 12 Coach of the Year.

Beat #9 Ole Miss 42-3 in the Peach Bowl.

# Texas Longhorns – Charlie Strong

## Coach Ranking: #25

**Overall Record:** 43-23 in 6 seasons
**Record at Texas:** 6-7 in 1 season
**2014 Results:** 6-7, 5-4 in the Big 12 (T-4th in the Big 12)
**Returning Starters in 2015:** 8 on offense (including QB), 5 on defense
**Salary:** $5 Million          **Age:** 55          **Job Security Grade:** B

COACH'S BIO:
Charlie Strong grew up in Arkansas and starred as a safety at Central Arkansas (NAIA) in the early 1980s. For 27 seasons (1983-2009), Strong built an impressive resume as an assistant coach. His stops included four years under **Steve Spurrier** at Florida (where he was promoted to assistant head coach in 1994), four years as the DL coach at Notre Dame under **Lou Holtz** and **Bob Davie** (1995-1998), and four years as Holtz's defensive coordinator at South Carolina (1999-2002). He returned to Florida as DC for **Ron Zook** in 2003. Zook was fired during the 2004 season and Strong served as the Gators' interim head coach for the bowl game. **Urban Meyer** was then hired as Florida's new head coach and retained Strong. After five more years as Florida's DC, Strong was hired as Louisville's head coach in 2010. He led the Cardinals to a bowl game in all four seasons there, won the Big East title twice, and went 12-1 in 2013. Texas hired Strong to replace Mack Brown after the 2013 season.

2014 REVIEW:
Before the 2014 season began, Strong sent a clear message about the high standards he's setting at Texas by dismissing nine players for violating the team's "core values." Entering the year ranked No. 24, Strong's debut season was a disappointing one as the Longhorns finished with a losing record for the first time since 2010. It was the *way* they lost that was most troubling as five of their seven losses were by 21 points or more.

| 2014 RESULTS:   6-7 (5-4 in the Big 12) | Final Ranking: NR | |
|---|---|---|
| North Texas | W 38-7 | (93,201) |
| BYU | L 7-41 | (93,463) |
| vs. #12 UCLA (in Arlington, TX) | L 17-20 | (60,479) |
| at Kansas | W 23-0 | (36,904) |
| #7 Baylor | L 7-28 | (93,727) |
| vs. #11 Oklahoma | L 26-31 | (92,100) |
| Iowa State | W 48-45 | (92,017) |
| at #11 Kansas State | L 0-23 | (52,879) |
| at Texas Tech | W 34-13 | (60,961) |
| #23 West Virginia | W 33-16 | (95,714) |
| at Oklahoma State | W 28-7 | (52,495) |
| #4 TCU | L 10-48 | (96,496) |
| vs. Arkansas (Texas Bowl) | L 7-31 | (71,115) |

**OFFENSE:**

In 2009, Texas led the Big 12 in scoring with 39 points a game and the Longhorns rode that firepower to a 13-1 record. Since that time, Texas has failed to make its way back into the upper half of the Big 12 in scoring. The offensive woes continued in Charlie Strong's debut season, culminating with just 59 yards of total offense in the bowl game against Arkansas. Some of the trouble was due to bad luck. Starting QB **David Ash** suffered a concussion that ended his career in the season-opening win against North Texas. Sophomore **Tyrone Swoopes** was thrown into the starting role and never quite looked comfortable, throwing nearly as many interceptions (11) as TDs (13). To breathe new life into the offense, Strong and offensive coordinator **Joe Wickline** are switching from the multiple-set pro-style system they ran last year to the wide-open spread offense Strong originally intended to install. This should be a better fit for whoever wins the starting QB job in 2015 as Swoopes and the two other QB contenders, sophomore **Jerrod Heard** and true freshman **Kai Locksley**, are all dual-threat QBs. To help with the transition to the spread, Strong hired **Jay Norvell** (Oklahoma's co-OC last year) as the new WR coach. Eight starters are back on this offense and the transition to a more wide-open system should create more big-play opportunities for a squad that has plenty of talent.

**DEFENSE:**

Strong's specialty has always been defense and he didn't waste any time improving this group. Texas went from 57th nationally in points allowed to 32nd in 2014. Though only five starters are back on this side of the ball, expect the progress to continue as the Longhorns get more familiar with defensive coordinator **Vance Bedford**'s aggressive 4-3 system (which also implements some 3-4 as necessary). Bedford was Strong's DC at Louisville also. Their final year there, Louisville fielded the nation's No. 1-ranked defense in yards allowed.

**RECRUITING:**

Texas landed the Big 12's top-ranked 2015 recruiting class, which was rated No. 10 nationally. Strong said he expects four-star athlete Kai Locksley to compete for the starting QB job as a true freshman.

**RUMOR MILL:**

It's been rumored that several NFL teams are interested in hiring Charlie Strong, but that interest appears to be one-sided. Strong says he loves the mentoring that comes with the college game and that he's never thought about a move to the NFL.

**NOTEWORTHY:**

Strong hired **Jeff Traylor** to be his new TE coach this offseason. Traylor spent the last 15 years as one of the most successful high school coaches in Texas. At Gilmer High, he won 175 games, 12 district titles, and three state championships. On his way to an undefeated state championship in 2014, Traylor's offense averaged 59.4 points a game, the second-most points in the history of Texas high school football. Traylor's experience developing high-powered offenses is no doubt a key reason for this hiring.

**2015 OUTLOOK:**

**Sept. 5**   **at Notre Dame Fighting Irish** – The last time these teams met (1996), Strong was the DL coach on Lou Holtz's staff at Notre Dame. The Longhorns are 2-8 against the Irish.

**Sept. 12**   **Rice Owls** – Rice has had three-straight winning seasons, but 2015 is expected to be a rebuilding year for the Owls as they return just 10 starters. Texas has dominated this series with a 71-21-1 all-time record.

**Sept. 19**   **California Golden Bears** – Cal head coach Sonny Dykes is trying to rebuild this program and with 17 starters back, this could be a dangerous opponent. Texas last played Cal in the 2011 Holiday Bowl, a game the Longhorns won 21-10. Cal runs the Air Raid offense, so this game will give the Texas defense an early look at an offense they'll face often in the Big 12.

**Sept. 26**   **Oklahoma State Cowboys** – Starting Big 12 play with a win would be huge for Texas. Both these teams are trying to rebound from mediocre 2014 seasons.

**Oct. 3**   **at TCU Horned Frogs** – After last year's ugly 48-10 loss, Texas is now 1-2 against TCU since the Horned Frogs joined the Big 12.

**Oct. 10**   **vs. Oklahoma Sooners (in Dallas)** – Despite outgaining the Sooners by 250 yards last year, Texas dropped its fourth game in five years to OU. If there's one way to prove this program is heading in the right direction, it's winning the Red River Rivalry. That makes this a *MUST-WIN* game for Strong.

**Oct. 24**   **Kansas State Wildcats** – K-State has dominated this series in recent history, winning seven of the last eight meetings. However, the last time they played in Austin (2013), the Longhorns won 31-21.

**Oct. 31**   **at Iowa State Cyclones** – Last year's three-point win over the Cyclones extended Texas' winning streak to four in this series. Texas is 11-1 all-time against Iowa State.

**Nov. 7**   **Kansas Jayhawks** – Since the Big 12 was formed in 1996, Texas has *never* lost to Kansas. Don't expect 2015 to be the year that streak ends.

**Nov. 14**   **at West Virginia Mountaineers** – Despite giving up 448 yards to West Virginia's Air Raid offense last year, Texas pulled out a 33-16 win at home.

**Nov. 26**   **Texas Tech Red Raiders** – This game will be played on Thanksgiving. The Longhorns are 11-1 in their last 12 meetings with Texas Tech.

**Dec. 5**   **at Baylor Bears** – Baylor has won four of the last five meetings in this series and that's a trend Strong must find a way to reverse.

**BOTTOM LINE:**
Charlie Strong-coached teams always have stout defenses, but in the high-scoring Big 12, teams must also be able to keep up in a shootout. Strong recognizes this and he's hoping the spread offense will generate more points for the Longhorns in 2015 and beyond. Texas looks like a team that is still a year or two away from competing for a Big 12 title, but the priority this season will be to get back on the positive side of the win-loss column. A Top-25 finish is certainly a possibility with this talented group.

## Charlie Strong's Year-by-Year Coaching Record:

### Florida: 0-1 (0-0 in the SEC)
2004   0-1 (0-0)         Final Ranking: #25

Ron Zook was fired during the season and Strong coached the Gators as the interim head coach in the bowl game. Florida lost to #14 Miami (FL) in the Peach Bowl 10-27.

### Louisville: 37-15 (20-9 in the Big East/American Conference)
2010   7-6 (3-4)         Final Ranking: NR

Beat Southern Miss 31-28 in the Beef 'O' Brady's Bowl.

2011   7-6 (5-2)         Final Ranking: NR

Big East Co-Champions.

Lost to NC State 24-31 in the Belk Bowl.

2012   11-2 (5-2)        Final Ranking: #13

Big East Co-Champions.

Beat #4 Florida 33-23 in the Sugar Bowl.

2013   12-1 (7-1)        Final Ranking: #15

Beat Miami (FL) 36-9 in the Russell Athletic Bowl.

### Texas: 6-7 (5-4 in the Big 12)
2014   6-7 (5-4)         Final Ranking: NR

Lost to Arkansas 7-31 in the Texas Bowl.

# Texas Tech Red Raiders – Kliff Kingsbury

## Coach Ranking: #75

**Overall Record:** 12-13 in 2 seasons
**Record at Texas Tech:** 12-13 in 2 seasons
**2014 Results:** 4-8, 2-7 in the Big 12 (8th in the Big 12)
**Returning Starters in 2015:** 9 on offense (including QB), 8 on defense
**Salary:** $3.1 Million      **Age:** 36      **Job Security Grade:** B

**COACH'S BIO:**
Kliff Kingsbury grew up the son of a high school football coach in New Braunfels, Texas. After passing for more than 3,000 yards his senior season and leading his team to the state semifinals, Kingsbury went to Texas Tech, where **Spike Dykes** was head coach, in 1998. In 2000, **Mike Leach** became Tech's head coach and Kingsbury would become a three-year starter in Leach's Air Raid offense. As a senior in 2002, Kingsbury won the Sammy Baugh Trophy and was named the AP's National Offensive Player of the Year. He spent three years playing in the NFL, one year in NFL Europe, and one year in the CFL. In 2008, Kingsbury began his coaching career when he joined **Kevin Sumlin**'s staff at Houston. He worked his way up to co-offensive coordinator by 2010. When Texas A&M hired Sumlin in 2012, he named Kingsbury his OC. In 2013, Texas Tech hired Kingsbury to be its new head coach, replacing **Tommy Tuberville**.

**2014 REVIEW:**
After an 8-5 debut season, expectations were high for Kingsbury and the Red Raiders heading into 2014. However, injuries on offense and inexperience on defense resulted in a big step back for the Red Raiders. Texas Tech did show a glimmer of hope in the season finale when it played No. 7 Baylor down to the wire and lost by just two points.

| 2014 RESULTS:   4-8 (2-7 in the Big 12) | Final Ranking: NR | |
|---|---|---|
| Central Arkansas | W 42–35 | (60,778) |
| at UTEP | W 30–26 | (35,422) |
| Arkansas | L 28–49 | (60,277) |
| at #24 Oklahoma State | L 35–45 | (55,958) |
| at #23 Kansas State | L 13–45 | (52,726) |
| West Virginia | L 34–37 | (58,502) |
| Kansas | W 34–21 | (54,071) |
| at #10 TCU | L 27–82 | (45,122) |
| Texas | L 13–34 | (60,961) |
| Oklahoma | L 30–42 | (59,014) |
| at Iowa State | W 34–31 | (50,877) |
| vs. #7 **Baylor** (in Arlington, TX) | L 46–48 | (54,179) |

**OFFENSE:**

After a breakout season as a true freshman, QB **Davis Webb** was mentioned as a dark-horse Heisman candidate heading into 2014. Stumbling out to a 2-4 start squashed any Heisman hopes for the young QB and Webb suffered a season-ending injury in Week 8 against TCU. Freshman **Patrick Mahomes** stepped in and performed well. His six TDs and 598 passing yards in the season finale against No. 7 Baylor, a game Tech nearly won, has created a QB competition between Webb and Mahomes heading into 2015. Whoever the QB is this year, expect Kingsbury's Air Raid offense to once again put up big passing numbers. For the second-consecutive season, nine starters return on offense, including four offensive linemen. **Eric Morris** will be entering his third season as offensive coordinator for Tech, but Kingsbury handles the play-calling duties himself. The Red Raiders have ranked in the Top 5 nationally in passing yards each of the past two seasons.

**DEFENSE:**

Offense wasn't the problem for Texas Tech last year, it was the atrocious defense. Only one team in *all* of college football (1-11 Georgia State) gave up more points per game than the Red Raiders in 2014. Opposing offenses pretty much did whatever they wanted against Tech, which ranked 98th nationally in pass defense and 124th in run defense. Even with just four returning starters, there's no good excuse for such a poor defensive performance. Not surprisingly, Kingsbury is bringing in a new defensive coordinator to overhaul this unit. **David Gibbs** spent the last two seasons as Houston's DC, where he engineered a dramatic turnaround. He took over a Houston defense that ranked 110th in points allowed and improved it to No. 20 in 2013 and No. 15 in 2014. Gibbs runs a multiple-front defense with a lot of zone coverage in the secondary and he makes forcing turnovers a top priority. Houston led the nation in takeaways in 2013 and ranked No. 11 in 2014. Gibbs also served as Houston's interim head coach in the Cougars' come-from-behind victory over Pittsburgh in last season's Armed Forces Bowl. This was a big hire for Texas Tech as Gibbs was also reportedly being courted for the DC job at Colorado, his alma mater. With eight starters back and Gibbs taking over the defense, look for the Red Raiders to make some much-needed improvements on this side of the ball.

**RECRUITING:**

After signing 36 recruits in a huge 2014 class, Kingsbury chose quality over quantity in 2015. Tech's 19-signee class was rated the third best in the Big 12. Kingsbury is improving the talent-level at Texas Tech with each recruiting cycle. His first class ranked No. 46 nationally, his 2014 class ranked No. 41, and his 2015 class landed at No. 33.

**RUMOR MILL:**

After his debut season, Texas Tech gave Kliff Kingsbury a $1 million raise and extended his contract through the 2020 season. Following a disappointing 2014 campaign, some criticized the extension for being premature.

**2015 OUTLOOK:**

Sept. 5    **Sam Houston State Bearkats** – Last year, the Red Raiders survived a scare from another FCS school, Central Arkansas, to open the season.

Sept. 12    **UTEP Miners** – Last year's win over UTEP was Texas Tech's sixth in a row over the Miners.

Sept. 19    **at Arkansas Razorbacks** – Texas Tech got embarrassed at home last year against the Razorbacks and this time the Red Raiders travel to Fayetteville to face what should be an even better Arkansas team.

Sept. 26    **TCU Horned Frogs** – The 82 points Tech gave up to TCU last year were the most points ever allowed by one team in a Big 12 conference game. This will be a chance for the Tech defense to prove it's no longer the joke of the conference.

Oct. 3    **vs. Baylor Bears (in Arlington, TX)** – "The Texas Shootout" has lived up to its name in Kingsbury's first two seasons as these teams combined for 191 points and 2,392 yards of offense in those two meetings.

Oct. 10    **Iowa State Cyclones** – Kingsbury is 2-0 against Iowa State, but they've both been tight games decided by a TD or less.

Oct. 17    **at Kansas Jayhawks** – New Kansas head coach David Beaty was the WR coach at Texas A&M when Kingsbury was the OC there in 2012. Texas Tech is 15-1 all-time against Kansas.

Oct. 24    **at Oklahoma Sooners** – The Red Raiders are currently riding a three-game losing streak against the Sooners.

Oct. 31    **Oklahoma State Cowboys** – The Cowboys have dominated this series in recent years. Texas Tech hasn't defeated Oklahoma State since Mike Leach was still head coach back in 2008.

Nov. 7    **at West Virginia Mountaineers** – This is the type of game Texas Tech *MUST WIN* if it's going to climb out of the bottom half of the Big 12.

Nov. 14    **Kansas State Wildcats** – Mike Leach went 5-1 against K-State, but since he was fired in 2009, Texas Tech has gone 0-4 against the Wildcats.

Nov. 26    **at Texas Longhorns** – Texas has dominated this series, winning the last six meetings by an average score of 36-18.

**BOTTOM LINE:**
In his debut season, Kingsbury got off to a 7-0 start and a No. 10 ranking the polls. Since that time, the Red Raiders have gone 5-13. Kingsbury needs to right this ship quickly and regain some momentum. The defense should be better in 2015 with David Gibbs as the DC, but with Arkansas on the nonconference schedule it may be tough for Tech to get the six wins it needs for a bowl invite.

## Kliff Kingsbury's Year-by-Year Coaching Record:

**Texas Tech: 12-13 (6-12 in the Big 12)**
2013    8-5 (4-5)        **Final Ranking: NR**
       Beat #16 Arizona State 37-23 in the Holiday Bowl.
2014    4-8 (2-7)        **Final Ranking: NR**

# West Virginia Mountaineers – Dana Holgorsen

## Coach Ranking: #46

**Overall Record:** 28-23 in 4 seasons
**Record at West Virginia:** 28-23 in 4 seasons
**2014 Results:** 7-6, 5-4 in the Big 12 (T-4th in the Big 12)
**Returning Starters in 2015:** 7 on offense (including QB), 8 on defense
**Salary:** $3.1 Million      **Age:** 44      **Job Security Grade:** C

COACH'S BIO:
Dana Holgorsen grew up in Mount Pleasant, Iowa, and played WR at Iowa Wesleyan (NAIA) in the early 1990s. His head coach at Iowa Wesleyan was **Hal Mumme** and his offensive coordinator was **Mike Leach**. This was where Mumme and Leach created the Air Raid offense. After graduating, Holgorsen joined Mumme's and Leach's coaching staff at Valdosta State (Division II) as an assistant from 1993-1995. Holgorsen then made stops as an assistant at Mississippi College (Division II) and Wingate (Division II) before reuniting with Leach when Leach became the head coach at Texas Tech in 2000. At Texas Tech, Holgorsen worked his way up to co-offensive coordinator in 2005 and sole OC in 2007. He was then hired by **Kevin Sumlin** to be the OC at Houston from 2008-2009. He became **Mike Gundy**'s OC at Oklahoma State in 2010 and was named the head coach at West Virginia in 2011. Holgorsen led the Mountaineers to the Big East championship in his first season there.

2014 REVIEW:
Holgorsen entered 2014 on the hot seat after a 4-8 season in 2013. Faced with a must-win-now situation, the Mountaineers fought their way to a 6-2 start that included an upset win over No. 4 Baylor. West Virginia then lost four of its final five games, with three of those losses coming by a TD or less. Though WVU hasn't returned to the level it traditionally expects, there were clear signs of improvement last season.

| 2014 RESULTS:   7-6 (5-4 in the Big 12) | Final Ranking: NR | |
|---|---|---|
| vs. #2 Alabama (in Atlanta, GA) | L 23–33 | (70,502) |
| #22 (FCS) Towson | W 54–0 | (56,414) |
| at Maryland | W 40–37 | (48,154) |
| #4 Oklahoma | L 33–45 | (61,908) |
| Kansas | W 33–14 | (52,164) |
| at Texas Tech | W 37–34 | (58,502) |
| #4 Baylor | W 41–27 | (60,758) |
| at Oklahoma State | W 34–10 | (59,124) |
| #10 TCU | L 30–31 | (61,190) |
| at Texas | L 16–33 | (95,714) |
| #12 Kansas State | L 20–26 | (47,683) |
| at Iowa State | W 37–24 | (50,059) |
| vs. Texas A&M (Liberty Bowl) | L 37–45 | (51,282) |

## OFFENSE:

In 2013, Dana Holgorsen's Air Raid offense uncharacteristically fell into the bottom half of the nation in total offense. The Mountaineers rebounded in 2014 by climbing to No. 12 nationally in that category. More balance helped the offense last season as West Virginia racked up its most rushing yards in a season (2,376) since Holgorsen arrived while still passing for more than 4,000 yards. The offense sputtered a bit late in the year and losing QB **Clint Trickett** to a season-ending injury against Kansas State was a devastating blow. **Skyler Howard** stepped in to replace Trickett late in the season, but struggled to find consistency. Howard will have to beat out three other talented QBs to retain the starting position in 2015. Last year's offensive coordinator, **Shannon Dawson**, is leaving for the OC job at Kentucky and though he came to West Virginia with Holgorsen in 2011, this shouldn't be a major shakeup since Holgorsen handles the play-calling duties himself. Adequate replacements for Trickett at QB and big-play WR **Kevin White** must be found quickly if WVU wants to avoid a step back in offensive production this season.

## DEFENSE:

Since joining the Big 12 in 2012, West Virginia's defense has ranked in the bottom half of the conference each season in points allowed, but progress is being made. Last year was **Tony Gibson**'s first year as defensive coordinator and he took this squad from ninth in total defense to sixth in the Big 12. Gibson runs a unique 3-3-5 defensive scheme, which likes to stack ("hide") LBs behind the down linemen and create confusion for the offense with various stunts and blitzes. Having four returning starters in the secondary should keep the improvement trend going for this squad. Gibson needs to start creating turnovers with this defense. In 2014, the Mountaineers ranked 116th nationally in takeaways.

## RECRUITING:

For the fourth year in a row, Holgorsen landed a Top-40 recruiting class. Rated the Big 12's fourth-best 2015 recruiting class and No. 36 nationally, West Virginia signed three four-star players (two at DB and one at WR). Holgorsen has done a good job establishing quality recruiting pipelines in Ohio and Florida to go along with West Virginia.

## RUMOR MILL:

Rumors were rampant that Holgorsen was about to be fired after going 4-8 in 2013, but AD **Oliver Luck** stood by him. Luck has now moved on to a position with the NCAA and a new AD has arrived in **Shane Lyons**. New ADs are usually quick to make changes as they seek to put their personal stamp on a program. Last year's winning season bought Holgorsen some time and his current contract runs through 2017, but there's no question his seat is still warm heading into 2015.

## NOTEWORTHY:

Following his mentor **Mike Leach**'s philosophy, Holgorsen stresses the importance of keeping his offense simple. In fact, he says the entire offense can be installed in as little as three days. From there, it's repetition, repetition, and more repetition. According to Holgorsen and Leach, that simplicity is one of the keys to making the Air Raid offense work.

**2015 OUTLOOK:**

**Sept. 5**      **Georgia Southern Eagles** – Georgia Southern is a more dangerous team than the casual fan may realize. In their first year at the FBS level in 2014, the Eagles went undefeated in the Sun Belt and finished 9-3 overall.

**Sept. 12**      **Liberty Flames** – Liberty is coached by Turner Gill, the former head coach at Buffalo and Kansas. In his three years at Liberty, Gill has won the Big South Conference all three years and the Flames made it into the second round of the FCS playoffs last season.

**Sept. 26**      **Maryland Terrapins** – Holgorsen is 3-1 in this cross-conference rivalry game and he's now 4-1 against current Big Ten schools.

**Oct. 3**      **at Oklahoma Sooners** – Holgorsen is 0-3 against Bob Stoops. New Oklahoma OC Lincoln Riley spent five years coaching with Holgorsen at Texas Tech.

**Oct. 10**      **Oklahoma State Cowboys** – Before taking the West Virginia job, Holgorsen spent 2010 as Mike Gundy's OC at Oklahoma State. Holgorsen is 2-1 against his former boss.

**Oct. 17**      **at Baylor Bears** – West Virginia handed Baylor its only Big 12 loss last season and Holgorsen is now 2-1 against Art Briles.

**Oct. 29**      **at TCU Horned Frogs** – The Mountaineers nearly knocked off TCU last year in Morgantown. This year, they'll travel to Fort Worth for a Thursday-night rematch. TCU co-OC Doug Meacham was the TE coach at Oklahoma State when Holgorsen was the OC there.

**Nov. 7**      **Texas Tech Red Raiders** – Holgorsen coached Kliff Kingsbury as a player at Texas Tech and he was the OC at Houston when Kingsbury became an assistant there. Since joining the Big 12, WVU has struggled during the back-half of the season. This will be the first of five winnable conference games for the Mountaineers and if they're going to finish the season strong, they *MUST WIN* this one.

**Nov. 14**      **Texas Longhorns** – Charlie Strong's defense held West Virginia to just 16 points last year and the Mountaineers now enter this matchup on a two-game losing streak against the Longhorns.

**Nov. 21**      **at Kansas Jayhawks** – The last time West Virginia traveled to Lawrence (2013), the Jayhawks pulled off a 31-19 upset.

**Nov. 28**      **Iowa State Cyclones** – Holgorsen is 2-1 against the Cyclones. That lone loss occurred in Morgantown two years ago.

**Dec. 5**      **at Kansas State Wildcats** – In his three seasons, there are only two Big 12 teams Holgorsen hasn't been able to beat: Bob Stoops' Oklahoma Sooners and Bill Snyder's Kansas State Wildcats.

**BOTTOM LINE:**
The Mountaineers played in several close games last season. They nearly knocked off No. 10 TCU, No. 12 Kansas State, and even played No. 2 Alabama tight for most of the season-opener. This year's schedule is softer and if they can pull off an upset or two against the four top-tier Big 12 teams they face in the middle of the schedule (as they've done in previous seasons), this team should be taking another step forward with eight wins or more in 2014.

## Dana Holgorsen's Year-by-Year Coaching Record:

<u>**West Virginia: 28-23 (16-18 in the Big East and Big 12)**</u>
2011    10–3 (5–2)              Final Ranking: #17
        Big East Champions.
        Beat #14 Clemson 70-33 in the Orange Bowl.
2012    7–6 (4–5)              Final Ranking: NR
        West Virginia leaves the Big East and joins the Big 12.
        Lost to Syracuse 14-38 in the Pinstripe Bowl
2013    4–8 (2–7)              **Final Ranking: NR**
2014    7–6 (5–4)              **Final Ranking: NR**
        Lost to Texas A&M 37-24 in the Liberty Bowl.

# 2015 PAC-12 PREVIEW

## Five Things You Need to Know about the Pac-12 in 2015:

**The Battle at the Top:** The SEC West is often called the nation's toughest division, but it was the Pac-12 South that finished 2014 with more ranked teams (five) than any other division. The South Division will be extremely tough once again and **UCLA** looks to be in the best position to win it *if* **Jim Mora** can find a reliable QB. In the North, **Oregon** is the favorite to repeat, but **Stanford** has a lot more talent than last season's 8-5 record showed.

**New to the Pac-12:** It's unclear what was the bigger surprise to college football fans, the fact that **Mike Riley** decided to leave **Oregon State** for **Nebraska** or that **Gary Anderson** decided to leave **Wisconsin** for Oregon State. Either way, the end result is that the Beavers landed one of the nation's top up-and-coming coaches. Anderson will be making some fundamental changes at Oregon State and this transition may take some time.

**Coach on the Rise:** The Pac-12 saw several coaches have breakout or bounce-back seasons in 2014. In fact, **Jim Mora**, **Steve Sarkisian**, **Rich Rodriguez**, and **Kyle Whittingham** all upped their stock last year. Flying under the radar a bit was **Cal's Sonny Dykes**. After an awful debut season with the Bears, Dykes came within a TD of bowl eligibility and landed a much stronger recruiting class.

**Keep an Eye On:** **Mike Leach**, one of the most innovative offensive coaches in the game and the co-creator of the "Air Raid" offense is now trying to figure out ways to *run* the ball in 2015. **Washington State** had the nation's top passing offense last year, but a nonexistent running game resulted in a 3-9 season. Leach knows he needs to find a way to move the ball on the ground and the Air Raid guru plans to add in more option and even some QB-under-center formations in 2015. It'll be very interesting to see how these tweaks impact Leach's famous offense.

**Coaches on the Hot Seat:** The Pac-12 coach closest to the hot seat heading into 2015 is **Colorado's Mike MacIntyre**, but winning just five games should be enough to keep the Buffs from conducting their third coaching search in six years.

## 2015 Projected Standings for the ACC:

**North Division:**
1. Oregon
2. Stanford
3. Washington
4. Washington State
5. California
6. Oregon State

**South Division:**
1. UCLA
2. Arizona State
3. USC
4. Arizona
5. Utah
6. Colorado

# Ranking the Pac-12's Coaches:

1. **David Shaw** – Stanford (42-12 in 4 seasons)
2. **Chris Petersen** – Washington (100-18 in 9 seasons)
3. **Mark Helfrich** – Oregon (24-4 in 2 seasons)
4. **Jim Mora** – UCLA (29-11 in 3 seasons)
5. **Todd Graham** – Arizona State (77-41 in 9 seasons)
6. **Rich Rodriguez** – Arizona (146-98-2 in 21 seasons)
7. **Mike Leach** – Washington State (96-68 in 13 seasons)
8. **Steve Sarkisian** – USC (43-33 in 6 seasons)
9. **Gary Anderson** – Oregon State (49-38 in 7 seasons)
10. **Kyle Whittingham** – Utah (85-43 in 10 seasons)
11. **Sonny Dykes** – California (28-33 in 5 seasons)
12. **Mike MacIntyre** – Colorado (22-39 in 5 seasons)

# 2014 Pac-12 Coach of the Year:
(Selected by the Pac-12 coaches)
Rich Rodriguez, Arizona

# 2014 Pac-12 Standings:

| North Division | (Conference) | (All Games) |
|---|---|---|
| #2 Oregon | 8–1 | 13–2 |
| Stanford | 5–4 | 8–5 |
| Washington | 4–5 | 8–6 |
| California | 3–6 | 5–7 |
| Oregon State | 2–7 | 5–7 |
| Washington State | 2–7 | 3–9 |
| | | |
| South Division | | |
| #19 Arizona | 7–2 | 10–4 |
| #10 UCLA | 6–3 | 10–3 |
| #12 Arizona State | 6–3 | 10–3 |
| #20 USC | 6–3 | 9–4 |
| #21 Utah | 5–4 | 9–4 |
| Colorado | 0–9 | 2–10 |

*Championship Game*: Oregon 51, Arizona 13

**2014 Pac-12 Bowl Record:** 6-3 (2nd place among all 10 conferences)

# California Golden Bears – Sonny Dykes

## Coach Ranking: #65

**Overall Record:** 28-33 in 5 seasons
**Record at California:** 6-18 in 2 seasons
**2014 Results:** 5-7, 3-6 in the Pac-12 (4th in the Pac-12 North)
**Returning Starters in 2015:** 8 on offense (including QB), 9 on defense
**Salary:** $1.8 Million     **Age:** 45     **Job Security Grade:** B

COACH'S BIO:
Sonny Dykes is the son of **Spike Dykes**, who was the head coach at Texas Tech from 1987-1999. Sonny was a first baseman for the Texas Tech baseball team in college and got his coaching start as a high school baseball coach in 1994. He began coaching football as a high school assistant the following fall and then moved to the junior college level in 1995. After two seasons as a juco assistant, he was hired as a graduate assistant for Kentucky under **Hal Mumme**. In 2000, Dykes was hired by **Mike Leach** to coach WRs at Texas Tech. He was promoted to co-offensive coordinator in 2005 and held that role for two seasons. In 2007, **Mike Stoops** hired Dykes to be his OC at Arizona. After three seasons in Arizona, Dykes became the head coach at Louisiana Tech in 2010. He improved Louisiana Tech's record all three seasons there and led the Bulldogs to a WAC championship in 2011. He was named Cal's new head coach after the 2012 season, replacing **Jeff Tedford**.

2014 REVIEW:
After going 1-11 in his debut season, expectations were low for Sonny Dykes and the Bears heading into 2014. A fast 4-1 start surprised many in the Pac-12 and Cal fell just short of bowl eligibility by losing its season finale against BYU. It was a successful second season for Dykes as he pulled Cal out of the North Division cellar.

| 2014 RESULTS:   5-7 (3-6 in the Pac-12) | Final Ranking: NR | |
|---|---|---|
| at Northwestern | W 31–24 | (34,228) |
| Sacramento State | W 55–14 | (48,145) |
| at Arizona | L 45–49 | (45,595) |
| Colorado | W 59–56 2OT | (39,821) |
| at Washington State | W 60–59 | (30,020) |
| Washington | L 7–31 | (44,449) |
| UCLA | L 34–36 | (49,257) |
| vs. #6 Oregon (in Santa Clara, CA) | L 41–59 | (55,575) |
| at Oregon State | W 45–31 | (42,479) |
| at USC | L 30–38 | (64,615) |
| Stanford | L 17–38 | (56,483) |
| BYU | L 35–42 | (47,856) |

## OFFENSE:

Dykes learned the Air Raid offense directly from its creators, **Hal Mumme** and **Mike Leach**, at Kentucky and he eventually became Leach's co-offensive coordinator at Texas Tech. He has brought this up-tempo pass-happy spread system to Cal, where it's being called the "Bear Raid" offense. Dykes' version of the Air Raid system is fairly well balanced. Last year, the Bears ran the ball 45% of the time and racked up nearly 1,800 rushing yards. Those numbers paled in comparison to Cal's 4,152 passing yards in 2014, but the more balanced approach helped the Bears score 38.3 points a game, which was No. 11 in the nation. This offense made tremendous strides last year as Cal went from dead last in the Pac-12 in scoring in 2013 (23 points a game) to No. 2 in the conference in 2014. With junior **Jared Goff** returning for his third season as the starting QB (he passed for 3,973 yards, 35 TDs and just 7 INTs in 2014) and seven other returning starters surrounding him, this offense should be even more potent in Year 3 with Dykes' system. **Tony Franklin** returns for his third season as Cal's OC. Franklin was also Dykes' OC at Louisiana Tech.

## DEFENSE:

When a program is most known for its offense, the defense often suffers and that's certainly been the case at Cal. After giving up 45.9 points a game in 2013 (125th in the nation), Dykes brought in **Art Kaufman** to be his new defensive coordinator in 2014. Though the defense improved a bit, it still gave up more points than any other team in the Pac-12 (39.8 points a game). The Bears will have nine starters back in 2015 and this will be their second year in Kaufman's system, which is an adaptable scheme based out of a 4-3. With a more experienced group, Cal should be better on this side of the ball. No matter how good the offense may be, there's only so far this program can rise if the defense continues to give up 500 yards and 40 points a game.

## RECRUITING:

Nothing improves recruiting efforts faster than winning and Cal's jump from one win to five wins captured the attention of several highly-touted recruits. Dykes' recruiting class climbed from a national ranking of No. 54 in 2014 to No. 35 in 2015. While the state of California is this staff's top priority, they're also using their ties to Texas and the South to reel in a few prospects from those talent-rich regions.

## RUMOR MILL:

At the time Cal hired Dykes after the 2012 season, he was also mentioned as a candidate for openings at Arkansas, NC State, and Kentucky. Yet, after his 1-11 debut season with the Bears, some were already placing Dykes on the hot seat. He silenced most his critics in 2014, showing that his program is on the right track.

## NOTEWORTHY:

Cal OC Tony Franklin worked with Hal Mumme, Mike Leach, and Sonny Dykes during his time at Kentucky (1997-2000) and he's widely considered one of the nation's top experts on the Air Raid offense. He's a sought-after offensive consultant for high school and college coaches all over the country. In 2012, he was a nominee for the Broyles Award, which goes to the nation's top assistant coach.

**2015 OUTLOOK:**

**Sept. 5**  **Grambling State Tigers** – Dykes is 4-0 all-time against FCS opponents, including a 20-6 win over Grambling State when he was at Louisiana Tech in 2010. The Tigers went 7-5 last season.

**Sept. 12**  **San Diego State Aztecs** – Cal is 6-7 all-time against the MWC. The Bears haven't played San Diego State since 1996.

**Sept. 19**  **at Texas Longhorns** – It'll be interesting to see how the Bear Raid offense does against Charlie Strong's stout defense at Texas. Cal is 0-5 all-time against the Longhorns.

**Sept. 26**  **at Washington Huskies** – Cal has lost six-straight games to this North Division opponent. The Bears were held to a season-low seven points in last year's game as five fumbles (three lost) cost them big.

**Oct. 3**  **Washington State Cougars** – Dykes and Leach coached for eight years together at Kentucky and Texas Tech. Dykes was Leach's co-OC at Texas Tech in 2005 and 2006. Cal won this game 60-59 last year, but the defense gave up an NCAA-record 734 passing yards to Leach's Air Raid offense.

**Oct. 10**  **at Utah Utes** – These schools last met in 2012, a 49-27 Utah win. This series is tied at 1-1 since Utah joined the Pac-12. This is the type of road game the Bears must find a way to win if they want to go bowling in 2015. For that reason, this is a *MUST-WIN* game for Cal.

**Oct. 22**  **at UCLA Bruins** – UCLA's come-from-behind win last year was the Bruins' first win at Berkeley since 1998. The home team is now 13-2 in this series since 2000.

**Oct. 31**  **USC Trojans** – The Trojans have won 11-straight games in this series. In last year's game, USC had a 31-9 halftime lead before Cal stormed back and made things interesting. USC ended up winning 38-30.

**Nov. 7**  **at Oregon Ducks** – Oregon has won the last six games in this series.

**Nov. 14**  **Oregon State Beavers** – The Bears rushed for a season-high 269 yards in last year's 45-31 win over Oregon State. Dykes went 2-1 against Gary Anderson when Dykes was at Louisiana Tech and Anderson was at Utah State.

**Nov. 21**  **at Stanford Cardinal** – Stanford owns a five-game winning streak in this historic rivalry and Dykes could send a big message to the Pac-12 North by breaking that streak.

**Nov. 28**  **Arizona State Sun Devils** – Cal has won eight of the last 10 in this series, but Arizona State won 27-17 the last time these teams met, in 2012. Last year, the Bears lost six of their last seven games and they can't let that happen again if they want to make it to a bowl game.

**BOTTOM LINE:**
The Cal Bears took a nice step forward in 2014 by showing they could beat the three lower-tier Pac-12 teams they played against. This year, it's time to take the next step and the Bears need to show they can pull off a win or two against the upper-echelon teams in this conference. The offense should once again be one of the highest-scoring in the country. Even a minor improvement on defense could be enough to get Cal to the six wins needed for bowl eligibility.

Sonny Dykes' Year-by-Year Coaching Record:

<u>Louisiana Tech: 22-15 (14-7 in the WAC)</u>
| 2010 | 5–7 (4–4) | Final Ranking: NR |
|------|-----------|-------------------|
| 2011 | 8–5 (6–1) | Final Ranking: NR |

WAC Champions.
Dykes named the WAC Coach of the Year.
Lost to #15 TCU 24-31 in the Poinsettia Bowl.
| 2012 | 9–3 (4–2) | Final Ranking: NR |

<u>California: 6-18 (3-15 in the Pac-12)</u>
| 2013 | 1–11 (0–9) | Final Ranking: NR |
|------|------------|-------------------|
| 2014 | 5–7 (3–6) | Final Ranking: NR |

# Oregon Ducks – Mark Helfrich

## Coach Ranking: #20

**Overall Record:** 24-4 in 2 seasons
**Record at Oregon:** 24-4 in 2 seasons
**2014 Results:** 13-2, 8-1 in the Pac-12 (Pac-12 Champions)
**Returning Starters in 2015:** 7 on offense, 5 on defense
**Salary:** $3.2 Million        **Age:** 41        **Job Security Grade:** A

**COACH'S BIO:**
Mark Helfrich grew up an Oregon Ducks fan in the coastal town of Coos Bay,
Oregon. After a successful high school career, he was a four-year starter at QB for
Southern Oregon (NAIA) and was named an All-American his senior year (1995).
He then spent the fall of 1996 coaching RBs at Southern Oregon and the spring of
1997 playing QB and serving as the assistant offensive coordinator for the Vienna
Vikings, a European Football League team. Helfrich spent the fall of 1997 as a
graduate assistant at Oregon. From 1998-2005, he served as **Dirk Koetter**'s OC, first
at Boise State and then at Arizona State. In 2006, **Dan Hawkins** hired Helfrich to be
his OC at Colorado, which made the 32-year-old the youngest OC at a BCS school.
In 2009, **Chip Kelly** hired Helfrich as Oregon's OC and when Kelly made the move
to the NFL, Helfrich was promoted to head coach in 2013.

**2014 REVIEW:**
The Ducks entered 2014 with high expectations and didn't disappoint. Oregon
made it to the first-ever CFP National Championship Game while racking up the
program's most wins ever in a single season. In the process, QB **Marcus Mariota**
became the school's first Heisman Trophy winner.

**2014 RESULTS:   13-2 (8-1 in the Pac-12)**          Final Ranking: #2

| | | |
|---|---|---|
| South Dakota | W 62–13 | (57,388) |
| #7 Michigan State | W 46–27 | (59,456) |
| Wyoming | W 48–14 | (56,533) |
| **at Washington State** | W 38–31 | (32,952) |
| **Arizona** | L 24–31 | (56,032) |
| **at #18 UCLA** | W 42–30 | (80,139) |
| **Washington** | W 45–20 | (57,858) |
| **at California** (in Santa Clara, CA) | W 59–41 | (55,575) |
| **Stanford** | W 45–16 | (58,974) |
| **at #17 Utah** | W 51–27 | (47,528) |
| **Colorado** | W 44–10 | (55,898) |
| **at Oregon State** | W 47–19 | (45,722) |
| **vs. #8 Arizona** (Pac-12 Championship) | W 51–13 | (45,618) |
| vs. #2 Florida State (CFP Semifinal) | W 59–20 | (91,322) |
| vs. #5 Ohio State (CFP Natl. Championship) | L 20–42 | (85,689) |

**OFFENSE:**

When **Chip Kelly** left for the NFL after the 2012 season, the big question on everyone's mind was whether the explosive Oregon offense he created would take a step back under a new head coach. Helfrich has answered that question loud and clear. During Kelly's four seasons, the Ducks averaged 482 yards a game. In Helfrich's two seasons, the offense has actually taken a step *forward* with 555 yards a game. Oregon runs a no-huddle spread-option offense that keeps the defense off-balance with its extremely fast pace. In 2014, the Ducks averaged 74.5 offensive plays a game while racking up 8,205 yards of total offense – the second-most total yards in a season ever by an FCS team. Now the question becomes: how will Oregon's offense look in the post-**Marcus Mariota** era? Mariota accounted for more than 13,000 yards of total offense during his three seasons as the Ducks' dual-threat QB. While it's unrealistic to expect anyone to match Mariota's combination of arm strength, accuracy, speed, and decision-making ability (he had 42 TD passes and just four interceptions in 2014), Helfrich and offensive coordinator **Scott Frost** will try to fill Mariota's big shoes with **Vernon Adams**, a transfer from FCS powerhouse Eastern Washington. In 2014, Adams was the runner-up for the Walter Payton Award (the Heisman of the FCS) despite missing four games with a broken foot. Don't be surprised if Oregon leans more on sophomore RB **Royce Freeman**, a powerful back who rushed for 1,365 yards as a freshman last year. While the offense probably won't slow down much, a step back is expected without Mariota in 2015.

**DEFENSE:**

**Nick Aliotti** had been Oregon's defensive coordinator for 15 years before retiring after the 2013 season. There were worries about how the transition to a new DC would go after such a long and successful tenure under Aliotti. As Oregon likes to do, the Ducks promoted from within and made Aliotti's longtime assistant and former Oregon LB, **Don Pellum**, the new DC. The Ducks run a "bend-but-don't-break" defensive scheme out of a hybrid 3-4 look. The focus on keeping points off the board worked well in 2014. Despite finishing in the back half of the Pac-12 in yards allowed, the Ducks finished No. 2 in points allowed. This year, Pellum must replace three all-conference starters in the secondary.

**RECRUITING:**

Though Helfrich hasn't been able to out-recruit USC and UCLA since taking over as head coach, he has made sure Oregon's recruiting classes stay near the top of the Pac-12. His 2015 class was ranked No. 3 in the conference and No. 16 in the nation. However, his most-valued recruit wasn't a blue-chip prep star, but a graduate transfer from an FCS school: QB Vernon Adams from Eastern Washington.

**RUMOR MILL:**

In February, Oregon gave Helfrich a five-year, $17.5 million contract extension that will run through the 2020 season. The contract includes an automatic one-year rollover extension for each time Helfrich wins 11 games or more. Scott Frost, Oregon's OC since 2013, was rumored to be a top candidate for the Nebraska job this past offseason, but the Huskers ended up hiring Oregon State head coach **Mike Riley**. Frost was the QB on Nebraska's 1997 National Championship team.

**2015 OUTLOOK:**

**Sept. 5**     **Eastern Washington Eagles** – In a very unique situation, Oregon will open the season against the FCS school that QB Vernon Adams starred at for the past three seasons.

**Sept. 12**     **at Michigan State Spartans** – Oregon beat Michigan State 46-27 last year, but the game was closer than the final score made it look. Oregon has won five of its last seven games against the Big Ten. This game should be a good indicator of whether or not the Ducks have a team capable of making another CFP run in 2015. That makes this a *MUST-WIN* early-season showdown for Helfrich.

**Sept. 19**     **Georgia State Panthers** – Oregon is 3-0 all-time against Sun Belt teams. Georgia State went 1-11 last year.

**Sept. 26**     **Utah Utes** – Oregon capitalized on four turnovers in last year's lopsided win over Utah. Helfrich is 2-0 against the Utes.

**Oct. 3**     **at Colorado Buffaloes** – Since Colorado joined the Pac-12 in 2011, Oregon has dominated this series. The Ducks have won all four meetings by an average of 43.5 points a game.

**Oct. 10**     **Washington State Cougars** – Washington State went toe-to-toe with Oregon last year, but the Ducks held on to win and extended their winning streak to 11 games in this series.

**Oct. 17**     **at Washington Huskies** – Washington coach Chris Petersen was Oregon's WR coach from 1995-2000. The Ducks have an 11-game winning streak active in this series and they've won all 11 of those games by 17 points or more.

**Oct. 29**     **at Arizona State Sun Devils** – These cross-division teams haven't met since 2012. The Ducks enter this Thursday-night game having won the last eight against the Sun Devils. Helfrich coached at Arizona State from 2001-2005.

**Nov. 7**     **California Golden Bears** – Oregon has won six straight against Cal, but the Ducks need to make sure they're not looking past this game. With 17 starters back and a third season in Sonny Dykes' "Bear Raid" system, Cal could be a surprise team in the North Division.

**Nov. 14**     **at Stanford Cardinal** – Since the Chip Kelly/Mark Helfrich era began at Oregon in 2009, this series is tied at 3-3. The Ducks lost the last time they traveled to Stanford, in 2013.

**Nov. 21**     **USC Trojans** – This game could be a preview of the Pac-12 Championship. It will be the first meeting between these two teams since 2012. This series is even at 4-4 since 2005.

**Nov. 27**     **Oregon State Beavers** – This game will be played the Friday after Thanksgiving. Oregon has dominated "The Civil War" in recent years, winning the last seven games in this series.

**BOTTOM LINE:**
Having to replace a three-year starter and Heisman Trophy winner at QB certainly makes the Ducks more vulnerable than they've been the last couple seasons, but there's enough talent here for a repeat Pac-12 Championship and another trip to the College Football Playoff.

## Mark Helfrich's Year-by-Year Coaching Record:

<u>Oregon: 24-4 (15-3 in the Pac-12)</u>
2013    11-2 (7-2)                Final Ranking: #9
         Pac-12 North Co-Champions.
         Beat Texas 30-7 in the Alamo Bowl.
2014    13-2 (8-1)                Final Ranking: #2
         Pac-12 Champions.
         Beat #8 Arizona 51-13 in the Pac-12 Championship Game.
         Beat #2 Florida State 59-20 in the CFP Semifinal Game.
         Lost to #5 Ohio State 20-42 in the CFP National Championship Game.

# Oregon State Beavers – Gary Anderson

## Coach Ranking: #39

**Overall Record:** 49-38 in 7 seasons (1 season in Division 1-AA)
**2014 Results:** Oregon State went 5-7, 2-7 in the Pac-12 (T-5th in the Pac-12 North)
At Wisconsin, Anderson went 10-3, 7-1 in the Big Ten
**Returning Starters in 2015:** 8 on offense, 2 on defense
**Salary:** $2.5 Million      **Age:** 51      **Job Security Grade:** A

COACH'S BIO:
Gary Anderson grew up in Salt Lake City and after earning All-American honors in junior college, he played center for Utah from 1985-1986. In a coaching career that began in 1988, Anderson worked his way up as an assistant at the junior college and FCS levels and even spent one season (1994) as the head coach at Park City (Utah) High School before landing a job on **Ron McBride**'s staff at his alma mater in 1997. In 2003, he left Utah to become the head coach at Southern Utah (Division 1-AA) but Anderson stayed for just one 4-7 season before returning to Utah as the DL coach on **Urban Meyer**'s staff. He was promoted to defensive coordinator when **Kyle Whittingham** became head coach of the Utes in 2005. In 2009, Anderson was named head coach at Utah State and turned around a program that had won just six games in the three seasons before he arrived. After leading Utah State to a WAC championship in 2012, he left for Wisconsin and won the Big Ten West Division in 2014. Anderson surprised the college football world by leaving Wisconsin for Oregon State this past offseason.

2014 REVIEW:
Last year, Oregon State fell short of bowl eligibility for the third time in five seasons. After going 5-7 in 2014, **Mike Riley** shocked Oregon State fans by leaving his hometown school after 14 seasons (12 consecutive) to accept the Nebraska job. Meanwhile, Gary Anderson spent 2014 going 10-3 and guiding the Wisconsin Badgers to a Big Ten West Division title in his second season there.

**2014 RESULTS:    5-7 (2-7 in the Pac-12)          Final Ranking: NR**

| | | |
|---|---|---|
| Portland State | W 29–14 | (40,309) |
| at Hawaii | W 38–30 | (29,050) |
| San Diego State | W 28–7 | (41,339) |
| **at #18 USC** | L 10–35 | (74,521) |
| **at Colorado** | W 36–31 | (36,415) |
| **#20 Utah** | L 23–29 2OT | (40,479) |
| **at Stanford** | L 14–38 | (48,401) |
| **California** | L 31–45 | (42,479) |
| **Washington State** | L 32–39 | (44,377) |
| **#7 Arizona State** | W 35–27 | (40,525) |
| **at Washington** | L 13–37 | (65,036) |
| **#3 Oregon** | L 19–47 | (45,722) |

## OFFENSE:

Changes are on the way for Oregon State's offense and after finishing at the bottom of the Pac-12 in scoring (89th in the nation) last season, those changes should be welcomed by Beaver fans. **Mike Riley** ran a pass-first pro-style offense that liked to put the ball in the air 55%-60% of the time. While Gary Anderson will be bringing in an offense that would still be considered "pro style" in terms of the formations used and the type of QB preferred, it's definitely a more physical, run-first brand of the pro-style offense. At Wisconsin, Anderson's offense ran the ball 67% of the time last year and finished No. 4 nationally in rushing yards. Anderson may not rely on the run quite so much – especially early on – at Oregon State, but he definitely prefers to have a team that can run downhill on opponents. Anderson's offensive coordinator will be **Dave Baldwin**, who spent the last two years as the OC at Colorado State. Baldwin's offense was more balanced at Colorado State, but the last time he was Anderson's OC (in 2011 at Utah State), his offense ran the ball 68% of the time. Though the Beavers will have eight starters back on offense, including all five offensive linemen, it will likely take some time to transition this offense – both physically and mentally – from a pass-first finesse style to a run-first ground-and-pound system.

## DEFENSE:

While some defenses are built on a bend-but-don't-break philosophy, which is content with allowing big yards as long as the defense doesn't give up big points, Oregon State had the opposite problem in 2014. The Beavers were ranked fourth in the Pac-12 in yards allowed, but when it came to keeping points off the board – the stat that matters most – Oregon State was ninth in the conference and 98th in the nation, giving up 31.6 points a game. At Wisconsin, Anderson's defense gave up just 18.2 points a game during his two seasons there and finished No. 4 nationally in total defense last year. Anderson's defensive coordinator will be **Kalani Sitake**, who spent the last six seasons as the DC at Utah. Anderson and Sitake originally planned to base their defense out of the 4-3 Oregon State was already familiar with, but after evaluating personnel in the spring, they switched to a 3-4 system, which is what Anderson ran at Wisconsin. This is a good time to hit the reset button on this defense. Only two defensive starters are returning in 2015, which is tied for the fewest number of returning starters for any defense in *all* of the FBS.

## RECRUITING:

As is often the case when a new head coach is hired and a new staff must scramble to complete its first recruiting class, Anderson's first class at Oregon State was small. In fact, it tied for the smallest in the Pac-12, with just 19 signees. The Beavers were ranked No. 11 in the Pac-12 and No. 64 in the nation. A $42-million project to improve and expand Oregon State's facilities should soon give the Beavers some additional help in the Pac-12 recruiting wars.

## RUMOR MILL:

Anderson blindsided Wisconsin by leaving for the Oregon State job. The Beavers gave Anderson a six-year contract that will pay him a base salary of $2.45 million in 2015 and he'll receive a $100,000 raise each year of the contract. Wisconsin paid Anderson $2.3 million in 2014. Oregon State paid Mike Riley $1.5 million in 2014.

**2015 OUTLOOK:**

**Sept. 4**    **Weber State Wildcats** – Anderson is 1-1 all-time against this FCS program. He lost 13-3 while at Southern Utah in 2003 and won 54-17 while at Utah State in 2011. Weber State went 2-10 last year.

**Sept. 12**    **at Michigan Wolverines** – Though Anderson may be somewhat familiar with Michigan from his two seasons in the Big Ten, he never faced the Wolverines while at Wisconsin and Michigan will have a new head coach as well in Jim Harbaugh.

**Sept. 19**    **San Jose State Spartans** – San Jose State went 3-9 last year, but the Spartans will have 15 starters back in 2015. Oregon State is 12-3 all-time against the MWC and Anderson went 4-0 against San Jose State while at Utah State.

**Sept. 25**    **Stanford Cardinal** – This Friday-night game will be a tough way to open Pac-12 play as Oregon State's inexperienced defense must try to match up with Stanford's experienced and physical offense. Stanford has won the last five games in this series.

**Oct. 10**    **at Arizona Wildcats** – Oregon State has gone 12-2 in its last 14 meetings against Arizona. These teams last played in 2012, a 38-35 win by the Beavers.

**Oct. 17**    **at Washington State Cougars** – These teams tied for last place in the Pac-12 North last season. To ensure that Oregon State doesn't take a step back and land at the bottom of the division in 2015, this will be a *MUST-WIN* game for Anderson.

**Oct. 24**    **Colorado Buffaloes** – Colorado has won just four conference games since joining the Pac-12 four years ago. Anderson went 3-0 against Mike MacIntyre when MacIntyre was at San Jose State and Anderson was at Utah State.

**Oct. 31**    **at Utah Utes** – Anderson will return to his hometown to face his alma mater in this one. He spent 11 seasons coaching at Utah, including four seasons as Kyle Whittingham's DC and assistant head coach. Anderson went 1-1 against the Utes while at Utah State.

**Nov. 7**    **UCLA Bruins** – These teams last met in 2012, a 27-20 Oregon State win.

**Nov. 14**    **at California Golden Bears** – Under Sonny Dykes, Cal looks like a program on the rise and the Beavers don't want to finish below the Bears in the Pac-12 North standings for the second-straight year.

**Nov. 21**    **Washington Huskies** – While at Utah State, Anderson went 0-2 against Chris Petersen when Petersen was at Boise State.

**Nov. 27**    **at Oregon Ducks** – Oregon State has lost the last seven games in this rivalry. No matter what type of first season Anderson has, breaking that streak on the Friday after Thanksgiving would create big momentum for this program heading into the future.

**BOTTOM LINE:**
As Gary Anderson takes over a program that has suffered through three losing seasons over the past five years, nobody is expecting an instant turnaround. Anderson will be shifting Oregon State into a more physical team on both sides of the ball and that transition will likely take some time.

## Gary Anderson's Year-by-Year Coaching Record:

**Sothern Utah: 4-7 (0-0 in the Division 1-AA Playoffs)**
2003    4-7 (0-0)           Final Ranking: NR

**Utah State: 26-24 (16-13 in the WAC)**
2009    4–8 (3–5)           Final Ranking: NR
2010    4–8 (2–6)           Final Ranking: NR
2011    7–6 (5–2)           Final Ranking: NR
          Lost to Ohio 23-24 in the Potato Bowl.
2012    11–2 (6–0)          Final Ranking: #16
          WAC Champions.
          Beat Toledo 41-15 in the Potato Bowl.

**Wisconsin: 19-7 (13-3 in the Big Ten)**
2013    9–4 (6–2)           Final Ranking: #21
          Lost to #8 South Carolina 24-34 in the Capital One Bowl.
2014    10–3 (7–1)          Final Ranking: #17
          Big Ten West Division Champions.
          Lost to #6 Ohio State 0-59 in the Big Ten Championship Game.
          Wisconsin beat #19 Auburn 34-31 in OT in the Outback Bowl, but Anderson had already left to accept the Oregon State job. Wisconsin finished the season ranked #13.

# Stanford Cardinal – David Shaw

## Coach Ranking: #17

**Overall Record:** 42-12 in 4 seasons
**Record at Stanford:** 42-12 in 4 seasons
**2014 Results:** 8-5, 5-4 in the Pac-12 (2nd in the Pac-12 North)
**Returning Starters in 2015:** 9 on offense (including QB), 4 on defense
**Salary:** $2 Million          **Age:** 43          **Job Security Grade:** A

COACH'S BIO:
There are good reasons that Stanford feels like the perfect fit for David Shaw. His father, **Willie Shaw**, coached there for six seasons and David played WR there from 1991-1994, under head coaches **Dennis Green** and **Bill Walsh**. David Shaw was a three-sport college athlete who also played on Stanford's basketball and track teams. After graduating, he began a coaching career that included NFL stops with the Philadelphia Eagles under **Ray Rhodes**, the Oakland Raiders under **Jon Gruden**, and the Baltimore Ravens under **Brian Billick**. In 2006, he joined **Jim Harbaugh**'s staff at the University of San Diego (FCS) and followed Harbaugh to Stanford in 2007. Shaw was Stanford's offensive coordinator from 2007-2010 and when Harbaugh left for the NFL, Shaw was promoted to head coach. He was named the Pac-12 Coach of the Year during his first two seasons as the Cardinal head coach.

2014 REVIEW:
Stanford entered the 2014 season ranked No. 11, but faced a tough schedule and went 1-5 against ranked opponents. The Cardinal broke its streak of four seasons with 11 or more wins. The season did end on a positive three-game stretch that included a win in the "Big Game" over Cal, a convincing win over No. 9 UCLA, and Shaw's second bowl win in three years.

| 2014 RESULTS:   8-5 (5-4 in the Pac-12) | Final Ranking: NR | |
|---|---|---|
| UC Davis | W 45-0 | (49,509) |
| **#14 USC** | L 10-13 | (50,814) |
| Army | W 35-0 | (49,680) |
| **at Washington** | W 20-13 | (66,512) |
| at #9 Notre Dame | L 14-17 | (80,795) |
| **Washington State** | W 34-17 | (44,135) |
| at #17 Arizona State | L 10-26 | (59,012) |
| **Oregon State** | W 38-14 | (48,401) |
| at #5 Oregon | L 16-45 | (58,974) |
| **#25 Utah** | L 17-20 2OT | (44,635) |
| at California | W 38-17 | (56,483) |
| **at #9 UCLA** | W 31-10 | (70,658) |
| vs. Maryland (Foster Farms Bowl) | W 45-21 | (34,780) |

**OFFENSE:**
Stanford runs a multiple-set pro-style offense that, in the past, has relied on a steady running game behind a physical offensive line and fullback. Last year, however, the offense threw the ball more than it typically does. After running the ball 65% of the time in 2013, the Cardinal cut its number of rushes down to 55% in 2014. It also marked the first time during the Shaw era that Stanford did not have a 1,000-yard rusher. The result was an offense that fell from seventh in the Pac-12 in scoring to 11th. Stanford's offensive coordinator is **Mike Bloomgren**, who has also been the OL coach since 2011. With nine starters back, including QB **Kevin Hogan** and four offensive linemen, Shaw and Bloomgren will have a much more experienced squad in 2015. The key will be finding a potent threat at RB. Many are still hoping for a breakout season from senior **Barry Sanders Jr.**, but **Christian McCaffrey** showed a lot of explosiveness as a true freshman last year, averaging more than 7 yards per carry and 14 yards per catch. Overall, this should be a much more productive offense in 2015.

**DEFENSE:**
**Derek Mason** had been Stanford's defensive coordinator and associate head coach from 2011-2013, but he left to become Vanderbilt's head coach last season. Once again, Stanford promoted from within and named **Lance Anderson** the new DC. Anderson was **Jim Harbaugh**'s DL coach at the University of San Diego and he's been a member of the Stanford staff since 2007. The transition from Mason to Anderson went as smoothly as one could hope for. The Cardinal stuck with its same 3-4 defensive scheme and led the Pac-12 in points allowed for the third season in a row. This year will be more challenging as Anderson must replace his entire defensive line, including two All-Pac-12 players, and two more All-Pac-12 players in the secondary.

**RECRUITING:**
Shaw's 2015 recruiting class took a step back from the highly-rated class of 2014 (No. 2 in the Pac-12), but the 2015 class still landed at No. 25 nationally and No. 5 in the conference. Several members of Shaw's monster 2012 class, which was ranked No. 1 in the Pac-12 and No. 7 in the nation, will be seniors on this year's roster.

**RUMOR MILL:**
Shaw's name comes up often as a candidate for head coaching jobs in the NFL. Rumors of NFL interest were particularly loud at the end of the 2013 season when the Houston Texans reportedly had Shaw high on their list of targets. Shaw said that while he takes the rumors as a compliment, he's not interested in the NFL and Stanford is where he wants to be. In December of 2012, Stanford and Shaw agreed to what was described as a "long-term" contract extension, but the university did not release the exact duration of the contract.

**NOTEWORTHY:**
Stanford has faced six or more ranked teams during each of its past three seasons. Though Shaw went 1-5 against ranked teams in 2014, he went 11-2 against ranked teams from 2012-2013.

**2015 OUTLOOK:**

**Sept. 5**   **at Northwestern Wildcats** – This will be Stanford's first regular season game against a Big Ten team since 1996. The last five times the Cardinal faced a Big Ten team, it was in bowl games. Shaw is 2-1 against the Big Ten.

**Sept. 12**   **UCF Knights** – This will be Stanford's first game against a school from the recently-formed American Athletic Conference. UCF went 9-4 and won its second-straight AAC title in 2014.

**Sept. 19**   **at USC Trojans** – For the second year in a row, Stanford will open up the Pac-12 schedule against this cross-division rival. After winning his first two games against USC, Shaw has lost the last two.

**Sept. 25**   **at Oregon State Beavers** – Shaw is 4-0 against Oregon State. The Beavers will be bringing in a new head coach this year in Gary Anderson.

**Oct. 3**   **Arizona Wildcats** – These cross-division teams last met in 2012, which was Rich Rodriguez's first season at Arizona. Shaw is 2-0 against the Wildcats.

**Oct. 15**   **UCLA Bruins** – Last year, Stanford dominated UCLA and cost the Bruins a trip to the Pac-12 Championship. UCLA will be looking for revenge in this Thursday-night showdown. Shaw is 5-0 against UCLA, including his victory in the 2012 Pac-12 Championship Game.

**Oct. 24**   **Washington Huskies** – Shaw is 3-1 against Washington, but the last three meetings in this series have been decided by seven points or less.

**Oct. 31**   **at Washington State Cougars** – Stanford has won the last seven games in this series. Last year, the Cardinal defense held Mike Leach's Air Raid offense to a season-low 266 total yards.

**Nov. 7**   **at Colorado Buffaloes** – These teams haven't played since 2012. Shaw is 2-0 against the Buffaloes and he won those two games by a combined score of 96-7.

**Nov. 14**   **Oregon Ducks** – Over the past four seasons, the winner of this game has won the Pac-12 North Division. That's expected to be the case again this year, which makes it a *MUST-WIN* game for Shaw and the Cardinal. Shaw is 2-2 against Oregon.

**Nov. 21**   **California Golden Bears** – Shaw has dominated this rivalry. He's 4-0 in the "Big Game" and he's won those four games by a combined score of 153-61. This will be the 118th meeting between these rivals. Stanford leads the all-time series 60-46-11.

**Nov. 28**   **Notre Dame Fighting Irish** – The home team has won each of the last four games in this series. Shaw is 2-2 against the Irish.

**BOTTOM LINE:**
Stanford is anxious to prove that last year's five-loss season was a short-term blip for a program that has reached elite status nationally. Offensively, the Cardinal should be improved and they have the talent to get back to the Pac-12 Championship. Defensively, major holes will need to be filled quickly as Stanford's schedule is once again tough from the start.

## David Shaw's Year-by-Year Coaching Record:

Stanford: 42-12 (28-8 in the Pac-12)

2011    11–2 (8–1)              Final Ranking: #7
        Pac-12 North Division Co-Champions.
        Shaw named Pac-12 Coach of the Year.
        Lost to #3 Oklahoma State 38-41 in OT in the Fiesta Bowl.

2012    12–2 (8–1)              Final Ranking: #6
        Pac-12 Champions.
        Shaw named Pac-12 Coach of the Year.
        Beat #17 UCLA 27-24 in the Pac-12 Championship Game.
        Beat Wisconsin 20-14 in the Rose Bowl.

2013    11–3 (7–2)              Final Ranking: #10
        Pac-12 Champions.
        Beat #11 Arizona State 38-14 in the Pac-12 Championship Game.
        Lost to #4 Michigan State 20-24 in the Rose Bowl.

2014    8–5 (5–4)               Final Ranking: NR
        Beat Maryland 45-21 in the Foster Farms Bowl.

# Washington Huskies – Chris Petersen

## Coach Ranking: #19

**Overall Record:** 100-18 in 9 seasons
**Record at Washington:** 8-6 in 1 season
**2014 Results:** 8-6, 4-5 in the Pac-12 (3rd in the Pac-12 North)
**Returning Starters in 2015:** 6 on offense (including QB), 4 on defense
**Salary:** $3.7 Million     **Age:** 50     **Job Security Grade:** A

**COACH'S BIO:**
Chris Petersen grew up in Yuba City, California, and after playing for two seasons at a junior college, he transferred to UC Davis (Division II) and set multiple school records as a QB. He was an assistant coach at UC Davis from 1987-1991 and then spent one season as the QB coach for Pittsburgh under **Paul Hackett**. After two seasons as the QB coach at Portland State (Division II), **Mike Bellotti** hired Petersen to be Oregon's WR coach. Petersen spent six seasons at Oregon and was then hired by **Dan Hawkins** to be Boise State's offensive coordinator in 2001. When Hawkins left for the Colorado job in 2006, Petersen was promoted to head coach. In eight seasons at Boise State, he led the Broncos to 92 victories, five conference championships, and two BCS bowl victories. He was hired by Washington after the 2013 season. Petersen is the only two-time winner of the Bear Bryant Award for National Coach of the Year.

**2014 REVIEW:**
The transition from **Steve Sarkisian** to Chris Petersen was fairly smooth in 2014 as the Huskies won eight regular season games for the second-consecutive year. Washington hadn't done that since 2000-2001 under **Rick Neuheisel**.

| 2014 RESULTS:   8-6 (4-5 in the Pac-12) | Final Ranking: NR | |
|---|---|---|
| at Hawaii | W 17–16 | (36,411) |
| #2 (FCS) Eastern Washington | W 59–52 | (62,861) |
| Illinois | W 44–19 | (62,325) |
| Georgia State | W 45–14 | (64,608) |
| #16 Stanford | L 13–20 | (66,512) |
| at California | W 31–7 | (44,449) |
| at #9 Oregon | L 20–45 | (57,858) |
| #14 Arizona State | L 10–24 | (64,666) |
| at Colorado | W 38–23 | (35,633) |
| #18 UCLA | L 30–44 | (65,547) |
| at #17 Arizona | L 26–27 | (47,757) |
| Oregon State | W 37–13 | (65,036) |
| at Washington State | W 31–13 | (32,952) |
| vs. Oklahoma State (Cactus Bowl) | L 22–30 | (35,409) |

**OFFENSE:**

At Boise State, Chris Petersen earned a reputation for having an innovative offense. In Petersen's debut season at Washington, the explosiveness so common in Boise was missing in Seattle. The Huskies finished No. 9 in the Pac-12 in scoring and they tied at No. 10 in yards per game. Petersen and offensive coordinator **Jonathan Smith** (Petersen's QB coach at Boise State from 2012-2013) run a shotgun/pistol-heavy offense that can be complicated for new QBs to pick up. Petersen made the decision to simplify the offense midway through the 2014 season and progress was steadily made. During their final five games of the regular season, the Huskies averaged nearly 100 yards more per game than they averaged during their first eight games. At Boise State, Petersen's and Smith's offense ran the ball 55% of the time in 2012 and 2013. Last year at Washington, they ran it 60% of the time. The increased reliance on the running game was likely a result of simplifying the offense while also adapting to the personnel they inherited from **Steve Sarkisian**. The progress this offense made at the end of 2014 carried over into spring ball and Petersen is hoping Washington's offense in 2015 looks more like the offenses he had at Boise State. The biggest challenge this year will be replacing four starters along the offensive line.

**DEFENSE:**

Defensive coordinator **Pete Kwiatkowski** followed Petersen from Boise State and implemented a bend-but-don't-break 3-4 defense in his first year at Washington. His strategy worked well. Though Washington's defense did plenty of "bending" by giving up 411 yards a game, it didn't "break" when it mattered most and the Huskies finished No. 3 in the Pac-12 in points allowed. It'll take an outstanding coaching performance by Kwiatkowski to avoid a letdown in 2015 as the Huskies must replace seven starters on defense, including four All-Pac-12 players in the front seven.

**RECRUITING:**

Petersen's 2015 recruiting class was ranked No. 6 in the Pac-12 and No. 27 nationally. It included two four-star offensive tackles and the nation's No. 5-rated pro-style QB in **Jake Browning**, who enrolled early and could compete for the starting job this fall.

**RUMOR MILL:**

For years at Boise State, Petersen was rumored to be a leading candidate for high-profile job openings across the nation. In 2013, he was reportedly one of the top choices for USC as a replacement for **Lane Kiffin**, but Petersen withdrew from consideration after some initial talks. In an interesting chain of events, USC hired **Steve Sarkisian** from Washington and Petersen stepped in to fill Sarkisian's vacated spot with the Huskies.

**NOTEWORTHY:**

In his final four seasons at Boise State, Petersen faced a *total* of six ranked teams and went 4-2 in those games. Last year at Washington, he faced five ranked teams and went 0-5 against them.

**2015 OUTLOOK:**

**Sept. 4**    **at Boise State Broncos** – Petersen will kick off the season by returning to the blue carpet he called home for 13 years (eight years as head coach of the Broncos). Washington beat Boise State 38-6 in 2013, when Petersen was coaching there. The Huskies are 4-6 all-time against the MWC.

**Sept. 12**    **Sacramento State Hornets** – This FCS team went 7-5 last year.

**Sept. 19**    **Utah State Aggies** – While at Boise State, Petersen went 6-0 against Utah State and won those six games by an *average* of 34 points each. The Aggies went 10-4 last season.

**Sept. 26**    **California Golden Bears** – Washington has won six-straight games in this series, capped off by last year's 31-7 blowout.

**Oct. 8**    **at USC Trojans** – This Thursday-night showdown will pit new coach versus former coach as Petersen takes on Steve Sarkisian. If there's any bad blood about the way Sarkisian left UW, this will be the Huskies' opportunity for payback. For those reasons, and because Washington needs to knock off an upper-echelon Pac-12 team, this is Petersen's *MUST-WIN* game of the season. The Huskies are 2-9 against the Trojans since 2002. Petersen and Sarkisian are 1-1 against each other.

**Oct. 17**    **Oregon Ducks** – Washington has lost 11-straight games to this North Division rival. Petersen was 2-0 against Oregon while at Boise State, but lost to the Ducks for the first time last year. Petersen was Oregon's WR coach from 1995-2000.

**Oct. 24**    **at Stanford Cardinal** – Stanford's defense held Washington to a season-low 179 yards of total offense last year. The Huskies are 2-8 in their last 10 meetings with the Cardinal.

**Oct. 31**    **Arizona Wildcats** – Arizona kicked the game-winning FG with three seconds left to beat the Huskies last year. The home team has won the last seven games in this series.

**Nov. 7**    **Utah Utes** – This will be Petersen's first game against Utah as Washington's coach. At Boise State, he went 2-0 against the Utes, winning those games by a combined score of 62-6.

**Nov. 14**    **at Arizona State Sun Devils** – The Huskies have lost their last nine games in this series. Petersen is 1-1 against Arizona State with the one victory occurring while he was at Boise State in 2011.

**Nov. 21**    **at Oregon State Beavers** – Washington has won the last three games in this series. Petersen is 3-0 all-time against the Beavers.

**Nov. 27**    **Washington State Cougars** – The 108th Apple Cup will be played on the Friday after Thanksgiving. The Huskies have won five out of the last six in this rivalry.

**BOTTOM LINE:**
Petersen picked up exactly where Sarkisian left off with an eight-win season and a third-place finish in the North Division. The one-year honeymoon is over and expectations will turn up in 2015. Petersen knows this is a proud program hungry to return to the top of the Pac-12. While the Huskies may not be ready to take that big of a step just yet, a 10-win season for the first time since 2000 is the next rung on the ladder.

## Chris Petersen's Year-by-Year Coaching Record:

### Boise State: 92-12 (57-6 in the WAC and MWC)

2006  13–0 (8–0)          Final Ranking: #5
WAC Champions.
Petersen wins the Bear Bryant Award for National Coach of the Year.
Beat #10 Oklahoma 43-42 in the Fiesta Bowl.

2007  10–3 (7–1)          Final Ranking: NR
Lost to East Carolina 38-41 in the Hawaii Bowl.

2008  12–1 (8–0)          Final Ranking: #11
WAC Champions.
Lost to #11 TCU 16-17 in the Poinsettia Bowl.

2009  14–0 (8–0)          Final Ranking: #4
WAC Champions.
Petersen wins the Bear Bryant Award for National Coach of the Year.
Beat #3 TCU 17-10 in the Fiesta Bowl.

2010  12–1 (7–1)          Final Ranking: #7
WAC Co-Champions.
Petersen wins the Bobby Dodd Award for National Coach of the Year.
Beat #19 Utah 26-3 in the Las Vegas Bowl.

2011  12–1 (6–1)          Final Ranking: #6
Boise State leaves the WAC and joins the Mountain West Conference.
Beat Arizona State 56-24 in the Las Vegas Bowl.

2012  11–2 (7–1)          Final Ranking: #14
MWC Co-Champions.
Beat Washington 28-26 in the Las Vegas Bowl.

2013  8–4 (6–2)          Final Ranking: NR
Boise State lost to Oregon State 23-38 in the Hawaii Bowl, but Petersen had
already left to accept the Washington job.

### Washington: 8-6 (4-5 in the Pac-12)

2014  8-6 (4-5)          Final Ranking: NR
Lost to Oklahoma State 22-30 in the Cactus Bowl.

# Washington State Cougars – Mike Leach

## Coach Ranking: #33

**Overall Record:** 96-68 in 13 seasons
**Record at Washington State:** 12-25 in 3 seasons
**2014 Results:** 3-9, 2-7 in the Pac-12 (T-5th in the Pac-12 North)
**Returning Starters in 2015:** 7 on offense, 7 on defense
**Salary:** $2.75 Million      **Age:** 54      **Job Security Grade:** B

**COACH'S BIO:**

Mike Leach grew up in Cody, Wyoming, attended college at BYU, and originally planned on becoming a lawyer; but after earning his law degree from Pepperdine University, he couldn't shake his desire to coach football instead. He landed his first coaching job as an OL assistant at Cal Poly (Division II) in 1987. He then spent the 1988 season coaching LBs at College of the Desert (junior college) and the spring of 1989 as the head coach for Pori, Finland, in the European League. In 1989, he was hired by new head coach **Hal Mumme** at the tiny NAIA college of Iowa Wesleyan. Leach was named offensive coordinator and the two created what would become known as the "Air Raid" offense. Their success at Iowa Wesleyan led Leach and Mumme to tenures at Valdosta State (Division II) and then Kentucky in 1997. Leach parted ways with Mumme when **Bob Stoops** hired him to become Oklahoma's OC in 1999. Leach became Texas Tech's head coach in 2000. He led the Red Raiders to bowl games in all 10 of his seasons there and was named the Big 12 Coach of the Year in 2008. Amidst controversial allegations, Texas Tech fired Leach the day before he was due an $800,000 bonus in December of 2009. Washington State hired Leach to replace **Paul Wulff** after the 2011 season.

**2014 REVIEW:**

In 2013, Leach led Washington State to its first bowl game in 10 years, but back-to-back losses to open 2014 ruined any positive momentum the Cougars may have been carrying into the season. Leach's team could never get back on track and Wazzu took a surprising step back in 2014.

| 2014 RESULTS:   3-9 (2-7 in the Pac-12) | Final Ranking: NR | |
|---|---|---|
| vs. Rutgers (in Seattle) | L 38–41 | (30,927) |
| at Nevada | L 13–24 | (26,023) |
| Portland State | W 59–21 | (30,874) |
| #2 Oregon | L 31–38 | (32,952) |
| at Utah | W 28–27 | (45,859) |
| California | L 59–60 | (30,020) |
| at #25 Stanford | L 17–34 | (44,135) |
| #15 Arizona | L 37–59 | (32,952) |
| USC | L 17–44 | (25,012) |
| at Oregon State | W 39–32 | (44,377) |
| at #13 Arizona State | L 31–52 | (51,428) |
| Washington | L 13–31 | (32,952) |

**OFFENSE:**

Leach helped invent the Air Raid offense; an up-tempo, pass-first, pass-often, spread-formation offense that has worked its way throughout the college football world over the last 15 years. It's not surprising that Leach, widely considered one of the best offensive minds in football, is his own offensive coordinator and handles all the play-calling duties. In 2014, Washington State averaged 518 yards a game, which ranked No. 7 in the nation in total offense. However, racking up big yardage didn't always translate to big points. Despite having the Pac-12's second-most potent offense in terms of yards gained, Wazzu's 32 points a game ranked in the back-half of the conference in scoring. (During his final two seasons at Texas Tech, Leach's offense averaged 42 points a game.) A big reason for the discrepancy between yards and scoring was the almost nonexistent running game Washington State had last season. Though the Cougars had the nation's No. 1 pass offense, they had the nation's *worst* rushing offense. Leach has always favored the pass over the run (passing the ball 70% or more of the time), but his offense works best when there's at least *some* kind of rushing threat. His last two teams at Texas Tech rushed for an average of more than 1,300 yards a season. Wazzu rushed for just 478 yards in 2014. The running game was emphasized more in the spring and in 2015 you can expect to see more read-option and the QB taking some snaps from under center. The entire offensive line will be returning this year, which should also help the running game. If there's one thing you can count on from a Mike Leach offense, it's that whoever he starts at QB will put up big-time passing numbers.

**DEFENSE:**

After finishing No. 10 in the Pac-12 in points allowed each of the past three seasons, Leach is making some changes on defense. The Cougars finished 117th nationally in points allowed last year and Leach is replacing defensive coordinator **Mike Breske** and OLB coach **Paul Volero**. Both had arrived at Wazzu with Leach. The new DC is **Alex Grinch**, 36, who spent the last three seasons as **Gary Pinkel**'s safeties coach at Missouri. The new OLB coach is **Roy Manning**, 33, who spent the last two years coaching OLBs and CBs for **Brady Hoke** at Michigan. Grinch and Manning are younger coaches who bring a high-energy approach to the defense. The Cougars will continue to operate out of a 3-4 base defense, but they'll shift to four-man fronts and nickel packages based on what they see from the offense.

**RECRUITING:**

Leach's 2015 recruiting class was ranked No. 9 in the Pac-12 and No. 44 in the nation. Headlined by **Shalom Luani**, the nation's top-rated juco safety, this was Leach's highest-rated class since arriving at Washington State.

**RUMOR MILL:**

Leach's name comes up often as a candidate for head coach openings across the nation. In 2012, he was rumored to be a top candidate for the NC State job that went to **Dave Doeren** and last year he was linked to the Houston opening that went to **Tom Herman**. In both cases, Leach quickly shot down the rumors and reiterated that he was happy where he was. Washington State gave Leach a two-year contract extension in November of 2013. His current contract runs through the 2018 season.

**2015 OUTLOOK:**

**Sept. 5**  **Portland State Vikings** – Leach is 11-0 against FCS schools and the Cougars beat Portland State 59-21 last year.

**Sept. 12**  **at Rutgers Scarlet Knights** – Washington State gave up a fourth-quarter lead in last year's season-opening loss to Rutgers. This game should provide an early glimpse of whether the Wazzu running game has improved. Last year, the Cougars rushed for just 6 yards against the Scarlet Knights.

**Sept. 19**  **Wyoming Cowboys** – New Wazzu DC Alex Grinch coached Wyoming's secondary from 2009-2011. This will be Leach's first time coaching against his home-state college. The Cougars have lost three of their last four games against MWC opponents.

**Oct. 3**  **at California Golden Bears** – Fans who like to see the ball in the air will love this game. Last year, these teams combined for 1,261 passing yards in Cal's 60-59 win. Dykes was Leach's WR coach at Texas Tech from 2000-2006 and also served as Leach's co-OC in 2005 and 2006. With these two teams both trying to climb out of the bottom half of the North Division (and recruiting players for the same Air Raid offense), this is a *MUST-WIN* game for Leach and the Cougars.

**Oct. 10**  **at Oregon Ducks** – Leach is 0-3 against Oregon, but the margin has gotten tighter each season, culminating with last year's seven-point loss.

**Oct. 17**  **Oregon State Beavers** – Last year was Leach's first win over Oregon State and Wazzu should have the advantage again this year. The Beavers return just *two* starters on defense, tied for the fewest in the FBS.

**Oct. 24**  **at Arizona Wildcats** – Despite outgaining Arizona by nearly 100 yards last year, the Cougars found a way to lose this game by 22 points. Leach is 1-1 against Rich Rodriguez.

**Oct. 31**  **Stanford Cardinal** – Stanford's defense has held Leach's offense to just 17 points in all three previous meetings. Last year, the Cardinal held Wazzu to a season-low 266 yards and minus-26 rushing yards.

**Nov. 7**  **Arizona State Sun Devils** – Leach is 0-3 against Arizona State and he's lost those three games by an average of 31 points each.

**Nov. 14**  **at UCLA Bruins** – These teams last met in 2012, a game UCLA won 44-36.

**Nov. 21**  **Colorado Buffaloes** – When Colorado beat Washington State in 2012 (the last meeting between these schools), it was the Buffaloes' only win of the season. Dating back to his time at Texas Tech, Leach is 1-4 all-time against Colorado.

**Nov. 27**  **at Washington Huskies** – After beating Washington in 2012, Leach has lost the last two in this rivalry. The 108th Apple Cup will be played on the Friday after Thanksgiving.

**BOTTOM LINE:**
Leach's track record has earned the right to some patience in this rebuilding effort, but last year's 3-9 season was a surprising step backwards. Year 4 is a crucial year for new coaches as they now have their systems fully installed and a roster made up mostly of players they've recruited. Wazzu needs a bowl game in 2015.

## Mike Leach's Year-by-Year Coaching Record:

### Texas Tech: 84-43 (47-44 in the Big 12)

2000    7–6 (3–5)              Final Ranking: NR
        Lost to East Carolina 27-40 in the GallergyFurniture.com Bowl.
2001    7–5 (4–4)              Final Ranking: NR
        Lost to Iowa 16-19 in the Alamo Bowl.
2002    9–5 (5–3)              Final Ranking: NR
        Beat Clemson 55-15 in the Tangerine Bowl.
2003    8–5 (4–4)              Final Ranking: NR
        Beat Navy 38-14 in the Houston Bowl.
2004    8–4 (5–3)              Final Ranking: #17
        Beat #4 California 45-31 in the Holiday Bowl.
2005    9–3 (6–2)              Final Ranking: #19
        Lost to #13 Alabama 10-13 in the Cotton Bowl Classic.
2006    8–5 (4–4)              Final Ranking: NR
        Beat Minnesota 44-41 in OT in the Insight Bowl.
2007    9–4 (4–4)              Final Ranking: #22
        Beat #21 Virginia 31-28 in the Gator Bowl.
2008    11–2 (7–1)             Final Ranking: #12
        Big 12 South Division Co-Champions.
        Leach named Big 12 Coach of the Year.
        Leach wins the Woody Hayes Trophy for National Coach of the Year.
        Lost to #20 Ole Miss 34-47 in the Cotton Bowl Classic.
2009    8–4 (5–3)              Final Ranking: NR
        Texas Tech beat Michigan State 41-31 in the Alamo Bowl and finished the
        season ranked #21, but Leach was fired before the bowl game.

### Washington State: 12-25 (7-20 in the Pac-12)

2012    3–9 (1–8)              Final Ranking: NR
2013    6–7 (4–5)              Final Ranking: NR
        Lost to Colorado State 45-48 in the New Mexico Bowl.
2014    3–9 (2–7)              Final Ranking: NR

# Arizona Wildcats – Rich Rodriguez

## Coach Ranking: #32

**Overall Record:** 146-98–2 in 21 seasons (8 seasons in NAIA)
**Record at Arizona:** 26-14 in 3 seasons
**2014 Results:** 10-4, 7-2 in the Pac-12 (Pac-12 South Champions)
**Returning Starters in 2015:** 7 on offense (including QB), 5 on defense
**Salary:** $3.3 Million      **Age:** 52      **Job Security Grade:** A

**COACH'S BIO:**
Rich Rodriguez grew up in the small coal-mining town of Grant Town, West Virginia. He walked on to **Don Nehlen**'s West Virginia football team in 1981 and was a three-year letterwinner as a DB for the Mountaineers. He spent four years as an assistant coach before being named head coach at Salem University (NAIA) in 1988. He was just 24 at the time, which made him the nation's youngest college football coach, but the school discontinued its football program after his one season there. From 1990-1996, Rodriguez was the head coach at Glenville State (NAIA), where he won four conference titles and an NAIA National Coach of the Year award. In 1997, **Tommy Bowden** hired Rodriguez to be his offensive coordinator at Tulane and the two went to Clemson in 1999. West Virginia hired Rodriguez as its head coach in 2001 and he spent seven seasons guiding the Mountaineers to six bowl games and five Big East championships. Rodriguez shocked many college football fans when he left his alma mater for Michigan in 2008. He was fired after three seasons at Michigan and spent 2011 in the broadcast booth. In 2012, Rodriguez replaced **Mike Stoops** as the new head coach at Arizona.

**2014 REVIEW:**
In 2014, Arizona won its first Pac-12 South Division title and finished the year ranked for the first time since 1998. It was also the school's second 10-win season in program history. Rodriguez was named the Pac-12 Coach of the Year.

| **2014 RESULTS:** 10-4 (7-3 in the Pac-12) | Final Ranking: #17 | |
|---|---|---|
| UNLV | W 58–13 | (50,103) |
| at UTSA | W 26–23 | (33,472) |
| Nevada | W 35–28 | (48,504) |
| **California** | W 49–45 | (45,595) |
| **at #2 Oregon** | W 31–24 | (56,032) |
| **USC** | L 26–28 | (56,754) |
| **at Washington State** | W 59–37 | (32,952) |
| **at #25 UCLA** | L 7–17 | (80,246) |
| **Colorado** | W 38–20 | (50,177) |
| **Washington** | W 27–26 | (47,757) |
| **at #20 Utah** | W 42–10 | (45,824) |
| **#13 Arizona State** | W 42–35 | (56,083) |
| **vs. #3 Oregon** (Pac-12 Championship) | L 13–51 | (45,618) |
| **vs. #21 Boise State** (Fiesta Bowl) | L 30–38 | (66,896) |

**OFFENSE:**

Rodriguez is one of the creators of the modern spread-option offense. He was one of the first coaches to utilize the read option and emphasize the running game out of the no-huddle shotgun-spread formation. In recent years, Rodriguez has done a good job of adapting to his personnel – especially the running ability of his QB – in determining his run-to-pass ratio. After running the ball 63% of the time in 2013 (with QB **B.J. Denker** rushing for nearly 1,000 yards), Rodriguez balanced his offense at 50-50 between the run and the pass in 2014. As a freshman last season, QB **Anu Solomon** passed for 3,793 yards while rushing for 291 yards (a light rushing total for a typical spread-option dual-threat QB). The balanced approach resulted in an offense that averaged 34.5 points a game and ranked No. 30 nationally in scoring. Along with Solomon at QB, the Wildcats will also return last year's leading rusher (sophomore RB **Nick Wilson**) and leading receiver (junior WR **Cayleb Jones**), so they'll be in great shape at the skill positions. It's up front that will be a concern as Rodriguez must find new starters at center and at both offensive tackle spots. Rodriguez has two co-offensive coordinators, **Calvin Magee** and **Rod Smith**, but he handles the play-calling himself.

**DEFENSE:**

After 11 seasons at West Virginia (10 as the defensive coordinator), **Jeff Casteel** reunited with Rodriguez at Arizona in 2012. As the DC for the Wildcats, Casteel runs a unique 3-3-5 defense. This defense likes to stack ("hide") LBs behind the defensive linemen and then use blitzes and stunts to attack offensive gaps with those LBs. This scheme can be very confusing for an offense, but it can also be very risky for the defense. To be successful, this system depends heavily on the right calls from the DC. (If the DC picks the wrong gap to attack with one or more of his LBs, the defense will find itself way out of position.) Casteel, a two-time Broyles Award nominee (which goes to the top assistant coach in America), is a master with the 3-3-5 defense and the five-DB formation makes it an effective strategy against modern spread offenses. Arizona's defense had an up-and-down season last year. They had a nice stretch against Utah and Arizona State to close the regular season, but then gave up more than 600 yards against Oregon in the Pac-12 Championship. This squad needs to be more consistent if it wants to climb out of the back-half of the conference. In 2015, Casteel must replace six starters, including three DBs, but his defense will be anchored by junior LB **Scooby Wright III**, who led the nation in tackles and won the Nagurski, Lombardi, and Bednarik awards (all given to the nation's top defensive player) last season.

**RECRUITING:**

After signing large classes of 32 recruits in 2013 and 31 recruits in 2014, Arizona signed a standard 25 recruits in 2015. The class was ranked No. 42 in the nation.

**RUMOR MILL:**

Rodriguez was rumored to be a top candidate to replace **Charlie Strong** at Louisville after the 2013 season, but the Cardinals hired **Bobby Petrino** and Arizona gave Rodriguez a two-year contract extension. Rodriguez's name comes up often in high-profile coaching searches, but he continues to reiterate that he's happy at Arizona. His current contract runs through the 2019 season.

**2015 OUTLOOK:**

Sept. 3    **UTSA Roadrunners** – For the third year in a row, Arizona will face UTSA in the nonconference schedule. Rodriguez is 2-3 against Larry Coker and all three losses occurred when Coker was at Miami (FL) and Rodriguez was at West Virginia.

Sept. 12    **at Nevada Wolf Pack** – Rodriguez is 2-0 against Nevada since arriving at Arizona, but those two wins have been by a *total* of just eight points. Last year's loss to Boise State in the Fiesta Bowl broke Arizona's five-game winning streak against MWC teams.

Sept. 19    **Northern Arizona Lumberjacks** – The last time these teams played, in 2013, Arizona easily won 35-0. This FCS team went 7-5 last year.

Sept. 26    **UCLA Bruins** – Rodriguez is 0-3 against Jim Mora and the Bruins. Last year, UCLA held the Wildcats to 255 yards of total offense – the fewest yards gained in a game by Arizona since Rodriguez arrived in 2012.

Oct. 3    **at Stanford Cardinal** – The good news is that Arizona doesn't have to play Oregon from the North Division this year. The bad news is that Stanford replaces the Ducks on the schedule. Stanford has a three-game winning streak in this series. The last time these teams played (2012), the Cardinal squeaked by with a 54-48 OT win.

Oct. 10    **Oregon State Beavers** – Arizona is just 2-12 in its last 14 games against Oregon State. Rodriguez lost in his only game against the Beavers, 38-35 in 2012.

Oct. 17    **at Colorado Buffaloes** – Rodriguez is 3-0 against this South Division foe and last year's 18-point win was the closest of those three games.

Oct. 24    **Washington State Cougars** – Interestingly, the home team has *lost* the last three games in this series. Rodriguez is 1-1 against Mike Leach.

Oct. 31    **at Washington Huskies** – In this series, the home team has won the last seven-straight games. Rodriguez is 2-1 against Washington and 1-0 against Chris Petersen.

Nov. 7    **at USC Trojans** – Arizona is 2-11 against USC since 2001. One of those wins occurred in Rodriguez's debut season (2012). Rodriguez is 1-2 against Steve Sarkisian and both of those wins occurred while Sarkisian was at Washington.

Nov. 14    **Utah Utes** – Rodriguez is 3-1 against Kyle Whittingham and the Utes. The only loss occurred while Rodriguez was at Michigan in 2008.

Nov. 21    **at Arizona State Sun Devils** – Both Rodriguez and Todd Graham arrived at these archrival schools in 2012. Both have their programs on the rise and fighting for South Division titles. And both know this is a *MUST-WIN* game in 2015. Rodriguez is 1-2 so far against Graham.

**BOTTOM LINE:**
The Wildcats won one of the toughest divisions in all of college football last year despite losing to both USC and UCLA. The Wildcats can't rely on that type of luck again and they'll need to win one (or both) of their games against the L.A. schools if they want to repeat as South Division champs. It'll be interesting to see how Rodriguez and the Wildcats handle having a big target on their backs in 2015.

## Rich Rodriguez's Year-by-Year Coaching Record:

### Salem: 2-8 (0-0 in the NAIA Playoffs)
1988    2-8 (0-0)              Final Ranking: NA
Salem discontinued its football program after this season.

### Glenville State: 43-28-2 (0-0 in the NAIA Playoffs)
1990    1-7-1 (0-0)           Final Ranking: NA
1991    4-5-1 (0-0)           Final Ranking: NA
1992    6-4 (0-0)             Final Ranking: NA
1993    10-3 (2-1)            Final Ranking: NA
NAIA Runners-Up.
Rodriguez named NAIA National Coach of the Year.
Lost to East Central (OK) 35-49 in the NAIA Championship Game.
1994    8-3 (0-1)             Final Ranking: NA
Lost to Montana Western 38-48 in the NAIA Division I quarterfinals.
1995    8-2 (0-0)             Final Ranking: NA
1996    6-4 (0-0)             Final Ranking: NA

### West Virginia: 60-26 (34-14 in the Big East)
2001    3-8 (1-6)             Final Ranking: NR
2002    9-4 (6-1)             Final Ranking: #20
Lost to Virginia 22-48 in the Continental Tire Bowl.
2003    8-5 (6-1)             Final Ranking: NR
Big East Co-Champions.
Rodriguez named Big East Coach of the Year.
Lost to #24 Maryland 7-41 in the Gator Bowl.
2004    8-4 (4-2)             Final Ranking: NR
Big East Co-Champions.
Lost to #15 Florida State 18-30 in the Gator Bowl.
2005    11-1 (7-0)            Final Ranking: #5
Big East Champions.
Rodriguez named Big East Coach of the Year.
Beat #8 Georgia 38-35 in the Sugar Bowl.
2006    11-2 (5-2)            Final Ranking: #10
Beat #25 Georgia Tech 38-35 in the Gator Bowl.
2007    10-2 (5-2)            Final Ranking: #9
Big East Co-Champions.
West Virginia beat #3 Oklahoma 48-28 in the Fiesta Bowl, but Rodriguez had already left to accept the Michigan job. West Virginia finished the year ranked #6.

### Michigan: 15-22 (6-18 in the Big Ten)
2008    3-9 (2-6)             Final Ranking: NR
2009    5-7 (1-7)             Final Ranking: NR
2010    7-6 (3-5)             Final Ranking: NR
Lost to #21 Mississippi State 14-52 in the Gator Bowl.

## Arizona: 26-14 (15-12 in the Pac-12)

2012    8–5 (4–5)          **Final Ranking: NR**
Beat Nevada 49-48 in the New Mexico Bowl.

2013    8–5 (4–5)          **Final Ranking: NR**
Beat Boston College 42-19 in the AdvoCare V100 Bowl.

2014    10–4 (7–2)        **Final Ranking: #17**
Pac-12 South Division Champions.
Rodriguez named Pac-12 Coach of the Year.
Lost to #3 Oregon 13-51 in the Pac-12 Championship Game.
Lost to #21 Boise State 30-38 in the Fiesta Bowl.

# Arizona State Sun Devils – Todd Graham

## Coach Ranking: #31

**Overall Record:** 77-41 in 9 seasons
**Record at Arizona State:** 28-12 in 3 seasons
**2014 Results:** 10-3, 6-3 in the Pac-12 (T-2nd in the Pac-12 South)
**Returning Starters in 2015:** 7 on offense, 9 on defense
**Salary:** $2.7 Million      **Age:** 50      **Job Security Grade:** A

COACH'S BIO:
Todd Graham grew up in Mesquite, Texas, and was an all-state DB at North Mesquite High School. In college, he was a two-time NAIA All-American at East Central University (Oklahoma). From 1988-1990, Graham was a high school assistant coach in his hometown of Mesquite. He returned to East Central University as the defensive coordinator in 1991 and helped lead his alma mater to an NAIA National Championship. He spent the 1994 season as a high school head coach in Oklahoma and then began a six-year stint (1995-2000) as the head coach at Allen High School (Texas), where he led the previously-struggling program to five playoff berths. In 2001, **Rich Rodriguez** hired Graham to be his LB coach at West Virginia and promoted him to co-DC the following year. Graham served as **Steve Kragthorpe**'s DC at Tulsa from 2003-2005 and he was hired as head coach at Rice in 2006. Graham then spent four seasons (2007-2010) as Tulsa's head coach, where he won three C-USA West Division titles. He spent the 2011 season as the head coach at Pittsburgh, but left for Arizona State just one year later. Graham was named the Pac-12 Coach of the Year in 2013 after winning the South Division title.

2014 REVIEW:
Despite falling just short of repeating as Pac-12 South champions in 2014, Graham led the Sun Devils to 10 wins for the second year in a row. That hadn't happened at Arizona State since 1973. The Sun Devils finished 2014 in a three-way tie (with UCLA and USC) for second in one of the nation's toughest divisions.

| 2014 RESULTS: 10-3 (6-3 in the Pac-12) | Final Ranking: #12 | |
|---|---|---|
| Weber State | W 45–14 | (52,133) |
| at New Mexico | W 58–23 | (25,742) |
| at Colorado | W 38–24 | (38,547) |
| #11 UCLA | L 27–62 | (60,876) |
| at #16 USC | W 38–34 | (70,115) |
| #23 Stanford | W 26–10 | (59,012) |
| at Washington | W 24–10 | (64,666) |
| #18 Utah | W 19–16 OT | (53,754) |
| #8 Notre Dame | W 55–31 | (65,870) |
| at Oregon State | L 27–35 | (40,525) |
| Washington State | W 52–31 | (51,428) |
| at #12 Arizona | L 35–42 | (56,083) |
| vs. Duke (Sun Bowl) | W 36–31 | (47,809) |

**OFFENSE:**
**Mike Norvell** has three titles at Arizona State. He's the offensive coordinator, the QB coach, and the "deputy head coach." He originally joined Graham's staff in 2007 at Tulsa and he was Graham's OC at Pittsburgh. Norvell runs a two-back spread offense that prefers to have a QB with some mobility, but the QB doesn't need to be a featured runner in this system. Like so many coaches who implement the spread, Norvell runs it at a fast pace and without a huddle. In Norvell's system, the Sun Devils typically run the ball 60% of the time, but they were more balanced in 2014 (52% rushes, 48% passes). Arizona State slipped a bit in points per game last year (from 39.7 to 36.9), but the offense still ranked as one of the nation's Top 20 in scoring (for the third season in a row). The Sun Devils will have seven starters back on offense, including multi-talented RB **D.J. Foster**. Though they must replace three-year starter **Taylor Kelly** at QB, **Mike Bercovici** looked sharp when he stepped in for an injured Kelly last season. Norvell's offense always puts up big points and with plenty of talent returning, 2015 should be no different.

**DEFENSE:**
Graham faced a major test on defense in 2014 as the Sun Devils had to replace nine starters, eight of whom were All-Pac-12 players. To answer the challenge, Graham brought in his longtime friend and coaching colleague, **Keith Patterson**, to be the new co-defensive coordinator. Patterson and Graham were college teammates and have coached together on multiple high school and college staffs through the years. Patterson had spent 2012 and 2013 running West Virginia's defense. The other co-DC is **Chris Ball**, who arrived at ASU with Graham and was promoted to co-DC in 2013. Despite the huge personnel losses, Arizona State managed to finish near the middle of the Pac-12 in most defensive categories and led the conference in interceptions last year. The Sun Devils run a unique 3-4-4 base defense that confuses offenses with its multiple looks. With nine starters back, the defense will go from being a major question mark heading into 2014 to a major strength for this team in 2015.

**RECRUITING:**
Arizona State landed eight four-star prospects on its way to signing the nation's 20th-ranked recruiting class. The class was ranked No. 4 in the Pac-12 and it was the school's highest-rated recruiting class since 2008. As recruiting efforts pick up, one gets the sense that Graham is on his way to building a Pac-12 dynasty at ASU.

**RUMOR MILL:**
Arizona State's deputy head coach and OC, Mike Norvell, is considered one of the nation's top assistant coaches in line for a head coaching position. As he continues to lead high-powered offenses with the Sun Devils, don't be surprised to see this 33-year-old coach moving on to a head coaching job soon.

**NOTEWORTHY:**
Arizona State gave Graham a one-year contract extension and a $300,000 raise following the 2013 season. Graham's contract currently runs through the 2018 season. If Graham takes Arizona State to the Pac-12 Championship Game, he'll earn a $270,000 bonus.

## 2015 OUTLOOK:

**Sept. 5**    **vs. Texas A&M Aggies (in Houston)** – When Graham was at Tulsa and Kevin Sumlin was at Houston, Graham went 1-2 against Sumlin. Though this is considered a "neutral site" game, the Sun Devils know they'll be walking into a very pro-Aggie environment. Arizona State is 0-4 all-time against the SEC.

**Sept. 12**   **Cal Poly Mustangs** – Graham is 7-0 all-time against FCS schools. Cal Poly went 7-5 last year.

**Sept. 18**   **New Mexico Lobos** – Graham is 3-0 against New Mexico and he's won those three games by an average of 37 points each.

**Sep. 26**    **USC Trojans** – Opening up Pac-12 play with a win over USC would go a long way toward winning the South Division. Arizona State beat USC with a 46-yard Hail Mary TD pass as time expired last season. That brought Graham's record to 2-1 against USC and 2-0 against Sarkisian.

**Oct. 3**     **at UCLA Bruins** – Graham is 1-2 against Jim Mora, but his lone victory occurred the last time the Sun Devils traveled to the Rose Bowl (2013). Arizona State had 4 turnovers and UCLA had none in last year's lopsided win for the Bruins.

**Oct. 10**    **Colorado Buffaloes** – Arizona State is 4-0 against Colorado since the Buffaloes joined the Pac-12 in 2011. The Sun Devils have won those four games by an average of 31 points each.

**Oct. 17**    **at Utah Utes** – Graham is 3-1 against Kyle Whittingham. The one loss occurred in 2011 when Graham was coaching Pittsburgh.

**Oct. 29**    **Oregon Ducks** – This Thursday-night showdown could be a preview of the Pac-12 Championship Game. The last time these teams played, Oregon won 43-21 during Graham's first season at ASU (2012).

**Nov. 7**     **at Washington State Cougars** – Washington State outgained Arizona State 622-330 yards in last year's game, but the Sun Devils capitalized off of 5 turnovers and beat the Cougars by 21 points. Graham is 3-0 against Mike Leach and he's won those games by an average of 31 points each.

**Nov. 14**    **Washington Huskies** – Arizona State has won nine-straight games in this series. Dating back to his time at Tulsa, Graham is 1-1 against Chris Petersen.

**Nov. 21**    **Arizona Wildcats** – This is quickly becoming one of the nation's must-watch rivalries. Last year, this game was for the South Division championship and that may be the case again this year. Graham was Rodriguez's LB coach and co-DC at West Virginia. This is a *MUST-WIN* game for Graham, who is 2-1 against the Wildcats.

**Nov. 28**    **at California Golden Bears** – These teams last played in 2012, when Arizona State broke a four-game losing streak to the Bears.

## BOTTOM LINE:
Arizona State will once again be one of the most dangerous teams in the tough Pac-12 South Division. We'll know early on just how good this team is as the Sun Devils must face Texas A&M, USC, and UCLA within the first five weeks of the season. If Graham can survive that stretch and make it to 5-0, this team could make a run right into the College Football Playoff.

## Todd Graham's Year-by-Year Coaching Record:

### Rice: 7-6 (6-2 in Conference USA)
2006    7-6 (6-2)          Final Ranking: NR
Graham named C-USA Coach of the Year.
Lost to Troy 17-41 in the New Orleans Bowl.

### Tulsa: 36-17 (22-12 in Conference USA)
2007    10–4 (6–3)        Final Ranking: NR
Conference USA West Division Champions.
Lost to UCF 25-44 in the C-USA Championship Game.
Beat Bowling Green 63-7 in the GMAC Bowl.
2008    11–3 (7–2)        Final Ranking: NR
Conference USA West Division Champions.
Lost to East Carolina 24-27 in the C-USA Championship Game.
Beat #22 Ball State 45-13 in the GMAC Bowl.
2009    5–7 (3–5)        Final Ranking: NR
2010    10–3 (6–2)        Final Ranking: #24
Conference USA West Division Co-Champions.
Beat #25 Hawaii 62-35 in the Hawaii Bowl.

### Pittsburgh: 6-6 (4-3 in Big East)
2011    6–6 (4–3)        Final Ranking: NR
Pittsburgh lost to SMU 6-28 in the BBVA Compass Bowl, but Graham had already left to accept the Arizona State job.

### Arizona State: 28-12 (19-8 in Pac-12)
2012    8–5 (5–4)        Final Ranking: NR
Beat Navy 62-28 in the Fight Hunger Bowl.
2013    10–4 (8–1)        Final Ranking: #20
Pac-12 South Division Champions.
Graham named Pac-12 Coach of the Year.
Lost to #7 Stanford 14-38 in the Pac-12 Championship Game.
Lost to Texas Tech 23-37 in the Holiday Bowl.
2014    10–3 (6–3)        Final Ranking: #12
Beat Duke 36-31 in the Sun Bowl.

# Colorado Buffaloes – Mike MacIntyre

## Coach Ranking: #83

**Overall Record:** 22-39 in 5 seasons
**Record at Colorado:** 6-18 in 2 seasons
**2014 Results:** 2-10, 0-9 in the Pac-12 (6th in the Pac-12 South)
**Returning Starters in 2015:** 7 on offense (including QB), 9 on defense
**Salary:** $2 Million      **Age:** 50      **Job Security Grade:** C

**COACH'S BIO:**
Mike MacIntyre's father, **George MacIntyre**, was the head coach at Vanderbilt from 1979-1985 and he was the Bobby Dodd Coach of the Year in 1982. Mike played for his father during the 1984 and 1985 seasons at Vanderbilt, but transferred to Georgia Tech when his father resigned from Vandy. Mike started coaching in 1990 and worked his way up with notable stops under **Ray Goff** at Georgia (1990-1991), **David Cutcliffe** at Ole Miss (1999-2002), **Bill Parcells** with the Dallas Cowboys (2003-2006), and **Eric Mangini** with the New York Jets (2007). MacIntyre reunited with Cutcliffe as Duke's defensive coordinator from 2008-2009 and was named the AFCA Assistant Coach of the Year in 2009. In 2010, MacIntyre became the head coach at San Jose State, a team that had gone 2-10 the year before he arrived. By his third season there, MacIntyre led the Spartans to a 10-2 record and a Top-25 ranking. He was hired by Colorado to replace **Jon Embree** after the 2012 season.

**2014 REVIEW:**
Though not long ago it was one of the nation's elite programs, Colorado hasn't had a winning season since 2005. MacIntyre's 4-8 debut season in 2013 gave fans hope that this program was headed back to its winning ways. However, the Buffs took a disappointing step back in 2014 and failed to win a conference game for the first time since 1915.

| 2014 RESULTS:   2-10 (0-9 in the Pac-12) | Final Ranking: NR | |
|---|---|---|
| vs. Colorado State (in Denver) | L 17–31 | (63,363) |
| at Massachusetts | W 41–38 | (10,227) |
| #16 Arizona State | L 24–38 | (38,547) |
| Hawaii | W 21–12 | (39,478) |
| at California | L 56–59 2OT | (39,821) |
| Oregon State | L 31–36 | (36,415) |
| at #22 USC | L 28–56 | (74,756) |
| #25 UCLA | L 37–40 2OT | (37,442) |
| Washington | L 23–38 | (35,633) |
| at #21 Arizona | L 20–38 | (50,177) |
| at #3 Oregon | L 10–44 | (55,898) |
| Utah | L 34–38 | (39,155) |

**OFFENSE:**

When MacIntyre and offensive coordinator **Brian Lindgren** came to Colorado from San Jose State, they brought with them a pistol-based offense that had racked up 35 points a game with the Spartans. However, the Buffaloes have now transitioned into a more traditional shotgun-spread offense that includes plenty of read option. Colorado has made steady offensive progress since MacIntyre arrived. The Buffs went from averaging 17.8 points a game in 2012 to 25.4 points a game in 2013 to 28.5 points a game in 2014. Though Colorado still ranks in the bottom-half of the nation in scoring, progress is being made. With junior **Sefo Liufau** returning for his third season as the starting QB and six other offensive starters, progress should continue to be made for this offense. To reach its potential, this offense needs to establish a reliable rushing attack. Despite running the ball 45% of the time last year, the Buffs finished 77th nationally in rushing yards.

**DEFENSE:**

Since joining the Pac-12 in 2011, Colorado has ranked last or next-to-last in the conference every year in points allowed. Last year, the Buffs finished 119th in the nation in points allowed. MacIntyre has seen enough and he's replacing defensive coordinator **Kent Baer** (who he brought with him from San Jose State) with **Jim Leavitt**. This is a big hire for the Buffs. Leavitt was South Florida's head coach from 1996-2009 and he spent the last four seasons as **Jim Harbaugh**'s LB coach with the San Francisco 49ers. You can expect to see multiple defensive looks from Leavitt in 2015. Colorado ran a 4-3 under Baer and Leavitt ran a 4-3 when he was at South Florida, but he was working out of a 3-4 in San Francisco. In the spring, Leavitt experimented with a 4-3, 3-4, and 4-2-5 in an effort to find the right fit for the personnel he's inheriting. Leavitt is known for having one of the best defensive minds in the game and for being a very demanding coach. His first order of business is to bring a hard-working, tough-minded attitude to Colorado's defense, which has nine starters returning in 2015.

**RECRUITING:**

Perpetual losing and a desperate need for facilities upgrades have hampered Colorado's recruiting efforts over the past few years. The Buffs have landed the Pac-12's lowest-ranked recruiting class each of the past three seasons. The good news for Colorado is that a $156 million facilities upgrade is underway. This project will take the program from having some of the worst facilities in the conference to having some the best, which should make a big impact on recruiting.

**RUMOR MILL:**

The job MacIntyre did at San Jose State warrants patience at Colorado, but that patience is wearing thin for a fan base that is tired of losing. Previous head coach **Jon Embree** was fired after just two seasons. Coach MacIntyre can't afford another step backwards in 2015.

**NOTEWORTHY:**

The hiring of new DC Jim Leavitt was criticized by some this offseason. Leavitt was fired from South Florida following an ugly situation in 2009 when he was accused of striking a player during halftime of a game. Leavitt denied the accusation.

**2015 OUTLOOK:**

**Sept. 3**    **at Hawaii Rainbow Warriors** – Dating back to his time at San Jose State, MacIntyre is 2-1 against Hawaii. Since 2012, Colorado is 2-3 against MWC teams.

**Sept. 12**    **Massachusetts Minutemen** – Last year was UMass' first season in the FBS. The Minutemen went 3-9.

**Sept. 19**    **vs. Colorado State Rams (in Denver)** – These teams have traded victories each year since 2011, which means Colorado is due for a win if that trend continues. If MacIntyre hopes to turn the corner and have a winning season, he *MUST WIN* this rivalry game over first-year head coach Mike Bobo. Dating back to his time at San Jose State, MacIntyre is 3-1 against Colorado State.

**Sept. 26**    **Nicholls State Colonels** – This FCS team went 0-12 last year. Colorado has a decent shot at going 4-0 in the nonconference schedule, which would go a long way toward bowl eligibility.

**Oct. 3**    **Oregon Ducks** – Since joining the Pac-12 in 2011, Colorado has lost all four games against Oregon by a combined score of 216-42.

**Oct. 10**    **at Arizona State Sun Devils** – Despite outgaining Arizona State by 119 yards last year, the Buffs couldn't overcome three turnovers in their 38-24 loss.

**Oct. 17**    **Arizona Wildcats** – Colorado has lost three-straight games to Arizona. Last year's 18-point loss was the closest of those three losses.

**Oct. 24**    **at Oregon State Beavers** – MacIntyre went 0-3 against Gary Anderson when Anderson was at Utah State and MacIntyre was at San Jose State.

**Oct. 31**    **at UCLA Bruins** – The Buffs scored 17 fourth-quarter points to send this game into OT last year, but the Bruins pulled off the win in double OT.

**Nov. 7**    **Stanford Cardinal** – Colorado lost to Stanford 48-0 the last time these teams played, in 2012.

**Nov. 13**    **USC Trojans** – Colorado is still looking for its first win over USC. The Buffs are 0-9 all-time against the Trojans.

**Nov. 21**    **at Washington State Cougars** – The last time these teams played (2012), Colorado's win over Washington State was the Buffaloes' only win of the year.

**Nov. 28**    **at Utah Utes** – Last year, Utah returned an interception in the fourth quarter to beat Colorado for the third year in a row. The last time Colorado beat Utah, in 2011, marked the last time the Buffs won a South Division game.

**BOTTOM LINE:**
MacIntyre enters 2015 on a seat that is warming up. Drawing both Oregon and Stanford from the North Division makes the road to a bowl game even tougher for Colorado, but having a manageable nonconference schedule and a 13th game (an allowed extra game due to the fact that they travel to Hawaii) gives the Buffs a better chance to reach the six wins required for bowl eligibility. At the very least, MacIntyre needs to win five games in order to give Colorado fans some sense that the program is moving in the right direction.

## Mike MacIntyre's Year-by-Year Coaching Record:

<u>San Jose State: 16-21 (8-13 in the WAC)</u>
| 2010 | 1–11 (0–8) | Final Ranking: NR |
| 2011 | 5–7 (3–4) | Final Ranking: NR |
| 2012 | 10–2 (5–1) | Final Ranking: #24 |

San Jose State beat Bowling Green 29-20 in the Military Bowl, but MacIntyre had already left to accept the Colorado job. San Jose State finished the year ranked #21.

<u>Colorado: 22-39 (1-17 in the Pac-12)</u>
| 2013 | 4–8 (1–8) | Final Ranking: NR |
| 2014 | 2–10 (0–9) | Final Ranking: NR |

# UCLA Bruins – Jim Mora

## Coach Ranking: #27

**Overall Record:** 29-11 in 3 seasons, 31-33 in 4 NFL seasons
**Record at UCLA:** 29-11 in 3 seasons
**2014 Results:** 10-3, 6-3 in the Pac-12 (T-2$^{nd}$ in the Pac-12 South)
**Returning Starters in 2015:** 10 on offense, 8 on defense
**Salary:** $3.25 Million    **Age:** 53    **Job Security Grade:** A

**COACH'S BIO:**
Jim Mora has followed in the footsteps of his father, **Jim Mora, Sr.**, who is best known for his coaching stints with the NFL's New Orleans Saints and Indianapolis Colts. After playing four years at Washington, the younger Mora immediately joined **Don James'** staff with the Huskies as a graduate assistant in 1984. He then started working his way up the NFL coaching ranks with stops at San Diego, New Orleans, and San Francisco. He was named head coach of the Atlanta Falcons in 2004 and led his team to the NFC Championship his first season there. He was fired after three seasons and then served as defensive coordinator for the Seattle Seahawks in 2007 and 2008. In 2009, Mora was promoted to head coach of the Seahawks, but he was fired after one season. After two years in the broadcast booth, Mora returned to the sidelines when UCLA hired him to replace **Rick Neuheisel** after the 2011 season.

**2014 REVIEW:**
UCLA entered 2014 with a No. 7 preseason ranking, but fell out of the rankings with back-to-back losses in early October. Mora regrouped his team and had the Bruins playing for a Pac-12 South title heading into its regular season finale against Stanford. Though the Cardinal's victory over UCLA kept the Bruins out of the Pac-12 Championship, the season ended on a high note with an Alamo Bowl victory over Kansas State. UCLA finished the season ranked in the Top 10 for the first time since 1998.

| 2014 RESULTS:   10-3 (6-3 in the Pac-12) | Final Ranking: #10 | |
|---|---|---|
| at Virginia | W 28-20 | (44,749) |
| Memphis | W 42-35 | (72,098) |
| vs. Texas (in Arlington, TX) | W 20-17 | (60,479) |
| at #15 Arizona State | W 62-27 | (60,876) |
| Utah | L 28-30 | (74,329) |
| #12 Oregon | L 30-42 | (80,139) |
| at California | W 36-34 | (49,257) |
| at Colorado | W 40-37 2OT | (37,442) |
| #14 Arizona | W 17-7 | (80,246) |
| at Washington | W 44-30 | (65,547) |
| #24 USC | W 38-20 | (82,431) |
| Stanford | L 10-31 | (70,658) |
| vs. #11 Kansas State (Alamo Bowl) | W 40-35 | (60,517) |

**OFFENSE:**
When Mora arrived at UCLA, he brought in **Noel Mazzone** to be his offensive coordinator. Mazzone is a spread-offense expert who teaches what he calls the "NZone Spread Offensive System" to high school coaches all over the nation. He runs a tough-minded version of the spread offense that emphasizes a physical running game. The Bruins run the ball 55%-60% of the time in Mazzone's system and they've averaged 35 points a game over the past three seasons. Last year, UCLA had the No. 2 rushing offense in the Pac-12. This year, the Bruins return 10 offensive starters (the most in the Pac-12), but they must replace QB **Brett Hundley**, who is leaving for the NFL after three years as UCLA's starter. There's a four-man competition for the starting QB spot and whoever emerges as the starter will be surrounded by experienced talent.

**DEFENSE:**
Mora brought a defensive mentality to UCLA and the Bruins have steadily improved on defense each year since he arrived. In yards allowed, they finished eighth in the Pac-12 in 2012, fifth in 2013, and third last year. For the third season in a row, Mora will be bringing in a new defensive coordinator in 2015. The new DC is **Tom Bradley**, who spent 12 seasons as Penn State's DC under **Joe Paterno** and served as Penn State's interim head coach for four games after Paterno was fired during the 2011 season. He then spent two years in the broadcast booth before returning to coaching last season as the DL coach at West Virginia. Bradley ran a 4-3 defense for years at Penn State, but he coached in West Virginia's 3-3-5 last season. The Bruins expect a smooth transition from the 3-4 they've previously been based out of to a multiple look this season. The UCLA defense ran plenty of four-man-front nickel packages last season against spread offenses and they should be comfortable operating out of Bradley's new scheme. Two-time All-Pac-12 LB **Myles Jack** leads a group of eight returning starters on this squad.

**RECRUITING:**
Mora landed another big-time recruiting class in 2015. It featured three five-star prospects and was ranked No. 2 in the Pac-12 and No. 12 in the nation. The 2015 class included the nation's No. 1-rated pro-style QB, **Josh Rosen**, who enrolled early and is expected to compete for the starting job this fall.

**RUMOR MILL:**
In December of 2013, rumors were flying that Mora might be headed to his alma mater, Washington, but UCLA stepped up and signed Mora to a six-year contract extension while promising to give his assistants raises and improve UCLA's facilities. Washington ended up hiring **Chris Petersen**. Mora's current contract runs through the 2019 season.

**NOTEWORTHY:**
Mora has guided the Bruins to nine or more wins in each of his three seasons at UCLA. That marks the first time in program history that UCLA has won nine or more games in three-consecutive seasons.

**2015 OUTLOOK:**

**Sept. 5**    **Virginia Cavaliers** – The Bruins relied on three defensive TDs to beat Virginia in a close game last year.

**Sept. 12**    **at UNLV Rebels** – UCLA is 10-4 all-time against the MWC. This will be the first-ever meeting between these two programs.

**Sept. 19**    **BYU Cougars** – The Bruins are 7-3 all-time against BYU, but the last time these teams played, the Cougars embarrassed UCLA with a 59-0 win in 2008.

**Sept. 26**    **at Arizona Wildcats** – Mora is 3-0 against Arizona. Last year, the Bruins had one of their best defensive performances in this game by holding Rich Rodriguez's high-powered offense to just 255 yards and a season-low seven points.

**Oct. 3**    **Arizona State Sun Devils** – Current Bruins OC Noel Mazzone was Arizona State's OC for the two seasons prior to arriving at UCLA in 2012. The Bruins gave up a season-high 626 yards in this game last year, but still managed to win the game by 35 points. Mora is 2-1 against Arizona State.

**Oct. 15**    **at Stanford Cardinal** – Mora is 0-4 against Stanford and last year's 31-10 loss ended up costing the Bruins a trip to the Pac-12 Championship. Mora needs to find a way to reverse his losing streak against the Cardinal.

**Oct. 22**    **California Golden Bears** – This will be the second of two-straight Thursday-night games for UCLA. The home team is 13-2 in this series since 2000.

**Oct. 31**    **Colorado Buffaloes** – Last year's double-OT win over brought Mora's record to 3-0 against Colorado.

**Nov. 7**    **at Oregon State Beavers** – The last time these two teams met, Oregon State handed Mora a 27-20 loss in his debut season at UCLA (2012).

**Nov. 14**    **Washington State Cougars** – UCLA has won five-straight games in this series. The last time these teams met, the Bruins won 44-36 in 2012.

**Nov. 21**    **at Utah Utes** – Last year's 30-28 Utah win was Mora's first loss to this South Division foe. This hard-fought game has been decided by a TD or less in each the past three seasons.

**Nov. 28**    **at USC Trojans** – Mora is 3-0 against UCLA's cross-town archrival, but this should be the best USC team he has faced. It's likely that the Pac-12 South Division title will be decided here, which makes this Mora's *MUST-WIN* game of the season.

**BOTTOM LINE:**
Coming off back-to-back 10-win seasons and with 18 starters returning, UCLA looks poised to take the next step. The Pac-12 South Division should once again be one of the toughest divisions in the country, but if the Bruins can find the right QB on offense and if the defense can transition smoothly to Tom Bradley's system, this team should be fighting for the South Division title when they face USC in the regular-season finale. Winning the Pac-12 would likely mean a spot in the College Football Playoff.

## Jim Mora's Year-by-Year Coaching Record:

<u>Atlanta Falcons: 26-22 (1-1 in the NFL Playoffs)</u>
2004   11-5 (1-1)                **NFC South Champions**
       Mora named NFC Coach of the Year.
       Lost to Philadelphia 10-27 in the NFC Championship Game.
2005   8-8 (0-0)                **3rd in the NFC South**
2006   7-9 (0-0)                **3rd in the NFC South**

<u>Seattle Seahawks: 5-11 (0-0 in the NFL Playoffs)</u>
2009   5-11 (0-0)               **3rd in the NFC West**

<u>UCLA: 29-11 (18-9 in the Pac-12)</u>
2012   9–5 (6–3)                **Final Ranking: NR**
       Pac-12 South Division Champions.
       Lost to #8 Stanford 24-27 in the Pac-12 Championship Game.
       Lost to Baylor 26-49 in the Holiday Bowl.
2013   10–3 (6–3)               **Final Ranking: #16**
       Beat Virginia Tech 42-12 in the Sun Bowl.
2014   10–3 (6–3)               **Final Ranking: #10**
       Beat #11 Kansas State 40-35 in the Alamo Bowl.

# USC Trojans – Steve Sarkisian

## Coach Ranking: #38

**Overall Record:** 43-33 in 6 seasons
**Record at USC:** 9-4 in 1 season
**2014 Results:** 9-4, 6-3 in the Pac-12 (T-2nd in the Pac-12 South)
**Returning Starters in 2015:** 7 on offense (including QB), 7 on defense
**Salary:** $3.75 Million*     **Age:** 41     **Job Security Grade:** B

**COACH'S BIO:**
Steve Sarkisian grew up in Torrance, California, and originally enrolled at USC to play baseball. After a semester with the Trojan baseball team, he transferred to El Camino Junior College, where he played football and baseball. He was a juco All-American QB at El Camino, which led to a two-year career at BYU. He was named the WAC Offensive Player of the Year as a senior in 1996. After three seasons playing in the CFL, Sarkisian became the QB coach at El Camino in 2000. He was hired by **Pete Carroll** to join USC's staff in 2001. He helped lead the Trojans to the National Championship as QB coach in 2003 and then spent one season as the QB coach of the Oakland Raiders under **Norv Turner**. Sarkisian returned to USC in 2005 and worked his way up to offensive coordinator in 2007. Washington hired Sarkisian to be its head coach in 2009. Sarkisian took over a Washington team that had gone 0-12 the year before he arrived. He led the Huskies to four bowl games in five years. He was hired by USC after the 2013 season to replace **Lane Kiffin** (and interim head coach **Ed Orgeron**).

**2014 REVIEW:**
It was a roller-coaster of a debut season for Sarkisian at USC. The Trojans entered the year ranked No. 15, but Sarkisian found his seat warming up fast after USC suffered an ugly loss to cross-town rival UCLA and fell to 7-4. However, Sarkisian rebounded with a blowout win over Notre Dame and then capped off the year by leading the Trojans to their first bowl victory over a Power 5 team since 2009.

| 2014 RESULTS:   9-4 (6-3 in the Pac-12) | Final Ranking: #20 | |
|---|---|---|
| Fresno State | W 52–13 | (76,037) |
| at #13 Stanford | W 13–10 | (50,814) |
| at Boston College | L 31–37 | (41,632) |
| Oregon State | W 35–10 | (74,521) |
| Arizona State | L 34–38 | (70,115) |
| at #10 Arizona | W 28–26 | (56,754) |
| Colorado | W 56–28 | (74,756) |
| at #19 Utah | L 21–24 | (47,619) |
| at Washington State | W 44–17 | (25,012) |
| California | W 38–30 | (64,615) |
| at #11 UCLA | L 20–38 | (82,431) |
| Notre Dame | W 49–14 | (79,586) |
| vs. #25 Nebraska (Holiday Bowl) | W 45–42 | (55,789) |

## OFFENSE:

When Sarkisian accepted the USC job, he retained **Clay Helton** to continue as the offensive coordinator. Helton had been USC's QB coach since 2010 and he was promoted to OC by previous head coach **Lane Kiffin** before the 2013 season. He also served as USC's interim head coach for the 2013 Las Vegas Bowl victory. Even though Helton stayed on as the OC, Sarkisian handles the play-calling duties and the Trojans dramatically changed their offense last season. USC transitioned from a pro-style West Coast system under Kiffin to the no-huddle shotgun-spread offense Sarkisian wants to implement. The Trojans picked up the pace in 2014, running 15% more plays per game. This up-tempo approach led to more points as USC improved from No. 60 nationally in scoring under Kiffin to No. 23 under Sarkisian last year. Senior QB **Cody Kessler** will be back for his third season as the starter and all five offensive linemen are returning as well. USC's 2015 offense should be one of the nation's Top 20 scoring offenses (which is where Sarkisian had Washington's offense in his final season there).

## DEFENSE:

Sarkisian brought **Justin Wilcox** with him to serve as defensive coordinator. Wilcox had been Sarkisian's DC at Washington in 2012 and 2013. Last year, he transitioned the Trojans from the 5-2 hybrid defense they were running under previous DC **Clancy Pendergast** to a 3-4 hybrid scheme. The defensive systems aren't all that different from a personnel perspective as they both rely on versatile outside LBs who can play on the line or off of it as needed. Philosophically, however, Wilcox seems to favor a bend-but-don't-break style of defense. The result was that although USC gave up 73 more yards a game last year under Wilcox than they did under Pendergast in 2013, they didn't suffer a dramatic drop in points allowed (they went from allowing 21.2 points a game in 2013 to 25.2 points a game in 2014). It's also important to point out that a faster-moving offense forces the defense to defend more plays. The Trojans allowed just 0.3 more yards per *play* in 2014. This year's defense has seven starters back, but Wilcox must replace three All-Pac 12 players in the front seven. That won't be easy, but a second season in Wilcox's system should mean a better overall defensive performance for the Trojans in 2015.

## RECRUITING:

Sarkisian carried his end-of-the-year momentum onto the recruiting trail and landed a monster class in 2015. The Trojans signed the nation's No. 2-ranked recruiting class. It included four five-star prospects, which tied USC with Florida State's four and was second only to Alabama's six. Sarkisian has quickly proven that his staff can reel in the nation's elite-level recruits.

## RUMOR MILL:

Three-straight 7-6 seasons at Washington had some impatient UW fans referring to Sarkisian as "Seven Win Sark" and that unflattering nickname reemerged in 2014 after an ugly loss to UCLA dropped USC's record to 7-4. However, Sarkisian answered his critics with two big wins to close out the year. New hires will always be second-guessed and Sarkisian is well aware of the giant expectations at USC. It seems clear that he is operating with very little room for error in 2015 and beyond.

**2015 OUTLOOK:**

**Sept. 5**    **Arkansas State Red Wolves** – This will be USC's first-ever game against a Sun Belt Conference opponent. Arkansas State went 7-6 last year.

**Sept. 12**    **Idaho Vandals** – This will be USC's second-ever game against a Sun Belt Conference opponent as the Trojans ease into the 2015 season. Idaho has gone 2-21 over the past two seasons.

**Sept. 19**    **Stanford Cardinal** – USC has defeated Stanford by three points each of the last two seasons. Dating back to his time at Washington, Sarkisian is 2-4 against the Cardinal and both those wins occurred after David Shaw became head coach at Stanford in 2011.

**Sept. 26**    **at Arizona State Sun Devils** – Sarkisian is 0-4 against Arizona State and USC has lost three of its last four against the Sun Devils.

**Oct. 8**    **Washington Huskies** – This Thursday-night showdown will match Sarkisian against his former team. Sarkisian and Chris Petersen went 1-1 against each other when Sarkisian was at Washington and Petersen was at Boise State.

**Oct. 17**    **at Notre Dame Fighting Irish** – Last year's win over Notre Dame broke USC's two-game losing streak in this historic rivalry. The Trojans have won 10 of the last 13 against the Irish, but all three losses have occurred since Brian Kelly arrived at Notre Dame in 2010.

**Oct. 24**    **Utah Utes** – Last year, Utah scored in the final seconds to beat USC for the first time since joining the Pac-12. Sarkisian is 2-1 against Kyle Whittingham.

**Oct. 31**    **at California Golden Bears** – Though the Trojans ended up winning this game 38-30 last year, they were up 31-9 at halftime. Sarkisian is a perfect 6-0 against Cal.

**Nov. 7**    **Arizona Wildcats** – The Trojans held the Wildcats to just 77 yards rushing in last year's 28-26 win. That marked the fewest rushing yards gained by Arizona since Rich Rodriguez arrived with his spread-option offense. Sarkisian is 2-0 against Rodriguez.

**Nov. 13**    **at Colorado Buffaloes** – USC is 9-0 all-time against Colorado. Since the Buffaloes joined the Pac-12 in 2011, the Trojans have won this annual game by an average score of 49-20.

**Nov. 21**    **at Oregon Ducks** – These final two games could make-or-break USC's season. Sarkisian is 0-5 all-time against Oregon. These teams last met in 2012 and the Ducks have won three of the last four meetings.

**Nov. 28**    **UCLA Bruins** – USC has lost three-straight games in this rivalry and Sarkisian is 0-2 against Jim Mora. The Pac-12 South Division title may be on the line in this *MUST-WIN* game for Sarkisian.

**BOTTOM LINE:**
After the first two games of the season, USC will face one of the toughest schedules in the country. The Trojans must play the top two teams in the Pac-12 North (Stanford and Oregon), a loaded Notre Dame team, and four South Division opponents that finished last season ranked. USC has the *starting* talent (maybe not the depth, yet) to compete for a spot in the College Football Playoff, but the brutal schedule will make it very tough for this team to win 10 or more games.

## Steve Sarkisian's Year-by-Year Coaching Record:

### Washington: 34-29 (24-21 in the Pac-12)
2009   5–7 (4–5)         **Final Ranking: NR**
2010   7–6 (5–4)         **Final Ranking: NR**
       Beat #16 Nebraska 19-7 in the Holiday Bowl.
2011   7–6 (5–4)         **Final Ranking: NR**
       Lost to #15 Baylor 56-67 in the Alamo Bowl.
2012   7–6 (5–4)         **Final Ranking: NR**
       Lost to #20 Boise State 26-28 in the Las Vegas Bowl.
2013   8–4 (5–4)         **Final Ranking: NR**
       Washington beat BYU 31-16 in the Fight Hunger Bowl, but Sarkisian had already left to accept the USC job. Washington finished the year ranked #25.

### USC: 9-4 (6-3 in the Pac-12)
2014   9-4 (6-3)         **Final Ranking: #20**
       Beat #25 Nebraska 45-42 in the Holiday Bowl.

# Utah Utes – Kyle Whittingham

## Coach Ranking: #40

**Overall Record:** 85-43 in 10 seasons
**Record at Utah:** 85-43 in 10 seasons
**2014 Results:** 9-4, 5-4 in the Pac-12 (5th in the Pac-12 South)
**Returning Starters in 2015:** 7 on offense (including QB), 7 on defense
**Salary:** $2.6 Million      **Age:** 55      **Job Security Grade:** B

COACH'S BIO:
Kyle Whittingham was raised in Provo, Utah, and played LB at BYU. As a senior in 1981, he was named the WAC Defensive Player of the Year. Whittingham spent three years in the NFL and USFL before starting his coaching career as a graduate assistant at BYU in 1985. He spent the 1987 season as the defensive coordinator at Eastern Utah (junior college) and was then hired as the LB coach at Idaho State (Division 1-AA) in 1988. Whittingham was promoted to DC at Idaho State in 1992 and spent two seasons in that role. In 1994, Whittingham's father, **Fred Whittingham** (who was Utah's DC at the time), hired him to become the DL coach for the Utes. Fred left for an NFL position in 1995 and Kyle was promoted to DC by Utah head coach **Ron McBride**. When **Urban Meyer** became Utah's head coach in 2003, he retained Whittingham as DC and Whittingham was promoted to head coach when Meyer left for Florida in 2005. Whittingham was named the National Coach of the Year after finishing the 2008 season undefeated.

2014 REVIEW:
After back-to-back losing seasons and facing a schedule that included a road trip to Michigan and games against Oregon and Stanford from the Pac-12 North, there were many who thought 2014 might be Whittingham's last at Utah. Instead, Whittingham proved his doubters wrong by pulling off several upsets and leading the Utes to a Top-20 finish for the first time since 2009.

**2014 RESULTS:    9-4 (5-4 in the Pac-12)**          **Final Ranking: #20**

| | | |
|---|---|---|
| Idaho State | W 56–14 | (45,925) |
| Fresno State | W 59–27 | (45,864) |
| at Michigan | W 26–10 | (103,890) |
| **Washington State** | L 27–28 | (45,859) |
| **at #8 UCLA** | W 30–28 | (74,329) |
| **at Oregon State** | W 29–23 2OT | (40,479) |
| **#20 USC** | W 24–21 | (47,619) |
| **at #15 Arizona State** | L 16–19 OT | (53,754) |
| **#5 Oregon** | L 27–51 | (47,528) |
| **at Stanford** | W 20–17 2OT | (44,635) |
| **#15 Arizona** | L 10–42 | (45,824) |
| **at Colorado** | W 38–34 | (39,155) |
| vs. Colorado State (Las Vegas Bowl) | W 45–10 | (33,067) |

**OFFENSE:**

Utah's offense has been stuck in the back-half of the Pac-12 since joining the conference in 2011. Whittingham tried to shake things up last year by demoting 2013's co-offensive coordinators, **Dennis Erickson** and **Brian Johnson**, and hiring former Wyoming head coach and Missouri OC **Dave Christenson** to take over the offense. Christensen made slight improvements in scoring (the Utes rose from 10th in the Pac-12 to eighth), but Utah couldn't retain him as OC and Christensen has left to become the OL coach and running game coordinator at Texas A&M. For 2014, Whittingham will go back to using co-OCs in **Aaron Roderick** and **Jim Harding**, who were both promoted from within. This will be the eighth change at OC in Whittingham's 11 years here. Roderick and Harding will be trying to rev up Utah's spread-option offense and having RB **Devontae Booker** back (who almost went pro after rushing for 1,512 yards last season) and six other returning starters should make their job a little easier. Still, it's hard to expect a lot from an offense that has been stuck near the bottom of the Pac-12 for the past four years.

**DEFENSE:**

Whittingham has built his program on defense and for the past six years, **Kalani Sitake** has been the defensive coordinator leading Utah's 4-3/Nickel defense. However, Utah is losing Sitake to **Gary Anderson**'s new staff at Oregon State. Following Sitake to the Beavers is DL coach **Ilaisa Tuiaki**. These are two big blows to Whittingham's staff. In 2014, the Utes led the nation in sacks and they had the Pac-12's second-best defense in yards allowed, behind only Stanford. For his new DC, Whittingham convinced veteran pro and college coach **John Pease** to come out of retirement after spending the last four years out of coaching. Pease last worked as Utah's DL coach in 2010. Seven starters return and no major schematic changes are expected, but it will be interesting to see how the Utes respond to a new DC calling the shots.

**RECRUITING:**

Utah's 2015 recruiting class was ranked No. 10 in the Pac-12 and No. 45 nationally. This was a solid step up compared to the 2014 class, which was ranked No. 67.

**RUMOR MILL:**

Whittingham entered 2014 on the hot seat and despite going 9-4, rumors about his future with Utah spilled into the offseason. There was rampant speculation in December that Whittingham was leaving Utah largely because of tension with athletic director **Chris Hill**. After both coordinators, Sitake and Christensen, left the program following the bowl game, it looked like Whittingham would soon be following. Not only was he mentioned as a potential candidate for the nation's most notable openings at the time – Pittsburgh, Wisconsin, and Michigan – but there was also speculation that Whittingham would return to his alma mater, BYU. (Those rumors picked up steam despite the fact that BYU already has a 10-year head coach of its own in **Bronco Mendenhall**.) In the end, Whittingham and Hill came to terms on a new contract. Whittingham signed a four-year extension that included a $400,000 raise and runs through the 2018 season. Despite the fresh contract extension, it's hard to disregard all the speculation about Whittingham's shaky future with the Utes.

**2015 OUTLOOK:**

**Sept. 3**    **Michigan Wolverines** – The nation will be watching this Thursday-night showdown as it marks Jim Harbaugh's debut game as Michigan's head coach. It's also the first time the Wolverines will be playing *at* Utah. Whittingham is 2-0 against Michigan with wins in 2008 and 2014.

**Sept. 11**    **Utah State Aggies** – Whittingham is 6-1 in this in-state series. The last time these teams played, the Utes won 30-26 in 2013. Utah State went 10-4 last year.

**Sept. 19**    **at Fresno State Bulldogs** – Last year's 59-27 Utah win was the first game between these two schools since 1999. Fresno State won the MWC West Division last year. Utah is 3-0 against the MWC since leaving the conference in 2011.

**Sept. 26**    **at Oregon Ducks** – This is a tough way to open up Pac-12 play. Whittingham is 0-3 against this North Division opponent.

**Oct. 10**    **California Golden Bears** – Whittingham is 2-1 against Cal, but this will be his first time coaching against Sonny Dykes' "Bear Raid" offense.

**Oct. 17**    **Arizona State Sun Devils** – Arizona State has won all four games in this series since Utah joined the Pac-12 in 2011, but the last two games were decided by a *total* of just four points. Whittingham is 1-3 against Todd Graham and the one win occurred while Graham was coaching Pittsburgh in 2011.

**Oct. 24**    **at USC Trojans** – Utah scored a TD in the final seconds to beat USC last year. It was Utah's first win against the Trojans since joining the Pac-12.

**Oct. 31**    **Oregon State Beavers** – The Utes will see some familiar faces on the Oregon State sidelines this year. Previous DC Kalani Sitake and DL coach Ilaisa Tuiaki are now on Oregon State's staff. Whittingham is 3-3 against Oregon State.

**Nov. 7**    **at Washington Huskies** – Whittingham is 0-2 against Washington and he went 0-2 against Chris Petersen when Petersen was coaching Boise State.

**Nov. 14**    **at Arizona Wildcats** – The Utes have lost three-straight games in this South Division series. Whittingham is 1-2 against Rich Rodriguez, with the one win occurring while Rodriguez was at Michigan in 2008.

**Nov. 21**    **UCLA Bruins** – Utah beat UCLA with a FG in the final minute of the game last year. It was Whittingham's first win against Jim Mora. Whittingham is now 3-3 against UCLA.

**Nov. 28**    **Colorado Buffaloes** – Whittingham is 3-1 in the "Rumble in the Rockies" series. His only loss occurred in 2011. Whittingham is 3-0 against Mike MacIntyre. With the difficult schedule Utah is facing, the Utes may be fighting for a bowl berth in this season finale. That makes this a *MUST-WIN* game for Whittingham.

**BOTTOM LINE:**
Whittingham pulled out two double-OT wins and two last-minute wins in 2014. He'll need a lot more of that magic in 2015 as this team faces another tough schedule and must adjust to new coordinators on both sides of the ball. It'll be difficult for Utah to avoid taking a step back this season.

## Kyle Whittingham's Year-by-Year Coaching Record:

<u>Utah: 85-43 (49-35 in the Mountain West and Pac-12)</u>

2004   1-0 (0-0)          Final Ranking: #4
Whittingham was the co-head coach with Urban Meyer (who was in the process of leaving for the Florida job) in Utah's 35-7 win over #20 Pittsburgh in the Fiesta Bowl.

2005   7-5 (4-4)          Final Ranking: NR
Beat #24 Georgia Tech 38-10 in the Emerald Bowl.

2006   8-5 (5-3)          Final Ranking: NR
Beat Tulsa 25-13 in the Armed Forces Bowl.

2007   9-4 (5-3)          Final Ranking: NR
Beat Navy 35-32 in the Poinsettia Bowl.

2008   13-0 (8-0)         Final Ranking: #2
Mountain West Conference Champions.
Whittingham named National Coach of the Year.
Whittingham named Mountain West Conference Coach of the Year.
Beat #4 Alabama 31-17 in the Sugar Bowl.

2009   10-3 (6-2)         Final Ranking: #18
Beat California 37-27 in the Poinsettia Bowl.

2010   10-3 (7-1)         Final Ranking: #23
Lost to #10 Boise State 3-26 in the Las Vegas Bowl.

2011   8-5 (4-5)          Final Ranking: NR
Utah leaves the Mountain West Conference and joins the Pac-12.
Beat Georgia Tech 30-27 in OT in the Sun Bowl.

2012   5-7 (3-6)          Final Ranking: NR
2013   5-7 (2-7)          Final Ranking: NR
2014   9-4 (5-4)          Final Ranking: #20
Beat Colorado State 45-10 in the Las Vegas Bowl.

For instant coaching news, the latest coaching rumors, and some great motivation from college football's greatest coaches, follow us on Twitter at:

# @CoachesAlmanac

# 2015 SEC PREVIEW

## Five Things You Need to Know about the SEC in 2015:

**The Battle at the Top:** It may hard to believe, but the SEC West, top-to-bottom, should be even better in 2015 than it was in 2014. In the projected standings below, a strong case could be made for any of the top six teams in the West winning the division and landing in the College Football Playoff. With so much competition, this could be a year where the division winner emerges with two losses. With **Tennessee** on the rise, the SEC East race is also looking more competitive.

**New to the SEC:** Florida's hiring of **Jim McElwain** may not have wowed the college football world, but he has an outstanding resume and proved he could build a winner quickly at **Colorado State**.

**Coaches on the Rise:** **Butch Jones** at **Tennessee** and **Brett Bielema** at **Arkansas** both have their programs improving quickly. These two teams look ready to take the next step and could make some big noise in their division races this year.

**Keep an Eye On:** **Gus Malzahn** at **Ole Miss** and **Kevin Sumlin** at **Texas A&M** have realized that offense alone isn't enough to win consistently in the SEC. This offseason, they went out and hired two of the best defensive coordinators in the game. Malzahn hired **Will Muschamp** and Sumlin convinced **John Chavis** to leave LSU. It'll be very interesting to see how quickly these DCs can make an impact at two programs that need instant results on the defensive side of the ball.

**Coaches on the Hot Seat:** Overall, the SEC has a roster of coaches that are very secure heading into 2015. The lone exception is **Derek Mason** at **Vanderbilt**. Everyone knew he was walking into a tough situation replacing **James Franklin**, but a complete 180 from nine wins to nine *losses* puts him on the hot seat in Year 2 of his tenure.

## 2015 Projected Standings for the SEC:

**East Division:**
1. Georgia
2. Tennessee
3. Missouri
4. South Carolina
5. Kentucky
6. Florida
7. Vanderbilt

**West Division:**
1. Alabama
2. Auburn
3. LSU
4. Ole Miss
5. Arkansas
6. Texas A&M
7. Mississippi State

# Ranking the SEC's Coaches:

1. **Nick Saban** – Alabama (177-59-1 in 19 seasons)
2. **Les Miles** – LSU (131-50 in 14 seasons)
3. **Mark Richt** – Georgia (136-48 in 14 seasons)
4. **Gus Malzahn** – Auburn (29-10 in 3 seasons)
5. **Steve Spurrier** – South Carolina (226-85-2 in 25 seasons)
6. **Gary Pinkel** – Missouri (186-103-3 in 24 seasons)
7. **Kevin Sumlin** – Texas A&M (63-28 in 7 seasons)
8. **Hugh Freeze** – Ole Miss (54-22 in 6 seasons)
9. **Brett Bielema** – Arkansas (78-39 in 9 seasons)
10. **Dan Mullen** – Mississippi State (46-31 in 6 seasons)
11. **Butch Jones** – Tennessee (62-40 in 8 seasons)
12. **Jim McElwain** – Florida (22-16 in 3 seasons)
13. **Mark Stoops** – Kentucky (7-17 in 2 seasons)
14. **Derek Mason** – Vanderbilt (3-9 in 1 season)

# 2014 SEC Coach of the Year:
(Selected by the SEC coaches)
Gary Pinkel, Missouri

# 2014 SEC Standings:

| East Division | (Conference) | (All Games) |
| --- | --- | --- |
| #5 Florida State | 8-0 | 13-1 |
| #14 Missouri | 7-1 | 11-3 |
| #9 Georgia | 6-2 | 10-3 |
| Florida | 4-4 | 7-5 |
| Tennessee | 3-5 | 7-6 |
| South Carolina | 3-5 | 7-6 |
| Kentucky | 2-6 | 5-7 |
| Vanderbilt | 0-8 | 3-9 |
| | | |
| West Division | | |
| #4 Alabama | 7-1 | 12-2 |
| #11 Mississippi State | 6-2 | 10-3 |
| #17 Ole Miss | 5-3 | 9-4 |
| #22 Auburn | 4-4 | 8-5 |
| LSU | 4-4 | 8-5 |
| Texas A&M | 3-5 | 8-5 |
| Arkansas | 2-6 | 7-6 |

*Championship Game*: Alabama 42, Missouri 13

**2014 SEC Bowl Record:** 7-5 (3rd place among all 10 conferences)

# Florida Gators – Jim McElwain

## Coach Ranking: #41

**Overall Record:** 22-16 in 3 seasons
**2014 Results:** Florida went 7-5, 4-4 in the SEC (3rd in the SEC East)
At Colorado State, McElwain went 10-2, 6-2 in the MWC
**Returning Starters in 2015:** 4 on offense (including QB), 6 on defense
**Salary:** $3.5 Million     **Age:** 52     **Job Security Grade:** B

**COACH'S BIO:**

Jim McElwain grew up in Missoula, Montana, where he was an all-state quarterback in high school. He played quarterback in college at Eastern Washington (Division 1-AA) from 1980-1983 and returned to his alma mater as a graduate assistant coach in 1985. He remained on the staff until 1994. McElwain then rose up the coaching ranks with notable stops as Michigan State's assistant head coach under **John L. Smith** (2003-2005), the QB coach for the Oakland Raiders under **Art Shell** (2006), and offensive coordinator at Alabama under **Nick Saban** from 2008-2011, helping Bama win two National Championships. He was the head coach at Colorado State from 2012-2014 and turned around the struggling program, which had won just three games in each of the three seasons prior to McElwain's arrival. He improved Colorado State each year with four wins, eight wins, and then 10 wins last year.

**2014 REVIEW:**

**Will Muschamp** entered his fourth season as the head coach of the Gators coming off a miserable 4-8 campaign in 2013. The Gators stumbled out of the gate with a 3-3 start that included a blowout loss to Missouri at home. Muschamp was fired after the loss to South Carolina, but finished out the regular season and nearly knocked off top-ranked Florida State. Meanwhile, Jim McElwain was busy leading Colorado State to its first 10-win season since **Sonny Lubick's** 2002 squad. The Gators won the Birmingham Bowl with interim head coach **D.J. Durkin**.

| 2014 RESULTS:   7-5 (4-4 in the SEC) | Final Ranking: NR | |
|---|---|---|
| Idaho | Canceled | (N/A) |
| Eastern Michigan | W 65-0 | (81,049) |
| **Kentucky** | W 36-30 3OT | (88,334) |
| **at #3 Alabama** | L 21-42 | (101,821) |
| **at Tennessee** | W 10-9 | (102,455) |
| **LSU** | L 27-30 | (88,014) |
| **Missouri** | L 13-42 | (89,117) |
| **vs. #9 Georgia** (in Jacksonville) | W 38-20 | (83,004) |
| **at Vanderbilt** | W 34-10 | (35,191) |
| **South Carolina** | L 20-23 OT | (85,088) |
| #14 (FCS) Eastern Kentucky | W 52-3 | (83,399) |
| at #1 Florida State | L 19-24 | (82,485) |
| vs. East Carolina (Birmingham Bowl) | W 28-20 | (30,083) |

**OFFENSE:**

Will **Muschamp** was fired largely because his offense was unable to rack up big points, but it's worth noting that last year's Gators averaged more points per game than SEC foes like Ole Miss, Missouri, and LSU. Still, the program expected more firepower. Incoming head coach Jim McElwain built explosive offenses at Colorado State. His Rams averaged 497.8 yards a game last season, the best in the Mountain West Conference. McElwain says he'll strive for balance with a multiple-set offense at Florida, but his first priority is adapting to the talent he has. In other words, he plans to play to his team's strengths, whether that be in the running or passing game. With just four starters back on offense, it may be tough to find many strengths early in the season. McElwain's offensive coordinator will be **Doug Nussmeier**, who filled that role at Michigan last year and at Alabama from 2012-2013.

**DEFENSE:**

Muschamp is a brilliant defensive coach and it will be tough to live up to the standards he set on this side of the ball. However, McElwain pulled off a very impressive hire by bringing in **Geoff Collins** as his defensive coordinator. Collins spent the last four seasons as Mississippi State's DC. His "Psycho Defense" at Mississippi State ranked 10th nationally in points allowed last year. McElwain also hired former Miami (FL) head coach **Randy Shannon** to be his associate head coach, co-defensive coordinator, and LB coach. Shannon spent the last two seasons as associate head coach and LB coach at Arkansas. Together, Collins and Shannon will transition Florida from Muschamp's 3-4/4-3 blend to an attacking 4-3 defense. With six starters returning and plenty of talent, the defense should be solid as long as the transition to the new scheme and staff goes smoothly.

**RECRUITING:**

For a school that has grown accustomed to signing recruiting classes that rank in the Top 10 nationally, signing the No. 10-ranked class in the *conference* was a major disappointment. However, a new head coach's first recruiting class is always a challenge. McElwain still reeled in two five-star prospects on Signing Day and ended up with a class that ranked just outside the nation's Top 20.

**RUMOR MILL:**

Gator fans will need to be patient during McElwain's first season as it will be one of transition on both sides of the ball. One thing is certain: this staff will need to sign a monster recruiting class in 2016. Even when Muschamp's teams struggled on the field, he still managed to recruit elite-level talent.

**NOTEWORTHY:**

McElwain says his time under **Nick Saban** at Alabama taught him what it takes to build a great football program, beyond just the Xs and Os. Based on McElwain's fast turnaround at Colorado State, it would appear that Saban did indeed pass along some of the secrets to building a successful program. With a new regime, a vital factor for success is getting the players to buy into the new vision quickly. He was able to do that at Colorado State.

## 2015 OUTLOOK:

**Sept. 5**  **New Mexico State Aggies** – The Gators open the season at home against a Sun Belt team that went 2-10 last year.

**Sept. 12**  **East Carolina Pirates** – This is a rematch of last year's Birmingham Bowl, a game the Gators won 28-20 with an interim head coach.

**Sept. 19**  **Kentucky Wildcats** – A win to open SEC play would show the players are buying into the new staff's vision. A loss here would send Gator fans into a panic. Florida hasn't lost to Kentucky since 1986, but the Wildcats are improving under Mark Stoops.

**Sept. 26**  **Tennessee Volunteers** – During his four-year tenure, Muschamp never lost to Tennessee. McElwain will try to keep that winning streak going against a Tennessee team on the rise.

**Oct. 3**  **Ole Miss Rebels** – These schools haven't played each other since 2008, when Ole Miss gave Urban Meyer's Gators the only loss of their National Championship season.

**Oct. 10**  **at Missouri Tigers** – If there was a single game that sealed Muschamp's fate, last year's 42-13 loss to Mizzou in Gainesville was it. Florida has now lost two-straight games to the Tigers. A win here would send a message to the SEC East that things are changing at Florida. That makes this a *MUST-WIN* game for McElwain and the Gators.

**Oct. 17**  **LSU Tigers** – The Gators have lost the last two games against their cross-division rivals.

**Oct. 31**  **vs. Georgia Bulldogs (in Jacksonville)** – Florida's win over Georgia cost the Bulldogs the SEC East title last year. The Bulldogs will be gunning for revenge in 2015. Prior to last year's victory, Florida had lost three in a row to Georgia.

**Nov. 7**  **Vanderbilt Commodores** – The Gators are 23-1 in their last 24 meetings with Vandy.

**Nov. 14**  **at South Carolina Gamecocks** – South Carolina head coach Steve Spurrier has won the last two games against Florida, his alma mater, but his overall record is an even 5-5 in this series.

**Nov. 21**  **Florida Atlantic Owls** – The Owls will be highly-motivated to knock off an in-state Power 5 school, but Florida is *much* more talented and shouldn't have trouble with this Sun Belt team.

**Nov. 28**  **Florida State Seminoles** – Florida State has owned this rivalry in recent years, winning four of the last five matchups.

## BOTTOM LINE:

Gator fans aren't in a patient mood, but it will likely take some time for Florida to transition into the program McElwain wants it to become. That doesn't mean this team should be content with mediocrity in 2015. Though the Gators may not be ready to win an East Division title just yet, there's enough talent stockpiled here that anything less than matching last year's seven wins will be a disappointment for McElwain's debut season.

## Jim McElwain's Year-by-Year Coaching Record:

**Colorado State: 22-16 (14-10 in the Mountain West)**
2012   4-8 (3-5)          **Final Ranking: NR**
2013   8-6 (5-3)          **Final Ranking: NR**
        Beat Washington State 48-45 in the New Mexico Bowl.
2014   10-2 (6-2)         **Final Ranking: #21**
        McElwain named MWC Coach of the Year.
        Colorado State lost to #23 Utah 10-45 in the Las Vegas Bowl and finished the season unranked, but McElwain had already left to accept the Florida job.

# Georgia Bulldogs – Mark Richt

## Coach Ranking: #7

**Overall Record:** 136-48 in 14 seasons
**Record at Georgia:** 136-48 in 14 seasons
**2014 Results:** 10-3, 6-2 in the SEC (2nd in the SEC East)
**Returning Starters in 2015:** 7 on offense, 5 on defense
**Salary:** $4 Million          **Age:** 54          **Job Security Grade:** A

**COACH'S BIO:**
Born in Omaha, Nebraska, Mark Richt was a high school quarterback in Boca Raton, Florida. In college, he was the backup quarterback to **Jim Kelly** at Miami (FL), where **Howard Schnellenberger** was head coach. He graduated in 1982 and served as a graduate and volunteer assistant coach for **Bobby Bowden** at Florida State from 1985-1988. After one season as the offensive coordinator at East Carolina, Richt returned to Florida State as the QB coach in 1990 and was promoted to OC in 1994. At Florida State, Richt coached two Heisman Trophy-winning QBs, **Charlie Ward** and **Chris Weinke**, and helped the Seminoles win two National Championships (1993 and 1999). He left FSU to become the head coach at Georgia in 2001.

**2014 REVIEW:**
After a disappointing injury-laden 8-5 season in 2013, Georgia bounced back and finished 2014 ranked once again in the Top 10. The midseason loss to rival Florida ended up costing the Bulldogs the SEC East title, which went to Missouri, a team Georgia whipped 34-0 in Columbia. An overtime loss at home to in-state rival Georgia Tech ruined any shot at a New Year's Six bowl game, but Richt rallied his team for an impressive win over No. 20 Louisville to close out the year. The 2014 season marked Coach Richt's eighth Top-10 finish in 14 years.

**2014 RESULTS:  10-3 (6-2 in the SEC)**          **Final Ranking: #9**

| | | |
|---|---|---|
| #16 Clemson | W 45–21 | (92,746) |
| at #24 South Carolina | L 35–38 | (84,232) |
| Troy | W 66–0 | (92,746) |
| Tennessee | W 35–32 | (92,746) |
| Vanderbilt | W 44–17 | (92,746) |
| at #23 Missouri | W 34–0 | (71,168) |
| at Arkansas (in Little Rock) | W 45–32 | (54,959) |
| vs. Florida (in Jacksonville) | L 20–38 | (83,004) |
| at Kentucky | W 63–31 | (60,152) |
| #9 Auburn | W 34–7 | (92,746) |
| Charleston Southern | W 55–9 | (92,746) |
| #16 Georgia Tech | L 24–30 OT | (92,746) |
| vs. #20 Louisville (Belk Bowl) | W 37–14 | (45,671) |

**OFFENSE:**
Georgia relies on a run-first pro-style offense that operates mostly out of traditional two-back and shotgun sets. Despite having to replace record-breaking QB **Aaron Murray**, Georgia led the SEC in scoring last season. It was the running game that carried the load and even though RB **Todd Gurley** missed half the season due to injuries and a suspension, freshman **Nick Chubb** stepped up and rushed for more than 1,500 yards. The Bulldogs ran the ball 63% of the time in 2014. With Gurley headed to the NFL, Chubb is expected to carry the ball even more this year. Four returning starters on the o-line should help the running game thrive again. A big staff shakeup will be a key storyline to watch in 2015. After spending all 14 years on Richt's Georgia staff (and eight as the offensive coordinator), **Mike Bobo** left to accept the head coaching position at Colorado State. After such a long and successful run together, it'll be interesting to see how the Georgia offense handles its transition to a new OC. Richt hired **Brian Schottenheimer**, who has spent the last nine years as an offensive coordinator in the NFL for the Jets and Rams, as Bobo's replacement. Richt calls Schottenheimer's NFL background "a perfect fit" for the offensive style he wants at Georgia. After spending the last 14 years on NFL sidelines, how smoothly Schottenheimer's transition to the college game goes will determine whether this offense can maintain its high level of play.

**DEFENSE:**
After serving as the defensive coordinator for Florida State's National Championship team in 2013, **Jeremy Pruitt** became Georgia's DC last year. His results were outstanding. Pruitt's 3-4/4-3 hybrid defense took the Bulldogs from an abysmal 79th in points allowed in 2013 to 16th in 2014. The Bulldogs also finished the season ranked No. 4 nationally in turnover margin. This impressive performance will be tough to duplicate in 2015 with just five defensive starters returning (and no returning starters on the d-line), but perhaps Pruitt has what it takes to make Georgia a top-rated defense for years to come.

**RECRUITING:**
Mark Richt has had no trouble bringing in stellar recruiting classes and his 2015 class ranked in the Top 10 for the second year in a row. This year's class quickly addressed a need area for the Bulldogs. Richt signed one five-star-rated and *five* four-star-rated defensive line prospects.

**RUMOR MILL:**
Richt's seat was warming up after his 8-5 season in 2013, but he quieted that talk with an impressive rebound and another Top-10 finish. Georgia gave Richt a two-year extension and a raise this past offseason. His contract now runs through the 2019 season. While it's difficult to complain about a coach who regularly churns out 10-win seasons, if there's one thing Richt hasn't done yet, it's put together a *complete* season. For whatever reason, it seems that the Bulldogs find a way to lose one or two games a year that they shouldn't. Florida was the prime example from 2014.

**2015 OUTLOOK:**

**Sept. 5**    **Louisiana-Monroe Warhawks** – Though ULM is 1-16 all-time against ranked opponents, they did knock off Arkansas in 2012 and barely lost to Texas A&M 21-16 last year.

**Sept. 12**    **at Vanderbilt Commodores** – Richt is 12-2 against Vandy and that trend shouldn't be changing any time soon.

**Sept. 19**    **South Carolina Gamecocks** – Steve Spurrier gave Richt one of his two SEC East losses last year and the Bulldogs will be looking for revenge in 2015. Richt is 8-6 against the Gamecocks.

**Sept. 26**    **Southern University Jaguars** – Richt has never lost to an FCS school and that streak should remain intact with this game.

**Oct. 3**    **Alabama Crimson Tide** – The Bulldogs catch Alabama on the West Division rotation and this game will undoubtedly be a big-time showdown. These two teams last met in the 2012 SEC Championship game, a classic battle that Bama held on to win 32-28. Richt is 3-2 all-time against the Tide and he's 2-4 against Nick Saban (dating back to Saban's time at LSU).

**Oct. 10**    **at Tennessee Volunteers** – Richt is 10-4 against Tennessee, but these games are getting closer. The last two Georgia wins in this series were decided by three points each. With the Vols on the rise, this is a *MUST-WIN* game for Richt and the Bulldogs.

**Oct. 17**    **Missouri Tigers** – The last time the Tigers came into Athens, they gave the Bulldogs a 41-26 beat-down. Georgia returned the favor last year.

**Oct. 31**    **vs. Florida Gators (in Jacksonville)** – Florida is the only SEC school Richt has a losing record against, at 5-9. Last year's loss to the Gators cost the Bulldogs the SEC East title. A losing record against your rival is fuel for the critics.

**Nov. 7**    **Kentucky Wildcats** – Richt will be looking for his sixth-straight win over Kentucky.

**Nov. 14**    **at Auburn Tigers** – Last year's 34-7 win over Auburn should have the Tigers gunning for revenge in 2015. This is a dangerous late-season road game that occurs after Georgia's SEC East schedule is already complete.

**Nov. 21**    **Georgia Southern Eagles** – Georgia Southern went 9-3 overall and undefeated in the Sun Belt last year. Though he's 3-0 against the Eagles, Richt knows this can be a dangerous team. The Georgia Southern option attack should help the Bulldogs prepare for Georgia Tech's similar style the following week.

**Nov. 28**    **at Georgia Tech Yellow Jackets** – Though Richt has dominated this in-state rivalry (he's 12-2 against the Jackets), Paul Johnson's flexbone offense is never easy to stop, as the Bulldogs found out last year.

**BOTTOM LINE:**

Georgia was the most talented team in the SEC East last year, but they let the division title slip away. If the defense plays near the same level as last year's unit and the offense transitions smoothly to its new OC, the Bulldogs should once again be gunning for nothing less than a return to the SEC Championship game. And with an SEC title comes a likely College Football Playoff spot.

## Mark Richt's Year-by-Year Coaching Record:

<u>Georgia: 136-48 (78-34 in the SEC)</u>

2001    8-4 (5-3)          Final Ranking: #22
Lost to Boston College 16-20 in the Music City Bowl.

2002    13-1 (7-1)          Final Ranking: #3
SEC Champions.
Richt named SEC Coach of the Year.
Beat #22 Arkansas 30-3 in the SEC Championship Game.
Beat #16 Florida State 26-13 in the Sugar Bowl.

2003    11-3 (6-2)          Final Ranking: #6
SEC East Champions.
Lost to #3 LSU 13-34 in the SEC Championship Game.
Beat #12 Purdue 34-27 in OT in the Citrus Bowl.

2004    10-2 (6-2)          Final Ranking: #6
Beat #16 Wisconsin 24-21 in the Outback Bowl.

2005    10-3 (6-2)          Final Ranking: #10
SEC Champions.
Richt named SEC Coach of the Year.
Beat #3 LSU 34-14 in the SEC Championship Game.
Lost to #11 West Virginia 35-38 in the Sugar Bowl.

2006    9-4 (4-4)          Final Ranking: #23
Beat #14 Virginia Tech 31-24 in the Chick-fil-A Bowl.

2007    11-2 (6-2)          Final Ranking: #2
SEC East Co-Champions.
Beat #10 Hawaii 41-10 in the Sugar Bowl.

2008    10-3 (6-2)          Final Ranking: #10
Beat #19 Michigan State 24-12 in the Capital One Bowl.

2009    8-5 (4-4)          Final Ranking: NR
Beat Texas A&M 44-20 in the Independence Bowl.

2010    6-7 (3-5)          Final Ranking: NR
Lost to #25 UCF 6-10 in the Liberty Bowl.

2011    10-4 (7-1)          Final Ranking: #18
SEC East Champions.
Lost to #1 LSU 10-42 in the SEC Championship Game.
Lost to #12 Michigan State 30-33 in triple OT in the Outback Bowl.

2012    12-2 (7-1)          Final Ranking: #4
SEC East Champions.
Lost to #2 Alabama 28-32 in the SEC Championship Game.
Beat #23 Nebraska 45-31 in the Capital One Bowl.

2013    8-5 (5-3)          Final Ranking: NR
Lost to Nebraska 19-24 in the Gator Bowl.

2014    10-3 (6-2)          Final Ranking: #9
Beat #20 Louisville 37-14 in the Belk Bowl.

# Kentucky Wildcats – Mark Stoops

## Coach Ranking: #64

**Overall Record:** 7-17 in 2 seasons
**Record at Kentucky:** 7-17 in 2 seasons
**2014 Results:** 5-7, 2-6 in the SEC (6th in the SEC East)
**Returning Starters in 2015:** 7 on offense (including QB), 7 on defense
**Salary:** $2.7 Million　　**Age:** 48　　**Job Security Grade:** A

**COACH'S BIO:**

Mark Stoops grew up in Youngstown, Ohio, and played football for his father, **Ron Stoops**, a longtime defensive coordinator at Youngstown's Cardinal Mooney High School. In college, he played under another coaching legend, Iowa's **Hayden Fry**. After serving as a graduate assistant for two years on Fry's staff at Iowa, Stoops spent four years as a high school athletic director and coach. He then reentered the college coaching ranks in 1995 and quickly worked his way up at South Florida, Wyoming, Houston, and Miami (FL) before joining his brother, **Mike Stoops**, to serve as defensive coordinator at Arizona from 2004-2009. He was hired by **Jimbo Fisher** to be the DC at Florida State in 2010. There, he inherited college football's 108th-ranked defense and built it up to the nation's No. 2-ranked defense in just three seasons. He was hired as Kentucky's head coach in 2013.

**2014 REVIEW:**

Last year was a tale of two seasons for Mark Stoops' team. After the Wildcats went 2-10 and failed to win a conference game in 2013, Kentucky stormed out to a 5-1 start in 2014. The second half of the season was not so impressive. The Wildcats lost all six of their remaining games, including a heartbreaking loss to in-state rival Louisville in the final game of the regular season (Kentucky had the lead with less than four minutes to play before Louisville came back to win). The Wildcats' 5-7 record kept them out of a bowl game for the fourth-straight year, but the program is clearly headed in the right direction under Stoops.

**2014 RESULTS:　5-7 (2-6 in the SEC)**　　**Final Ranking: NR**

| | | |
|---|---|---|
| Tennessee–Martin | W 59–14 | (50,398) |
| Ohio | W 20–3 | (51,910) |
| at Florida | L 30–36 3OT | (88,334) |
| Vanderbilt | W 17–7 | (56,940) |
| South Carolina | W 45–38 | (62,135) |
| Louisiana–Monroe | W 48–14 | (56,676) |
| at LSU | L 3–41 | (101,581) |
| #1 Mississippi State | L 31–45 | (64,791) |
| at Missouri | L 10–20 | (62,004) |
| #17 Georgia | L 31–63 | (60,152) |
| at Tennessee | L 16–50 | (102,455) |
| at #24 Louisville | L 40–44 | (55,118) |

**OFFENSE:**

**Neal Brown** was Kentucky's offensive coordinator for Stoops' first two seasons here, but Brown is leaving to accept the head coaching job at Troy. His replacement is **Shannon Dawson**. This is an impressive hire for Kentucky. Dawson spent the last three seasons as the OC at West Virginia. Last year, West Virginia's offense averaged 500 yards per game (12th nationally in this category) and it ranked 11th nationally in passing yards. Davis' fast-paced Air Raid offense piled up the points and passing yards, but it also ranked fourth in the Big 12 in rushing yards. It's this type of balance that makes Davis' system especially difficult to stop. This should be a fairly easy transition for Kentucky as the Wildcats were already running an Air Raid offense under Brown. It also helps that QB **Patrick Towles** will be returning as the starter after passing for more than 2,700 yards as a sophomore in 2014.

**DEFENSE:**

Kentucky had a lot of trouble keeping points off the board with its hybrid nickel defense last season. The Wildcats ranked second-to-last in the SEC in points allowed. They entered 2014 with a lot of inexperience at the DL and LB spots, so it wasn't too surprising that their run defense caused them the most trouble throughout the year. Still, poor defensive football is not something you'd expect from Mark Stoops and his defensive coordinator **D.J. Elliot** (who came with Stoops from Florida State). Seven starters will be back this year, but it's the d-line that is once again the most inexperienced unit on this team. Stoops was hired largely for his defensive expertise and it's time for this defense to start living up to those expectations. Transitions take time, but the Kentucky defense needs to climb out of the SEC cellar.

**RECRUITING:**

The 2013 and 2014 recruiting classes under Stoops were the best back-to-back classes in school history. Instead of focusing solely on the Southern states, Stoops is finding greener pastures to the north, in his home state of Ohio. The Wildcats signed a smaller class in 2015. As a result, the class fell from No. 22 nationally to No. 39.

**RUMOR MILL:**

This turnaround job is already starting to gain nationwide attention as Stoops' name came up as a candidate for the Michigan opening last season. Kentucky knows it's got someone leading this program in the right direction and the school locked up Stoops with a contract extension that now stretches through the 2019 season.

**NOTEWORTHY:**

Stoops' record speaks for itself; going from two wins to five wins tells us this program is trending upward. The next step is to put together a full season of quality football. Last year's squad couldn't regain its momentum once it began a midseason slide.

**2015 OUTLOOK:**

Sept. 5    **Louisiana-Lafayette Ragin' Cajuns** – This game might not be the cakewalk one would expect when an SEC team hosts a Sun Belt team. The Ragin' Cajuns have put together four-consecutive nine-win seasons.

Sept. 12    **at South Carolina Gamecocks** – Last year's upset win over South Carolina let the rest of the conference know that Kentucky was no longer the pushover of the SEC East.

Sept. 19    **Florida Gators** – Had Kentucky pulled off this triple-OT thriller last season, they would've gone to a bowl game. It also would have broken the Wildcats' *28-game* losing streak to the Gators.

Sept. 26    **Missouri Tigers** – The Tigers are 3-0 against Kentucky since joining the SEC.

Oct. 3    **Eastern Kentucky Colonels** – There might be some bad blood between these two teams after an alleged bar fight involving players from both teams occurred in the offseason. Regardless of any extra motivation, the Wildcats should have no trouble handling this FCS school.

Oct. 15    **Auburn Tigers** – Kentucky draws Auburn in its SEC West schedule rotation. These teams last met in 2010, a 37-34 win for the Tigers.

Oct. 24    **at Mississippi State Bulldogs** – With the rise of Mississippi State, this annual cross-division matchup has become a much tougher game for Kentucky. The Wildcats have lost six-straight games in this series.

Oct. 31    **Tennessee Volunteers** – Butch Jones was hired by Tennessee at the same time Stoops was hired by Kentucky. So far, Stoops is 0-2 against Jones as both programs try to fight their way into SEC East contention.

Nov. 7    **at Georgia Bulldogs** – Stoops' first two meetings with Georgia have resulted in blowout losses of 32 and 42 points.

Nov. 14    **at Vanderbilt Commodores** – Last year's win over Vanderbilt was Kentucky's first SEC victory since 2011.

Nov. 21    **Charlotte 49ers** – Charlotte is making the move to FBS as a member of Conference USA. Last year, the 49ers went 5-6 as an FCS school.

Nov. 28    **Louisville Cardinals** – This is a *MUST-WIN* game for Stoops. He needs to establish Kentucky as the premier football program in the state and that means taking control of this rivalry, which Louisville has dominated since 2010.

**BOTTOM LINE:**
The next step for this turnaround effort is six wins and a bowl game. Last year's three-win improvement will be hard to match, but with Stoops' recruits growing up and a more evened-out schedule, six or seven wins is a realistic goal.

## Mark Stoops' Year-by-Year Coaching Record:

<u>**Kentucky: 7-17 (2-14 in the SEC)**</u>
| | | |
|---|---|---|
| 2013 | 2-10 (0-8) | Final Ranking: NR |
| 2014 | 5-7 (2-6) | Final Ranking: NR |

# Missouri Tigers – Gary Pinkel

## Coach Ranking: #16

**Overall Record:** 186-103-3 in 24 seasons
**Record at Missouri:** 113-66 in 14 seasons
**2014 Results:** 11-3, 7-1 in the SEC (SEC East Champions)
**Returning Starters in 2015:** 7 on offense (including QB), 6 on defense
**Salary:** $4 Million          **Age:** 63          **Job Security Grade:** A

**COACH'S BIO:**
Gary Pinkel grew up in Akron, Ohio, and was an All-American TE at Kent State. The team was led by future Hall of Fame coach **Don James** and Pinkel's teammates at Kent State included **Nick Saban** and legendary LB **Jack Lambert**. After graduating in 1974, Pinkel immediately joined the Kent State coaching staff and then followed Don James to Washington in 1976. After a two-year stint as WR coach at Bowling Green, Pinkel coached on James' Washington staff from 1979-1990 and served as offensive coordinator from 1984-1990. In 1991, he was hired as Toledo's head coach, replacing Nick Saban (who left to become the defensive coordinator for the Cleveland Browns). Pinkel was hired by Mizzou in 2001 and in 14 seasons there, he's won five division titles (three in the Big 12 North and two in the SEC East). He's won more games than any other coach at Missouri.

**2014 REVIEW:**
In 2013, Missouri surprised the college football world with a 12-2 record, its first SEC East title, and a finish at No. 5 in the polls. With just four starters returning on both sides of the ball, 2014 was supposed to be a difficult rebuilding year for the Tigers. Instead, Mizzou claimed its second-straight SEC East crown and finished No. 11 in the coaches' poll. This was a tremendous coaching job and it sent a message to the SEC that 2013 was no fluke. The SEC coaches voted Pinkel the conference's Coach of the Year for his 2014 performance.

| 2014 RESULTS:   11-3 (7-1 in the SEC) | Final Ranking: #11 | |
|---|---|---|
| #10 (FCS) South Dakota State | W 38–18 | (60,589) |
| at Toledo | W 49–24 | (24,196) |
| UCF | W 38–10 | (60,348) |
| Indiana | L 27–31 | (66,455) |
| at #13 South Carolina | W 21–20 | (83,493) |
| #13 Georgia | L 0–34 | (71,168) |
| at Florida | W 42–13 | (89,117) |
| Vanderbilt | W 24–14 | (65,264) |
| Kentucky | W 20–10 | (62,004) |
| at #24 Texas A&M | W 34–27 | (104,756) |
| at Tennessee | W 29–21 | (95,821) |
| Arkansas | W 21–14 | (71,168) |
| vs. #1 Alabama (SEC Championship) | L 13-42 | (73,526) |
| vs. Minnesota (Citrus Bowl) | W 33–17 | (48,624) |

**OFFENSE:**

Gary Pinkel decided to install the spread offense back in 2005. Two years later, Missouri finished the year ranked No. 4 and just missed a shot at the National Championship. In 2013, **Josh Henson** was promoted to offensive coordinator. Fearing that defenses were catching up with the standard spread offense, Henson made a few tweaks to the system and the Tigers averaged 39 points a game that season (13th nationally in scoring). However, that offensive production took a big step back in 2014. The Tigers fell to second-to-last in the SEC in scoring with just 27.4 points a game. A big reason for that decline was inexperienced personnel – just one skill position starter returned last season. With QB **Matty Mauk** and six other starters back this year, the 2015 offense should be much more potent.

**DEFENSE:**

Despite entering the year with just four returning starters, defensive coordinator **Dave Steckel** produced a defense that ranked 19th nationally in points allowed. This outstanding coaching job made Steckel one of five finalists for the Frank Broyles Award, which goes to the nation's top assistant coach. It also led to a new job as Steckel is leaving to become the head coach at Missouri State (FCS) after spending the last 14 years with Pinkel at Mizzou (he's spent the last six as the DC). **Barry Odom** will be his replacement in 2015. Odom spent the last three seasons turning around Memphis' defense. At Memphis, he inherited a defense that ranked 117th in the nation. Last year's squad ranked No. 11 in points allowed. This transition should be a smooth one. Before taking the DC job at Memphis, Odom spent nine years on Pinkel's Missouri staff. He was also a LB for the Tigers from 1996-1999.

**RECRUITING:**

Once again, Missouri landed a class that ranked near the bottom of the SEC, at No. 12. However, this class came in ranked No. 25 nationally as recruits appear to be realizing the 2013 season was no fluke for the Tigers.

**RUMOR MILL:**

When the Washington job opened up prior to last season, Pinkel's name came up quickly as an ideal candidate. After all, he'd spent 12 years coaching there under **Don Nelson**. But Pinkel adamantly stated that he wasn't going anywhere. "I'm a Missouri Tiger, and I'm going to stay a Missouri Tiger," Pinkel said. In April, Mizzou gave Pinkel an $800,000 raise and a contract extension. His contract now runs through the 2021 season.

**NOTEWORTHY:**

Pinkel has somewhat quietly become the winningest coach ever at Mizzou. His recruiting classes have ranked near the bottom of the SEC since joining the conference, but he finds a way to win regardless. One of the secrets to that success might be staff continuity. Amazingly, in Pinkel's 14 years at Mizzou, only five coaches have left the program (and one of those departures was due to retirement). How does he do it? Pinkel treats his staff well and is known for being loyal to them. He encourages his assistants to be home by 7:30 each night so they can spend time with their families, which is very rare in this profession.

## 2015 OUTLOOK:

**Sept. 5**  **Southeast Missouri State RedHawks** – The last time this FCS school came into Columbia, they left with a 52-3 loss in 2008.

**Sept. 12**  **at Arkansas State Red Wolves** – This will mark the fourth time these two schools have met since 2004. Pinkel's Tigers dominated the previous meetings, but this will be the first time the game is being played in Arkansas State's home stadium.

**Sept. 19**  **Connecticut Huskies** – This will be the first-ever meeting between these two schools. UConn is coming off an abysmal 2-10 season.

**Sept. 26**  **at Kentucky Wildcats** – Since joining the SEC, Pinkel is 3-0 against the Wildcats and he's won these games by an average of three TDs each.

**Oct. 3**  **South Carolina Gamecocks** – In 2013, South Carolina knocked off No. 5 Missouri in double OT. Last year, the Tigers returned the favor with a one-point win.

**Oct. 10**  **Florida Gators** – Last year's 42-13 beat-down of Florida in Gainesville was an embarrassing day for the Gators and some believe Will Muschamp's fate was decided at that moment. The Tigers will need to be ready for an inspired Florida team this year.

**Oct. 17**  **at Georgia Bulldogs** – Georgia blew out the Tigers last season in an uncharacteristic coaching performance for Pinkel. Yet, Missouri still ended up winning the SEC East. They won't be that lucky again and if the Tigers want to make it three-straight division titles, this game is a *MUST-WIN*.

**Oct. 24**  **at Vanderbilt Commodores** – When the Tigers went into Nashville two years ago, they rolled out with a 51-28 victory, and that was a much better Vandy team than the one they'll face this year.

**Nov. 5**  **Mississippi State Bulldogs** – This will be the first meeting between these two schools since Missouri joined the SEC.

**Nov. 14**  **vs. BYU Cougars (in Kansas City)** – This "neutral site" game should feel like a home game for the Tigers.

**Nov. 21**  **Tennessee Volunteers** – Pinkel is 3-0 against Tennessee, but this should be the best Vols squad he has faced.

**Nov. 28**  **at Arkansas Razorbacks** – They're calling this new annual matchup the "Battle Line Rivalry" and last year Missouri had to come from behind to pull this one off and lock up their trip to the SEC Championship.

## BOTTOM LINE:

When the Tigers first joined the SEC in 2012, they limped through a 5-7 record that had many wondering if they were in over their heads in this league. After back-to-back SEC East titles, nobody's wondering anymore. The Tigers may have had the luxury of flying under the radar the past two seasons, but that won't happen again. Missouri now has a target on its back and teams like Georgia, South Carolina, and Florida will be underlining the Mizzou game. On paper, the Tigers enter 2015 with a much more experienced team compared to last season, but the SEC East as a whole is improving. It'll be very difficult to match last year's 11 wins, but it's clearly not safe to bet against Missouri.

## Gary Pinkel's Year-by-Year Coaching Record:

### Toledo: 73-37-3 (53-23-2 in the MAC)
1991   5-5-1 (4-3-1)     Final Ranking: NR
1992   8-3 (5-3)     Final Ranking: NR
1993   4-7 (3-5)     Final Ranking: NR
1994   6-4-1 (4-3-1)     Final Ranking: NR
1995   11-0-1 (7-0-1)     Final Ranking: #24
      MAC Champions.
      Pinkel named MAC Coach of the Year.
      Beat Nevada 40-37 in the Las Vegas Bowl.
1996   7-4 (6-2)     Final Ranking: NR
1997   9-3 (7-1)     Final Ranking: NR
      MAC West Champions.
      Lost to Marshall 14-34 in the MAC Championship Game.
1998   7-5 (6-2)     Final Ranking: NR
      MAC West Champions.
      Lost to Marshall 17-23 in the MAC Championship Game.
1999   6-5 (5-3)     Final Ranking: NR
2000   10-1 (6-1)     Final Ranking: NR
      MAC West Co-Champions.

### Missouri: 113-66 (63-50 in the Big 12 and SEC)
2001   4-7 (3-5)     Final Ranking: NR
2002   5-7 (2-6)     Final Ranking: NR
2003   8-5 (4-4)     Final Ranking: NR
      Lost to Arkansas 14-27 in the Independence Bowl.
2004   5-6 (3-5)     Final Ranking: NR
2005   7-5 (4-4)     Final Ranking: NR
      Beat South Carolina 38-31 in the Independence Bowl.
2006   8-5 (4-4)     Final Ranking: NR
      Lost to #24 Oregon State 38-39 in the Sun Bowl.
2007   12-2 (7-1)     Final Ranking: #4
      Big 12 North Division Champions.
      Lost to #9 Oklahoma 17-38 in Big 12 Championship Game.
      Beat #25 Arkansas 38-7 in the Cotton Bowl.
2008   10-4 (5-3)     Final Ranking: #16
      Big 12 North Division Champions.
      Lost to #4 Oklahoma 21-62 in Big 12 Championship Game.
      Beat #22 Northwestern 30-23 in OT in the Alamo Bowl.
2009   8-5 (4-4)     Final Ranking: NR
      Lost to Navy 13-35 in the Texas Bowl.
2010   10-3 (6-2)     Final Ranking: #18
      Big 12 North Co-Champions.
      Lost to Iowa 24-27 in the Insight Bowl.
2011   8-5 (5-4)     Final Ranking: NR
      Beat North Carolina 41-24 in the Independence Bowl.

**Missouri (continued)**

2012   5–7 (2–6)          Final Ranking: NR
       Missouri joins the SEC.

2013   12–2 (7–1)        Final Ranking: #5
       SEC East Champions.
       Lost to #3 Auburn 42-59 in the SEC Championship Game.
       Beat #13 Oklahoma State 41-31 in the Cotton Bowl.

2014   11–3 (7–1)        Final Ranking: #11
       SEC East Champions.
       Pinkel named SEC Coach of the Year.
       Lost to #1 Alabama 13-42 in the SEC Championship Game.
       Beat Minnesota 33-17 in the Citrus Bowl.

# South Carolina Gamecocks – Steve Spurrier

## Coach Ranking: #12

**Overall Record:** 226-85-2 in 25 seasons, 12-20 in 2 NFL seasons, 35-19 in 3 USFL seasons

**Record at South Carolina:** 84-45 in 10 seasons

**2014 Results:** 7-6, 3-5 in the SEC (T-4th in the SEC East)

**Returning Starters in 2015:** 4 on offense, 8 on defense

**Salary:** $4 Million        **Age:** 70        **Job Security Grade:** B

**COACH'S BIO:**

Growing up in Johnson City, Tennessee, Steve Spurrier was an all-state baseball, basketball, and football player in high school. He played QB for **Ray Graves** at Florida from 1963-1966 and won the 1966 Heisman Trophy. After a 10-year NFL career as a punter and QB for the 49ers and Buccaneers, Spurrier began his coaching career with stops as an assistant at Florida (QBs in 1978), Georgia Tech (QBs in 1979), and Duke (offensive coordinator from 1980-1982). At the age of 37, Spurrier became the youngest head coach in pro football when he was hired to coach the Tampa Bay Bandits of the newly-created USFL in 1983. He coached there until the league dissolved in 1985. He was hired as Duke's head coach in 1987 and led the Blue Devils to an ACC championship in 1989. He was hired by Florida in 1990 and led the Gators to six SEC championships and a National Championship in 1996. In 2002, Spurrier tried his hand again at coaching pro football and lasted two seasons with the Washington Redskins before resigning. He was hired as South Carolina's head coach in 2005.

**2014 REVIEW:**

After three-consecutive 11-win seasons, Spurrier entered his 10th year at South Carolina with high expectations and a No. 9 preseason ranking. An ugly season-opening loss to Texas A&M and a four-game SEC losing streak later in the year made 2014 the most disappointing season of the Spurrier era at South Carolina.

**2014 RESULTS:    7-6 (3-5 in the SEC)**          Final Ranking: NR

| | | |
|---|---|---|
| #21 Texas A&M | L 28–52 | (82,847) |
| East Carolina | W 33–23 | (80,899) |
| #6 Georgia | W 38–35 | (84,232) |
| at Vanderbilt | W 48–34 | (34,441) |
| Missouri | L 20–21 | (83,493) |
| at Kentucky | L 38–45 | (62,135) |
| Furman | W 41–10 | (78,101) |
| at #5 Auburn | L 35–42 | (87,451) |
| Tennessee | L 42–45 OT | (81,891) |
| at Florida | W 23–20 OT | (85,088) |
| South Alabama | W 37–12 | (78,201) |
| at #21 Clemson | L 17–35 | (82,720) |
| vs. Miami (FL) (Independence Bowl) | W 24–21 | (38,242) |

**OFFENSE:**
Dating back to his days of running the "Fun 'n' Gun" offense at Florida, Spurrier has long been known as an offensive mastermind. His offense looks a little more "ordinary" these days – not because he's no longer innovative, but because the rest of the college football world now implements many of the aspects that once made his offense so unique. Spurrier's multiple-set, shotgun-heavy, pass-happy system may be more common across the college football landscape than it once was, but the "Old Ball Coach" is still one of the best play-callers in the business. Prior to 2014, Spurrier's offenses had been trending towards more balance, but they relied heavily on the pass last season as the Gamecocks racked up the second-most passing yards in the SEC. Spurrier employs co-offensive coordinators in **Steve Spurrier Jr.** and **Shawn Elliot**. Last year, Spurrier delegated some of the play-calling duties to his assistants, but he says he's taking back full control of the play-calling in 2015. With a new QB to break in and only four offensive starters returning, Spurrier will have his work cut out for him this season.

**DEFENSE:**
After leading the nation's 12th-best defense (points allowed) in 2013, defensive coordinator **Lorenzo Ward** had to replace five starters – including All-Americans **Jadeveon Clowney** and **Kelcy Quarles** on the d-line – in 2014. Adding some 3-4 looks to South Carolina's 4-2-5 base defense couldn't make up for the loss of such tremendous talent and the defense fell to No. 91 nationally. After the ugly reversal in 2014, Spurrier has hired **Jon Hoke** (the older brother of former Michigan coach **Brady Hoke**) to be co-DC with Ward in 2015. Hoke spent the last six seasons coaching DBs for the Chicago Bears. From 1999-2001, Hoke was Spurrier's DC at Florida (stepping in when **Bob Stoops** left to take the Oklahoma job). In this new setup, Hoke will be in charge of the pass defense and Ward will be in charge of stopping the run. This year's squad returns eight starters, including three defensive linemen, which should make it easier to operate out of the four-man front South Carolina has preferred in the past. Expect this unit to make some much-needed improvement in 2015.

**RECRUITING:**
Spurrier will be 70 when the Gamecocks take the field this fall, which makes him the third-oldest head coach in the FBS (behind only Kansas State's **Bill Snyder** and Ohio's **Frank Solich**). A coach's age can be a disadvantage in recruiting if recruits worry about the coach's impending retirement plans. Though Spurrier still reeled in the nation's 19th-ranked recruiting class, it ranked 11 spots behind in-state rival Clemson.

**RUMOR MILL:**
Spurrier admitted that he thought about retiring after last season and even discussed the issue with South Carolina athletic director **Ray Tanner**. Ultimately, Spurrier chalked up such thoughts to disappointment in how the 2014 season turned out and later said he has "four or five more years" left in him. Spurrier's high energy level certainly doesn't look like a coach running on fumes, but another disappointing season like 2014 could prompt the Old Ball Coach to speed up his retirement plans.

**2015 OUTLOOK:**

| | |
|---|---|
| Sept. 3 | **at North Carolina Tar Heels (in Charlotte, NC)** – This Thursday-night matchup to kick off the season will mark the third time these border-state schools have met during the Spurrier era. Dating back to his time at Duke, Spurrier is a perfect 5-0 against UNC. |
| Sept. 12 | **Kentucky Wildcats** – Last year's loss to Kentucky was Spurrier's second in five years. Before the 2010 loss, he was a perfect 17-0 against the Wildcats. |
| Sept. 19 | **at Georgia Bulldogs** – While at Florida, Spurrier dominated the Bulldogs with an 11-1 record. Since coming to South Carolina, he is 5-5 against Mark Richt. |
| Sept. 26 | **UCF Knights** – This won't be a cakewalk non-conference game. UCF finished 9-4 last year and 12-1 the year before. |
| Oct. 3 | **at Missouri Tigers** – Last year's loss was Spurrier's first to the Tigers since they joined the SEC. |
| Oct. 10 | **LSU Tigers** – Spurrier is still looking for his first win over Les Miles as he's lost all three previous matchups. |
| Oct. 17 | **Vanderbilt Commodores** – Spurrier has won the last six meetings against Vanderbilt and he's 20-2 against the Commodores dating back to his time at Florida. |
| Oct. 31 | **at Texas A&M Aggies** – Last year's season-opening blowout loss to the Aggies was devastating to the Gamecocks and they'll be looking for payback in this rematch. This will mark the second-ever meeting between these two schools. |
| Nov. 7 | **at Tennessee Volunteers** – Butch Jones is 2-0 against Spurrier since becoming head coach at Tennessee. With the Vols on the rise and South Carolina taking a step back last season, the Gamecocks really need a win here. |
| Nov. 14 | **Florida Gators** – In his 10 years at South Carolina, Spurrier is an even 5-5 against his alma mater. Interestingly, Spurrier has won his last five SEC-conference finales. |
| Nov. 21 | **The Citadel Bulldogs** – Spurrier has met this FCS school while at all three of his head coaching stops. He's 3-0 against the Bulldogs. |
| Nov. 28 | **Clemson Tigers** – Last season's loss to Clemson broke a five-game winning streak for Spurrier and the Gamecocks against their in-state rivals. Clemson also beat South Carolina in the recruiting wars last year. That makes this a *MUST-WIN* game for South Carolina in 2015. |

**BOTTOM LINE:**
A fast start will be critical if South Carolina wants to shake off the rust of last year's disappointing effort. The Gamecocks lost four games in 2014 in which they were either tied or leading at the start of the fourth quarter. This year's team needs to prove it can pull off the close games and that starts with making big improvements on defense.

## Steve Spurrier's Year-by-Year Coaching Record:

### Tampa Bay Bandits: 35-19 (0-2 in the USFL Playoffs)
1983  11-7 (0-0)          3rd in the Central Division
1984  14-4 (0-1)          2nd in the Southern Division
       Lost to Birmingham 17-36 in the Eastern Conference semifinal game.
1985  10-8 (0-1)          5th in the Eastern Conference
       Lost to Oakland 27-30 in the USFL quarterfinals.

### Duke: 20-13-1 (11-9-1 in the ACC)
1987  5–6 (2–5)           Final Ranking: NR
1988  7–3–1 (3–3–1)       Final Ranking: NR
       Spurrier named ACC Coach of the Year.
1989  8–4 (6–1)           Final Ranking: NR
       ACC Co-Champions.
       Spurrier named ACC Coach of the Year.
       Lost to #24 Texas Tech 21-49 in the All-American Bowl.

### Florida: 122-27-1 (87-12 in the SEC)
1990  9–2 (6–1)           Final Ranking: #13
       Spurrier named SEC Coach of the Year.
       Florida was ineligible for the SEC title or a bowl game.
1991  10-2 (7–0)          Final Ranking: #7
       SEC Champions.
       Spurrier named SEC Coach of the Year.
       Lost to #18 Notre Dame 28-39 in the Sugar Bowl.
1992  9–4 (6–2)           Final Ranking: #10
       SEC East Co-Champions.
       Lost to #2 Alabama 21-28 in the SEC Championship Game.
       Beat #12 NC State 27-10 in the Gator Bowl.
1993  11–2 (7–1)          Final Ranking: #4
       SEC Champions.
       Beat #17 Alabama 28-13 in the SEC Championship Game.
       Beat #3 West Virginia 41-7 in the Sugar Bowl.
1994  10–2–1 (7–1)        Final Ranking: #7
       SEC Champions.
       Spurrier named SEC Coach of the Year.
       Beat #3 Alabama 24-23 in the SEC Championship Game.
       Lost to #7 Florida State 17-23 in the Sugar Bowl.
1995  12–1 (8–0)          Final Ranking: #2
       SEC Champions.
       Spurrier named SEC Coach of the Year. Beat #23 Arkansas 34-3 in the SEC
       Championship Game.
       Lost to #1 Nebraska 24-62 in the Bowl Alliance National Championship
       Game.

## Florida (continued)

**1996    12-1 (8-0)            Final Ranking: #1**
National Champions.
SEC Champions.
Spurrier named SEC Coach of the Year.
Beat #11 Alabama 45-30 in the SEC Championship Game.
Beat #1 Florida State 52-20 in the Bowl Alliance National Championship Game.

**1997    10-2 (6-2)            Final Ranking: #4**
Beat #11 Penn State 21-6 in the Citrus Bowl.

**1998    10-2 (7-1)            Final Ranking: #5**
Beat #18 Syracuse 31-10 in the Orange Bowl.

**1999    9-4 (7-1)             Final Ranking: #12**
SEC East Division Champions.
Lost to #7 Alabama 7-34 in the SEC Championship Game.
Lost to #9 Michigan State 34-37 in the Citrus Bowl.

**2000    10-3 (7-1)            Final Ranking: #10**
SEC Champions.
Beat #18 Auburn 28-6 in the SEC Championship Game.
Lost to #2 Miami (FL) 20-37 in the Sugar Bowl.

**2001    10-2 (6-2)            Final Ranking: #3**
Beat #6 Maryland 56-23 in the Orange Bowl.

## Washington Redskins: 12-20 (0-0 in the NFL Playoffs)

**2002    7-9 (0-0)            3rd in the NFC East**
**2003    5-11 (0-0)           3rd in the NFC East**

## South Carolina: 84-45 (44-36 in the SEC)

**2005    7-5 (5-3)            Final Ranking: NR**
Spurrier named SEC Coach of the Year.
Lost to Missouri 31-38 in the Independence Bowl.

**2006    8-5 (3-5)            Final Ranking: NR**
Beat Houston 44-36 in the Liberty Bowl.

**2007    6-6 (3-5)            Final Ranking: NR**
**2008    7-6 (4-4)            Final Ranking: NR**
Lost to Iowa 10-31 in the Outback Bowl.

**2009    7-6 (3-5)            Final Ranking: NR**
Lost to Connecticut 7-20 in the PapaJohns.com Bowl.

**2010    9-5 (5-3)            Final Ranking: #22**
SEC East Champions.
Spurrier named SEC Coach of the Year.
Lost to #2 Auburn 17-56 in the SEC Championship Game.
Lost to #23 Florida State 17-23 in the Chick-fil-A Bowl.

**2011    11-2 (6-2)           Final Ranking: #8**
Beat #21 Nebraska 30-13 in the Capital One Bowl.

**2012    11-2 (6-2)           Final Ranking: #7**
Beat #19 Michigan 33-28 in the Outback Bowl.

<u>**South Carolina (continued)**</u>

2013  **11–2 (6–2)**        **Final Ranking: #4**
Beat #19 Wisconsin 34-24 in the Capital One Bowl.

2014  **7–6 (3–5)**        **Final Ranking: NR**
Beat Miami (FL) 24-21 in the Independence Bowl.

# Tennessee Volunteers – Butch Jones

## Coach Ranking: #36

**Overall Record:** 62-40 in 8 seasons
**Record at Tennessee:** 12-13 in 2 seasons
**2014 Results:** 7-6, 3-5 in the SEC (T-4th in SEC East)
**Returning Starters in 2015:** 10 on offense (including QB), 8 on defense
**Salary:** $3 Million      **Age:** 47      **Job Security Grade:** A

**COACH'S BIO:**

Butch Jones grew up in Saugatuck, Michigan, and played at Ferris St. (Division II) for two years before a knee injury ended his playing career. While still in college, Jones began his coaching career as an intern for the Tampa Bay Buccaneers. After graduating in 1990, he joined the Rutgers coaching staff as a graduate assistant. He returned to Ferris State as the offensive coordinator in 1995 and then joined the Central Michigan staff in 1998. He worked his way up to OC in 2002 and retained that position when **Brian Kelly** was hired as Central Michigan's head coach in 2004. In 2005, Jones joined **Rich Rodriguez**'s staff at West Virginia and served as WR coach for two seasons there. Jones was hired as Central Michigan's head coach in 2007 (replacing Brian Kelly, who left for the Cincinnati job). After winning two MAC championships, he was hired by Cincinnati to (again) replace Brian Kelly (who this time left for the Notre Dame job) in 2010. He won two Big East titles at Cincinnati and was hired by Tennessee to replace **Derek Dooley** in 2013.

**2014 REVIEW:**

Butch Jones entered his second season at Tennessee with a young team (just five returning starters on each side of the ball) facing one of the nation's toughest schedules. He responded by ending Tennessee's four-year streak of losing seasons and leading the Volunteers to their first bowl victory since the **Phil Fulmer** era. Last year's team played its best football later in the year, winning four of its last five games.

**2014 RESULTS:   7-6 (3-5 in the SEC)**     **Final Ranking: NR**

| | | |
|---|---|---|
| Utah State | W 38-7 | (102,455) |
| Arkansas State | W 34-19 | (99,538) |
| at #4 Oklahoma | L 10-34 | (85,622) |
| at #12 Georgia | L 32-35 | (92,746) |
| Florida | L 9-10 | (102,455) |
| #13 (FCS) Chattanooga | W 45-10 | (93,097) |
| at #3 Ole Miss | L 3-34 | (62,081) |
| #4 Alabama | L 20-34 | (102,455) |
| at South Carolina | W 45-42 OT | (81,891) |
| Kentucky | W 50-16 | (102,455) |
| #19 Missouri | L 21-29 | (95,821) |
| at Vanderbilt | W 24-17 | (40,350) |
| vs. Iowa (TaxSlayer Bowl) | W 45-28 | (56,310) |

**OFFENSE:**

Butch Jones runs an up-tempo spread offense. Like Ohio State's **Urban Meyer**, Jones refers to his system as the "power spread" due to its emphasis on the power running game out of the spread formation. Last year's OC, **Mike Bajakian**, left to become the QB coach for the Tampa Bay Buccaneers. Bajakian had been Jones' OC for all eight of his seasons as a head coach. His replacement is Jones' longtime friend **Mike DeBord**, who was the head coach at Central Michigan from 2000-2003, where Jones served as *his* OC. DeBord had two stints as the OC at Michigan under **Lloyd Carr** and most recently coached TEs for the Chicago Bears under **Lovie Smith** from 2010-2012, but he's been off the sidelines since then. DeBord inherits a talented offense with 10 starters coming back, including junior QB **Joshua Dobbs**.

**DEFENSE:**

**John Jancek** has been Jones' defensive coordinator for the past six seasons. Before joining Jones at Cincinnati, he was one of **Mark Richt's** co-defensive coordinators at Georgia in 2009. He also served as **Brian Kelly's** DC at Central Michigan in 2004. Like the offense, this unit was very young heading into 2014. Yet, despite having just three senior starters, Jancek's defense finished as one of the nation's Top 40 in points allowed. The defense (a 4-3 base) should only improve this season with eight starters back and several emerging stars.

**RECRUITING:**

When a coach is hired from a "mid-major" school located far from his new school's region, there are obvious concerns about how well he will be able to recruit. Butch Jones has answered those concerns. In 2014, he signed 32 new recruits and landed the No. 7-ranked class in the country. That's impressive for a top-tier program, but Tennessee was coming off its fourth-straight losing season at the time. What's more, Jones got 14 of those recruits to enroll in the spring, which gave them an opportunity to make a significant impact right away. This past offseason, he signed an even stronger class, which ranked as the nation's No. 4 class. Ten of the 29 recruits were early enrollees. Jones is quickly establishing himself as one of the best recruiters in the nation.

**RUMOR MILL:**

As a coach on the rise who grew up in Michigan, it wasn't surprising to hear Butch Jones' name come up as a candidate for the Michigan job before the Wolverines hired **Jim Harbaugh**. When Jones took the Tennessee job two years ago, he reportedly turned down offers from Colorado and Purdue at the same time. With the quick turnaround he's engineering, don't be surprised to see Jones as a hot target for future openings across the nation.

**NOTEWORTHY:**

Jones faced an interesting challenge last season with a young team and a grueling schedule. To avoid physical and mental burnout, he implemented "No Sweat Thursdays." While most schools practice on Thursdays, Jones told his players *not* to break a sweat on this day and they instead focused on rest, meetings, and walkthroughs. The technique must have worked because Tennessee played its best football in the second half of the season.

**2015 OUTLOOK:**

**Sept. 5**   **Bowling Green Falcons** – This game was supposed to be against UAB, but the Blazers abruptly discontinued their football program. Bowling Green will be the replacement. The Falcons won the MAC East last year and finished 8-6.

**Sept. 12**   **Oklahoma Sooners** – Tennessee is looking for payback after Oklahoma beat the Vols 34-10 last year in Norman. Knocking off the Sooners would announce to the nation that Tennessee is back.

**Sept. 19**   **Western Carolina Catamounts** – A week after a showdown with Oklahoma and a week before starting SEC play makes this the perfect spot to play an FCS school.

**Sept. 26**   **at Florida Gators** – This a *MUST-WIN* game for Tennessee because the Volunteers need to get off to a faster start in SEC play. They lost their first four SEC games last year.

**Oct. 3**   **Arkansas Razorbacks** – This is not an easy draw from the SEC West as Arkansas looks to be turning things around. The last time these two teams played, the Razorbacks blew away Tennessee 49-7 back in 2011.

**Oct. 10**   **Georgia Bulldogs** – Georgia has won the last five meetings in this series, but the previous two games were decided by just three points each. Jones needs to knock off the Bulldogs at home if he wants to win the East Division.

**Oct. 24**   **at Alabama Crimson Tide** – This traditional SEC rivalry has been dominated by Bama over the past decade. The Vols will be looking for their first win in the series since 2006.

**Oct. 31**   **at Kentucky Wildcats** – Kentucky is a program on the rise heading into 2015 and Tennessee needs to make it four-straight wins against this division rival.

**Nov. 7**   **South Carolina Gamecocks** – After last year's OT win, Butch Jones is now 2-0 against Steve Spurrier.

**Nov. 14**   **North Texas Mean Green** – These schools actually played once before, back in 1975. North Texas won that game 21-14. This isn't 1975 and Tennessee should overpower this Conference USA opponent. The Mean Green went 4-8 last season.

**Nov. 21**   **at Missouri Tigers** – After winning back-to-back SEC East titles, Missouri is the team to beat in this division. Since joining the SEC, the Tigers are 3-0 against the Vols.

**Nov. 28**   **Vanderbilt Commodores** – Butch Jones knows he needs to dominate this in-state rivalry. He's 1-1 against Vanderbilt heading into 2015.

**BOTTOM LINE:**
Butch Jones has brought an aura of positive energy and confidence back to Tennessee. The Volunteers are starting to show some swagger and the momentum they picked up late last year should carry over to 2015. This team is loaded with young talent. On paper, it looks like the Vols may be a year away from a serious run at an SEC title, but don't be shocked if that run gets started a year earlier than expected. This team could surprise a lot of people in 2015.

## Butch Jones' Year-by-Year Coaching Record:

<u>Central Michigan: 27-13 (20-3 in the MAC)</u>
2007   8–6 (7–1)                 **Final Ranking: NR**
         MAC Champions.
         Beat Miami (OH), 35-10, in the MAC Championship Game.
         Lost to Purdue 48-51 in the Motor City Bowl.
2008   8–5 (6–2)                 **Final Ranking: NR**
         Lost to Florida Atlantic 21-24 in the Motor City Bowl.
2009   11–2 (8–0)                **Final Ranking: #23**
         MAC Champions.
         Beat Ohio, 20-10, in the MAC Championship Game.
         Central Michigan beat Troy 44-41 in double OT in the GMAC Bowl, but
         Jones had already left to accept the Cincinnati job.

<u>Cincinnati: 23-14 (12-9 in the Big East)</u>
2010   4–8 (2–5)                 **Final Ranking: NR**
2011   10–3 (5–2)                **Final Ranking: #21**
         Big East Co-Champions.
         Beat Vanderbilt 31-24 in the Liberty Bowl.
2012   9–3 (5–2)                 **Final Ranking: #22**
         Big East Co-Champions.
         Cincinnati beat Duke 48-34 in the Belk Bowl, but Jones had already left to
         accept the Tennessee job.

<u>Tennessee: 12-13 (5-11 in the SEC)</u>
2013   5–7 (2–6)                 **Final Ranking: NR**
2014   7–6 (3–5)                 **Final Ranking: NR**
         Beat Iowa 45-28 in the TaxSlayer Bowl.

# Vanderbilt Commodores – Derek Mason

## Coach Ranking: #106

**Overall Record:** 3-9 in 1 season
**Record at Vanderbilt:** 3-9 in 1 season
**2014 Results:** 3-9, 0-8 in the SEC (7th in the SEC East)
**Returning Starters in 2015:** 9 on offense (including QB), 9 on defense
**Salary:** $2.25 Million*     **Age:** 45     **Job Security Grade:** C

**COACH'S BIO:**

Derek Mason grew up in Phoenix and played cornerback at Northern Arizona from 1989-1992. He worked his way up the coaching ranks as an assistant at multiple schools in the 1990s and 2000s. In 2007, he joined **Brad Childress'** staff with the Minnesota Vikings, where he coached DBs from 2007-2009. He was hired by **Jim Harbaugh** to coach DBs at Stanford in 2010 and was promoted to co-defensive coordinator and assistant head coach by **David Shaw** in 2011. He was Stanford's sole defensive coordinator from 2012-2013. In 2012, Mason was a finalist for the Broyles Award, which goes to the nation's top assistant coach. He was hired by Vanderbilt to be its head coach in January of 2014.

**2014 REVIEW:**

Nobody expected replacing **James Franklin** as Vanderbilt's head coach to be easy. Franklin led the Commodores to back-to-back nine-win seasons in 2012 and 2013. Prior to Franklin's arrival, Vanderbilt had only one nine-win season in its entire 100-plus year history. With just 10 starters returning and a recruiting class that scattered when Franklin announced he was leaving, it was not surprising that Vanderbilt took a step back in a difficult transition year. Just how big a step back they took was surprising. The Commodores were embarrassed at home in their opener against Temple, which set the tone for a season in which Vanderbilt failed to beat a single SEC opponent. Coach Mason cleaned house in the offseason by firing several coaches on his staff, including both his offensive and defensive coordinators.

| 2014 RESULTS: 3-9 (0-8 in the SEC) | Final Ranking: NR | |
|---|---|---|
| Temple | L 7–37 | (31,731) |
| #15 Ole Miss | L 3–41 | (43,260) |
| Massachusetts | W 34–31 | (33,386) |
| #14 South Carolina | L 34–48 | (34,441) |
| at Kentucky | L 7–17 | (56,940) |
| at #13 Georgia | L 17–44 | (92,746) |
| #24 (FCS) Charleston Southern | W 21–20 | (26,738) |
| at Missouri | L 14–24 | (65,264) |
| Old Dominion | W 42–28 | (28,966) |
| Florida | L 10–34 | (35,191) |
| at #4 Mississippi State | L 0–51 | (60,493) |
| Tennessee | L 17–24 | (40,350) |

## OFFENSE:

Vanderbilt fielded one of the worst offenses in all of college football last year, averaging just 17.2 points a game. As a result, Mason fired offensive coordinator (and former UCLA head coach) **Karl Dorrell** and replaced him with **Andy Ludwig**. Ludwig has spent the last two years as Wisconsin's offensive coordinator, where he led a run-first pro-style offense that ranked in the nation's Top 10 in rushing yards both seasons. In 2014, Wisconsin racked up 468.9 yards and 34.6 points per game, making it one of the nation's Top 30 offenses in both categories. Mason is hoping Ludwig can bring some of that Wisconsin efficiency and physicality to Vanderbilt. With nine starters back, he'll have a good shot at instantly moving this offense in the right direction.

## DEFENSE:

When an incoming head coach is best known for his defensive expertise, it's expected that his defense will rank better than 106th nationally in points allowed. Mason understands this line of thinking and responded to last year's ugly effort by firing defensive coordinator **David Kotulski**. Mason will take over the DC position himself this season. The Commodores struggled with their transition from a 4-3 to a 3-4 defense last year, but with nine starters returning in 2015, this squad should be much better.

## RECRUITING:

When **James Franklin** announced he was leaving Vanderbilt to accept the Penn State job, recruits fled Vandy. Five key commitments followed Franklin to Penn State, two more signed with in-state rival Tennessee, and another fled for SEC East rival Kentucky. Yet, Mason still managed to sign a class that ranked No. 45 nationally. This was a big turnaround from where the class stood in early January. Mason signed another Top-50 class in 2015, which is quite an accomplishment for a program coming off a winless conference record. If his team starts winning games, Mason could become one of the SEC's top recruiters.

## RUMOR MILL:

A drop-off of some kind after Franklin's departure was fully expected, but following up a nine-win season with a nine-*loss* season is a sure way to put yourself on the hot seat. It's worth remembering that **Robbie Caldwell** only lasted one season at Vanderbilt, resigning after his first year produced a 2-10 record in 2010. In an era of impatience, Mason needs to reverse course quickly.

## NOTEWORTHY:

Mason made another key hire in the offseason when he brought in a new strength and conditioning coach. **James Dobson** was Nebraska's strength coach under **Bo Pelini** from 2008-2014. During that time, the Cornhuskers had a reputation for fielding top-conditioned teams that regularly outplayed opponents in the fourth quarter. Mason also deserves some credit for not losing this team emotionally down the stretch of a miserable season. They played Tennessee very tough in the final game last year.

**2015 OUTLOOK:**

**Sept. 5**   **Western Kentucky Hilltoppers** – This won't be an easy game for Vanderbilt as Western Kentucky finished 8-5 last season. Another home-opening loss to a nonconference foe would be devastating.

**Sept. 12**   **Georgia Bulldogs** – Mark Richt has dominated this series with a 12-2 record against Vanderbilt during his 14 seasons at Georgia.

**Sept. 19**   **Austin Peay Governors** – Last year, the Commodores slipped past their FCS opponent with a one-point win over Charleston Southern. They know they can't take this game lightly.

**Sept. 26**   **at Ole Miss Rebels** – Vanderbilt lost by a combined score of 92-3 against both the SEC schools from the state of Mississippi last year.

**Oct. 3**   **at Middle Tennessee Blue Raiders** – This is a *MUST-WIN* game for Mason. He can't let Vanderbilt lose to an in-state mid-major opponent.

**Oct. 17**   **at South Carolina Gamecocks** – Dating back to his days at Florida, South Carolina head coach Steve Spurrier is 20-2 against Vanderbilt.

**Oct. 24**   **Missouri Tigers** – The Commodores played Mizzou tough in Columbia last year, losing by just 10. They're hoping this year they can close the gap with the Tigers coming to Nashville.

**Oct. 31**   **at Houston Cougars** – This is not a great nonconference game to have on your schedule. The Commodores don't stand to gain much if they knock off a mid-major Houston team that is breaking in a new head coach, but it's an embarrassing loss if they can't pull off the win.

**Nov. 7**   **at Florida Gators** – The last time Vanderbilt traveled to Gainesville, it pulled off a convincing 34-17 win in 2013.

**Nov. 14**   **Kentucky Wildcats** – This November home game is Vanderbilt's best shot at beating an SEC opponent in 2015.

**Nov. 21**   **Texas A&M Aggies** – These two schools met for the first time ever in 2013. Texas A&M won 56-24.

**Nov. 28**   **at Tennessee Volunteers** – Last year's seven-point loss to Tennessee was Vanderbilt's closest conference game.

**BOTTOM LINE:**
After an ugly debut season, Derek Mason is hitting the reset button by revamping his coaching staff. With 18 starters back, the Commodores are positioned to pull off a few surprises. Year 2 is a key evaluation season for new coaches and if Mason can't improve on the 2014 effort, he may have trouble holding onto this job.

## Derek Mason's Year-by-Year Coaching Record:

**Vanderbilt: 3-9 (0-8 in the SEC)**
2014   3-9 (0-8)          Final Ranking: NR

# Alabama Crimson Tide – Nick Saban

## Coach Ranking: #2

**Overall Record:** 177-59-1 in 19 seasons, 15-17 in 2 NFL seasons
**Record at Alabama:** 86-17 in 8 seasons
**2014 Results:** 12-2, 7-1 in the SEC (SEC Champions)
**Returning Starters in 2015:** 4 on offense, 7 on defense
**Salary:** $7.2 Million        **Age:** 63        **Job Security Grade:** A

COACH'S BIO:
Nick Saban grew up just outside of Fairmont, West Virginia, and played DB for **Don James** at Kent State. He joined the Kent State coaching staff as a graduate assistant in 1972 and began his fast ascent up the coaching ladder with notable stops on **Earl Bruce**'s staff at Ohio State (1980-1981) and **Jerry Glanville**'s staff with the Houston Oilers (1988-1989). He became the head coach at Toledo in 1990 and led the Rockets to a share of the MAC Championship in his one season there. Saban was then hired by **Bill Belichick** to be the defensive coordinator for the Cleveland Browns from 1991-1994. He became the head coach at Michigan State in 1995 and left for the LSU job in 2000. Saban returned to the NFL as head coach of the Miami Dolphins from 2005-2006, but left to become the head coach at Alabama in 2007. Saban has won six conference titles and four National Championships.

2014 REVIEW:
After losing its final two games of 2013 (the "Kick Six" game against Auburn and an upset loss to Oklahoma in the Sugar Bowl), Alabama bounced back to win its third SEC championship under Saban. The Crimson Tide overcame an upset loss to Ole Miss in October to win eight-straight games and enter the first ever College Football Playoff as the committee's No. 1-ranked team. Alabama lost to eventual champion Ohio State in the semifinal game.

| 2014 RESULTS:   12-2 (7-1 in the SEC) | Final Ranking: #4 | |
|---|---|---|
| vs. West Virginia (in Atlanta) | W 33–23 | (70,502) |
| Florida Atlantic | W 41–0 | (100,306) |
| Southern Miss | W 52–12 | (101,821) |
| Florida | W 42–21 | (101,821) |
| at #11 Ole Miss | L 17–23 | (61,826) |
| at Arkansas | W 14–13 | (72,337) |
| #21 Texas A&M | W 59–0 | (101,821) |
| at Tennessee | W 34–20 | (102,455) |
| at #14 LSU | W 20–13 OT | (102,321) |
| #1 Mississippi State | W 25–20 | (101,821) |
| Western Carolina | W 48–14 | (101,325) |
| #15 Auburn | W 55–44 | (101,821) |
| vs. #14 Missouri (SEC Championship) | W 42–13 | (73,526) |
| vs. #5 Ohio State (CFP Semifinal) | L 35–42 | (74,682) |

**OFFENSE:**

Nick Saban surprised many by hiring **Lane Kiffin** to be his new offensive coordinator last season. Kiffin had spent the previous four years as USC's head coach (he was fired after five games in 2013). Prior to that, he served as Tennessee's head coach for just one season after being fired by the Oakland Raiders four games into the 2008 season. Saban's Kiffin experiment was a huge success. Despite entering the season with big questions at the QB spot, Kiffin's offense racked up 6,783 yards, the most yards *ever* in Alabama football history. Kiffin came to Alabama known for his West Coast pro-style offense that passed the ball more than it ran it at USC, but last year he adapted to Saban's run-first mentality and ran the ball 55% of the time. He opened up the Tide offense with more spread and shotgun formations and he also sped up the pace by running plenty of no-huddle. The Tide ran 14% more plays per game in 2014 compared to 2013. Kiffin was reportedly a candidate for the OC job with the San Francisco 49ers this past offseason, but decided to stay at Alabama for another year. With just four starters returning and a new QB in 2015, he'll have his work cut out for him.

**DEFENSE:**

Saban has built this college football dynasty with a defense-first mentality and defensive coordinator **Kirby Smart** has made sure that Alabama's multiple 3-4 defense is one of the nation's best every year. Smart has been the DC since 2008 and Alabama has finished all seven of those seasons ranked in the Top 10 nationally in points allowed. That's an incredible statistic that proves just how consistently great Bama has been on this side of the ball. It's no wonder that the 39-year-old Smart is one the highest paid assistant coaches in all of college football ($1.35 million in 2014). With seven starters back in 2015, expect the defensive dominance to continue.

**RECRUITING:**

Saban dominates the college football world on the field *and* on the recruiting trail. In 2015, he landed the nation's No. 1-ranked class for the *fifth* year in a row.

**RUMOR MILL:**

Every year, Saban is mentioned as a candidate for vacant NFL head coaching jobs. The speculation is that **Bill Belichick**'s protégé still feels badly about his two-year performance with the Miami Dolphins and wants to redeem himself at the NFL level. As the highest paid coach in college football and with a seemingly unstoppable recruiting machine in place, it's getting more and more difficult to buy into the rumors that Saban might head to the NFL.

**NOTEWORTHY:**

Saban calls his coaching philosophy "the process." Similar to the approach used by legendary basketball coach **John Wooden**, "the process" is a relentless focus not on end results, like wins and championships, but instead a focus on the little things that need to be done – and done right – every day in order to achieve the desired result. It's a focus on only the things *you* can control. Saban's philosophy is clearly working.

## 2015 OUTLOOK:

**Sept. 5**   **vs. Wisconsin Badgers (in Arlington, TX)** – Alabama has started each of the last three seasons with a neutral site "kickoff" game. The Tide has won all three. Wisconsin kicked off last year by nearly beating LSU in Houston. Saban is 4-1 against the Big Ten since he arrived at Alabama. Last year's CFP semifinal loss to Ohio State was his lone loss to the Big Ten.

**Sept. 12**   **Middle Tennessee Blue Raiders** – This Conference USA team went 6-6 last season.

**Sept. 19**   **Ole Miss Rebels** – Ole Miss may have caught Alabama off guard in this game last year, but the Tide will be looking to make a statement in the rematch this season.

**Sept. 26**   **Louisiana-Monroe Warhawks** – These two teams met in Saban's first year at Alabama. ULM upset the Tide 21-14 in that 2007 matchup.

**Oct. 3**   **at Georgia Bulldogs** – This huge game will be a rematch of the 2012 SEC Championship – a down-to-the-wire game that Bama held on to win 32-28. Saban is 4-2 against Mark Richt, a record that dates back to his tenure at LSU.

**Oct. 10**   **Arkansas Razorbacks** – Arkansas nearly pulled off a big upset in this game last season, but Alabama emerged with a one-point win.

**Oct. 17**   **at Texas A&M Aggies** – Alabama embarrassed A&M with a 59-0 stomping last year. Expect College Station to be an extremely hostile environment when these teams meet again.

**Oct. 24**   **Tennessee Volunteers** – Alabama has now won eight straight in the "Third Saturday in October" rivalry. Tennessee is improving and the Crimson Tide will need to make sure they're not looking ahead to LSU.

**Nov. 7**   **LSU Tigers** – This is becoming one of the best games of the college football season each year. Three of the last eight meetings have been decided in OT. Saban is 6-3 against Les Miles.

**Nov. 14**   **at Mississippi State Bulldogs** – Saban is 6-0 against Dan Mullen, though last year's five-point win gives reason to believe that Mullen and the Bulldogs might be closing the gap.

**Nov. 21**   **Charleston Southern Buccaneers** – Saban has scheduled an FCS school in each of the past six seasons prior to the Auburn game. He's won all six of those games by an average of 43 points each.

**Nov. 28**   **at Auburn Tigers** – As it often is, this is Alabama's *MUST-WIN* game in 2015. Saban is 5-3 against Auburn since arriving at Alabama. He is 1-1 against Gus Malzahn.

## BOTTOM LINE:

On paper, Alabama looks like a team that will take a step back in 2015. They have just 11 starters returning (the third-fewest in the SEC) and one would expect this to be a rebuilding year for the Crimson Tide. However, with the tremendous amount of talent Saban recruits every year, his team doesn't need to *rebuild*, it can simply *reload*. Expect a motivated Alabama team in 2015 with the goal being nothing less than another National Championship.

## Nick Saban's Year-by-Year Coaching Record:

<u>Toledo: 9-2 (7-1 in the MAC)</u>
1990    9-2 (7–1)                Final Ranking: NR
        MAC Co-Champions.

<u>Michigan State: 34-24-1 (23-16-1 in the Big Ten)</u>
1995    6–5–1 (4–3–1)           Final Ranking: NR
        Lost to LSU 26-45 in the Independence Bowl.
1996    6–6 (5–3)               Final Ranking: NR
        Lost to Stanford 0-38 in the Sun Bowl.
1997    7–5 (4–4)               Final Ranking: NR
        Lost to #21 Washington 23-51 in the Aloha Bowl.
1998    6–6 (4–4)               Final Ranking: NR
1999    9–2 (6–2)               Final Ranking: #9
        Michigan State beat #10 Florida 37-34 in the Citrus Bowl, but Saban had already left to accept the LSU job. Michigan State finished the year ranked #7.

<u>LSU: 48-16 (28-12 in the SEC)</u>
2000    8–4 (5–3)               Final Ranking: #22
        Beat #15 Georgia Tech 28-14 in the Peach Bowl.
2001    10–3 (5–3)              Final Ranking: #7
        SEC Champions.
        Beat #2 Tennessee 31-20 in the SEC Championship Game.
        Beat #7 Illinois 47-34 in the Sugar Bowl.
2002    8–5 (5–3)               Final Ranking: NR
        SEC West Co-Champions.
        Lost to #9 Texas 20-35 in the Cotton Bowl.
2003    13–1 (7–1)              Final Ranking: #1
        National Champions.
        SEC Champions.
        Saban named National Coach of the Year.
        Saban named SEC Coach of the Year.
        Beat #5 Georgia 34-13 in the SEC Championship Game.
        Beat #3 Oklahoma 21-14 in the BCS National Championship Game.
2004    9–3 (6–2)               Final Ranking: #16
        Lost to #11 Iowa 25-30 in the Citrus Bowl.

<u>Miami Dolphins: 15-17 (0-0 in the NFL Playoffs)</u>
2005    9-7 (0-0)               2nd in the AFC East
2006    6-10 (0-0)              4th in the AFC East

## Alabama: 86-17 (50-11 in the SEC)

**2007**   **2-6 (1-4)**         **Final Ranking: NR**
Beat Colorado 30-24 in the Independence Bowl.
Record was originally 7-6, but five victories were later vacated due to the participation of ineligible players.

**2008**   **12-2 (8-0)**       **Final Ranking: #6**
SEC West Champions.
Saban named National Coach of the Year.
Saban named SEC Coach of the Year.
Lost to #2 Florida 20-31 in the SEC Championship Game.
Lost to #4 Utah 17-31 in the Sugar Bowl.

**2009**   **14-0 (8-0)**       **Final Ranking: #1**
National Champions.
SEC Champions.
Saban named SEC Coach of the Year.
Beat #1 Florida 32-13 in the SEC Championship Game.
Beat #2 Texas 37-21 in the BCS National Championship Game.

**2010**   **10-3 (5-3)**       **Final Ranking: #10**
Beat #7 Michigan State 49-7 in the Citrus Bowl.

**2011**   **12-1 (7-1)**       **Final Ranking: #1**
National Champions.
Beat #1 LSU 21-0 in the BCS National Championship Game.

**2012**   **13-1 (7-1)**       **Final Ranking: #1**
National Champions.
SEC Champions.
Beat #3 Georgia 32-28 in the SEC Championship Game.
Beat #1 Notre Dame 42-14 in the BCS National Championship Game.

**2013**   **11-2 (7-1)**       **Final Ranking: #7**
SEC West Co-Champions.
Lost to #11 Oklahoma 31-45 in the Sugar Bowl.

**2014**   **12-2 (7-1)**       **Final Ranking: #4**
SEC Champions.
Beat #14 Missouri 42-13 in the SEC Championship Game.
Lost to #5 Ohio State 35-42 in the CFP Semifinal Game.

# Arkansas Razorbacks – Bret Bielema

## Coach Ranking: #24

**Overall Record:** 78-39 in 9 seasons
**Record at Arkansas:** 10-15 in 2 seasons
**2014 Results:** 7-6, 2-6 in the SEC (7th in the SEC West)
**Returning Starters in 2015:** 9 on offense (including QB), 6 on defense
**Salary:** $4 Million      **Age:** 45      **Job Security Grade:** A

**COACH'S BIO:**
Bret Bielema walked on as a defensive lineman at Iowa in 1989 and by his senior season he was a team captain for **Hayden Fry's** Hawkeyes. After a year playing in the Arena Football League, Bielema joined Fry's coaching staff in 1994 as a graduate assistant. He was promoted to LB coach in 1996 and would keep that position when **Kirk Ferentz** was hired to replace the retiring Fry in 1999. Bielema left Iowa to serve as the co-defensive coordinator under **Bill Snyder** at Kansas State from 2002-2003, where his defenses ranked in the Top 10 nationally. In 2004, **Barry Alvarez** hired Bielema to be his DC at Wisconsin and in 2006 he was hired to replace the retiring Alvarez as head coach. He spent seven seasons as Wisconsin's head coach and led the Badgers to three-straight Big Ten championships from 2010-2012. Arkansas surprised the college football world by convincing Bielema to leave Wisconsin and become the Razorbacks' new head coach after the 2012 season.

**2014 REVIEW:**
Arkansas entered 2014 needing to give some indication that the Bielema era was headed in the right direction after dropping nine-straight games to close out 2013. Though Arkansas finished at the bottom of the SEC West for the second year in a row, this team showed clear progress in 2014 with the school's first winning season since **Bobby Petrino** was fired following his off-the-field troubles in 2011. The Razorbacks played their best football down the stretch and ended the year with a 31-7 stomping of their old Southwest Conference rivals in the Texas Bowl.

| **2014 RESULTS:   7-6 (2-6 in the SEC)** | **Final Ranking: NR** | |
|---|---|---|
| at #6 Auburn | L 21–45 | (87,451) |
| Nicholls State | W 73-7 | (63,108) |
| at Texas Tech | W 49–28 | (60,277) |
| Northern Illinois | W 52–14 | (67,204) |
| vs. #6 Texas A&M (in Arlington, TX) | L 28–35 OT | (68,113) |
| #7 Alabama | L 13–14 | (72,337) |
| #10 Georgia (in Little Rock) | L 32–45 | (54,959) |
| UAB | W 45–17 | (61,800) |
| at #1 Mississippi State | L 10–17 | (63,207) |
| #20 LSU | W 17–0 | (70,165) |
| #8 Ole Miss | W 30–0 | (64,510) |
| at #17 Missouri | L 14–21 | (71,168) |
| vs. Texas (Texas Bowl) | W 31–7 | (71,115) |

**OFFENSE:**
Bielema brought with him from Wisconsin a smash-mouth pro-style offense that aims to wear down opponents with a bruising running game. Arkansas fans understood it would take time to recruit the right type of players (especially on the offensive line) to execute this offense and last season showed that progress was being made. The Razorbacks controlled the line of scrimmage throughout much of the year. This season, Arkansas has nine starters returning on offense (including four offensive linemen and QB **Brandon Allen**), but they'll also be making the transition to a new offensive coordinator. **Jim Chaney**, who spent the past two seasons here at Arkansas, is leaving to become the OC at Pittsburgh. His replacement is **Dan Enos**, who left his position as head coach at Central Michigan. Enos ran a balanced pro-style offense at CMU, which ranked near the middle of the MAC in almost every category last year. A former Michigan State QB, Enos has a good reputation for developing QBs. With the experience coming back in 2015, this unit should have no problem carrying last year's late-season momentum into the new season.

**DEFENSE:**
After the 2013 season, Bielema hired **Robb Smith** from Rutgers to be his new defensive coordinator and Smith upgraded the defense from an SEC ranking of No. 12 to No. 4 in points allowed. Smith's 4-3 scheme improved as the year went on, allowing an average of just nine points a game in their final five games of the season. The Razorback defense finished the year ranked No. 10 nationally in yards allowed. This squad won't have as much experience heading into this season, but they may be more talented overall.

**RECRUITING:**
For the third year in a row, Bielema brought in a Top-30 recruiting class and Arkansas once again focused on bringing in four-star talent in the trenches.

**RUMOR MILL:**
Bielema reportedly turned down the Nebraska job this past offseason and Arkansas promptly gave him a two-year contract extension and an $800,000 raise. His new contract runs through the 2020 season and will pay him an average annual salary of $4.25 million with additional performance incentives of up to $1 million per year. This makes Bielema one of the top-paid coaches in the nation. Bielema interviewed with the Miami Dolphins when he was still at Wisconsin and if Iowa decides to part ways with **Kirk Ferentz** anytime soon, you can bet that Bielema will be at the top of his alma mater's list of targets.

**NOTEWORTHY:**
The Razorbacks played so well in the second half of last season that expectations have risen considerably heading into 2015. With higher expectations comes a different set of challenges for a coach who has officially crossed over from *rebuild* mode to *compete-for-a-title* mode. Bielema proved he could handle high expectations in Wisconsin. The same should be expected in Arkansas.

## 2015 OUTLOOK:

**Sept. 5**    **UTEP Miners** – UTEP went 7-6 last season, but the Miners were 2-5 in games outside of El Paso.

**Sept. 12**    **Toledo Rockets (in Little Rock)** – Arkansas is 2-0 all-time against MAC schools, including last season's 52-14 win over Northern Illinois.

**Sept. 19**    **Texas Tech Red Raiders** – The Red Raiders have 17 starters back and should be better than the 4-8 team that Arkansas beat 49-28 last year.

**Sept. 26**    **vs. Texas A&M Aggies (in Arlington, TX)** – The Aggies won this game by 48 points the year before Bielema was hired, they won by 12 in 2013, and last year they squeaked by with a seven-point win in OT. Bielema is closing the gap in this rivalry and if Arkansas is truly ready to compete for an SEC West title, this will be a *MUST-WIN* game to start the SEC schedule.

**Oct. 3**    **at Tennessee Volunteers** – The Razorbacks replace Georgia with Tennessee in their SEC East rotation game. These teams last met in 2011 and Arkansas blew away Tennessee 49-7. Expect this year's game to be much closer.

**Oct. 10**    **at Alabama Crimson Tide** – Alabama squeaked out a one-point win against Arkansas last season, which gave the Tide its eighth-straight win over the Razorbacks.

**Oct. 24**    **Auburn Tigers** – Getting Auburn at home and midway through the season should help the Razorbacks be better-prepared for the Tigers than they were in last year's season opener.

**Oct. 31**    **UT Martin Skyhawks** – Scheduling an FCS opponent here is the perfect spot to break up two brutal four-game stretches.

**Nov. 7**    **at Ole Miss Rebels** – Last season's 30-0 win over the Rebels made Bielema only the second coach ever to shut out a Hugh Freeze-coached team. Expect Ole Miss to have a few tricks up its sleeve for Arkansas' defense this year.

**Nov. 14**    **at LSU Tigers** – This border rivalry is always nasty and after Bielema handed Les Miles the only shutout loss of his career last season, you can expect an extremely hostile environment when Arkansas travels to Death Valley.

**Nov. 21**    **Mississippi State Bulldogs** – Bielema has lost his two games against Dan Mullen by seven points each. Mississippi State has now won the last three meetings in this series after Arkansas went 15-2 in the 17 meetings before that.

**Nov. 28**    **Missouri Tigers** – Last year, Mizzou came from behind to win the first matchup in this newly-titled "Battle Line Rivalry."

## BOTTOM LINE:

Expectations are high for an Arkansas team that finished red hot in 2014 and returns 15 starters for 2015. The transition period is over and Bielema should now be able to run the type of offense and defense he envisioned bringing to Fayetteville. With the rise of Ole Miss and Mississippi State, one has to wonder if there is room for *another* Top-10-level program in the SEC West. The Razorbacks intend to find out this season.

## Bret Bielema's Year-by-Year Coaching Record:

### Wisconsin: 68-24 (37-19 in the Big Ten)
2006   12–1 (7-1)          Final Ranking: #5
         Bielema named Big Ten Coach of the Year.
         Beat #12 Arkansas 17-14 in the Citrus Bowl.
2007   9–4 (5–3)          Final Ranking: #21
         Lost to #16 Tennessee 17-21 in the Outback Bowl.
2008   7–6 (3–5)          Final Ranking: NR
         Lost to Florida State 13-42 in the Citrus Bowl.
2009   10–3 (5–3)        Final Ranking: #16
         Beat #14 Miami (FL) 20-14 in the Citrus Bowl.
2010   11–2 (7–1)        Final Ranking: #7
         Big Ten Champions.
         Lost to #4 TCU 19-21 in the Rose Bowl.
2011   11–3 (6–2)        Final Ranking: #10
         Big Ten Champions.
         Beat #11 Michigan State 42-39 in the Big Ten Championship Game.
         Lost to #6 Oregon 38-45 in the Rose Bowl.
2012   8–5 (4–4)          Final Ranking: #23
         Big Ten Champions.
         Beat #14 Nebraska 70-31 in the Big Ten Championship Game.
         Wisconsin lost to #8 Stanford 14-20 in the Rose Bowl, but Bielema had already left to accept the Arkansas job.

### Arkansas: 10-15 (2-14 in the SEC)
2013   3–9 (0–8)          Final Ranking: NR
2014   7–6 (2–6)          Final Ranking: NR
         Beat Texas 31-7 in the Texas Bowl.

# Auburn Tigers – Gus Malzahn

## Coach Ranking: #9

**Overall Record:** 29-10 in 3 seasons
**Record at Auburn:** 20-7 in 2 seasons
**2014 Results:** 8-5, 4-4 in the SEC (T-4th in SEC West)
**Returning Starters in 2015:** 4 on offense, 8 on defense
**Salary:** $3.9 Million      **Age:** 49      **Job Security Grade:** A

**COACH'S BIO:**
Gus Malzahn got his coaching start at the high school level in Arkansas. In 1992, after one year as an assistant, he was named the head coach at Hughes High School and made it to the state championship in his third season there. He then built a powerhouse program at Shiloh Christian where he won state championships in 1998 and 1999 while gaining national attention for his no-huddle spread offense. He went to Springdale High in 2001. There, he won a state championship and earned a national Top-10 ranking in 2005. **Houston Nutt** hired Malzahn to be his offensive coordinator at Arkansas in 2006. From 2007-2008, he was **Todd Graham's** OC and assistant head coach at Tulsa, where he led one of the nation's top-ranked offenses. **Gene Chizik** hired Malzahn to be Auburn's OC in 2009 and the Tigers won a National Championship in 2010. Malzahn accepted the head coaching job at Arkansas State in 2012. After one season there, he became Auburn's head coach in 2013. In his first season as Auburn's head coach, he led the Tigers to an SEC championship and a No. 2 final ranking.

**2014 REVIEW:**
After winning the SEC and playing in the National Championship Game, Auburn had high hopes heading into 2014. The Tigers raced out to a 7-1 start and a No. 3 ranking before dropping two of their last three SEC games. An overtime loss to Wisconsin in the Outback Bowl put the finishing touches on a surprising late-season skid.

| **2014 RESULTS:   8-5 (4-4 in the SEC)** | **Final Ranking: #22** | |
|---|---|---|
| Arkansas | W 45–21 | (87,451) |
| San Jose State | W 59–13 | (87,451) |
| at #20 Kansas State | W 20–14 | (53,046) |
| Louisiana Tech | W 45–17 | (87,451) |
| #15 LSU | W 41–7 | (87,451) |
| at #3 Mississippi State | L 23–38 | (62,945) |
| South Carolina | W 42–35 | (87,451) |
| at #7 Ole Miss | W 35–31 | (62,090) |
| Texas A&M | L 38–41 | (87,451) |
| at #16 Georgia | L 7–34 | (92,746) |
| Samford | W 31–7 | (87,451) |
| at #1 Alabama | L 44–55 | (101,821) |
| vs. #17 Wisconsin (Outback Bowl) | L 31–34 OT | (44,023) |

**OFFENSE:**
While Gus Malzahn has two co-offensive coordinators in **Rhett Lashlee** and **Dameyune Craig**, Malzahn is the man who calls the plays. Recognized as an offensive mastermind, he wrote the book (*literally*) on the "hurry-up no-huddle" offense. Malzahn's version of the spread relies heavily on the run. He ran the ball 72% of the time in 2013 and 65% of the time in 2014. The Tigers have finished second in the SEC in total offense each of the past two seasons. With just four starters returning, one would expect this offense to suffer some growing pains in 2015. However, Malzahn has proven in the past that he can rack up the points with just about anyone. Junior QB **Jeremy Johnson** is expected to fit right in with this system.

**DEFENSE:**
When a team is known best for its offensive fireworks, the defense usually takes a back seat. In fact, one drawback to the no-huddle offense is that the defense doesn't get as much time to rest between each series. Auburn's defense has ranked in the bottom half of the SEC in Malzahn's first two seasons here. To change his team's defensive mentality, Malzahn hired **Will Muschamp** to be his new defensive coordinator. This may have been college football's biggest offseason hire as Muschamp is recognized as one of the top defensive minds in the game. He was fired as Florida's head coach last year due to the Gators' lack of offensive production. His defense, on the other hand, ranked in the Top 10 nationally each year during his Florida tenure. Eight starters are back in 2015 and while the Tigers will have to transition from a 4-2-5 defense to Muschamp's 3-4/4-3 blend, Auburn should make major improvements on this side of the ball.

**RECRUITING:**
Malzahn is proving he can recruit with the best in the nation as he's now landed back-to-back Top-10 recruiting classes. Adding Will Muschamp to his staff is a big plus as Muschamp has a long-established reputation for being one of the nation's best recruiters.

**RUMOR MILL:**
Over the past two years, several NFL teams, including the Cleveland Browns and Miami Dolphins, have reportedly been interested in Malzahn. However, there may be more hesitation from NFL franchises about bringing in a hurry-up offense guru now that **Chip Kelly** has failed to win a playoff game in his first two years with that style in Philadelphia. Malzahn himself has admitted that he thinks he's a better fit for the college game.

**NOTEWORTHY:**
We know Malzahn's high-energy, high-speed style can quickly build up and reenergize a program. The question now becomes, can he *maintain* a program? The longest Malzahn has ever stayed at one school was his five-year stint at Shiloh Christian High School. Entering Year 3 as head coach of the Tigers presents a new set of challenges for this offensive guru.

## 2015 OUTLOOK:

**Sept. 5**    **vs. Louisville Cardinals (in Atlanta)** – Auburn played at this same site in the Chick-fil-A Kickoff game against Clemson in 2012. They lost 26-19 to start what would be Gene Chizik's fourth and final season with the Tigers. Louisville went 9-4 last year in Bobby Petrino's first season back with the Cardinals.

**Sept. 12**    **Jacksonville State Gamecocks** – This should be an easy win for the Tigers as they get ready for a trip to Death Valley.

**Sept. 19**    **at LSU Tigers** – Les Miles handed Malzahn his only regular-season loss of 2013. Last year, Auburn paid back the favor with a 41-7 stomping of LSU.

**Sept. 26**    **Mississippi State Bulldogs** – The home team has won four in a row in this series.

**Oct. 3**    **San Jose State Spartans** – The Spartans will visit Auburn for the second year in a row. Last season, the Tigers won easily 59-13.

**Oct. 15**    **at Kentucky Wildcats** – Auburn draws Kentucky from the SEC East for this Thursday-night game. The Tigers have lost to the Wildcats just once in their last 17 meetings.

**Oct. 24**    **at Arkansas Razorbacks** – Last year's convincing season-opening win over Arkansas looked more impressive at the end of the year as the Razorbacks went on to break a two-year streak of losing seasons. Arkansas should be an improved team again this year.

**Oct. 31**    **Ole Miss Rebels** – Last season's win over the Rebels was Malzahn's fourth victory over a Top-10 team in his two seasons at Auburn. Malzahn is 2-0 against Hugh Freeze.

**Nov. 7**    **at Texas A&M Aggies** – The home loss to Texas A&M last year knocked the Tigers out of playoff contention and deflated their energy for the rest of the season. Malzahn is 1-1 against Kevin Sumlin.

**Nov. 14**    **Georgia Bulldogs** – Georgia embarrassed Auburn with a 34-7 rout last year and Malzahn is now 1-1 against Mark Richt.

**Nov. 21**    **Idaho Vandals** – The state of Alabama doesn't get to watch very good football the week before the Iron Bowl as both Auburn and Alabama schedule glorified practices the week before their showdown. Idaho has won just one game each of the past three seasons.

**Nov. 28**    **Alabama Crimson Tide** – Not only is this one of the best rivalries in all of college football, but the winner of this game has won the SEC West championship in six of the last seven seasons. This is the *MUST-WIN* game of the season for both teams.

## BOTTOM LINE:

Having just four starters back on offense is a big problem for most schools. It won't be for a Gus Malzahn-coached team, where offensive production has never been an issue. It's the defensive side of the ball that Auburn must improve. With Will Muschamp joining the staff and eight starters returning for this unit, expect the Tiger defense to be much better in 2015. Last year's five-loss record isn't a good indicator of how talented this team is. Auburn should once again be competing for the SEC championship and a spot in the playoffs.

## Gus Malzahn's Year-by-Year Coaching Record:

**Arkansas State: 9-3 (7-1 in the Sun Belt)**
2012    9-3 (7-1)          **Final Ranking: NR**
          Sun Belt Conference Champions.
          Arkansas State beat Kent State 17-13 in the GoDaddy.com Bowl, but Malzahn had already left to accept the Auburn job.

**Auburn: 20-7 (11-5 in the SEC)**
2013    12-2 (7-1)          **Final Ranking: #2**
          SEC Champions.
          Malzahn named National Coach of the Year.
          Malzahn named SEC Coach of the Year.
          Beat #5 Missouri 59-42 in the SEC Championship Game.
          Lost to #1 Florida State 31-34 in the BCS National Championship Game.
2014    8-5 (4-4)          **Final Ranking: #22**
          Lost to #17 Wisconsin 31-34 in OT in the Outback Bowl.

# LSU Tigers – Les Miles

## Coach Ranking: #5

**Overall Record:** 131-50 in 14 seasons
**Record at LSU:** 103-29 in 10 seasons
**2014 Results:** 8-5, 4-4 in the SEC (T-4th in the SEC West)
**Returning Starters in 2015:** 9 on offense (including QB), 6 on defense
**Salary:** $4.4 Million      **Age:** 61      **Job Security Grade:** B

**COACH'S BIO:**

Les Miles grew up in Elyria, Ohio, where he was an all-state lineman in high school. He played his college ball at Michigan under legendary head coach **Bo Schembechler** in the 1970s. He became a graduate assistant at Michigan in 1980 and was hired as **Bill McCartney's** OL coach at Colorado in 1982. Miles returned to Michigan to coach the offensive line from 1987-1994 (under Schembechler and then **Gary Moeller**). After a three-year stint as **Bob Simmons'** offensive coordinator at Oklahoma State, Miles moved to the NFL to coach tight ends for the Dallas Cowboys from 1998-2000 (under **Chan Gailey** and **Dave Campo**). In 2001, he was hired as the head coach at Oklahoma State, a school that had been to just one bowl game in the previous 12 years. He led Oklahoma State to three-straight bowl games before accepting the LSU job in 2005, replacing **Nick Saban** (who left for the NFL).

**2014 REVIEW:**

Heading into 2014, LSU lost more underclassmen to the NFL draft than any other team in the country (it the second year in a row that LSU held this distinction). The departure of talent caught up with the Tigers and they snapped a four-year streak of winning 10 games or more. A three-game stretch that included an upset win over No. 3 Ole Miss, an overtime loss to No. 4 Alabama, and a shutout loss to unranked Arkansas in back-to-back-to-back weeks summed up the up-and-down season. The Tigers struggled to find consistency in a year that ended with a surprising loss to unranked Notre Dame in the Music City Bowl.

**2014 RESULTS:   8-5 (4-4 in the SEC)**          **Final Ranking: NR**

| | | |
|---|---|---|
| vs. #14 Wisconsin (in Houston) | W 28–24 | (71,599) |
| Sam Houston State | W 56–0 | (100,338) |
| Louisiana–Monroe | W 31–0 | (101,194) |
| **Mississippi State** | L 29–34 | (102,321) |
| New Mexico State | W 63–7 | (101,987) |
| at #5 Auburn | L 7–41 | (87,451) |
| at Florida | W 30–27 | (88,014) |
| Kentucky | W 41–3 | (101,581) |
| #3 Ole Miss | W 10–7 | (102,321) |
| #4 Alabama | L 13–20 OT | (102,321) |
| at Arkansas | L 0–17 | (70,165) |
| at Texas A&M | W 23–17 | (105,829) |
| vs. Notre Dame (Music City Bowl) | L 28–31 | (60,149) |

**OFFENSE:**

LSU runs a physical pro-style offense that emphasizes the running game. The Tigers ran the ball nearly 70% of the time in 2014 and they were comfortable running out a more traditional I-formation as well as a shotgun set. After serving five seasons as the Baltimore Ravens' offensive coordinator, **Cam Cameron** was hired to the same position at LSU in 2013. With two inexperienced QBs and a seasoned offensive line, it wasn't surprising to see LSU rely heavily on its bruising ground game last year. The Tigers ranked 25th nationally in rushing. But despite the powerful rushing attack, LSU ranked 76th in scoring offense. Why the discrepancy? Because LSU's pass offense fell from 45th in 2013 to 116th in 2014. Miles did what he had to do with a young team in 2014. While the overall offense took a step back, the Tigers should tout an even stronger running game and a more balanced overall attack in 2015. Freshman RB **Leonard Fournette** proved he was the real deal last season and he'll get a lot more touches this year. Questions remain at the QB spot with no clear starter, but the experience gained in 2014 means the passing game should be better. As one of college football's highest-paid assistants, Cam Cameron will make $1.5 million in 2015, which is the third and final year of his current contract with LSU.

**DEFENSE:**

The Tigers employ a fast and aggressive defensive style with a standard four-man front. Experience up front was a major concern heading into 2014 and though the Tigers struggled with the run early in the season, they made marked improvement as the year went on, giving up just 95 rushing yards per game in November. LSU's pass defense was one of the nation's best last year and only three other teams allowed fewer points per game than the Tigers. A stellar coaching job. However, defensive coordinator **John Chavis** is leaving LSU for the same position at Texas A&M after six years with the Tigers. This move sent shockwaves through the SEC. Chavis' replacement is Alabama LB coach (and former Clemson DC) **Kevin Steele**. To help with the big shoes he's filling, Miles also hired former Ole Miss and USC head coach **Ed Orgeron** to coach the d-line. Six starters are back on this defense, which should help Steele and Orgeron pick up where last year's squad left off.

**RECRUITING:**

Year-after-year, Miles brings in incredible recruiting classes. It undoubtedly helps that LSU is the school-of-choice in a state loaded with football talent. The 2015 class wasn't quite as highly-touted as 2014's No. 2-ranked class, but it was still rated as the nation's No. 5 class on Signing Day. Adding Ed Orgeron to the staff should ensure that LSU keeps dominating the recruiting wars. Orgeron is widely recognized as one of the best recruiters in the country.

**RUMOR MILL:**

Now that Michigan has hired **Jim Harbaugh**, LSU fans can stop worrying about Miles' name coming up every time the Wolverines lose a game. Miles gets a pass for last year's 8-5 record due to the inexperience he had coming into the season, but a *big* turnaround is fully expected in 2015.

**2015 OUTLOOK:**

**Sept. 5**    **McNeese State Cowboys** – Miles is 10-0 against FCS teams and beat McNeese State 32-10 in 2010. The Cowboys went 6-5 last year.

**Sept. 12**    **at Mississippi State Bulldogs** - Starting the SEC West schedule off with a bang, this will be the perfect opportunity for Miles and company to show they're back in the national-title hunt. Last year was Miles' first loss ever to Mississippi State.

**Sept. 19**    **Auburn Tigers** – This is a huge September showdown with another SEC West power trying to bounce back from an 8-5 season of its own. Auburn embarrassed LSU last year with a 41-7 stomping last year. Miles is 7-3 against Auburn and 1-1 against Gus Malzahn.

**Sept. 26**    **at Syracuse Orange** – This is not an easy road trip and it has the dangerous potential to be a "letdown" game for the Tigers.

**Oct. 3**    **Eastern Michigan Eagles** – LSU is 5-1 all-time against MAC schools. The only loss occurred back in 1986.

**Oct. 10**    **at South Carolina Gamecocks** – These schools last played in 2012 and Miles led the Tigers to an upset win over Spurrier's No. 3-ranked Gamecocks. Miles has won all three previous matchups against South Carolina.

**Oct. 17**    **Florida Gators** – The Gators always play LSU tough and this year should be no different. Miles is 6-4 against Florida and just five *total* points separate these two teams over those 10 games (Florida has outscored LSU 215-210 over those 10 games).

**Oct. 24**    **Western Kentucky Hilltoppers** – WKU isn't the glorified practice many fans might be expecting, but LSU should overpower the Hilltoppers. Since arriving at LSU, Miles is 5-0 against Conference USA schools.

**Nov. 7**    **at Alabama Crimson Tide** – This is one of college football's annual must-watch games as two great programs and coaches collide. Last year's OT loss to Bama dropped Miles' record to 3-6 against Nick Saban.

**Nov. 14**    **Arkansas Razorbacks** – This is a *MUST-WIN* game for LSU. The Tigers were shut out by their border rivals last year (the only shutout loss of Miles' career) and the Razorbacks look like a team ready to push its way back into SEC West contention. Miles is 6-4 against Arkansas and this game has been decided by an average of seven points each during the Miles era.

**Nov. 21**    **at Ole Miss Rebels** – Ole Miss will be looking for revenge in this renewed rivalry. Miles is 7-4 against Ole Miss, with one of those losses occurring while he was at Oklahoma State.

**Nov. 28**    **Texas A&M Aggies** – LSU has won all three games against the Aggies since they joined the SEC.

**BOTTOM LINE:**
The SEC West schedule will be brutal once again, but that means LSU could still make the playoffs with a loss. With six players who could've entered the NFL Draft deciding to come back, the 2015 season has a chance to be very special in Baton Rouge.

## Les Miles' Year-by-Year Coaching Record:

#### Oklahoma State: 28-21 (16-16 in the Big 12)
| | | |
|---|---|---|
| 2001 | 4-7 (2-6) | Final Ranking: NR |
| 2002 | 8-5 (5-3) | Final Ranking: NR |

Beat Southern Miss 33-23 in the Houston Bowl.

| | | |
|---|---|---|
| 2003 | 9-4 (5-3) | Final Ranking: NR |

Lost to #16 Ole Miss 28-31 in the Cotton Bowl.

| | | |
|---|---|---|
| 2004 | 7-5 (4-4) | Final Ranking: NR |

Lost to #22 Ohio State 7–33 in the Alamo Bowl.

#### LSU: 103-29 (56-24 in the SEC)
| | | |
|---|---|---|
| 2005 | 11-2 (7-1) | Final Ranking: #5 |

SEC West Champions.
Lost to #13 Georgia 14-34 in the SEC Championship Game.
Beat #9 Miami (FL) 40-3 in the Peach Bowl.

| | | |
|---|---|---|
| 2006 | 11-2 (6-2) | Final Ranking: #3 |

Beat #11 Notre Dame 41–14 in the Sugar Bowl.

| | | |
|---|---|---|
| 2007 | 12-2 (6-2) | Final Ranking: #1 |

National Champions.
SEC Champions. Beat #14 Tennessee 21-14 in the SEC Championship Game.
Beat #1 Ohio State 38–24 in the BCS National Championship Game.

| | | |
|---|---|---|
| 2008 | 8-5 (3-5) | Final Ranking: NR |

Beat #14 Georgia Tech 38-3 in the Chick-fil-A Bowl.

| | | |
|---|---|---|
| 2009 | 9-4 (5-3) | Final Ranking: #17 |

Lost to #11 Penn State 17–19 in the Capital One Bowl.

| | | |
|---|---|---|
| 2010 | 11-2 (6-2) | Final Ranking: #8 |

Beat #18 Texas A&M 41-24 in the Cotton Bowl.

| | | |
|---|---|---|
| 2011 | 13-1 (8-0) | Final Ranking: #2 |

SEC Champions.
Miles named the National Coach of the Year.
Beat #2 Alabama 9-6 in OT in the regular season, but lost in a rematch with Alabama in the BCS National Championship Game 0-21.

| | | |
|---|---|---|
| 2012 | 10-3 (6-2) | Final Ranking: #12 |

Lost to #15 Clemson 24-25 in the Chick-fil-A Bowl.

| | | |
|---|---|---|
| 2013 | 10-3 (5-3) | Final Ranking: #14 |

Beat Iowa 21-14 in the Outback Bowl.

| | | |
|---|---|---|
| 2014 | 8-5 (4-4) | Final Ranking: NR |

Lost to Notre Dame 28-31 in the Music City Bowl.

# Mississippi State Bulldogs – Dan Mullen

## Coach Ranking: #35

**Overall Record:** 46-31 in 6 seasons
**Record at Mississippi State:** 46-31 in 6 seasons
**2014 Results:** 10-3, 6-2 in the SEC (2nd in the SEC West)
**Returning Starters in 2015:** 5 on offense (including QB), 4 on defense
**Salary:** $4 Million      **Age:** 43      **Job Security Grade:** A

COACH'S BIO:

As a player, Dan Mullen helped lead Trinity High School in Manchester, New Hampshire, to the 1988 state championship and he was an all-conference TE at Ursinus College (Division III) in Pennsylvania. After graduating, he immediately began working his way up the coaching ranks and was eventually hired as a graduate assistant at Notre Dame in 1999 (under **Bob Davie**). It was there that he formed a friendship with fellow assistant coach **Urban Meyer**. When Meyer was hired as the head coach at Bowling Green, Mullen followed as the QB coach. He made the moves with Meyer to Utah and Florida as well. At Florida, Mullen was the offensive coordinator from 2005-2008, where he helped the Gators win two National Championships (2006 and 2008). He was hired as Mississippi State's head coach in 2009. The AP voted Mullen the SEC Coach of the Year in 2014.

2014 REVIEW:

The 2014 season was a magical ride for Mississippi State that ended on a sour note. During an amazing stretch that began in September, the Bulldogs knocked off three-consecutive Top-10 opponents and rose to No. 1 in the nation. They held that top ranking for three weeks before losing a heartbreaker to No. 4 Alabama. Two weeks later, archrival Ole Miss would upset Mississippi State and ruin any chance the Bulldogs had of making it into the College Football Playoff. Despite a 453-yard passing effort by QB **Dak Prescott**, Mississippi State fell to No. 10 Georgia Tech in the Orange Bowl as the defense couldn't slow down the Jackets' option attack.

| 2014 RESULTS:   10-3 (6-2 in the SEC) | Final Ranking: #11 | |
|---|---|---|
| Southern Miss | W 49-0 | (61,889) |
| Alabama-Birmingham | W 47-34 | (57,704) |
| at South Alabama | W 35-3 | (38,129) |
| at #8 LSU | W 34-29 | (102,321) |
| #6 Texas A&M | W 48-31 | (61,133) |
| #2 Auburn | W 38-23 | (62,945) |
| at Kentucky | W 45-31 | (64,791) |
| Arkansas | W 17-10 | (62,307) |
| Tennessee–Martin | W 45-16 | (61,421) |
| at #4 Alabama | L 20-25 | (101,821) |
| Vanderbilt | W 51-0 | (60,493) |
| at #18 Ole Miss | L 17-31 | (62,058) |
| vs. #10 Georgia Tech (Orange Bowl) | L 34-49 | (58,211) |

**OFFENSE:**

Dan Mullen and **Urban Meyer** are largely credited with creating the offensive system now widely known as the spread-option offense. Ideally-suited for a dual-threat QB, **Dak Prescott** has been a perfect fit for this system. Last season, Prescott passed for 3,449 yards while rushing for 986 yards and he'll return for his senior season in 2015. However, the Bulldogs will lose six starters from this explosive group, including breakout RB **Josh Robinson**, who declared for the NFL draft. Mullen used two co-offensive coordinators last season. **Billy Gonzales** was the passing game coordinator and **John Hevesy** was the running game coordinator. This setup worked well for Mullen, who handles the offensive play calling himself. The Bulldogs ranked 10th in the nation last year in yards per game, but it's going to be tough to match that firepower with just five starters back in 2015.

**DEFENSE:**

After spending the last four years running Mississippi State's "Psycho Defense," **Geoff Collins** is leaving the Bulldogs to become the defensive coordinator at Florida. This is a big loss for Mississippi State, which became one of the top defenses in the SEC under Collins. His departure seemed to catch Mullen by surprise, who said after the announcement, "I hope our guys have opportunities to go be head coaches more than leaving for lateral positions." Collins left before the Orange Bowl and his absence showed as the Bulldogs gave up 577 yards to Georgia Tech. Mullen is bringing back **Manny Diaz**, who served as the Bulldogs' DC in 2010, to replace Collins. Diaz was the DC at Texas from 2011-2013 and despite leading the top defense in the Big 12 in 2011, he was fired early in 2013 after Texas gave up a school-record 550 rushing yards to BYU in an ugly loss. Last year, Diaz was the DC at Louisiana Tech, where his defense finished the season ranked No. 39 in points allowed. Only four starters are returning this season and losing Collins is a significant blow to this unit.

**RECRUITING:**

The good news is that Mullen signed a recruiting class that was ranked No. 18 nationally. The bad news is that this class was ranked eighth in the SEC. Fans were hoping that Mullen could parlay last season's success into a recruiting class that ranked in the upper half of the SEC.

**RUMOR MILL:**

Mullen's name came up quickly as a candidate for the Florida job after **Will Muschamp** was fired, but rumor has it there was friction between Mullen and Florida athletic director **Jeremy Foley**, which kept Mullen from being seriously considered for the job. There were also reports that Mullen was very high on Michigan's list before they were able to lure **Jim Harbaugh**. With Mullen expected to remain one of the top candidates for any big-time job that opens up in the future, Mississippi State gave him a $1 million raise and a four-year contract extension (the most allowed by state law) this past offseason.

## 2015 OUTLOOK:

**Sept. 5**    **at Southern Miss Golden Eagles** – The Bulldogs had no trouble beating this in-state opponent last season in Starkville 49-0. The result shouldn't be much different on the road this year. Southern Miss finished 3-9 in 2014.

**Sept. 12**    **LSU Tigers** – LSU was blindsided at home by Mississippi State last season and they'll be looking for payback this year. Last year was Mullen's first victory ever against Les Miles and the Tigers.

**Sept. 19**    **Northwestern State Demons** – This FCS school went 6-6 last year.

**Sept. 26**    **at Auburn Tigers** – Mullen is 2-4 against Auburn and he's 1-1 against Gus Malzahn.

**Oct. 3**    **at Texas A&M Aggies** – Last year's victory over A&M was Mullen's first in three meetings against Kevin Sumlin's Aggies. Mullen went 1-1 against Sumlin when Sumlin was at Houston.

**Oct. 10**    **Troy Trojans** – When these teams last met (2013), the Bulldogs won 62-7. Troy went 3-9 last year.

**Oct. 17**    **Louisiana Tech Bulldogs** – Returning Mississippi State DC Manny Diaz was Louisiana Tech's DC last season.

**Oct. 24**    **Kentucky Wildcats** – Mullen is a perfect 6-0 against the Wildcats.

**Nov. 5**    **at Missouri Tigers** – This will be the first meeting between these two schools since Mizzou joined the SEC.

**Nov. 14**    **Alabama Crimson Tide** – Mullen is still looking for his first win against Nick Saban. Last season's five-point loss was by far his best effort as Alabama won the previous five meetings by an average of 22 points each.

**Nov. 21**    **at Arkansas Razorbacks** – After losing his first three meetings with Arkansas, Mullen has reversed the trend and won the last three.

**Nov. 28**    **Ole Miss Rebels** – Mullen is 4-2 against this archrival, but last year's loss to the Rebels stung badly, likely costing the Bulldogs an invitation to the College Football Playoff. One gets the sense that the state of Mississippi may not be big enough for *two* elite-level programs, especially in the ultra-competitive SEC West. That makes this a *MUST-WIN* game for Mullen in 2015.

## BOTTOM LINE:

Even with Dak Prescott back, it's going to be very tough for Mississippi State to duplicate last year's success. Ten wins as an SEC West team is an outstanding feat, but with just nine starters returning (only three other schools in *all* of college football have fewer starters back next season), a step back is expected for the Bulldogs.

## Dan Mullen's Year-by-Year Coaching Record:

<u>Mississippi State: 46-31 (22-26 in the SEC)</u>
| | | |
|---|---|---|
| 2009 | 5–7 (3–5) | Final Ranking: NR |
| 2010 | 9–4 (4–4) | Final Ranking: #15 |

Beat Michigan 52-14, in the Gator Bowl.

| | | |
|---|---|---|
| 2011 | 7–6 (2–6) | Final Ranking: NR |

Beat Wake Forest 23-17 in the Music City Bowl.

| | | |
|---|---|---|
| 2012 | 8–5 (4–4) | Final Ranking: NR |

Lost to #21 Northwestern 20-34 in the Gator Bowl.

| | | |
|---|---|---|
| 2013 | 7–6 (3–5) | Final Ranking: NR |

Beat Rice 44-7 in the Liberty Bowl.

| | | |
|---|---|---|
| 2014 | 10–3 (6–2) | Final Ranking: #11 |

Mullen named SEC Coach of the Year by the AP.
Mullen named National Coach of the Year by the Maxwell Football Club.
Lost to #10 Georgia Tech 34-49 in the Orange Bowl.

# Ole Miss Rebels – Hugh Freeze

## Coach Ranking: #23

**Overall Record:** 54-22 in 6 seasons (2 seasons in NAIA)
**Record at Ole Miss:** 24-15 in 3 seasons
**2014 Results:** 9-4, 5-3 in the SEC (3rd in the SEC West)
**Returning Starters in 2015:** 9 on offense, 7 on defense
**Salary:** $4.3 Million      **Age:** 45      **Job Security Grade:** A

**COACH'S BIO:**
The 2009 hit movie *The Blind Side* told the inspiring true story of high school football player **Michael Oher**. What wasn't made clear in the movie was that Oher's coach at Briarcrest Christian School in Memphis was one of the most successful coaches in the South, making six-straight state championship appearances, winning two state titles, and being named the high school Coach of the Year four times during his 10-year tenure from 1995-2004. That coach was Hugh Freeze and after racking up a 99-23 record at the high school level, Freeze joined **Ed Orgeron's** staff at Ole Miss as the recruiting coordinator and TE coach from 2005-2007. In 2008, he took over as head coach at Lambuth, a struggling NAIA school in Tennessee. After 20 wins in two seasons, he was hired as Arkansas State's offensive coordinator in 2010 and promoted to head coach in 2011. Freeze went 10-2 and won the Sun Belt Conference in his debut season at Arkansas State. Ole Miss hired Freeze after the Rebels finished 2-10 under **Houston Nutt** in 2011.

**2014 REVIEW:**
Ole Miss sprinted out to a 7-0 start for the first time since 1962 and climbed to No. 3 in the polls before losing back-to-back games by a combined seven points. Though the Rebels were crushed by TCU in the Peach Bowl on New Year's Eve, the 2014 season will be remembered best by Ole Miss fans for their Egg Bowl victory over archrival Mississippi State, an upset win that cost the No. 4-ranked Bulldogs a spot in the College Football Playoff.

**2014 RESULTS:   9-4 (5-3 in the SEC)**      Final Ranking: #17

| | | |
|---|---|---|
| vs. Boise State (in Atlanta) | W 35–13 | (32,823) |
| at Vanderbilt | W 41–3 | (43,260) |
| Louisiana–Lafayette | W 56–15 | (60,937) |
| Memphis | W 24–3 | (61,291) |
| #3 Alabama | W 23–17 | (61,826) |
| at #14 Texas A&M | W 35–20 | (110,633) |
| Tennessee | W 34–3 | (62,081) |
| at #24 LSU | L 7–10 | (102,321) |
| #4 Auburn | L 31–35 | (62,090) |
| Presbyterian | W 48–0 | (60,546) |
| at Arkansas | L 0–30 | (64,510) |
| #4 Mississippi State | W 31–17 | (62,058) |
| vs. #6 TCU (Peach Bowl) | L 3–42 | (65,706) |

**OFFENSE:**
There are striking similarities between longtime friends Hugh Freeze and Auburn's **Gus Malzahn**. Both coaches first gained national recognition for building high school powerhouses with an innovative no-huddle spread offense. They were both hired as SEC head coaches after one season as head coach at Arkansas State. Both coaches employ two co-offensive coordinators (**Dan Werner** and **Matt Luke** at Ole Miss), while handling the offensive play-calling duties themselves. And both coaches continue to run no-huddle spread offenses. However, Freeze slowed down his offense a bit in 2014. The Rebels still operated without a huddle, but they took more time at the line of scrimmage to read defenses. As a result, Ole Miss ran about 10% fewer plays in 2014 compared to the previous year. Interestingly, their yards-per-play average was an identical 6.0 for both seasons. Fewer plays meant fewer total yards and Mississippi's total offense fell from 21st in the nation to 54th in 2014. The Rebels have to replace **Bo Wallace** at QB, but they return nine starters (including all five offensive linemen) and they are loaded with talent. As long as the QB transition goes smoothly, this offense should have more firepower in 2015.

**DEFENSE:**
Slowing down the pace of the offense last year was intended to help out the defense, which it certainly seemed to do. Ole Miss was ranked No. 1 in the nation in points allowed last season. This represented a dramatic one-year improvement as this defense ranked near the middle of the SEC in 2013. Co-defensive coordinators **Dave Wommack** and **Jason Jones** run a 4-2-5 defense that can radically change its look from week-to-week based on the offense it faces. Wommack was the DC at seven different schools prior to Ole Miss and he's been Freeze's DC since their time at Arkansas State. The Rebels will have to replace two All-Americans (CB **Senquez Golson** and S **Cody Prewitt**) in the secondary, but they'll have seven starters back on this defense.

**RECRUITING:**
In 2013, Hugh Freeze and his staff shocked the college football world on Signing Day by landing *four* five-star recruits and the nation's 8th-ranked recruiting class. Ole Miss has shown that 2013 was no one-year fluke by landing the No. 15 class in 2014 and the No. 17 class in 2015.

**RUMOR MILL:**
Shortly after rumors circulated that Freeze was a top candidate for the vacant Florida job, Ole Miss stepped in to give him a $1.2 million raise and a four-year contract extension (the largest extension allowed by state law in Mississippi) that will keep him the head Rebel through 2018. The commitment seems mutual as Freeze has publicly stated that he hopes to retire at Ole Miss.

**NOTEWORTHY:**
Hugh Freeze is not only recognized as a brilliant offensive coach and one of the nation's best recruiters, but he's also a master motivator. His style is rooted in positive reinforcement and he's established a reputation for delivering classic pre-game speeches.

## 2015 OUTLOOK:

**Sept. 5**  **Tennessee-Martin Skyhawks** – Ole Miss eases into the year with this FCS opponent. The Skyhawks went 6-6 in 2014.

**Sept. 12**  **Fresno State Bulldogs** – Fresno State won the MWC West Division last season, though it finished the year 6-8.

**Sept. 19**  **at Alabama Crimson Tide** – Ole Miss gave Alabama its only SEC loss last season and this will be a crucial early-season showdown in the West Division. Freeze is 1-2 against Nick Saban.

**Sept. 26**  **Vanderbilt Commodores** – Having Vanderbilt as the annual East Division matchup looks a lot easier now that James Franklin is gone and the Commodores are rebuilding.

**Oct. 3**  **at Florida Gators** – With a new head coach and just 10 starters returning for the Gators, Ole Miss may be catching Florida at the perfect time on this East Division draw. This will be Freeze's first game against the Gators.

**Oct. 10**  **New Mexico State Aggies** – New Mexico State went 2-10 last season and shouldn't give the Rebels much trouble.

**Oct. 17**  **at Memphis Tigers** – Freeze won his two previous games against Memphis (including a 2011 game while he was at Arkansas State) by a combined score of 71-6. Last year, Memphis went 10-3 and finished the season ranked No. 25.

**Oct. 24**  **Texas A&M Aggies** – Last year's win was Freeze's first victory over Kevin Sumlin and the Aggies. He is now 1-2 in this series. This will mark the start of a brutal five-game stretch to close the season.

**Oct. 31**  **at Auburn Tigers** – When Freeze left Arkansas State for Ole Miss, he recommended that Arkansas State hire Gus Malzahn as his replacement. After last year's loss to Auburn, Freeze is now 0-2 against Malzahn.

**Nov. 7**  **Arkansas Razorbacks** – Only two college coaches have scored a shutout victory against Hugh Freeze, Nick Saban's Crimson Tide in 2013 and Bret Bielema's Razorbacks last year.

**Nov. 21**  **LSU Tigers** – Last year's loss to LSU, which ended when the Tigers intercepted a Bo Wallace pass at the one-yard-line, still stings and Ole Miss will be looking for payback. Expect a great atmosphere for this one.

**Nov. 28**  **at Mississippi State Bulldogs** – Last season's Egg Bowl victory over Mississippi State knocked the Bulldogs out of the playoffs. Freeze is now 2-1 in this rivalry, which is the *MUST-WIN* game of the year for both teams.

## BOTTOM LINE:

Freeze won seven games in Year 1 at Ole Miss, eight games in Year 2, and nine games last year. Will Year 4 bring 10 wins or more? Though the Rebels will have to break in a new QB, all the blue-chip athletes they've been recruiting are growing up and this will be the most talented Ole Miss team Freeze has had. The Rebels have the coaching staff and the talent to make a playoff run in 2015 *if* they survive the brutal five-game stretch to close out the season.

## Hugh Freeze's Year-by-Year Coaching Record:

<u>Lambuth: 20-5 (1-2 in the NAIA Playoffs)</u>
2008    8–4 (0-1)              Final Ranking: NA
        Lost to Lindenwood 48-65 in first round of the NAIA Playoffs.
2009    12–1 (1-1)             Final Ranking: NA
        Lost to St. Xavier 10-52 in the NAIA quarterfinals.

<u>Arkansas State: 10-2 (8-0 in the Sun Belt)</u>
2011    10–2 (8-0)            Final Ranking: NR
        Sun Belt Champions.
        Freeze becomes the 14th coach in history to win 10 games in his first season
        as an FBS head coach.
        Arkansas State lost to Northern Illinois 20-38 in the GoDaddy.com Bowl,
        but Freeze had already left to accept the Ole Miss job.

<u>Ole Miss: 24-15 (11-13 in the SEC)</u>
2012    7–6 (3-5)             Final Ranking: NR
        Beat Pittsburgh 38-17 in the BBVA Compass Bowl.
2013    8–5 (3-5)             Final Ranking: NR
        Beat Georgia Tech 25-17 in the Music City Bowl.
2014    9–4 (5-3)             Final Ranking: #17
        Lost to #6 TCU 3-42 in the Peach Bowl.

# Texas A&M Aggies – Kevin Sumlin

## Coach Ranking: #21

**Overall Record:** 63-28 in 7 seasons
**Record at Texas A&M:** 28-11 in 3 seasons
**2014 Results:** 8-5, 3-5 in the SEC (6th in the SEC West)
**Returning Starters in 2015:** 8 on offense (including QB), 7 on defense
**Salary:** $5 Million          **Age:** 51          **Job Security Grade:** B

**COACH'S BIO:**
Kevin Sumlin was a four-year starter at LB for Purdue from 1983-1986. He was a graduate assistant at Washington State from 1988-1990 (under head coaches **Dennis Erickson** and **Mike Price**). As a player at Purdue, his defensive coordinator was **Joe Tiller** and when Tiller was hired as Wyoming's head coach in 1991, Sumlin joined his staff as WR coach. After two years there, Sumlin coached WRs and then QBs at Minnesota from 1993-1997. He reunited with Tiller at Purdue from 1998-2000. In 2001, Sumlin was hired by **R.C. Slocum** at Texas A&M and was promoted to offensive coordinator in 2002. After Slocum was fired at A&M, Sumlin was quickly hired by **Bob Stoops** at Oklahoma, where he coached from 2003-2007. Sumlin was the OC for the Sooners during his final two seasons there. Houston hired Sumlin as its head coach in 2008 and during his four years there, he was named Conference USA Coach of the Year twice and led the Cougars to a Top-20 finish in 2011. Texas A&M hired Sumlin to be its head coach in 2012. He was named the SEC Coach of the Year after going 11-2 in his debut season.

**2014 REVIEW:**
The Aggies entered 2014 looking to prove their offense could still rack up big points without Heisman Trophy-winning QB **Johnny Manziel**, who left early for the NFL. After an impressive 5-0 start, Texas A&M lost three games in a row and Sumlin replaced starting QB **Kenny Hill** with true freshman **Kyle Allen**. Allen went 3-2 in his five starts at the end of the season.

**2014 RESULTS:   8-5 (3-5 in the SEC)**          **Final Ranking: NR**

| | | |
|---|---|---|
| at #9 South Carolina | W 52–28 | (82,847) |
| Lamar | W 73–3 | (104,728) |
| Rice | W 38–10 | (103,867) |
| at SMU | W 58–6 | (34,820) |
| vs. Arkansas (in Arlington, TX) | W 35–28 OT | (68,113) |
| at #12 Mississippi State | L 31–48 | (61,133) |
| #3 Ole Miss | L 20–35 | (110,633) |
| at #7 Alabama | L 0–59 | (101,821) |
| Louisiana–Monroe | W 21–16 | (100,922) |
| at #3 Auburn | W 41–38 | (87,451) |
| Missouri | L 27–34 | (104,756) |
| LSU | L 17–23 | (105,829) |
| vs. West Virginia (Liberty Bowl) | W 45–37 | (51,282) |

**OFFENSE:**

Texas A&M runs a balanced version of the Air Raid offense and third-year offensive coordinator **Jake Spavital** knows this system well. In his five seasons prior to joining the A&M staff, Spavital coached with **Gus Malzahn** at Tulsa, Sumlin at Houston, and **Dana Holgorsen** at Oklahoma State and West Virginia. After leading the SEC in scoring in 2013, the Aggies dropped from 44.2 points per game to 35.2 points per game in 2014. That scoring pace was enough to rank a respectable No. 28 nationally, but those numbers aren't the type of production Sumlin's offenses are used to. In fact, dating back to his tenure at Houston, 2014 marked the first time *ever* that a Sumlin-coached team landed outside the nation's Top 15 in scoring offense. The lack of firepower can largely be blamed on inconsistency at QB. Sophomore **Kenny Hill** started strong, but was benched after the ugly loss to Alabama and true freshman **Kyle Allen** finished the season as the starter. Hill is now transferring and Allen will be the starter heading into 2015 if he can fight off incoming blue-chip recruit **Kyler Murray**. Eight starters are back in 2015, which means the Aggie offense should return to its big-scoring ways.

**DEFENSE:**

Great coaches can recognize when something isn't working and quickly make the necessary adjustments to right the ship. Sumlin, one of the nation's top offensive gurus, has recognized that offensive firepower alone isn't enough to win championships, especially in the SEC. After finishing last in the SEC in total defense each of the past two seasons, Sumlin went out and hired **John Chavis** to be his new defensive coordinator. This big hire surprised many in the SEC. Chavis spent the last six seasons as LSU's DC, where his squads have consistently ranked as some of the best in the nation. His defense in 2014 ranked No. 1 in the SEC in total defense. Chavis will be sticking with a 4-3 base defense at Texas A&M, but he'll be shifting the Aggie defense from a read-and-react style to a more aggressive attacking style. While bringing in Chavis doesn't guarantee a worst-to-first turnaround, it certainly sends a message to the SEC that defense will become more of a priority at Texas A&M. With seven starters back, expect the Aggie defense to quickly climb out of the SEC's cellar in 2015.

**RECRUITING:**

The John Chavis hire also had an immediate impact on recruiting. Five-star DT and Under Armor All-American Game MVP **Daylon Mack** had decommitted from the Aggies in January, but when Chavis was hired as the new DC, he *re*committed to Texas A&M. Sumlin signed the nation's 11th-ranked recruiting class in 2015.

**RUMOR MILL:**

In what is becoming an annual tradition, Sumlin was once again a top target for NFL franchises looking for a new head coach this past offseason. He was reportedly contacted by three teams in December and told them he was staying at Texas A&M. Sumlin was rumored to be one of USC's top targets the previous year, but he chose to stay at A&M and the Trojans hired **Steve Sarkisian**. Aggie fans should get used to the fact that Sumlin will likely be a top coaching candidate for open jobs each offseason.

**2015 OUTLOOK:**

**Sept. 5**    **vs. Arizona State Sun Devils (in Houston)** – The Aggies open the season in a "neutral" environment that will feel an awful lot like a hometown crowd. Sumlin went 2-1 against ASU head coach Todd Graham when Graham was at Tulsa and Sumlin was at Houston.

**Sept. 12**    **Ball State Cardinals** – This MAC team went 5-7 in 2014, but they have 18 starters returning this season.

**Sept. 19**    **Nevada Wolf Pack** – Nevada's third-year head coach, Brian Polian, was Sumlin's special teams coordinator and TE coach at A&M in 2012.

**Sept. 26**    **vs. Arkansas Razorbacks (in Arlington, TX)** – The Aggies pulled this game off in OT last season and Arkansas should be better this year. Expect this one to be another great matchup.

**Oct. 3**    **Mississippi State Bulldogs** – Last year's loss to the Bulldogs was Sumlin's first against Dan Mullen since coming to A&M. While at Houston, Sumlin went 1-1 against Mullen's Bulldogs.

**Oct. 17**    **Alabama Crimson Tide** – Last year's 59-0 blowout loss to the Tide was the most lopsided loss of Sumlin's coaching career and it marked the only time he's *ever* been shut out. Expect a highly-motivated Aggie team for this one.

**Oct. 24**    **at Ole Miss Rebels** – This will be A&M's first true road game of the season and it'll be interesting to see how they handle it so late in the year.

**Oct. 31**    **South Carolina Gamecocks** – South Carolina's high expectations heading into 2014 were squashed quickly in its season-opening blowout loss to the Aggies last year. Sumlin is now 1-0 against Steve Spurrier.

**Nov. 7**    **Auburn Tigers** – The Aggies shocked then-No. 3 Auburn late last season. Sumlin is 1-1 against Gus Malzahn and these two teams have averaged 41 points each in their previous two meetings.

**Nov. 14**    **Western Carolina Catamounts** – A&M closes its home schedule with an FCS opponent in what should be an easy win.

**Nov. 21**    **at Vanderbilt Commodores** – The Aggies get Vanderbilt in their SEC East rotation game. Texas A&M beat Vandy 56-24 the last time they met, in 2013.

**Nov. 28**    **at LSU Tigers** – Sumlin is 0-3 against Les Miles' Tigers. This makes LSU the only SEC West team Texas A&M has failed to beat since joining the conference in 2012. This new border rivalry is a *MUST-WIN* game for Sumlin and the Aggies.

**BOTTOM LINE:**
With just three true road games and drawing Vanderbilt from the SEC East, Texas A&M's schedule is about as good as it can get for an SEC West school. (Of course, the schedule is still nowhere near "soft" in this grueling division.) With 15 starters back, a more experienced starting QB, and a new commitment to improving the defense, Texas A&M should reverse the two-year decline it's been on. Expect this team to be right back in the hunt for the SEC West title.

## Kevin Sumlin's Year-by-Year Coaching Record:

<u>Houston: 35-17 (24-8 in Conference USA)</u>
2008    8–5 (6–2)                Final Ranking: NR
        Beat Air Force 34-28 in the Armed Forces Bowl.
2009    10–4 (6–2)               Final Ranking: NR
        C-USA West Division Champions.
        Sumlin named C-USA Coach of the Year.
        Lost to ECU 32-38 in the C-USA Championship Game.
        Lost to Air Force 20-47 in the Armed Forces Bowl.
2010    5–7 (4–4)                Final Ranking: NR
2011    12–1 (8–0)               Final Ranking: #17
        C-USA West Division Champions.
        Sumlin named C-USA Coach of the Year.
        Lost to Southern Miss 28-49 in the C-USA Championship Game.
        Houston beat #20 Penn State 30-14 in the Cotton Bowl, but Sumlin had
        already left to accept the Texas A&M job. Houston finished the year ranked
        #14.

<u>Texas A&M: 28-11 (13-11 in the SEC)</u>
2012    11–2 (6–2)               Final Ranking: #5
        Sumlin named SEC Coach of the Year.
        Beat #12 Oklahoma 41-13 in the Cotton Bowl.
2013    9–4 (4–4)                Final Ranking: #18
        Beat #22 Duke 52-48 in the Chick-fil-A Bowl.
2014    8–5 (3–5)                Final Ranking: NR
        Beat West Virginia 45-37 in the Liberty Bowl.

# 2015 AMERICAN PREVIEW

## Five Things You Need to Know about the AAC in 2015:

**The Battle at the Top:** Last year, the 11-team AAC didn't have a conference championship game and the result was a three-way tie at the top between **Cincinnati**, **Memphis**, and **UCF**. This year, those three teams will again be the favorites, but the league's new arrival, **Navy**, is just dangerous enough to sneak into the West Division race. With a new head coach at **Houston**, the Cougars also have the talent to compete for an AAC title right away.

**New to the AAC:** Three of the nation's most sought-after offensive coordinators have been hired by AAC-West programs. **Houston** hired **Tom Herman**, who was **Urban Meyer's** OC at **Ohio State**. SMU hired **Chad Morris**, who was was **Dabo Swinney's** OC at **Clemson**. **Tulsa** hired **Philip Montgomery**, who was **Art Briles'** OC at **Baylor**. All three of these big-time hires will be fun to watch. Herman walks into the best win-now opportunity at Houston while Morris and Montgomery will face bigger rebuilding jobs at SMU and Tulsa.

**Coaches on the Rise:** **Justin Fuente** rightfully received accolades for leading a **Memphis** team that hadn't had a winning season since 2007 to a Top-25 finish last year. Another coach on the rise is **Matt Rhule** at **Temple**. He quietly led the Owls to a 6-6 record after his 2-10 debut season in 2013.

**Keep an Eye On:** A big reason for Memphis' turnaround has been the Tiger defense, which was No. 11 in the nation in points allowed last year. However, after three seasons as Memphis' defensive coordinator, **Barry Odom** is headed to the same position at his alma mater, **Missouri**. Memphis is promoting LB coach **Galen Scott** to the DC role and he'll have some big shoes to fill.

**Coaches on the Hot Seat:** With the West Division replacing half of its head coaches this past offseason, the American will have a fairly-secure roster of coaches heading into 2015. However, **Bob Diaco** needs to speed up the turnaround effort at **UConn**, **South Florida's Willie Taggart** needs a bowl game, and **Tulane's Curtis Johnson** can't afford another step back in 2015.

## 2015 Projected Standings for the AAC:

**East Division:**
1. Cincinnati
2. UCF
3. East Carolina
4. Temple
5. South Florida
6. Connecticut

**West Division:**
1. Memphis
2. Houston
3. Navy
4. SMU
5. Tulsa
6. Tulane

# Ranking the AAC's Coaches:

1. **George O'Leary** – UCF (133-93 in 19 seasons)
2. **Tommy Tuberville** – Cincinnati (148-85 in 19 seasons)
3. **Justin Fuente** – Memphis (17-20 in 3 seasons)
4. **Ken Niumatalolo** – Navy (57-35 in 7 seasons)
5. **Ruffin McNeill** – East Carolina (38-27 in 5 seasons)
6. **Tom Herman** – Houston (First Year Head Coach)
7. **Chad Morris** – SMU (First Year Head Coach)
8. **Philip Montgomery** – Tulsa (First Year Head Coach)
9. **Matt Rhule** – Temple (8-16 in 2 seasons)
10. **Willie Taggart** – South Florida (22-38 in 5 seasons)
11. **Curtis Johnson** – Tulane (12-25 in 3 seasons)
12. **Bob Diaco** – Connecticut (2-10 in 1 season)

# 2014 AAC Coach of the Year:
(Selected by the AAC coaches)
Justin Fuente, Memphis

# 2014 AAC Standings:

|  | (Conference) | (All Games) |
|---|---|---|
| #25 Memphis | 7–1 | 10–3 |
| Cincinnati | 7–1 | 9–4 |
| UCF | 7–1 | 9–4 |
| East Carolina | 5–3 | 8–5 |
| Houston | 5–3 | 8–5 |
| Temple | 4–4 | 6–6 |
| South Florida | 3–5 | 4–8 |
| Tulsa | 2–6 | 2–10 |
| Tulane | 2–6 | 3–9 |
| SMU | 1–7 | 1–11 |
| Connecticut | 1–7 | 2–10 |

**2014 AAC Bowl Record:** 2-3 (Tied for 6th place among all 10 conferences)

# Cincinnati Bearcats – Tommy Tuberville

## Coach Ranking: #44

**Overall Record:** 148-85 in 19 seasons
**Record at Cincinnati:** 18-8 in 2 seasons
**2014 Results:** 9-4, 7-1 in the AAC (AAC Co-Champions)
**Returning Starters in 2015:** 8 on offense (including QB), 4 on defense
**Salary:** $2.2 Million    **Age:** 60    **Job Security Grade:** B

**2015 SCHEDULE:**
(Conference games in bold.)

| | |
|---|---|
| Sept. 5 | Alabama A&M Bulldogs |
| Sept. 12 | **Temple Owls** |
| Sept. 19 | at Miami (OH) RedHawks |
| Sept. 24 | **at Memphis Tigers** |
| Oct. 1 | Miami (FL) Hurricanes |
| Oct. 17 | at BYU Cougars |
| Oct. 24 | **UConn Huskies** |
| Oct. 31 | **UCF Knights** |
| Nov. 7 | **at Houston Cougars** |
| Nov. 14 | **Tulsa Golden Hurricane** |
| Nov. 20 | **at South Florida Bulls** |
| Nov. 28 | **at East Carolina Pirates** |

**2014 RESULTS:   9-4 (7-1 in the AAC)**    **Final Ranking: NR**

| | | |
|---|---|---|
| Toledo | W 58–34 | (31,912) |
| Miami (OH) | W 31–24 | (41,926) |
| at #22 Ohio State | L 28–50 | (108,362) |
| **Memphis** | L 14–41 | (25,456) |
| at Miami (FL) | L 34–55 | (43,953) |
| **at SMU** | W 41–3 | (16,849) |
| **South Florida** | W 34–17 | (30,024) |
| **at Tulane** | W 38–14 | (21,414) |
| **East Carolina** | W 54–46 | (19,113) |
| **at Connecticut** | W 41–0 | (24,012) |
| **at Temple** | W 14–6 | (21,255) |
| **Houston** | W 38–31 | (24,606) |
| vs. Virginia Tech (Military Bowl) | L 17–33 | (34,277) |

## Tommy Tuberville's Year-by-Year Coaching Record:

### Ole Miss: 25-20 (12-20 in the SEC)
1995   6–5 (3–5)              Final Ranking: NR
1996   5–6 (2–6)              Final Ranking: NR
1997   8–4 (4–4)              Final Ranking: #22
       Tuberville named SEC Coach of the Year.
       Beat Marshall 34-31 in the Motor City Bowl.
1998   6–5 (3–5)              Final Ranking: NR
       Ole Miss beat Texas Tech 35-18 in the Independence Bowl, but Tuberville
       had already left to accept the Auburn job.

### Auburn: 85-40 (52-30 in the SEC)
1999   5–6 (2–6)              Final Ranking: NR
2000   9–4 (6–2)              Final Ranking: #18
       SEC West Champions.
       Lost to #7 Florida 6-28 in the SEC Championship Game.
       Lost to #17 Michigan 28-31 in the Citrus Bowl.
2001   7–5 (5–3)              Final Ranking: NR
       SEC West Co-Champions.
       Lost to North Carolina 10-16 in the Peach Bowl.
2002   9–4 (5–3)              Final Ranking: #14
       SEC West Co-Champions.
       Beat #10 Penn State 13-9 in the Capital One Bowl.
2003   8–5 (5–3)              Final Ranking: NR
       Beat Wisconsin 28-14 in the Music City Bowl.
2004   13–0 (8–0)             Final Ranking: #2
       SEC Champions.
       Tuberville named National Coach of the Year.
       Tuberville named SEC Coach of the Year.
       Beat #15 Tennessee 38-28 in the SEC Championship Game.
       Beat #9 Virginia Tech 16-13 in the Sugar Bowl.
2005   9–3 (7–1)              Final Ranking: #14
       SEC West Co-Champions.
       Lost to #21 Wisconsin 10-24 in the Capital One Bowl.
2006   11–2 (6–2)             Final Ranking: #8
       Beat #22 Nebraska 17-14 in the Cotton Bowl Classic.
2007   9–4 (5–3)              Final Ranking: #14
       Beat #15 Clemson 23-20 in OT in the Peach Bowl.
2008   5–7 (2–6)             Final Ranking: NR

### Texas Tech: 20-17 (9-17 in the Big 12)
2010   8–5 (3–5)              Final Ranking: NR
       Beat Northwestern 45-38 in the TicketCity Bowl.
2011   5–7 (2–7)              Final Ranking: NR
2012   7–5 (4–5)              Final Ranking: NR
       Texas Tech beat Minnesota 34-231 in the Meineke Car Care Bowl of Texas,
       but Tuberville had already left to accept the Cincinnati job.

<u>**Cincinnati: 18-8 (12-3 in the AAC)**</u>
2013  9–4 (6–2)              **Final Ranking: NR**
    Lost to North Carolina 17-39 in the Belk Bowl.
2014  9–4 (7–1)              **Final Ranking: NR**
    AAC Co-Champions.
    Lost to Virginia Tech 17-33 in the Military Bowl.

# Connecticut Huskies – Bob Diaco

## Coach Ranking: #109

**Overall Record:** 2-10 in 1 season
**Record at Connecticut:** 2-10 in 1 season
**2014 Results:** 2-10, 1-7 in the AAC (T-10th in the AAC)
**Returning Starters in 2015:** 6 on offense, 8 on defense
**Salary:** $1.5 Million      **Age:** 42      **Job Security Grade:** B

**2015 SCHEDULE:**
(Conference games in bold.)

| | |
|---|---|
| Sept. 3 | Villanova Wildcats |
| Sept. 12 | Army Black Knights |
| Sept. 19 | at Missouri Tigers |
| Sept. 26 | **Navy Midshipmen** |
| Oct. 2 | at BYU Cougars |
| Oct. 10 | **at UCF Knights** |
| Oct. 17 | **South Florida Bulls** |
| Oct. 24 | **at Cincinnati Bearcats** |
| Oct. 30 | **East Carolina Pirates** |
| Nov. 7 | **at Tulane Green Wave** |
| Nov. 21 | **Houston Cougars** |
| Nov. 28 | **at Temple Owls** |

| 2014 RESULTS:   2-10 (1-7 in the AAC) | Final Ranking: NR | |
|---|---|---|
| BYU | L 10–35 | (35,150) |
| Stony Brook | W 19–16 | (23,543) |
| Boise State | L 21–38 | (30,098) |
| **at South Florida** | L 14–17 | (28,273) |
| **Temple** | L 10–36 | (27,755) |
| **at Tulane** | L 3–12 | (23,076) |
| **at #18 East Carolina** | L 21–31 | (40,152) |
| **UCF** | W 37–29 | (28,751) |
| vs. Army (in New York City) | L 21–35 | (27,453) |
| **Cincinnati** | L 0–41 | (24,012) |
| **at Memphis** | L 10–41 | (35,102) |
| **SMU** | L 20–27 | (22,921) |

**Bob Diaco's Year-by-Year Coaching Record:**

**Connecticut: 2-10 (1-7 in the AAC)**

| 2014 | 2-10 (1-7) | Final Ranking: NR |
|---|---|---|

# East Carolina Pirates – Ruffin McNeill

## Coach Ranking: #62

**Overall Record:** 38-27 in 5 seasons
**Record at East Carolina:** 37-27 in 5 seasons
**2014 Results:** 8-5, 5-3 in the AAC (T-4th in the AAC)
**Returning Starters in 2015:** 6 on offense, 5 on defense
**Salary:** $1.25 Million     **Age:** 56      **Job Security Grade:** A

**2015 SCHEDULE:**
(Conference games in bold.)

| | |
|---|---|
| Sept. 5 | Towson Tigers |
| Sept. 12 | at Florida Gators |
| Sept. 19 | **at Navy Midshipmen** |
| Sept. 26 | Virginia Tech Hokies |
| Oct. 3 | **at SMU Mustangs** |
| Oct. 10 | at BYU Cougars |
| Oct. 17 | **Tulsa Golden Hurricane** |
| Oct. 22 | **Temple Owls** |
| Oct. 30 | **at UConn Huskies** |
| Nov. 7 | **South Florida Bulls** |
| Nov. 19 | **at UCF Knights** |
| Nov. 28 | **Cincinnati Bearcats** |

**2014 RESULTS:   8-5 (5-3 in the AAC)**     Final Ranking: NR

| | | |
|---|---|---|
| North Carolina Central | W 52–7 | (42,758) |
| at #21 South Carolina | L 23–33 | (80,899) |
| at #17 Virginia Tech | W 28–21 | (63,267) |
| North Carolina | W 70–41 | (51,082) |
| **SMU** | W 45–24 | (45,029) |
| **at South Florida** | W 28–17 | (31,567) |
| **Connecticut** | W 31–21 | (40,152) |
| **at Temple** | L 10–20 | (22,130) |
| **at Cincinnati** | L 46–54 | (19,113) |
| Tulane | W 34–6 | (48,433) |
| **at Tulsa** | W 49–32 | (15,126) |
| **UCF** | L 30–32 | (41,259) |
| vs. Florida (Birmingham Bowl) | L 20–28 | (30,083) |

## Ruffin McNeill's Year-by-Year Coaching Record:

### Texas Tech: 1-0 (0-0 in the Big 12)
2009   1-0 (0-0)                 Final Ranking: #21
McNeill was the interim head coach for the bowl game after Mike Leach was fired.
Beat Michigan State 41-31 in the Alamo Bowl.

### East Carolina: 37-27 (27-13 in C-USA and the AAC)
2010   6–7 (5–3)                 Final Ranking: NR
Lost to Maryland 20-51 in the Military Bowl.
2011   5–7 (4–4)                 Final Ranking: NR
2012   8–5 (7–1)                 Final Ranking: NR
C-USA East Division Co-Champions.
Lost to Louisiana-Lafayette 34-43 in the New Orleans Bowl.
2013   10–3 (6–2)                Final Ranking: NR
Beat Ohio 37-20 in the Beef 'O' Brady's Bowl.
2014   8–5 (5–3)                 Final Ranking: NR
East Carolina leaves C-USA and joins the American Athletic Conference.
Lost to Florida 20-28 in the Birmingham Bowl.

# South Florida Bulls – Willie Taggart

## Coach Ranking: #93

**Overall Record:** 22-38 in 5 seasons
**Record at South Florida:** 6-18 in 2 seasons
**2014 Results:** 4-8, 3-5 in the AAC (7th in the AAC)
**Returning Starters in 2015:** 5 on offense (including QB), 7 on defense
**Salary:** $1.1 Million     **Age:** 39     **Job Security Grade:** B

**2015 SCHEDULE:**
(Conference games in bold.)

| Sept. 5 | Florida A&M Rattlers |
| Sept. 12 | at Florida State Seminoles |
| Sept. 19 | at Maryland Terrapins |
| Oct. 2 | **Memphis Tigers** |
| Oct. 10 | Syracuse Orange |
| Oct. 17 | **at UConn Huskies** |
| Oct. 24 | **SMU Mustangs** |
| Oct. 31 | **at Navy Midshipmen** |
| Nov. 7 | **at East Carolina Pirates** |
| Nov. 14 | **Temple Owls** |
| Nov. 20 | **Cincinnati Bearcats** |
| Nov. 27 | **at UCF Knights** |

**2014 RESULTS:   4-8 (3-5 in the AAC)**          **Final Ranking: NR**

| | | |
|---|---|---|
| Western Carolina | W 36–31 | (31,642) |
| Maryland | L 17–24 | (28,915) |
| NC State | L 17–49 | (27,269) |
| **Connecticut** | W 17–14 | (28,273) |
| at #19 Wisconsin | L 10–27 | (78,111) |
| **#19 East Carolina** | L 17–28 | (31,567) |
| **at Tulsa** | W 38–30 | (18,744) |
| **at Cincinnati** | L 17–34 | (30,024) |
| **Houston** | L 3–27 | (29,782) |
| **at SMU** | W 14–13 | (19,463) |
| **at Memphis** | L 20–31 | (34,635) |
| **UCF** | L 0–16 | (36,963) |

## Willie Taggart's Year-by-Year Coaching Record:

### Western Kentucky: 16-20 (13-11 in the Sun Belt)
2010    2–10 (2–6)          **Final Ranking: NR**
2011    7–5 (7–1)           **Final Ranking: NR**
2012    7–5 (4–4)           **Final Ranking: NR**
      Western Kentucky lost to Central Michigan 21-24 in the Little Caesars Pizza Bowl, but Taggart had already left to accept the South Florida job.

### South Florida: 6-18 (5-11 in the AAC)
2013    2–10 (2–6)          **Final Ranking: NR**
2014    4–8 (3–5)           **Final Ranking: NR**

# Temple Owls – Matt Rhule

## Coach Ranking: #92

**Overall Record:** 8-16 in 2 seasons
**Record at Temple:** 8-16 in 2 seasons
**2014 Results:** 6-6, 4-4 in the AAC (6th in the AAC)
**Returning Starters in 2015:** 8 on offense (including QB), 11 on defense
**Salary:** $1.3 Million*     **Age:** 40     **Job Security Grade:** A

**2015 SCHEDULE:**
(Conference games in bold.)

| | |
|---|---|
| Sept. 5 | Penn State Nittany Lions |
| Sept. 12 | **at Cincinnati Bearcats** |
| Sept. 19 | at Massachusetts Minutemen |
| Oct. 2 | at Charlotte 49ers |
| Oct. 10 | **Tulane Green Wave** |
| Oct. 17 | **UCF Knights** |
| Oct. 22 | **at East Carolina Pirates** |
| Oct. 31 | Notre Dame Fighting Irish |
| Nov. 6 | **at SMU Mustangs** |
| Nov. 14 | **at South Florida Bulls** |
| Nov. 21 | **Memphis Tigers** |
| Nov. 28 | **UConn Huskies** |

**2014 RESULTS:   6-6 (4-4 in the AAC)**      **Final Ranking: NR**

| | | |
|---|---|---|
| at Vanderbilt | W 37-7 | (31,731) |
| Navy | L 24-31 | (28,408) |
| Delaware State | W 59-0 | (19,202) |
| **at Connecticut** | W 36-10 | (27,755) |
| **Tulsa** | W 35-24 | (25,340) |
| **at Houston** | L 10-31 | (21,471) |
| **at UCF** | L 14-34 | (39,554) |
| **#21 East Carolina** | W 20-10 | (22,130) |
| **Memphis** | L 13-16 | (23,882) |
| at Penn State | L 13-30 | (100,173) |
| **Cincinnati** | L 6-14 | (21,255) |
| **at Tulane** | W 10-3 | (20,612) |

## Matt Rhule's Year-by-Year Coaching Record:

**Temple: 8-16 (5-11 in the AAC)**

| | | |
|---|---|---|
| 2013 | 2-10 (1-7) | Final Ranking: NR |
| 2014 | 6-6 (4-4) | Final Ranking: NR |

# UCF Knights – George O'Leary

## Coach Ranking: #37

**Overall Record:** 133-93 in 19 seasons
**Record at UCF:** 81-60 in 10 seasons
**2014 Results:** 9-4, 7-1 in the AAC (AAC Co-Champions)
**Returning Starters in 2015:** 5 on offense (including QB), 4 on defense
**Salary:** $1.8 Million          **Age:** 69          **Job Security Grade:** A

**2015 SCHEDULE:**
(Conference games in bold.)

| | |
|---|---|
| Sept. 3 | FIU Golden Panthers |
| Sept. 12 | at Stanford Cardinal |
| Sept. 19 | Furman Paladins |
| Sept. 26 | at South Carolina Gamecocks |
| Oct. 3 | **at Tulane Green Wave** |
| Oct. 10 | **UConn Huskies** |
| Oct. 17 | **at Temple Owls** |
| Oct. 24 | **Houston Cougars** |
| Oct. 31 | **at Cincinnati Bearcats** |
| Nov. 7 | **at Tulsa Golden Hurricane** |
| Nov. 19 | **East Carolina Pirates** |
| Nov. 27 | **South Florida Bulls** |

**2014 RESULTS:   9-4 (7-1 in the AAC)**          **Final Ranking: NR**

| | | |
|---|---|---|
| vs. Penn State (in Dublin, Ireland) | L 24–26 | (53,304) |
| at #20 Missouri | L 10–38 | (60,348) |
| #12 (FCS) Bethune-Cookman | W 41–7 | (44,510) |
| **at Houston** | W 17–12 | (26,685) |
| BYU | W 31–24 OT | (41,547) |
| **Tulane** | W 20–13 | (35,015) |
| **Temple** | W 34–14 | (39,554) |
| **at Connecticut** | L 29–37 | (28,751) |
| **Tulsa** | W 31–7 | (35,323) |
| **SMU** | W 53–7 | (30,920) |
| **at South Florida** | W 16–0 | (36,963) |
| **at East Carolina** | W 32–30 | (41,259) |
| vs. NC State (St. Petersburg Bowl) | L 27–34 | (26,675) |

## George O'Leary's Year-by-Year Coaching Record:

Georgia Tech: 52-33 (36-22 in the ACC)
1994   0–3 (0–2)          Final Ranking: NR
O'Leary replaced Bill Lewis eight games into the season.
1995   6–5 (5–3)          Final Ranking: NR
1996   5–6 (4–4)          Final Ranking: NR
1997   7–5 (5–3)          Final Ranking: #25
Beat West Virginia 35-30 in the Carquest Bowl.
1998   10–2 (7–1)         Final Ranking: #9
ACC Co-Champions.
O'Leary named ACC Coach of the Year.
Beat #17 Notre Dame 35-28 in the Gator Bowl.
1999   8–4 (5–3)          Final Ranking: #20
Lost to #23 Miami (FL) 13-28 in the Gator Bowl.
2000   9–3 (6–2)          Final Ranking: #17
O'Leary named ACC Coach of the Year.
Lost to LSU 21-30 in the Peach Bowl.
2001   7–5 (4–4)          Final Ranking: #24
Georgia Tech beat #11 Stanford 24-14 in the Seattle Bowl, but O'Leary had already left to accept the Notre Dame job.
O'Leary resigned at Notre Dame before ever coaching a game there after inaccuracies were discovered in his resume.

UCF: 81-60 (58-30 in the MAC, C-USA and the AAC)
2004   0–11 (0–8)        Final Ranking: NR
2005   8–5 (7–1)          Final Ranking: NR
UCF leaves the MAC and joins Conference USA.
C-USA Eastern Division Champions.
O'Leary named C-USA Coach of the Year.
Lost to Tulsa 27-44 in the C-USA Championship Game.
Lost to Nevada 48-49 in OT in the Hawaii Bowl.
2006   4–8 (3–5)          Final Ranking: NR
2007   10–4 (7–1)         Final Ranking: NR
C-USA Champions.
O'Leary named C-USA Coach of the Year.
Beat Tulsa 44-25 in the C-USA Championship Game.
Lost to Mississippi State 3-10 in the Liberty Bowl.
2008   4–8 (3–5)          Final Ranking: NR
2009   8–5 (6–2)          Final Ranking: NR
Lost to Rutgers 24-45 in the St. Petersburg Bowl.
2010   11–3 (7–1)         Final Ranking: #20
C-USA Champions.
O'Leary named C-USA Coach of the Year.
Beat SMU 17-7 in the C-USA Championship Game.
Beat Georgia 10-6 in the Liberty Bowl.
2011   5–7 (3–5)          Final Ranking: NR

**UCF (continued):**

2012   10–4 (7–1)           **Final Ranking: NR**
         C-USA Eastern Division Co-Champions.
         Beat Ball State 38-17 in the Beef 'O' Brady's Bowl.

2013   12–1 (8–0) 1st      **Final Ranking: #10**
         UCF leaves C-USA and joins the American Athletic Conference.
         AAC Champions.
         O'Leary named AAC Coach of the Year.
         Beat #6 Baylor 52-42 in the Fiesta Bowl.

2014   9–4 (7–1)            **Final Ranking: NR**
         AAC Co-Champions.
         Lost to NC State 27-34 in the BITCOIN St. Petersburg Bowl.

# Houston Cougars – Tom Herman

## Coach Ranking: #67

**Overall Record:** 0-0

**2014 Results:** Houston went 8-5, 5-3 in the AAC (T-4th in the AAC)
Herman was Ohio State's offensive coordinator from 2012-2014
**Returning Starters in 2015:** 6 on offense (including QB), 7 on defense
**Salary:** $1.4 Million      **Age:** 40      **Job Security Grade:** A

**2015 SCHEDULE:**
(Conference games in bold.)

| | |
|---|---|
| Sept. 5 | Tennessee Tech Golden Eagles |
| Sept. 12 | at Louisville Cardinals |
| Sept. 26 | Texas State Bobcats |
| Oct. 3 | **at Tulsa Golden Hurricane** |
| Oct. 8 | **SMU Mustangs** |
| Oct. 16 | **at Tulane Green Wave** |
| Oct. 24 | **at UCF Knights** |
| Oct. 31 | Vanderbilt Commodores |
| Nov. 7 | **Cincinnati Bearcats** |
| Nov. 14 | **Memphis Tigers** |
| Nov. 21 | **at Connecticut Huskies** |
| Nov. 27 | **Navy Midshipmen** |

**2014 RESULTS:   8-5 (5-3 in the AAC)**          **Final Ranking: NR**

| | | |
|---|---|---|
| UTSA | L 7–27 | (40,755) |
| Grambling State | W 47–0 | (30,081) |
| at #25 BYU | L 25–33 | (57,630) |
| UNLV | W 47–14 | (23,408) |
| **UCF** | L 12–17 | (26,685) |
| **at Memphis** | W 28–24 | (32,784) |
| **Temple** | W 31–10 | (21,471) |
| **at South Florida** | W 27–3 | (29,782) |
| **Tulane** | L 24–31 | (32,205) |
| **Tulsa** | W 38–28 | (23,572) |
| **at SMU** | W 35–9 | (15,446) |
| **at Cincinnati** | L 31–38 | (24,606) |
| vs. Pittsburgh (Armed Forces Bowl) | W 35–34 | (37,888) |

# Memphis Tigers – Justin Fuente

## Coach Ranking: #59

**Overall Record:** 17-20 in 3 seasons
**Record at Memphis:** 17-20 in 3 seasons
**2014 Results:** Houston went 10-3, 7-1 in the AAC (AAC Co-Champs)
**Returning Starters in 2015:** 8 on offense (including QB), 3 on defense
**Salary:** $1.4 Million      **Age:** 39      **Job Security Grade:** A

**2015 SCHEDULE:**
(Conference games in bold.)

| | |
|---|---|
| Sept. 5 | Missouri State Bears |
| Sept. 12 | at Kansas Jayhawks |
| Sept. 19 | at Bowling Green Falcons |
| Sept. 24 | **Cincinnati Bearcats** |
| Oct. 2 | **at South Florida Bulls** |
| Oct. 17 | Ole Miss Rebels |
| Oct. 23 | **at Tulsa Golden Hurricane** |
| Oct. 31 | **Tulane Green Wave** |
| Nov. 7 | **Navy Midshipmen** |
| Nov. 14 | **at Houston Cougars** |
| Nov. 21 | **at Temple Owls** |
| Nov. 28 | **SMU Mustangs** |

**2014 RESULTS:** 10-3 (7-1 in the AAC)      **Final Ranking: #25**

| | | |
|---|---|---|
| Austin Peay | W 63-0 | (27,361) |
| at #11 UCLA | L 35-42 | (72,098) |
| Middle Tennessee | W 36-17 | (46,378) |
| at #10 Ole Miss | L 3-24 | (61,291) |
| **at Cincinnati** | W 41-14 | (25,456) |
| **Houston** | L 24-28 | (32,784) |
| **at SMU** | W 48-10 | (19,498) |
| **Tulsa** | W 40-20 | (26,846) |
| **at Temple** | W 16-13 | (23,882) |
| **at Tulane** | W 38-7 | (28,614) |
| **South Florida** | W 31-20 | (34,635) |
| **Connecticut** | W 41-10 | (35,102) |
| vs. BYU (Miami Beach Bowl) | W 55-48 2OT | (20,761) |

## Justin Fuente's Year-by-Year Coaching Record:

<u>Memphis: 17-20 (12-12 in Conference USA and the AAC)</u>
2012    4–8 (4–4)              Final Ranking: NR
2013    3–9 (1–7)              Final Ranking: NR
        Memphis leaves C-USA and joins the American Athletic Conference.
2014    10–3 (7–1)             Final Ranking: #25
        AAC Co-Champions.
        Beat BYU 55-48 in double OT in the Miami Beach Bowl.

# Navy Midshipmen – Ken Niumatalolo

## Coach Ranking: #60

**Overall Record:** 57-35 in 7 seasons
**Record at Navy:** 57-35 in 7 seasons
**2014 Results:** 8-5 (Independent)
**Returning Starters in 2015:** 5 on offense (including QB), 6 on defense
**Salary:** $1.6 Million      **Age:** 50      **Job Security Grade:** A

**2015 SCHEDULE:**
(Conference games in bold.)

| | |
|---|---|
| Sept. 5 | Colgate Raiders |
| Sept. 19 | **East Carolina Pirates** |
| Sept. 26 | **at UConn Huskies** |
| Oct. 3 | Air Force Falcons |
| Oct. 10 | at Notre Dame Fighting Irish |
| Oct. 24 | **Tulane Green Wave** |
| Oct. 31 | **South Florida Bulls** |
| Nov. 7 | **at Memphis Tigers** |
| Nov. 14 | **SMU Mustangs** |
| Nov. 21 | **at Tulsa Golden Hurricane** |
| Nov. 28 | **at Houston Cougars** |
| Dec. 12 | vs. Army Black Knights (in Philadelphia) |

**2014 RESULTS:  8-5**     **Final Ranking: NR**

| | | |
|---|---|---|
| vs. #6 Ohio State  (in Baltimore) | L 17–34 | (57,579) |
| at Temple | W 31–24 | (28,408) |
| at Texas State | W 35–21 | (32,007) |
| Rutgers | L 24–31 | (33,655) |
| Western Kentucky | L 27–36 | (30,537) |
| at Air Force | L 21–30 | (37,731) |
| Virginia Military Institute | W 51–14 | (33,812) |
| San Jose State | W 41–31 | (30,612) |
| vs. #10 Notre Dame (in Landover, MD) | L 39–49 | (36,807) |
| Georgia Southern | W 52–19 | (33,894) |
| at South Alabama | W 42–40 | (14,571) |
| vs. Army (in Baltimore) | W 17–10 | (70,935) |
| vs. San Diego State (Poinsettia Bowl) | W 17–16 | (33,077) |

## Ken Niumatalolo's Year-by-Year Coaching Record:

<u>Navy: 57-35 (Independent Prior to 2015)</u>
2007    0–1 (Ind.)              Final Ranking: NR
        Niumatalolo got an early start on the job and coached Navy in its 32-35 loss
        to Utah in the Poinsettia Bowl.
2008    8–5 (Ind.)              Final Ranking: NR
        Lost to Wake Forest 19-29 in the EagleBank Bowl.
2009    10–4 (Ind.)             Final Ranking: NR
        Beat Missouri 35-13 in the Texas Bowl.
2010    9–4 (Ind.)              Final Ranking: NR
        Lost to San Diego State 14-35 in the Poinsettia Bowl.
2011    5–7 (Ind.)              Final Ranking: NR
2012    8–5 (Ind.)              Final Ranking: NR
        Lost to Arizona State 28-61 in the Fight Hunger Bowl.
2013    9–4 (Ind.)              Final Ranking: NR
        Beat Middle Tennessee 24-6 in the Armed Forces Bowl.
2014    8–5 (Ind.)              Final Ranking: NR
        Beat San Diego State 17-16 in the Poinsettia Bowl.

# SMU Mustangs – Chad Morris

## Coach Ranking: #68

**Overall Record:** 0-0
**2014 Results:** SMU went 1-11, 1-7 in the AAC (T-10th in the AAC)
Morris was Clemson's offensive coordinator from 2011-2014
**Returning Starters in 2015:** 8 on offense (including QB), 7 on defense
**Salary:** $2 Million*      **Age:** 46      **Job Security Grade:** A

**2015 SCHEDULE:**
(Conference games in bold.)

| | |
|---|---|
| Sept. 4 | Baylor Bears |
| Sept. 12 | North Texas Mean Green |
| Sept. 19 | at TCU Horned Frogs |
| Sept. 26 | James Madison Dukes |
| Oct. 3 | **East Carolina Pirates** |
| Oct. 8 | **at Houston Cougars** |
| Oct. 24 | **at South Florida Bulls** |
| Oct. 31 | **Tulsa Golden Hurricane** |
| Nov. 6 | **Temple Owls** |
| Nov. 14 | **at Navy Midshipmen** |
| Nov. 21 | **Tulane Green Wave** |
| Nov. 28 | **at Memphis Tigers** |

**2014 RESULTS:   1-11 (1-7 in the AAC)**       **Final Ranking: NR**

| | | |
|---|---|---|
| at #10 Baylor | L 0–45 | (45,733) |
| at North Texas | L 6–43 | (22,398) |
| #6 Texas A&M | L 6–58 | (34,820) |
| TCU | L 0–56 | (23,093) |
| **at #22 East Carolina** | L 24–45 | (45,029) |
| **Cincinnati** | L 3–41 | (16,849) |
| **Memphis** | L 10–48 | (19,498) |
| **at Tulsa** | L 28–38 | (14,269) |
| **South Florida** | L 13–14 | (19,463) |
| **at UCF** | L 7–53 | (30,920) |
| **Houston** | L 9–35 | (15,446) |
| **at Connecticut** | W 27–20 | (22,921) |

# Tulane Green Wave – Curtis Johnson

## Coach Ranking: #98

**Overall Record:** 12-25 in 3 seasons
**Record at Tulane:** 12-25 in 3 seasons
**2014 Results:** 3-9, 2-6 in the AAC (T-8th in the AAC)
**Returning Starters in 2015:** 8 on offense (including QB), 7 on defense
**Salary:** $900,000*       **Age:** 53       **Job Security Grade:** B

**2015 SCHEDULE:**
(Conference games in bold.)

| | |
|---|---|
| Sept. 3 | Duke Blue Devils |
| Sept. 12 | at Georgia Tech Yellow Jackets |
| Sept. 19 | Maine Black Bears |
| Oct. 3 | **UCF Knights** |
| Oct. 10 | **at Temple Owls** |
| Oct. 16 | **Houston Cougars** |
| Oct. 24 | **at Navy Midshipmen** |
| Oct. 31 | **at Memphis Tigers** |
| Nov. 7 | **UConn Huskies** |
| Nov. 14 | at Army Black Knights |
| Nov. 21 | **at SMU Mustangs** |
| Nov. 28 | **Tulsa Golden Hurricane** |

**2014 RESULTS:   3-9 (2-6 in the AAC)**      **Final Ranking: NR**

| | | |
|---|---|---|
| at Tulsa | L 31–38 2OT | (19,032) |
| Georgia Tech | L 21–38 | (30,000) |
| #3 (FCS) Southeastern Louisiana | W 35–20 | (26,358) |
| at Duke | L 13–47 | (20,197) |
| at Rutgers | L 6–31 | (48,361) |
| **Connecticut** | W 12–3 | (23,076) |
| **at UCF** | L 13–20 | (35,015) |
| **Cincinnati** | L 14–38 | (21,414) |
| **at Houston** | W 31–24 | (32,205) |
| **Memphis** | L 7–38 | (28,614) |
| **at East Carolina** | L 6–34 | (48,433) |
| **Temple** | L 3–10 | (20,612) |

## Curtis Johnson's Year-by-Year Coaching Record:

<u>Tulane: 12-25 (9-15 in Conference USA and the AAC)</u>
2012   2–10 (2–6)              Final Ranking: NR
2013   7–6 (5–3)              Final Ranking: NR
       Lost to Louisiana-Lafayette 21-24 in the New Orleans Bowl.
2014   3–9 (2–6)              Final Ranking: NR
       Tulane leaves C-USA and joins the American Athletic Conference.

# Tulsa Golden Hurricane – Philip Montgomery

## Coach Ranking: #77

**Overall Record:** 0-0

**2014 Results:** Tulsa went 2-10, 2-6 in the AAC (T-8th in the AAC)
Montgomery was Baylor's offensive coordinator from 2006-2014

**Returning Starters in 2015:** 10 on offense (including QB), 7 on defense

**Salary:** $800,000*        **Age:** 43        **Job Security Grade:** A

**2015 SCHEDULE:**
(Conference games in bold.)

| | |
|---|---|
| Sept. 5 | Florida Atlantic Owls |
| Sept. 12 | at New Mexico Lobos |
| Sept. 19 | at Oklahoma Sooners |
| Oct. 3 | **Houston Cougars** |
| Oct. 10 | Louisiana-Monroe Warhawks |
| Oct. 17 | **at East Carolina Pirates** |
| Oct. 23 | **Memphis Tigers** |
| Oct. 31 | **at SMU Mustangs** |
| Nov. 7 | **UCF Knights** |
| Nov. 14 | **at Cincinnati Bearcats** |
| Nov. 21 | **Navy Midshipmen** |
| Nov. 28 | **at Tulane Green Wave** |

**2014 RESULTS:   2-10 (2-6 in the AAC)**          **Final Ranking: NR**

| | | |
|---|---|---|
| Tulane | W 38–31 2OT | (19,032) |
| #4 Oklahoma | L 7–52 | (29,357) |
| at Florida Atlantic | L 21–50 | (14,112) |
| Texas State | L 34–37 3OT | (21,353) |
| at Colorado State | L 17–42 | (25,806) |
| **at Temple** | L 24–35 | (25,340) |
| **South Florida** | L 30–38 | (18,744) |
| **at Memphis** | L 20–40 | (26,846) |
| **SMU** | W 38–28 | (14,269) |
| **at UCF** | L 7–31 | (35,323) |
| **at Houston** | L 28–38 | (23,572) |
| **East Carolina** | L 32–49 | (15,126) |

Should the Mid-Major programs receive just as much coverage as the Power 5 programs in next year's edition of the *College Football Coaches Almanac*? Let me know what you think.

Email: **info@coachesalmanac.com**

Twitter: **@CoachesAlmanac**

# 2015 CONFERENCE-USA PREVIEW

## Five Things You Need to Know about the C-USA in 2015:

**The Battle at the Top:** **Western Kentucky** finished 2014 with five-straight wins and with 16 starters returning, **Jeff Brohm** shouldn't have much trouble carrying that momentum into 2015. The C-USA schedule-makers have set it up to where the East Division title will likely be decided in the final week of the regular season when WKU travels to **Marshall**. In the East, expect **Louisiana Tech** and **Rice** to once again battle for the top spot.

**New to C-USA:** There won't be any new head coaches in Conference USA this season, but there is a new team in the **Charlotte 49ers**. This football program was started from scratch in 2013 and trying to transition this quickly to the FBS level may have been overly-ambitious. Charlotte went 5-6 last year with a schedule that consisted of only FCS, Division II, and Division III schools.

**Coaches on the Rise:** In his debut season last year, **Jeff Brohm** led Western Kentucky to its first bowl victory ever. Another coach who may soon find himself as a hot candidate for top job openings is **Bobby Wilder**, who is brilliantly managing Old Dominion's football rebirth.

**Keep an Eye On:** Conference USA media members voted **Bill Clark** the league's 2014 Coach of the Year. In his first year as head coach, Clark led **UAB** to a 6-6 season even as the university announced the termination of its football program. In June, however, UAB reversed its decision and announced it would bring back the football program in 2016. Clark will return as head coach of the Blazers when the program resumes play.

**Coaches on the Hot Seat:** **Brad Lambert** is trying to build Charlotte from scratch, but the weak schedules in 2013 and 2014 didn't translate to confidence-builders. How patient will the 49ers be with this process? After losing his final five games of 2014, **Todd Monken** also enters 2015 on a warming seat at **Southern Miss**.

## 2015 Projected Standings for Conference USA:

**East Division:**
1. Western Kentucky
2. Marshall
3. Old Dominion
4. FIU
5. Middle Tennessee
6. Florida Atlantic
7. Charlotte

**West Division:**
1. Louisiana Tech
2. Rice
3. UTEP
4. UTSA
5. Southern Miss
6. North Texas

# Ranking Conference USA's Coaches:

1. **Doc Holliday** – Marshall (40-25 in 5 seasons)
2. **Skip Holtz** – Louisiana Tech (101-84 in 15 seasons)
3. **David Bailiff** – Rice (69-68 in 11 seasons)
4. **Larry Coker** – UTSA (83-38 in 10 seasons)
5. **Jeff Brohm** – Western Kentucky (8-5 in 1 season)
6. **Bobby Wilder** – Old Dominion (52-20 in 6 seasons)
7. **Rick Stockstill** – Middle Tennessee (57-55 in 9 seasons)
8. **Dan McCarney** – North Texas (78-112 in 16 seasons)
9. **Sean Kugler** – UTEP (9-16 in 2 seasons)
10. **Ron Turner** – FIU (47-80 in 11 seasons)
11. **Charlie Partridge** – Florida Atlantic (3-9 in 1 season)
12. **Todd Monken** – Southern Miss (4-20 in 2 seasons)
13. **Brad Lambert** – Charlotte (10-12 in 2 seasons)

# 2014 C-USA Coach of the Year:
(Selected by the Conference USA coaches)
Doc Holliday, Marshall

# 2014 C-USA Standings:

| East Division | (Conference) | (All Games) |
|---|---|---|
| #23 Marshall | 7–1 | 13–1 |
| Middle Tennessee | 5–3 | 6–6 |
| Western Kentucky | 4–4 | 8–5 |
| UAB | 4–4 | 6–6 |
| Old Dominion | 4–4 | 6–6 |
| FIU | 3–5 | 4–8 |
| Florida Atlantic | 2–6 | 3–9 |
| | | |
| West Division | | |
| Louisiana Tech | 7–1 | 9–5 |
| Rice | 5–3 | 8–5 |
| UTEP | 5–3 | 7–6 |
| UTSA | 3–5 | 4–8 |
| North Texas | 2–6 | 4–8 |
| Southern Miss | 1–7 | 3–9 |

*Championship Game*: Marshall 26, Louisiana Tech 23

**2014 C-USA Bowl Record:** 4-1 (1st place among all 10 conferences)

# Charlotte 49ers – Brad Lambert

## Coach Ranking: #124

**Overall Record:** 10-12 in 2 seasons (2 seasons in FCS)
**Record at Charlotte:** 10-12 in 2 seasons
**2014 Results:** 5-6 (FCS Independent)
**Returning Starters in 2015:** 9 on offense (including QB), 10 on defense
**Salary:** $250,000          **Age:** 50          **Job Security Grade:** C

**2015 SCHEDULE:**
(Conference games in bold.)

| | |
|---|---|
| Sept. 4 | at Georgia State Panthers |
| Sept. 12 | Presbyterian Blue Hose |
| Sept. 19 | **at Middle Tennessee Blue Raiders** |
| Sept. 26 | **Florida Atlantic Owls** |
| Oct. 2 | Temple Owls |
| Oct. 17 | **at Old Dominion Monarchs** |
| Oct. 24 | **Southern Miss Golden Eagles** |
| Oct. 31 | **Marshall Thundering Herd** |
| Nov. 7 | **at FIU Golden Panthers** |
| Nov. 14 | **UTSA Roadrunners** |
| Nov. 21 | at Kentucky Wildcats |
| Nov. 28 | **at Rice Owls** |

**2014 RESULTS:   5-6 (FCS)**                **Final Ranking: NR**

| | | |
|---|---|---|
| at Campbell | W 33–9 | (6,472) |
| Johnson C. Smith | W 56–0 | (15,875) |
| at North Carolina Central | W 40–28 | (4,006) |
| at Elon | L 13–20 | (11,203) |
| #25 (FCS) Charleston Southern | L 41–47 OT | (14,498) |
| at Gardner–Webb | L 24–27 | (7,892) |
| at The Citadel | L 56–63 2OT | (10,467) |
| James Madison | L 40–48 | (15,677) |
| #2 (FCS) Coastal Carolina | L 34–59 | (12,052) |
| #4 (Division III) Wesley | W 38–33 | (10,704) |
| Morehead State | W 52–14 | (10,826) |

**Brad Lambert's Year-by-Year Coaching Record:**

**Charlotte: 10-12 (0-0 in the FCS Playoffs)**
| | | |
|---|---|---|
| 2013 | 5–6 (0-0) | **Final Ranking: NR** |

This was Charlotte's first-ever season as a football program.

| | | |
|---|---|---|
| 2014 | 5–6 (0-0) | **Final Ranking: NR** |

# FIU Golden Panthers – Ron Turner

## Coach Ranking: #114

**Overall Record:** 47-80 in 11 seasons
**Record at FIU:** 5-19 in 2 seasons
**2014 Results:** 4-8, 3-5 in Conference USA (6th in the C-USA East)
**Returning Starters in 2015:** 8 on offense (including QB), 8 on defense
**Salary:** $550,000          **Age:** 61          **Job Security Grade:** B

**2015 SCHEDULE:**
(Conference games in bold.)

| | |
|---|---|
| Sept. 3 | at UCF Knights |
| Sept. 12 | at Indiana Hoosiers |
| Sept. 19 | North Carolina Central Eagles |
| Sept. 26 | **at Louisiana Tech Bulldogs** |
| Oct. 3 | at Massachusetts Minutemen |
| Oct. 10 | **UTEP Miners** |
| Oct. 17 | **at Middle Tennessee Blue Raiders** |
| Oct. 24 | **Old Dominion Monarchs** |
| Oct. 31 | **at Florida Atlantic Owls** |
| Nov. 7 | **Charlotte 49ers** |
| Nov. 14 | **at Marshall Thundering Herd** |
| Nov. 21 | **Western Kentucky Hilltoppers** |

**2014 RESULTS:   4-8 (3-5 in C-USA)**          **Final Ranking: NR**

| | | |
|---|---|---|
| #22 (FCS) Bethune-Cookman | L 12–14 | (14,053) |
| Wagner | W 34–3 | (9,981) |
| Pittsburgh | L 25–42 | (10,147) |
| Louisville | L 3–34 | (10,826) |
| **at UAB** | W 34–20 | (16,133) |
| **Florida Atlantic** | W 38–10 | (12,544) |
| **at UTSA** | L 13–16 | (25,318) |
| **#25 Marshall** | L 13–45 | (13,163) |
| **Rice** | L 17–31 | (12,097) |
| **at Old Dominion** | L 35–38 | (20,118) |
| **Middle Tennessee** | W 38–28 | (12,917) |
| **at North Texas** | L 14–17 | (14,824) |

## Ron Turner's Year-by-Year Coaching Record:

<u>San Jose State: 7-4 (4-2 in the Big West)</u>
| 1992 | 7-4 (4-2) | Final Ranking: NR |

<u>Illinois: 35-57 (20-44 in the Big Ten)</u>
| 1997 | 0–11 (0–8) | Final Ranking: NR |
| 1998 | 3–8 (2–6) | Final Ranking: NR |
| 1999 | 8–4 (4–4) | Final Ranking: #24 |

Beat Virginia 63-21 in the MicronPC Bowl.

| 2000 | 5–6 (2–6) | Final Ranking: NR |
| 2001 | 10–2 (7–1) | Final Ranking: #12 |

Big Ten Champions.
Lost to #12 LSU 34-47 in the Sugar Bowl.

| 2002 | 5–7 (4–4) | Final Ranking: NR |
| 2003 | 1–11 (0–8) | Final Ranking: NR |
| 2004 | 3–8 (1–7) | Final Ranking: NR |

<u>FIU: 5-19 (4-12 in Conference USA)</u>
| 2013 | 1–11 (1-7) | Final Ranking: NR |
| 2014 | 4–8 (3–5) | Final Ranking: NR |

# Florida Atlantic Owls – Charlie Partridge

## Coach Ranking: #115

**Overall Record:** 3-9 in 1 season
**Record at Florida Atlantic:** 3-9 in 1 season
**2014 Results:** 3-9, 2-6 in Conference USA (7th in the C-USA East)
**Returning Starters in 2015:** 6 on offense (including QB), 6 on defense
**Salary:** $500,000        **Age:** 41        **Job Security Grade:** B

**2015 SCHEDULE:**
(Conference games in bold.)

| | |
|---|---|
| Sept. 5 | at Tulsa Golden Hurricane |
| Sept. 11 | Miami (FL) Hurricanes |
| Sept. 19 | Buffalo Bulls |
| Sept. 26 | **at Charlotte 49ers** |
| Oct. 10 | **Rice Owls** |
| Oct. 17 | **Marshall Thundering Herd** |
| Oct. 24 | **at UTEP Miners** |
| Oct. 31 | **FIU Golden Panthers** |
| Nov. 7 | **at Western Kentucky Hilltoppers** |
| Nov. 14 | **Middle Tennessee Blue Raiders** |
| Nov. 21 | at Florida Gators |
| Nov. 28 | **at Old Dominion Monarchs** |

**2014 RESULTS:   3-9 (2-6 in C-USA)**          **Final Ranking: NR**

| | | |
|---|---|---|
| at #22 Nebraska | L 7–55 | (91,441) |
| at #2 Alabama | L 0–41 | (100,306) |
| Tulsa | W 50–21 | (14,112) |
| at Wyoming | L 19–20 | (21,226) |
| **UTSA** | W 41–37 | (13,928) |
| **at FIU** | L 10–38 | (12,544) |
| **Western Kentucky** | W 45–38 | (10,915) |
| at #23 Marshall | L 16–35 | (27,236) |
| **UAB** | L 28–31 | (17,724) |
| **at North Texas** | L 10–31 | (20,957) |
| **at Middle Tennessee** | L 34–35 | (12,243) |
| **Old Dominion** | L 28–31 | (9,566) |

**Charlie Partridge's Year-by-Year Coaching Record:**

<u>Florida Atlantic: 3-9 (2-6 in Conference USA)</u>
| | | |
|---|---|---|
| 2014 | 3-9 (2-6) | Final Ranking: NR |

# Marshall Thundering Herd – Doc Holliday

## Coach Ranking: #50

**Overall Record:** 40-25 in 5 seasons
**Record at Marshall:** 40-25 in 5 seasons
**2014 Results:** 13-1, 7-1 in Conference USA (C-USA Champions)
**Returning Starters in 2015:** 6 on offense, 5 on defense
**Salary:** $755,000      **Age:** 58      **Job Security Grade:** A

**2015 SCHEDULE:**
(Conference games in bold.)

| | |
|---|---|
| Sept. 6 | Purdue Boilermakers |
| Sept. 12 | at Ohio Bobcats |
| Sept. 19 | Norfolk State Spartans |
| Sept. 26 | at Kent State Golden Flashes |
| Oct. 3 | **Old Dominion Monarchs** |
| Oct. 9 | **Southern Miss Golden Eagles** |
| Oct. 17 | **at Florida Atlantic Owls** |
| Oct. 24 | **North Texas Mean Green** |
| Oct. 31 | **at Charlotte 49ers** |
| Nov. 7 | **at Middle Tennessee Blue Raiders** |
| Nov. 14 | **FIU Golden Panthers** |
| Nov. 27 | **at Western Kentucky Hilltoppers** |

**2014 RESULTS:   13-1 (7-1 in C-USA)**      **Final Ranking: #22**

| | | |
|---|---|---|
| at Miami (OH) | W 42–27 | (19,005) |
| Rhode Island | W 48–7 | (25,106) |
| Ohio | W 44–14 | (31,710) |
| at Akron | W 48–17 | (13,357) |
| **at Old Dominion** | W 56–14 | (20,118) |
| **Middle Tennessee** | W 49–24 | (30,210) |
| **at FIU** | W 45–13 | (13,163) |
| **Florida Atlantic** | W 35–16 | (27,236) |
| **at Southern Miss** | W 63–17 | (22,949) |
| **Rice** | W 41–14 | (30,680) |
| **at UAB** | W 23–18 | (28,355) |
| **Western Kentucky** | L 66–67 OT | (23,576) |
| **Louisiana Tech** (C-USA Championship) | W 26–23 | (23,711) |
| vs. Northern Illinois (Boca Raton Bowl) | W 52–23 | (29,419) |

**Doc Holliday's Year-by-Year Coaching Record:**

<u>Marshall: 40-25 (27-13 in Conference USA)</u>
2010  5–7 (4–4)              **Final Ranking: NR**
2011  7–6 (5–3)              **Final Ranking: NR**
      Beat FIU 20-10 in the Beef 'O' Brady's Bowl.
2012  5–7 (4–4)              **Final Ranking: NR**
2013  10–4 (7–1)             **Final Ranking: NR**
      C-USA East Division Champions.
      Lost to Rice 24-41 in the C-USA Championship Game.
      Beat Maryland 31-20 in the Military Bowl.
2014  13–1 (7–1)             **Final Ranking: #22**
      C-USA Champions.
      Holliday named C-USA Coach of the Year.
      Beat Louisiana Tech 26-23 in the C-USA Championship Game.
      Beat Northern Illinois 52-23 in the Boca Raton Bowl.

# Middle Tennessee Blue Raiders – Rick Stockstill

## Coach Ranking: #84

**Overall Record:** 57-55 in 9 seasons
**Record at Middle Tennessee:** 57-55 in 9 seasons
**2014 Results:** 6-6, 5-3 in Conference USA (2nd in the C-USA East)
**Returning Starters in 2015:** 6 on offense (including QB), 7 on defense
**Salary:** $800,000          **Age:** 57          **Job Security Grade:** B

### 2015 SCHEDULE:
(Conference games in bold.)

|  |  |
|------|----------|
| Sept. 5 | Jackson State Tigers |
| Sept. 12 | at Alabama Crimson Tide |
| Sept. 19 | **Charlotte 49ers** |
| Sept. 26 | at Illinois Fighting Illini |
| Oct. 3 | Vanderbilt Commodores |
| Oct. 10 | **at Western Kentucky Hilltoppers** |
| Oct. 17 | **FIU Golden Panthers** |
| Oct. 24 | **at Louisiana Tech Bulldogs** |
| Nov. 7 | **Marshall Thundering Herd** |
| Nov. 14 | **at Florida Atlantic Owls** |
| Nov. 21 | **North Texas Mean Green** |
| Nov. 28 | **at UTSA Roadrunners** |

### 2014 RESULTS:   6-6 (5-3 in C-USA)          Final Ranking: NR

| Opponent | Result | Attendance |
|----------|--------|-----------|
| Savannah State | W 61-7 | (15,605) |
| at Minnesota | L 24-35 | (47,223) |
| **Western Kentucky** | W 50-47 3OT | (24,911) |
| at Memphis | L 17-36 | (46,378) |
| **at Old Dominion** | W 41-28 | (20,118) |
| **Southern Miss** | W 37-31 | (14,022) |
| **at Marshall** | L 24-49 | (30,210) |
| **UAB** | W 34-22 | (18,717) |
| BYU | L 7-27 | (18,952) |
| **at FIU** | L 28-38 | (12,917) |
| **Florida Atlantic** | W 35-34 | (12,243) |
| **at UTEP** | L 21-24 | (27,455) |

## Rick Stockstill's Year-by-Year Coaching Record:

<u>Middle Tennessee: 57-55 (43-26 in the Sun Belt and Conference USA)</u>

2006   7–6 (6–1)             **Final Ranking: NR**
Sun Belt Conference Co-Champions.
Stockstill named Sun Belt Conference Coach of the Year.
Lost to Central Michigan 14-31 in the Motor City Bowl.

2007   5–7 (4–3)             **Final Ranking: NR**

2008   5–7 (3–4)             **Final Ranking: NR**

2009   10–3 (7–1)           **Final Ranking: NR**
Stockstill named Sun Belt Conference Coach of the Year.
Beat Southern Miss 42-32 in the New Orleans Bowl.

2010   6–7 (5–3)             **Final Ranking: NR**
Lost to Miami (OH) 21-35 in the GoDaddy.com Bowl.

2011   2–10 (1–7)           **Final Ranking: NR**

2012   8–4 (6–2)             **Final Ranking: NR**

2013   8–5 (6–2)             **Final Ranking: NR**
Middle Tennessee leaves the Sun Belt and joins Conference USA.
Lost to Navy 6-24 in the Armed Forces Bowl.

2014   6–6 (5–3)             **Final Ranking: NR**

# Old Dominion Monarchs – Bobby Wilder

## Coach Ranking: #79

**Overall Record:** 52-20 in 6 seasons (4 seasons in FCS)
**Record at Old Dominion:** 52-20 in 6 seasons
**2014 Results:** 6-6, 4-4 in Conference USA (T-3rd in the C-USA East)
**Returning Starters in 2015:** 8 on offense, 5 on defense
**Salary:** $550,000          **Age:** 51          **Job Security Grade:** A

**2015 SCHEDULE:**
(Conference games in bold.)

| | |
|---|---|
| Sept. 5 | at Eastern Michigan Eagles |
| Sept. 12 | Norfolk State Spartans |
| Sept. 19 | NC State Wolfpack |
| Sept. 26 | Appalachian State Mountaineers |
| Oct. 3 | **at Marshall Thundering Herd** |
| Oct. 17 | **Charlotte 49ers** |
| Oct. 24 | **at FIU Golden Panthers** |
| Oct. 31 | **Western Kentucky Hilltoppers** |
| Nov. 7 | **at UTSA Roadrunners** |
| Nov. 14 | **UTEP Miners** |
| Nov. 21 | **at Southern Miss Golden Eagles** |
| Nov. 28 | **Florida Atlantic Owls** |

**2014 RESULTS:   6-6 (4-4 in C-USA)**          **Final Ranking: NR**

| | | |
|---|---|---|
| Hampton | W 41–28 | (20,118) |
| at NC State | L 34–46 | (55,390) |
| Eastern Michigan | W 17–3 | (20,118) |
| **at Rice** | W 45–42 | (17,558) |
| **Middle Tennessee** | L 28–41 | (20,118) |
| **Marshall** | L 14–56 | (20,118) |
| **at UTEP** | L 35–42 | (25,509) |
| **at Western Kentucky** | L 51–66 | (17,886) |
| at Vanderbilt | L 28–42 | (28,966) |
| **FIU** | W 38–35 | (20,118) |
| **Louisiana Tech** | W 30–27 OT | (20,118) |
| **at Florida Atlantic** | W 31–28 | (9,566) |

**Bobby Wilder's Year-by-Year Coaching Record:**

<u>Old Dominion: 52-20 (4-4 in Conference USA)</u>
2009   9–2 (FCS)                 Final Ranking: NR
       This was Old Dominion's first season of football since 1941.
2010   8–3 (FCS)                 Final Ranking: NR
2011   10–3 (FCS)                Final Ranking: #10
       Lost to #3 Georgia Southern 48-55 in the second round of the FCS playoffs.
2012   11–2 (FCS)                Final Ranking: #6
       Lost to #6 Georgia Southern 35-49 in the FCS quarterfinals.
2013   8–4 (Ind.)                Final Ranking: NR
       Old Dominion moves up from FCS to FBS and competes as an Independent
       program.
2014   6–6 (4–4)                 Final Ranking: NR
       Old Dominion joins Conference USA.

# Western Kentucky Hilltoppers – Jeff Brohm

## Coach Ranking: #76

**Overall Record:** 8-5 in 1 season
**Record at Western Kentucky:** 8-5 in 1 season
**2014 Results:** 8-5, 4-4 in Conference USA (T-3rd in the C-USA East)
**Returning Starters in 2015:** 7 on offense (including QB), 9 on defense
**Salary:** $600,000          **Age:** 44          **Job Security Grade:** A

**2015 SCHEDULE:**
(Conference games in bold.)

| Sept. 5 | at Vanderbilt Commodores |
|---------|--------------------------|
| Sept. 10 | **Louisiana Tech Bulldogs** |
| Sept. 19 | at Indiana Hoosiers |
| Sept. 26 | Miami (OH) RedHawks |
| Oct. 3 | **at Rice Owls** |
| Oct. 10 | **Middle Tennessee Blue Raiders** |
| Oct. 15 | **at North Texas Mean Green** |
| Oct. 24 | at LSU Tigers |
| Oct. 31 | **at Old Dominion Monarchs** |
| Nov. 7 | **Florida Atlantic Owls** |
| Nov. 21 | **at FIU Golden Panthers** |
| Nov. 27 | **Marshall Thundering Herd** |

**2014 RESULTS:   8-5 (4-4 in C-USA)**          **Final Ranking: NR**

| | | |
|---|---|---|
| Bowling Green | W 59–31 | (17,215) |
| at Illinois | L 34–42 | (38,561) |
| **at Middle Tennessee** | L 47–50 3OT | (24,911) |
| at Navy | W 36–27 | (30,537) |
| **UAB** | L 39–42 | (14,923) |
| **at Florida Atlantic** | L 38–45 | (10,915) |
| **Old Dominion** | W 66–51 | (17,886) |
| **at Louisiana Tech** | L 10–59 | (20,011) |
| **UTEP** | W 35–27 | (18,472) |
| Army | W 52–24 | (16,819) |
| **UTSA** | W 45–7 | (12,518) |
| **at #19 Marshall** | W 67–66 OT | (23,576) |
| vs. Central Michigan (Bahamas Bowl) | W 49–48 | (13,667) |

## Jeff Brohm's Year-by-Year Coaching Record:

**Western Kentucky: 8-5 (4-4 in Conference USA)**

| 2014 | 8-5 (4-4) | **Final Ranking: NR** |
|------|-----------|------------------------|

Beat Central Michigan 49-48 in the Bahamas Bowl.

# Louisiana Tech Bulldogs – Skip Holtz

## Coach Ranking: #51

**Overall Record:** 101-84 in 15 seasons (5 seasons in Division 1-AA)
**Record at Louisiana Tech:** 13-13 in 2 seasons
**2014 Results:** 9-5, 7-1 in Conference USA (West Division Champions)
**Returning Starters in 2015:** 7 on offense, 5 on defense
**Salary:** $500,000 **Age:** 51 **Job Security Grade:** A

**2015 SCHEDULE:**
(Conference games in bold.)

| | |
|---|---|
| Sept. 5 | Southern Jaguars |
| Sept. 10 | **at Western Kentucky Hilltoppers** |
| Sept. 19 | at Kansas State Wildcats |
| Sept. 26 | **FIU Golden Panthers** |
| Oct. 3 | Louisiana-Lafayette Ragin' Cajuns |
| Oct. 10 | **at UTSA Roadrunners** |
| Oct. 17 | at Mississippi State Bulldogs |
| Oct. 24 | **Middle Tennessee Blue Raiders** |
| Oct. 30 | **at Rice Owls** |
| Nov. 7 | **North Texas Mean Green** |
| Nov. 21 | **at UTEP Miners** |
| Nov. 28 | **Southern Miss Golden Eagles** |

**2014 RESULTS:** 9-5 (7-1 in C-USA) **Final Ranking: NR**

| | | |
|---|---|---|
| at #4 Oklahoma | L 16–48 | (85,063) |
| at Louisiana–Lafayette | W 48–20 | (25,607) |
| **at North Texas** | W 42–21 | (16,998) |
| Northwestern State | L 27–30 | (26,004) |
| at #5 Auburn | L 17–45 | (87,451) |
| **UTEP** | W 55–3 | (18,157) |
| **UTSA** | W 27–20 | (18,071) |
| **at Southern Miss** | W 31–20 | (23,343) |
| **Western Kentucky** | W 59–10 | (20,011) |
| **at UAB** | W 40–24 | (9,457) |
| **at Old Dominion** | L 27–30 OT | (20,118) |
| **Rice** | W 76–31 | (18,029) |
| **at Marshall** (C-USA Championship) | L 23–26 | (23,711) |
| vs. Illinois (Heart of Dallas Bowl) | W 35–18 | (31,297) |

## Skip Holtz's Year-by-Year Coaching Record:

### Connecticut: 34-23 (1-1 in the Division 1-AA Playoffs)
| | | |
|---|---|---|
| 1994 | 4–7 (0-0) | Final Ranking: NR |
| 1995 | 8–3 (0-0) | Final Ranking: #23 |
| 1996 | 5–6 (0-0) | Final Ranking: NR |
| 1997 | 7–4 (0-0) | Final Ranking: NR |
| 1998 | 10–3 (1-1) | Final Ranking: #8 |

Lost to #2 Georgia Southern 30-52 in the Division 1-AA quarterfinals.

### East Carolina: 38-27 (28-12 in Conference USA)
2005    5–6 (4–4)            Final Ranking: NR
2006    7–6 (5–3)            Final Ranking: NR
Lost to South Florida 7-24 in the PappaJohns.com Bowl.
2007    8–5 (6–2)            Final Ranking: NR
Beat #22 Boise State 41-38 in the Hawaii Bowl.
2008    9–5 (6–2)            Final Ranking: NR
Conference USA Champions.
Holtz named Conference USA Coach of the Year.
Beat Tulsa 27-24 in the C-USA Championship Game.
Lost to Kentucky 19-25 in the Liberty Bowl.
2009    9–5 (7–1)            Final Ranking: NR
Conference USA Champions.
Beat #18 Houston 38-32 in the C-USA Championship Game.
Lost to Arkansas 17-20 in OT in the Liberty Bowl.

### South Florida: 16-21 (5-16 in the Big East)
2010    8–5 (3–4)            Final Ranking: NR
Beat Clemson 31-26 in the Meineke Car Care Bowl.
2011    5–7 (1–6)            Final Ranking: NR
2012    3–9 (1–6)            Final Ranking: NR

### Louisiana Tech: 13-13 (10-6 in Conference USA)
2013    4–8 (3–5)            Final Ranking: NR
2014    9–5 (7–1)            Final Ranking: NR
Conference USA West Division Champions.
Lost to Marshall 23-26 in the C-USA Championship Game.
Beat Illinois 35-18 in the Heart of Dallas Bowl.

# North Texas Mean Green – Dan McCarney

## Coach Ranking: #99

**Overall Record:** 78-112 in 16 seasons
**Record at North Texas:** 22-27 in 4 seasons
**2014 Results:** 4-8, 2-6 in Conference USA (5th in the C-USA West)
**Returning Starters in 2015:** 6 on offense (including QB), 6 on defense
**Salary:** $700,000          **Age:** 62          **Job Security Grade:** B

**2015 SCHEDULE:**
(Conference games in bold.)

| | |
|---|---|
| Sept. 12 | at SMU Mustangs |
| Sept. 19 | **Rice Owls** |
| Sept. 26 | at Iowa Hawkeyes |
| Oct. 3 | **at Southern Miss Golden Eagles** |
| Oct. 10 | Portland State Vikings |
| Oct. 15 | **Western Kentucky Hilltoppers** |
| Oct. 24 | **at Marshall Thundering Herd** |
| Oct. 31 | **UTSA Roadrunners** |
| Nov. 7 | **at Louisiana Tech Bulldogs** |
| Nov. 14 | at Tennessee Volunteers |
| Nov. 21 | **at Middle Tennessee Blue Raiders** |
| Nov. 28 | **UTEP Miners** |

**2014 RESULTS:    4-8 (2-6 in C-USA)**          **Final Ranking: NR**

| | | |
|---|---|---|
| at Texas | L 7–38 | (93,201) |
| SMU | W 43–6 | (22,398) |
| **Louisiana Tech** | L 21–42 | (16,998) |
| Nicholls State | W 77–3 | (21,323) |
| at Indiana | L 24–49 | (40,457) |
| **at UAB** | L 21–56 | (20,365) |
| **Southern Miss** | L 20–30 | (19,127) |
| **at Rice** | L 21–41 | (18,430) |
| **Florida Atlantic** | W 31–10 | (20,957) |
| **at UTEP** | L 17–35 | (24,222) |
| FIU | W 17–14 | (14,824) |
| **at UTSA** | L 27–34 | (24,012) |

## Dan McCarney's Year-by-Year Coaching Record:

### Iowa State: 56-85 (27-68 in the Big 12/Big 8)
| | | |
|---|---|---|
| 1995 | 3–8 (1–6) | Final Ranking: NR |
| 1996 | 2–9 (1–7) | Final Ranking: NR |

The Big 8 expands and becomes the Big 12.

| | | |
|---|---|---|
| 1997 | 1–10 (1–7) | Final Ranking: NR |
| 1998 | 3–8 (1–7) | Final Ranking: NR |
| 1999 | 4–7 (1–7) | Final Ranking: NR |
| 2000 | 9–3 (5–3) | Final Ranking: #23 |

Beat Pittsburgh 37-29 in the Insight.com Bowl.

| | | |
|---|---|---|
| 2001 | 7–5 (4–4) | Final Ranking: NR |

Lost to Alabama 13-14 in the Independence Bowl.

| | | |
|---|---|---|
| 2002 | 7–7 (4–4) | Final Ranking: NR |

Lost to #18 Boise State 16-34 in the Humanitarian Bowl.

| | | |
|---|---|---|
| 2003 | 2–10 (0–8) | Final Ranking: NR |
| 2004 | 7–5 (4–4) | Final Ranking: NR |

Big 12 North Division Co-Champions.
Beat Miami (OH) 17-13 in the Independence Bowl.

| | | |
|---|---|---|
| 2005 | 7–5 (4–4) | Final Ranking: NR |

Lost to #14 TCU in the Houston Bowl.

| | | |
|---|---|---|
| 2006 | 4–8 (1–7) | Final Ranking: NR |

### North Texas: 22-27 (15-17 in the Sun Belt and Conference USA)
| | | |
|---|---|---|
| 2011 | 5–7 (4–4) | Final Ranking: NR |
| 2012 | 4–8 (3–5) | Final Ranking: NR |
| 2013 | 9–4 (6–2) | Final Ranking: NR |

North Texas leaves the Sun Belt Conference and joins Conference USA.
Beat UNLV 36-14 in the Heart of Dallas Bowl.

| | | |
|---|---|---|
| 2014 | 4–8 (2–6) | Final Ranking: NR |

# Rice Owls – David Bailiff

## Coach Ranking: #71

**Overall Record:** 69-68 in 11 seasons (3 seasons in Division 1-AA)
**Record at Rice:** 48-53 in 8 seasons
**2014 Results:** 8-5, 5-3 in Conference USA (T-2nd in the C-USA West)
**Returning Starters in 2015:** 6 on offense (including QB), 4 on defense
**Salary:** $780,000          **Age:** 62          **Job Security Grade:** A

**2015 SCHEDULE:**
(Conference games in bold.)

| | |
|---|---|
| Sept. 5 | Wagner Seahawks |
| Sept. 12 | at Texas Longhorns |
| Sept. 19 | **at North Texas Mean Green** |
| Sept. 26 | at Baylor Bears |
| Oct. 3 | **Western Kentucky Hilltoppers** |
| Oct. 10 | **at Florida Atlantic Owls** |
| Oct. 24 | Army Black Knights |
| Oct. 30 | **Louisiana Tech Bulldogs** |
| Nov. 6 | **at UTEP Miners** |
| Nov. 14 | **Southern Miss Golden Eagles** |
| Nov. 21 | **at UTSA Roadrunners** |
| Nov. 28 | **Charlotte 49ers** |

**2014 RESULTS:   8-5 (5-3 in C-USA)**          **Final Ranking: NR**

| | | |
|---|---|---|
| at #17 Notre Dame | L 17–48 | (80,795) |
| at #7 Texas A&M | L 10–38 | (103,867) |
| **Old Dominion** | L 42–45 | (17,558) |
| **at Southern Miss** | W 41–23 | (24,756) |
| Hawaii | W 28–14 | (17,465) |
| at Army | W 41–21 | (37,011) |
| **North Texas** | W 41–21 | (18,430) |
| **at FIU** | W 31–17 | (12,097) |
| **UTSA** | W 17–7 | (19,464) |
| **at #21 Marshall** | L 14–41 | (30,680) |
| **UTEP** | W 31–13 | (18,164) |
| **at Louisiana Tech** | L 31–76 | (18,029) |
| vs. Fresno State (Hawaii Bowl) | W 30–6 | (25,365) |

## David Bailiff's Year-by-Year Coaching Record:

### Texas State: 21-15 (2-1 in the Division 1-AA Playoffs)
2004    5–6 (0-0)                 Final Ranking: NR
2005    11–3 (2-1)                Final Ranking: #4
        Lost to #2 Northern Iowa 37-40 in the Division 1-AA semifinals.
2006    5–6 (0-0)                 Final Ranking: NR

### Rice: 48-53 (34-30 in Conference USA)
2007    3–9 (3–5)                 Final Ranking: NR
2008    10–3 (7–1)                Final Ranking: NR
        Conference USA West Division Co-Champions.
        Bailiff named C-USA Coach of the Year.
        Beat Western Michigan 38-14 in the Texas Bowl.
2009    2–10 (2–6)                Final Ranking: NR
2010    4–8 (3–5)                 Final Ranking: NR
2011    4–8 (3–5)                 Final Ranking: NR
2012    7–6 (4–4 )                Final Ranking: NR
        Beat Air Force 33-14 in the Armed Forces Bowl.
2013    10–4 (7–1)                Final Ranking: NR
        Conference USA Champions.
        Bailiff named C-USA Coach of the Year.
        Beat Marshall 41-24 in the C-USA Championship Game.
        Lost to Mississippi State 7-44 in the Liberty Bowl.
2014    8–5 (5–3)                 Final Ranking: NR
        Beat Fresno State 30-6 in the Hawaii Bowl.

# Southern Miss Golden Eagles – Todd Monken

## Coach Ranking: #116

**Overall Record:** 4-20 in 2 seasons
**Record at Southern Miss:** 4-20 in 2 seasons
**2014 Results:** 3-9, 1-7 in Conference USA (6th in the C-USA West)
**Returning Starters in 2015:** 9 on offense (including QB), 4 on defense
**Salary:** $700,000          **Age:** 49          **Job Security Grade:** C

**2015 SCHEDULE:**
(Conference games in bold.)

| | |
|---|---|
| Sept. 5 | Mississippi State Bulldogs |
| Sept. 12 | Austin Peay Governors |
| Sept. 19 | at Texas State Bobcats |
| Sept. 26 | at Nebraska Cornhuskers |
| Oct. 3 | **North Texas Mean Green** |
| Oct. 9 | **at Marshall Thundering Herd** |
| Oct. 17 | **UTSA Roadrunners** |
| Oct. 24 | **at Charlotte 49ers** |
| Oct. 31 | **UTEP Miners** |
| Nov. 14 | **at Rice Owls** |
| Nov. 21 | **Old Dominion Monarchs** |
| Nov. 28 | **at Louisiana Tech Bulldogs** |

**2014 RESULTS:   3-9 (1-7 in C-USA)**          **Final Ranking: NR**

| | | |
|---|---|---|
| at Mississippi State | L 0–49 | (61,889) |
| Alcorn State | W 26–20 | (26,448) |
| at #3 Alabama | L 12–52 | (101,821) |
| Appalachian State | W 21–20 | (21,836) |
| **Rice** | L 23–41 | (24,756) |
| **at Middle Tennessee** | L 31–37 | (14,022) |
| **at North Texas** | W 30–20 | (19,127) |
| **Louisiana Tech** | L 20–31 | (23,343) |
| **at UTEP** | L 14–35 | (24,673) |
| **#23 Marshall** | L 17–63 | (22,949) |
| **at UTSA** | L 10–12 | (20,281) |
| **UAB** | L 24–45 | (17,103) |

**Todd Monken's Year-by-Year Coaching Record:**

**Southern Miss: 4-20 (2-14 in Conference USA)**

| | | |
|---|---|---|
| 2013 | 1–11 (1–7) | Final Ranking: NR |
| 2014 | 3–9 (1–7) | Final Ranking: NR |

# UTEP Miners – Sean Kugler

## Coach Ranking: #105

**Overall Record:** 9-16 in 2 seasons
**Record at UTEP:** 9-16 in 2 seasons
**2014 Results:** 7-6, 5-3 in Conference USA (T-2nd in the C-USA West)
**Returning Starters in 2015:** 6 on offense, 6 on defense
**Salary:** $500,000      **Age:** 49      **Job Security Grade:** A

**2015 SCHEDULE:**
(Conference games in bold.)

| | |
|---|---|
| Sept. 5 | at Arkansas Razorbacks |
| Sept. 12 | at Texas Tech Red Raiders |
| Sept. 19 | at New Mexico State Aggies |
| Sept. 26 | Incarnate Word Cardinals |
| Oct. 3 | **UTSA Roadrunners** |
| Oct. 10 | **at FIU Golden Panthers** |
| Oct. 24 | **Florida Atlantic Owls** |
| Oct. 31 | **at Southern Miss Golden Eagles** |
| Nov. 6 | **Rice Owls** |
| Nov. 14 | **at Old Dominion Monarchs** |
| Nov. 21 | **Louisiana Tech Bulldogs** |
| Nov. 28 | **at North Texas Mean Green** |

**2014 RESULTS:** 7-6 (5-3 in C-USA)      Final Ranking: NR

| | | |
|---|---|---|
| at New Mexico | W 31–24 | (25,802) |
| Texas Tech | L 26–30 | (35,422) |
| New Mexico State | W 42–24 | (32,979) |
| at #25 Kansas State | L 28–58 | (52,899) |
| **at Louisiana Tech** | L 3–55 | (18,157) |
| **Old Dominion** | W 42–35 | (25,509) |
| **at UTSA** | W 34–0 | (31,956) |
| **Southern Miss** | W 35–14 | (24,673) |
| **at Western Kentucky** | L 27–35 | (18,472) |
| **North Texas** | W 35–17 | (24,222) |
| **at Rice** | L 13–31 | (18,164) |
| **Middle Tennessee** | W 24–21 | (27,455) |
| vs. Utah State (New Mexico Bowl) | L 6–21 | (28,725) |

## Sean Kugler's Year-by-Year Coaching Record:

UTEP: 9-16 (6-10 in Conference USA)

| | | |
|---|---|---|
| 2013 | 2–10 (1–7) | Final Ranking: NR |
| 2014 | 7–6 (5–3) | Final Ranking: NR |

Lost to Utah State 6-21 in the New Mexico Bowl.

# UTSA Roadrunners – Larry Coker

## Coach Ranking: #72

**Overall Record:** 83-38 in 10 seasons (1 season in FCS)
**Record at UTSA:** 23-23 in 4 seasons
**2014 Results:** 4-8, 3-5 in Conference USA (4th in the C-USA West)
**Returning Starters in 2015:** 6 on offense, 6 on defense
**Salary:** $425,000        **Age:** 67        **Job Security Grade:** B

### 2015 SCHEDULE:
(Conference games in bold.)

| Sept. 3 | at Arizona Wildcats |
|---|---|
| Sept. 12 | Kansas State Wildcats |
| Sept. 19 | at Oklahoma State Cowboys |
| Sept. 26 | Colorado State Rams |
| Oct. 3 | **at UTEP Miners** |
| Oct. 10 | **Louisiana Tech Bulldogs** |
| Oct. 17 | **at Southern Miss Golden Eagles** |
| Oct. 31 | **at North Texas Mean Green** |
| Nov. 7 | **Old Dominion Monarchs** |
| Nov. 14 | **at Charlotte 49ers** |
| Nov. 21 | **Rice Owls** |
| Nov. 28 | **Middle Tennessee Blue Raiders** |

### 2014 RESULTS:   4-8 (3-5 in C-USA)        Final Ranking: NR

| | | |
|---|---|---|
| at Houston | W 27–7 | (40,755) |
| Arizona | L 23–26 | (33,472) |
| at Oklahoma State | L 13–43 | (54,577) |
| **at Florida Atlantic** | L 37–41 | (13,928) |
| New Mexico | L 9–21 | (30,419) |
| **FIU** | W 16–13 | (25,318) |
| **at Louisiana Tech** | L 20–27 | (18,071) |
| **UTEP** | L 0–34 | (31,956) |
| **at Rice** | L 7–17 | (19,464) |
| **Southern Miss** | W 12–10 | (20,281) |
| **at Western Kentucky** | L 7–45 | (12,518) |
| **North Texas** | W 34–27 | (24,012) |

## Larry Coker's Year-by-Year Coaching Record:

### Miami (FL): 60-15 (34-11 in the Big East and ACC)
2001    12–0 (7–0)            Final Ranking: #1
        National Champions.
        Big East Champions.
        Coker named National Coach of the Year.
        Coker named Big East Coach of the Year.
        Beat #4 Nebraska 37-14 in the BCS National Championship Game.
2002    12–1 (7–0)            Final Ranking: #2
        Big East Champions.
        Coker named Big East Coach of the Year.
        Lost to #2 Ohio State 24-31 in OT in the BCS National Championship Game.
2003    11–2 (6–1)            Final Ranking: #5
        Big East Champions.
        Beat #9 Florida State 16-14 in the Orange Bowl.
2004    9–3 (5–3)             Final Ranking: #11
        Miami leaves the Big East and joins the ACC.
        Beat #20 Florida 27-10 in the Peach Bowl.
2005    9–3 (6–2)             Final Ranking: #17
        Lost to #10 LSU 3-40 in the Peach Bowl.
2006    7–6 (3–5)             Final Ranking: NR

### UTSA: 23-23 (12-10 in the WAC and Conference USA)
2011    4–6 (FCS)            Final Ranking: NR
2012    8–4 (3–3)            Final Ranking: NR
        UTSA moved up from FCS to FBS and joined the WAC.
        UTSA was not bowl eligible due to the FCS-to-FBS transition period.
2013    7–5 (6–2)            Final Ranking: NR
        The WAC dissolves as a football conference and UTSA joins C-USA.
2014    4–8 (3–5)            Final Ranking: NR

# Army Black Knights – Jeff Monken

## Coach Ranking: #94

**Overall Record:** 42-24 in 5 seasons (4 seasons in FCS)
**Record at Army:** 4-8 in 1 season
**2014 Results:** 4-8 (Independent)
**Returning Starters in 2015:** 5 on offense, 4 on defense
**Salary:** $830,000          **Age:** 48          **Job Security Grade:** A

**2015 SCHEDULE:**

| | |
|---|---|
| Sept. 4 | Fordham Rams |
| Sept. 12 | at Connecticut Huskies |
| Sept. 19 | Wake Forest Demon Deacons |
| Sept. 26 | at Eastern Michigan Eagles |
| Oct. 3 | at Penn State Nittany Lions |
| Oct. 10 | Duke Blue Devils |
| Oct. 17 | Bucknell Bison |
| Oct. 24 | at Rice Owls |
| Nov. 7 | at Air Force Falcons |
| Nov. 14 | Tulane Green Wave |
| Nov. 21 | Rutgers Scarlet Knights |
| Dec. 12 | vs. Navy Midshipmen (in Philadelphia) |

**2014 RESULTS:  4-8**                **Final Ranking: NR**

| | | |
|---|---|---|
| Buffalo | W 47–39 | (28,643) |
| at #15 Stanford | L 0–35 | (49,680) |
| at Wake Forest | L 21–24 | (28,123) |
| at Yale | L 43–49 OT | (34,142) |
| Ball State | W 33–24 | (31,384) |
| Rice | L 21–41 | (37,011) |
| at Kent State | L 17–39 | (18,114) |
| Air Force | L 6–23 | (40,479) |
| vs. Connecticut (in New York City) | W 35–21 | (27,453) |
| at Western Kentucky | L 24–52 | (16,819) |
| #7 (FCS) Fordham | W 42–31 | (33,793) |
| Vs. Navy (in Baltimore) | L 10–17 | (70,935) |

# Jeff Monken's Year-by-Year Coaching Record:

<u>Georgia Southern: 38-16 (7-3 in the FCS Playoffs)</u>
2010    10–5 (3-1)              Final Ranking: #5
        Lost to #5 Delaware 10-27 in the FCS semifinals.
2011    11–3 (2–1)             Final Ranking: #3
        Lost to #4 North Dakota State 7-35 in the FCS semifinals.
2012    10–4 (2-1)             Final Ranking: #6
        Lost to #1 North Dakota State 20-23 in the FCS semifinals.
2013    7–4 (0-0)              Final Ranking: NR

<u>Army: 4-8 (Independent)</u>
2014    4-8 (Ind.)            Final Ranking: NR

# BYU Cougars – Bronco Mendenhall

## Coach Ranking: #61

**Overall Record:** 90-39 in 10 seasons
**Record at BYU:** 90-39 in 10 seasons
**2014 Results:** 8-5 (Independent)
**Returning Starters in 2015:** 8 on offense (including QB), 6 on defense
**Salary:** $2 Million*    **Age:** 49    **Job Security Grade:** B

**2015 SCHEDULE:**

| Sept. 5 | at Nebraska Cornhuskers |
| Sept. 12 | Boise State Broncos |
| Sept. 19 | at UCLA Bruins |
| Sept. 26 | at Michigan Wolverines |
| Oct. 2 | Connecticut Huskies |
| Oct. 10 | East Carolina Pirates |
| Oct. 16 | Cincinnati Bearcats |
| Oct. 24 | Wagner Seahawks |
| Nov. 6 | at San Jose State Spartans |
| Nov. 14 | vs. Missouri Tigers (in Kansas City) |
| Nov. 21 | Fresno State Bulldogs |
| Nov. 28 | at Utah State Aggies |

**2014 RESULTS:   8-5**                     **Final Ranking: NR**

| | | |
|---|---|---|
| at Connecticut | W 35–10 | (35,150) |
| at # 25 Texas | W 41–7 | (93,463) |
| Houston | W 33–25 | (57,630) |
| Virginia | W 41–33 | (59,023) |
| Utah State | L 20–35 | (64,090) |
| at UCF | L 24–31 OT | (41,547) |
| Nevada | L 35–42 | (56,355) |
| at Boise State | L 30–55 | (36,752) |
| at Middle Tennessee | W 27–7 | (18,952) |
| UNLV | W 42–23 | (53,622) |
| Savannah State | W 64–0 | (52,123) |
| at Cal | W 42–35 | (47,856) |
| vs. Memphis (Miami Beach Bowl) | L 48–55 2OT | (20,761) |

## Bronco Mendenhall's Year-by-Year Coaching Record:

**BYU: 90-39 (39-9 in the Mountain West)**

2005    6–6 (5–3)                Final Ranking: NR
Lost to Cal 28-35 in the Las Vegas Bowl.

2006    11–2 (8–0)               Final Ranking: #15
MWC Champions.
Mendenhall named the MWC Coach of the Year.
Beat Oregon 38-8 in the Las Vegas Bowl.

2007    11–2 (8–0)               Final Ranking: #14
MWC Champions.
Beat UCLA 17-16 in the Las Vegas Bowl.

2008    10–3 (6–2) 3rd           Final Ranking: #21
Lost to Arizona 21-31 in the Las Vegas Bowl.

2009    11–2 (7–1)               Final Ranking: #12
Beat #20 Oregon State 44-20 in the Las Vegas Bowl.

2010    7–6 (5–3)                Final Ranking: NR
Beat UTEP 52-24 in the New Mexico Bowl.

2011    10–3 (Ind.)              Final Ranking: #25
BYU leaves the Mountain West Conference and becomes an Independent program.
Beat Tulsa 24-21 in the Armed Forces Bowl.

2012    8–5 (Ind.)               Final Ranking: NR
Beat San Diego State 23-6 in the Poinsettia Bowl.

2013    8–5 (Ind.)               Final Ranking: NR
Lost to Washington 16-31 in the Fight Hunger Bowl.

2014    8–5 (Ind.)               Final Ranking: NR
Lost to Memphis 48-55 in 2OT in the Miami Beach Bowl.

Want the latest college football coaching news? Visit:

# CoachesAlmanac.com

# 2015 MAC PREVIEW

## Five Things You Need to Know about the MAC in 2015:

**The Battle at the Top:** **Northern Illinois** has won five-straight West Division titles and three of the last four MAC championships. Until proven otherwise, **Rod Carey's** Huskies are still the kings of this league. However, **Western Michigan** has emerged quickly as a serious threat for the West Division title and **Frank Solich** should have his best team in years at **Ohio.**

**New to the MAC:** One of this year's most intriguing new FBS head coaches is **Buffalo's Lance Leipold.** Leipold spent the last eight years winning six Division III National Championships at **Wisconsin-Whitewater.** It'll be very interesting to see whether his success at the Division-III level can be quickly replicated in the MAC. Also new to the MAC is **Central Michigan's John Bonamego,** who spent the last 16 years as an assistant in the NFL.

**Coach on the Rise:** Last year, **P.J. Fleck** led **Western Michigan** to the greatest one-year turnaround in the history of the MAC. The young coach's name came up quickly as a candidate for some high-profile job openings and WMU responded by giving him a six-year contract extension and a raise of more than $400,000. His new $800,000 salary makes him the highest-paid coach in the MAC.

**Keep an Eye On:** From 1998-2003, **Mark Whipple** led a Division 1-AA dynasty at **UMass.** He returned to the program last year and will have 19 starters back in 2015 (the most in the MAC). UMass is hoping Whipple can quickly bring the magic back to this once-thriving program. Don't be surprised if the Minutemen have their best season since joining the MAC back in 2012.

**Coaches on the Hot Seat:** When **Paul Haynes** arrived at **Kent State,** he took over a team that had won 11 games the previous year (2012). With a 4-8 debut season and a 2-9 record in 2014, Haynes is sliding in the wrong direction and he needs to right this ship quickly.

## 2015 Projected Standings for the MAC:

**East Division:**
1. Ohio
2. Bowling Green
3. Buffalo
4. Massachusetts
5. Akron
6. Kent State
7. Miami (OH)

**West Division:**
1. Northern Illinois
2. Western Michigan
3. Ball State
4. Toledo
5. Central Michigan
6. Eastern Michigan

## Ranking the MAC's Coaches:

1. **Frank Solich** – Ohio (130-75 in 16 seasons)
2. **Terry Bowden** – Akron (151-87-2 in 21 seasons)
3. **Lance Leipold** – Buffalo (109-6 in 8 seasons)
4. **Rod Carey** – Northern Illinois (23-6 in 2 seasons)
5. **P.J. Fleck** – Western Michigan (9-16 in 2 seasons)
6. **Matt Campbell** – Toledo (26-13 in 3 seasons)
7. **Dino Babers** – Bowling Green (27-13 in 3 seasons)
8. **Mark Whipple** – Massachusetts (124-68 in 17 seasons)
9. **Chuck Martin** – Miami (OH) (76-17 in 7 seasons)
10. **Pete Lembo** – Ball State (109-56 in 14 seasons)
11. **Chris Creighton** – Eastern Michigan (141-56 in 18 seasons)
12. **John Bonamego** – Central Michigan (First Year Head Coach)
13. **Paul Haynes** – Kent State (6-17 in 2 seasons)

## 2014 MAC Coach of the Year:
(Selected by the MAC coaches)
P.J. Fleck, Western Michigan

## 2014 MAC Standings:

| East Division | (Conference) | (All Games) |
|---|---|---|
| Bowling Green | 5–3 | 8–6 |
| Ohio | 4–4 | 6–6 |
| Buffalo | 3–4 | 5–6 |
| Akron | 3–5 | 5–7 |
| UMass | 3–5 | 3–9 |
| Miami (OH) | 2–6 | 2–10 |
| Kent State | 1–6 | 2–9 |
| *West Division* | | |
| Northern Illinois | 7–1 | 11–3 |
| Toledo | 7–1 | 9–4 |
| Western Michigan | 6–2 | 8–5 |
| Central Michigan | 5–3 | 7–6 |
| Ball State | 4–4 | 5–7 |
| Eastern Michigan | 1–7 | 2–10 |

*Championship Game*: Northern Illinois 51, Bowling Green 17

**2014 MAC Bowl Record:** 2-3 (Tied for 6th place among all 10 conferences)

# Akron Zips – Terry Bowden

## Coach Ranking: #82

**Overall Record:** 151-87-2 in 21 seasons (4 seasons in Division 1-AA, 6 seasons in Division II, 2 seasons in Division III)

**Record at Akron:** 11-25 in 3 seasons

**2014 Results:** 5-7, 3-5 in the MAC (T-4$^{th}$ in the MAC East)

**Returning Starters in 2015:** 6 on offense (including QB), 6 on defense

**Salary:** $410,000          **Age:** 59          **Job Security Grade:** B

**2015 SCHEDULE:**
(Conference games in bold.)

| | |
|---|---|
| Sept. 5 | at Oklahoma Sooners |
| Sept. 12 | Pittsburgh Panthers |
| Sept. 19 | Savannah State Tigers |
| Sept. 26 | at Louisiana-Lafayette Ragin' Cajuns |
| Oct. 3 | **Ohio Bobcats** |
| Oct. 10 | **at Eastern Michigan Eagles** |
| Oct. 17 | **at Bowling Green Falcons** |
| Oct. 31 | **Central Michigan Chippewas** |
| Nov. 7 | **at Massachusetts Minutemen** |
| Nov. 14 | **at Miami (OH) RedHawks** |
| Nov. 21 | **Buffalo Bulls** |
| Nov. 27 | **Kent State Golden Flashes** |

**2014 RESULTS:   5-7 (3-5 in the MAC)**          **Final Ranking: NR**

| | | |
|---|---|---|
| Howard | W 41–0 | (9,104) |
| at Penn State | L 3–21 | (97,354) |
| Marshall | L 17–48 | (13,357) |
| at Pittsburgh | W 21–10 | (40,059) |
| **Eastern Michigan** | W 31–6 | (8,416) |
| **Miami (OH)** | W 29–19 | (8,223) |
| **at Ohio** | L 20–23 | (20,018) |
| **at Ball State** | L 21–35 | (7,617) |
| **Bowling Green** | L 10–27 | (10,348) |
| **at Buffalo** | L 24–55 | (17,343) |
| **Massachusetts** | W 30–6 | (5,571) |
| **at Kent State** | L 24–27 | (5,118) |

## Terry Bowden's Year-by-Year Coaching Record:

### Salem: 19-13 (0-0 in the Division II Playoffs)
| 1983 | 3–7 (0-0) | Final Ranking: NR |
|------|-----------|-------------------|
| 1984 | 8–3 (0-0) | Final Ranking: NR |
| 1985 | 8–3 (0-0) | Final Ranking: NR |

### Samford: 45-23-1 (2-2 in the Division 1-AA Playoffs)
| 1987 | 9–1 (Div. III) | Final Ranking: NA |
|------|----------------|-------------------|
| 1988 | 5–6 (Div. III) | Final Ranking: NA |
| 1989 | 4–7 (0-0) | Final Ranking: NA |

Samford moves from Division III to Division 1-AA.

| 1990 | 6–4–1 (0-0) | Final Ranking: NA |
|------|-------------|-------------------|
| 1991 | 12–2 (2-1) | Final Ranking: NA |

Lost to Youngstown State 0-10 in the Division 1-AA semifinals.

| 1992 | 9–3 (0-1) | Final Ranking: #9 |
|------|-----------|-------------------|

Lost to #8 Delaware 21-56 in first round of the Division 1-AA playoffs.

### Auburn: 47-17-1 (30-14-1 in the SEC)
| 1993 | 11–0 (8–0) | Final Ranking: #4 |
|------|------------|-------------------|

Bowden named National Coach of the Year.
Bowden named SEC Coach of the Year.
Auburn was on probation and ineligible for postseason play.

| 1994 | 9–1–1 (6–1–1) | Final Ranking: #9 |
|------|---------------|-------------------|

Auburn was on probation and ineligible for postseason play.

| 1995 | 8–4 (5–3) | Final Ranking: #21 |
|------|-----------|--------------------|

Lost to Penn State 14-53 in the Outback Bowl.

| 1996 | 8–4 (4–4) | Final Ranking: #24 |
|------|-----------|--------------------|

Beat Army 32-29 in the Independence Bowl.

| 1997 | 10–3 (6–2) | Final Ranking: #11 |
|------|------------|--------------------|

SEC West Champions.
Lost to #3 Tennessee 29-30 in the SEC Championship Game.
Beat Clemson 21-17 in the Peach Bowl.

| 1998 | 1–5 (1–4) | Final Ranking: NR |
|------|-----------|-------------------|

Bowden resigned after a 1-5 start and Auburn finished the year 3-8.

### North Alabama: 29-9 (3-3 in the Division II Playoffs)
| 2009 | 11–2 (1-1) | Final Ranking: NA |
|------|------------|-------------------|

Lost to Carson-Newman 21-24 in the Division II quarterfinals.

| 2010 | 9–4 (1-1) | Final Ranking: NA |
|------|-----------|-------------------|

Lost to Delta State 21-47 in the second round of the Division II playoffs.

| 2011 | 9–3 (1-1) | Final Ranking: NA |
|------|-----------|-------------------|

Lost to Delta State 14-42 in the second round of the Division II playoffs.

### Akron: 11-25 (7-17 in the MAC)
| 2012 | 1–11 (0–8) | Final Ranking: NR |
|------|------------|-------------------|
| 2013 | 5–7 (4–4) | Final Ranking: NR |
| 2014 | 5–7 (3–5) | Final Ranking: NR |

# Bowling Green Falcons – Dino Babers

## Coach Ranking: #101

**Overall Record:** 27-13 in 3 seasons (2 seasons in FCS)
**Record at Bowling Green:** 8-6 in 1 season
**2014 Results:** 8-6, 5-3 in the MAC (MAC East Champions)
**Returning Starters in 2015:** 10 on offense (including QB), 4 on defense
**Salary:** $400,000      **Age:** 53      **Job Security Grade:** A

**2015 SCHEDULE:**
(Conference games in bold.)

| | |
|---|---|
| Sept. 5 | at Tennessee Volunteers |
| Sept. 12 | at Maryland Terrapins |
| Sept. 19 | Memphis Tigers |
| Sept. 26 | at Purdue Boilermakers |
| Oct. 3 | **at Buffalo Bulls** |
| Oct. 10 | **Massachusetts Minutemen** |
| Oct. 17 | **Akron Zips** |
| Oct. 24 | **at Kent State Golden Flashes** |
| Nov. 4 | **Ohio Bobcats** |
| Nov. 11 | **at Western Michigan Broncos** |
| Nov. 17 | **Toledo Rockets** |
| Nov. 24 | **at Ball State Cardinals** |

| **2014 RESULTS:** 8-6 (5-3 in the MAC) | **Final Ranking: NR** | |
|---|---|---|
| at Western Kentucky | L 31–59 | (17,215) |
| Virginia Military Institute | W 48–7 | (18,311) |
| Indiana | W 45–42 | (23,717) |
| at #19 Wisconsin | L 17–68 | (79,849) |
| **at Massachusetts** | W 47–42 | (17,000) |
| **Buffalo** | W 36–35 | (17,185) |
| **at Ohio** | W 31–13 | (24,311) |
| **Western Michigan** | L 14–26 | (15,201) |
| **at Akron** | W 27–10 | (10,348) |
| **Kent State** | W 30–20 | (8,417) |
| **at Toledo** | L 20–27 | (17,486) |
| **Ball State** | L 24–41 | (8,534) |
| **vs. Northern Illinois** (MAC Championship) | L 17–51 | (15,110) |
| vs. South Alabama (Camellia Bowl) | W 33–28 | (20,256) |

## Dino Babers' Year-by-Year Coaching Record:

### Eastern Illinois: 19-7 (1-2 in the FCS Playoffs)
2012    7–5 (0-1)           **Final Ranking: #25**
        Babers named the Ohio Valley Conference Coach of the Year.
        Lost to #19 South Dakota State 10-58 in the first round of the FCS playoffs.
2013    12–2 (1-1)          **Final Ranking: #4**
        Babers named the Ohio Valley Conference Coach of the Year.
        Lost to #5 Towson 39-49 in the FCS quarterfinals.

### Bowling Green: 8-6 (5-3 in the MAC)
2014    8–6 (5–3)          **Final Ranking: NR**
        MAC East Division Champions.
        Lost to Northern Illinois 17-51 in the MAC Championship Game.
        Beat South Alabama 33-28 in the Camellia Bowl.

# Buffalo Bulls – Lance Leipold

## Coach Ranking: #86

**Overall Record:** 109-6 in 8 seasons (8 seasons in Division III)
**2014 Results:** Buffalo went 5-6, 3-4 in the MAC (3rd in the MAC East)
Leipold was Wisconsin-Whitewater's head coach from 2007-2014
**Returning Starters in 2015:** 7 on offense (including QB), 4 on defense
**Salary:** $400,000        **Age:** 51        **Job Security Grade:** A

**2015 SCHEDULE:**
(Conference games in bold.)

| | |
|---|---|
| Sept. 5 | Albany Great Danes |
| Sept. 12 | at Penn State Nittany Lions |
| Sept. 19 | at Florida Atlantic Owls |
| Sept. 26 | Nevada Wolf Pack |
| Oct. 3 | **Bowling Green Falcons** |
| Oct. 17 | **at Central Michigan Chippewas** |
| Oct. 24 | **Ohio Bobcats** |
| Oct. 29 | **at Miami (OH) RedHawks** |
| Nov. 5 | **at Kent State Golden Flashes** |
| Nov. 11 | **Northern Illinois Huskies** |
| Nov. 21 | **at Akron Zips** |
| Nov. 27 | **Massachusetts Minutemen** |

**2014 RESULTS:**   5-6 (3-4 in the MAC)        **Final Ranking: NR**

| | | |
|---|---|---|
| Duquesne | W 38–28 | (20,329) |
| at Army | L 39–47 | (28,643) |
| #8 Baylor | L 21–63 | (24,714) |
| Norfolk State | W 36–7 | (21,139) |
| **Miami (OH)** | W 35–27 | (20,841) |
| **at Bowling Green** | L 35–36 | (17,185) |
| **at Eastern Michigan** | L 27–37 | (11,886) |
| **Central Michigan** | L 14–20 | (18,052) |
| **at Ohio** | L 14–37 | (15,405) |
| **Akron** | W 55–24 | (17,343) |
| **Kent State** | Canceled | (N/A) |
| **at Massachusetts** | W 41–21 | (13,417) |

## Lance Leipold's Year-by-Year Coaching Record:

<u>Wisconsin-Whitewater: 109-6 (34-1 in the Division III Playoffs)</u>
2007   **14–1 (5-0)**          **Final Ranking: NA**
Division III National Champions.
Leipold named Division III Coach of the Year.
Beat Mount Union 31-21 in the Division III National Championship Game.

2008   **13–2 (4–1)**          **Final Ranking: NA**
Lost to Mount Union 26-31 in the Division III National Championship Game.

2009   **15–0 (5-0)**          **Final Ranking: NA**
Division III National Champions.
Leipold named Division III Coach of the Year.
Beat Mount Union 38-28 in the Division III National Championship Game.

2010   **15–0 (5-0)**          **Final Ranking: NA**
Division III National Champions.
Leipold named Division III Coach of the Year.
Beat Mount Union 31-21 in the Division III National Championship Game.

2011   **15–0 (5-0)**          **Final Ranking: NA**
Division III National Champions.
Leipold named Division III Coach of the Year.
Beat Mount Union 13-10 in the Division III National Championship Game.

2012   **7–3 (0-0)**          **Final Ranking: NA**
2013   **15–0 (5-0)**          **Final Ranking: NA**
Division III National Champions.
Beat Mount Union 52-14 in the Division III National Championship Game.

2014   **15–0 (5-0)**          **Final Ranking: NA**
Division III National Champions.
Beat Mount Union 43-34 in the Division III National Championship Game.

# Kent State Golden Flashes – Paul Haynes

## Coach Ranking: #125

**Overall Record:** 6-17 in 2 seasons
**Record at Kent State:** 6-17 in 2 seasons
**2014 Results:** 2-9, 1-6 in the MAC (7th in the MAC East)
**Returning Starters in 2015:** 8 on offense (including QB), 8 on defense
**Salary:** $380,000     **Age:** 46     **Job Security Grade:** C

**2015 SCHEDULE:**
(Conference games in bold.)

| | |
|---|---|
| Sept. 4 | at Illinois Fighting Illini |
| Sept. 12 | Delaware State Hornets |
| Sept. 19 | at Minnesota Golden Gophers |
| Sept. 26 | Marshall Thundering Herd |
| Oct. 3 | **Miami (OH) RedHawks** |
| Oct. 10 | **at Toledo Rockets** |
| Oct. 17 | **at Massachusetts Minutemen** |
| Oct. 24 | **Bowling Green Falcons** |
| Nov. 5 | **Buffalo Bulls** |
| Nov. 10 | **at Ohio Bobcats** |
| Nov. 18 | **Central Michigan Chippewas** |
| Nov. 27 | **at Akron Zips** |

**2014 RESULTS:** 2-9 (1-6 in the MAC)     Final Ranking: NR

| | | |
|---|---|---|
| Ohio | L 14–17 | (22,754) |
| South Alabama | L 13–23 | (15,355) |
| at #22 Ohio State | L 0–66 | (104,404) |
| at Virginia | L 13–45 | (33,526) |
| **at Northern Illinois** | L 14–17 | (15,620) |
| **Massachusetts** | L 17–40 | (12,451) |
| Army | W 39–17 | (18,114) |
| **at Miami (OH)** | L 3–10 | (22,792) |
| **Toledo** | L 20–30 | (7,471) |
| **at Bowling Green** | L 20–30 | (8,417) |
| **at Buffalo** | Canceled | (N/A) |
| **Akron** | W 27–24 | (5,118) |

## Paul Haynes' Year-by-Year Coaching Record:

Kent State: 6-17 (4-11 in the MAC)

| | | |
|---|---|---|
| 2013 | 4–8 (3–5) | Final Ranking: NR |
| 2014 | 2–9 (1–6) | Final Ranking: NR |

# Massachusetts Minutemen – Mark Whipple

## Coach Ranking: #108

**Overall Record:** 124-68 in 17 seasons (6 seasons in Division II, 10 seasons in Division 1-AA)

**Record at Massachusetts:** 52-35 in 7 seasons

**2014 Results:** 3-9, 3-5 in the MAC (T-4th in the MAC East)

**Returning Starters in 2015:** 10 on offense (including QB), 9 on defense

**Salary:** $450,000     **Age:** 58     **Job Security Grade:** A

**2015 SCHEDULE:**
(Conference games in bold.)

| Sept. 12 | at Colorado Buffaloes |
|---|---|
| Sept. 19 | Temple Owls |
| Sept. 26 | at Notre Dame Fighting Irish |
| Oct. 3 | FIU Golden Panthers |
| Oct. 10 | **at Bowling Green Falcons** |
| Oct. 17 | **Kent State Golden Flashes** |
| Oct. 24 | **Toledo Rockets** |
| Oct. 31 | **at Ball State Cardinals** |
| Nov. 7 | **Akron Zips** |
| Nov. 14 | **at Eastern Michigan Eagles** |
| Nov. 21 | **Miami (OH) RedHawks** |
| Nov. 27 | **at Buffalo Bulls** |

**2014 RESULTS:** 3-9 (3-5 in the MAC)     **Final Ranking: NR**

| | | |
|---|---|---|
| Boston College | L 7–30 | (30,479) |
| Colorado | L 38–41 | (10,227) |
| at Vanderbilt | L 31–34 | (33,386) |
| at Penn State | L 7–48 | (99,155) |
| **Bowling Green** | L 42–47 | (17,000) |
| **at Miami (OH)** | L 41–42 | (15,970) |
| **at Kent State** | W 40–17 | (12,451) |
| **Eastern Michigan** | W 36–14 | (12,030) |
| **at Toledo** | L 35–42 | (20,104) |
| **Ball State** | W 24–10 | (13,374) |
| **at Akron** | L 6–30 | (5,571) |
| **Buffalo** | L 21–41 | (13,417) |

## Mark Whipple's Year-by-Year Coaching Record:

### New Haven: 48-17 (3-2 in the Division II Playoffs)
| | | |
|---|---|---|
| 1988 | 7–3 (0-0) | Final Ranking: NA |
| 1989 | 8–2 (0-0) | Final Ranking: NA |
| 1990 | 7–3 (0-0) | Final Ranking: NA |
| 1991 | 3–7 (0-0) | Final Ranking: NA |
| 1992 | 12–1 (2-1) | Final Ranking: NA |

Lost to Jacksonville State 35-46 in the Division II semifinals.

| | | |
|---|---|---|
| 1993 | 11–1 (1-1) | Final Ranking: NA |

Lost to Indiana (PA) 35-38 in the Division II quarterfinals.

### Brown: 24-16 (0-0 in the Division 1-AA Playoffs)
| | | |
|---|---|---|
| 1994 | 7–3 (0-0) | Final Ranking: NR |
| 1995 | 5–5 (0-0) | Final Ranking: NR |
| 1996 | 5–5 (0-0) | Final Ranking: NR |
| 1997 | 7–3 (0-0) | Final Ranking: NR |

### Massachusetts: 52-35 (5-2 in the Division 1-AA Playoffs, 3-5 in the MAC)
| | | |
|---|---|---|
| 1998 | 12–3 (4-0) | Final Ranking: #1 |

Division 1-AA National Champions.
Beat #1 Georgia Southern 55-42 in the Division 1-AA National Championship Game.

| | | |
|---|---|---|
| 1999 | 9–4 (1-1) | Final Ranking: #7 |

Lost to #2 Georgia Southern 21-38 in the Division 1-AA quarterfinals.

| | | |
|---|---|---|
| 2000 | 7–4 (0-0) | Final Ranking: NR |
| 2001 | 3–8 (0-0) | Final Ranking: NR |
| 2002 | 8–4 (0-0) | Final Ranking: NR |
| 2003 | 10–3 (0-1) | Final Ranking: #11 |

Lost to #6 Colgate 7-19 in first round of the Division 1-AA playoffs.

------

| | | |
|---|---|---|
| 2014 | 3–9 (3–5) | Final Ranking: NR |

Whipple returns to UMass after spending eight seasons as an assistant coach in the NFL.
UMass moved up to FBS and joined the MAC in 2012.

# Miami (Ohio) RedHawks – Chuck Martin

## Coach Ranking: #110

**Overall Record:** 76-17 in 7 seasons (6 seasons in Division II)
**Record at Miami (OH):** 2-10 in 1 season
**2014 Results:** 2-10, 2-6 in the MAC (6th in the MAC East)
**Returning Starters in 2015:** 4 on offense, 8 on defense
**Salary:** $450,000          **Age:** 47          **Job Security Grade:** B

**2015 SCHEDULE:**
(Conference games in bold.)

| | |
|---|---|
| Sept. 5 | Presbyterian Blue Hose |
| Sept. 12 | at Wisconsin Badgers |
| Sept. 19 | Cincinnati Bearcats |
| Sept. 26 | at Western Kentucky Hilltoppers |
| Oct. 3 | **at Kent State Golden Flashes** |
| Oct. 10 | **at Ohio Bobcats** |
| Oct. 17 | **Northern Illinois Huskies** |
| Oct. 24 | **at Western Michigan Broncos** |
| Oct. 29 | **Buffalo Bulls** |
| Nov. 7 | **Eastern Michigan Eagles** |
| Nov. 14 | **Akron Zips** |
| Nov. 21 | **at Massachusetts Minutemen** |

**2014 RESULTS:   2-10 (2-6 in the MAC)**          **Final Ranking: NR**

| | | |
|---|---|---|
| Marshall | L 27–42 | (19,005) |
| Eastern Kentucky | L 10–17 | (16,670) |
| at Michigan | L 10–34 | (102,824) |
| at Cincinnati | L 24–31 | (41,926) |
| **at Buffalo** | L 27–35 | (20,841) |
| **Massachusetts** | W 42–41 | (15,970) |
| **at Akron** | L 19–29 | (8,223) |
| **at Northern Illinois** | L 41–51 | (11,211) |
| **Kent State** | W 10–3 | (22,792) |
| **Western Michigan** | L 10–41 | (9,045) |
| **at Central Michigan** | L 27–34 | (7,689) |
| **Ohio** | L 21–24 | (11,956) |

## Chuck Martin's Year-by-Year Coaching Record:

### Grand Valley State: 74-7 (16-4 in the Division II Playoffs)
2004    10–3 (2-1)              **Final Ranking: NA**
Lost to North Dakota 15-19 in the Division II quarterfinals.
2005    13–0 (4–0)              **Final Ranking: NA**
Division II National Champions.
Martin named Division II Coach of the Year.
Beat Northwest Missouri State 21-17 in the Division II National Championship Game.
2006    15–0 (4–0)              **Final Ranking: NA**
Division II National Champions.
Martin named Division II Coach of the Year.
Beat Northwest Missouri State 17-14 in the Division II National Championship Game.
2007    12–1 (2-1)              **Final Ranking: NA**
Lost to Northwest Missouri State 16-34 in the Division II semifinals.
2008    11–1 (1-1)              **Final Ranking: NA**
Lost to Minnesota Duluth in double OT in the Division II quarterfinals.
2009    13–2 (3-1)              **Final Ranking: NA**
Lost to Northwest Missouri State 23-30 in the Division II National Championship Game.

### Miami (OH): 2-10 (2-6 in the MAC)
2014    2-10 (2-6)              **Final Ranking: NR**

# Ohio Bobcats – Frank Solich

## Coach Ranking: #78

**Overall Record:** 130-75 in 16 seasons
**Record at Ohio:** 72-56 in 10 seasons
**2014 Results:** 6-6, 4-4 in the MAC (2nd in the MAC East)
**Returning Starters in 2015:** 8 on offense (including QB), 7 on defense
**Salary:** $550,000 **Age:** 70 **Job Security Grade:** B

**2015 SCHEDULE:**
(Conference games in bold.)

| | |
|---|---|
| Sept. 3 | at Idaho Vandals |
| Sept. 12 | Marshall Thundering Herd |
| Sept. 19 | Southeastern Louisiana Lions |
| Sept. 26 | at Minnesota Golden Gophers |
| Oct. 3 | **at Akron Zips** |
| Oct. 10 | **Miami (OH) RedHawks** |
| Oct. 17 | **Western Michigan Broncos** |
| Oct. 24 | **at Buffalo Bulls** |
| Nov. 4 | **at Bowling Green Falcons** |
| Nov. 10 | **Kent State Golden Flashes** |
| Nov. 17 | **Ball State Cardinals** |
| Nov. 24 | **at Northern Illinois Huskies** |

**2014 RESULTS:** 6-6 (4-4 in the MAC) **Final Ranking:** NR

| | | |
|---|---|---|
| at Kent State | W 17–14 | (22,754) |
| at Kentucky | L 3–20 | (51,910) |
| at Marshall | L 14–44 | (31,710) |
| Idaho | W 36–24 | (25,211) |
| Eastern Illinois | W 34–19 | (23,027) |
| at Central Michigan | L 10–28 | (18,223) |
| Bowling Green | L 13–31 | (24,311) |
| Akron | W 23–20 | (20,018) |
| at Western Michigan | L 21–42 | (20,225) |
| Buffalo | W 37–14 | (15,405) |
| Northern Illinois | L 14–21 | (15,118) |
| at Miami (OH) | W 24–21 | (11,956) |

## Frank Solich's Year-by-Year Coaching Record:

### Nebraska: 58-19 (34-15 in the Big 12)

**1998**　9-4 (5-3)　　　　**Final Ranking: #19**
Lost to #5 Arizona 20-23 in the Holiday Bowl.

**1999**　12-1 (8-1)　　　　**Final Ranking: #2**
Big 12 Champions.
Solich named Big 12 Coach of the Year.
Beat #12 Texas 22-6 in the Big 12 Championship Game.
Beat #6 Tennessee 31-21 in the Fiesta Bowl.

**2000**　10-2 (6-2)　　　　**Final Ranking: #7**
Big 12 North Co-Champions.
Beat #18 Northwestern 66-17 in the Alamo Bowl.

**2001**　11-2 (7-1)　　　　**Final Ranking: #7**
Big 12 North Co-Champions.
Solich named Big 12 Coach of the Year.
Lost to #1 Miami (FL) 14-37 in the BCS National Championship Game.

**2002**　7-7 (3-5)　　　　**Final Ranking: NR**
Lost to Ole Miss 23-27 in the Independence Bowl.

**2003**　9-3 (5-3)　　　　**Final Ranking: #20**
Solich was fired after the regular season. Nebraska beat Michigan State 17-3 in the Alamo Bowl and finished the season ranked #18.

### Ohio: 72-56 (48-32 in the MAC)

**2005**　4-7 (3-5)　　　　**Final Ranking: NR**

**2006**　9-5 (7-1)　　　　**Final Ranking: NR**
MAC East Division Champions.
Solich named the MAC Coach of the Year.
Lost to Central Michigan 10-31 in the MAC Championship Game.
Lost to Southern Miss 7-28 in the GMAC Bowl.

**2007**　6-6 (4-4)　　　　**Final Ranking: NR**

**2008**　4-8 (3-5)　　　　**Final Ranking: NR**

**2009**　9-5 (7-1)　　　　**Final Ranking: NR**
MAC East Division Champions.
Lost to Central Michigan 10-20 in the MAC Championship Game.
Lost to Marshall 17-21 in the Little Caesars Pizza Bowl.

**2010**　8-5 (6-2)　　　　**Final Ranking: NR**
Lost to Troy 21-48 in the New Orleans Bowl.

**2011**　10-4 (6-2)　　　　**Final Ranking: NR**
MAC East Division Champions.
Lost to Northern Illinois 20-23 in the MAC Championship Game.
Beat Utah State 24-23 in the Famous Idaho Potato Bowl.

**2012**　9-4 (4-4)　　　　**Final Ranking: NR**
Beat Louisiana-Monroe 45-14 in the Independence Bowl.

**2013**　7-6 (4-4)　　　　**Final Ranking: NR**
Lost to East Carolina 20-37 in the Beef 'O' Brady's Bowl.

**2014**　6-6 (4-4)　　　　**Final Ranking: NR**

# Ball State Cardinals – Pete Lembo

## Coach Ranking: #112

**Overall Record:** 109-56 in 14 seasons (10 seasons in FCS)
**Record at Ball State:** 30-20 in 5 seasons
**2014 Results:** 5-7, 4-4 in the MAC (5th in the MAC West)
**Returning Starters in 2015:** 10 on offense (including QB), 8 on defense
**Salary:** $500,000          **Age:** 45          **Job Security Grade:** A

**2015 SCHEDULE:**
(Conference games in bold.)

| Sept. 3 | Virginia Military Institute Keydets |
|---|---|
| Sept. 12 | at Texas A&M Aggies |
| Sept. 19 | **at Eastern Michigan Eagles** |
| Sept. 26 | at Northwestern Wildcats |
| Oct. 3 | **Toledo Rockets** |
| Oct. 10 | **at Northern Illinois Huskies** |
| Oct. 17 | Georgia State Panthers |
| Oct. 24 | **Central Michigan Chippewas** |
| Oct. 31 | **Massachusetts Minutemen** |
| Nov. 5 | **at Western Michigan Broncos** |
| Nov. 17 | **at Ohio Bobcats** |
| Nov. 24 | **Bowling Green Falcons** |

**2014 RESULTS:   5-7 (4-4 in the MAC)**          **Final Ranking: NR**

| | | |
|---|---|---|
| Colgate | W 30–10 | (9,659) |
| at Iowa | L 13–17 | (64,210) |
| Indiana State | L 20–27 | (15,860) |
| **at Toledo** | L 23–34 | (17,229) |
| at Army | L 24–33 | (31,384) |
| **Western Michigan** | L 38–42 | (11,237) |
| **at Central Michigan** | W 32–29 | (13,337) |
| **Akron** | W 35–21 | (7,617) |
| **Northern Illinois** | L 21–35 | (6,642) |
| **at Massachusetts** | L 10–24 | (13,374) |
| **Eastern Michigan** | W 45–30 | (5,317) |
| **at Bowling Green** | W 41–24 | (8,534) |

## Pete Lembo's Year-by-Year Coaching Record:

### Lehigh: 44-14 (1-2 in the Division 1-AA Playoffs)
2001    11–1 (1-1)            Final Ranking: #5
        Lembo named Patriot League Coach of the Year.
        Lost to Furman 17-34 in the Division 1-AA quarterfinals.
2002    8–4 (0-0)            Final Ranking: NR
2003    8–3 (0-0)            Final Ranking: #23
2004    9–3 (0-1)            Final Ranking: #15
        Lost to James Madison 13-14 in the first round of the Division 1-AA playoffs.
2005    8–3 (0-0)            Final Ranking: NR

### Elon: 35-22 (0-1 in the FCS Playoffs)
2006    5–6 (0-0)            Final Ranking: NR
        Division 1-AA becomes the Football Championship Subdivision (FCS).
2007    7–4 (0-0)            Final Ranking: #23
        Lembo named Southern Conference Coach of the Year.
2008    8–4 (0-0)            Final Ranking: #17
2009    9–3 (0-1)            Final Ranking: #9
        Lost to #5 Richmond 13-16 in the first round of the FCS playoffs.
2010    6–5 (0-0)            Final Ranking: NR

### Ball State: 30-20 (21-11 in the MAC)
2011    6–6 (4–4)            Final Ranking: NR
2012    9–4 (6–2)            Final Ranking: NR
        Lost to UCF 17-38 in the Beef 'O' Brady's Bowl.
2013    10–3 (7–1)            Final Ranking: NR
        Lost to Arkansas State 20-23 in the GoDaddy Bowl.
2014    5–7 (4–4)            Final Ranking: NR

# Central Michigan Chippewas – John Bonamego
## Coach Ranking: #120

**Overall Record:** 0-0

**2014 Results:** CMU went 7-6, 5-3 in the MAC (4th in the MAC West) Bonamego spent the last two seasons as the special teams coordinator for the Detroit Lions

**Returning Starters in 2015:** 6 on offense (including QB), 6 on defense

**Salary:** $475,000          **Age:** 45          **Job Security Grade:** B

**2015 SCHEDULE:**
(Conference games in bold.)

| | |
|---|---|
| Sept. 3 | Oklahoma State Cowboys |
| Sept. 12 | Monmouth Hawks |
| Sept. 19 | at Syracuse Orange |
| Sept. 26 | at Michigan State Spartans |
| Oct. 3 | **Northern Illinois Huskies** |
| Oct. 10 | **at Western Michigan Broncos** |
| Oct. 17 | **Buffalo Bulls** |
| Oct. 24 | **at Ball State Cardinals** |
| Oct. 31 | **at Akron Zips** |
| Nov. 10 | **Toledo Rockets** |
| Nov. 18 | **at Kent State Golden Flashes** |
| Nov. 27 | **Eastern Michigan Eagles** |

**2014 RESULTS:   7-6 (5-3 in the MAC)**          **Final Ranking: NR**

| | | |
|---|---|---|
| Chattanooga | W 20–16 | (15,793) |
| at Purdue | W 38–17 | (36,410) |
| Syracuse | L 3–40 | (25,531) |
| at Kansas | L 10–24 | (34,822) |
| **at Toledo** | L 28–42 | (18,087) |
| **Ohio** | W 28–10 | (18,223) |
| **at Northern Illinois** | W 34–17 | (20,122) |
| **Ball State** | L 29–32 | (13,337) |
| **at Buffalo** | W 20–14 | (18,052) |
| **at Eastern Michigan** | W 38–7 | (19,613) |
| **Miami (OH)** | W 34–27 | (7,689) |
| **Western Michigan** | L 20–32 | (17,265) |
| vs. Western Kentucky (Bahamas Bowl) | L 48–49 | (13,667) |

# Eastern Michigan Eagles – Chris Creighton

## Coach Ranking: #119

**Overall Record:** 141-56 in 18 seasons (6 seasons in FCS, 7 seasons in Division III, 4 seasons in NAIA)

**Record at Eastern Michigan:** 2-10 in 1 season

**2014 Results:** 2-10, 1-7 in the MAC (6th in the MAC West)

**Returning Starters in 2015:** 5 on offense (including QB), 8 on defense

**Salary:** $425,000          **Age:** 46          **Job Security Grade:** B

**2015 SCHEDULE:**
(Conference games in bold.)

| | |
|---|---|
| Sept. 5 | Old Dominion Monarchs |
| Sept. 12 | at Wyoming Cowboys |
| Sept. 19 | **Ball State Cardinals** |
| Sept. 26 | Army Black Knights |
| Oct. 3 | at LSU Tigers |
| Oct. 10 | **Akron Zips** |
| Oct. 17 | **at Toledo Rockets** |
| Oct. 24 | **at Northern Illinois Huskies** |
| Oct. 29 | **Western Michigan Broncos** |
| Nov. 7 | **at Miami (OH) RedHawks** |
| Nov. 14 | **Massachusetts Minutemen** |
| Nov. 27 | **at Central Michigan Chippewas** |

**2014 RESULTS:**    2-10 (1-7 in the MAC)          Final Ranking: NR

| | | |
|---|---|---|
| Morgan State | W 31–28 | (8,748) |
| at Florida | L 0–65 | (81,049) |
| at Old Dominion | L 3–17 | (20,118) |
| at #11 Michigan State | L 14–73 | (73,846) |
| **at Akron** | L 6–31 | (8,416) |
| **Buffalo** | W 37–27 | (11,886) |
| **at Massachusetts** | L 14–36 | (12,030) |
| **Northern Illinois** | L 17–28 | (19,654) |
| **Central Michigan** | L 7–38 | (19,613) |
| **at Western Michigan** | L 7–51 | (12,985) |
| **at Ball State** | L 30–45 | (5,317) |
| Toledo | L 16–52 | (15,226) |

## Chris Creighton's Year-by-Year Coaching Record:

### Ottawa: 32-9 (0-2 in the NAIA Playoffs)
1997   9–2 (0-1)          Final Ranking: NA
Lost in first round of the NAIA playoffs.
1998   8–2 (0-0)          Final Ranking: NA
1999   6–3 (0-0)          Final Ranking: NA
2000   9–2 (0-1)          Final Ranking: NA
Lost to Huron 17-47 in the first round of the NAIA playoffs.

### Wabash: 63-15 (5-3 in the Division III Playoffs)
2001   8–2 (0-0)   6–1     Final Ranking: NA
2002   12–1 (2-1)        Final Ranking: NA
Lost to Mount Union 16-45 in the Division III quarterfinals.
2003   7–3 (0-0)          Final Ranking: NA
2004   6–4 (0-0)          Final Ranking: NA
2005   11–1 (1-1)        Final Ranking: NA
Lost to Capital 11-14 in the second round of the Division III playoffs.
2006   8–2 (0-0)          Final Ranking: NA
2007   11–2 (2-1)        Final Ranking: NA
Lost to Wisconsin-Whitewater 7-47 in the Division III quarterfinals.

### Drake: 42-22 (1-0 in the FCS Postseason)
2008   6–5 (0-0)          Final Ranking: NR
2009   8–3 (0-0)          Final Ranking: NR
2010   8–4 (1-0)          Final Ranking: NR
Beat CONADEIP (Mexican All-Star team) 17-7 in the Global Kilimanjaro Bowl.
2011   9–2 (0-0)          Final Ranking: NR
2012   8–3 (0-0)          Final Ranking: NR
2013   6–5 (0-0)          Final Ranking: NR

### Eastern Michigan: 2-10 (1-7 in the MAC)
2014   2-10 (1-7)        Final Ranking: NR

# Northern Illinois Huskies – Rod Carey

## Coach Ranking: #87

**Overall Record:** 23-6 in 2 seasons
**Record at Northern Illinois:** 23-6 in 2 seasons
**2014 Results:** 11-3, 7-1 in the MAC (MAC Champions)
**Returning Starters in 2015:** 6 on offense (including QB), 8 on defense
**Salary:** $400,000 **Age:** 44 **Job Security Grade:** A

**2015 SCHEDULE:**
(Conference games in bold.)

| Sept. 5 | UNLV Rebels |
|---|---|
| Sept. 12 | Murray State Racers |
| Sept. 19 | at Ohio State Buckeyes |
| Sept. 26 | at Boston College Eagles |
| Oct. 3 | **at Central Michigan Chippewas** |
| Oct. 10 | **Ball State Cardinals** |
| Oct. 17 | **at Miami (OH) RedHawks** |
| Oct. 24 | **Eastern Michigan Eagles** |
| Nov. 3 | **at Toledo Rockets** |
| Nov. 11 | **at Buffalo Bulls** |
| Nov. 18 | **Western Michigan Broncos** |
| Nov. 24 | **Ohio Bobcats** |

**2014 RESULTS:  11-3 (7-1 in the MAC)**     **Final Ranking: NR**

| | | |
|---|---|---|
| Presbyterian | W 55–3 | (12,398) |
| at Northwestern | W 23–15 | (41,139) |
| at UNLV | W 48–34 | (14,305) |
| at Arkansas | L 14–52 | (67,204) |
| **Kent State** | W 17–14 | (15,620) |
| **Central Michigan** | L 17–34 | (20,122) |
| **Miami (OH)** | W 51–41 | (11,211) |
| **at Eastern Michigan** | W 28–17 | (19,654) |
| **at Ball State** | W 35-21 | (6,642) |
| **Toledo** | W 27–24 | (8,462) |
| **at Ohio** | W 21–14 | (15,118) |
| **at Western Michigan** | W 31–21 | (11,195) |
| **vs. Bowling Green** (MAC Championship) | W 51–17 | (15,110) |
| vs. Marshall (Boca Raton Bowl) | L 23-52 | (29,419) |

## Rod Carey's Year-by-Year Coaching Record:

### Northern Illinois: 23-6 (15-1 in the MAC)
2012   0–1 (0-0)                   Final Ranking: #22
Carey got an early start on the job and coached Northern Illinois in its 10-31 loss to #13 Florida State in the Orange Bowl.

2013   12–2 (8–0)                  Final Ranking: NR
MAC West Division Champions.
Lost to Bowling Green 27-47 in the MAC Championship Game.
Lost to Utah State 14-21 in the Poinsettia Bowl.

2014   11–3 (7–1)                  Final Ranking: NR
MAC Champions.
Beat Bowling Green 51-17 in the MAC Championship Game.
Lost to Marshall 23-52 in the Boca Raton Bowl.

# Toledo Rockets – Matt Campbell

## Coach Ranking: #95

**Overall Record:** 26-13 in 3 seasons
**Record at Toledo:** 26-13 in 3 seasons
**2014 Results:** 9-4, 7-1 in the MAC (MAC West Co-Champions)
**Returning Starters in 2015:** 5 on offense (including QB), 8 on defense
**Salary:** $470,000      **Age:** 35      **Job Security Grade:** A

**2015 SCHEDULE:**
(Conference games in bold.)

| | |
|---|---|
| Sept. 3 | Stony Brook Sea Wolves |
| Sept. 12 | at Arkansas Razorbacks |
| Sept. 19 | Iowa State Cyclones |
| Sept. 26 | Arkansas State Red Wolves |
| Oct. 3 | **at Ball State Cardinals** |
| Oct. 10 | **Kent State Golden Flashes** |
| Oct. 17 | **Eastern Michigan Eagles** |
| Oct. 24 | **at Massachusetts Minutemen** |
| Nov. 3 | **Northern Illinois Huskies** |
| Nov. 10 | **at Central Michigan Chippewas** |
| Nov. 17 | **at Bowling Green Falcons** |
| Nov. 27 | **Western Michigan Broncos** |

**2014 RESULTS:  9-4 (7-1 in the MAC)**      **Final Ranking: NR**

| | | |
|---|---|---|
| #4 (FCS) New Hampshire | W 54–20 | (20,184) |
| #24 Missouri | L 24–49 | (24,196) |
| at Cincinnati | L 34–58 | (31,912) |
| **Ball State** | W 34–23 | (17,229) |
| **Central Michigan** | W 42–28 | (18,087) |
| **at Western Michigan** | W 20–19 OT | (11,493) |
| at Iowa State | L 30–37 | (52,281) |
| **Massachusetts** | W 42–35 | (20,104) |
| **at Kent State** | W 30–20 | (7,471) |
| **at Northern Illinois** | L 24–27 | (8,462) |
| **Bowling Green** | W 27–20 | (17,486) |
| **at Eastern Michigan** | W 52–16 | (15,226) |
| vs. Arkansas State (GoDaddy Bowl) | W 63–44 | (36,811) |

## Matt Campbell's Year-by-Year Coaching Record:

<u>Toledo: 26-13 (18-6 in the MAC)</u>
2011    1–0 (0–0)                 **Final Ranking: NR**
        Campbell got an early start on the job and coached Toledo to its 42-41 win over Air Force in the Military Bowl.
2012    9–4 (6–2)                 **Final Ranking: NR**
        Lost to #20 Utah State 15-41 in the Famous Idaho Potato Bowl.
2013    7–5 (5–3)                 **Final Ranking: NR**
2014    9–4 (7–1)                 **Final Ranking: NR**
        Beat Arkansas State 63-44 in the GoDaddy Bowl.

# Western Michigan Broncos – P.J. Fleck

## Coach Ranking: #88

**Overall Record:** 9-16 in 2 seasons
**Record at Western Michigan:** 9-16 in 2 seasons
**2014 Results:** 8-5, 6-2 in the MAC (3rd in the MAC West)
**Returning Starters in 2015:** 9 on offense (including QB), 7 on defense
**Salary:** $800,000          **Age:** 34          **Job Security Grade:** A

**2015 SCHEDULE:**
(Conference games in bold.)

| | |
|---|---|
| Sept. 4 | Michigan State Spartans |
| Sept. 12 | at Georgia Southern Eagles |
| Sept. 19 | Murray State Racers |
| Sept. 26 | at Ohio State Buckeyes |
| Oct. 10 | **Central Michigan Chippewas** |
| Oct. 17 | **at Ohio Bobcats** |
| Oct. 24 | **Miami (OH) RedHawks** |
| Oct. 29 | **at Eastern Michigan Eagles** |
| Nov. 5 | **Ball State Cardinals** |
| Nov. 11 | **Bowling Green Falcons** |
| Nov. 18 | **at Northern Illinois Huskies** |
| Nov. 27 | **at Toledo Rockets** |

**2014 RESULTS:**   8-5 (6-2 in the MAC)          **Final Ranking: NR**

| | | |
|---|---|---|
| at Purdue | L 34–43 | (37,031) |
| at Idaho | W 45–33 | (14,721) |
| Murray State | W 45–14 | (22,226) |
| at Virginia Tech | L 17–35 | (59,625) |
| Toledo | L 19-20 OT | (11,493) |
| at Ball State | W 42–38 | (11,237) |
| at Bowling Green | W 26–14 | (15,201) |
| Ohio | W 42–21 | (20,225) |
| at Miami (OH) | W 41–10 | (9,045) |
| Eastern Michigan | W 51–3 | (12,985) |
| at Central Michigan | W 32–20 | (17,265) |
| Northern Illinois | L 21-31 | (11,195) |
| vs. Air Force (Famous Idaho Potato Bowl) | L 24-38 | (18,223) |

## P.J. Fleck's Year-by-Year Coaching Record:

**Western Michigan: 9-16 (7-9 in the MAC)**

| | | |
|---|---|---|
| 2013 | 1–11 (1-7) | Final Ranking: NR |
| 2014 | 8-5 (6–2) | Final Ranking: NR |

Lost to Air Force 24-38 in the Famous Idaho Potato Bowl.

To receive FREE updates by email on the latest coaching news, rumors, rankings, contract changes, and emerging college football trends, sign up at:

# CoachesAlmanac.com/Updates

# 2015 MOUNTAIN WEST PREVIEW

## Five Things You Need to Know about the MWC in 2015:

**The Battle at the Top: Fresno State** won the West Division last year with a .500 record while four teams from the Mountain Division had 10 wins or more. The strength of the conference remains tilted to the Mountain Division and **Boise State** is the favorite to repeat.

**New to the MWC: Tony Sanchez** will become just the fourth coach in the modern era of college football to make the one-year leap straight from high school head coach to FBS head coach when he leads **UNLV** this fall. The previous coaches who made this move (**Bob Commings** at **Iowa**, **Todd Dodge** at **North Texas**, and **Gerry Faust** at **Notre Dame**) fell short of expectations. Sanchez spent the last six years coaching a nationally-recognized high school program that traveled all over the country while winning six-straight Nevada state titles and a National Championship in 2014. He'll face a major rebuilding job at UNLV.

**Coaches on the Rise:** In his first year as head coach at his alma mater, **Boise State**, 38-year-old **Bryan Harsin** won the Mountain West and capped off his 12-2 season with a Fiesta Bowl victory. The Broncos seem to have found the right man for picking up where **Chris Petersen** left off. The best coaching performance of 2014 in the MWC belongs to **Troy Calhoun** at **Air Force**. After a 2-10 season in 2013, Calhoun bounced back with a 10-3 season in 2014.

**Keep an Eye On:** After losing MWC Coach of the Year **Jim McElwain** to **Florida**, **Colorado State** made a big-time hire by bringing in longtime **Georgia** offensive coordinator **Mike Bobo**. His scheme should be a good fit with the personnel already at Colorado State and a smooth transition is expected.

**Coaches on the Hot Seat: Norm Chow's** rebuilding job is taking longer than expected at **Hawaii**, but this could be the year patience is rewarded and the Rainbow Warriors make it back to a bowl game. **San Jose State's** ugly six-game losing streak to end 2014 has caused **Ron Caragher's** seat to heat up as well.

## 2015 Projected Standings for the MWC:

**Mountain Division:**
1. Boise State
2. Utah State
3. Colorado State
4. Air Force
5. Wyoming
6. New Mexico

**West Division:**
1. Fresno State
2. San Diego State
3. Nevada
4. Hawaii
5. San Jose State
6. UNLV

# Ranking the MWC's Coaches:

1. **Bryan Harsin** – Boise State (19-7 in 2 seasons)
2. **Tim DeRuyter** – Fresno State (27-14 in 3 seasons)
3. **Troy Calhoun** – Air Force (59-44 in 8 seasons)
4. **Mike Bobo** – Colorado State (First Year Head Coach)
5. **Matt Wells** – Utah State (19-9 in 2 seasons)
6. **Craig Bohl** – Wyoming (108-40 in 12 seasons)
7. **Rocky Long** – San Diego State (97-89 in 15 seasons)
8. **Brian Polian** – Nevada (11-14 in 2 seasons)
9. **Bob Davie** – New Mexico (46-51 in 8 seasons)
10. **Norm Chow** – Hawaii (8-29 in 3 seasons)
11. **Tony Sanchez** – UNLV (First Year Head Coach)
12. **Ron Caragher** – San Jose State (53-37 in 8 seasons)

# 2014 MWC Coach of the Year:
(Selected by the MWC coaches and media members)
Jim McElwain, Colorado State

# 2014 MWC Standings:

| Mountain Division | (Conference) | (All Games) |
|---|---|---|
| #16 Boise State | 7–1 | 12–2 |
| Colorado State | 6–2 | 10–3 |
| Utah State | 6–2 | 10–4 |
| Air Force | 5–3 | 10–3 |
| New Mexico | 2–6 | 4–8 |
| Wyoming | 2–6 | 4–8 |
| | | |
| West Division | | |
| Fresno State | 5–3 | 6–8 |
| San Diego State | 5–3 | 7–6 |
| Nevada | 4–4 | 7–6 |
| Hawaii | 3–5 | 4–9 |
| San Jose State | 2–6 | 3–9 |
| UNLV | 1–7 | 2–11 |

*Championship Game*: Boise State 28, Fresno State 14

**2014 MWC Bowl Record:** 3-4 (5th place among all 10 conferences)

# Air Force Falcons – Troy Calhoun

## Coach Ranking: #54

**Overall Record:** 59-44 in 8 seasons
**Record at Air Force:** 59-44 in 8 seasons
**2014 Results:** 10-3, 5-3 in the MWC (4th in the MWC Mountain)
**Returning Starters in 2015:** 7 on offense, 4 on defense
**Salary:** $1 Million*     **Age:** 48     **Job Security Grade:** A

**2015 SCHEDULE:**
(Conference games in bold.)

| | |
|---|---|
| Sept. 5 | Morgan State Bears |
| Sept. 12 | **San Jose State Spartans** |
| Sept. 19 | at Michigan State Spartans |
| Oct. 3 | at Navy Midshipmen |
| Oct. 10 | **Wyoming Cowboys** |
| Oct. 17 | **at Colorado State Rams** |
| Oct. 24 | **Fresno State Bulldogs** |
| Oct. 31 | **at Hawaii Rainbow Warriors** |
| Nov. 7 | Army Black Knights |
| Nov. 14 | **Utah State Aggies** |
| Nov. 20 | **at Boise State Broncos** |
| Nov. 28 | **at New Mexico Lobos** |

**2014 RESULTS:** 10-3 (5-3 in the MWC)     **Final Ranking: NR**

| | | |
|---|---|---|
| Nicholls State | W 44–16 | (32,038) |
| **at Wyoming** | L 13–17 | (21,246) |
| at Georgia State | W 48–38 | (16,836) |
| **Boise State** | W 28–14 | (30,012) |
| Navy | W 30–21 | (37,731) |
| **at Utah State** | L 16–34 | (24,037) |
| **New Mexico** | W 35–31 | (25,017) |
| at Army | W 23–6 | (40,479) |
| **at UNLV** | W 48–21 | (13,481) |
| Nevada | W 45–38 OT | (11,519) |
| **at San Diego State** | L 14–30 | (28,626) |
| **#21 Colorado State** | W 27–24 | (32,650) |
| vs. Western Michigan (Potato Bowl) | W 38–24 | (18,223) |

## Troy Calhoun's Year-by-Year Coaching Record:

### Air Force: 59-44 (34-30 in the MWC)
2007   9–4 (6–2)              Final Ranking: NR
       Calhoun named MWC Coach of the Year.
       Lost to Cal 36-42 in the Armed Forces Bowl.
2008   8–5 (5–3)              Final Ranking: NR
       Lost to Houston 28-34 in the Armed Forces Bowl.
2009   8–5 (5–3)              Final Ranking: NR
       Beat #25 Houston 47-20 in the Armed Forces Bowl.
2010   9–4 (5–3)              Final Ranking: NR
       Beat Georgia Tech 14-7 in the Independence Bowl.
2011   7–6 (3–4)              Final Ranking: NR
       Lost to Toledo 41-42 in the Military Bowl.
2012   6–7 (5–3)              Final Ranking: NR
       Lost to Rice 14-33 in the Armed Forces Bowl.
2013   2–10 (0–8)             Final Ranking: NR
2014   10–3 (5–3)             Final Ranking: NR
       Beat Western Michigan 38-24 in the Famous Idaho Potato Bowl.

# Boise State Broncos – Bryan Harsin

## Coach Ranking: #48

**Overall Record:** 19-7 in 2 seasons
**Record at Boise State:** 12-2 in 1 season
**2014 Results:** 12-2, 7-1 in the MWC (Mountain West Champions)
**Returning Starters in 2015:** 8 on offense, 8 on defense
**Salary:** $1.1 Million      **Age:** 38      **Job Security Grade:** A

**2015 SCHEDULE:**
(Conference games in bold.)

| | |
|---|---|
| Sept. 4 | Washington Huskies |
| Sept. 12 | at BYU Cougars |
| Sept. 18 | Idaho State Bengals |
| Sept. 25 | at Virginia Cavaliers |
| Oct. 3 | **Hawaii Rainbow Warriors** |
| Oct. 10 | **at Colorado State Rams** |
| Oct. 16 | **at Utah State Aggies** |
| Oct. 24 | **Wyoming Cowboys** |
| Oct. 31 | **at UNLV Rebels** |
| Nov. 14 | **New Mexico Lobos** |
| Nov. 20 | **Air Force Falcons** |
| Nov. 27 | **at San Jose State Spartans** |

**2014 RESULTS:   12-2 (7-1 in the MWC)**      **Final Ranking: #16**

| | | |
|---|---|---|
| vs. #19 Ole Miss (in Atlanta) | L 13–35 | (32,823) |
| Colorado State | W 37–24 | (34,910) |
| at Connecticut | W 38–21 | (30,098) |
| Louisiana–Lafayette | W 34–9 | (33,337) |
| **at Air Force** | L 14–28 | (30,012) |
| **at Nevada** | W 51–46 | (32,327) |
| **Fresno State** | W 37–27 | (35,008) |
| BYU | W 55–30 | (36,752) |
| **at New Mexico** | W 60–49 | (21,089) |
| **San Diego State** | W 38–29 | (27,478) |
| **at Wyoming** | W 63–14 | (15,821) |
| **Utah State** | W 50–19 | (33,940) |
| **Fresno State** (MWC Championship) | W 28–14 | (26,101) |
| vs. #11 Arizona (Fiesta Bowl) | W 38–30 | (66,896) |

## Bryan Harsin's Year-by-Year Coaching Record:

### Arkansas State: 7-5 (5-2 in the Sun Belt)
2013    7-5 (5-2)                Final Ranking: NR
Sun Belt Conference Co-Champions.
Arkansas State beat Ball State 23-20 in the GoDaddy Bowl, but Harsin had already left to accept the Boise State job.

### Boise State: 12-2 (7-1 in the MWC)
2014    12-2 (7-1)               Final Ranking: #16
MWC Champions.
Beat Fresno State 28-14 in the MWC Championship Game.
Beat #11 Arizona State 38-30 in the Fiesta Bowl.

# Colorado State Rams – Mike Bobo

## Coach Ranking: #55

**Overall Record:** 0-0

**2014 Results:** Colorado State went 10-3, 6-2 in the MWC (T-2nd in the MWC Mountain)

Bobo was Georgia's offensive coordinator from 2007-2014

**Returning Starters in 2015:** 6 on offense, 7 on defense

**Salary:** $1.35 Million     **Age:** 41          **Job Security Grade:** A

**2015 SCHEDULE:**
(Conference games in bold.)

| | |
|---|---|
| Sept. 5 | Savannah State Tigers |
| Sept. 12 | Minnesota Golden Gophers |
| Sept. 19 | vs. Colorado Buffaloes (in Denver) |
| Sept. 26 | at UTSA Roadrunners |
| Oct. 3 | **at Utah State Aggies** |
| Oct. 10 | **Boise State Broncos** |
| Oct. 17 | **Air Force Falcons** |
| Oct. 31 | **San Diego State Aztecs** |
| Nov. 7 | **at Wyoming Cowboys** |
| Nov. 14 | **UNLV Rebels** |
| Nov. 21 | **at New Mexico Lobos** |
| Nov. 28 | **at Fresno State Bulldogs** |

**2014 RESULTS:   10-3 (6-2 in the MWC)**          **Final Ranking: NR**

| | | |
|---|---|---|
| vs. Colorado (in Denver) | W 31–17 | (63,363) |
| **at Boise State** | L 24–37 | (34,910) |
| UC Davis | W 49–21 | (21,202) |
| at Boston College | W 24–21 | (33,632) |
| Tulsa | W 42–17 | (25,806) |
| **at Nevada** | W 31–24 | (21,847) |
| **Utah State** | W 16–13 | (32,546) |
| **Wyoming** | W 45–31 | (32,529) |
| **at San Jose State** | W 38–31 | (17,887) |
| **Hawaii** | W 49–22 | (25,236) |
| **New Mexico** | W 58–20 | (22,131) |
| **at Air Force** | L 24–27 | (32,650) |
| vs. #23 Utah (Las Vegas Bowl) | L 10–45 | (33,067) |

# New Mexico Lobos – Bob Davie

## Coach Ranking: #113

**Overall Record:** 46-51 in 8 seasons
**Record at New Mexico:** 11-26 in 3 seasons
**2014 Results:** 4-8, 2-6 in the MWC (T-5th in the MWC Mountain)
**Returning Starters in 2015:** 7 on offense (including QB), 7 on defense
**Salary:** $770,000          **Age:** 60          **Job Security Grade:** B

**2015 SCHEDULE:**
(Conference games in bold.)

| | |
|---|---|
| Sept. 5 | Mississippi Valley State Delta Devils |
| Sept. 12 | Tulsa Golden Hurricane |
| Sept. 18 | at Arizona State Sun Devils |
| Sept. 26 | **at Wyoming Cowboys** |
| Oct. 3 | New Mexico State Aggies |
| Oct. 10 | **at Nevada Wolf Pack** |
| Oct. 17 | **Hawaii Rainbow Warriors** |
| Oct. 24 | **at San Jose State Spartans** |
| Nov. 7 | **Utah State Aggies** |
| Nov. 14 | **at Boise State Broncos** |
| Nov. 21 | **Colorado State Rams** |
| Nov. 28 | **Air Force Falcons** |

**2014 RESULTS:    4-8 (2-6 in the MWC)**          **Final Ranking: NR**

| | | |
|---|---|---|
| UTEP | L 24–31 | (25,802) |
| #17 Arizona State | L 23–58 | (25,742) |
| at New Mexico State | W 38–35 | (24,651) |
| **Fresno State** | L 24–35 | (21,005) |
| at UTSA | W 21–9 | (30,419) |
| **San Diego State** | L 14–24 | (19,497) |
| **at Air Force** | L 31–35 | (25,017) |
| **at UNLV** | W 31–28 | (13,419) |
| **Boise State** | L 49–60 | (21,089) |
| **at Utah State** | L 21–28 | (19,591) |
| **at #22 Colorado State** | L 20–58 | (22,131) |
| **Wyoming** | W 36–30 | (18,489) |

## Bob Davie's Year-by-Year Coaching Record:

### Notre Dame: 35-25 (Independent)
1997    7–6 (Ind.)              **Final Ranking: NR**
        Lost to #15 LSU 9-27 in the Independence Bowl.
1998    9–3 (Ind.)              **Final Ranking: #22**
        Lost to #12 Georgia Tech 28-35 in the Gator Bowl.
1999    5–7 (Ind.)              **Final Ranking: NR**
2000    9–3 (Ind.)              **Final Ranking: #15**
        Lost to #5 Oregon State 9-41 in the Fiesta Bowl.
2001    5–6 (Ind.)              **Final Ranking: NR**

### New Mexico: 11-26 (4-20 in the MWC)
2012    4–9 (1–7)              **Final Ranking: NR**
2013    3–9 (1–7)              **Final Ranking: NR**
2014    4–8 (2–6)              **Final Ranking: NR**

# Utah State Aggies – Matt Wells

## Coach Ranking: #58

**Overall Record:** 19-9 in 2 seasons
**Record at Utah State:** 19-9 in 2 seasons
**2014 Results:** 10-4, 6-2 in the MWC (T-2nd in the MWC Mountain)
**Returning Starters in 2015:** 9 on offense (including QB), 6 on defense
**Salary:** $575,000          **Age:** 42          **Job Security Grade:** A

**2015 SCHEDULE:**
(Conference games in bold.)

| | |
|---|---|
| Sept. 3 | Southern Utah Thunderbirds |
| Sept. 11 | at Utah Utes |
| Sept. 19 | at Washington Huskies |
| Oct. 3 | **Colorado State Rams** |
| Oct. 10 | **at Fresno State Bulldogs** |
| Oct. 16 | **Boise State Broncos** |
| Oct. 23 | **at San Diego State Aztecs** |
| Oct. 30 | **Wyoming Cowboys** |
| Nov. 7 | **at New Mexico Lobos** |
| Nov. 14 | **at Air Force Falcons** |
| Nov. 21 | **Nevada Wolf Pack** |
| Nov. 28 | BYU Cougars |

**2014 RESULTS:   10-4 (6-2 in the MWC)**          **Final Ranking: NR**

| | | |
|---|---|---|
| at Tennessee | L 7–38 | (102,455) |
| Idaho State | W 40–20 | (20,445) |
| Wake Forest | W 36–24 | (20,345) |
| at Arkansas State | L 14–21 OT | (29,029) |
| at #18 BYU | W 35–20 | (64,090) |
| **Air Force** | W 34–16 | (24,037) |
| **at Colorado State** | L 13–16 | (32,546) |
| **UNLV** | W 34–20 | (20,153) |
| **at Hawaii** | W 35–14 | (24,761) |
| **at Wyoming** | W 20–3 | (14,430) |
| **New Mexico** | W 28–21 | (19,591) |
| **San Jose State** | W 41–7 | (18,428) |
| **at #25 Boise State** | L 19–50 | (33,940) |
| vs. UTEP (New Mexico Bowl) | W 21–6 | (28,725) |

**Matt Wells' Year-by-Year Coaching Record:**

<u>Utah State: 19-9 (13-3 in the MWC)</u>
2013    9–5 (7–1)              **Final Ranking: NR**
        MWC Mountain Division Champions.
        Wells named MWC Coach of the Year.
        Lost to #24 Fresno State 17-24 in the MWC Championship Game.
        Beat #24 Northern Illinois 21-14 in the Poinsettia Bowl.
2014    10–4 (6–2)             **Final Ranking: NR**
        Beat UTEP 21-6 in the New Mexico Bowl.

# Wyoming Cowboys – Craig Bohl

## Coach Ranking: #85

**Overall Record:** 108-40 in 12 seasons (10 seasons in FCS, 1 season in Division II)

**Record at Wyoming:** 4-8 in 1 season

**2014 Results:** 4-8, 2-6 in the MWC (T-5th in the MWC Mountain)

**Returning Starters in 2015:** 6 on offense, 4 on defense

**Salary:** $830,000     **Age:** 57     **Job Security Grade:** A

**2015 SCHEDULE:**
(Conference games in bold.)

| | |
|---|---|
| Sept. 5 | North Dakota |
| Sept. 12 | Eastern Michigan Eagles |
| Sept. 19 | at Washington State Cougars |
| Sept. 26 | **New Mexico Lobos** |
| Oct. 3 | at Appalachian State Mountaineers |
| Oct. 10 | **at Air Force Falcons** |
| Oct. 17 | **Nevada Wolf Pack** |
| Oct. 24 | **at Boise State Broncos** |
| Oct. 30 | **at Utah State Aggies** |
| Nov. 7 | **Colorado State Rams** |
| Nov. 14 | **at San Diego State Aztecs** |
| Nov. 28 | **UNLV Rebels** |

**2014 RESULTS:  4-8 (2-6 in the MWC)**     **Final Ranking: NR**

| | | |
|---|---|---|
| #5 (FCS) Montana | W 17–12 | (25,243) |
| **Air Force** | W 17–13 | (21,246) |
| at #2 Oregon | L 14–48 | (56,533) |
| Florida Atlantic | W 20–19 | (21,226) |
| at #9 Michigan State | L 14–56 | (74,227) |
| **at Hawaii** | L 28–38 | (24,273) |
| **San Jose State** | L 20–27 OT | (19,627) |
| **at Colorado State** | L 31–45 | (32,529) |
| **at Fresno State** | W 45–17 | (32,164) |
| **Utah State** | L 3–20 | (14,430) |
| **Boise State** | L 14–63 | (15,821) |
| **at New Mexico** | L 30–36 | (18,489) |

## Craig Bohl's Year-by-Year Coaching Record:

### North Dakota State: 104-32 (13-1 in the FCS Playoffs)

2003    8–3 (Div. II)          Final Ranking: NA

2004    8–3 (0-0)              Final Ranking: #23

North Dakota State moves from Division II to the Football Championship Subdivision (FCS).

Ineligible for the FCS playoffs due to a four-year transition period.

2005    7–4 (0-0)              Final Ranking: NR

Ineligible for the FCS playoffs due to a four-year transition period.

2006    10–1 (0-0)            Final Ranking: #5

Ineligible for the FCS playoffs due to a four-year transition period.

2007    10–1 (0-0)            Final Ranking: #9

Ineligible for the FCS playoffs due to a four-year transition period.

2008    6–5 (0-0)              Final Ranking: NR

2009    3–8 (0-0)              Final Ranking: NR

2010    9–5 (2-1)              Final Ranking: #9

Lost to #1 Eastern Washington 31-38 in the FCS quarterfinals.

2011    14–1 (4-0)            Final Ranking: #1

FCS National Champions.

Beat #1 Sam Houston State 17-6 in the FCS National Championship Game.

2012    14–1 (4-0)            Final Ranking: #1

FCS National Champions.

Beat #5 Sam Houston State 39-13 in the FCS National Championship Game.

2013    15–0 (4-0)            Final Ranking: #1

FCS National Champions.

Beat #5 Towson 35-7 in the FCS National Championship Game.

### Wyoming: 4-8 (2-6 in the MWC)

2014    4-8 (2-6)              Final Ranking: NR

# Fresno State Bulldogs – Tim DeRuyter

## Coach Ranking: #53

**Overall Record:** 27-14 in 3 seasons
**Record at Fresno State:** 26-14 in 3 seasons
**2014 Results:** 6-8, 5-3 in the MWC (MWC West Champions)
**Returning Starters in 2015:** 7 on offense (including QB), 6 on defense
**Salary:** $1.4 Million        **Age:** 52        **Job Security Grade:** A

**2015 SCHEDULE:**
(Conference games in bold.)

| | |
|---|---|
| Sept. 3 | Abilene Christian Wildcats |
| Sept. 12 | at Ole Miss Rebels |
| Sept. 19 | Utah Utes |
| Sept. 26 | **at San Jose State Spartans** |
| Oct. 3 | **at San Diego State Aztecs** |
| Oct. 10 | **Utah State Aggies** |
| Oct. 16 | **UNLV Rebels** |
| Oct. 24 | **at Air Force Falcons** |
| Nov. 5 | **Nevada Wolf Pack** |
| Nov. 14 | **at Hawaii Rainbow Warriors** |
| Nov. 21 | at BYU Cougars |
| Nov. 28 | **Colorado State Rams** |

**2014 RESULTS:    6-8 (5-3 in the MWC)**          **Final Ranking: NR**

| | | |
|---|---|---|
| at #15 USC | L 13–52 | (76,037) |
| at Utah | L 27–59 | (45,864) |
| Nebraska | L 19–55 | (41,031) |
| Southern Utah | W 56–16 | (32,645) |
| **at New Mexico** | W 35–24 | (21,005) |
| **San Diego State** | W 24–13 | (33,894) |
| **at UNLV** | L 27–30 OT | (15,398) |
| at Boise State | L 27–37 | (35,008) |
| **Wyoming** | L 17–45 | (32,164) |
| **San Jose State** | W 38–24 | (36,909) |
| **at Nevada** | W 40–20 | (21,446) |
| **Hawaii** | W 28–21 | (32,580) |
| **at #22 Boise State** (MWC Championship) | L 14–28 | (26,101) |
| vs. Rice (Hawaii Bowl) | L 6–30 | (25,365) |

## Tim DeRuyter's Year-by-Year Coaching Record:

<u>Texas A&M: 1-0 (0-0 in the Big 12)</u>
2011    1-0 (0-0)                    Final Ranking: NA
DeRuyter was the interim head coach for the bowl game after Mike Sherman was fired.
Beat Northwestern 33-22 in the Meineke Car Care Bowl.

<u>Fresno State: 26-14 (19-5 in the MWC)</u>
2012    9–4 (7–1)                    Final Ranking: NR
MWC Co-Champions.
Lost to SMU 10-43 in the Hawaii Bowl.
2013    11–2 (7–1)                   Final Ranking: NR
MWC Champions.
Beat Utah State 24-17 in the MWC Championship Game.
Lost to USC 20-45 in the Las Vegas Bowl.
2014    6–8 (5–3)                    Final Ranking: NR
MWC West Division Champions.
Lost to #22 Boise State 14-28 in the MWC Championship Game.
Lost to Rice 6-30 in the Hawaii Bowl.

# Hawaii Rainbow Warriors – Norm Chow

## Coach Ranking: #117

**Overall Record:** 8-29 in 3 seasons
**Record at Hawaii:** 8-29 in 3 seasons
**2014 Results:** 4-9, 3-5 in the MWC (4th in the MWC West)
**Returning Starters in 2015:** 7 on offense (including QB), 6 on defense
**Salary:** $620,000 **Age:** 69 **Job Security Grade:** C

**2015 SCHEDULE:**
(Conference games in bold.)

| | |
|---|---|
| Sept. 3 | Colorado Buffaloes |
| Sept. 12 | at Ohio State Buckeyes |
| Sept. 19 | UC Davis Aggies |
| Sept. 26 | at Wisconsin Badgers |
| Oct. 3 | **at Boise State Broncos** |
| Oct. 10 | **San Diego State Aztecs** |
| Oct. 17 | **at New Mexico Lobos** |
| Oct. 24 | **at Nevada Wolf Pack** |
| Oct. 31 | **Air Force Falcons** |
| Nov. 7 | **at UNLV Rebels** |
| Nov. 14 | **Fresno State Bulldogs** |
| Nov. 21 | **San Jose State Spartans** |
| Nov. 28 | Louisiana-Monroe Warhawks |

**2014 RESULTS: 4-9 (3-5 in the MWC)** **Final Ranking: NR**

| | | |
|---|---|---|
| #25 Washington | L 16–17 | (36,411) |
| Oregon State | L 30–38 | (29,050) |
| #10 (FCS) Northern Iowa | W 27–24 | (24,999) |
| at Colorado | L 12–21 | (39,478) |
| **at Rice** | L 14–28 | (17,465) |
| **Wyoming** | W 38–28 | (20,495) |
| **at San Diego State** | L 10–20 | (35,686) |
| **Nevada** | L 18–26 | (27,061) |
| **Utah State** | L 14–35 | (19,799) |
| **at Colorado State** | L 22–49 | (25,236) |
| **at San Jose State** | W 13–0 | (17,962) |
| **UNLV** | W 37–35 | (25,604) |
| at Fresno State | L 21–28 | (32,580) |

## Norm Chow's Year-by-Year Coaching Record:

**Hawaii: 8-29 (4-20 in the MWC)**

| | | |
|---|---|---|
| 2012 | 3–9 (1–7) | **Final Ranking: NR** |
| 2013 | 1–11 (0–8) | **Final Ranking: NR** |
| 2014 | 4–9 (3–5) | **Final Ranking: NR** |

# Nevada Wolf Pack – Brian Polian

## Coach Ranking: #103

**Overall Record:** 11-14 in 2 seasons
**Record at Nevada:** 11-14 in 2 seasons
**2014 Results:** 7-6, 4-4 in the MWC (3rd in the MWC West)
**Returning Starters in 2015:** 7 on offense, 5 on defense
**Salary:** $575,000          **Age:** 40          **Job Security Grade:** A

**2015 SCHEDULE:**
(Conference games in bold.)

| | |
|---|---|
| Sept. 3 | UC Davis Aggies |
| Sept. 12 | Arizona Wildcats |
| Sept. 19 | at Texas A&M Aggies |
| Sept. 26 | at Buffalo Bulls |
| Oct. 3 | **UNLV Rebels** |
| Oct. 10 | **New Mexico Lobos** |
| Oct. 17 | **at Wyoming Cowboys** |
| Oct. 24 | **Hawaii Rainbow Warriors** |
| Nov. 5 | **at Fresno State Bulldogs** |
| Nov. 14 | **San Jose State Spartans** |
| Nov. 21 | **at Utah State Aggies** |
| Nov. 28 | **at San Diego State Aztecs** |

**2014 RESULTS:   7-6 (4-4 in the MWC)**      **Final Ranking: NR**

| | | |
|---|---|---|
| Southern Utah | W 28–19 | (21,021) |
| Washington State | W 24–13 | (26,023) |
| at Arizona | L 28–35 | (48,504) |
| **at San Jose State** | W 21–10 | (14,693) |
| **Boise State** | L 46–51 | (32,327) |
| **Colorado State** | L 24–31 | (21,847) |
| at BYU | W 42–35 | (56,355) |
| **at Hawaii** | W 26–18 | (27,061) |
| **San Diego State** | W 30–14 | (20,508) |
| **at Air Force** | L 38–45 OT | (11,519) |
| **Fresno State** | L 20–40 | (21,446) |
| **at UNLV** | W 49–27 | (20,151) |
| vs. Louisiana–Lafayette (New Orleans Bowl) | L 3–16 | (34,014) |

## Brian Polian's Year-by-Year Coaching Record:

**Nevada: 11-14 (7-9 in the MWC)**

| | | |
|---|---|---|
| 2013 | 4-8 (3-5) | Final Ranking: NR |
| 2014 | 7-6 (4-4) | Final Ranking: NR |

Lost to Louisiana-Lafayette 3-16 in the New Orleans Bowl.

# San Diego State Aztecs – Rocky Long

## Coach Ranking: #102

**Overall Record:** 97-89 in 15 seasons
**Record at San Diego State:** 32-20 in 4 seasons
**2014 Results:** 7-6, 5-3 in the MWC (MWC West Co-Champions)
**Returning Starters in 2015:** 7 on offense, 5 on defense
**Salary:** $800,000          **Age:** 65          **Job Security Grade:** B

**2015 SCHEDULE:**
(Conference games in bold.)

| | |
|---|---|
| Sept. 5 | San Diego Toreros |
| Sept. 12 | at California Golden Bears |
| Sept. 19 | South Alabama Jaguars |
| Sept. 26 | at Penn State Nittany Lions |
| Oct. 3 | **Fresno State Bulldogs** |
| Oct. 10 | **at Hawaii Rainbow Warriors** |
| Oct. 17 | **at San Jose State Spartans** |
| Oct. 23 | **Utah State Aggies** |
| Oct. 31 | **at Colorado State Rams** |
| Nov. 14 | **Wyoming Cowboys** |
| Nov. 21 | **at UNLV Rebels** |
| Nov. 28 | **Nevada Wolf Pack** |

**2014 RESULTS:   7-6 (5-3 in the MWC)**          **Final Ranking: NR**

| | | |
|---|---|---|
| #23 (FCS) Northern Arizona | W 38–7 | (30,761) |
| at #21 North Carolina | L 27–31 | (58,000) |
| at Oregon State | L 7–28 | (41,339) |
| **UNLV** | W 34–17 | (28,005) |
| **at Fresno State** | L 13–24 | (33,894) |
| **at New Mexico** | W 24–14 | (19,497) |
| **Hawaii** | W 20–10 | (35,686) |
| **at Nevada** | L 14–30 | (20,508) |
| Idaho | W 35–21 | (46,293) |
| **at Boise State** | L 29–38 | (27,478) |
| Air Force | W 30–14 | (28,626) |
| **San Jose State** | W 38–7 | (24,391) |
| Navy (Poinsettia Bowl) | L 16–17 | (33,077) |

## Rocky Long's Year-by-Year Coaching Record:

### New Mexico: 65-69 (40-34 in the WAC and MWC)
| | | |
|---|---|---|
| 1998 | 3–9 (1–7) | Final Ranking: NR |
| 1999 | 4–7 (3–4) | Final Ranking: NR |

New Mexico leaves the WAC and joins the Mountain West Conference.

| | | |
|---|---|---|
| 2000 | 5–7 (3–4) | Final Ranking: NR |
| 2001 | 6–5 (4–3) | Final Ranking: NR |
| 2002 | 7–7 (5–2) | Final Ranking: NR |

Lost to UCLA 13-27 in the Las Vegas Bowl.

| | | |
|---|---|---|
| 2003 | 8–5 (5–2) | Final Ranking: NR |

Lost to Oregon State 14-55 in the Las Vegas Bowl.

| | | |
|---|---|---|
| 2004 | 7–5 (5–2) | Final Ranking: NR |

Lost to Navy 19-34 in the Emerald Bowl.

| | | |
|---|---|---|
| 2005 | 6–5 (4–4) | Final Ranking: NR |
| 2006 | 6–7 (4–4) | Final Ranking: NR |

Lost to San Jose State 12-20 in the New Mexico Bowl.

| | | |
|---|---|---|
| 2007 | 9–4 (5–3) | Final Ranking: NR |

Beat Nevada 23-0 in the New Mexico Bowl.

| | | |
|---|---|---|
| 2008 | 4–8 (2–6) | Final Ranking: NR |

### San Diego State: 32-20 (22-9 in the MWC)
| | | |
|---|---|---|
| 2011 | 8–5 (4–3) | Final Ranking: NR |

Lost to Louisiana-Lafayette 30-32 in the New Orleans Bowl.

| | | |
|---|---|---|
| 2012 | 9–4 (7–1) | Final Ranking: NR |

MWC Co-Champions.
Lost to BYU 6-23 in the Poinsettia Bowl.

| | | |
|---|---|---|
| 2013 | 8–5 (6–2) | Final Ranking: NR |

Beat Buffalo 49-24 in the Famous Idaho Potato Bowl.

| | | |
|---|---|---|
| 2014 | 7–6 (5–3) | Final Ranking: NR |

Lost to Navy 16-17 in the Poinsettia Bowl.

# San Jose State Spartans – Ron Caragher

## Coach Ranking: #122

**Overall Record:** 53-37 in 8 seasons (6 seasons in FCS)
**Record at San Jose State:** 9-15 in 2 seasons
**2014 Results:** 3-9, 2-6 in the MWC (5th in the MWC West)
**Returning Starters in 2015:** 9 on offense (including QB), 6 on defense
**Salary:** $525,000          **Age:** 48          **Job Security Grade:** C

**2015 SCHEDULE:**
(Conference games in bold.)

| | |
|---|---|
| Sept. 3 | New Hampshire Wildcats |
| Sept. 12 | **at Air Force Falcons** |
| Sept. 19 | at Oregon State Beavers |
| Sept. 26 | **Fresno State Bulldogs** |
| Oct. 3 | at Auburn Tigers |
| Oct. 10 | **at UNLV Rebels** |
| Oct. 17 | **San Diego State Aztecs** |
| Oct. 24 | **New Mexico Lobos** |
| Nov. 6 | **BYU Cougars** |
| Nov. 14 | **at Nevada Wolf Pack** |
| Nov. 21 | **at Hawaii Rainbow Warriors** |
| Nov. 28 | **Boise State Broncos** |

**2014 RESULTS:   3-9 (2-6 in the MWC)**          **Final Ranking: NR**

| | | |
|---|---|---|
| North Dakota | W 42–10 | (10,371) |
| at #5 Auburn | L 13–59 | (87,451) |
| at Minnesota | L 7–24 | (47,739) |
| **Nevada** | L 10–21 | (14,693) |
| **UNLV** | W 33–10 | (14,427) |
| **at Wyoming** | W 27–20 OT | (19,627) |
| at Navy | L 31–41 | (30,612) |
| **Colorado State** | L 31–38 | (17,887) |
| **at Fresno State** | L 24–38 | (36,909) |
| **Hawaii** | L 0–13 | (17,962) |
| **at Utah State** | L 7–41 | (18,428) |
| **at San Diego State** | L 7–38 | (24,391) |

## Ron Caragher's Year-by-Year Coaching Record:

### University of San Diego: 44-22 (0-0 in FCS Postseason Games)
2007    9–2 (0-0)                   Final Ranking: NR
        Pioneer League Co-Champions.
2008    9–2 (0-0)                   Final Ranking: NR
2009    4–7 (0-0)                   Final Ranking: NR
2010    5–6 (0-0)                   Final Ranking: NR
2011    9–2 (0-0)                   Final Ranking: NR
        Pioneer League Co-Champions.
2012    8–3 (0-0)                   Final Ranking: NR
        Pioneer League Co-Champions.

### San Jose State: 9-15 (7-9 in the MWC)
2013    6–6 (5–3)                   Final Ranking: NR
2014    3–9 (2–6)                   Final Ranking: NR

# UNLV Rebels – Tony Sanchez

## Coach Ranking: #121

**Overall Record:** 0-0

**2014 Results:** UNLV went 2-11, 1-7 in the MWC (6th in the MWC West) At Bishop Gorman High School in Las Vegas, Sanchez went 15-0 (*USA Today* High School National Champions)

**Returning Starters in 2015:** 6 on offense (including QB), 5 on defense

**Salary:** $500,000          **Age:** 41          **Job Security Grade:** B

### 2015 SCHEDULE:
(Conference games in bold.)

| | |
|---|---|
| Sept. 5 | at Northern Illinois Huskies |
| Sept. 12 | UCLA Bruins |
| Sept. 19 | at Michigan Wolverines |
| Sept. 26 | Idaho State Bengals |
| Oct. 3 | **at Nevada Wolf Pack** |
| Oct. 10 | **San Jose State Spartans** |
| Oct. 16 | **at Fresno State Bulldogs** |
| Oct. 31 | **Boise State Broncos** |
| Nov. 7 | **Hawaii Rainbow Warriors** |
| Nov. 14 | **at Colorado State Rams** |
| Nov. 21 | **San Diego State Aztecs** |
| Nov. 28 | **at Wyoming Cowboys** |

**2014 RESULTS:   2-11 (1-7 in the MWC)**          **Final Ranking: NR**

| | | |
|---|---|---|
| at Arizona | L 13–58 | (50,103) |
| Northern Colorado | W 13–12 | (17,289) |
| Northern Illinois | L 34–48 | (14,305) |
| at Houston | L 14–47 | (23,408) |
| **at San Diego State** | L 17–34 | (28,005) |
| **at San Jose State** | L 10–33 | (14,427) |
| **Fresno State** | W 30–27 OT | (15,398) |
| **at Utah State** | L 20–34 | (20,153) |
| **New Mexico** | L 28–31 | (13,419) |
| **Air Force** | L 21–48 | (13,481) |
| **at BYU** | L 23–42 | (53,622) |
| **at Hawaii** | L 35–37 | (25,604) |
| **Nevada** | L 27–49 | (20,151) |

# 2015 SUN BELT PREVIEW

## Five Things You Need to Know about the Sun Belt in 2015:

**The Battle at the Top:** In **Georgia Southern's** first year as an FBS program, **Willie Fritz** led the Eagles to an undefeated Sun Belt Conference record and nearly pulled off upsets against **NC State** and **Georgia Tech**. It looks like the new kid on the block is already the king of the block and Georgia Southern is poised to repeat as SBC champs. Another recent addition to the SBC, **Appalachian State**, might be the Eagles' biggest challenge in 2015. The Mountaineers have 20 starters back (the most in the FBS) from a team that finished third in the conference last year.

**New to the SBC:** After 24 seasons, **Troy's Larry Blakeney** is retiring. Replacing the legend will be **Neal Brown**, who spent the last two seasons as **Kentucky's** offensive coordinator. Brown, 35, runs the Air Raid offense. Before his time at Kentucky, he was the OC at **Texas Tech**. Before that, he was Blakeney's OC at Troy.

**Coach on the Rise:** **Willie Fritz** is earning national attention for the job he did in his debut season at **Georgia Southern** and some big-time coaching offers may be coming his way soon.

**Keep an Eye On:** Some SBC schools are tired of losing their coaches to bigger programs and salaries are rising for the conference's top coaches. After **Arkansas State** lost **Hugh Freeze**, **Gus Malzahn**, and **Bryan Harsin** to bigger programs in three-consecutive seasons, the Red Wolves gave **Blake Anderson** a $700,000 salary with a hefty $3 million buyout. Meanwhile, **Louisiana-Lafayette** has made **Mark Hudspeth** the conference's highest-paid coach with a $1 million salary. **Neal Brown** will make close to $700,000 as **Troy's** new head coach. The other eight coaches in this conference make significantly less – an average of $390,000 a year.

**Coaches on the Hot Seat:** **Georgia Southern's** instant success in the Sun Belt has raised the expectations for every other coach in this conference. Coaches who now face a more impatient fan base include: **Georgia State's Trent Miles**, **Idaho's Paul Petrino**, **Louisiana-Monroe's Todd Berry**, and **New Mexico State's Doug Martin**. All four of these coaches may be fighting for their jobs in 2015.

## 2015 Projected Standings for the Sun Belt:

1. Georgia Southern
2. Appalachian State
3. Arkansas State
4. Texas State
5. Louisiana-Lafayette
6. Troy

7. Louisiana-Monroe
8. South Alabama
9. New Mexico State
10. Georgia State
11. Idaho

# Ranking the Sun Belt's Coaches:

1. **Willie Fritz** – Georgia Southern (146-65 in 18 seasons)
2. **Mark Hudspeth** – Louisiana-Lafayette (103-37 in 11 seasons)
3. **Dennis Franchione** – Texas State (210-126-2 in 29 seasons)
4. **Neal Brown** – Troy (First Year Head Coach)
5. **Blake Anderson** – Arkansas State (7-6 in 1 season)
6. **Joey Jones** – South Alabama (40-35 in 7 seasons)
7. **Scott Satterfield** – Appalachian State (11-13 in 2 seasons)
8. **Todd Berry** – Louisiana-Monroe (56-93 in 13 seasons)
9. **Doug Martin** – New Mexico State (33-73 in 9 seasons)
10. **Trent Miles** – Georgia State (21-59 in 7 seasons)
11. **Paul Petrino** – Idaho (2-21 in 2 seasons)

# 2014 Sun Belt Coach of the Year:
(Selected by the Sun Belt coaches and media members)
Willie Fritz, Georgia Southern

# 2014 Sun Belt Standings:

|                     | (Conference) | (All Games) |
|---------------------|--------------|-------------|
| Georgia Southern    | 8–0          | 9–3         |
| Louisiana–Lafayette | 7–1          | 9–4         |
| Appalachian State   | 6–2          | 7–5         |
| Texas State         | 5–3          | 7–5         |
| Arkansas State      | 5–3          | 7–6         |
| South Alabama       | 5–3          | 6–7         |
| Louisiana–Monroe    | 3–5          | 4–8         |
| Troy                | 3–5          | 3–9         |
| New Mexico State    | 1–7          | 2–10        |
| Idaho               | 1–7          | 1–10        |
| Georgia State       | 0–8          | 1–11        |

**2014 Sun Belt Bowl Record:** 1-2 (9th place among all 10 conferences)

# Appalachian St. Mountaineers – Scott Satterfield

## Coach Ranking: #111

**Overall Record:** 11-13 in 2 seasons (1 season in FCS)
**Record at Appalachian State:** 11-13 in 2 seasons
**2014 Results:** 7-5, 6-2 in the Sun Belt (3rd in the Sun Belt)
**Returning Starters in 2015:** 10 on offense (including QB), 10 on defense
**Salary:** $225,000 **Age:** 42 **Job Security Grade:** A

**2015 SCHEDULE:**
(Conference games in bold.)

| | |
|---|---|
| Sept. 5 | Howard Bison |
| Sept. 12 | at Clemson Tigers |
| Sept. 26 | at Old Dominion Monarchs |
| Oct. 3 | Wyoming Cowboys |
| Oct. 10 | **at Georgia State Panthers** |
| Oct. 17 | **at Louisiana-Monroe Warhawks** |
| Oct. 22 | **Georgia Southern Eagles** |
| Oct. 31 | **Troy Trojans** |
| Nov. 5 | **Arkansas State Red Wolves** |
| Nov. 14 | **at Idaho Vandals** |
| Nov. 28 | **Louisiana-Lafayette Ragin' Cajuns** |
| Dec. 5 | **at South Alabama Jaguars** |

**2014 RESULTS:** 7-5 (6-2 in the Sun Belt) **Final Ranking: NR**

| | | |
|---|---|---|
| at Michigan | L 14–52 | (106,811) |
| Campbell | W 66–0 | (25,861) |
| at Southern Miss | L 20–21 | (21,836) |
| **at Georgia Southern** | L 14–34 | (24,535) |
| **South Alabama** | L 21–47 | (24,215) |
| Liberty | L 48–55 OT | (26,058) |
| **at Troy** | W 53–14 | (15,664) |
| **Georgia State** | W 44–0 | (22,643) |
| **Louisiana–Monroe** | W 31–29 | (20,497) |
| **at Arkansas State** | W 37–32 | (20,016) |
| **at Louisiana–Lafayette** | W 35–16 | (20,638) |
| Idaho | W 45–28 | (19,721) |

## Scott Satterfield's Year-by-Year Coaching Record:

**Appalachian State: 11-13 (6-2 in the Sun Belt)**

| | | |
|---|---|---|
| 2013 | 4–8 (FCS) | Final Ranking: NR |
| 2014 | 7–5 (6–2) | Final Ranking: NR |

Appalachian State moves from FCS to FBS and joins the Sun Belt.
Ineligible for bowl game due to transition period. Will be eligible in 2015.

# Arkansas State Red Wolves – Blake Anderson

## Coach Ranking: #104

**Overall Record:** 7-6 in 1 season
**Record at Arkansas State:** 7-6 in 1 season
**2014 Results:** 7-6, 5-3 in the Sun Belt (T-4th in the Sun Belt)
**Returning Starters in 2015:** 9 on offense (including QB), 5 on defense
**Salary:** $700,000        **Age:** 46        **Job Security Grade:** A

**2015 SCHEDULE:**
(Conference games in bold.)

| | |
|---|---|
| Sept. 5 | at USC Trojans |
| Sept. 12 | Missouri Tigers |
| Sept. 19 | Missouri State Bears |
| Sept. 26 | at Toledo Rockets |
| Oct. 3 | **Idaho Vandals** |
| Oct. 13 | **at South Alabama Jaguars** |
| Oct. 20 | **Louisiana-Lafayette Ragin' Cajuns** |
| Oct. 31 | **Georgia State Panthers** |
| Nov. 5 | **at Appalachian State Mountaineers** |
| Nov. 14 | **at Louisiana-Monroe Warhawks** |
| Nov. 28 | **at New Mexico State Aggies** |
| Dec. 5 | **Texas State Bobcats** |

**2014 RESULTS:   7-6 (5-3 in the Sun Belt)**        **Final Ranking: NR**

| | | |
|---|---|---|
| #18 (FCS) Montana State | W 37–10 | (26,143) |
| at Tennessee | L 19–34 | (99,538) |
| at Miami (FL) | L 20–41 | (41,519) |
| Utah State | W 21–14 OT | (29,029) |
| **Louisiana–Monroe** | W 28–14 | (29,317) |
| **at Georgia State** | W 52–10 | (10,196) |
| **at Louisiana–Lafayette** | L 40–55 | (21,760) |
| **at Idaho** | W 44–28 | (11,082) |
| **South Alabama** | W 45–10 | (23,615) |
| **Appalachian State** | L 32–37 | (20,016) |
| **at Texas State** | L 27–45 | (12,264) |
| **New Mexico State** | W 68–35 | (21,043) |
| vs. Toledo (GoDaddy Bowl) | L 44–63 | (36,811) |

### Blake Anderson's Year-by-Year Coaching Record:

<u>Arkansas State: 7-6 (5-3 in the Sun Belt)</u>
2014    7–6 (5–3)        **Final Ranking: NR**
     Lost to Toledo 44-63 in the GoDaddy Bowl.

# Georgia Southern Eagles – Willie Fritz

## Coach Ranking: #73

**Overall Record:** 146-65 in 18 seasons (4 seasons in FCS, 13 seasons in Division II)

**Record at Georgia Southern:** 9-3 in 1 season

**2014 Results:** 9-3, 8-0 in the Sun Belt (Sun Belt Champions)

**Returning Starters in 2015:** 5 on offense (including QB), 7 on defense

**Salary:** $400,000          **Age:** 55          **Job Security Grade:** A

**2015 SCHEDULE:**
(Conference games in bold.)

| Sept. 5 | at West Virginia Mountaineers |
| Sept. 12 | Western Michigan Broncos |
| Sept. 19 | The Citadel Bulldogs |
| Sept. 26 | **at Idaho Vandals** |
| Oct. 3 | **at Louisiana-Monroe Warhawks** |
| Oct. 17 | **New Mexico State Aggies** |
| Oct. 22 | **at Appalachian State Mountaineers** |
| Oct. 29 | **Texas State Bobcats** |
| Nov. 14 | **at Troy Trojans** |
| Nov. 21 | at Georgia Bulldogs |
| Nov. 28 | **South Alabama Jaguars** |
| Dec. 5 | **Georgia State Panthers** |

| 2014 RESULTS: 9-3 (8-0 in the Sun Belt) | Final Ranking: NR | |
| --- | --- | --- |
| at NC State | L 23–24 | (54,273) |
| Savannah State | W 83–9 | (23,121) |
| at Georgia Tech | L 38–42 | (53,173) |
| **at South Alabama** | W 28–6 | (11,348) |
| **Appalachian State** | W 34–14 | (24,535) |
| **at New Mexico State** | W 36–28 | (10,256) |
| **Idaho** | W 47–24 | (23,250) |
| **at Georgia State** | W 69–31 | (28,427) |
| **Troy** | W 42–10 | (18,321) |
| **at Texas State** | W 28–25 | (16,772) |
| at Navy | L 19–52 | (33,894) |
| **Louisiana–Monroe** | W 22–16 | (16,283) |

## Willie Fritz's Year-by-Year Coaching Record:

### Central Missouri: 97-47 (1-1 in Division II Postseason Games)
1997    5–6 (0-0)              Final Ranking: NA
1998    8–3 (0-0)              Final Ranking: NA
1999    7–4 (0-0)              Final Ranking: NA
2000    7–4 (0-0)              Final Ranking: NA
2001    10–2 (1-0)             Final Ranking: NA
        Beat Minnesota-Duluth 48-17 in the Mineral Water Bowl.
2002    10–2 (0-1)             Final Ranking: NA
        Lost to Northern Colorado 28-49 in the first round of the Division II playoffs.
2003    9–2 (0-0)              Final Ranking: NA
2004    7–4 (0-0)              Final Ranking: NA
2005    7–3 (0-0)              Final Ranking: NA
2006    5–6 (0-0)              Final Ranking: NA
2007    7–4 (0-0)              Final Ranking: NA
2008    7–4 (0-0)              Final Ranking: NA
2009    8–3 (0-0)              Final Ranking: NA

### Sam Houston State: 40-14 (7-3 in the FCS Playoffs)
2010    6–5 (0-0)             Final Ranking: NR
2011    14–1 (3-1)            Final Ranking: #2
        Southland Conference Champions.
        Fritz named FCS National Coach of the Year.
        Lost to #4 North Dakota St. 6-17 in the FCS National Championship Game.
2012    11–4 (3-1)            Final Ranking: #2
        Southland Conference Co-Champions.
        Lost to #1 North Dakota St. 13-39 in the FCS National Championship Game.
2013    9–5 (1-1)             Final Ranking: #14
        Lost to Southeastern Louisiana 29-30 in the second round of the FCS playoffs.

### Georgia Southern: 9-3 (8-0 in the Sun Belt)
2014    9-3 (8-0)             Final Ranking: NR
        Georgia Southern moves from FCS to FBS and joins the Sun Belt.
        Sun Belt Conference Champions.
        Fritz named the Mid-Major Coach of the Year by the *CFCA*.
        Fritz named Sun Belt Conference Coach of the Year.
        Ineligible for bowl game due to transition period. Will be eligible in 2015.

# Georgia State Panthers – Trent Miles

## Coach Ranking: #127

**Overall Record:** 21-59 in 7 seasons (5 seasons in FCS)
**Record at Georgia State:** 1-23 in 2 seasons
**2014 Results:** 1-11, 0-8 in the Sun Belt (11th in the Sun Belt)
**Returning Starters in 2015:** 8 on offense (including QB), 9 on defense
**Salary:** $510,000        **Age:** 52        **Job Security Grade:** D

**2015 SCHEDULE:**
(Conference games in bold.)

| | |
|---|---|
| Sept. 4 | Charlotte 49ers |
| Sept. 12 | **at New Mexico State Aggies** |
| Sept. 19 | at Oregon Ducks |
| Oct. 3 | Liberty Flames |
| Oct. 10 | **Appalachian State Mountaineers** |
| Oct. 17 | at Ball State Cardinals |
| Oct. 31 | **at Arkansas State Red Wolves** |
| Nov. 7 | **Louisiana-Lafayette Ragin' Cajuns** |
| Nov. 14 | **at Texas State Bobcats** |
| Nov. 21 | **South Alabama Jaguars** |
| Nov. 27 | **Troy Trojans** |
| Dec. 5 | **at Georgia Southern Eagles** |

**2014 RESULTS:**    1-11 (0-8 in the Sun Belt)    **Final Ranking:** NR

| | | |
|---|---|---|
| Abilene Christian | W 38–37 | (10,140) |
| **New Mexico State** | L 31–34 | (10,126) |
| Air Force | L 38–48 | (16,836) |
| at Washington | L 14–45 | (64,608) |
| **at Louisiana–Lafayette** | L 31–34 | (24,816) |
| **Arkansas State** | L 10–52 | (10,196) |
| **at South Alabama** | L 27–30 | (13,186) |
| **Georgia Southern** | L 31–69 | (28,427) |
| **at Appalachian State** | L 0–44 | (22,643) |
| **at Troy** | L 21–45 | (16,148) |
| at Clemson | L 0–28 | (77,693) |
| **Texas State** | L 31–54 | (14,312) |

## Trent Miles' Year-by-Year Coaching Record:

<u>Indiana State: 20-36 (0-0 in the FCS Playoffs)</u>
| | | |
|---|---|---|
| 2008 | 0–12 (0-0) | Final Ranking: NR |
| 2009 | 1–10 (0-0) | Final Ranking: NR |
| 2010 | 6–5 (0-0) | Final Ranking: NR |

Miles named Missouri Valley Conference Coach of the Year.

| | | |
|---|---|---|
| 2011 | 6–5 (0-0) | Final Ranking: NR |
| 2012 | 7–4 (0-0) | Final Ranking: NR |

<u>Georgia State: 1-23 (0-15 in the Sun Belt)</u>
| | | |
|---|---|---|
| 2013 | 0–12 (0–7) | Final Ranking: NR |
| 2014 | 1–11 (0–8) | Final Ranking: NR |

# Idaho Vandals – Paul Petrino

## Coach Ranking: #128

**Overall Record:** 2-21 in 2 seasons
**Record at Idaho:** 2-21 in 2 seasons
**2014 Results:** 1-10, 1-7 in the Sun Belt (T-9th in the Sun Belt)
**Returning Starters in 2015:** 6 on offense (including QB), 7 on defense
**Salary:** $400,000          **Age:** 48          **Job Security Grade:** C

**2015 SCHEDULE:**
(Conference games in bold.)

| | |
|---|---|
| Sept. 3 | Ohio Bobcats |
| Sept. 12 | at USC Trojans |
| Sept. 19 | Wofford Terriers |
| Sept. 26 | **Georgia Southern Eagles** |
| Oct. 3 | **at Arkansas State Red Wolves** |
| Oct. 17 | **at Troy Trojans** |
| Oct. 24 | **Louisiana-Monroe Warhawks** |
| Oct. 31 | **at New Mexico State Aggies** |
| Nov. 7 | **at South Alabama Jaguars** |
| Nov. 14 | **Appalachian State Mountaineers** |
| Nov. 21 | at Auburn Tigers |
| Nov. 28 | **Texas State Bobcats** |

**2014 RESULTS:**   1-10 (1-7 in the Sun Belt)   Final Ranking: NR

| | | |
|---|---|---|
| at Florida | Canceled | (N/A) |
| **at Louisiana–Monroe** | L 31–38 | (16,694) |
| Western Michigan | L 33–45 | (14,721) |
| at Ohio | L 24–36 | (25,211) |
| **South Alabama** | L 10–34 | (14,887) |
| **at Texas State** | L 30–35 | (21,345) |
| **at Georgia Southern** | L 24–47 | (23,250) |
| **New Mexico State** | W 29–17 | (15,207) |
| **Arkansas State** | L 28–44 | (11,082) |
| at San Diego State | L 21–35 | (46,293) |
| **Troy** | L 17–34 | (8,535) |
| **at Appalachian State** | L 28–45 | (19,721) |

## Paul Petrino's Year-by-Year Coaching Record:

**Idaho: 2-21 (1-7 in the Sun Belt)**

| | | |
|---|---|---|
| 2013 | 1–11 (Ind.) | Final Ranking: NR |
| 2014 | 1–10 (1-7) | Final Ranking: NR |

Idaho joins the Sun Belt Conference after one season as an Independent program.

# Louisiana-Lafayette Ragin' Cajuns – Mark Hudspeth

## Coach Ranking: #74

**Overall Record:** 103-37 in 11 seasons (7 seasons in Division II)
**Record at Louisiana-Lafayette:** 36-16 in 4 seasons
**2014 Results:** 9-4, 7-1 in the Sun Belt (2nd in the Sun Belt)
**Returning Starters in 2015:** 6 on offense, 5 on defense
**Salary:** $1 Million          **Age:** 46          **Job Security Grade:** A

**2015 SCHEDULE:**
(Conference games in bold.)

| | |
|---|---|
| Sept. 5 | at Kentucky Wildcats |
| Sept. 12 | Northwestern State Demons |
| Sept. 26 | Akron Zips |
| Oct. 3 | at Louisiana Tech Bulldogs |
| Oct. 10 | **Texas State Bobcats** |
| Oct. 20 | **at Arkansas State Red Wolves** |
| Oct. 31 | **Louisiana-Monroe Warhawks** |
| Nov. 7 | **at Georgia State Panthers** |
| Nov. 12 | **at South Alabama Jaguars** |
| Nov. 21 | **New Mexico State Aggies** |
| Nov. 28 | **at Appalachian State Mountaineers** |
| Dec. 5 | **Troy Trojans** |

**2014 RESULTS:   9-4 (7-1 in the Sun Belt)        Final Ranking: NR**

| | | |
|---|---|---|
| Southern | W 45–6 | (36,170) |
| Louisiana Tech | L 20–48 | (25,607) |
| at #14 Ole Miss | L 15–56 | (60,937) |
| at Boise State | L 9–34 | (33,337) |
| **Georgia State** | W 34–31 | (24,816) |
| **at Texas State** | W 34–10 | (18,509) |
| **Arkansas State** | W 55–40 | (21,760) |
| **South Alabama** | W 19–9 | (25,861) |
| **at New Mexico State** | W 44–16 | (10,299) |
| **at Louisiana–Monroe** | W 34–27 | (19,544) |
| **Appalachian State** | L 16–35 | (20,638) |
| **at Troy** | W 42–23 | (12,241) |
| vs. Nevada (New Orleans Bowl) | W 16–3 | (34,014) |

## Mark Hudspeth's Year-by-Year Coaching Record:

### North Alabama: 66-21 (8-4 in the Division II Playoffs)
2002    4–7 (0-0)                Final Ranking: NA
2003    13–1 (2-1)               Final Ranking: NA
        Hudspeth named Gulf South Conference Coach of the Year.
        Lost to North Dakota 22-29 in the Division II semifinals.
2004    5–5 (0-0)                Final Ranking: NA
2005    11–3 (3-1)               Final Ranking: NA
        Lost to Northwest Missouri State 24-25 in the Division II semifinals.
2006    11–1 (1-1)               Final Ranking: NA
        Hudspeth named Gulf South Conference Coach of the Year.
        Lost to Delta State 10-27 in the Division II quarterfinals.
2007    10–2 (1-1)               Final Ranking: NA
        Lost to Valdosta State 27-37 in the Division II quarterfinals.
2008    12–2 (2-1)               Final Ranking: NA
        Lost to Northwest Missouri State 7-41 in the Division II semifinals.

### Louisiana-Lafayette: 36-16 (24-7 in the Sun Belt)
2011    9–4 (6–2)                Final Ranking: NR
        Beat San Diego State 32-30 in the New Orleans Bowl.
2012    9–4 (6–2)                Final Ranking: NR
        Beat East Carolina 43-34 in the New Orleans Bowl.
2013    9–4 (5–2)                Final Ranking: NR
        Sun Belt Conference Co-Champions.
        Beat Tulane 24-21 in the New Orleans Bowl.
2014    9–4 (7–1)                Final Ranking: NR
        Beat Nevada 16-3 in the New Orleans Bowl.

# Louisiana-Monroe Warhawks – Todd Berry

## Coach Ranking: #123

**Overall Record:** 56-93 in 13 seasons (4 seasons in Division 1-AA)
**Record at Louisiana-Monroe:** 27-34 in 5 seasons
**2014 Results:** 4-8, 3-5 in the Sun Belt (T-7th in the Sun Belt)
**Returning Starters in 2015:** 6 on offense, 8 on defense
**Salary:** $360,000          **Age:** 54          **Job Security Grade:** C

**2015 SCHEDULE:**
(Conference games in bold.)

| | |
|---|---|
| Sept. 5 | at Georgia Bulldogs |
| Sept. 12 | Nicholls State Colonels |
| Sept. 26 | at Alabama Crimson Tide |
| Oct. 3 | **Georgia Southern Eagles** |
| Oct. 10 | at Tulsa Golden Hurricane |
| Oct. 17 | **Appalachian State Mountaineers** |
| Oct. 24 | **at Idaho Vandals** |
| Oct. 31 | **Louisiana-Lafayette Ragin' Cajuns** |
| Nov. 7 | **at Troy Trojans** |
| Nov. 14 | **Arkansas State Red Wolves** |
| Nov. 19 | **at Texas State Bobcats** |
| Nov. 28 | at Hawaii Rainbow Warriors |
| Dec. 5 | **New Mexico State Aggies** |

**2014 RESULTS:    4-8 (3-5 in the Sun Belt)**      **Final Ranking: NR**

| | | |
|---|---|---|
| Wake Forest | W 17–10 | (21,003) |
| **Idaho** | W 38–31 | (16,694) |
| at #9 LSU | L 0–31 | (101,194) |
| **Troy** | W 22–20 | (18,544) |
| **at Arkansas State** | L 14–28 | (29,317) |
| at Kentucky | L 14–48 | (56,676) |
| **Texas State** | L 18–22 | (14,755) |
| at Texas A&M | L 16–21 | (100,922) |
| **at Appalachian State** | L 29–31 | (20,497) |
| **Louisiana–Lafayette** | L 27–34 | (19,544) |
| at New Mexico State | W 30–17 | (6,011) |
| at Georgia Southern | L 16–22 | (16,283) |

## Todd Berry's Year-by-Year Coaching Record:

### Illinois State: 24-24 (2-2 in the Division 1-AA Playoffs)
1996   3–8 (0-0)          Final Ranking: NR
1997   2–9 (0-0)          Final Ranking: NR
1998   8–4 (0-1)          Final Ranking: #16
       Berry named Gateway Conference Coach of the Year.
       Lost to #3 Northwestern State 28-48 in the first round of the Division 1-AA playoffs.
1999   11–3 (2-1)         Final Ranking: #3
       Berry named Gateway Conference Coach of the Year.
       Lost to #1 Georgia Southern 17-31 in the Division 1-AA semifinals.

### Army: 5-35 (4-22 in Conference USA)
2000   1–10 (1-6)         Final Ranking: NR
2001   3–8 (2-5)          Final Ranking: NR
2002   1–11 (1-7)         Final Ranking: NR
2003   0–6 (0-4)          Final Ranking: NR
       Berry was fired after a 0-6 start and Army finished the year 0-13.

### Louisiana-Monroe: 27-34 (20-19 in the Sun Belt)
2010   5–7 (4-4)          Final Ranking: NR
2011   4–8 (3-5)          Final Ranking: NR
2012   8–5 (6-2)          Final Ranking: NR
       Berry named Sun Belt Conference Coach of the Year.
       Lost to Ohio 14-45 in the Independence Bowl.
2013   6–6 (4-3)          Final Ranking: NR
2014   4–8 (3-5)          Final Ranking: NR

# New Mexico State Aggies – Doug Martin
## Coach Ranking: #126

**Overall Record:** 33-73 in 9 seasons
**Record at New Mexico State:** 4-20 in 2 seasons
**2014 Results:** 2-10, 1-7 in the Sun Belt (T-9th in the Sun Belt)
**Returning Starters in 2015:** 8 on offense (including QB), 9 on defense
**Salary:** $380,000        **Age:** 52        **Job Security Grade:** C

**2015 SCHEDULE:**
(Conference games in bold.)

| | |
|---|---|
| Sept. 5 | at Florida Gators |
| Sept. 12 | **Georgia State Panthers** |
| Sept. 19 | UTEP Miners |
| Oct. 3 | at New Mexico Lobos |
| Oct. 10 | at Ole Miss Rebels |
| Oct. 17 | **at Georgia Southern Eagles** |
| Oct. 24 | **Troy Trojans** |
| Oct. 31 | **Idaho Vandals** |
| Nov. 7 | **at Texas State Bobcats** |
| Nov. 21 | **at Louisiana-Lafayette Ragin' Cajuns** |
| Nov. 28 | **Arkansas State Red Wolves** |
| Dec. 5 | **at Louisiana-Monroe Warhawks** |

**2014 RESULTS:** 2-10 (1-7 in the Sun Belt)    **Final Ranking:** NR

| | | |
|---|---|---|
| Cal Poly | W 28–10 | (13,772) |
| **at Georgia State** | W 34–31 | (10,126) |
| at UTEP | L 24–42 | (32,979) |
| New Mexico | L 35–38 | (24,651) |
| at #17 LSU | L 7–63 | (101,987) |
| **Georgia Southern** | L 28–36 | (10,256) |
| **at Troy** | L 24–41 | (17,628) |
| **at Idaho** | L 17–29 | (15,207) |
| **Texas State** | L 29–37 | (8,623) |
| **Louisiana–Lafayette** | L 16–44 | (10,299) |
| **Louisiana–Monroe** | L 17–30 | (6,011) |
| **at Arkansas State** | L 35–68 | (21,043) |

## Doug Martin's Year-by-Year Coaching Record:

### Kent State: 29-53 (21-35 in the MAC)
| | | |
|---|---|---|
| 2004 | 5–6 (4–4) | Final Ranking: NR |
| 2005 | 1–10 (0–8) | Final Ranking: NR |
| 2006 | 6–6 (5–3) | Final Ranking: NR |
| 2007 | 3–9 (1–7) | Final Ranking: NR |
| 2008 | 4–8 (3–5) | Final Ranking: NR |
| 2009 | 5–7 (4–4) | Final Ranking: NR |
| 2010 | 5–7 (4–4) | Final Ranking: NR |

### New Mexico State: 4-20 (1-7 in the Sun Belt)
| | | |
|---|---|---|
| 2013 | 2–10 (Ind.) | Final Ranking: NR |
| 2014 | 2–10 (1–7) | Final Ranking: NR |

New Mexico State joins the Sun Belt Conference after one season as an Independent program.

# South Alabama Jaguars – Joey Jones
## Coach Ranking: #107

**Overall Record:** 40-35 in 7 seasons (3 seasons in FCS, 1 season in Division III)

**Record at South Alabama:** 37-28 in 6 seasons

**2014 Results:** 6-7, 5-3 in the Sun Belt (T-4th in the Sun Belt)

**Returning Starters in 2015:** 6 on offense (including QB), 2 on defense

**Salary:** $470,000          **Age:** 52          **Job Security Grade:** A

**2015 SCHEDULE:**
(Conference games in bold.)

| | |
|---|---|
| Sept. 5 | Gardner-Webb Bulldogs |
| Sept. 12 | at Nebraska Cornhuskers |
| Sept. 19 | at San Diego State Aztecs |
| Sept. 26 | NC State Wolfpack |
| Oct. 3 | **at Troy Trojans** |
| Oct. 13 | **Arkansas State Red Wolves** |
| Oct. 24 | **at Texas State Bobcats** |
| Nov. 7 | **Idaho Vandals** |
| Nov. 12 | **Louisiana-Lafayette Ragin' Cajuns** |
| Nov. 21 | **at Georgia State Panthers** |
| Nov. 28 | **at Georgia Southern Eagles** |
| Dec. 5 | **Appalachian State Mountaineers** |

**2014 RESULTS:   6-7 (5-3 in the Sun Belt)**          **Final Ranking: NR**

| | | |
|---|---|---|
| at Kent State | W 23–13 | (15,355) |
| Mississippi State | L 3–35 | (38,129) |
| **Georgia Southern** | L 6–28 | (11,348) |
| **at Idaho** | W 34–10 | (14,887) |
| **at Appalachian State** | W 47–21 | (24,215) |
| **Georgia State** | W 30–27 | (13,186) |
| **Troy** | W 27–13 | (17,146) |
| **at Louisiana–Lafayette** | L 9–19 | (25,861) |
| **at Arkansas State** | L 10–45 | (23,615) |
| **Texas State** | W 24–20 | (10,289) |
| at South Carolina | L 12–37 | (78,201) |
| Navy | L 40–42 | (14,571) |
| vs. Bowling Green (Camellia Bowl) | L 28–33 | (20,256) |

## Joey Jones' Year-by-Year Coaching Record:

**Birmingham-Southern: 3-7 (0-0 in the Division III Playoffs)**
2007     3-7 (0-0)                Final Ranking: NA

**South Alabama: 37-28 (10-13 in the Sun Belt)**
2009     7–0 (NA)                 Final Ranking: NA
         2009 was South Alabama's first season of football.
         Competes as an unclassified program.
2010     10–0 (NA)                Final Ranking: NA
         Competes as an unclassified program.
2011     6–4 (FCS)                Final Ranking: NR
         Competes as an FCS Independent program.
2012     2–11 (1–7)               Final Ranking: NR
         South Alabama moves from FCS to FBS and joins the Sun Belt.
2013     6–6 (4–3)                Final Ranking: NR
2014     6–7 (5–3)                Final Ranking: NR
         Lost to Bowling Green 28-33 in the Camellia Bowl.

# Texas State Bobcats – Dennis Franchione

## Coach Ranking: #89

**Overall Record:** 210-126-2 in 29 seasons (3 seasons in FCS, 1 season in Division II, 6 seasons in NAIA)

**Record at Texas State:** 36-34 in 6 seasons

**2014 Results:** 7-5, 5-3 in the Sun Belt (T-4th in the Sun Belt)

**Returning Starters in 2015:** 7 on offense (including QB), 5 on defense

**Salary:** $400,000        **Age:** 64        **Job Security Grade:** A

2015 SCHEDULE:
(Conference games in bold.)

| | |
|---|---|
| Sept. 5 | at Florida State Seminoles |
| Sept. 12 | Prairie View A&M Panthers |
| Sept. 19 | Southern Miss Golden Eagles |
| Sept. 26 | at Houston Cougars |
| Oct. 10 | **at Louisiana-Lafayette Ragin' Cajuns** |
| Oct. 24 | **South Alabama Jaguars** |
| Oct. 29 | **at Georgia Southern Eagles** |
| Nov. 7 | **New Mexico State Aggies** |
| Nov. 14 | **Georgia State Panthers** |
| Nov. 19 | **Louisiana-Monroe Warhawks** |
| Nov. 28 | **at Idaho Vandals** |
| Dec. 5 | **at Arkansas State Red Wolves** |

2014 RESULTS:   7-5 (5-3 in the Sun Belt)        Final Ranking: NR

| | | |
|---|---|---|
| Arkansas–Pine Bluff | W 65–0 | (17,813) |
| Navy | L 21–35 | (32,007) |
| at Illinois | L 35–42 | (41,019) |
| at Tulsa | W 37–34 3OT | (21,353) |
| **Idaho** | W 35–30 | (21,345) |
| **Louisiana–Lafayette** | L 10–34 | (18,509) |
| **at Louisiana–Monroe** | W 22–18 | (14,755) |
| **at New Mexico State** | W 37–29 | (8,623) |
| **Georgia Southern** | L 25–28 | (16,772) |
| **at South Alabama** | L 20–24 | (10,289) |
| **Arkansas State** | W 45–27 | (12,264) |
| **at Georgia State** | W 54–31 | (14,312) |

## Dennis Franchione's Year-by-Year Coaching Record:

### Southwestern College (KS): 14-4-2 (1-0 in NAIA Postseason Games)
1981    5–2–2 (0-0)                Final Ranking: NA
1982    9–2 (1-0)                  Final Ranking: NA
        Beat Oklahoma Panhandle State 15-0 in the Sunflower Bowl.

### Pittsburg State: 53-6 (6-5 in the NAIA and Division II Playoffs)
1985    8–2 (0-1)                  Final Ranking: NA
        Lost to Central Arkansas 22-32 in the NAIA quarterfinals.
1986    11–1 (1-1)                 Final Ranking: NA
        Franchione named NAIA National Coach of the Year.
        Lost to Cameron 6-17 in the NAIA semifinals.
1987    11–1 (2-1)                 Final Ranking: NA
        Franchione named NAIA National Coach of the Year.
        Lost to Cameron 10-20 in the NAIA semifinals.
1988    11–1 (2-1)                 Final Ranking: NA
        Lost to Adams State 10-13 in the NAIA semifinals.
1989    12–1 (1-1)                 Final Ranking: NA
        Pitt State moves from NAIA to NCAA Division II.
        Lost to Angelo State 21-24 in the Division II quarterfinals.

### Southwest Texas State: 13-9 (0-0 in Division 1-AA Playoffs)
1990    6–5 (0-0)                  Final Ranking: NR
1991    7–4 (0-0)                  Final Ranking: NR
        Southwest Texas State changed its name to Texas State-San Marcos in 2003
        and then to Texas State in 2013.

### New Mexico: 33-36 (21-27 in the WAC)
1992    3–8 (2–6)                  Final Ranking: NR
1993    6–5 (4–4)                  Final Ranking: NR
1994    5–7 (4–4)                  Final Ranking: NR
1995    4–7 (2–6)                  Final Ranking: NR
1996    6–5 (3–5)                  Final Ranking: NR
1997    9–4 (6–2)                  Final Ranking: NR
        WAC Mountain Division Champions.
        Lost to #17 Colorado State 13-41 in the WAC Championship Game.
        Lost to Arizona 14-20 in the Insight.com Bowl.

### TCU: 25-10 (16-7 in the WAC)
1998    7–5 (4–4)                  Final Ranking: NR
        Beat USC 28-19 in the Sun Bowl.
1999    8–4 (5–2)                  Final Ranking: NR
        WAC Co-Champions
        Beat #19 East Carolina 28-14 in the Mobile Alabama Bowl.

## TCU (continued):

2000    10-1 (7-1)              Final Ranking: #13
WAC Co-Champions.
TCU lost to Southern Miss 21-28 in the Mobile Alabama Bowl, but Franchione had already left to accept the Alabama job.
TCU finished the season ranked #21.

## Alabama: 17-8 (10-6 in the SEC)

2001    7-5 (4-4)              Final Ranking: NR
Beat Iowa State 14-13 in the Independence Bowl.

2002    10-3 (6-2)             Final Ranking: #11
Alabama finished first in the SEC West, but was ineligible for a conference title or postseason play due to NCAA probation.

## Texas A&M: 32-28 (19-21 in the Big 12)

2003    4-8 (2-6)              Final Ranking: NR

2004    7-5 (5-3)              Final Ranking: NR
Lost to #15 Tennessee 7-38 in the Cotton Bowl Classic.

2005    5-6 (3-5)              Final Ranking: NR

2006    9-4 (5-3)              Final Ranking: NR
Lost to #20 Cal 10-45 in the Holiday Bowl.

2007    7-5 (4-4)              Final Ranking: NR
Franchione resigned prior to the bowl game. Texas A&M lost to Penn State 17-24 in the Alamo Bowl and finished the season 7-6.

## Texas State: 36-34 *includes 1990-1991* (15-18 in the Sun Belt and WAC)

2011    6-6 (FCS)             Final Ranking: NR
Competes as an FCS Independent program.

2012    4-8 (2-4)              Final Ranking: NR
Texas State moves from FCS to FBS and joins the WAC.

2013    6-6 (2-5)              Final Ranking: NR
The WAC dissolves as a football conference and Texas State joins the Sun Belt.

2014    7-5 (5-3)              Final Ranking: NR

# Troy Trojans – Neal Brown

## Coach Ranking: #97

**Overall Record:** 0-0

**2014 Results:** Troy went 3-9, 3-5 in the Sun Belt (T-7th in the Sun Belt)
Brown was Kentucky's offensive coordinator from 2013-2014

**Returning Starters in 2015:** 7 on offense (including QB), 6 on defense

**Salary:** $660,000          **Age:** 35          **Job Security Grade:** A

**2015 SCHEDULE:**
(Conference games in bold.)

| | |
|---|---|
| Sept. 5 | at NC State Wolfpack |
| Sept. 12 | Charleston Southern Buccaneers |
| Sept. 19 | at Wisconsin Badgers |
| Oct. 3 | **South Alabama Jaguars** |
| Oct. 10 | at Mississippi State Bulldogs |
| Oct. 17 | **Idaho Vandals** |
| Oct. 24 | **at New Mexico State Aggies** |
| Oct. 31 | **at Appalachian State Mountaineers** |
| Nov. 7 | **Louisiana-Monroe Warhawks** |
| Nov. 14 | **Georgia Southern Eagles** |
| Nov. 27 | **at Georgia State Panthers** |
| Dec. 5 | **at Louisiana-Lafayette Ragin' Cajuns** |

**2014 RESULTS:**   3-9 (3-5 in the Sun Belt)        **Final Ranking: NR**

| | | |
|---|---|---|
| at UAB | L 10–48 | (27,133) |
| Duke | L 17–34 | (21,331) |
| Abilene Christian | L 35–38 | (17,320) |
| at #13 Georgia | L 0–66 | (92,746) |
| **at Louisiana–Monroe** | L 20–22 | (18,544) |
| **New Mexico State** | W 41–24 | (17,628) |
| **Appalachian State** | L 14–53 | (15,664) |
| **at South Alabama** | L 13–27 | (17,146) |
| **at Georgia Southern** | L 10–42 | (18,321) |
| **Georgia State** | W 45–21 | (16,148) |
| **at Idaho** | W 34–17 | (8,535) |
| **Louisiana–Lafayette** | L 23–42 | (12,241) |

Would you like to share any comments, questions, or suggestions regarding the *College Football Coaches Almanac and Preview*? I'd love to hear from you.

Email: **info@coachesalmanac.com**

Twitter: **@CoachesAlmanac**

And don't forget to stop by **CoachesAlmanac.com**, where the coaching news and discussion never stops.

# Resources and Acknowledgments

I'd like to acknowledge – and highly recommend – the excellent resources I refer to most when researching coaches and their programs.

**Statistics:** *CFBStats.com, Yahoo! Sports*

**Salaries and Contracts:** *USA Today, ESPN.com, FootballScoop, CoachesHotSeat.com*

**Historical Records:** *CFBDataWarehouse.com, ESPN College Football Encyclopedia, Phil Steele's College Football Previews, mcubed.net, Wikipedia*

**Recruiting Rankings and Ratings:** *247Sports.com*

**Schedules:** *FBSchedules.com*

**Returning Personnel:** *PhilSteele.com, ESPN.com, AthlonSports.com*

**News and Rumors:** *Sports Illustrated, BleacherReport.com, FootballScoop, ESPN.com, Yahoo! Sports, Fox Sports, CBS Sports, Sporting News*

**Football Strategy:** *SmartFootball.com, Grantland, American Football Monthly*

On a personal note, I want to thank Kevin Cumiskey, Garret Donnelly, Kyle Donnelly, Travis Donnelly, John Goetz, Joe Hornback, Jason Kazar, Devon Krusich, and Ryan Modin for taking the time to offer their invaluable feedback and thoughtful advice as I wrote this book. I can't tell you how much I appreciate the ideas each of you shared, the time you spent evaluating this book, and the encouragement you offered me during the writing process.

Most of all, I want to thank my wife, my first editor, and my Chief Encouragement Officer, Laura. Without your wisdom, encouragement, love, and support, this book would not exist. I can't thank you enough!

# About the Author

**Darrin Donnelly** is an entrepreneur and writer with more than 20 years of experience as a published sports journalist. Donnelly and his material have been featured in publications such as *Sports Illustrated*, *The Wall Street Journal*, *Fast Company Magazine*, *ESPN The Magazine*, and newspapers, websites, and radio outlets all over the world. He lives at the intersection of the Big 12, SEC, and Big Ten (in the suburbs of Kansas City) with his wife, Laura, and their three children, Patrick, Katie, and Tommy.

You can contact him directly at: **info@coachesalmanac.com**

Made in the USA
Middletown, DE
26 August 2015